DR. MANDELL'S ULTIMATE PC DESK REFERENCE

Dr. Steven Mandell

alpha books

A Division of Macmillan Computer Publishing
A Prentice Hall Macmillan Company
201 West 103rd St., Indianapolis, Indiana 46290 USA

International Standard Book Number: 1-56761-533-3

Library of Congress Catalog Card Number: 94-78132

97 96 95 8 7 6 5 4 3 2 1

Interpretation of the printing code: the rightmost number of the first series of numbers is the year of the book's printing; the rightmost number of the second series of numbers is the number of the book's printing. For example, a printing code of 95-1 shows that the first printing of the book occurred in 1995.

Printed in the United States of America

Publisher
Marie Butler-Knight

Product Development Manager
Faithe Wempen

Acquisitions Manager
Barry Pruett

Managing Editor
Elizabeth Keaffaber

Development Editor
Heather Stith

Production Editor
Michelle Shaw

Copy Editor
Barry Childs-Helton

Cover Designer
Jay Corpus

Designer
Barbara Kordesh

Indexer
Bront Davis

Production Team
Gary Adair, Dan Caparo, Brad Chinn, Kim Cofer, Lisa Daugherty, Jennifer Eberhardt, David Garratt, Joe Millay, Erika Millen, Beth Rago, Karen Walsh, Robert Wolf

Special thanks to Discovery Computing, Inc. for ensuring the technical accuracy of this book.

CONTENTS

Introduction

If terms such as megabytes, serial port, and non-interlaced are only slightly more decipherable than a Chinese menu, then this book is definitely appropriate for you. It can help you understand fundamental computer concepts. If you are familiar with computers, but are not using the full power of the technology, this book introduces ideas that could help you in becoming a "power user." Even if you use a computer often, this book can help clarify answers to your questions about computer issues, the ever-changing technology, and the numbers that describe it.

This book is designed to explain not only the terminology and the functions of computers, but also the numbers and the alphabet soup of acronyms—SCSI, RAM, CRT, CD-ROM, DAT, QIC, LCD, CPU, VGA, WYSIWYG, and so on—that you'll encounter when buying software, reading computer magazines, or talking to computer salespeople. The material has been written and organized to help you make informed decisions with respect to personal computing. It can help you "go online," try new applications, get acquainted with a computer magazine, care for your system, and shop wisely for hardware and software.

Using This Book

Our purpose is to provide a book you can use as a resource. The book is designed for two approaches: You can read through it from beginning to end, or you can look up only the topics that interest you. Each numbered topic is self-contained and includes references to related topics. The references include titles and topic numbers. Within each major section, topics are numbered consecutively, making it easy for you to locate a particular topic by its number. The software reviews are listed alphabetically by software title; an index of contents at the beginning of the Software Review section will help you find what you need.

The topics are grouped according to general subject into six parts. Part One, "Hardware Fundamentals," defines terms associated with the inner workings of a computer, memory, and storage. It also discusses keyboards, mice, monitors, printers, and other devices used for entering items into the computer and seeing the results of processing. This section includes guidelines for evaluating the various devices. Part Two, "Buying and Caring for Your Computer," gives some general guidelines for purchasing computers and taking care of the equipment and disks.

Part Three, "Software Fundamentals," tells about operating systems (programs that enable the computer to manage itself), user interfaces (the methods you use to tell a computer what you want done), and using computer programming languages. It also lists some guidelines for evaluating software, and describes programs such as word processors, spreadsheets, databases, and graphics programs. Part Four, "Communication," is an in-depth discussion of using your computer to communicate; its topics range from connecting your computer to telephone lines to using information services. Part Five, "Issues and Challenges," deals with some often problematic issues associated with computer use; such as, ethics, piracy, privacy, viruses, and ergonomics.

Each Part is introduced by a Contents Index, which contains an alphabetical listing of the topics covered. You can skim this "mini-index" to find topics you're interested in.

Commercial software is reviewed in Part Six. The rating system is simple—on a scale of one to five, five is the highest rating. Look for the rating icon (a stack of diskettes) in the left margin:

The above, for example, indicates a rating of 3, which is average. If you don't have an exact software title you're interested in, check out the Parts Page for this section. It lists all the reviewed programs by category, such as games or education.

At the end of the book are a number of lists for using the book or locating resources. These are as follows:

- a description of some common computer problems, and what to do about them
- company names, addresses, and telephone numbers of hardware manufacturers
- a list of popular computer magazines, with addresses and telephone numbers
- a glossary of major terms
- a complete index

By using the lists and the cross-references, you can find the meanings of unfamiliar terms and read about related subjects. Any material that seems too technical for your purposes now can be skipped and read later when you need it. Remember, however, that throughout most topics, there are tips that may be useful to you now. The very nature of computers is that they evolve rapidly; new becomes old very quickly. This book should provide enough general material that you can evaluate the products on the market today, and quickly grasp the concepts behind tomorrow's products. And now, as you begin to read, you can start right off with the hardware fundamentals—or turn to the index at the back of the book to find your own starting point.

Part 1 Contents Index

HARDWARE FUNDAMENTALS

Hardware consists of the physical components that make up a computer system. These are the items you can actually touch. Instead of the hammers and wrenches you might normally think of as hardware, a computer system includes this hardware:

- the computer (system unit) with a given amount of memory
- a hard disk drive
- a floppy disk drive
- a monitor
- a keyboard
- a mouse
- a printer

The topics in this section describe the internal workings of the computer itself, as well as what the computer does with the programs and data you feed it. This section also covers the various input and output devices you will use to process the data. Although the material may seem difficult to understand, the more you read about it and use it, the easier it is to absorb. By the way, when we use the term *high-end*, we are referring to the more powerful—and usually more expensive—equipment in a group. The term *low-end* describes the less powerful—and less expensive—models.

1.1 ANALOG VERSUS DIGITAL

Why is the term *digital* used in conjunction with computers? When you think of digits, you think of distinct units such as fingers or toes or the numerals 0 to 9. Thus, the word *digit* is an apt term to use for describing computers, because the two digits of the binary number system, 1 and 0, are used (respectively) to represent the two distinct states of electricity—"on" and "off"—in which computers operate. The components in the circuitry can hold a state so the computer can "remember" what it is doing, or they can cause a state to be recorded on a storage medium, such as a hard disk or a floppy disk.

On the other hand, *analog* devices (such as watches with dials) do not operate directly in "on" and "off" states. Instead, they measure changes in a condition (such as time, pressure, length, temperature, voltage, or volume) in a continuous pattern or wave. An analog dial represents every possible value for the condition being measured, although you must estimate the value to some degree.

Most analog computers today are used for special scientific and engineering purposes, although some computer devices (such as monitors) receive analog signals that must be changed to digital signals for computer processing to occur.

(See 1.2 Data Representation; 1.12 Memory and Storage; 1.13 Addresses; 1.46 Monitors.)

1.2 DATA REPRESENTATION

Codes are commonly used for representing data. A computer uses a code because it cannot understand the symbols of our alphabet. Because all computer activity is based upon the two states of electricity—on and off, or conducting and non-conducting—a computer's code needs only two symbols.

The binary number system is ideal for representing data in this manner because it consists of only two digits, 0 (zero) for off and 1 (one) for on. These two digits are commonly referred to as *bits*, short for BInary digiTs. In contrast, the decimal system we use for most of our calculating is based on ten digits, 0 through 9.

The computer uses the binary system to do arithmetic computations such as addition, subtraction, and multiplication. For example, the computer calculates the decimal equation 2 + 2 = 4 (one 2 plus one 2 equals one 4) as 10 + 10 = 100; the binary place positions are ones, twos, fours, eights, sixteens, and so on—as opposed to the decimal place positions of ones, tens, hundreds, thousands, etc. Multiplication can be done by a series of additions: in decimal numbers, 2 x 3 = 6, but the computer would figure 10 + 10 + 10 = 110. Multiplication can also be done by shifting digits to the left. Shifting a binary digit to the left multiplies it by a power of 2. For example, shifting the binary number 10 to the left by one digit (making it 100) multiplies it by 2. Subtraction and division are more complicated.

So far so good, but how does a computer handle alphabetic input? If there are only two digits, how is it possible to encode 26 lowercase letters, 26 capital letters, 10 digits (0 through 9), and all of the characters such as *, #, and @—plus the codes for Delete, Enter, Tab, Shift, Space, and the other special keys on the computer keyboard?

In the 1-bit code, there are only two choices. In the 2-bit code, there are four choices: two in the left position and two in the right position, or 2 x 2 = 4. How many choices are there with three positions? Each position has two choices, so 2 x 2 x 2 = 8. The codes would be 000, 001, 010, 011, 100, 101, 110, and 111. With four positions, there are 16 possible codes: 2 x 2 x 2 x 2 = 16. You can see how a pattern is forming. The more positions, the more items can be coded. Five bits provide 32 codes, the number of codes needed to encode the 26 letters of the alphabet with 6 left over.

In computer coding, data are often stored in blocks of eight bits. Each block is called a *byte*. An 8-bit byte makes 256 codes. This is more than enough to write the uppercase and lowercase letters, ten digits, special characters, and commands such as those activated by the Spacebar and the Enter key. Pressing a key on the keyboard generates the code number for that key and converts it to a binary number, which is then input into the computer. For example, one coding system codes an uppercase letter B this way:

1100 0010

When you enter a B via a computer keyboard, the computer knows that you have pressed the B key along with the Shift key (instead of, say, a G key). The computer then sends the code on to the monitor, where you see the B displayed on the screen. The computer does not understand the symbol B, but it can interpret the code made up of 1s and 0s. On a particular system, the same code always stands for the B. Thus, a computer can handle the binary digits directly—as when it adds two numbers—and it can handle text that has been encoded into binary form. As we shall see later, it also uses the binary format in creating images and handling sound.

Because computers use the binary number system, many specifications are given in multiples of two. For example, there are 32-bit computers (32 is 2 to the fifth power, or 2^5) and 8-bit buses (8 is 2 to the third power, or 2^3). If your computer is a 16-bit computer, it can handle 16 bits—two bytes—at a time. A 32-bit computer handles 32 bits at a time. (Other devices such as video cards or expansion slots may also be described in terms of how many bits they can handle.) The larger the amount of data handled at one time, the faster the computer or device operates.

(See 1.3 Bits, Bytes, and Characters; 1.4 Computer Codes; 1.8 Microprocessors; 1.10 How a Computer Works; 1.18 Ports, Slots, and Bays.)

1.3 Bits, Bytes, and Characters

The smallest unit of information a computer can handle is the *bit*. The word stands for BInary digiT, and it can hold only one of two values, 0 or 1. Bits are usually grouped in sets of 8 consecutive bits called *bytes*. On most systems, each byte is capable of storing one character, which is a letter, a number, punctuation, graphics symbol, or key command (such as Tab or Shift).

Bytes can be counted in large units used for describing the size of computer memory and storage. A *kilobyte*, abbreviated KB or K, is equal to 1,024 bytes. A *megabyte* (abbreviated MB or M) is equal to just over 1 million (1,048,576) bytes; a *gigabyte* (GB) is equal to 1 billion bytes.

Although a computer can be described as having so many kilobytes of memory, the actual memory chips in that computer may have capacities measured in units called *kilobits* or *megabits*. This difference in memory measurements is due to the way the computer handles memory. Each memory chip in a set of eight or nine holds just one of the bits in a particular byte.

(See 1.2 Data Representation; 1.12 Memory and Storage.)

1.4 COMPUTER CODES

Programs and numbers are used in binary format, as described under the "Data Representation" topic. A major format for storing data is the text format *ASCII*: each character of data is assigned a specific code number. ASCII stands for American Standard Code for Information Interchange, and is a *de facto* standard for coding data.

ASCII (pronounced *ask-ee*) codes a character with 7 bits, which gives it the capacity for 128 unique symbols. It also provides a decimal number code for the character. For example, the ASCII code for the letter H is the bit code 1001000 or the decimal number 72. An 8-bit version of ASCII, called ASCII-8 or *extended ASCII*, is designed to use the extra bit in a byte. This version has an additional 128 characters, used to represent mathematical symbols and special symbols for drawing pictures, among others. IBM has defined the extended characters and their ASCII codes; though these are not standardized, most IBM-compatible PCs recognize them.

ASCII is often used in microcomputers. Word processing programs usually offer an option that enables the user to store text as ASCII files, though ASCII is not always the default storage format. Often a file stored in ASCII can be used with a program different from the one used to create the file. Not all data, however, is stored in ASCII format. Other formats are used for storing graphical data (like that found in a graphical user interface, for example).

(See 1.2 Data Representation; 2.9 Standards; 3.28 Files.)

1.5 The Motherboard

A printed circuit board is a rectangular plate designed to hold chips and other electronic components. Some of the circuitry that connects the various chips is actually imprinted on the board. The *motherboard*, just one of several types of printed circuit boards, holds all the main circuitry of a computer. On IBM PCs, the motherboard is called the *system board*; on IBM PS/2 computers, it is referred to as the *planar board*.

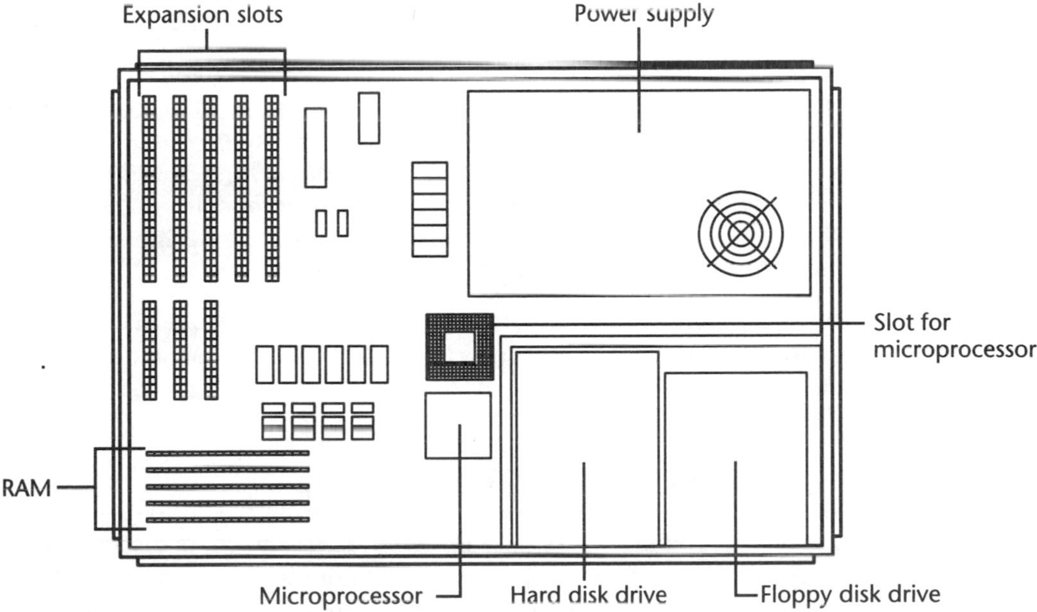

An inside look at your basic motherboard.

The motherboard holds the *central processing unit (CPU)*, memory chips, serial and parallel ports, and controllers required to control standard devices such as the monitor, keyboard, and disk drive. It also holds the internal power supply unit (which lowers the line voltage of electricity to a level the computer can handle), a fan or other cooling unit, and a battery, which maintains the time and date even when the computer is turned off.

Part of the motherboard is dedicated to the *expansion bus*, which contains connectors for installing additional printed circuit boards (also known as *add-ons*), add-on cards, or *expansion cards*. You can insert cards for adding memory and storage, for example, or cards that enable the computer to use printers, modems, voice-recognition units, and music synthesizers. Although the motherboard is flat, the expansion cards stand on their sides in special sockets called *slots*. There is a limit to the number of cards that can be added. Most older computers had expansion cards for everything; today, the standard functions are built directly onto the motherboard.

Any chips other than the CPU located on the motherboard can access the CPU directly without going through the expansion bus. For this reason, you should fill up the motherboard completely before attaching add-on boards. If you want to add memory to your system, you usually can insert memory chips directly onto the motherboard. Using a separate memory board, on the other hand, may slow down the system because of the varying operating speeds among the components.

Some systems can be upgraded by replacing the existing motherboard with one that has a more powerful microprocessor. Upgrading in this manner is more expensive than adding individual components—and involves more work—but you do avoid potential compatibility problems between updated high-speed units and the existing components on the motherboard. All of the components—the CPU, expansion bus, ROM, and memory—on the new motherboard are designed to work properly together for greater speed and performance.

(See 1.6 Chips and Semiconductors; 1.8 Microprocessors; 1.11 Buses; 1.15 RAM; 1.17 ROM; 1.18 Ports, Slots, and Bays; 1.20 Controllers and Drivers; 1.21 Add-ins and Add-ons; 2.12 Obsolescence.)

1.6 Chips and Semiconductors

Miniaturization of computers was only possible when scientists discovered how to put the electronic circuitry on tiny pieces of semiconducting material such as silicon or gallium. A *semiconductor* is a material that is neither a good conductor of electricity (such as copper) nor a good insulator (such as rubber). Adding precise amounts of other materials to a semiconductor can make it act like any of the tiny components needed in electric circuits. In fact, there may be millions of these electronic components etched on a single semiconductor *chip*. Other terms for the tiny chip are *microchip* and *integrated circuit*—so called because all its components can be placed together on one piece of material where they can work together efficiently.

Semiconductors are used to make both microprocessor chips and memory chips. There are sound chips that produce tones, clicks, and beeps. There are clock chips that govern the timing that the microprocessor chips need to execute instructions and retrieve data. There are ROM chips that contain instructions for governing access to data, managing other chips, providing a drawing capability, and many other tasks. Many of these chips would easily fit on a dime; they are less than 1/4-inch square. Others are as large as a small postage stamp.

For protection against dust, fingerprints, and other foreign matter, the chips are housed in plastic or ceramic packages, some of which have tiny windows on one side through which you can see the chip. Tiny pins, or legs, extending from the chip packages connect them to the motherboard or printed circuit board. Some packages—for example, Intel microprocessors—are square, and their many pins are arranged in concentric squares. Chips like these are called *PGAs*, or *pin-grid arrays*. Others, called *DIPs* or *dual in-line packages*, are rectangular and somewhat buglike in appearance; the term *spider legs* is often used in reference to their pins. Single in-line packages (SIPs) have just one row of legs.

Advances in chip technology are basically geared toward adding more transistors to the chips. Thus, even more components can be added to the same size chip. For example, today's microprocessor chips hold many more transistors for actual processing than did older chips; yet they also hold additional components. These include *coprocessors* (processors that take over some specialized processing from the main CPU) and *memory caches*, which increase the speed with which the CPU can get the data needed for processing. This means more functions can occur directly on the microprocessor rather than off the chip, which would take more time. The principle is that the smaller the distance electricity must travel, the faster the processing.

In the future, expect chip technology to advance to multi-layered chips (that is, a stack of chips); in addition, multi-chip modules could put RAM, video, and input/output functions all in one processor package. Superchips will increase the speed of processing for multimedia, speech recognition, artificial intelligence, and virtual reality. They could also emulate a number of hardware devices such as modems, fax modems, network cards, sound cards, and video cards.

There is a physical limit, however, on just how closely the chip components can be packed. When the paths that the electrons follow are too close together, the electrons can interfere with each other—and even jump into the wrong path. To get past this barrier, chip engineers will use *photonics* instead of electronics to build chips. Photons are the basic particles of light; photonics will use light to carry information—in fact, more information than electronics can carry, and faster. In addition, the components of a photonics chip can be packed more densely than those of an electronics chip, because light beams can pass through each other without affecting the physics—or the path—of the beam. AT&T's Bell Laboratories have already produced demonstrations of photonics computers.

(See 1.7 The Making of a Microchip; 1.8 Microprocessors; 1.15 RAM; 1.17 ROM; 1.22 Sound Cards; 1.23 Video Boards; 1.43 Speech Recognition; 3.45 Multimedia Applications; 3.47 Virtual Reality; 4.3 Modems; 4.5 Computer Networks: Wide Area Networks; 5.19 Automation and Applied Intelligence.)

1.7 THE MAKING OF A MICROCHIP

Many computer chips are smaller than a small postage stamp or even your little fingernail. This section explains how chip manufacturers pack so much information in such a tiny space.

You know that when you turn on a light in your house, the circuit draws electricity from the electric line that leads into your house. If you turn on a flashlight, the circuit draws electricity from batteries. The power from the electric line or the batteries causes particles called *electrons* to move through metal wires. Electrons are found in particles called *atoms* that make up everything in the universe. These electrons are stuck in orbit around the center of the atom, much as the earth revolves around the sun. Some electrons, however, move freely—and can even squeeze between atoms. When the electrons squeeze through the atoms of the metal filament in a light bulb, the filament glows.

There is enough space between the atoms in a metal such as a light bulb's filament for electrons to move easily; thus, metals are called *conductors* of electricity. When you turn on the light switch or the flashlight, the electrons do not move into your body and shock you because the plastic around the metal wiring in either device keeps the electrons in line. Plastic is a poor conductor of electrons—that is, an *insulator* of electricity.

Let's look at the flashlight alone: when you flick its switch, you turn it either on or off. That means you either connect or disconnect the *circuit*, or path, that carries the electrons to the metal filament in the bulb. When the circuit is connected, the plus end (or + terminal) of the battery pulls electrons into it, while the negative end (or – terminal) pushes electrons away from it. This causes the electrons to move through the filament and make it glow. When the circuit is disconnected, electrons cannot move through the wire because there is air space between the negative end of the terminal and the wire leading to the filament. Since air is an insulator, electrons do not move through it.

Some materials, called *semiconductors,* can be made to act as either conductors or insulators. Pure silicon is one such semiconductor. The silicon atoms are found in both glass and sand. When layered with both insulating materials and conducting materials, silicon can act as either an insulator or a conductor, whichever is desired. These layers create transistors and paths among the transistors.

Very simply, *transistors* are electrical switches that turn the conduction of electrons either on or off. The electrons flow through paths (or *traces* of very fine wire) leading to and from the transistors. A strip of silicon called a *gate* sits between the trace leading onto the transistor and the trace leading away from the transistor. The gate normally keeps electrons from jumping from one trace to the other, thus blocking the path of electricity. The gate has a trace of its own, however, and if the trace gives the gate a charge, electricity can flow through the gate—turning on the transistor and letting electricity continue down the path. The transistors, traces, and gates can be configured to provide various predictable logical outputs that enable the computer to add, make a choice, or store an item.

Because one or more of these circuits can be embedded on a chip, the result is often called an *integrated circuit*. The problem is getting thousands of these transistors and paths onto the surface of a tiny chip of silicon to make up the complex integrated circuit a computer needs. Rather than trying to lay down the thousands of components individually, it is easier to coat the whole chip with a substance and then remove it where it is not needed. This is done through a *photoresist etching* method.

Engineers draw the circuits using computers. Each layer of the large master chip design is reduced by a photographic process to microscopic size. The result is a "mask" for each layer through which the circuits will be etched upon a wafer of silicon. The silicon used to make computer chips is purified from common rocks and sand, and then *doped* with chemicals to give it either a positive or a negative charge. In its molten form, the silicon is cast into cylindrical ingots in a process similar to candle-dipping. The ingots are sliced into circular wafers, each 4 to 6 inches in diameter and thinner than a credit card. Each wafer is sterilized and polished.

Because a single speck of dust can ruin a chip, the chips are manufactured in *clean rooms* in which the air is filtered and workers must wear special coveralls (facetiously called "bunny suits") to decrease the chances of dust contamination. (These rooms are many times cleaner than hospital rooms.) Then the wafers are subjected to repeated layering and etching away until all circuits are formed.

Electrically positive wafers, for example, are encased in an open glass tube and placed in an extremely hot oxidation furnace. As oxygen reacts with the silicon of the wafer, a thin layer of silicon dioxide is formed which does not conduct electricity well. The wafers are then coated with the gelatin-like *photoresist* substance and placed under the mask. Exposure to ultraviolet light changes the photoresist substance so that appropriate areas can be washed away in a solvent. The silicon dioxide exposed by the solvent is etched away by hot gases. The silicon underneath is doped to make it electrically negative, thus forming a circuit pathway. This process is repeated using a different mask for each layer, thus creating the pathways for electricity to follow. After the last layer is etched, the wafer is covered with aluminum to connect the components of the circuits.

A testing machine checks each chip to see if the electrical circuits behave as planned, and marks defective chips with ink. Then a diamond saw cuts the wafer into the individual chips. A robot picks up each good chip and places it on a drop of adhesive in a ceramic or plastic carrier. (The robot's vision system detects the ink spots that mark defective chips, thus the robot can ignore those chips.) Another robotic machine wires sections of the chip called *bonding pads* to electrical leads on the carrier, using aluminum or gold wire finer than human hair. A robot clamps a lid rimmed with solder onto the carrier, and then sends it through a hot furnace. As the solder melts, it seals the chip hermetically inside the carrier. The chip is now ready to be placed inside a computer.

(See 1.6 Chips and Semiconductors; 1.8 Microprocessors; 1.9 Instructions of a Computer: CISC Versus RISC; 1.15 RAM; 1.17 ROM.)

1.8 MICROPROCESSORS

An ad says a particular manufacturer offers a 486 DX2/66 system, a description that is meaningless unless you know that the numbers refer to the type of microprocessor the system contains. The *microprocessor* (sometimes shortened to "processor") is also known as the *central processing unit*, or *CPU*, of a microcomputer. Its function is so vital that it is often called the brain or heart of a computer.

The microprocessor is actually a tiny silicon chip that contains all of the arithmetic and logic circuitry needed for processing data (in a section called the ALU, or *arithmetic-logic unit*) and the circuitry used for directing the sequence of operations and the activities of the computer (in a section called the *control unit*). The chip is packaged in a dirt-free plastic or ceramic case with a set of tiny legs or pins that plug into the motherboard of a microcomputer. (You will find microprocessors in other digital devices, too, such as clock radios, fuel-injection systems, and washing machines.) The major parts of the microprocessor and their functions follow:

CONTROL UNIT

- Maintains order and controls the activity in the computer.
- Directs communication and coordinates operations between the microprocessor and other devices in a computer system.
- Directs sequence of computer operations.
- Interprets instructions from programs.
- Produces signals that act as commands to carry out the instructions.
- Finds data items to be processed.

- Keeps track of instructions already executed.
- Directs the results of processing to storage or output devices.

Arithmetic-Logic Unit (ALU)

- Performs calculations.
- Determines whether a number is negative, positive, or zero.
- Conducts logic operations that compare values for equality—that is, equal to, greater than, and less than.
- Conducts logic operations for AND, NOT, and OR gates.

Microprocessors are identified in three primary ways—model (usually identified by a number), bandwidth (or bit architecture), and clock speed; each of these will be defined momentarily. Programs written for use with high-end microprocessors will not run on less powerful microprocessors, though lower-end programs are usually compatible with high-end microprocessors. The two largest manufacturers of microprocessors are Intel and Motorola.

Intel, which supplies IBM and Tandy, has become very well known for its 80286, 80386, and 80486 microprocessor chips. These model numbers are often shortened to 286, 386, and 486. (Preceded by an "i," as in "i486," they refer to Intel-brand chips.) Variations on these numbers describe different capabilities of chip designs; they include 386SL, 386SX, 386DX, 486SX, 486DX, and Pentium. Apart from the chips used in Apple Macintosh computers, Intel chips have become the industry standard. (Clones of Intel chips are available from Advanced Micro Devices. Other microprocessors are available from Cyrix.)

The Apple Macintosh computers use 68000, 68020, 68030, or 68040 microprocessors manufactured by the Motorola Corporation. The most recent and most powerful Apple computers, the Power Macs, use the Power PC 601 microprocessor, one result of an alliance Apple, Motorola, and IBM formed to increase compatibility between the Macintosh and IBM platforms. Motorola also supplies workstation manufacturers such as Hewlett-Packard and NeXT.

A higher model number does not always mean a higher-quality CPU, because CPU power also depends on the bit architecture and the clock speed of the microprocessor. *Bit architecture* describes the size of the *registers*, storage areas within the microprocessor. All data must be represented in a register—either as the actual data, or as the address of the memory location where the data is stored—before it can be manipulated.

The most common architectures today in microcomputers are 16-bit and 32-bit designs. A 16-bit CPU can handle 16 bits, or 2 bytes, of data at a time. A 32-bit CPU can handle 32 bits, or 4 bytes, of data at once. The more data a CPU can handle, the faster the computer operates. If you see computers advertised with more than one bit number, the larger number refers to the *register width* (the number of bits the computer can process at one time), and the smaller number refers to the *bus width* (the number of bits that travel through the buses at one time). The bit architecture is sometimes called the *bandwidth* or the *word size*.

Clock speed is the speed at which the CPU executes an instruction. It is described in terms of a frequency or megahertz rating. *Mega* means million; *hertz* means one cycle, or pulse, per second. A *megahertz*, abbreviated *MHz*, is equal to one million cycles, or ticks, per second. The CPU requires a fixed number of these ticks to execute each instruction. The fewer clock cycles per instruction, the better. Pulses from an internal clock or quartz crystal regulate this speed and synchronize the various components of the computer. The faster the clock—that is, the higher the megahertz rating of a CPU—the faster the computer.

Clock speeds of most personal computers range from 25 to over 100MHz; the most common are 25 and 33. Intel is also manufacturing clock-doubled and clock-tripled microprocessors, but this refers only to actual processing inside the chip. Interaction with other components occurs at regular clock speed. The speed of a microprocessor is sometimes described in *million instructions per second*, or *MIPS*. MIPS shows roughly the number of instructions a computer can execute in one second, but it does not describe the speed of a computer when other factors, such as the speed of input and output, are considered.

In some computers, a specialized processing unit called a *coprocessor* takes over certain types of processing operations from the microprocessor, thus helping to increase the speed of processing. For example, a *math coprocessor*, such as the 80387SX used in 386SX computers, performs mathematical operations. Computer manufacturers include a coprocessor or two on the motherboards of some models; computers lacking a coprocessor may have a space on the motherboard into which you can insert one. A coprocessor can dramatically improve a computer's performance—especially when you are running graphics, engineering, scientific, and statistical analysis applications. If the software you are running is not written to take advantage of a coprocessor, however, the extra hardware is useless.

A new type of coprocessor, the *digital signal processor (DSP)*, has been developed especially to manipulate real-time digital data such as sound and video. Unlike the CPU, which processes all kinds of data in a variety of ways, the DSP is dedicated to a single processing task. Although most frequently associated with sound and video cards, the DSP also is used in data and voice modems, voice recognition, data compression, medical imaging, and video conferencing. It can be reprogrammed with a software upgrade without removing it from the computer.

(See 1.9 Instructions of a Computer: CISC Versus RISC; 1.11 Buses; 1.22 Sound Cards; 1.23 Video Boards; 2.3 Which Computer? The Platforms; 2.7 Configuration and Compatibility; 2.8 Portables; 2.10 Multimedia Standards; 2.12 Obsolescence.)

1.9 Instructions of a Computer: CISC Versus RISC

To a computer, an instruction is not a general command such as "format this letter with a left margin of 1.5 inches and a right margin of 1 inch," or even "let tax = price * .06." An *instruction* would be one of many tiny electronic steps that it would take a computer to do the job. The instructions used for doing the job collectively are called the *instruction set*; they are designed into the microprocessor's circuitry. Basically, the on/off patterns formed by the transistors determine the path the electricity follows to execute these instructions.

By using the instruction set (through programming languages), programmers produce software that harnesses the computer's power to achieve the desired results. When a program is executed, the computer's microprocessor uses the instruction set to do any arithmetic and logic functions, as well as to control the sequence of all operations in the program. It can add, subtract, multiply, or divide numbers through simple manipulations of bits. It can solve logic functions such as AND, OR, and NOT by comparing data bit by bit. It can move data around to new locations. It also controls the storage of data, instructions, and intermediate and final results of processing.

Instruction sets approaching 300 instructions on a 32-bit microprocessor occupy a lot of space on the chip, leaving less room for other components and slowing processing speeds. A newer development, the *Reduced Instruction Set Computer* (*RISC*, pronounced *risk*), uses a very simple and small instruction set. The principle of the simplified format is that the CPU can do its work more efficiently, thus increasing speed. In addition, the CPU employs *pipelining*, in which it handles more than one instruction at once. For example, an item can be stored while the arithmetic-logic unit is doing a calculation and the control unit is decoding the next instruction. (Conventional microprocessors are now called *CISC* chips—pronounced *sisk*—to differentiate them from RISC chips; the acronym stands for *Complex Instruction Set Computer*.)

Because RISC CPUs have fewer instructions than CISC chips, they require fewer transistors. Thus, they produce less heat and take up less space on the microprocessor chip. This leaves more room for other items such as memory caches and coprocessors that can increase processing speed. Experts disagree about the values of RISC and CISC architectures; they note that conventional microprocessors are becoming so fast and cheap as to neutralize the value of RISC machines. In addition, the designers of RISC machines are increasing the number of instructions present on the microprocessor, thus decreasing the margin of difference between CISC and RISC.

Several companies, notably IBM and Hewlett-Packard, are developing families of computers that use the RISC concept. In fact, the most popular RISC-based chip, the PowerPC, is found in the new Power Macintosh computers. It is based on the IBM Power Optimization with Enhanced RISC (POWER) architecture, and is the result of a 1991 agreement among IBM, Apple, and Motorola.

(See 1.8 Microprocessors; 1.10 How a Computer Works.)

1.10 How a Computer Works

The transistors, traces, and gates on a chip are configured to provide various predictable logical outputs. The plan for this configuration is a predetermined instruction set that enables the computer to add, make a choice, or store an item. This basic set of instructions varies among the different types of microprocessors, and determines how processing occurs.

Processing is a digital operation called the *machine cycle*. After data and instructions are moved to memory, the CPU waits for instructions on what to do next. Upon the command to begin processing, the control unit gets one instruction from memory and decodes it (or examines it to decide what it means). It sends electronic signals to the ALU (arithmetic-logic unit) and memory; these state that the instruction should be carried out.

Data and instructions may be moved into a *memory cache* (an area in RAM designed to improve the speed of data retrieval), and from there, into registers in the ALU. The ALU then manipulates the data; the result is stored in a register and may be transferred back to memory. The part of the machine cycle in which the control unit gets and interprets the instruction is called *I-time*, or *instruction time*; the part of the machine cycle in which the ALU acts and the result is stored is called *E-time*, or *execution time*.

A single machine cycle may consist of a number of smaller instructions that must be synchronized with all others. Each microprocessor has an internal clock that regulates this synchronization with fixed-rate pulses. The fewer clock cycles per instruction, the better. *Clock speed* is expressed in megahertz (MHz). A megahertz is equal to one million ticks per second. Clock speed for microcomputers ranges from 8MHz on early, very slow machines to over 100MHz on today's speedy microprocessors.

(See 1.1 Analog Versus Digital; 1.6 Chips and Semiconductors; 1.8 Microprocessors; 1.9 Instructions of a Computer: CISC Versus RISC; 1.12 Memory and Storage; 1.15 RAM.)

1.11 Buses

A *bus* is a collection of wires through which data is sent from one part of the computer to another. In a computer, the bus is both the "vehicle" and the route by which data are transmitted.

The size of a bus, described in terms of its width, determines how much data can be sent at one time. A 16-bit bus can send 16 bits of data; a 32-bit bus can send 32 bits of data. Generally, the larger the bus width, the faster the computer. Like microprocessors, the bus has a clock speed measured in MHz. If the clock speed of the bus is much slower than that of the microprocessor, however, execution of programs may slow down.

A bus in a personal computer may refer to more than one type of route. For example, the *data bus* connects the CPU with any RAM located on the motherboard. The *expansion bus* lets all of the various computer components—such as expansion boards (or adapter cards) and external devices such as printers—communicate with the CPU.

The component that controls the device and enables the computer to communicate with it is called the *controller*. Each controller is designed to connect to a particular type of device, as well as to a particular type of bus. In personal computers, the controller is often a single chip inserted into the motherboard. A computer comes outfitted with standard controllers for the monitor, keyboard, and disk drives. Additional devices may require that you insert expansion boards containing the appropriate controllers.

There are a number of expansion buses. Each defines a different *protocol* for regulating data traffic; each has different physical connectors. Always check to be sure that the devices you purchase are compatible with the bus your computer has. Common buses for IBM-compatible computers are identified by specific design standards. These include the Industry Standard Architecture (ISA) bus, the Micro Channel Architecture (MCA) bus, and the Extended Industry Standard Architecture (EISA) bus. Descriptions of several follow.

- The ISA buses were designed for the IBM PC/XT and IBM PC/AT computers, and are thus called XT and AT buses. The XT bus, or 8-bit ISA, is an early design and all but obsolete. The AT bus, or 16-bit ISA, is the *de facto* industry standard, but is being replaced by more powerful buses compatible with the high-end chips.

- The 32-bit MCA bus is used in high-end PS/2 computers with Intel 386 or 486 microprocessors. It cannot be used with expansion boards designed for the AT bus (16-bit ISA).
- The EISA bus, designed by a group of IBM competitors, is similar to the MCA, but it will accept expansion boards designed for the AT bus. Being a 32-bit bus, it transfers twice the amount of data at each pulse of the clock, even though it operates at the same speed as the ISA. Its cost is high; thus, it is used mainly in file servers and high-end business machines.
- The local bus, now usually 32 bits wide, is the bus the CPU sits on. Used most often for video and drive-controller circuitry, it requires an appropriate motherboard design. The local bus video display card is inserted into one slot; the local bus disk controller is inserted into the other. This method attaches the video card directly to the CPU and RAM, rather than routing the video signal through the expansion bus. The local bus is also designed to operate at the microprocessor's clock speed. The point is to speed up the display of graphical data—necessary because graphics require large amounts of data. The result is greater speed in operating programs such as Microsoft Windows 3.1. As yet, there is no standard for the local bus, but the Video Electronics Standards Association (VESA) has announced its standard called VESA Local Bus (VL-Bus) to be used with an ISA or EISA system. The standard should permit interchanging of local-bus adapter cards.
- Competing with the local-bus design is the Peripheral Component Interconnect, or PCI, used on Pentium machines. PCI can use a 64-bit data path; it is often faster than VESA. It features *plug-and-play*; devices connected through it configure themselves to your system automatically, without your help.

For Macintosh computers, there are the ADB (Apple Desktop Bus) and NuBus expansion buses. The ADB bus has a port into which you can *daisy-chain* (connect sequentially) a number of devices. For example, the keyboard is connected to the ADB port, and the mouse is attached to the keyboard. A single ADB port can support up to 16 input devices at once. On the Macintosh, the local-bus concept is called the *processor direct slot*.

Now that you've read all of this material about buses, you really don't have to worry about it: computers already have built-in buses that are appropriate for the applications they are intended to run.

(See 1.3 Bits, Bytes, and Characters; 1.5 The Motherboard; 1.8 Microprocessors; 1.15 RAM; 1.18 Ports, Slots, and Bays; 1.19 PC Cards; 1.20 Controllers and Drivers; 1.21 Add-ins and Add-ons.)

1.12 Memory and Storage

Data and programs are put into two basic holding areas: memory and storage. *Memory*—also called *main memory*, *main system memory*, *primary memory*, *internal memory*, or *primary storage*—consists of semiconductor chips inside the computer. Being able to hold programs in memory was a major breakthrough that led to the manufacture and sale of computers for business use. The idea—called the *stored-program* concept—enabled programmers to feed a program into a computer via punched tape or punched cards, rather than depending on operators to flip switches and replug wires each time a new program was needed.

Memory chips are designed to store data in locations called *bit cells*, which are capable of being either "on" or "off." Because of the way data is coded, a bit cell holds information whether it is on or off. (Each **1** represents an "on" state; each **0** represents an "off" state.) Data and programs held in memory can be used, or *accessed*, over and over again. This operation is called *reading*. In most memory, new instructions and new data can be stored over old instructions and data, replacing them. This operation is called *writing*.

Each program or bit of information that you use in a computer must be present in memory before the computer can use it. In addition, before they can be processed, any data or instructions (or the addresses thereof) must be represented in a special temporary holding area located in the CPU called a register. A *register* is a kind of high-speed loading zone, where data and instructions are parked only temporarily while the CPU is using them. It can receive information, hold it, and transfer it rapidly as directed by the CPU. Once the CPU is finished with the immediate data and instructions, it sends them back to memory.

Storage, also called *secondary storage* or *mass storage*, uses disks or tapes to hold or store data. You can instruct the computer to read from or write items to the disks or tapes, referred to as *storage media*. Storage is generally permanent until erased or written over—or until it deteriorates or is damaged by heat or magnets. If you want to save the form letter you wrote for Christmas until you are ready to print copies, you will command the computer to write, or *save*, it to a hard disk or a floppy disk. Computer storage was intended to eliminate the mass of paperwork, but somehow the nature of computers—and the ease with which many drafts of paper copies can be generated—has yet to decrease the proliferation of paper.

(See 1.6 Chips and Semiconductors; 1.7 The Making of a Microchip; 1.13 Addresses; 1.14 Access Time; 1.15 RAM; 1.17 ROM; 1.19 PC Cards; 1.24 Floppy Disks; 1.25 Hard Disks; 1.26 Tapes; 1.27 CD-ROMs and Optical Storage; 1.29 RAM Disks; 1.32 Caching; 2.19 Caring for Your Disks; 3.29 Memory-Resident Programs.)

1.13 ADDRESSES

In order to direct computer operations, the control unit of the CPU must be able to locate each instruction and data item in memory. Therefore, each location in memory is assigned an *address*. Programmers can use these addresses to specify particular bytes of data.

Addresses are also used to specify the location of items stored on disks. Disks are divided into *tracks* and *sectors*, each of which is used to indicate the address of a particular byte. You, as the user, do not usually have to worry about addresses, though you may see the word **address** appear in some on-screen messages that tell you an error has occurred.

(See 1.12 Memory and Storage; 1.14 Access Time; 1.15 RAM; 1.24 Floppy Disks; 1.25 Hard Disks.)

1.14 ACCESS TIME

As it relates to computer usage, the word *access* has a number of meanings. As a noun, it means a privilege to read and use information stored on a computer. For example, a nurse "has access" to the computerized medical records of her patients. The word *access* can also be used as a verb meaning "to use." For example, a program can access items in memory; a user can access files.

When the computer itself does the accessing, the word *access* has one of two customary meanings:

- As a noun, it means the act of reading data from (or writing data to) memory or a storage device.
- As a verb, it means to read data from (or write data to) memory or a storage device; this is the context in which we use the word *access* in this topic.

The amount of time it takes a program or device to locate a single piece of data and make it available for processing is called the *access time*; for memory, this time is measured in *nanoseconds* (billionths of a second). For example, some types of RAM chips have access times of 50 nanoseconds.

The speed of disk drives is also described in terms of access time, only the unit of measure is the *millisecond* (thousandths of a second). Access time is made up of two components: seek time and transfer rate. *Seek time* is the time it takes for the read/write head to locate a sector on the disk. The *transfer rate* is the time needed to move data from one place to another. The access time of a hard disk drive is generally well under 20 milliseconds.

(See 1.15 RAM; 1.24 Floppy Disks; 1.25 Hard Disks; 1.26 Tapes; 1.27 CD-ROMs and Optical Storage; 1.28 Flopticals.)

1.15 RAM

Memory is located on tiny chips protected in chip carriers and connected to a printed circuit board such as the motherboard. There are two types of memory: *random-access memory* (*RAM*, pronounced like the animal) and *read-only memory* (*ROM*, which rhymes with *mom*).

The instructions and data needed for processing must be held in RAM before they can be used. When you load a program from a disk, parts of it are sent to RAM to be used right away. When you are using a word processing program, the words you type are kept in RAM while you work. Some of the words—the ones that you are working on currently—may be kept temporarily in an area of RAM called a *buffer* or *cache*, a kind of holding tank for data. As you go on to other parts of your file, those words are sent to ordinary RAM and new ones are held in the buffer.

Data is more accessible in buffers than in ordinary RAM. Buffers are also useful during printing; data can be sent to the printer's RAM buffer so that you can keep working with other data at the computer.

As the name *random-access memory* suggests, the CPU can access items stored in RAM easily and in any order (randomly). To get data or use instructions, the CPU must be able to find them in memory. Each item in memory is put into a special place. Each place has an *address*, a built-in and unique number that names its location.

Once an item is stored at a certain spot, it can be read over and over again without being erased. The same instructions can be read again and again to process the grades of 100 students, for example, and the same data can be read over and over in a single program to figure bills at the grocery store. New data can be written over old data in RAM, in effect erasing the old data. This is often referred to as the *nondestructive-read/destructive-write* characteristic of RAM. RAM is not a permanent form of storage. It relies on continuous electrical current; if the power fails or is turned off, the items in RAM are lost. Thus, RAM is described as *volatile*. That is why you save your work onto a disk.

There are two basic types of RAM chips: DRAM and SRAM. *DRAM* (pronounced as *dee-ram*) is short for *dynamic RAM*. *SRAM* (pronounced as *ess-ram*) is short for *static RAM*. The difference between the two lies in how often each needs to be *refreshed*, or recharged, per second. Without being refreshed, RAM would lose the data stored in it. DRAM, the more common type of RAM, needs to be refreshed thousands of times per second. SRAM needs to be refreshed much less often. It is faster, but more expensive than DRAM, and is used only for special purposes such as *cache memory*, a temporary area used to help speed the execution of a program.

Every computer comes with a certain amount of RAM, measured in *kilobytes* (abbreviated KB or K). A computer that has 640KB of memory can hold over 640,000 characters of information. Most computers have a standard 4MB of RAM, but many current computer uses require 8MB and even 16MB of RAM.

RAM chips can be added to a computer to increase the amount of memory. RAM comes in two basic packages: *single inline packages (SIPs)* and *dual inline packages (DIPs)*. Another common package is the *SIMM*, or *single inline memory module*, a cartridge of up to nine memory chips. SIMMs can contain 1MB, 2MB, 4MB, 8MB, 16MB, or 32MB of RAM. It is best to fill up the motherboard with chips before adding a separate memory expansion board; the chips on the board can access the CPU directly without going through the expansion bus.

How do you know if you need more memory? Your computer will act slow, or even "freeze up." You may see an **OUT OF MEMORY** message displayed on the monitor screen, and you'll probably have to restart the computer. Any data you didn't save is gone.

(See 1.3 Bits, Bytes, and Characters; 1.16 Memory Management; 1.29 RAM Disks; 1.32 Caching.)

1.16 Memory Management

Back in the early days of personal computing, engineers believed that 1MB (that is, 1024KB) of RAM was all that would ever be needed by personal computer users. The first 640KB of memory, called *conventional memory*, is available to users. The remaining 384KB, called *upper memory*, is used for special system functions. But soon users were wanting to create complex graphics and large spreadsheets; there wasn't enough memory to do all that. So the engineers had to figure out how to trick the computer into using more memory. On early PCs using microprocessors such as the 8088 and 8086, this limit could be overcome by installing either an expanded memory specification (EMS) system or the enhanced version, known as the enhanced expanded memory specification (EEMS).

An *expanded memory* system consists of extra physical memory and the software needed to access the extra memory. A fairly recent alternative to expanded memory is *extended memory*, a concept used commonly for *RAM disks* (sections of memory set up to act as "phantom" disk drives). It is a type of memory utilization available on Intel 80386 and 80486 microprocessors. Extended memory enables a single program to access up to 16MB of physical memory, and it can also emulate expanded memory. With MS-DOS 5.0 and 6.0, you can run DOS from extended memory, thus freeing up more of the 640KB of conventional memory for other applications. (The *de facto* standard for extended memory is Microsoft XMS—Extended Memory Specification.) The difference between the two types of memory lies in how they are configured and used.

Some operating systems, as well as the latest version of Microsoft Windows, support *virtual memory*, a capability that is characteristic of newer chips such as Intel's 80486 and Pentium, and the Motorola Power PC. Virtual memory is the concept of an imaginary memory area that enlarges the set of addresses in memory a program can use. In using virtual memory, the operating system keeps only portions of a program or programs in real memory addresses at any one time. The remaining portions of the programs are kept in storage. Because only a portion of any program is in memory, more programs can be executed within a given time period.

This technique creates the illusion that memory is virtually unlimited. When instructions or data that are not in memory are needed, the portion of the program containing them is directly accessed and transferred from storage to memory. Another portion of a program—still in memory, but no longer needed—is overwritten. This process is known as *swapping*. In order for swapping to take place in an orderly fashion, virtual memory is divided into chunks called *pages*. Each page is typically 256 bytes long and contains 256 addresses. When the operating system calls forth a page, the virtual addresses become real addresses.

Software, whether as part of an operating system or in the form of a special memory-management program, governs how the computer uses these forms of memory. Some software enables a computer to load programs "high"—that is, in the upper memory portion of that first 1MB of RAM. Other programs govern the use of extended and expanded memory. The software helps determine the *mode* that the microprocessor supports. *Real mode* imitates the early Intel 8088 and 8086 microprocessors; it limits programs to the 1MB of conventional memory. Real mode is no longer supported by software such as Windows 3.1. *Protected mode* allows your PC to access extended memory. *Standard mode* includes conventional memory and extended memory. *Enhanced mode* is the sum of conventional memory, extended memory, and expanded memory.

Today, if you buy a 386SX or higher IBM-compatible PC with 4MB of RAM, you will get the 640KB of conventional memory, the 384KB of upper memory, and about 3MB of extended memory. You do not need expanded memory. By using a program such as QEMM-386 (Quarterdeck Expanded Memory Emulator), you can force your computer to simulate expanded memory within existing extended memory. Through its Optimize program, QEMM-386 configures memory for you automatically. In this manner, you can use programs that call for expanded memory (provided you do not run them under Windows 3.1), or load items into unused portions of upper memory. Other "memory makers" are 386Max from Qualitas and MEMMAKER in DOS 6 or higher. To see how your memory is configured, you can use the DOS MEM command.

With a Macintosh, wonder of wonders, you do not have to worry about all this memory usage. Macintoshes can directly address an infinite amount of memory.

(See 1.3 Bits, Bytes, and Characters; 1.15 RAM; 1.29 RAM Disks; 1.32 Caching; 2.3 Which Computer? The Platforms; 2.7 Configuration and Compatibility; 3.6 DOS Versions; 3.9 Microsoft Windows; 3.10 OS/2; Software Review section: QEMM-386.)

1.17 ROM

Read-only memory (ROM) is one of the two types of memory placed on chips made of semiconductor material. Like RAM, read-only memory can be accessed randomly; unlike RAM, items in ROM can be read, but not changed or erased. For all practical purposes, new items cannot be written into ROM.

ROM usually holds the basic instructions needed to start the computer, though some of these instructions are read from a hard or floppy disk. ROM programs also perform diagnostic tests and other technical jobs. In addition, ROM can hold instructions that translate programs written in a computer programming language called BASIC into codes the computer can understand. ROM chips are used in printers (for holding fonts) and in calculators, as well as inside computers.

A common ROM chip is the *ROM BIOS*, which stands for *ROM basic input/output system*. The BIOS is built-in software that controls many computer operations. For example, it contains code needed to control the keyboard, monitor, disk drives, some communication, and a miscellany of other functions. The BIOS also makes it possible for the computer to *boot* itself, or start up, once you turn it on. This capability is called the *bootstrap loader*. All ROM is slower than RAM, however, so many manufacturers design their systems to copy the ROM programs into RAM when the computer is booted. This operation is called *shadowing*; it increases processing speed. It takes up RAM space, however, so some computers enable you to choose whether you want shadowing to occur.

There are several types of ROM chips. The basic ROM chip provides read capabilities, but it cannot be written to. A version of ROM that can be programmed is *programmable read-only memory (PROM)*. PROM chips can be programmed by the manufacturer especially for you, or shipped blank to another company that does the programming. Once the chip is programmed, its contents are unalterable.

PROM provides the advantages of ROM along with the flexibility to meet your needs. The problem with it is that mistakes programmed into the unit cannot be corrected. To overcome this drawback, *erasable programmable read-only memory (EPROM)* has been developed; such a chip can be erased when it is submitted to a special process such as being bathed in ultraviolet light. *EEPROM (electrically erasable programmable read-only memory)* is a type of PROM that can be erased by exposing it to an electrical charge. PROM, EPROM, and EEPROM are written with a device called a *PROM programmer*, or *PROM burner*, although a special type of EEPROM, called *flash memory*, can be rewritten while inside the computer. One advantage of flash memory is that you can download upgrades directly via modem or from a floppy.

By their very nature, ROM chips protect valuable data and programs. Data in ROM is hard-wired; it cannot be changed or deleted by stored-program instructions. In addition, ROM chips cannot be copied easily. Thus, ROM software is called *firmware*. (Building instructions into ROM makes the distinction between hardware and software somewhat fuzzy.)

(See 1.12 Memory and Storage; 1.15 RAM; 1.19 PC Cards; 1.20 Controllers and Drivers.)

1.18 Ports, Slots, and Bays

In order to attach devices to your computer, you need some way to plug them into the computer. Devices such as printers, some disk drives, mice, and scanners are located outside the computer. Many are attached with a cable plugged into the back of the computer. Some external devices are attached to an add-on card that has been inserted inside the computer. Other devices, such as the different types of drives, are placed inside the computer.

The areas inside the computer into which disk or tape drives are put are called *bays*. Only disk and tape drives can be installed in bays. Most commonly, the bays hold a hard disk drive, a CD-ROM drive, or a floppy disk drive. Some bays are hidden from view, and cannot be used for removable media such as floppy disks. You do not see the drives in these bays. Other bays are *exposed*, or accessible, because you can use removable media such as floppy disks. In some cases, the entire drive can be removed from the bay and replaced with another type of drive (such as a magneto-optical disk drive). Computers with this option are handy for multimedia uses.

The inside of a computer also contains *expansion slots* into which *expansion boards* can be installed. The bus that connects these boards to the CPU is called the *expansion bus*. For IBM PCs and compatibles, this is commonly an ISA or EISA bus; Macintosh computers use the Apple Desktop Bus (ADB) or the NuBus design as the expansion bus. Boards for video, sound, and memory can be installed in the slots. In addition, some expansion cards provide connection points for external disk drives, tape drives, and some mice. Expansion slots may be one of three sizes: half, three-quarter, and full. In general, the need for slots has decreased because many components are now integrated onto the motherboard. The result is high performance, less heat production, and lower cost.

With the increased popularity of notebook computers has come the need for a reduction in the size of expansion cards. The solution is the PCMCIA slot, which holds expansion cards only slightly thicker than credit cards. (See topic 1.19, "PC Cards," that follows.)

Devices such as printers, keyboards, mice, and scanners are attached to *ports*—sockets where you plug in the cable attached to the external device. Ports can be different sizes—in other words, they can have a different number and arrangement of pinholes. There are serial ports, parallel ports, and SCSI ports. Some computers label the ports for specific devices (for example, mouse or printer). Expansion cards also may contain ports.

Serial ports such as the RS-232C, RS-422, and RS-423 are commonly used for connecting modems or mice. They are called serial ports because the cable attached carries data bit by bit, in single file. *Parallel ports* are generally used for connecting printers. The cables attached to parallel ports carry more than one bit at a time, much as four northbound freeway lanes can carry four cars traveling side by side. The maximum cable length is shorter than that for serial ports. The common parallel port is a type DB-25, which uses a 25-pin connector. Computers may be designed to handle only two serial ports and three parallel ports. Trying to add more may present conflicts among the devices.

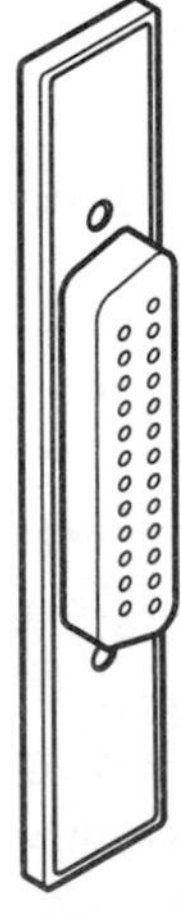

An example of a parallel port.

SCSI (Small Computer System Interface) ports support high transmission speeds, and they let you *daisy-chain* (link together) up to seven devices at the same port. SCSI (pronounced *scuzzy*) is a *parallel interface* that is standard on Macintosh computers, most high-end new IBM machines, and many UNIX systems. It is used to connect disk drives and printers to the computer. SCSI devices can be attached to other IBM PCs and compatibles when a SCSI board is installed in an expansion slot.

A new interface, called SCSI-2, can be used with bus architectures such as MCA and EISA. It is very fast, and may become a standard interface on new computers. (A competing interface called FireWire could replace SCSI serial ports, and ADB in future Macintosh computers. FireWire is a very high-speed serial data bus. It allows real-time transfer of multiple large video files, supports many configurations, and works with many kinds of devices at once.)

The concept of connecting devices with the computer is often referred to as the *interface*. Disk drives are most generally attached to the IBM computers and compatibles through ST-506, IDE, and ESDI interfaces. The *ST-506* is the old standard used on the PC/XT and PC/AT. *IDE*, which stands for *Integrated Drive Electronics*, is a low-cost interface in which the controller is integrated into the drive. *ESDI (Enhanced Small Device Interface)* supports fast data rates and large storage capacities. It requires an ESDI controller.

MIDI (musical instrument digital interface) is the protocol for connecting devices such as electronic keyboards, guitars, and other instruments. Some computers, such as the Commodore Amiga and Atari STE series, have this interface built in. MS-DOS machines will need it added. When you plug a keyboard into MIDI, you can play a tune and have the sounds you play stored, retrieved, and manipulated. The MIDI representation of a sound has values for a note's pitch, length, and volume. It may also imitate a particular instrument and include vibrato. This MIDI standard is supported by most synthesizers. In addition, a number of software programs conform to the MIDI standard.

The connectors that plug into these interfaces are given the interface names. For example, a Centronics connector plugs into a Centronics interface socket, and a SCSI connector plugs into a SCSI interface socket. If the connector has clips or screws, be sure to use them to ensure a firm fit.

Some interfaces, although approved as standards by ANSI or other committees, are available in enough variations that two interfaces of the same name may not be compatible. For example, SCSI supports several types of connectors. For this reason, you should always be sure that any device you want to buy is not only compatible with the interfaces on your computer, but also has the proper controller.

(See 1.11 Buses; 1.19 PC Cards; 1.21 Add-ins and Add-ons; 1.22 Sound Cards; 1.23 Video Boards; 1.24 Floppy Disks; 1.25 Hard Disks; 1.27 CD-ROMs and Optical Storage; 2.9 Standards.)

1.19 PC CARDS

A *PC card* is about the size of four to six credit cards stacked on top of each other. There are pins in one end for plugging the card into the computer. Many PC cards are used as *flash memory* in which the storage consists of special semiconductor memory that retains data even when the computer's power is turned off. The system treats a flash memory card as if it were RAM memory. That is, programs on PC cards are not transferred to the computer's RAM, but instead are read by a device called a *PC card reader* and executed directly from the card. This technique is referred to as *XIP (eXecute-In-Place)*. The cards can also be configured with software, disk drives, modems, or other peripherals.

Although PC cards are available for any style of personal computer, they are especially suited to notebook computers for several reasons. Except for the very miniature hard disk drives, they have no moving parts to fail. They are rugged enough to withstand being dropped, are lightweight, and require much less power than normal hard disk drives.

Standards, of course, help ensure that any card can be used in any slot. The standard for PC cards is *PCMCIA (Personal Computer Memory Card International Association)*, named for the organization that sets the specifications for both the cards and the *bus*, or slot. There are three types of PCMCIA cards. All three are the length and width of a credit card; each has a 68-pin interface. *Type I* cards are the thinnest at 3.3 mm and usually are reserved for use as RAM and various forms of ROM. The thicker *Type II* cards (5.0 mm) are used for input/output devices such as modems, fax modems, combination modems, and LAN adapter cards. *Type III* cards, the thickest at 10.5 mm, can hold miniature hard disk drives or radio communication hardware. Type II cards and slots are the most commonly used. Type III slots can accept Type II and Type I cards and Type II slots can accept Type I cards, but larger cards cannot be used in smaller slots. Although the PCMCIA technology is still somewhat expensive, the standards help to bring the costs down; increasing numbers of computers probably will be equipped with the cards.

(See 1.11 Buses; 1.12 Memory and Storage; 1.17 ROM.)

1.20 Controllers and Drivers

It's not enough that keyboards, printers, disk drives, mice, monitors, and other peripheral devices need connectors, interfaces, slots, and ports: they also need controllers and drivers. So what is the difference between a controller and a driver, and what does each do? The basic difference is that a controller is hardware and a driver is software.

The *controller* governs the transfer of data from a computer to the peripheral device and vice versa. In personal computers, controllers are often single chips placed on the motherboard. Each computer comes with standard controllers for the keyboard, monitor, and disk drives. When you attach an additional device, however, you may need to install an expansion board that contains the controller for the new device. Any controllers should be compatible with the expansion bus.

The *driver* is a program that controls a device. It translates general commands from programs into exact instructions for the specific peripheral device. Many drivers—for example, the keyboard driver—are built into the operating system when you buy your computer. The drivers for equipment that you add to your system may need to be installed.

The driver may already be contained in the controller chip. A driver acts as a go-between for the device and the program. It is needed because each device has its own special commands and each program uses generic commands. The driver receives the generic commands from the program and translates them into specialized commands for the device. Most word processing programs come with drivers for the most popular printers, for example. You will need to choose which printer you have from a menu so the word processing program can activate the proper driver. The concept of a driver enables manufacturers of peripheral equipment to concentrate on designing the product and its functions without worrying about its compatibility; the driver can take care of compatibility.

Knowing about controllers and drivers is especially important if you are ordering equipment by mail. You want to be sure the device you order is compatible with the equipment you have, and has a controller and driver.

(See 1.6 Chips and Semiconductors; 1.18 Ports, Slots, and Bays; 1.21 Add-ins and Add-ons; 2.15 Buying by Mail; 3.2 Operating Systems.)

1.21 Add-ins and Add-ons

Items that you add to the computer's inner circuitry or to a program are often called *add-ins* and *add-ons*. When used synonymously, both the add-in and the add-on refer to a product or a component you add to your computer or other device when you want to complement another product and increase the capabilities of your computer. They can increase memory or add graphics or communication capabilities to a computer. Both can be hardware or software products.

Although some people use the terms to mean the same thing, the technical usage applies to different products. The term *add-in* is often applied to chips you install on a board that is already located inside the computer. Memory chips and coprocessor chips are add-ins that plug directly into the motherboard. The term *add-on* almost always describes a circuit board, cartridge, or program that is installed to increase the capabilities of the computer or software.

A number of circuit boards (or *expansion cards*, as they are also called) can be added to a computer. The primary ones are memory boards, sound cards, video boards, accelerator boards, disk controllers, and modem boards. You can also use boards for attaching scanners, mice, fax capabilities, and light pens to your system. Memory boards contain memory chips, often in modules called SIMMs, that increase the amount of memory in a computer. The acronym *SIMM* stands for *single in-line memory module*, which consists of up to nine memory chips packaged as a single unit.

Accelerator boards are designed to increase the computer's performance, usually by adding a faster microprocessor or a special processing unit for mathematics or graphics. For example, a special accelerator board called a *coprocessor board* may contain a math coprocessor along with some RAM. A *video board* affects the quality of monitor output. There are also *video accelerator* boards with high-speed video RAM (VRAM, pronounced *vee-ram*), and video processors that can be used if you want to increase the performance of Microsoft Windows or other GUIs. In order to have certain qualities of sound output from DOS machines (IBM computers and compatibles), you may need to add a *digital-to-analog converter*, or *DAC*, on a printed circuit board—essentially a sound card.

When you add a circuit board to a computer, you may have to adjust its configuration to fit a particular computer or application. This task may require that you set tiny switches called *DIP switches* located on a package called a dual in-line package. The DIP switches are toggle switches, meaning they have two possible positions, either on or off. With newer computers and operating systems, you can configure your computer through software rather than by physically setting DIP switches. The latest (and most user-friendly) controller/driver technology is *plug-and-play*: expansion boards and their devices configure themselves to your system automatically.

(See 1.11 Buses; 1.12 Memory and Storage; 1.18 Ports, Slots, and Bays; 1.22 Sound Cards; 1.23 Video Boards; 1.42 Camera and Video Input.)

1.22 Sound Cards

If your automobile already scolds you when you forget to latch your seat belt, you may not appreciate owning a computer that talks to you. But sound capabilities not only make playing games more fun, they are essential for reaping the full benefits of multimedia. Sound can also help you create interesting, attention-keeping business presentations. For years, Macintosh computers have been outfitted with sound capabilities beyond beeps and clicks, but IBM/DOS computers still require adapter cards for sound.

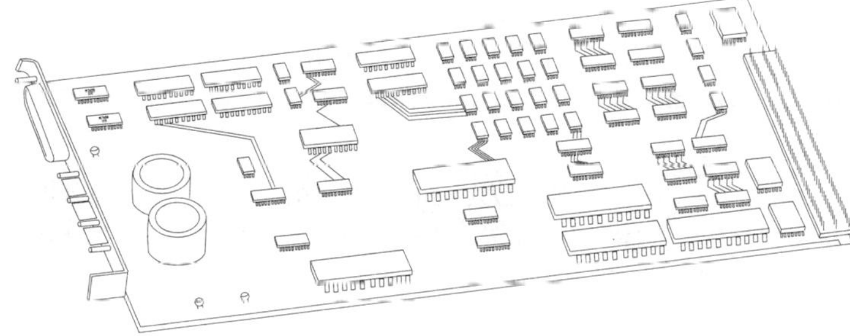

In order to use sound, your computer needs to have a sound card installed.

Sound adapter cards enable you to record and play back digital sound, using hard drive storage and *waveform* sound (stored as WAV files). To do this, you use a microphone for recording and a speaker for playback. The concept is the digital equivalent of tape recording. A WAV file represents the actual recording of each sound wave. It provides a method of converting analog sound to digital sound referred to as wave-table synthesis.

Sound cards also let you use the built-in music synthesizer circuitry, which really acts like a keyboard instrument. The synthesizer is accessed by MIDI commands (.MID files). A MIDI file is a compact sequence of instructions (such as note on, note off, change pitch, change volume, or change instrument) that control the synthesizer, making it create electronic sounds. The MIDI interface is already standard in drum machines, keyboards, and other electronic sound machines.

Many sound cards also contain a *digital signal processor (DSP)*. The DSP deals with the mathematical algorithms that read files, manipulate notes, and create additional sounds. It may also provide capabilities for speech recognition and multitasking (in which it allows more than one type of sound at the same time).

Remember that 16-bit cards capable of 44KHz (kilohertz) speed provide higher quality sound than the slower 8-bit (or even some slower 16-bit) cards. A sound card can also play both MIDI sounds and waveform sounds at the same time because the sounds are derived by different methods. Microsoft Windows 3.1 supports both types of sound files; it also gives you a number of options for controlling sound. In addition, you can buy special software that lets you edit and refine almost any kind of sound. Thus, you can create a "soundtrack" for animation and presentations that includes a variety of sound effects, music, and voices.

For multimedia purposes, it is wise to buy the sound card before buying the CD-ROM drive, as the sound card may determine which CD-ROM drive is compatible. Also be sure the sound card is compatible with any MIDI software you want to buy. Shop for the future, looking for a SCSI interface (or the ability to add a SCSI interface); choose a card with many voices and ranges. Most buyers also want cards that can both play and record, are compatible with both the Microsoft Windows Sound System and the sound card standard, Sound Blaster from Creative Labs.

(See 1.8 Microprocessors; 1.11 Buses; 1.18 Ports, Slots, and Bays; 1.21 Add-ins and Add-ons; 2.10 Multimedia Standards; 3.45 Multimedia Applications; Software Review section: Audioshop, Power Chords.)

1.23 Video Boards

Your system's video monitor determines the maximum resolution and the number of colors you see on a screen, but special software is needed for governing the use of those pixels and colors. Whether software or logic circuitry, this capability is stored in chips often located on a *video board*. Also called *video adapter*, *display*, or *graphics card*, this optional hardware is plugged into the motherboard or an expansion slot. The graphics board and the monitor work together, thus the monitor must have the number of pixels required to support the resolution a particular board offers. Signals from the software are sent through the card, which accepts the digital signals and converts them to signals and voltages the monitor can use.

The Macintosh is already a high-quality, graphics-based computer. Accordingly, much of the following discussion about video circuitry applies mainly to the video adapter boards used in IBM computers and compatibles.

The first display adapter, *monochrome display adapter (MDA)* for IBM-compatible PCs, supported high-resolution monochrome text, but did not support graphics or colors. In 1981, IBM introduced a graphics system called *color graphics adapter (CGA)*, which was designed primarily for use with computer games. The resolution was not sharp enough for use during extended text editing sessions. The highest graphics mode supported only two colors, but at lower resolutions, more colors were available. CGA was followed by *EGA (enhanced graphics adapter)* and *VGA (video graphics array)*. IBM's two highest video resolution standards, *8514/A* and *extended VGA (XGA)*, expand the capabilities of VGA. In addition, VESA (Video Electronic Standards Association)—a consortium of manufacturers led by NEC—introduced a protocol to compete with the later IBM standards: *SVGA (Super VGA)*, also known as *VGA plus*.

Each successive graphics capability supports more colors at higher resolutions. Standard VGA boards offer a resolution of 640-by-480 pixels. SVGA boards support resolutions of 640-by-480, 800-by-600, and 1,024-by-768 pixels, as well as 1,280-by-960 and 1,280-by-1,024 on accelerated SVGA boards.

The video adapter board also controls the *depth* of resolution. As the depth (expressed as the number of bits per pixel) increases, so does the number of colors the screen can display. The standard VGA board supports 4 bits per pixel; thus, a total of 16 different colors can be displayed simultaneously at 640-by-480 resolution. With a VGA board that supports 8 bits per pixel, 256 colors are available. Some of the higher-resolution boards offer 16- and 24-bit color modes. Displays at these resolutions offer almost photo-quality images.

VGA cards are backwardly compatible with software designed for CGA and EGA graphics levels. If a monitor has only the required number of pixels for a CGA board, however, it cannot provide higher resolutions—even if a VGA board were installed. In addition, VGA boards provide analog signals, and monitors that accept only digital signals cannot use VGA. Your monitor also produces graphics at a certain *refresh rate*, but the video board must support this refresh rate. Video boards that support high refresh rates (70Hz and over) will help reduce or eliminate annoying flicker. The amount of memory on a board determines how many colors the board can display at a particular resolution. Most boards come with 512KB of memory, but for 256 colors at the highest resolution, look for boards with at least 1 megabyte of memory.

Two types of memory may be found on a video board. The first is DRAM, like that found in your computer system. The other is *VRAM* (pronounced *vee-ram*), or *video RAM*, which is a RAM designed especially for video adapters. Unlike DRAM, it can be accessed by two different devices simultaneously. Thus, the monitor can access VRAM for current screen displays at the same time a graphics processor provides new data. VRAM provides better graphics performance than DRAM, but is more expensive. In speed, DRAM technology has all but caught up with VRAM.

Some video adapter boards contain *graphics coprocessors* (or *graphics processors*) that improve the speed of video operations, but your software or its driver must support the coprocessor in order for you to take advantage of it. Coprocessors generally support *vector graphics*—that is, graphics that use geometric formulas to produce images; they are of little help with *bit-mapped graphics* (represented by columns and rows of dots).

Because graphic images are made up of pixels, you may notice that the edges of curved and diagonal images have a "stair-step" appearance sometimes called *jaggies*. A feature of video cards known as *anti-aliasing* blends the colors of the images wherever there is an edge between two contrasting colors. With this feature, you see an illusion of smoothness, though the edges may appear fuzzy.

IBM computers and compatibles come with graphics capabilities included. (For all practical purposes, CGA and EGA are obsolete; either VGA or SVGA is commonly sold with a computer.) Most adapters offer at least two video modes: text and graphics. In *text mode*, the monitor displays only ASCII characters. In *graphics mode*, the displays are bit-mapped images. Computers with earlier graphics standards can be upgraded with the installation of a more current graphics board, as long as the monitor used with the system supports the upgraded version. Before buying anything but a standard video board, be sure drivers are available that will allow your software to work with the adapter. Some manufacturers of video adapter boards for DOS machines are ATI Technologies, Hercules Computer Technology, Diamond Computer Systems, Everex Systems, Matrox Electronic Systems, NEC Technologies, and Focus Information Systems.

The Macintosh Classic computers come with high-resolution monitors capable of graphics displays. Apple differentiates the video cards for its modular Macintosh color systems by the number of colors they can display. A 4-bit board can display 16 colors, an 8-bit board can display 256 colors, and a 24-bit board can deliver 16.7 million colors (more than your eyes can ever differentiate). Since the Macintosh is graphics-based, there is no choice between text modes and graphics modes. Usually a modular Mac's graphics capabilities can be upgraded by plugging a video board called a *video accelerator* into a NuBus slot inside the computer. (SuperMac, Radius, and RasterOps manufacture video accelerators.) High-quality video cards for graphic-arts applications include the RasterOps ProColor 32 and Lapis video cards.

Some of today's blazing-fast video cards can support 3-D modeling, animation, movies, and other complex functions. Special boards can even capture video from your VCR, camera, or videodisc player. These all include data-compression capabilities, without which the functions would be all but impossible on a computer.

(See 1.11 Buses; 1.21 Add-ins and Add-ons; 1.30 Data Compression; 1.33 Resolution; 1.34 Pixels; 1.42 Camera and Video Input; 1.46 Monitors; 3.36 Graphics Software; 3.38 Paint and Draw Programs.)

1.24 Floppy Disks

Because RAM is volatile, data and programs must reside in *permanent storage* if they are to be kept for future use. A common form of storage is the *floppy disk*, a circular platter made of a plastic material with a coating that can be magnetized. Data is stored on it as magnetized spots. Each pattern of spots matches the byte code for the character or item being stored. The data is recorded on a floppy disk in concentric *tracks* you cannot see. The disk surface is smooth. Each track is divided into *sectors*; if you could see these, they would make a pattern of wedges radiating from the center of the disk.

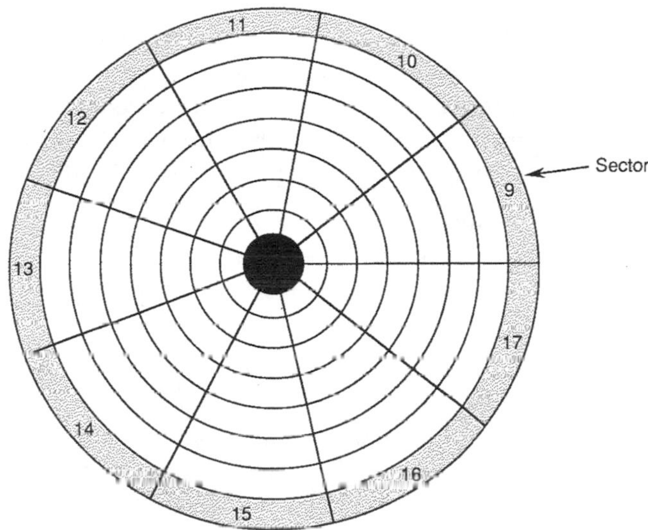

Floppy disks are laid out in tracks and sectors for easy data storage.

Floppy disks are used for *direct-access storage*, which means that data can be read at any point on the disk without passing through other, unneeded data. The user puts a floppy disk into a disk drive that spins it past a *read/write head*, which is actually an electromagnet. The drive spins the disk only when the information it contains is being accessed. When the head is *reading*, it detects the magnetized spots, changes them into electrical pulses, and sends them to the CPU. When *writing*, the head magnetizes spots on the disk. The head finds the right track and sector to read or write the data. This way, the drive finds the data without searching through the whole disk.

Disk drives are *internal* (built into the computer) or *external* (located in a separate case that is attached to the computer). They are designed to accept a particular size and density of floppy disk; you should know the specifications of the disk drive and read the package the disks come in.

A box of floppy disks might have the following information printed on it: "3.25-inch, double-sided, high-density, for use with high-density drives, 2MB, 1.44MB formatted capacity, and 135 tpi." This information not only describes the disks themselves, but also indicates generally what kind of disk drive you must use with the disks. The following paragraphs explain each characteristic.

Floppy disks measure 5.25 inches or 3.5 inches square as encased. The 5.25-inch disks have flexible vinyl jackets and can be easily dented or bent (if you value your data, they should not be); openings in the jacket expose part of the disk so the disk drive can access the data. It is important never to touch these exposed areas; you could damage data. The oval cutout is the *read/write notch* that allows the disk drive to read or write data. The small round hole is the *sector-aligning hole* that helps the drive align the disk to locate the desired data. The 3.5-inch disks, also called *diskettes* or *microfloppies*, are encased in hard plastic. A small spring-activated shutter covers the read/write notch where the disk drive accesses the disk.

Diskettes manufactured today are *double-sided*; data can be recorded on both sides. The 3.5-inch drives have two read/write heads—one for each side of the disk—and they use both sides of the disk automatically. You should always insert the disk into the disk drive with the label side up.

Disks come in a variety of densities: single, double, high, and extra-high. The *density* of a storage medium describes how much data can be packed on it. To use a disk with anything other than single-density, you must have a drive that supports the density level. *Single-density* disks are practically obsolete, however, and most of today's disks are *high-density*. High-density 5.25-inch disks can store 1.2MB of data, and high-density 3.5-inch disks can store 1.44MB of data. Some floppies can store 2.88MB of data.

The unit *tracks per inch* or *tpi* describes the density of tracks on a diskette; a common number is 135 tpi. The tracks are also divided into *sectors*. A brand-new disk, called a *blank disk*, is not divided this way. You must *format* it to match the way your microcomputer's operating system stores data. (Formatting is called *initializing* in the Macintosh computer manuals.) The formatting erases all book-keeping information on the disk, checks to be sure the sectors are reliable (not scratched or damaged in any other way), and creates *directories* or address tables that enable a drive to find data. (A drive cannot use an unformatted diskette, but formatting takes up space. Thus the amount of space left in which to store data is called the *formatted capacity*. You'll notice, for example, that a box of high-density 3.5-inch diskettes states that each diskette has 2.0MB of unformatted space—or *total capacity*—and 1.44MB of formatted space. A high-density 5.25-inch diskette has 1.2MB of formatted space.)

Disks formatted by one operating system usually cannot be read by another operating system. The exception is the *FDHD (floppy drive high-density)*, a 3.5-inch disk drive for Apple Macintosh computers that can read DOS-formatted floppy disks—provided they were formatted on FDHD drives (which are often called *SuperDrives*).

When you format a disk, any data already stored on it is essentially unavailable. Because the formatting process is selective in what it erases, however, you may be able to recover most of the data lost if you format a used disk by mistake. A computer specialist or a disk-recovery program can help you with this task.

Floppy disks have a built-in mechanism with which you can prevent loss of data or accidental reformatting. The 5.25-inch disks have a *write-enable*, or *write-protect, notch* located on the side of the jacket. When this notch is uncovered, data can be written onto the disk. If the notch is covered with a piece of tape, the disk is *write-protected*: no data can be written to or erased from the disk. The *write-protect tab* on a 3.5-inch disk is located in the top corner of the disk. It is a small plastic square (usually black) positioned within a small rectangular opening. When this piece of plastic is at the bottom of the rectangular opening, data can be written onto the disk. To protect data, you simply slide the plastic square to the top of the opening.

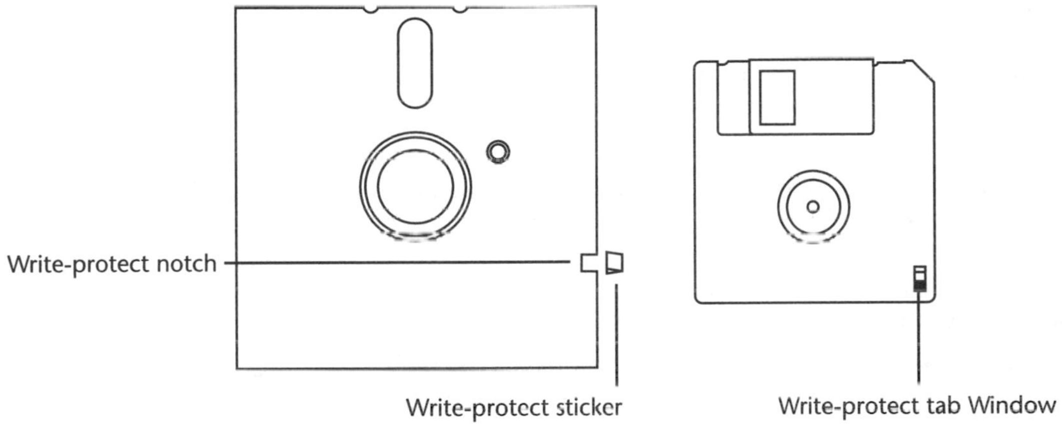

Write-protecting your floppy disks can prevent you (or someone else) from accidentally erasing or formatting over data.

The software you buy usually comes on floppy disks. Some software packages contain two sizes of disks; others contain one size and include a coupon to send in for the size disk you need. Some software, such as shareware, may still come only on the 5.25-inch disks, so you may want both 3.5-inch and 5.25-inch floppy disk drives in your computer. Software is rarely run directly from floppies on today's computers. As the price of hard disk drives decreased and they became more common, software programs got larger, making them impractical to use from floppies. Today floppies are used primarily for distributing software, backing up data and programs, and transporting files.

Most computers have at least one floppy drive included as standard equipment. The disk drive can be *full-height* or *half-height* on IBM PCs and compatibles. It's always a good idea to buy high-quality disks to help prevent disk failures and head crashing. In addition, if you are using a particular disk on a daily basis, it is a good idea to mark it with a date and transfer all the data to a new disk after three months.

(See 1.12 Memory and Storage; 1.13 Addresses; 1.28 Flopticals; 1.30 Data Compression; 2.8 Portables; 2.19 Caring for Your Disks.)

1.25 Hard Disks

Most new computers today, even notebooks, come with hard disk drives installed. The units work somewhat like floppy disk drives; read/write heads read and write data to and from the disk. Unlike a floppy disk, however, a hard disk consists of two or more rigid, metallic, circular platters. In addition, the hard disk spins as long as the power is on. As rigid disks can be spun faster without wobbling, hard disk drives are much faster than floppy disk drives. Speeds of hard drives are measured in *milliseconds (ms)*; lower numbers mean higher speeds. A speed of 85 milliseconds, for example, is slow for a hard drive; 40 ms is better, and 13 to 20 ms is fast—and desirable.

Each platter in a hard disk has two *read/write heads*, one for each side of the platter. The read/write heads cannot move independently of each other, however, because they are all attached to a single *access arm*. Each platter has the same number of *tracks*. All of the number-1 tracks on all the disk surfaces form a *cylinder*, the number-2 tracks on all surfaces form another cylinder, and so on.

The number of cylinders per hard disk equals the number of tracks per surface. When the read/write heads are reading, they detect the magnetized spots and change them into electrical pulses that are sent to the CPU. When writing, the heads magnetize spots on the disk. Most drives have *self-parking* heads so that the heads can't move and damage the disk when the computer or drive is moved.

In general, the hard disk and its drive are sealed, well protected against dust and inaccessible to the user. Some hard disk drives use removable cartridges in which the disk is sealed in a plastic or metal casing, a handy option if you need to lock up data for security reasons. Also available are completely removable hard drives. Some of these drives are rugged, designed with shock sensors, mechanical head locks, and other safety features to withstand hours in your pocket or a fall off your desk. If your computer does not have a hard disk drive, you can buy what is called a *hard card*—an expansion board that adds hard-disk capabilities to a computer. There are also external hard drives that you plug into your computer.

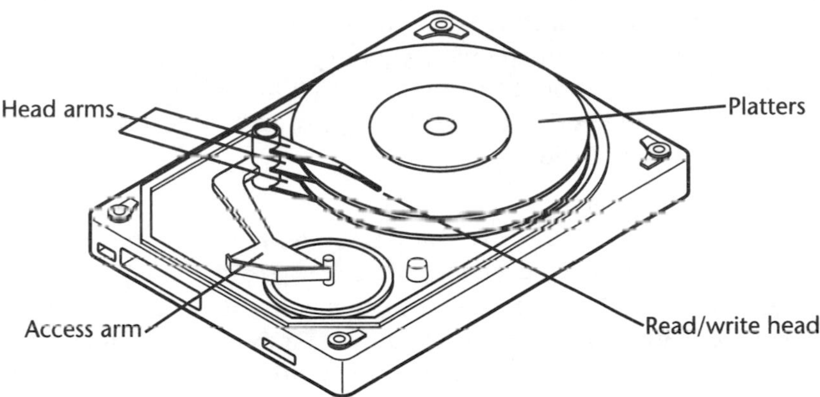

An inside look at a hard drive.

A hard disk drive allows fast access to data and holds very large amounts of data. It is almost essential for much software, including children's programs that have high-quality graphics and realistic sound. Disk capacities of 200MB up to 1.37GB are common. In fact, few manufacturers are producing hard drives of less than 200MB. Bigger hard drives are faster. Graphic artists and multimedia users will most likely need a 600MB hard drive. The access time should be 20 milliseconds or less for a computer that runs at 20MHz or faster; if your microprocessor is slower, however, the hard disk drive should be slower, too.

Today's drives also come with 64KB to 256KB caches that help increase speed. The drives come in various sizes, designed to fit in desktop systems, in notebook computers, and in *sub-notebook* and *palmtop* computers. Even the smallest of these drives have incredible amounts—up to 120MB—of storage space.

Most drives for IBM-type computers are *IDE (Integrated Drive Electronics)* or *enhanced IDE* drives. Macintosh computers use the speedy SCSI interfaces for hard drives. SCSI is available for IBM-type computers, too. You may see a reference to a *Winchester drive*, a term sometimes applied to any hard disk drive. The Winchester drive, developed by IBM, was the first popular hard disk drive technology and is used in most hard disk drives today.

Although the early hard disk drives were somewhat temperamental, today's drives are reliable and much cheaper. Hard disks do not eliminate the need for floppy disk drives, however; you still need a way to transfer new software from floppy disks onto the hard disk. In addition, backup is recommended for the data and programs on hard disk drives, partially as protection against viruses and partly as protection against machine failure. Items can be backed up individually onto floppy disks or, if you want to spend a little extra money for a tape drive, the contents of the entire hard disk can be regularly copied onto tape. Another handy (but expensive) form of backup is the *Bernoulli box*, a removable-cartridge option that uses both floppy and hard disk technologies. The actual medium is flexible, typically holding 44MB or 90MB of data. Both the drive and the cartridges are expensive compared to other disk technologies. Drives cost $1,200 to $2,500, and cartridges cost $90 to $150 each.

Probably the computer you buy will be already set up with a hard disk. If you plan to buy a new hard disk drive for your system, be sure the computer's power supply can handle it. Also check a figure called *Mean Time Between Failures (MTBF)*, which describes the mean time that a disk drive can go without failing. Approximately 300,000 to 500,000 hours is common today, and times of up to 800,000 hours (91 years) are available. (Most drive failures occur within the first 90 days of use.) As with any other piece of hardware you buy, be sure the cables, port or slot, drive, and the disk controller all work together properly.

(See 1.12 Memory and Storage; 1.13 Addresses; 1.18 Ports, Slots, and Bays; 1.19 PC Cards; 1.24 Floppy Disks; 1.28 Flopticals; 1.30 Data Compression; 1.31 Interleaving; 1.32 Caching; 2.17 Caring for Your Computer; 3.30 Utilities; 5.9 Security Measures.)

1.26 TAPES

Magnetic tapes are used in *tape backup* systems or *archiving* systems for microcomputers. (*Backing up* data means to make copies as insurance against loss or hard-disk failure. *Archiving* means to save data such as financial files or a finished report that you may need someday.) If you have many programs and large data files on a hard disk, it is a good idea to back up the entire contents of the disk onto tape to ensure against hard-drive failure. Tape backup systems operate very rapidly, so the job can be done quickly. Tapes provide *sequential access* to data, which means a tape must be searched from beginning to end, in order, if specific data is to be located. Sequential access makes data retrieval slow.

The tape itself is a magnetically coated strip of plastic, similar to tapes used for storing music. Data is recorded by magnetizing small spots on the tape's surface. Each pattern of spots matches the byte code for the character or item being stored. You cannot see the magnetized spots. The machine that reads and writes data onto a magnetic tape is called a *tape drive*. The drive moves the tape past a *read/write head* that is an electromagnet. When the head is reading, it detects the magnetized spots and changes them into electrical pulses that are sent to the CPU. When writing, the head magnetizes spots on the tape.

A tape has a very large storage capacity and is much cheaper than a disk. Most tapes designed for use with microcomputers are enclosed in plastic cartridges (or smaller versions called *minicartridges*). There are several types: *quarter-inch cartridges (QIC)*, *8-mm helical-scan* cartridges, and *4-mm DAT (digital audio tape)*. QIC tapes are those most widely used for personal computer backup systems. They are standardized and come in full-size cartridges and minicartridges. Helical-scan cartridges and DAT tapes use the same technology as VCR tapes, but DAT tapes are smaller. A DAT cartridge is slightly larger than a credit card; it can hold very large amounts of data. Tape drives for quarter-inch cartridges are less expensive than drives for helical-scan and DAT tapes.

Tape drives can be installed internally or attached as an external peripheral. Colorado Memory Systems, Inc., CMS Enhancements, Inc., Maynard Electronics, Inc., and Tallgrass Technologies Corporation are among the companies that manufacture tape drives. Many manufacturers build tape drive units capable of *data compression*, which increases the amount of material a tape can hold.

(See 1.12 Memory and Storage; 1.14 Access Time; 1.30 Data Compression.)

1.27 CD-ROMs and Optical Storage

Optical disks, or laser disks, need laser beams, thin beams of concentrated light, to store and read data. The beam produces pits in a thin layer of metal or polymer on the disk. Another laser beam in the optical disk drive shines on the disk and detects the pits by the changes in the way the light is reflected. Unlike floppy disks, optical disks can better withstand wear, fingerprints, and dust. They can store a great deal of data—more than 800 times the amount on typical floppies—and they store text, graphics, video, and sound all in one. They are slower than magnetic disks and you do need to purchase special drives to use the various types of optical disks. There are three types of optical disks: CD-ROM, WORM, and erasable optical. Each is suited to a particular purpose, and each requires its own type of disk drive.

You probably know already about the compact discs (CDs) that are used for sound recording. The CD-ROM (compact disc-read-only memory) is like a compact disc, and is also like ROM memory in a computer because items on it cannot be changed. CD-ROMs hold very large amounts of data (more than 680MB); they are therefore used for storing information like that found in encyclopedias and dictionaries. (Increasingly, software—especially game software—is being sold on CD-ROMs.) When you purchase a CD-ROM, it already has the information recorded on it, and your CD-ROM drive (called a CD-ROM *reader*) only reads the data from the disk.

One advantage of the CD-ROM drive is that usually it can play audio CDs. CD-ROM readers are more expensive than CD players, however, because they are built to be more rugged, have better interfaces, and must be able to read data much more accurately. Like CD players, they may come in "jukebox" form, able to hold (and switch among) several disks.

WORM stands for *write once, read many*. Data can be written to this disk just one time, but the data can be read many times. So far, there has been no evidence of deterioration of the WORM disks or the data stored on them. For this reason, WORM disks are used by libraries for mass archive storage. Because WORM disks hold so much data, you can save your work often and can read previous drafts through WORM software, even though all the drafts have been saved under the same name. WORM disks cannot be read by CD-ROM drives, and WORM drives are more expensive than CD-ROM drives.

Erasable *optical* disks, also called *magneto-optical* disks, can be written to, read, and erased. Because they are rewritable, these disks are ideal for use when you are creating documents. Erasable optical-disk drives are the most expensive type of optical disk drives on the market. Their speed is comparable to that of floppy drives, but much slower than that of hard disk drives. The drives write using magnetic technology and read using laser technology. They are reliable and safe from disk crashes. The disks hold up to 1GB each.

CD-ROM disks are relatively standardized, but as yet there are no standards for the other types of optical disks. WORM disks recorded with one manufacturer's WORM drive may not be readable on another's WORM drive, and the same is true for magneto-optical disks.

Access time is improving on today's optical disk drives, and more are capable of *continuous read*, which means animations do not jerk and data transfer is better. For multimedia purposes, consider a CD-ROM drive of under 200ms, at least. That is, look for *double-* or *triple-speed* drives. Remember that you'll want the drive to keep up with new software being released.

You should also consider a couple of other factors. Look for front-mounted jacks for earphones. Also check for dust-protection features. To eliminate the problem of dust preventing the read head from doing its job, many manufacturers of optical disk drives are including self-cleaning lenses and double-sealed drive enclosures. As the SCSI interface (common on CD-ROM drives) has many variations, be sure to check that the connection on the drive you want to buy is compatible with your computer. The price you pay for any one of these drives is not based on the amount of data it can handle, but on the speed with which it handles the access.

(See 1.12 Memory and Storage; 2.10 Multimedia Standards; 3.45 Multimedia Applications; 5.9 Security Measures; Software Review section: Compton's Multimedia Encyclopedia.)

1.28 Flopticals

Floptical disks look about the same as the standard 3.5-inch floppy disk, but if you open the metal shutter, you will see that the disk inside looks more like a CD-ROM disk than a floppy. Flopticals are a lot more expensive than floppies, running from $25 to almost $50 each (compared with the cost of a floppy at about $2 to $5), but then you can store about 21MB on one; a high-density floppy can store only 1.2 to 1.44MB.

Floptical technology combines normal magnetic recording with optical-alignment mechanisms. Each disk has been stamped with grooves that allow laser light to precisely align the read write heads with the proper tracks and sectors. This precision enables a floptical to hold a great deal of data. Capacity is increased not only by the number of tracks per inch, but also by the number of bits that can be squeezed together side by side. Once the proper track and sector is located, the read/write mechanism reads or writes the data as it would on an ordinary floppy disk. The floptical is coated with the same magnetic material as a floppy disk.

One problem with flopticals is that it takes about 25 minutes to format one. On the plus side, flopticals provide faster access than floppy disk drives. In addition, today's floptical disk drives will read from and write to ordinary 3.5-inch floppy disks, but at the same storage capacity as a normal floppy disk drive. Most users buy floptical disk drives for backup and archiving purposes, but you can add a floptical disk drive to an older IBM/DOS computer in order to use 3.5-inch disks. Other users find flopticals handy for storing graphics and sound files that normally take up a lot of space on another type of storage device.

(See 1.12 Memory and Storage; 1.24 Floppy Disks; 1.27 CD-ROMs and Optical Storage; 5.9 Security Measures.)

1.29 RAM Disks

Accessing data on disks is relatively slow compared to the speed at which a microprocessor can manipulate data. To approach a microprocessor's speed, software engineers have developed a software means of using RAM to simulate a disk drive. The result is called a *RAM disk*. The computer sets aside storage space in RAM to function like a disk, and then treats the configured RAM just as if it were a disk drive. Configuring RAM to act as a disk drive is sometimes done through the operating system. On an IBM system, you would set up the drive by editing the CONFIG.SYS file (the DOS documentation explains how to do it). On a Macintosh system, the RAM disk is like any other application: it merely runs when it is selected. (RAM disks are also available as third-party utilities, and were once purchased on separate cards that included extra RAM chips.)

The advantage of using RAM disks is speed. Data stored in RAM can be transferred from one part of RAM to another much faster than it can be transferred from a hard disk to RAM. Thus, a RAM disk is especially useful for applications that require frequent disk access, such as occasions when you need to open and close several files often during a computer session. The disadvantage of RAM disks is that they require a continuous power supply. As with any RAM memory, when the power supply is discontinued, data is erased from the RAM disk. Some manufacturers provide battery backup units for use with RAM disks in case of power failure. As CPUs and hard-drive access speed up, RAM disks are becoming obsolete. They hardly seem worth the risk of data loss.

(See 1.12 Memory and Storage; 1.15 RAM.)

1.30 DATA COMPRESSION

Data compression is a method of packing data into less space than normal, and in fact, is sometimes called data packing. It is especially useful for communications because it enables devices to send the same amount of data in fewer bits. A few of the methods have been standardized.

Large software packages come compressed onto floppy disks, and must be *decompressed* during installation onto the hard drive. The installation program takes care of this process. Data compression is frequently the solution if your computer's hard disk is too small, though special software is needed for this purpose. The software to compress data may come as a software package or as a data-compression system on an expansion board called a *compression board*. Data compression shrinks the data automatically while reading it to storage (eliminating unnecessary information), and unpacks the data (restoring it to its full form) when reading it into RAM. There are a number of methods for packing data, but because of the special mathematics being used, packed files can be read only by the program that packed them.

Data compression is also used for telecommunications to increase speed and decrease costs. Common compression formats for this purpose on IBM computers and compatibles are ARC and ZIP—and on the Macintosh computers, StuffIt. Many high-speed modems use a compression protocol called *MNP (Microcom Networking Protocol)*.

All of the preceding techniques are basically for text compression, however. The leading standards in image compression are *JPEG* (pronounced *jay-peg*) for still pictures and *MPEG* (*em-peg*) for moving images. JPEG finds ways of removing nonessential material from a single image, and MPEG looks for redundancies in neighboring images in a series of video frames. MPEG records a few frames in detail, describing others by the way they differ from the detailed frames. On playback, some information is missing from the images, but the eye is fooled into seeing detail that does not exist.

(See 1.24 Floppy Disks; 1.25 Hard Disks; 1.42 Camera and Video Input; 3.28 Files; 3.30 Utilities; 4.4 Communication Software.)

1.31 Interleaving

Interleaving is a method that makes both storage and memory more efficient. When used in reference to disks, it describes the way the sectors on a disk are organized. Rather than formatting the disk so that the sectors are consecutively numbered all around the disk, interleaving formats the disk so that the sectors are staggered; intervening sectors occur between consecutively numbered sectors.

Interleaving is useful because of the way the disk drive accesses data. A disk drive can access only one sector at a time, but since the disk is constantly spinning, it may have already spun past the next sector to be accessed. Therefore, it must make a complete rotation to access the next section of a file. If the sectors are numbered alternately, on the other hand, the disk will be positioned to access the data.

Sectors are numbered consecutively skipping over no sectors, one sector, or two sectors. You can change the *interleave factor* in some operating systems, but in doing so, you will probably destroy all the data on the disk. There are special utility programs that enable you to change the interleaving factor without destroying data.

Interleaving is also a method of sectioning memory. This technique makes the CPU more efficient because it is often faster than the memory chips. Thus, instead of waiting for memory to "catch up," the CPU can access data by alternating its access operations between sections of memory.

(See 1.12 Memory and Storage; 1.15 RAM; 1.25 Hard Disks.)

1.32 Caching

Caching is a method that improves the access time to memory or storage. *Cache* (pronounced *cash*) *memory* is a portion of memory (usually 256KB) used to speed the processing operations of a computer. It is also called a *high-speed buffer*, *instruction cache*, *cache store*, or *RAM cache*. It can be made up of the higher-speed SRAM rather than the slower and cheaper DRAM used for most memory. The computer can access items stored in cache memory much faster than it can access items in normal RAM. Thus, the data and instructions that are accessed most often in a program are transferred to cache memory. The program simply looks ahead, tries to anticipate what instructions and data must be accessed often, and places these in cache memory for faster access by the CPU. Some memory caches are built into the microprocessor—for example, the Intel 80486 microprocessor has 8KB of primary cache memory. Cache memory helps the speed of memory keep up with the speed of the microprocessor.

Disk caching is similar to memory caching, only it makes use of conventional DRAM memory. The disk cache is basically a *terminate-and-stay-resident program (TSR)*. Essentially, it keeps the most recently used data from a disk stored in a *memory buffer*, a temporary 256KB-to-2MB storage area in RAM. When a program needs to access data from a disk, it first checks the *disk cache*, or *RAM disk*, to see if the data it needs is there. Using a memory cache or a disk cache can dramatically improve speeds because accessing data in any kind of RAM is much faster than accessing data from a disk.

(See 1.8 Microprocessors; 1.12 Memory and Storage; 1.15 RAM; 1.29 RAM Disks; 3.29 Memory-Resident Programs.)

1.33 RESOLUTION

Resolution means clarity or sharpness. The term is used in describing the capabilities of scanners, video boards, mice, and other input devices, as well as the images produced by monitors and printers. The resolution of printers and scanners is indicated in *dots per inch (dpi)*. A printer that is advertised with 300 dpi will print 300 dots in a line 1 inch long. The resolution of a monitor, on the other hand, is described in *pixels*, or dots, over the entire screen. For example, a resolution of 640-by-480 means that there are 640 pixels on each of 480 lines. The more pixels per line, the higher the resolution.

The maximum resolution of a monitor is determined by the monitor itself, not by the video card. A video card that governs a resolution lower than that which the monitor supports, however, does not let you take advantage of the greatest resolution possible with that monitor. Similarly, using a high-resolution video card does not improve output on a low-resolution monitor.

Although resolution is often described as high, medium, or low, the actual range of these descriptions changes as the technology improves. In addition, other factors can influence the clarity or sharpness of an image. For example, a monitor display can look sharp if it has a small *dot pitch* (distance between pixels), a high *refresh rate* (the speed with which the image is re-energized or redrawn), and well-controlled *convergence* (the degree to which the dots in a pixel come together). A printer or scanner with an *optical*, or base, resolution of 300 dpi can appear to have a higher resolution through a process called *interpolation*—a method of increasing resolution through special software algorithms used to "guess" where the extra dots would be placed if, in fact, the resolution *were* 600 dpi.

(See 1.23 Video Boards; 1.34 Pixels; 1.35 Gray Scaling; 1.41 Scanners; 1.46 Monitors; 1.48 Flat-Panel Displays; 1.49 Printers; 1.50 Print Quality; 3.36 Graphics Software.)

1.34 Pixels

The word *pixel* is short for *picture element*. A pixel is a single point in a graphic image. Pixels are arranged in rows and columns in the display screen, but appear to be connected. Each pixel may be represented by more than one bit. The more bits per pixel, the more colors or shades of gray the monitor can display. An 8-bit color monitor uses 8 bits per pixel, thus can display 256 different colors or shades of gray.

On color monitors, each pixel is actually made up of three dots—one each of red, blue, and green. The degree to which the dots converge at the same point determines how fuzzy the pixels look. All monitors have some *convergence* errors, but some have less noticeable problems than others.

(See 1.33 Resolution; 1.35 Gray Scaling; 1.46 Monitors; 1.47 Evaluating a Monitor; 1.48 Flat-Panel Displays.)

1.35 Gray Scaling

Gray scaling is a term associated with monitors and scanners. It describes the use of shades of gray to represent an image. Shades of gray are created by activating one, two, three, or more of the bits in one pixel. In black-and-white photographs, you would see an unlimited number of shades of gray (called *continuous tone*), but computer equipment can only represent a few—typically 16 to 256—in the process called gray scaling.

Gray scaling requires a great deal of memory, but improves the monitor's output. If you are using an optical scanner capable of gray scaling, your monitor or printer should also be capable of gray scaling; otherwise, gray scaling is useless. Most color monitors can display gray scaling, but not with as high a quality as dedicated gray-scale monitors.

Typical monochrome monitors, on the other hand, simulate gray scaling by the density and pattern of single pixels. A black-and-white newspaper photograph can illustrate how this technique works. If you look closely at the photograph, you will see that it is made up of tiny black dots whose density determines the light and dark spots of the photograph. On a monitor, the technique is called *dithering*.

(See 1.33 Resolution; 1.41 Scanners; 1.46 Monitors; 1.47 Evaluating a Monitor; 1.49 Printers.)

1.36 CURSORS

A *cursor* is a vital part of input operations that depend on a screen; it indicates your location on the screen. It is generally a solid, highlighted rectangle, a blinking underline character, or a vertical line that shows where the next character will be displayed on the screen; sometimes it is called the text cursor. You can move the cursor throughout the screen by using the arrow keys or a mouse. The arrow keys are often called *cursor-control keys*. Some programs have a *status line* that indicates the cursor position. For example, the status line in a word processor may show that the cursor is in line 5, column 15.

Other cursors called *pointers* are designed for special purposes. The pointer moves as you move a mouse. These pointers are sometimes called *mouse cursors*, because they are used for selecting items with a mouse. They are usually operational at the same time as the text cursor. The Macintosh, a graphics-based system, for example, has a number of pointers, including the arrow and the I-beam. The arrow, for example, enables you to select options from the menu or on the ruler at the top of the screen; the I-beam shows the movement of the mouse so you can go to a new location on the screen, and is helpful in marking blocks of text. In some spreadsheet programs, the pointer is a long solid rectangle that highlights the particular value, formula, or label you are working on.

(See 1.37 Keyboards; 1.38 Mice and Trackballs; 1.46 Monitors.)

1.37 KEYBOARDS

The *keyboard* lets you input words, numbers, and commands. You use the keyboard much like a regular typewriter. When you use a keyboard, what you are doing is normally called *keyboarding*, or *keying in*, rather than typing. Each press of a key is called a *keystroke*. When you hold down a key on the computer keyboard, its character or function is repeated until you release it. Because of this feature, be sure that you hold down a key just long enough for the character to appear on the screen or for the computer to receive the command.

There are two basic arrangements of keys for typing: QWERTY and Dvorak. The name QWERTY derives from the first six characters from the left on the top row of letter keys. The *Dvorak* keyboard was designed so that the most frequently used keys are in the middle row of the keyboard. A number of computers enable you to choose between the two keyboards. Although the Dvorak is designed for speed, the QWERTY layout continues to dominate because most people have already learned to type on QWERTY typewriters.

Most of the keys on a computer keyboard work the same way as a typewriter's keys. The **Spacebar** makes a blank space. Use it just as you would use the one on a typewriter, to put spaces between words and sentences. Pressing the **Shift** key with a letter key makes a capital letter. Pressing the Shift key with a number or symbol key produces the symbol shown on the top half of the key. If you want to type all capital letters, press the **Caps Lock** key. Press Caps Lock again to stop typing all capital letters. (The Caps Lock key is called a *toggle* key because it has only two positions, and you can switch back and forth between the two settings.) Caps Lock affects only the letter keys. You must still use the Shift key if you want to type an exclamation mark rather than a 1, for example. The **Tab** key operates similarly to the typewriter's Tab key: When you press it, the cursor moves to the next tab stop that has been set.

You see that the keyboard also has special keys described as follows:

- The **Enter** key has two purposes. It can act like a *carriage return* lever or key on a typewriter by moving the cursor to a new line for making lists or starting new paragraphs. It also is used to tell the computer to go ahead and process the data or commands that have been typed. On Macintosh computers, the Enter key is labeled **Return**.
- The **Backspace** key (**Delete** key on Macintosh computers) lets you erase a character. It moves the cursor to the left, erasing each character as it moves.
- The **Esc** key is used to escape, or leave, whatever you are starting to do.
- The **arrow** keys are used to move the cursor up, down, to the left, or to the right, without removing characters as the cursor moves.
- The **Home** key, in combination with other keys, returns the cursor to the beginning of a document or line, or the top of the screen.
- The **End** key puts the cursor at the end of a document, line, or screen.
- The **Page Up** key scrolls to a previous screenful of work.
- The **Page Down** key scrolls to the next screenful of work.
- Some computers have a **Print Screen** key that enables you to print a paper copy of whatever is currently displayed on the screen; the user need not type special key combination codes.

- Pressing the **Help** key (which may be the F1 function key) results in a display of instructions for doing a task you don't understand.

Most desktop computers also have *numeric keypads* located next to their alphabetic keyboards. Keypads are used like the keys on a calculator for simple math functions and numeric data entry. They contain the characters **0** through **9**, a decimal point, arithmetic functions, an **Enter** key, and a **Num Lock** key that enables you to use the keys for cursor control.

Most keyboards, excepting some of Apple's products, also have function keys labeled **F1**, **F2**, **F3**, and so on. These keys provide a method by which you issue commands to the computer. They may be used, for example, to start a print job, save a program, or display a menu.

Other keys such as the **Control** key and Apple **Command** (flower) key are used in combination with other keys to provide shortcuts or choose a menu command. For example, pressing the **P** key by itself yields the letter *p* on the screen, but pressing the **P** key with the **Control** key may start the printer. Pressing the **Shift** and Apple **Command** (flower) keys with the **B** key might enable you to produce boldfaced characters. Always read the software manuals to learn the functions of a key or combination of keys; the functions may vary from program to program. Some manufacturers, including FuncKey Enterprises, sell *templates*, or overlays, for your keyboard that define the functions of special keys and key combinations. The templates are available for popular programs such as WordPerfect.

Keyboards for microcomputers are available in one of two forms. They can be built into the computer casing or detached from it. Laptop, notebook, and palmtop computers have keyboards designed in the computer casing. Some early desktop computers had the keyboard in the same unit as the computer. Detached keyboards on desktop models may be either connected to the computer by a cord or operated remotely by batteries. Battery-operated keyboards are linked with the CPU through infrared or radio-frequency transmitters.

The angle of the keyboard is important. Keyboards that are part of the machine's enclosure cannot be adjusted; typing for long periods of time on these can be tiresome. Detachable keyboards usually adjust to two or more positions. Keyboard touch is another consideration. Most microcomputers have standard touch-sensitive keys similar to electronic typewriter keys. The feel of the keys and the "thipping" sound vary from keyboard to keyboard, but the standard touch-sensitive keys on most computers make a quieter noise than typewriter keys. Some systems let you adjust your keyboard to respond to a light or heavy typing touch. If you don't like the keyboard that comes with your system, you can purchase a keyboard separately from third-party companies.

The keys on most desktop models travel 4 mm to the bottom as you depress them, but on some of the new notebook computers, the depth of depression is as slight as 2 mm. Otherwise, the keyboards on laptop and notebook computers approximate the keyboards on desktop models. The spacing is generally the same between keys, as is their size, but the location of function keys may vary among the different brands. Of necessity, separate numeric keypads are not included, but they can be purchased as external devices to plug into the computer. Most notebook computers have an embedded numeric keypad mode; you can change the function of a set of existing keys to perform "calculator" functions.

(See 1.36 Cursors; 2.8 Portables; 2.17 Caring for Your Computer; 5.16 Ergonomics.)

1.38 Mice and Trackballs

You can buy a number of different input tools that enable you to bypass the keyboard while entering commands or using graphics software. Among the most commonly used are the mouse and its variation, the trackball. These devices let you use natural arm or hand motions to move the cursor. They sense your motions and change the signals into electrical pulses, which they send through cables to the computer. The mouse has increased in use with the growing popularity of *graphical user interfaces (GUIs)* such as Microsoft Windows. It is standard equipment on all Macintosh computers, which have used a GUI from the very beginning.

The *mouse* is a small plastic object about the size of a bar of soap. You roll it over a smooth surface such as a *mouse pad* in order to move the cursor on the screen. A mouse usually has a ball bearing about the size of a medium-sized marble underneath it that senses your motions. (Some mice operate by light sensors rather than ball bearings. These *optical mice*, or *pucks*, must be used with a special gridded mat that provides a frame of reference corresponding to the screen.) You also push or hold down the one, two, or three buttons on the mouse to send commands through its "tail" (which is plugged into the computer) to the CPU. Moving the cursor to a particular location on the screen and then pressing the button to activate a command is referred to as *pointing and clicking*. Holding down a button while moving the mouse is called *dragging*; you can use this method to select large amounts of text, use a menu bar, or move an icon. In graphics programs, the mouse can be used somewhat like a pen, pencil, or paintbrush to draw images on the screen. Generally, you can adjust the mouse to respond quickly or slowly to tracking and clicking by using a menu.

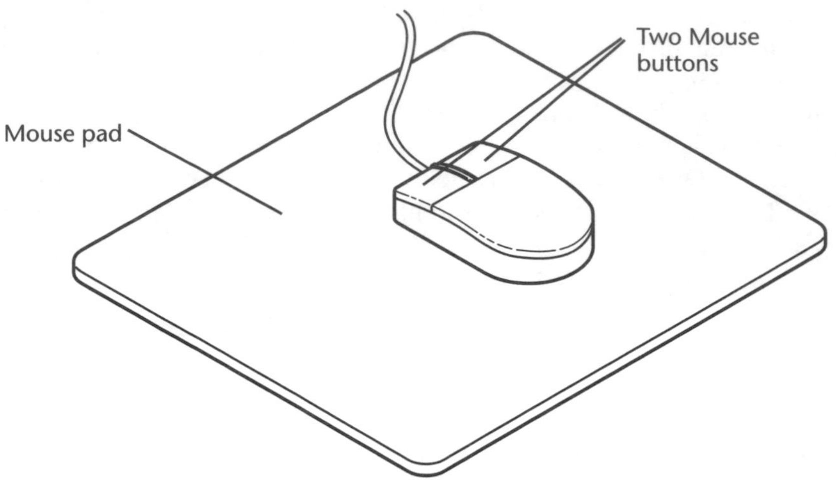

A mouse.

In reading about mice, you may be surprised to see the devices described in terms of resolution since they actually do not display images. Mouse resolution tells the number of pixels that can be detected with each inch of mouse movement and is usually described in dots per inch. With a high-resolution mouse, you can identify points on the screen more accurately but you also will have to move the mouse a greater distance to move the cursor. Some mice have several resolution options.

There are two types of mouse attachments. One is the serial mouse that plugs into an unused serial port in the back of the computer. The other—the bus mouse—attaches to a card inserted in an unused slot inside the computer. Mice for Macintosh computers operate through the *ADB (Apple Desktop Bus)* port, usually by being plugged into the keyboard.

If you have played video games, you may be familiar with the *trackball* or *tracker ball*—a roller-bearing mouse, upside down. The ball bearing, about the size of a Ping-Pong ball or large marble, rests on top of a base. Rather than move the whole device, you simply spin the ball with the palm of your hand, your thumb, or your fingers. Under the ball are sensors that pick up your motions and send the signals to the computer. Like mice, trackballs include from one to three buttons.

Trackballs eliminate the numerous "swiping" motions often needed to move the cursor from one side of the screen to the other without sliding the mouse clear across the length of the desk. They require less space than mice; because of the popularity of GUIs, increasingly trackballs are built into the keyboards of notebook computers.

Detachable trackballs are also available especially for use with portables. Many users claim that trackballs give them a finer degree of cursor control.

An alternative to these devices is the *voice mouse*, which lets you speak commands such as "File, open" rather than manually operate a mouse. The voice mouse is a software technique that requires a system equipped with a sound card and a microphone. A second option, the *mouse pad*, is not to be confused with the mat on which you roll a mouse. It is a small area in the keyboard that detects your touch and sends signals to the computer to move the cursor accordingly. No mechanical roller device is necessary. A third mouse option is the *mouse pen*, which is held like a pen and rolled.

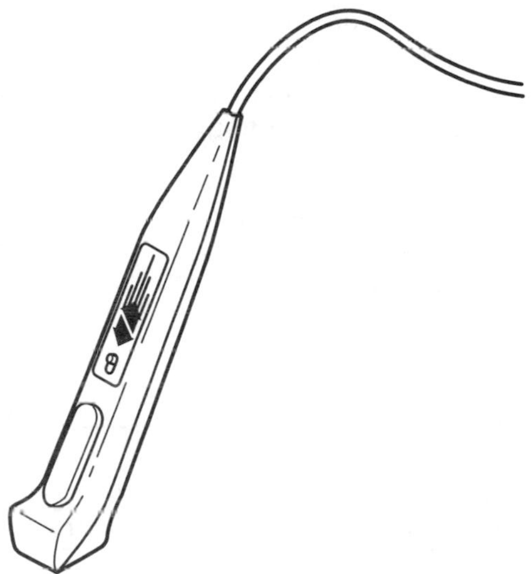

A mouse pen.

Before buying mice or trackballs, test the ones you like by sitting down at the computer and trying them. You cannot administer a true test while standing. Although the mouse can be picked up and repositioned rather than moved in one stroke, you may want to test how far you must move the mouse to move an arrow pointer one inch on the screen. In addition, any mouse package you purchase should include *mouse-driver* software for controlling device operation.

(See 1.18 Ports, Slots, and Bays; 1.20 Controllers and Drivers; 1.21 Add-ins and Add-ons; 1.33 Resolution; 1.36 Cursors; 1.39 Joysticks and Light Pens; 1.40 Graphics Tablets; 2.8 Portables; 2.17 Caring for Your Computer; 3.3 Telling the Computer What to Do: User Interfaces; 3.36 Graphics Software.)

1.39 Joysticks and Light Pens

Two other devices that rely on natural hand or arm movements are joysticks and light pens. Joysticks are used primarily with games and graphics software, but are found occasionally on some CAD/CAM systems. A *joystick* is a lever mounted on a base that holds two buttons called *triggers*. These buttons operate much as the buttons do on mice and trackballs. The joystick may remind you of a floor-mounted gearshift on a car. Unlike the gearshift, which slides into preset positions, a joystick moves freely.

A *light pen* is a pen-shaped object with a light-sensitive cell at its end. It is used in conjunction with the screen. You touch it to the screen to select items from menus or alter graphs and other drawings. Unlike joysticks and trackballs, which are often used for entertainment applications, light pens are used more often in highly technical fields for working on graphics, maps, and engineering plans. They are more precise than mice because the light-sensitive detector can recognize individual pixels.

(See 1.20 Controllers and Drivers; 1.36 Cursors; 1.38 Mice and Trackballs; 1.40 Graphics Tablets; 1.46 Monitors; 3.36 Graphics Software; 3.37 Presentation Graphics; 3.38 Paint and Draw Programs.)

1.40 Graphics Tablets

Graphics tablets, also called *digitizers*, are flat, boardlike surfaces directly connected to a computer display. You draw on the tablet using a stylus or a puck, during which the image is transmitted to the display. The graphics tablet puck is a cursor device similar to a mouse that has a window through which crosshairs are visible. The puck may have as many as 16 buttons. The stylus has an electronic nib, rather than an ink-dispensing nib. Your hand movements using a stylus may be smoother and less jerky than they would be with the puck (or even with a mouse or joystick), because you already know how to write smoothly with a pen and paper. Most current graphics tablets support a *mouse-emulation mode* that enables you to use the stylus or puck as you would the mouse.

The tablet itself contains electronics that enable it to detect your movements with the stylus or puck and transfer the signals it picks up to the computer. There is a one-to-one correspondence between each point on the graphics tablet and each point on the display screen. A graphics tablet enables you to employ colors, textures, and patterns when creating images. It can be especially effective if you need to trace drawings.

(See 1.36 Cursors; 1.38 Mice and Trackballs; 1.46 Monitors; 3.36 Graphics Software; 3.38 Paint and Draw Programs.)

1.41 SCANNERS

Scanners, sometimes called *optical scanners*, are devices that read printed material (in a manner similar to that of copy machines) so it can be put in computer-readable form without your having to retype, redraw, reprint, or rephotograph the material. They work by illuminating the image and measuring the light being reflected from it. Scanners have become very popular for use with microcomputers, especially since desktop publishing applications have made their debut. They are available for color, conventional black-and-white, and gray-scaling purposes. (Color scanners support gray scaling and black-and-white modes, so you may want to pay more now for the more versatile option, rather than having to buy a second scanner later.)

A scanner *digitizes* an image or text—that is, it divides the image into a grid of boxes in which each box is represented by a zero or a one, depending on whether the box is filled in. The result is a *bit map*, which can be stored or displayed on a screen. The denser the bit map, the higher the resolution. Scanner resolutions range from 70 *dpi (dots per inch)* to 600 dpi. Low-resolution scanning is usually faster than high-resolution scanning, but may be less accurate. A scanner that supports several resolutions will enable you to select the resolution that works best for each type of job.

To manipulate the bit-mapped images once they are inside your computer, special software is required. You can edit either text or pictures. To edit text that has been entered by scanning, you need *optical-character recognition (OCR)* software. On machines that support ASCII characters, the software translates a bit-mapped character image into an ASCII character that can then be edited with word processing software. Scanners, especially the low-cost ones, do not recognize all typefaces; even with the best of scanners, you should proofread the material. Sometimes, capital Os are mistaken for zeroes, and so on. Some OCR software checks for spelling and flags suspicious words. If you are using OCR software from a manufacturer other than the scanner's maker, be sure the two are compatible.

Because a scanned image is already bit-mapped, usually you can edit pictures with graphics software. Always be sure that the scanning software can save an image in the file format your graphics or desktop publishing program supports. During editing, you can reduce or enlarge the image, add or subtract sections, redraw parts, and so on. Editing should be judged by the way the image looks in its final form, whether hard copy or soft copy. For example, if the image will be printed in a paper newsletter, print a sample copy of the image before you finish editing. In addition, you may want to experiment with originals versus photocopies. Remember that scanned images require a great deal of memory. An 8.5-by-11-inch photograph, for example, scanned at 300 dpi in 256 shades of gray, requires over 8MB of memory.

Scanners come in a number of forms. Some are small *hand-held* devices that you move across a page. Typically these scan a width of only four inches at a time, and are difficult to use if you need to scan an entire page or a large photograph. These small scanners are sometimes called *half-page* scanners. Their advantage has been cost, but considering the decreasing cost of *full-page* scanners (and the alignment problems of using hand-held models), you may be better off buying a full-page scanner unless you have a specific need for a portable hand-held device.

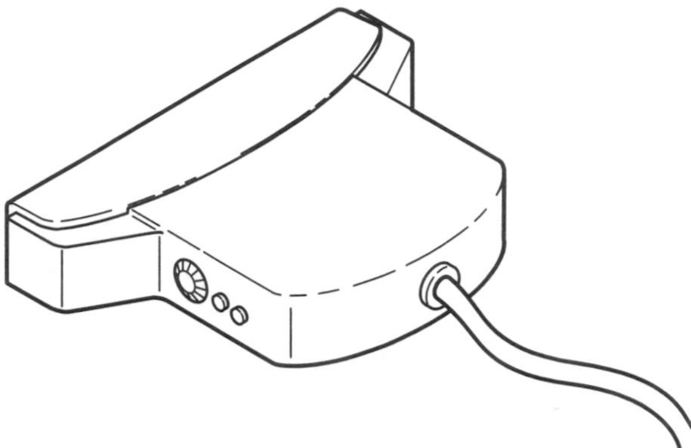

Hand-held scanners are inexpensive, but they can be difficult to use.

Two common types of full-page scanners are sheet-fed and flatbed models. *Sheet-fed* scanners work somewhat the opposite of printers. Rather than transferring the digitized data in the computer to paper that slides out of a printer, the scanner reads the image on the paper copy you feed in, translating it into computer-usable form. Small sheet-fed scanners, 12.5-by-3 inches, are designed for portable use. A *flatbed* scanner resembles a copy machine. The page is laid upside down on a glass, and is then read by a scanning device that moves under the glass. The advantage of the flatbed scanner is, of course, that you can scan material from books and periodicals as well as from single sheets of paper.

The scanner is attached to your computer either through a *port*, such as the SCSI port, or by installing an *interface card* in one of your computer's slots. The scanning software may be installed automatically or by loading from a disk. Many OCR and image-manipulation systems consist of both logic circuitry (on special add-on boards) and software loaded into the computer's memory.

Before buying a scanner, check its accuracy in reading text. Also check a scanned image for clarity, *banding* (appearance of unwanted lines or "ribbons" across an image), and *artifacts* (blips or other unwanted marks). You may also want to check the color or grays of the screen or printer output against the original scanned image.

Scanned images and text should not be used indiscriminately. Material found in published sources is copyrighted, and the copyright holders are becoming increasingly vigilant about unauthorized use of their material. Instead, use your own photographs, original art, or clip art—or write for permission to use the work.

(See 1.18 Ports, Slots, and Bays; 1.21 Add-ins and Add-ons; 1.33 Resolution; 1.35 Gray Scaling; 3.28 Files; 3.36 Graphics Software; 5.11 Copyright and Piracy.)

1.42 Camera and Video Input

With a digital camera, you can shoot pictures and download the results via cable into your computer. Using your graphics software, you can edit the pictures and prepare them for desktop publishing or multimedia presentations. (You'll have to check to be sure the file formats of the cameras are compatible with the file formats of your graphics program.) The quality of photos taken with conventional cameras is greater than the quality of digital photos. Camera memory may be small, and you cannot selectively erase photos in some brands. The camera is convenient, however, and fun to use. (By the way, for cheaper still-photography input, you can have your regular camera film processed onto a CD-ROM for use with a CD-ROM drive.)

Digital cameras take still shots; for multimedia, you may want to use movies. For this purpose, you can install a *video-capture board*, also called a *motion-capture board*. One of the hardest jobs a personal computer can do, however, is to deal with motion video. Like film, video consists of a sequence of still frames that are played at high speed to create the illusion of motion. Film rates are 24 frames per second. For a computer to duplicate this speed in 16-bit color for full-screen display at 640-by-480 resolution, it would need a great deal of memory and speed. In addition, a 10-minute film would take up all of a 1GB hard drive.

To deal with the vast amount of data, the video-capture board uses *compression/decompression (CODEC) algorithms*—either from software or from a coprocessor chip such as a *digital signal processor (DSP)*. It can accept video and audio from video cameras, VCRs, or videodisc players. Using the software that comes with the board, you can control the brightness, contrast, and sharpness of the image. Special filters for improving the image may also be available. After the video is stored on your hard drive, you can use special *film-editing* software to edit the movie for presentation.

(See 1.8 Microprocessors; 1.21 Add-Ins and Add-Ons; 1.30 Data Compression; 2.10 Multimedia Standards; 3.39 Moving Pictures; 3.45 Multimedia Applications.)

1.43 Speech Recognition

Speech recognition, also called *voice recognition*, is the capability of a computer system to accept spoken input. It implies that the computer can take dictation, but cannot understand the meaning of what is being said.

Speech processing changes the analog input of speech into a representation of speech. It generally involves comparing a spoken sound against stored speech models. To use speech processing, you talk into a microphone, which converts the changes in air pressure from that speech into voltage variations. The system samples the variations and then digitizes them.

Research in speech recognition occurs in three major areas: speaker-dependence versus speaker-independence, discrete words versus continuous speech, and vocabulary size and grammar complexity. A *speaker-dependent* system is one in which you must "train" the system to recognize your voice, but once the system accepts a voice, it also recognizes a large vocabulary. A *speaker-independent* system recognizes many voices, but few words. The distinctions between the two will fade as systems are invented that recognize many words and many speakers. With today's voice-recognition systems, you must speak clearly and pause slightly between words. This is called *discrete speech*. Only experimental systems accept flowing, or conversational, speech of any vocabulary beyond 50 words or so.

Speech recognition systems are expensive; thus they are used primarily for specialized applications. As costs go down and capabilities improve, voice interfaces will enable you—the everyday computer user—to command the computer by speaking rather than by using key commands or a mouse. Good speech recognition systems will also enable you to compute over the telephone, and they may change the way you receive information and buy merchandise.

(See 1.1 Analog Versus Digital; 5.18 Computers for People with Disabilities: Meeting Special Needs.)

1.44 Pen-Based Computing

Notepad computers, or interactive tablets, are basically electronic pen-and-paper systems. They allow much more direct interaction with programs and data on the screen than using mice and menus. To input data, you use a liquid-crystal screen pad and a special electronic stylus, which may be wireless or attached to the notepad with a cable. The stylus acts as a pen, paintbrush, or mouse, depending on the job. Using a stylus as the input device eliminates the constant hand movement back and forth between the mouse and the keyboard in GUIs.

Many notepads are designed to accept input normally written on forms. An electronic version of the form appears on the screen, after which you enter names, check off boxes, or circle answers to data requested on the form. Once you have marked or printed the input onto the screen with the stylus, the computer changes your figures into computer characters. Then you can edit the material. A mistake is simply crossed out, after which it deletes itself. A command can be issued or a file opened by tapping the stylus at a menu choice. The catch is, you must print, and on most systems, you must also stay within the box or line indicated.

A notepad detects the presence of the stylus (which emits a faint signal from its tip). As you write, the screen grows darker where the stylus touches it. To recognize printing, the notepad uses built-in *pattern-recognition* software. You must train the system to recognize your writing. This is done by repeatedly writing words and characters, a job that takes anywhere from a half hour to 90 minutes. Like other small computers, the notepad contains memory and has a hard disk drive or memory chips for permanent storage.

Ease of communication with other devices will be an important factor in notepad computing. A notepad does not contain a floppy drive, thus must be plugged into a desktop or laptop model microcomputer to load programs or data. (The computer to which the data is sent from the notebook is often referred to as a *docking station.*) Notepads will be usable with modems, and eventually will be capable of handling faxes and telephone calls. The most advanced will incorporate cellular phone circuitry so you could get data, faxes, and phone calls at almost any location.

Devices such as notepads meant for personal use are often called *personal interactive electronics (PIE)* or *personal digital assistants (PDAs)*. Various companies may refer to their notepads as *tablets*, *stylus computers*, *pen-based computers*, *pen PCs*, and *electronic slates*. Some of these notepads use pen-based operating systems available from Microsoft and GO Corporation. In addition, some digitizing tablets such as Handwriter from the Communication Intelligence Corporation (CIC) provide pen computing for desktop computer systems.

Apple's Newton MessagePad is a popular pen-based computer.

(See 2.7 Configuration and Compatibility; 2.8 Portables.)

1.45 SENSOR INPUT

Sensor input is used widely in studying volcanoes, weather, earthquakes, and other natural phenomena. Sensing devices pick up the data—for example, slight movement of the earth, a shift in wind direction, or a change in temperature. Either through communication lines or by simply dumping all at once, the sensing equipment sends the data to computers that compile and chart the data, keeping track of variations from the norms. Sensor input is widely used in factories and medical facilities as well.

Most people saw little use for sensors and computers in their homes, however, until architects started designing "smart houses." These homes have systems that regulate temperature, lighting, entertainment, and communications. Most of the ideas are too impractical and expensive for the average person to implement, but builders are beginning to embed some of the more practical ones—temperature control and lighting control—in new homes at reasonable costs.

Today, many home computer hobbyists link their systems to thermometers, light detectors, or motion detectors to help control energy use and deter vandalism. Input from these detectors is also called sensor input. Once the data is transmitted to the computer, the computer records it, and takes action if it is warranted by changes in the data. For example, some homeowners have their microcomputers attached to alarm systems. Sensors identify potential intrusions into a home. The computer reads these signals and, as appropriate, sounds an alarm or places a call to a police station. The computer output generated by changes in sensor input is referred to as a *control signal*. As computers and televisions evolve from today's standard machines into whole-house systems, more and more homeowners will be using sensor input for at least minimum-home energy regulation.

(See 4.1 Telecommunications.)

1.46 Monitors

The most common output device, the *monitor*, shows output on a screen much like a television. Without one, you could not see your input. You see your location on the screen by looking for the cursor. The cursor may be a square, an underline bar, or a vertical line. It usually blinks. As you type, the cursor moves ahead of each character that appears on the screen.

Monitors are fast: they display output almost as soon as you ask for it. The output can be directly edited—that is, mistakes made during data entry can be seen on the screen and corrected before a paper copy is printed. Thus, monitors are suitable for inquiry and response applications. Monitors show only a small portion of the data at a time, however; their output, called *soft copy*, is not portable or permanent.

You may have heard someone refer to a monitor as a CRT or a VDT. The acronym *CRT* refers to *cathode ray tube*, the technology upon which most monitors are based. Monitors used with large computers such as mainframes and minicomputers are often called *video display terminals*, or *VDTs*. A VDT setup usually includes a keyboard, as well.

Some computers—such as Macintosh Classics, laptops, and notebook models—have the video display built into the computer unit. Most, however, require the purchase of a separate monitor. (Television sets are usually not adequate for use with computers because the on-screen lettering is generally fuzzy, colors are hard to control, and images such as circles are often distorted.)

The CRT itself is a funnel-shaped glass tube that is sealed in order to hold a vacuum; most of the air has been pumped out of the tube. At the back, or small end, of the tube is a *cathode*, a device that moves an electron beam back and forth toward the front, or large end, of the tube. Each time the beam makes a pass across the screen, it lights up the phosphor dots of the *pixels* on the inside of the screen, thus illuminating the active portions of the screen. Once a spot is lit, however, it does not stay lit; it must be constantly *refreshed*. The beam sweeps from left to right, top to bottom, very rapidly redrawing the lines of pixels and creating the images. The beam redraws the screen at a typical rate of 60 times per second, or 60Hz (hertz). This is the monitor's vertical *refresh rate*. The horizontal refresh rate, or *line rate*, is quoted in kilohertz (KHz) and describes the speed with which each line is drawn.

The color a monitor displays depends on the phosphor coating on the tube. *Monochrome* monitors show a single color (such as black, white, green, amber, or blue) on a background that is black or a shade of gray. They generally flicker less than color monitors. A high-quality monochrome monitor that shows black characters against a white background is referred to as a *paper-white* display. A monitor that can display an image in many shades of gray is called a *gray-scaling* monitor.

Color monitors, on the other hand, are coated with phosphors in the three primary colors: red, green, and blue. There are three cathodes, and each shoots at a different color in the triangle. Thus, there are three separate color signals, one for each of three colors—red, green, and blue; that is why such a monitor is called an *RGB (red-green-blue)* color monitor. Depending on which phosphors are activated, different colors and intensities appear on the screen. A *shadow mask*, a thin metal screen with very tiny holes arranged in a matrix, is placed near the CRT's inner face. It is used to increase the accuracy of *convergence*, in which the color signals line up with each other.

The Sony Trinitron uses a different masking technology called an *aperture grille*, which consists of vertical slits rather than round holes. One cathode, rather than three, shoots three beams in Trinitron tubes. The Trinitron is flat vertically, and slightly rounded horizontally. The main problem with Trinitron tubes is that you see one or two black lines across the screen. These lines are shadows of the wires used to support or stiffen the aperture grille.

RGB monitors produce very high-quality output. They cost more than monochrome monitors and are fun to use with games, paint software, and graphs. Some color monitors may not show text as clearly as monochrome monitors do, however.

(See 1.1 Analog Versus Digital; 1.23 Video Boards; 1.33 Resolution; 1.34 Pixels; 1.35 Gray Scaling; 1.36 Cursors; 1.47 Evaluating a Monitor; 1.48 Flat-Panel Displays; 2.10 Multimedia Standards; 2.17 Caring for Your Computer; 5.16 Ergonomics; 5.17 Safety Issues; Software Review section: After Dark.)

1.47 Evaluating a Monitor

When evaluating a monitor, you'll run into a number of terms—resolution, dot pitch, refresh rates, bandwidth, multiscanning, and so on—that can seem quite confusing. It helps to know what the terms mean, and they are described in this section. Before buying a monitor, you should read the reviews and look at the displays produced by highly rated monitors in order to have a reference point for evaluation.

Monitors offer varying levels of image *resolution*, or clarity. The resolution is determined by the number of image points, or *pixels* (picture elements) on the screen. The greater the number of pixels suitable for a particular screen size, the better the resolution will be. Common numbers of pixels are 640-by-480 and 1,024-by-768. A monitor described as 640-by-480 has pixels are arranged in 480 lines of 640 pixels each. The distance between the pixels affects clarity, too. This distance is called *dot pitch* and it is measured in millimeters. The smaller the dot pitch, the closer the pixels and the sharper the image. A monitor with a larger dot pitch will show blocky images. The dot pitch of a good quality monitor should be no more than .28 for smaller monitors and .31 millimeters for larger monitors, in high resolutions.

Maximum resolution and possible colors are determined by the monitor, but special software is needed for governing the use of the pixels and colors. This software, or *logic circuitry*, is stored in chips on a *video adapter card* that is plugged into an *expansion slot* (or connector) in a computer that permits the installation of such cards. The video adapter card and the monitor work together; the monitor must have the number of pixels required to support the resolution that a particular card offers. If a monitor has only the required number of pixels for a CGA card, it cannot provide VGA resolution, even if a VGA card were installed. (You'll get the best results if you buy the monitor and the adapter card together as a system.)

You may notice that some monitors have an annoying flicker. Screen flicker results from a slow refresh rate, or from a technique called *interlacing* that refreshes only every other line of the screen, redrawing the remaining lines on the next pass. This technique is used to increase resolution while saving costs. (On the same monitor, resolution may be non-interlaced at 1024-by-768 and interlaced at 1280-by-1024.) You may notice the problem especially in a program like *Windows* because the great amount of white background space makes flicker obvious. To avoid flicker, buy a non-interlaced monitor that supports a high refresh rate of 70Hz or 72Hz, paired with a video card capable of the same—and be sure the card is in *non-interlaced mode*. (Slow flicker, or an objectionable waver, is called *swim*, and will be noticed within 10 seconds or so. *Drift* occurs more slowly, over 60 seconds. *Jitter*, where the entire image shakes, is easily detectable and should be avoided.)

Vertical refresh rates go as high as 100Hz, but you should also check the minimum scanning numbers. Otherwise, you may not be able to use the monitor with older video standards, or with software that does not support high resolution. A *multiscanning*, or *multisync*, monitor will adjust to whatever signals a video card sends as long as the range of the video card does not exceed that of the monitor. Buying a multiscanning monitor gives you more options for later purchase of a video card that supports higher resolution. For compatibility with a wide range of applications—both older and up-to-date—a monitor with a vertical refresh rate of 50Hz to 100Hz and a horizontal range of 20KHz to 75KHz provides an ideal scanning range. Another figure to consider is the *bandwidth*, which tells the speed with which new information can arrive at the screen. Bandwidth for monitors is measured in megahertz. VGA video has a bandwidth of 25MHz to 28MHz, and XGA runs at 45MHz to 47MHz.

Which brings us to analog versus digital monitors. Actually, all monitors are analog devices, so the terms *analog* and *digital* refer to the type of *signals* a monitor can receive from its video adapter card. Digital monitors—which accept MDA (monochrome), CGA, and EGA video signals—support less resolution than analog monitors do. VGA and Super VGA video cards require an analog monitor. Multiscanning monitors are capable of accepting either type of signal. *Multifrequency* monitors accept signals at two or more preset frequencies.

Monitors are available in several screen dimensions. The dimensions are measured as television screens are—in inches diagonally across the screen from one corner to the opposite corner. Most are 15-inch displays or smaller, but large-screen models are available that show displays of 16, 17, 19, 20, or 21 inches. The larger the screen, the more benefit you get from high resolution. You'll see more of a file, or be able to put more applications on your screen at once with a 17-inch monitor. On a 14-inch screen, a high resolution of 1,024-by-768 or more would simply make the image very small and hard to read. You should know that you might notice flicker in your peripheral vision when using a large screen. Large-screen monitors are heavy, too, weighing up to 50 pounds or more. Many large-screen monitors display material in *portrait* fashion, referring to the fact that a portrait painting is usually hung so that the vertical is greater than the horizontal dimension. Called *full-page* monitors, they can display an entire page of text, which is handy if you are doing word processing or desktop publishing jobs. (Monitors that have a greater horizontal dimension than vertical measurement are called *landscape* monitors. Large-screen monitors of this orientation can comfortably display two full pages side by side.) Monitors of the 19- to 21-inch range are very expensive; they are used primarily by professional designers and desktop publishers.

Generally, images do not fill the entire display area on a monitor. A monitor should have knobs for sizing and positioning the image both horizontally and vertically. Some monitors use a technique known as *autosizing* to deliver a consistent image size across the various applications and operating environments. Autosizing adjusts the size and position of the display automatically at the start of each new application. The settings can be predefined in the monitor or preset by you, the user. Autosizing is an expensive option. (Sizing options are more important to the PC user than to the Macintosh user.)

Make sure there is a way to control the brightness, contrast, and focus of the display. Controlling these features permits you to adjust the display to suit the lighting conditions of the room in which you are working. Glare can be a stubborn nuisance, too. Flatter screens (on flat technology monitors, not referring to flat-panel displays) eliminate most glare and distortion, and many monitors now incorporate some kind of anti-glare coating or etching either inside or outside the glass. Snap-on glare covers are available for most monitors as well. (Glare reduction features can reduce the sharpness of the image.) Tilt-and-swivel monitor stands enable you to eliminate glare and neck-muscle tension by moving the monitor to a better viewing angle.

After reading about all these monitor options, you should know that the best way to judge a monitor for its quality, clarity, and glare is simply to look at it. Eliminate any prospective monitors that show fuzzy lettering, bleeding colors, or poor contrast. On a clear screen such as an empty word processor screen, look for evenness of tone without a noticeable dark spot. If you are really picky, look at the pixels through a magnifying glass to check for convergence or a halo effect. (Convergence is upset when white pixels show bits of color, indicating that the electron beams have misconverged. The halo effect occurs when the area around a color is lit with color that has spilled over.) Check to see whether straight lines bow in or out at the center of the screen—and whether the images are as sharp and clear at the edges as they are at the center of the screen. Also, check to see whether an image leaves a trail as you scroll or move an arrow with the mouse. You will have to judge your own reaction to flicker, as it affects people differently. If you are unsure about judging an expensive monitor, you can buy video display testing programs such as DisplayMate by Sonera Technology that can help you evaluate a monitor for speed, color accuracy, distortion, and other features.

Most computer system manufacturers offer a choice of monitors, but monitors can be purchased separately from companies such as NEC Technologies. Be sure the monitor has the standard 15-pin mini D-sub connecting cable for connecting it to the computer (for Macintosh compatibility, full-size 15-pin D-sub) and a plug for the electrical outlet. (A large monitor may have a *BNC* connector option, a sophisticated cable that reduces *line noise*—that is, unwanted signals or interference—at very high scanning frequencies.) See topic 5.17, "Safety Issues," for information about monitor emissions and energy use.

(See 1.1 Analog Versus Digital; 1.23 Video Boards; 1.33 Resolution; 1.34 Pixels; 1.35 Gray Scaling; 1.36 Cursors; 1.46 Monitors; 1.48 Flat-Panel Displays; 2.10 Multimedia Standards; 2.17 Caring for Your Computer; 5.16 Ergonomics; 5.17 Safety Issues; Software Review section: After Dark.)

1.48 FLAT-PANEL DISPLAYS

Flat-panel displays are used mainly on laptop, notebook, and pen-based computers. Their display looks like the display on a digital watch. They are less bulky and require less power than the cathode-ray tubes (CRTs) used in most monitors. On some earlier displays, the image appeared faint when viewed at an angle or in direct lighting, but flat-panel displays are continually being improved—and are available in color, as well.

Most flat-panel displays use *liquid crystal display*, or *LCD*, technology. LCD does not give off light of its own. An LCD screen has two sheets of polarizing material with a liquid crystal solution between them. The crystals act as pixels. When an electric current passes through the liquid, the crystals align so that light cannot pass through them. Each crystal either lets light pass through or blocks light, somewhat like a shutter. This creates the character display. Most LCD screens are backlit by an internal light source to make them easier to read in bright environments. This means that the background is illuminated to make the foreground characters sharper in contrast with the background. Thus, the screen display is brighter and clearer. LCD technology usually produces bluish letters on a grayish-white background. Some LCD displays can display 16 or more colors.

LCD displays have been improved by several technologies. In *active-matrix* LCD, the screen is refreshed more often than in regular LCD. A technique called *supertwist* twists the light waves for improved background to character contrast. Page-white display, offering the greatest contrasts between the images and the background, is produced by *dual supertwist*. A special type of active-matrix LCD technology called *thin film transistors (TFT)* provides the best resolution of all the flat-panel technologies, though it is also the most expensive of them. In TFT, each pixel consists of from one to four transistors. A pixel consisting of three transistors, for example, has one each for red, green, and blue.

LCD technologies use the least power of all the flat-panel displays, an important consideration for battery-operated notebook and laptop computers. Two other technologies have been used successfully, although expensively, in portable computers. One—the *gas plasma display*—uses electric current to ionize gases, causing them to glow. This technology is similar to the technique used in neon signs. The display is usually orange on a black background. The other technology—*electroluminescent display (ELD)*—is similar to gas plasma, but has layers of phosphor rather than gas. Most computers with gas plasma or ELD displays need to be plugged into wall outlets.

Flat-panel displays are capable of gray scaling. Although normally a large number of gray-scale steps indicates high-quality output, this ratio may in fact produce a fuzzier image on current flat-panel displays.

(See 1.34 Pixels; 1.35 Gray Scaling; 2.8 Portables.)

1.49 Printers

Printers make *hard copy*, sometimes called a *printout*, that is permanent and easy to carry around. Hard copy can also act as backup for data stored on disks and tapes, although it is not space-efficient. Printers are attached to microcomputer systems through ports of various types: parallel, serial, SCSI, or AppleTalk network. The two types of printers are impact and non-impact.

Printers that print images with a striking motion are called *impact* printers. They strike together an inked ribbon, the paper, and the plastic or metal parts that hold the characters. There are many types of impact printers—some printing a character at a time, others printing a line at a time. The most common impact printer for microcomputers is the *dot-matrix* printer, which uses the tips of wires in the print head to create characters from patterns of dots.

Non-impact printers do not print characters by striking ribbon, paper, and character elements together. Instead, they use heat, laser, or photographic methods to make the image. Most of these printers are not only much faster and quieter than dot-matrix printers, they also offer a wide choice of print styles. They cost more than impact printers, however, and need special cartridges of ink or toner that add to their cost. Some also require special paper. Most are very quiet and can be used in situations where printer noise would be a problem. Non-impact printers form characters made up of dots. The dots, however, are much harder to detect than those made by dot-matrix impact printers. The most common types are *thermal*, *ink-jet*, and *laser*.

Most printers use standard *letter-size* (8.5-by-11-inch) and *legal-size* (8.5-by-14-inch) paper, although some have a wide carriage for larger fan-fold paper. In addition, many printers are adapted for heavy stock paper, envelopes, transparencies and labels. Special envelope printers have been designed for handling envelopes and postcards.

Printers accept paper either by the sheet, often called *cut-sheet* paper, or from *fan-fold stacks*. Most printers are *friction-fed*, using rubber or plastic rollers to grab each sheet of paper and draw it into the printer. They normally have paper trays that hold from 50 to 250 sheets at a time. Dot-matrix printers, on the other hand, are often *tractor-feed* printers, using teeth or pins on wheels attached to both sides of the printer. These teeth catch into holes along both sides of special continuous paper folded accordion-style into a fan-fold stack. As the wheels rotate, the teeth draw the paper into the printer. When printing is finished, you tear the sheets apart along perforated edges, and remove the strips that contain the holes. Tractor-feed printers often have a lever you can adjust to feed in regular paper a sheet at a time. You can often adapt a tractor-feed printer to accept sheets of paper by attaching a *sheet feeder*. This piece of equipment is basically a molded plastic bin that allows for automatic feeding and stacking of individual sheets of paper.

You can attach a *printer fax* to non-impact printers such as the Hewlett-Packard LaserJet or DeskJet. This equipment will enable you to receive and send documents by facsimile. Faxed copies you receive will be printed on ordinary printer paper. The printer faxes will store incoming faxes in memory, even when your computer and printer are turned off. You may need a scanner, however, for inputting hard copy to send faxes. In addition, most fax products require 1MB or 2MB of extra free memory on the printer.

When you shop for a printer, it may help to take along an example of the type of output you will be producing—labels, forms, newsletters, spreadsheets, and so on. Carefully compare the quality of output you want against a range of print samples that show the variety of fonts, solid blacks, and shadings each printer produces.

Knowing how you plan to use the printer will help you choose a printer with enough memory for your purposes. If you plan to use lots of complex graphics and desktop publishing applications, choose a laser printer with at least 1MB RAM rather than the standard 512KB RAM. If you are considering *PostScript fonts* (whose page-description language enables them to be sized easily and accurately), you will need at least 2MB realistically; buying more memory at the outset is less expensive than adding it later. Be sure to get a list of *resident fonts* so you'll know exactly what variety is offered in the typefaces you consider.

Always be sure your software works with the printer you plan to buy. If you use old software occasionally, check whether the printer *emulates* any older-style printers. Be sure the interface is correct: Most printers use parallel interfaces, for example, but Macintosh computers have serial printer ports. Find out the number of sheets the paper tray can hold, the ports offered, and the cost of consumables such as special paper, ribbons, or toner. Remember that you will pay more for faster speeds and higher print quality. Except for laser printers, however, the printers discussed here are within most budgets—and even laser printers are becoming inexpensive enough to be the choice for many people.

Some printers are designed to be used with notebook computers, and are called *notebook printers*. They can operate on a battery pack, printing up to 25 pages (for example) on battery power. They may offer different fonts, and can often print on anything from letterheads to transparencies. One example is the Citizen PN48 Notebook Printer, designed to be used with IBM-compatible laptop or notebook computers.

Usually you select the printer's *device driver* from the software you are using. Because the software cannot list all brands and models of printers, you may need to indicate which printer your printer acts like, or emulates. Almost all dot-matrix printers emulate Epson or IBM dot-matrix printers; the industry standard for ink-jet printers is the Hewlett-Packard DeskJet— and for lasers, the Hewlett-Packard LaserJet.

Some printers are designed with *memory buffers* that can accept an entire document for printing, enabling you to work on another job at the computer while the printer is printing. Many word processors and other applications also provide a program called a *print spooler (Simultaneous Peripheral Operation OnLine)* that does the same job; it uses a portion of the computer's RAM to store the print data, then spools it out to the printer as needed.

(See 1.18 Ports, Slots, and Bays; 1.20 Controllers and Drivers; 1.33 Resolution; 1.50 Print Quality; 1.51 Dot-Matrix Impact Printers; 1.52 Ink-Jet Printers; 1.53 Laser Printers; 1.54 Page-Description Languages; 1.55 Typefaces and Fonts; 1.56 Color Printing; 2.17 Caring for Your Computer; 3.33 Desktop Publishing.)

1.50 Print Quality

Printers are often characterized by the quality of their output. *Draft-quality (DQ)* printers—usually dot-matrix—produce a hard copy that is legible and good enough for the first draft (or version) of a document. *Near-letter quality (NLQ)* printers generate an output that nearly resembles the appearance of a typewritten document. Dot-matrix printers often have an *NLQ mode* that produces print quality suitable for school assignments, letters, and informal communications. Some lower-quality non-impact printers also produce NLQ output. The best quality is *letter-quality (LQ)*, which is suitable for formal communication such as business letters and dissertations.

The quality of a printer's output is measured in *dots per inch (dpi)*. Most laser and ink-jet printers produce LQ output, commonly at 300 dpi. Printers that produce 600 dpi output (generally laser printers) are sometimes described as *near-typeset quality* printers. Even laser printers with 1200-dpi resolution, however, cannot match the high-resolution *imagesetters* (1270 and 2540 dpi) used in professional print shops. (If you need print quality of this caliber, you can enlist the services of a desktop publishing *service bureau.* You may need PostScript files to send your work to a professional print shop.) When shopping for a printer, look for printers with *equal vertical and horizontal resolution*—300 dpi-by-300 dpi, for example—unless you don't mind circles that look like ovals and squares that look like rectangles.

(See 1.33 Resolution; 1.49 Printers; 1.51 Dot-Matrix Impact Printers; 1.52 Ink-Jet Printers; 1.53 Laser Printers; 1.54 Page-Description Languages; 1.56 Color Printing; 1.57 Plotters; 3.33 Desktop Publishing.)

1.51 Dot-Matrix Impact Printers

Dot-matrix impact printers (also called *wire-matrix* printers) work by striking the pins in a *print element*, or *print head*, against an inked ribbon to put a character on paper. The pins, which are fine steel wires, are formed into a vertical line or a rectangle; different combinations of pins shoot out to shape the characters. The software regulates which pins are activated to form a particular character. Most dot-matrix printers sold today have 24-pin heads.

Dot-matrix printers are capable of graphic output; usually they supply several fonts. This type of printer is convenient for printing multiple forms; it can strike through several layers of paper and carbons. Often dot-matrix machines offer two or three qualities of print—from *draft* to *near-letter quality (NLQ)* output—though their near-letter quality ranges from only 72 to 150 dpi. Although draft-quality printing is fairly rapid at 500 characters per second (cps), it can take a minute or more to print out only one page of text in NLQ mode.

Dot-matrix printers make a racket, although most companies are working hard to reduce printer noise by combining sound-absorption materials with quieter mechanical parts. Their vibrations can scoot them off a smooth table, and the mechanical jerking of the print action can cause banding, or uneven distribution of the lines across the page. Despite the drawbacks of noise and print quality, the cost of printing one page with dot-matrix technology remains at less than a penny, while the cost of using laser or other non-impact technology is about three cents per page. Paper and replacement ribbons are the main expenses associated with dot-matrix printers.

Most dot-matrix printers are outfitted with sprockets to accept fan-fold paper. The sprocket rollers can be adjusted to accept many widths of forms and labels. Sheet feeders are usually available. The printers have options for advancing an entire page at a time, called *form feed (FF)*, and for advancing a line at a time, called *line feed (LF)*. The feeds can be used to position hand-fed single sheets of paper and eject a page when printing finishes in mid-page.

(See 1.33 Resolution; 1.49 Printers; 1.50 Print Quality; 1.55 Typefaces and Fonts; 1.56 Color Printing.)

1.52 Ink-Jet Printers

In an *ink-jet printer*, nozzles arranged in a vertical row shoot streams of ink toward the paper. There are several types of ink-jet technology, but the most common is *drop-on-demand*. In this method, the nozzle creates a droplet (the drop part) and the software governs which nozzles shoot droplets when (the demand part). In most drop-on-demand ink-jets, the circuitry creates heat in either a small piezoelectric crystal at the end of each nozzle or in the ink chamber. As the crystal expands and contracts, it squeezes out a dot of ink with enough force to hit the paper. If the ink is heated in the chamber, a bubble is formed (hence the name *bubble-jet* for some types of ink-jet printers) forcing an ink droplet out of the nozzle. Some drop-on-demand ink-jets work by electrical charge instead of heat.

Keep in mind that these nozzles are hair-fine. On early ink-jet printers, ink easily clogged the nozzles, creating frustration and messes. Clogging is no longer the problem it was in the past, but changing the ink cartridges can still be messy on some machines. In addition, the ink may smudge immediately after printing (or if it gets wet). The ink tends to *bleed*, or *wick*, a bit on some types of paper, and may create *satellites*, which are fine mists of ink around the dots. New ink compositions have diminished these problems, but even so, be sure to test any special paper you plan to use (such as letterheads) before buying a particular ink-jet printer. You may want to use high-quality glossy paper, or choose a different printer.

Ink-jet printers are quiet. Most accept cut-sheet paper, although some have wide carriages and tractor-feed action. They can produce one to two pages per minute, but speed is often cited as a drawback of this type of printer. In fact, it may take up to 10 minutes for an ink-jet printer to warm up, and almost a minute to print a page. Ink-jets cannot print multiple copies at once. Costs per page are estimated anywhere from two to seven cents. Ink cartridges are $20 to $50; they may print only 200 to 300 pages before they need replacing. Most ink-jet printers offer several fonts, and accept additional fonts via cartridges that are inserted into the printer. Some accept downloaded fonts from a disk. Ink-jet printers are often used for low-end desktop publishing purposes because they do have the ability to print graphics as well as text and the quality of output is fairly high.

(See 1.33 Resolution; 1.49 Printers; 1.50 Print Quality; 1.55 Typefaces and Fonts; 1.56 Color Printing; 3.33 Desktop Publishing.)

1.53 LASER PRINTERS

The technique employed in a *laser printer* does not use striking or squirting to put characters on paper. Instead, laser beams make images on a rotating drum. The laser beam changes the electrical charge on the drum wherever it hits. The drum then spins through a reservoir holding a powder called *toner*, which is charged with the opposite polarity of the charged spots on the drum. The toner—basically tiny iron filings—adheres to the charged spots on the drum, from which it is then fused to ordinary paper by heat and pressure. (This is also the way copy machines work.) An entire page is transferred to the drum at once, thus laser printers are sometimes called *page printers*. Some "laser" printers use liquid crystals or light-emitting diodes rather than actual laser beams to expose the drum.

Laser printers are controlled through *page-description languages*, which describe the layout and contents of a printed page. The best known of these are Adobe PostScript and Hewlett-Packard PCL (Printer Control Language). PostScript is the de facto standard for Apple Macintosh printers, and PCL is generally found on IBM equipment. It is possible to connect a PostScript printer to an IBM computer, but some IBM software does not support the PostScript standard. Check before you buy.

Laser printers operate at speeds of 4 to 6 text pages per minute at the low end to 20 text pages per minute for business machines. Printing complex graphics with a laser printer may be slow, because of the time needed to load a page into the printer's memory. The print quality is very high, however, and fonts are available in nearly unlimited variety—either internally, in cartridges, or from software. On the down side, laser printers are still expensive, (though some are now affordable for home use at less than $800 each). They use more power than ink-jet printers, and a replacement toner cartridge is expensive at $60 and up. One cartridge can print around 3,000 pages, however, depending upon the density and frequency of graphics printing. As no special paper is required, costs are estimated at 2.5 to 3.5 cents per page.

(See 1.33 Resolution; 1.49 Printers; 1.50 Print Quality; 1.54 Page-Description Languages; 1.55 Typefaces and Fonts; 1.56 Color Printing; 5.17 Safety Issues.)

1.54 PAGE-DESCRIPTION LANGUAGES

Page-description languages are used to control laser printers. Also called *imaging models*, they are used for printing preparation. They describe the page layout and contents of each page. The two common page-description languages are Adobe

PostScript, which is associated with Apple Macintosh printers, and Hewlett-Packard PCL (Printer Control Language), which is found on IBM-compatible machines.

PostScript was developed by Adobe Systems primarily for use with laser printers, although it can be adapted for use with other types of devices. It is an *object-oriented language,* which means it treats pictures and fonts as geometrical *objects* rather than as bit maps. The method is called *vector graphics*; the fonts are called *outline fonts* because the outline of each character is geometrically defined. The fonts are also called *scalable* fonts, because you can change their size with special PostScript commands. Once a typeface is defined, PostScript can produce a multitude of type sizes and variations within. In contrast, printers that rely on bit map technology must contain a complete set of bit maps for each size and font. In addition, the print quality of object-oriented graphics improves with a higher-resolution printer, whereas bit-mapped graphics look exactly the same as they would with lower-resolution printers. As an added bonus, object-oriented images take up less memory than bit-mapped graphics.

Most PostScript fonts are *printer* fonts; you cannot see them on-screen unless you are using *type-manager software* such as that from Adobe. PostScript machines generally offer 35 fonts, with more (up to 7000) available at additional cost. The latest version of PostScript is Level 2. PostScript remains the predominant page-description language for graphics applications, but clones are being developed that increase the competition. In addition, a number of products—such as *PostScript-emulation* cartridges and type-manager software—can bring your non-PostScript laser printer's capabilities closer to the PostScript standard. Some of these products can be used with dot-matrix and ink-jet printers.

Almost all software products for IBM computers and compatibles contain a Hewlett-Packard (HP) driver that enables printing on an HP-compatible printer. You should beware of compatibility, however. There are several versions of PCL; a printer may be compatible with one and not another. In addition, a printer that claims compatibility may not be able to accept Hewlett-Packard font cartridges. Older PCLs are based on bit maps, but newer versions support scalable fonts through a technology named Intellifont. Many laser printers now offer a smoothing feature called *anti-aliasing* that improves the appearance of bit-mapped fonts at higher resolutions.

An option for Macintosh computers is the QuickDraw laser printer, which uses the Macintosh's underlying graphics display system called QuickDraw. QuickDraw printers are less expensive than PostScript printers; although typically they have been less versatile than PostScript printers, that is changing. Adobe, the company known for fonts and print managers, offers a utility that enables non-PostScript printers to use some of the PostScript fonts. In addition, Apple's TrueType software, built into System 7, provides outline fonts for both PostScript and non-PostScript printers. (Windows 3.1 also supports TrueType.) The true PostScript language, however, remains the standard page-description language if you will be using professional printing services to print your documents.

(See 1.49 Printers; 1.50 Print Quality; 1.53 Laser Printers; 1.55 Typefaces and Fonts; 3.8 System 7.5; 3.33 Desktop Publishing; Software Review section: Adobe Type Manager.)

1.55 TYPEFACES AND FONTS

Some people use the terms typeface and font incorrectly to mean the same thing. A *typeface* is simply the design for a set of characters. That is, it describes how the type is drawn. Examples include Times, Helvetica, Gothic, and Courier. There are two general categories of typeface: serif and sans serif. *Serifs* are small decorative marks that look like tiny flags and feet used to embellish characters. Characters without these embellishments are described as *sans serif*. Times is a serif typeface, and Helvetica is a sans serif typeface.

Typefaces also are described in terms of *pitch*—the number of characters that can fit in an inch. Some typefaces are of *fixed pitch*, meaning each character gets exactly the same width on a line as any other (a holdover from typewriters); other typefaces are *proportional*, meaning the amount of space a character takes up on a line varies with the shape of the characters. Courier is a fixed-pitch typeface, and Times is a proportional typeface. In Courier, a **W** takes up the same amount of space as a period (**.**), but in Times, the period (**.**) takes up much less space.

Font is a more complex—and precise—concept than typeface. A font is a specific set of characters that have a number of attributes, including the typeface, but also size, style, and weight. Within the Helvetica typeface, for example, there are many sizes to choose from. Type size is measured in points (a *point* is about 1/72 of an inch), so 9-point Helvetica looks smaller than 12-point Helvetica. The *style* of the print can be changed from plain to *italic*, and the *weight* can be changed from plain to **boldface** (some systems include *light* and *extra bold* weights, too). Thus, "Helvetica" is the name of a typeface, but "14-point Helvetica bold" is the name of a font.

Some fonts are *resident*, or *internal*; they come with the printer. PostScript machines, for example, generally offer 35 fonts, four styles each of typefaces such as Helvetica, Courier, Times, Bookman, New Century Schoolbook, Palatino, and

Avant Garde. Other fonts can be added by inserting ROM cartridges or *font cards* (printed circuit boards) into the printer. Fonts downloaded into the printer's memory from software are called *soft fonts*. These take time to download—and take up a lot of memory space—but unlike resident fonts or font cartridges, soft fonts can be erased from a printer's memory.

Computers and related devices use two methods to represent fonts. One method is by *bit-mapping*, in which each character is represented by an arrangement of dots. Each font requires a different set of bit-mapped images, and therefore takes up a lot of memory. The other method of representing fonts—rapidly becoming popular—is by *vector graphics*, in which the shape or outline of a character is defined geometrically. The advantage of this method is that each typeface can be displayed in any size. Thus, fonts described geometrically are called *scalable*, or *outline*, fonts. The programs that create the different sizes by algorithm are called *type managers*, or font managers.

Scalable fonts show off the qualities of high-resolution printers, but do not look very good on low-resolution devices; almost all computer systems use bit-mapped fonts for screen display. Another drawback of scalable fonts is that each character must be generated as it is needed. Thus, the computations require a powerful microprocessor for acceptable speed. The font files are smaller, however, and require less memory for use. The PostScript system is a scalable font system.

An increasingly popular scalable font format is TrueType, a new standard from Microsoft and Apple. TrueType is included in the Macintosh System 7 and in Microsoft Windows 3.1. In this format, you see any size and style on both the printed copy and the screen. TrueType fonts work on any printer, and many versions provide high-quality fonts at low prices.

Font cartridges for both laser printers and ink-jet printers are available from the printer companies, but other companies produce special *cartridge libraries* as part of their product line. Font managers such as Adobe Type Manager enable you to see on-screen the fonts that are resident in the printer, and also let you use soft fonts (some included in the package, others available in accessory packages). Some vendors, including Adobe, Agfa Compugraphic, and NEC Technologies offer CD-ROM disks containing entire font libraries, often over 1,000 possible selections.

(See 1.49 Printers; 1.52 Ink-Jet Printers; 1.53 Laser Printers; 1.54 Page-Description Languages; 3.8 System 7.5; 3.31 Word Processors; 3.33 Desktop Publishing; 3.36 Graphics Software; Software Review section: Adobe Type Manager.)

1.56 COLOR PRINTING

Look at a newsletter in black and white, and look at the same newsletter with color added. The color attracts attention every time. The simplest way to add color is to use a color ribbon with dot-matrix printers to highlight text and enhance graphics. For around $150 to $200, you can purchase a color dot-matrix printer to which you can add a *multicolor* ribbon (red, blue, yellow, and black). These printers are able to move the ribbon up and down to select a particular color. The colors on the ribbon can also be combined for printing orange, purple, and green. Thus, with software that supports color printing, you can typically print documents in six colors plus black.

Dot-matrix printers offer relatively poor resolution and color saturation, however, in comparison with the higher-quality color output of ink-jet, laser, and other non-impact printers. Even so, the sophisticated technology used in these printers makes some of them quite expensive.

The primary challenges of improving color printing are: creating brilliant colors, printing solid blocks of consistent color, matching colors between the monitor and the printer, printing as fast as monochrome (at the same cost), and using any kind and weight of paper. Being able to buy a high-quality color printer for under $10,000 is a relatively recent development—even then, prices hover around $7,000. Despite the high costs now, I'm discussing these printers because I anticipate their costs will be reduced dramatically in the next several years. (By the way, your software must support colors no matter which printing system you buy.)

Color non-impact printers simply cannot hold all the colors of ink necessary to print in all colors. Like monitors, however, printers use a few primary colors to mix (or *dither*) into the many colors desired.

Monitors are light sources, but printers produce output that reflects light. Thus, monitors mix the primary *additive* colors (red, green, and blue—*RGB*) to form other colors; printers use the primary *subtractive* colors (cyan, magenta, and yellow—*CMY*) for color printing. The subtractive primaries combine to form the entire color *gamut* of a printer. For example, magenta plus yellow yields red, yellow plus cyan yields green, and cyan plus magenta yields blue. Equal amounts of the subtractive primaries form black, but most printers include a separate black color (designated as *K* in the printing industry) for a truer black printout. The *four-color* model is referred to as *CMYK*. Under the CMYK model, only seven colors are possible. To produce other colors, shades, and tints, the printer uses *dithering*, which breaks a color pixel into an array of dots. Each dot may be any one of the seven colors, or left blank.

You can see how the more dots there are, the greater the number of color combinations the printer can produce. The problem with using a large matrix (such as 8-by-8 dots) for dithering is that resolution is reduced. In addition, the *dot-distribution pattern* can have a substantial impact on the appearance of the page; bad dot distribution can create blurs or unwanted lines. Dither patterns vary from printer to printer.

Another problem of color printing is *color matching*. Colors vary from monitor to monitor; the printed colors may not match the colors you see on the monitor. In turn, the color generated on hard-copy output is dependent on the printing device's color system, not on the color you see on your monitor. Some printer manufacturers, notably Hewlett-Packard and Tektronix, emphasize monitor/printer color matching, especially in the Macintosh environment. A Mac user can even specify the type of monitor being used; the printer will adjust all color printouts according to the characteristics of the selected monitor.

Programs such as Cachet by Electronics for Imaging, Inc., and PostScript Level 2 by Adobe, help you deal with the problem of color matching. If you will be doing a lot of color work that will be printed at a print shop, however, you may want to look into the Pantone Matching System. Pantone provides numbered, solid-ink samples of 747 Pantone colors on coated and uncoated stock (Pantone Color Formula Guide), and definitions of the primary-color mixes required to simulate the Pantone colors on a printer (the Pantone Process Color Simulation Guide). A *Pantone-certified* printer uses *color-simulation formulas* specific to that particular printer's ink and printing process. Some computer programs, such as Aldus PageMaker, support Pantone colors. However, even with these color standards in place, you will still get variations in the accuracy of color printers, due to the number of variables that remain. These include paper quality, condition of the equipment, ink quality, ink flow, color registration, and the order in which the printer applies the colors to the page. (By the way, Pantone Inc. plans to introduce a six-color process that will greatly improve color matching and reproduction.)

Color ink-jet printers, which use four liquid-ink cartridges to hold the colored inks, offer the best value, good color rendition, and medium- to high-resolution output for most personal computer users. The prices range from $700 to around $1,500. People who need professional-quality color output have three basic—and expensive—options: the color laser printer, thermal-wax printers, and phase-change ink-jet printers.

A *color laser printer* uses a photographic process for color printing. The printer lays down each of the subtractive colors separately, and thus must demonstrate careful alignment to create clean, crisp images. Although color laser printers can use ordinary paper to print much higher-quality output than ink-jet printers, the $10,000-plus (which is what color laser printers cost) will buy you lots of specially coated paper for your less-costly color ink-jet.

Thermal-wax transfer printing uses heat to transfer inks from special ink ribbons directly to paper or transparency film. The colored-wax inks come on plastic ribbons in page-size blocks; each of the three subtractive colors is available, and often black, as well. A print head melts the wax required for the image. As printing occurs, the melted wax adheres to the paper, and the unmelted wax remains on the ribbon. This process makes three or four passes over the same sheet of paper in order to print the various colors; the alignment of the paper (*registration*) must be accurate or else the image becomes fuzzy. These printers perform best with extremely smooth papers. Some thermal-wax transfer color printers are under $5,000, but most are more costly. Some industry pundits believe that phase-change ink-jet printers will soon replace thermal-wax printers.

The *phase-change ink-jet* printer uses inks that are solid at room temperature. Once the inks are heated, they become liquid and can be shot out through the ink-jet print head. The ink solidifies almost immediately on contact with the paper, due to the temperature differences between the ink reservoirs and the paper. The inks produce bright colors without bleeding—on a variety of paper weights and finishes, even tissue paper. Phase-change ink-jet printers are usually priced under $10,000.

There is another type of printer that may become widely used in the future. It is the *continuous-tone* printer. Unlike the other color printers discussed here, continuous-tone printers blend the colors during printing, avoiding the dots of dithering. Most use a print process called *dye-sublimation* which heats the dye, changing it to a gas that diffuses in the chemical coating on the special paper (where the dye reverts to a solid). Price ranges are high—from $5,000 to over $39,000—but the technology may eventually be adapted for home computer use.

Manufacturers of color non-impact printers are Seiko Instruments USA, Inc.; Epson; Hewlett-Packard Co.; Tektronix Inc.; Canon USA; Colorocs; QMS, Inc.; Eastman Kodak; Nikon; Sharp Electronics Corp.; and Mitsubishi International Corp.

(See 1.35 Gray Scaling; 1.49 Printers; 1.50 Print Quality; 1.51 Dot-Matrix Impact Printers; 1.52 Ink-Jet Printers; 1.53 Laser Printers; 1.57 Plotters; 3.33 Desktop Publishing.)

1.57 Plotters

Plotters work with your computer and software much as printers do, to make paper copies of your work. A plotter uses pens to make hard copies of images such as bar charts, graphs, engineering drawings, maps, and other useful pictures. Many plotters use a variety of pens—felt-tip, ballpoint, liquid roller, nylon-tip, and fine drafting pens. Four, six, or even eight colors can be used. Before buying a plotter, be sure that the type of pens you need are always restocked. Getting a plotter with Hewlett-Packard-compatible pens basically ensures that you will always be able to get the pens you need.

The two types of plotters are the flatbed plotter and the drum plotter. A *flatbed* plotter looks like a table with pens mounted on a track. On some plotters, the pens move; on others, the table holding the paper moves. *Drum* plotters draw on paper that is rolled on a cylinder. *Plotters* produce high-quality output, and handle larger paper sizes than printers.

(See 1.49 Printers; 3.36 Graphics Software.)

1.58 Voice Synthesizers

A *voice synthesizer* uses phonemes to create spoken words. A *phoneme* is the smallest combination of letters that can generate a sound. The voice synthesizer analyzes the letters in a word, determines which phonemes are created by the letters, and combines the phonemes into words. The program also uses rules for *tone and accents* (stress) to make the speech seem more realistic. Many voice synthesizers have poor sound quality, but research is improving this problem. Someday, listeners will be unable to distinguish between human speech and synthesized voices.

Voice synthesizers can help people with special needs to lead meaningful and productive lives. For example, the Kurzweil Reading Machine, designed by Ray Kurzweil to aid the blind, scans a printed page and reads aloud. Other systems, called *screen readers*, direct all of a microcomputer's keyboard input and screen text to the voice synthesizer. A screen reader is generally a *terminate-and-stay-resident (TSR)* program. Once the program is loaded, another program can be loaded on top of it. This way, popular off-the-shelf software can be used without any special preparation by its manufacturer. Job Acquisition with Speech screen-reader software by Henter-Joyce can drive synthesizers that are compatible with DOS machines. OutSPOKEN by Berkeley Systems is a screen reader for the Macintosh.

The CD-ROM may revolutionize computer systems for the blind. Such a disk can hold an entire reference work, and thus eliminate the expense and volume of Braille reference works. The CD-ROMs can be used with many speech synthesizers.

(See 1.27 CD-ROMs and Optical Storage; 3.45 Multimedia Applications; 5.18 Computers for People with Disabilities: Meeting Special Needs; Software Review section: Monologue, outSPOKEN.)

PART 2 CONTENTS INDEX

BUYING AND CARING FOR YOUR COMPUTER

For a number of reasons, buying a microcomputer and software can be a difficult and time-consuming task. As with stereo components and other appliances, there are many models of microcomputers. Choosing one out of 150 models can seem impossible. Even the price range is wide—from a few hundred dollars to well over $10,000 for a *high-end* machine (that is, one that has great capabilities). Add to that choice the hundreds of peripheral devices, add-ons, and software packages from which to select, and the task seems complex and confusing indeed.

The purchase of a computer is a major investment for most people, so care must be taken not to make expensive mistakes. Spend time learning about the different systems on the market—and analyzing what you want to *do* with a computer—before making a decision. Otherwise, your computer purchase may end up in the closet gathering dust.

The suggestions offered in this section deal with the overall aspects of buying computers. Under most of the topics, you will find additional suggestions regarding software and particular pieces of equipment.

2.1 THE MAIN CATEGORIES OF COMPUTERS

If you are purchasing a computer for yourself or your small business, one of the decisions has probably been made for you already. Most likely you will buy a *microcomputer*. A microcomputer is a small, single-user computer that is governed by a microprocessor. It can be linked into a network of other microcomputers and equipment that can be shared (such as printers), which is convenient for small businesses with limited financial resources. Microcomputers (sometimes called *personal computers*) are ranked in size from the powerful desktop-size workstation to the tiny palmtop.

Along with microcomputers, the other types of computers on the market—minicomputers, mainframes, and supercomputers—are categorized according to size, capability, price range, and speed of operation. Unlike microcomputers, their expense makes them unsuitable for home use and for most small businesses.

The *minicomputer* (actually the size of a refrigerator or closet) got its name in comparison with the large-scale mainframe computers that dominated the market when it was introduced in the 1960s. It provides capabilities similar to those of a mainframe, but has a smaller capacity, and supports fewer users and devices. Its cost, anywhere from a few thousand dollars to over $100,000, is its primary advantage for small- to medium-sized businesses. Colleges became early and continuing users of minicomputers; many of these machines support the operations of retail chain stores and hospitals.

A *mainframe* computer supports thousands of users and peripherals concurrently, and processes great quantities of data at very high speeds. It can occupy an entire floor of a large office building. The computer alone can cost from $50,000 to over $5 million and requires expensive installation and maintenance procedures. These include heavy-duty electrical wiring, air conditioning, and security features. Mainframes are typically found in organizations such as large corporations, banks, and airlines. You might use your microcomputer to access a mainframe in order to transfer money from your savings to your checking account, for example, or to make airline reservations.

The most powerful and most expensive computer is the *supercomputer*, which is distinguished from the mainframe not by the number of users or equipment it can support, but by its incredibly fast processing power. Supercomputers carry price tags to match their capabilities, costing from $5 million to over $20 million. Therefore, only the largest organizations tend to use these systems. Among them are large research and science facilities, and giant corporations or federal agencies that study weather forecasting, oil exploration, energy conservation, seismology, nuclear reactor safety, and cryptography. In addition, supercomputers are used for simulations in nuclear energy research, stress tests in aircraft design, and special effects in films.

(See 2.2 Purchasing Computers: The Big Picture; 2.7 Configuration and Compatibility; 2.8 Portables.)

2.2 Purchasing Computers: The Big Picture

Although you will be choosing from just one category of computers—microcomputers—there is a wide variety of options within that category. Experts often recommend that you choose the software first, and then match the hardware to the requirements of that software. This approach is a good general policy because the software determines how much memory you need, what kind of operating system is necessary, and whether you need high-quality graphics capabilities. Even so, there may be other factors involved in the final decision. For example, you may need several software packages or a portable computer to accomplish the jobs you want to do. In addition, most of the new computers sold today have more than enough capabilities and memory for normal home use, such as school work, financial planning, letter writing, games, and hobby databases. Further, some special uses (such as desktop publishing and multimedia) and some popular software (such as Microsoft Windows and Windows applications) work better with more than the minimum requirements listed on the package.

Use the following list of guidelines before looking at specifications for your new system:

- **Know what you want to do with your computer and software.** Do you want to write papers, analyze financial data, file data, create graphs and charts, publish a newsletter, or use the same data interchangeably among several programs? Do you want to run a particular software package? Will you use multimedia and graphics-intensive programs? Do you need to carry your computer with you for your work?
- **Know about how much room you will need to store and run software.** If you are planning on putting 200 computer games on a hard disk drive, you want to be sure you'll have a large enough drive.
- **Know about how much data you will be using at once.** Will you normally be using ten pages or fifty pages of text? A day's figures or a month's figures of financial data? Text or complex drawings? Both software and data determine how much memory, speed, and storage you need.
- **Know the functions and names of basic hardware devices.**
- **Know some basic functions of various types of software packages.**
- **Test different computers and programs.** Read the reviews in computer books and magazines. Test programs with data similar to what you will be entering. Decide how important "user friendliness" is to you.
- **Determine whether the computer you're considering will meet your future needs.** Will you be able to use it for different tasks? Is it easily upgradeable? Does it have room to grow?
- **Decide whether the hardware and software must be compatible with certain other computers.** You may want to buy a computer that is compatible with those you use at work, or with those your clients use. Or you may want to base your choice on what computer your children are using at school.
- **Be sure that the system and all the equipment and software you want to use will work together.** Printers, for example, require certain types of connections. Be sure you have the right number of the proper connections, and that those connections won't be needed for some other piece of equipment.
- **If you get software, a driver, or other items bundled with your purchase, be sure you are getting the latest version.** This is important because earlier versions of some products do not work with the latest versions of other products.

- **Check with friends, computer magazines, and users' groups for further information about the software and hardware you are considering.**
- **Find out how much is included in the basic package, and get firm prices.** The price may include the CPU only, or the CPU, monitor, keyboard, and disk drive. You may need additional cash outlays for cards that drive a printer or produce sound.
- **Find out about warranties, service, and return policies.**
- **Set price limits, but don't be too price-conscious.** By identifying your intended uses, you already will have defined some price limits.

(See 1.12 Memory and Storage; 2.3 Which Computer? The Platforms; 2.6 Open Versus Proprietary; 2.7 Configuration and Compatibility; 2.8 Portables; 2.10 Multimedia Standards; 2.11 Used or New?; 2.12 Obsolescence; 3.25 Evaluating Software; 5.17 Safety Issues; 5.18 Computers for People with Disabilities: Meeting Special Needs.)

2.3 Which Computer? The Platforms

Once you know some of the brand names of computers, you may wonder what the differences are among them. Computers commonly used in homes today conform to just a few *platforms*. A platform defines the standard around which a system can be developed—for example, two common platforms are the Apple Macintosh computer with a Motorola 68040 microprocessor, and the IBM-compatible PC (personal computer) with an Intel 80486 microprocessor. (The initials *PC* are commonly used to identify IBM-type computers, while Macintoshes are commonly referred to as *Macs*.) IBM-compatible machines are sometimes called *clones*. Other platforms include the Apple II line and the Commodore Amiga. The Apple II computers have been popular in schools. The Amiga is a high-performance computer with television-quality animation and graphics. The following sections talk about the Macintosh and IBM-compatible platforms in more detail.

The Macintosh Platform

All computers in the Macintosh platform also include the current version of its operating system, which is called System. When you start up a Macintosh computer, the screen greets you and then stops at a display called the Desktop. From there, you use the mouse to point at the *icon* (or picture) of a file or program you want to use. To see what jobs you can do, you can click the mouse button to pull down one of the items in the menu bar at the top of the screen. Once you decide what you want to do, you simply use the mouse to highlight that icon, and click the mouse button twice to open the file or program. If you open a document, the program opens automatically with that document. This picture-oriented approach to using a computer is called a *graphical user interface*, or GUI, pronounced "gooey."

With a little instruction, a novice can sit down at a Macintosh and start using it instinctively without memorizing anything. Thus, the Macintosh computers are often described as *user-friendly*. There are no cryptic codes to memorize, and none of the arcane file-naming conventions used so often in the PC arena/platform.

With the GUI, all Macintosh programs have a consistent look and feel; once you have learned how to operate one Macintosh program, it's easy to learn the basic conventions of another. In addition, the words and text generally appear on the screen the same way they will when printed on paper. This feature is called WYSIWYG, an acronym for "What You See Is What You Get," and it can be very helpful when you are experimenting with graphics and fonts.

Now, some seasoned computer users might snicker a bit when they hear you are using a Macintosh. After all, using a mouse and little pictures and menus is not what they'd call "real" computing. In the area of sheer computing speed, at least, they may have a point. A GUI requires more memory, and may run more slowly than the command-line user interfaces, although recent Macintoshes are much speedier. Some people feel that using the mouse and the menus can be cumbersome and slow; others make the same complaint about having to type commands.

Macintosh computers not only feature a friendly user interface, they are generally easier to set up than IBM-compatible (PC) computers, and software and hardware compatibility is less of a problem. (This concept is called *plug-and-play* because little other preparation is needed besides plugging in the device.) Network capabilities, sound, and graphics are already built into the Macintosh computers. You can buy Macintosh computers as a package, but it is also possible to buy separate pieces from different manufacturers. The benefit to Macintosh computers is that Apple defines most of the hardware standards for peripherals and other equipment designed for use with the Mac, so compatibility is usually not a problem.

The PC (IBM-Compatible) Platform

The PC platform can be further refined by the *system software* it uses: MS-DOS or PC-DOS; DOS with Windows; or OS/2. (Some people even include the basic configuration—tower, desktop, notebook—in the platform description.)

In the past, the most noticeable difference between the Macintosh and IBM platforms has been the method by which you command the computer to do a job.

When you start up a PC in the DOS operating system, all that appears on the screen is this: **C:>**. This is called a *prompt*, but it doesn't really prompt, or tell, you to do anything because there are no on-screen instructions. You must know what to do next in order to use the computer. This means typing in a command, so you can see why this type of *user interface* (i.e., method of letting a user communicate with a computer) is called *command-line* user interface. You could type something such as **TYPE FILE1.DAT |MORE** or **COPY C:FILE2.DAT A:\XYZ** to tell the computer's operating system (PC-DOS or MS-DOS) what you want to do. The catch is that you have to know exactly which command to type, and type it accurately.

Computer and software manufacturers now have realized that many people will not use a computer unless it is easy and natural to use. Thus, GUIs have become available for PCs, too. One of the best known is Windows, by Microsoft Corporation, but some computer manufacturers are providing their own GUIs with their new machines. Examples include Presentation Manager in IBM's OS/2 operating system, and Deskmate on Tandy's machines. Experts predict that all operating systems will include GUI features in the future.

IBM PCs and compatibles are usually less expensive than the Macintoshes—until you consider the extras you may need to buy. DOS machines can be bought as a package, but it is also possible to buy separate pieces from different manufacturers. The monitor may come from NEC and the modem from Hayes, for example. If you are planning to buy pieces from two or more manufacturers, you face a plethora of options for monitors, storage, and other equipment. This is often where the confusion begins about what to buy. It may be better to buy your first computer as a package—perhaps with the exception of the modem and peripherals, such as a printer—until you know more about computers and have used one for a while.

(See 1.8 Microprocessors; 2.6 Open Versus Proprietary; 2.8 Portables; 2.10 Multimedia Standards; 3.2 Operating Systems; 3.4 Telling the Computer What to Do: User Interfaces; 3.6 DOS Versions; 3.8 System 7.5; 3.9 Microsoft Windows; 3.10 OS/2.)

2.4 Power Macs and Apple Macintosh Computers

All Macintosh computers use microprocessors from the Motorola company, so that with a few exceptions, programs written for one Macintosh computer will run on the later Macintosh computers. Computers in the Macintosh line include the following models:

- The Performa is designed for mass-market sales, so you can find it in office-supply stores and other general stores as well as stores that specialize in computers.
- The LC, targeted for the education market, will soon be available only through schools.
- The PowerBook is Apple's popular notebook computer. A variation of the PowerBook is the Macintosh Duo System, which consists of a PowerBook Duo (a small portable) you can insert into the Macintosh Duo Dock, which is equipped with a desktop monitor and keyboard.

The PowerBook is Apple's offering in the notebook computer market.

- The Quadra is a high-end computer designed with graphics, desktop publishing, engineering, and other power-intensive jobs. High-end Quadras can be adapted to use software designed for MS-DOS and Windows machines.

Each family of Macintosh computers includes models that range from less powerful to more powerful; one measure of this power is *clock speed* in megahertz. Macs use the Motorola 68030 or 68040 microprocessor chip; high-end models have faster microprocessors. For example, the Performa uses a 25MHz 68030 chip; the higher-end Quadra 950 uses a 33MHz 68040 chip.

Apple has produced a number of different models over the years, some of which are no longer on the market. You may find used Macintosh computers with names like the Classic, Lisa, and Centris (which was absorbed into the Quadra family). Apple's newest Macintosh is the Power Macintosh, which uses the Motorola PowerPC 601 microprocessors. These very speedy chips were developed as a result of an agreement among Apple, Motorola, and IBM.

The PowerPC is designed to be used with both System 7.xx *and* DOS/Windows software—a first step in the direction of compatibility between the Mac and PC platforms. (To perform in this manner, however, the computer must be equipped with additional RAM and a software program called SoftWindows by Insignia Solutions.) Apple advertises the Power Macintosh as a business computer, in order to make inroads into corporations that have in the past used all IBM-compatible machines.

Three Power Macintosh models available at this time are the 6100/60, the 7100/66, and the 8100/80. Chips running at 100 MHz and 133 MHz are also available. PowerPC 603 chips will be used in notebook computers. In the future, Apple is expected to exchange the slower NuBus bus for PCI, which is three times faster (a fast *data bus*, i.e., data pathway, is another way of measuring a computer's power). Existing Macintosh software is being rewritten to take advantage of the PowerPC's capabilities, but Power Macs run other Macintosh software in an *emulation mode* (in which they imitate, or run like, the other models such as Quadras). There can be a trade-off between speed and compatibility.

New "fat" applications have "smart" installers that know on which Mac they are being installed, and configure themselves appropriately. PowerPCs will be supporting such advanced features as virtual memory, full-scale live video, fast 3-D graphics, two-way video conferences, speech recognition, handwriting recognition, and interactive cable television connections.

Apple's Newton MessagePads pioneered *pen-based* systems, which allow a user to hand-write commands. Although the Newtons were the laughingstock of computing for a while—*character recognition* remains a technical challenge—each succeeding model has improved, and pen-based systems are becoming quite popular.

(See 1.44 Pen-Based Computing, 2.3 Which Computer? The Platforms; 2.5 IBM and IBM-Compatible Computers; 2.6 Open Versus Proprietary; 2.7 Configuration and Compatibility; 2.8 Portables.)

2.5 IBM and IBM-Compatible Computers

The IBM-compatible PCs use Intel microprocessors, starting with the first PC (introduced in 1981) which used the 8088, and increasing in power to the 80486 microprocessor used in the current line of entry-level and low-end IBM computers. Rather than continue using numbers to identify microprocessors, however, Intel decided on *Pentium* as the name for its most recent and most powerful microprocessor for personal computers. The Pentium runs at 66 MHz or more, has 3.1 million transistors, and can do two things at once.

You'll find IBM models by such names as ValuePoint, PS/2, ThinkPad, and Aptiva. The ValuePoint computers are designed for mass-market sales and are IBM's low-end models. The PS/2 computers are the IBM business machines, which use the Pentium processors, and the ThinkPads are notebook and pen-based systems. The latest IBM model is their multimedia machine, Aptiva. Older IBM models include the XT and the AT.

Because IBM opened its designs to third-party manufacturers, many companies today make IBM-compatible computers. Most of these computers use Intel microprocessors, though a few use chips made by AMD (Advanced Micro Devices) and Cyrix. The computers are called "compatible" because they can run software designed for IBM microcomputers. Manufacturers of IBM-compatible computers include Dell, Gateway 2000, Tandy, Toshiba, Zenith, Acer Corporation, Compaq, CompuAdd, Everex, NEC, and many more. If you are in the market for a workstation, you may want to look at Sun Computer, Hewlett-Packard Corporation, and NeXT, which can perform three-dimensional imagery and animation.

It is no wonder that IBM computers have become the norm in business use: first, IBM had already established its mainframes and minicomputers in business and industry, and second, once microcomputers became popular, the availability of IBM-compatibles was widespread.

(See 1.44 Pen-Based Computing, 2.3 Which Computer? The Platforms; 2.4 Power Macs and Apple Macintosh Computers; 2.6 Open Versus Proprietary; 2.7 Configuration and Compatibility; 2.8 Portables.)

2.6 Open Versus Proprietary

The words *open* and *proprietary* describe the way a manufacturer presents its computers' *architecture*, or design, to the market. The process begins with *design specifications*—officially approved standards and privately designed features of the architecture. An architecture is *open* if its design specifications are public. Anyone can design add-on products for a machine with open architecture; buyers will find a variety of choices and prices for products they can install themselves. (A warning about installation: Installing a device yourself may void the warranty on your original computer or even on the new piece of equipment. Be sure to check the fine print each time you buy a new product.) The disadvantage of open architecture is that other manufacturers can duplicate the product, as personal computer manufacturers did when they "cloned" the IBM PC.

A *proprietary* design, on the other hand, is privately owned and controlled; sometimes it is called *closed*. The concept implies that the company is keeping secret the specifics that would enable other companies to duplicate a product. Macintosh computers are proprietary machines. Even the case on the Macintosh Classic machines was designed to discourage users from opening it and inserting products made by other manufacturers. Increasingly, closed or proprietary systems are seen as a disadvantage; consumers want the option of buying equipment from various manufacturers, and will avoid systems that prevent it. A proprietary system, however, can be "friendlier" to the user because there are fewer decisions to make. Manufacturers of proprietary systems also have a great deal of control over the quality of the system and the consistency of the user interface. (Apple is working on licensing its designs to a number of companies to produce Macintosh compatibles.)

(See 2.2 Purchasing Computers: The Big Picture; 2.3 Which Computer? The Platforms; 2.7 Configuration and Compatibility; 2.9 Standards; 2.13 Warranties, Service, and Legal Rights.)

2.7 Configuration and Compatibility

The *configuration* of a computer system describes the system's components—hardware or software or both—and how they are arranged. For example, a typical new Macintosh system would include the computer with a hard disk drive and a floppy disk drive, the monitor, a keyboard, a mouse, and the System 7 operating system. The computer in this setup is normally called a *desktop* model, a type of computer that can easily fit on a desk but is cumbersome to carry around. Desktop models are the type you set up and leave in place. The various brands and models of desktops take up varying amounts of space (in computer lingo, the *footprint*). For example, a Macintosh Classic computer takes up less space than the IBM PS/2, and so you say that it has a smaller footprint.

The two other types of configurations are tower and portable. A *tower* configuration is one in which the power supply, motherboard, and mass storage devices are stacked in a case or cabinet that is taller than it is wide. It is often part of a high-end system designed as a workstation, which is a powerful microcomputer generally used for engineering, graphics, and desktop-publishing applications. (To add confusion here, the term *workstation* also means the desk area, cubicle, or other physical location of your computer equipment, chair, and other work supplies. This location is often a member or node in a network of computers.) Desktop models, in contrast, have these same components arranged in a box that is wider and deeper than it is tall (in general, this means a bigger footprint). Portable computers (discussed in detail later in this book) are small enough to carry comfortably with you.

Much of the software on the market requires a minimum configuration in order to work properly. For example, Windows requires a minimum of 2MB of RAM, a fast microprocessor (at least a 386 or 386SX is recommended), and plenty of hard disk space. Most dealers and users recommend at least 8MB of RAM and a 486 microprocessor; minimum configurations may not provide optimum conditions for Windows to work efficiently as an operating environment.

Part of the configuration is the *power supply*. This component delivers electrical power from the outlet to the computer. Most personal computers plug into standard electrical outlets; the power supply pulls the required amount of current, and regulates the voltage to some degree. It changes the high-voltage alternating current into low-voltage direct current. In general, the more powerful the computer, the more wattage the power supply must deliver. Any time you change the configuration of your system, you need to be sure the power supply can handle the new equipment. The power supply can be upgraded, if necessary. Common power supplies are 140W, 150W, and 200W (W standing for watts).

Configuration also describes the jobs you need to do to make a particular hardware device or program work with your computer. For example, a graphics program may need to know what type of video adapter the computer has; a word processor may need to know what printer you are using. You configure a device by setting switches—for example, the DIP switches in printers—or by making choices from the menus in software. (Physically setting DIP switches is becoming obsolete.) You can even configure the speed with which a cursor blinks, or the rate at which a key repeats itself when it is held down. You specify these configurations either by typing commands (in the DOS operating system) or by choosing options from the Control Panel program in the Macintosh or Windows environment. "Plug-and-play" devices skip this complexity, and configure themselves to your system automatically.

If a system is configured correctly, all its components should be compatible. *Compatibility* means a device or program is capable of working with another device or program. The concept is important for both hardware and software. For example, a word processor designed for the IBM PC is compatible with a Dell computer if it can be run on the Dell with no problems. A printer is compatible with a computer if it can be connected to it and used to print material sent from the computer. A printer can achieve compatibility by making the software believe that it is actually another printer; this is called *emulation*. Software products can be compatible, too. For example, a lesser-known database program may be designed to be compatible with a better-known product, in which case it can accept files from or send files to the better-known program.

IBM PCs are generally software-compatible, which means they can use the same software without modification, and share the same data. Some software developers are writing software specifically for the 80486 microprocessors, however, and these programs are not compatible with earlier microprocessors.

Despite recent developments such as the PowerPC, Macintosh computers have not been compatible with IBM and other PC lines. Macs have different microprocessors, different operating systems, and different file formats. Thus, it is difficult to share data between the two types of computers. It is possible to buy software called a *file transfer program* that enables you to transfer files from an IBM computer or compatible to a Macintosh, and vice versa. One example is the MacLink Plus/PC set of programs by DataViz, with which you can transfer files from the most popular programs running under Macintosh, MS-DOS, or Windows. Another method of bridging the Macintosh-IBM difference is to use an emulator program, which enables a Macintosh to emulate an IBM PC. This property is valuable in a business setting where most microcomputers are IBMs and compatibles. (Note discussions elsewhere of the Power Macs and Soft Windows for running DOS/Windows.)

By the way, in reference to IBM PCs, the word *clone* implies that a product is an exact duplicate of another. Thus, an IBM PC clone should have most, if not all, the same components that an actual IBM computer has. An IBM-compatible, on the other hand, is capable of running the same software that an IBM PC can run, but it is not necessarily the same inside. Not all computers advertised as IBM-compatible can run every piece of software designed for IBM PCs; always check whether your software will run on the machine you want to buy.

(See 1.8 Microprocessors; 2.3 Which Computer? The Platforms; 2.8 Portables; 2.9 Standards; 2.10 Multimedia Standards; Software Review section: MacLink Plus/PC, Universal Soft PC.)

2.8 Portables

Portable computers are lightweight microcomputers that are small enough to be carried from place to place easily. The largest of the portable computers is called the transportable, or *luggable*, computer. This category generally weighs more than 17 pounds and is equal in power to the majority of desktop models. Nearly all luggables have high-density hard disk drives, and can be equipped for multimedia. They require an external power source to operate.

Smaller portable machines are categorized as laptops and notebooks. The difference lies mainly in weight: laptop computers generally weigh 8 to 12 pounds, whereas notebooks weigh less than 8 pounds. Notebook computers that weigh from 3 to 5 pounds are sometimes called *sub-notebooks*. (You may see slightly different weight ranges assigned to each group of portables, but these are the standard ranges.) The terms *laptop* and *notebook* are often used to mean the same thing, but some sources refer to notebooks as subsets of laptops. Some experts say that laptops per se have all but disappeared.

Laptop computers used to be a novelty. Up until now, they have lagged behind the technology of desktop models, and were used primarily for the special needs that computing-on-the-run salespeople or students might have. They were not serious contenders as replacements for desktop PCs. In fact, most of their data had to be downloaded into PCs for serious computing to take place. Thus, the small size of laptops was not enough to win over serious PC users.

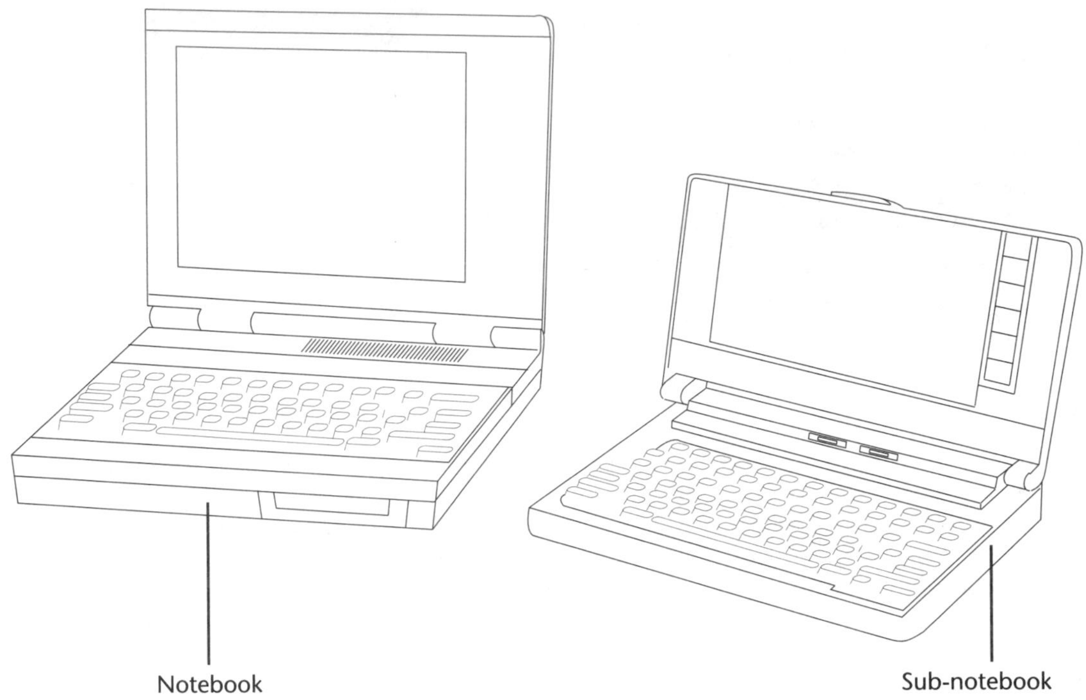

Today's notebooks fit a lot of processing power into a compact package.

Today, notebook computers are powerful enough to be your only personal computer, and are less expensive than their predecessors. For example, the 386SX and higher notebooks are powerful enough to handle Microsoft Windows, a graphical user interface that remains popular among users of DOS-based desktop computers with 80386 or 80486 chips. This fact is significant; it means people who are accustomed to using Windows on their desktop PCs can use the same applications and files on their notebook computers.

The principal difference between the laptops and desktop models is the display. A regular desktop model uses a television-like screen that is almost as deep as it is wide. The laptop uses a flat-panel technology, usually liquid-crystal display (LCD). The image is still not as sharp as images on high-quality desktop monitors, but it is improving rapidly. Most portables' screens display images at a level of resolution that rivals VGA, and many laptops can be connected to a regular monitor. Some can use both the regular monitor and the flat-panel display simultaneously. Many manufacturers provide a mechanism for connecting a laptop computer easily to a desktop display. This procedure is called *docking*.

Despite their reduced size, many notebooks offer a feel that is consistent with that of their larger cousins. Notebooks' keyboards often feature normal spacing between the keys, and normal-sized keys that depress about the same distance as those on a desktop keyboard. The location of function keys may vary with each notebook; choose the model that puts them in the location most convenient for you. Some notebook models include a *trackball* that performs the functions of a mouse in a more limited space. For example, the trackball on Macintosh PowerBooks is placed in the center front of the keyboard. You can rest your palms on the flat areas on either side of the trackball as you type, and rotate the trackball.

The hard disk drives are miniaturized, yet these 2.5- or 1.8-inch drives have capacities of 60MB or higher. Access time to data on the drives has also improved compared with that of earlier laptops. Because most machines have a standard 2MB of RAM, many users who want to run Windows (and other memory-hogging software) add RAM for a total of 4MB to 8MB. Additional memory and capabilities such as modems are usually added at *PCMCIA slots*, which accept the credit card-sized expansion boards. In addition, you can use cables to connect your notebook computer to a monitor, printer, tape drive, external modem, full-sized keyboard, or desktop computer. Almost all notebook computer manufacturers offer a fax modem with their computers, so you will not need an external modem—and maybe not even a printer, as you can use the fax modem to print a document through a fax machine.

Battery life on small portable computers is still a problem. The battery generally runs from two to three hours before it needs recharging. New, low-power microprocessors such as the Intel 386SL add to battery life, freezing power usage to the minimum without shutting down a program, until you are ready to work again. Many laptops have power-conservation methods included in the software that allow you to enter a standby mode, or use a suspend/resume mode that shuts down everything but RAM until you are ready to resume working. Even then, the battery life is often only seven to eight hours. (When you shop for a notebook to use with Windows, be sure the computer you are considering can suspend without disabling Windows.) Recharge time can run into a couple of hours, too. Some models offer interchangeable batteries, but changing the batteries can be difficult. The Dell laptop lets you change batteries without shutting down the system, as it incorporates a tiny internal battery that operates for a couple of minutes.

Some market analysts predict that notebooks will account for over half of all personal computers sold by the second half of the 1990s. Manufacturers who want to be successful in the notebook market must move their products quickly from conception to production, and be ready to change plans quickly to incorporate new technology. A particular screen or a microprocessor can become outdated very quickly. Examples of notebook and laptop computers include the Macintosh PowerBooks by Apple, AT&T Safari, Compaq Contura Aero, NEC Ultralite Versa, Everex, Tempo LX, Texas Instruments TravelMate, Zeos Contenda, IBM ThinkPad, Toshiba Portégé, Zenith Mastersport 386SL, Gateway 2000 Colorbook, and Dell Latitude.

Although there are computers smaller than notebooks, commonly called *palmtops*, any model smaller than a notebook computer has a relatively cramped keyboard with tiny keys that are hard to use with any speed. They are handy for use as electronic address and memo machines, but some include Lotus 1-2-3, data-communication software, file managers, and a financial calculator. The Hewlett-Packard 95LX, Atari Portfolio, and Poqet PC Classic are popular models. Simple electronic organizers include the Sharp Wizard, the Zenith 2DS-112, and the Casio B.O.S.S. (You can also read about the pen-based portable systems in the sections on Pen-based Computing and Gesture-based Interface.)

(See 1.12 Memory and Storage; 1.15 RAM; 1.25 Hard Disks; 1.37 Keyboards; 1.38 Mice and Trackballs; 1.44 Pen-Based Computing; 1.48 Flat-Panel Displays; 2.7 Configuration and Compatibility; 3.9 Microsoft Windows; 4.3 Modems.)

2.9 STANDARDS

Without specific standards, it would be impossible for almost any type of communication to occur. You would have to buy all of your hardware and software from the same manufacturer. Some standards are industry-wide, such as the standards for electrical installations and communications, and have been set by a specific standards organization. Others are *de facto standards*, accepted simply because they are widely used and recognized by manufacturers *as* standards.

Standards enable manufacturers to produce equipment that will work with any IBM PC or compatible, or any Macintosh system, for example. Buying standard equipment also enables you to buy products from various manufacturers and be reasonably sure that the equipment will run with your machine.

Organizations that approve industry standards include ANSI (the American National Standards Institute, which is primarily concerned with standards for software and programming languages), IEEE (the Institute of Electrical and Electronics Engineers, which sets standards for electrical interfaces), and ISO (International Standards Organization). ANSI was founded in 1918 to support all industries, and its members now include all the large computer companies. The object of ANSI is to set standards, not only for the computer industry, but also for a wide range of other technical areas including electrical specifications and communications protocols. Some standards set by ANSI are ANSI FORTRAN, the version of the FORTRAN computer language approved by the ANSI committee, and FDDI, the main set of protocols for transmitting data over fiber-optic cables.

Standards have been set for character-set codes, video cards and graphics, programming languages, buses, and interfaces. For example, microcomputers use ASCII codes for representing English characters as numbers. The standard ASCII set uses seven bits for each character. Although ASCII is not always the default storage format for many programs, most programs such as word processors have an option to store files in ASCII form, which enables you to transfer the files to noncompatible computers and programs.

Materials such as tapes have standards, too, so that when you buy any brand of tape cartridge, for example, you can be sure it will work on your tape drive. QIC (quarter-inch cartridge) tapes are among the most popular tapes used with personal computer systems. A consortium of manufacturers, the Quarter-Inch Cartridge Drive Standards, Inc., established the various QIC standards. Tapes have varying qualities, however, and generally you get what you pay for. Floppy disks and CD-ROMs are standardized, too, so that any blank floppy can be formatted to suit your system (provided the densities are compatible), and most CD-ROM titles can be played on your CD-ROM drive. (WORM and erasable optical disks are not standardized yet.)

Protocols for sending data over telephone lines are approved standards, too. For example, in the United States, the standard for sending data at 300 baud is Bell 103, and the standard for sending data at 1,200 bps (bits per second) is Bell 212A. The CCITT (Comité Consultatif International Téléphonique et Télégraphique) sets international standards for error-detection and recovery methods, modems, network and electronic-mail transmissions, and data-compression techniques for fax and modem transmissions.

Standards can change in response to technical advances. Metal telephone wires, for example, can send data at a maximum rate of 56,000 bps, but these lines are being replaced by fiber-optic cables, which are capable of much faster rates. Thus, countries all over the world may be changing their standards to fit the new technology. One such suggested standard is broadband ISDN (B-ISDN) for sending voice, video, and data at the same time over fiber-optic telephone lines. The data rates for B-ISDN range up to 1,500,000 bps.

Other standards include the following:

- RS-232C (EIA-232D is its new name) and its successors, RS-422 and RS-423, standard interfaces for connecting serial devices (set by IEEE)

- SCSI (Small Computer Systems Interface), a parallel interface standard
- MIDI (Musical Instrument Digital Interface), a standard for representing sounds
- NuBus expansion bus for Macintosh computers starting with the Macintosh II
- Centronics interface for parallel ports
- ESDI (Enhanced Small Device Interface), a standard for connecting disk drives to computers
- SVGA (Super Video Graphics Array), a standard for graphics display on video monitors
- EPA Energy Star Standard, which requires power-management circuitry that trims an idle computer's energy drain to 30 watts
- Swedish MPR-II for monitor emissions
- TWAIN, for scanning images directly into TWAIN-compliant applications

Although some standards are ANSI-approved, there are enough variations on these standards that you cannot always be assured that two products with the same standard are compatible. For example, SCSI supports several types of connectors. Also, many devices are described as being "standard" when (in fact) a consortium of manufacturers is pushing to establish their products—rather than those of competitors—as standard, but this effort has not succeeded yet. Consider that an organization called VESA (Video Electronics Standards Association) is trying to get the SVGA high-resolution graphics specifications accepted as the industry standard, but competing "standards" exist: TI 34010 from Texas Instruments and, from IBM, XGA (Extended Graphics Array) and 8514/A.

De facto standards apply to formats, programming languages, operating systems, and protocols that are recognized because they are widely used, not because they are approved by a particular standards organization. For example, IBM has defined an extended ASCII code that uses 8 bits and allows for 128 additional characters. Extended ASCII is not officially standardized, but most PC-compatibles recognize the code.

De facto standards for laser printers include the Adobe PostScript page-description language and the Hewlett-Packard Printer Control Language. The following examples are other de facto standards:

- Hayes command set for controlling modems
- Xmodem Communications Protocol

- IBM PC BIOS (Basic Input/Output System)
- AT bus (used on older PCs)
- Kermit, a file-transfer protocol
- Sound Blaster for sound boards

If this talk about standards is confusing, you should remember that you will often see these standards listed in advertisements for various machines and software. It is probably best to go with a standard that seems to be widely accepted, rather than one with only a few adherents; note, however, that widely *accepted* standards are not always the *best*. Your dealer should be able to help you identify standards that will keep everything in your system compatible.

(See 2.6 Open Versus Proprietary; 2.10 Multimedia Standards.)

2.10 Multimedia Standards

Multimedia refers to a capability of transferring information through more than one medium at a time—for example, simultaneous text, video, and audio. Such a capability is designed as a multisensory method of improving—and speeding—the user's understanding, usually of instructional material.

The technology began to catch on in the mid-1980s when corporations used interactive laser videodiscs for in-house training. Multimedia computer applications include sound, color video images, and interactive components. Commonly, the user accesses such applications from CD-ROMs or through networks. For example, a laser-disc encyclopedia could include voices, pictures, and music to expand upon the text and charts. You could also ask questions of the encyclopedia to clarify points you do not understand. A tutorial that teaches physiology, for example, might include interactive components and animated sequences that help medical students understand the design of the human body almost as if they were manipulating a real body. Students can make up their own multimedia applications, too—for example, while reading about the Civil War, a user might choose songs and images to combine with oral and written text to present to a class.

There are really no standards for multimedia at this time, although a group of manufacturers—including Tandy Corp., NEC Technologies, CompuAdd Computer Corp., and Philips Consumer Electronics Corp.—have formed a marketing organization called the Multimedia PC Marketing Council. The standard they have developed is called the Multimedia PC (the latest being MPC-2), and vendors use an MPC logo on products and upgrade kits designed for multimedia applications. Experts warn, however, that standards set today will be rapidly outdated. Here are some of the minimum standards—actually somewhat greater than the MPC standards—that experts recommend for IBM computers and compatibles:

- a computer with (at minimum) a 66MHz 486DX2 microprocessor
- double-speed CD-ROM drive with 300KB-per-second data-transfer rate
- 8MB of RAM
- 320MB hard disk drive
- 3.5-inch high-density floppy disk drive
- graphical user interface, such as Multimedia with Windows
- 14-inch, 256-color, Super VGA monitor
- 16-bit stereo Sound-Blaster-compatible sound card with MIDI interface
- microphone
- headphones or speakers
- mouse
- 14,400-bit-per-second fax modem
- an authoring program

There are also *multimedia boards*, such as the VGA Broadcaster (IEV Corp.), with which you can capture analog input from a videodisc player, a camera, or a VCR, and also transfer your computer's output to videotape or television.

Although you can compile the components for a multimedia system from various manufacturers, many of today's systems are advertised specifically for multimedia. A number of companies—including CompuAdd, Creative Labs, and Media Vision—offer upgrade kits that bring an IBM PC or compatible system up to multimedia standards with CD-ROM drives, sound boards, and software. NEC even makes a multimedia expansion chassis for portable computers.

Apple was actually a multimedia pioneer, with music and video capabilities built into its Macintosh computers. The Macintosh was designed originally as a multimedia computer; if you own a Macintosh, you may need to purchase only a CD-ROM drive. In addition, Macintosh computers are outfitted with an operating-system extension called QuickTime that lets you manipulate moving images. The main considerations for utilizing multimedia on a Macintosh are memory, operating system, and processor speed. The minimum requirements for a video action capability, for example, would be 7MB of RAM, System 7, and an LC model or higher.

Space and speed for full-motion video are the major problems with multimedia. A television shows 30 distinct images per second. Multimedia video images that would approach this speed create storage problems for computers, although there are a number of ways to solve the problem. The size of the images can be reduced, the number of colors can be reduced, or files can be compressed.

Some critics say that multimedia is a solution without a problem. In other words, it does not answer an existing need, and users must find a way to use the technology to its best potential. Other experts believe that as the method catches on, people will discover more ways to use it. You should know that the developers of many multimedia data packages have put their products together in a hurry to get them on the market, and some show little thought or planning. It's best to read reviews and talk with current users to see whether a particular package is worth buying or would be put out in your next garage sale. Some packages are like many videos and movies: They will quickly drive you to boredom. Others are well worth the price.

(See 1.22 Sound Cards; 1.27 CD-ROMs and Optical Storage; 1.30 Data Compression; 1.38 Mice and Trackballs; 2.7 Configuration and Compatibility; 3.9 Microsoft Windows; 3.45 Multimedia Applications; 3.46 Software for Multimedia Management: Hypertext and Authoring Tools.)

2.11 Used or New?

A quick scan through a newspaper's classified ads may tempt you to call parties who offer used computer equipment for sale. Some used equipment is advertised as almost new, and you wonder why the owner is so quick to get rid of it. Maybe the user quickly graduated to a more powerful machine, does not use the computer, or needs the money. In any case, you could get a real bargain.

You can also buy used equipment through user groups, auctions, and computer swap meets. If you purchase from companies that specialize in selling used equipment, however, you may get some kind of guarantee—often money back—for each piece of equipment. Used computers, recycled software, or both are available through the Boston Computer Exchange, Purple Mountain Computers, American Computer Exchange, Second Source, National Computer Exchange, United Computer Exchange, and Recycled Software.

There are a few things to remember about used equipment before you make a purchase:

- First, *caveat emptor*—let the buyer beware.
- Second, used equipment is often being sold because it is outdated. If you know what software you want to use, be sure that it will work on the equipment you are considering. It would be a mistake to buy an underpowered or severely outdated computer.
- Third, though you may not know whether the equipment has been abused, you will want to avoid equipment that shows obvious signs of abuse—dirt, sticky substances, broken parts, and so on. Until you actually try to use the equipment, you won't know whether someone has stuck a foreign object into the floppy disk drive, or the hard disk drive crashed when the computer was dropped. Therefore you should ask to try out the equipment before buying it. Make sure you test the connections for any other equipment you plan to add to the system. Examine the floppy disk drive carefully; make sure it can initialize a new disk, read some good disks you brought from home, and eject a disk smoothly.
- Fourth, even though the computer has nothing wrong with it now, it may be old enough that its chips or disk drive could fail soon. Repairs can be expensive.
- And fifth, if you are considering upgrading a used machine to meet the demands of current software, you may be in for a surprise. The highest upgrade possible for your machine may not be enough to run the software, and some methods of upgrading can cause compatibility problems among the software and other necessary components. The rule is that simply replacing a few chips on a motherboard will not create a system that is capable of reliable operation and greater speeds. An upgrade may require a new motherboard (for example, installing a 386SX in a 286 computer) or a special upgrade board. Even then, you will probably need more memory—and you may discover that slow peripherals such as the hard drive limit the performance of your upgraded machine. (Before attempting a motherboard upgrade, be sure the new board will fit into the old casing, and that all the connectors on the board match the connector holes in the case.)

Buying used equipment does have advantages, however; the major one is price. You could be learning how to use a second-hand computer at a price you can afford now, while you save the money you need to buy a more expensive, powerful machine later. If you don't mind rudimentary text and graphics displays, you can use an old machine for lightweight jobs. Used computers can enable you to put a computer on each of your children's desks, too. If you are trying to match the computer platform your children use at school (unless they are using Macs), you have no other choice than to buy used: the Apple IIe and Apple IIGS computers some schools use are no longer being sold. Before buying a used computer, however, be sure you know the prices of new equipment; you could easily put more money into buying, repairing, and upgrading older computers than into buying a brand-new multimedia machine.

Buying a new machine does not guarantee that your new system will be trouble-free. You may need to take the equipment back to the store within a few days with a problem. The general rule, however, is that new equipment presents no problems, and if there are problems, you have warranties that help ensure a well-running system. You will also have powerful sound, graphics, and even animation on new computers. And if you think children don't need the computing power that adults do, here's what the experts say: children enjoy programs with high-resolution graphics, animation, sound capabilities, and even voice output, and all of these features require considerable computing power and memory.

(See 2.2 Purchasing Computers: The Big Picture; 2.7 Configuration and Compatibility; 2.12 Obsolescence; 2.22 Users' Groups.)

2.12 Obsolescence

No matter what computer ads may say, a computer is not obsolete as long as it meets your needs. The truth is that many computers being sold today are a great deal more powerful than the average user needs them to be. That said, obsolescence is a real concern of many potential computer buyers and current computer owners. Here are some things to keep in mind when dealing with this issue:

- **A computer is not an investment.** Like cars, computers only depreciate in monetary value. Realize that a computer's real value lies in its capability to make your life easier by helping you perform tasks.
- **Computers continue to improve and computer prices continue to fall.** If your dream machine is a little out of your price range right now, waiting for prices to drop is a much better strategy than buying a cheaper system that will quickly cease to be useful to you. But if you're waiting so that you can buy a system with greater capabilities (that you don't really need) for about the same amount of money as you'd spend now, you're just preventing yourself from realizing the benefits of technology.
- **Once you have your computer, it's possible to upgrade it.** Some components are easier to upgrade than others, however, and some upgrades create problems with compatibility. For example, it is possible to insert a microprocessor upgrade, but other components may not work correctly with that

upgrade. Memory upgrades can be tricky, too. Be sure that you match the speed of the new chips to that of the old. If you are watching costs, it is best to splurge on the microprocessor, and add memory or a better graphics card to your computer later. You should look for a computer that is expandable, with plenty of expansion slots and ports to add the equipment you may want. In fact, you should check regularly to see whether drivers for your video card or hard drive have been upgraded so that you can install the most recent versions for greater computer speed and performance. Computer magazines would be one of your best sources for finding out what upgrades are available.

If you have truly matched your software and hardware to your needs, you should be able to use your computer—with perhaps a few additions—for five to ten years. In addition, most software manufacturers will want to be sure that their software products run on a wide range of machines, including older models. Eventually, however, you may want to run new applications that are simply not possible on the old machines. Then you will be looking at buying your next computer system.

(See 1.8 Microprocessors; 1.15 RAM; 1.18 Ports, Slots, and Bays; 1.23 Video Boards; 2.10 Multimedia Standards; 2.11 Used or New?)

2.13 Warranties, Service, and Legal Rights

A person selling a product may give a guarantee that the product will be of a certain kind, or operate in a certain way. The seller may lead the customer to believe that this product will function as advertised. If the product then fails to live up to the advertisement, the merchant has breached the warranty.

Warranties are covered by the Uniform Commercial Code, which promotes uniformity among state courts in their legal treatment of commercial transactions. (The Uniform Commercial Code dictates, for example, that a seller agrees to ship a product by a certain date, at a specified price, and with a specified warranty.) There are two types of warranties: implied and express. An *implied* warranty suggests that a contract for the sale of goods automatically contains certain warranties that exist by law. These need not be stated verbally or included in written warranties. The implied warranty of merchantability exists if the seller is considered a merchant. It guarantees that the product will function properly for a reasonable amount of time. The implied warranty of fitness is created when the purchaser communicates to the supplier the specific purpose for which the product will be used. If the goods then fail to meet this purpose, then the supplier has breached the warranty.

The *express* warranty is created when the seller makes any promise or statement of fact about the goods being sold which the purchaser uses as a basis for buying the goods. Thus, the seller warrants, or guarantees, that the product will meet the purchaser's needs. A contract may attempt to limit or disclaim all warranties. If the goods fail to conform to the express warranty, the buyer is entitled to a reduced price for the goods as compensatory damages.

Each computer product you buy should be covered by a warranty. In fact, the first things you should see when you unpack your equipment are the packing list and the warranty. In addition, you should have a specified amount of time during which you can return the product for refund, usually a 30-day money-back guarantee. Warranties are valid for a specific time period, usually one to five years. (There is a current trend toward longer warranties.) Within its time frame, a warranty provides for the replacement of particular faulty parts or the entire unit, excepting obvious user abuse, at any time. The warranties should be firm and in writing. Ask the dealer if the system maker's warranty covers the entire computer, including the hard disk drive. If the dealer squirms, some of the parts in the computer may have been replaced with cheap components. Be sure that all parts—original and dealer-installed—are covered by warranties. Also be sure that the warranty applies to the entire computer; some dealers warrant the disk drives separately, and for a much shorter period (such as 90 days).

Remember that warranties can be voided if you attempt to add memory or other components to your system by yourself. This principle applies as well to such items as generic printer consumables and "remanufactured" toner cartridges for laser printers: If a remanufactured cartridge is faulty, the printer's manufacturer most likely will not honor the warranty—though the remanufacturer *should* have a warranty. Failure to follow certain procedures—such as returning equipment in its original packaging, or not getting a return authorization number when using mail order—may also void a warranty. In addition, any attempts to make a case for breaches of warranty may cost more than the items you bought.

You may get added protection through your credit-card company. Using a premium credit card can get you double the amount of warranty coverage. In addition, there may be theft or damage protection, or both. Be sure to check with your credit-card company about its policies and conditions before placing an order. Paying by credit card can help you in case you have exhausted the usual channels to get a problem corrected. Most credit-card companies have offices in every state; they will pursue a fraudulent supplier for you, as long as you have followed their guidelines for reporting problems to the vendor and the credit company.

You may wonder about the extended warranties that many retailers offer. These warranties can often make up for small profit margins. Generally, the more warranties sold, the lower the sales prices of the equipment can be, and low prices are what attract customers in the first place. Retailers generally count on customers buying extended warranties as an afterthought. You may never need an extended warranty, however; a large percentage of equipment failures occur early, when the manufacturer's warranty is still in effect. Without an early failure, you may be able to use your equipment for years without problems, and when a problem does finally occur, even your extended warranty may have expired. Rather than buying an extended warranty, buy products with a solid record of reliability, and put some money aside in a repair fund, just in case your equipment fails after the manufacturer's warranty has expired.

When you need to have your computer repaired, you should find out exactly what the charges will be. Sometimes, the cost of the parts is in inverse proportion with the time needed to make the repair. Be sure to ask whether new parts or refurbished parts will be used. Also, find out how long the repair will take. Ask if the company provides equipment for you to use while yours is being repaired or serviced. Usually, you will take faulty equipment back to your dealer for repair, but you may need to take it to the manufacturer's local service site. If you have ordered equipment by mail, you may need to return it by mail, for which there may be added charges. Many mail-order companies now provide free on-site repairs during warranty, and they have been known to ship a new board overnight and talk the user through installing it.

(See 2.11 Used or New?; 2.14 Where to Buy; 2.15 Buying by Mail.)

2.14 WHERE TO BUY

You can purchase your computer and peripheral equipment from several sources: microcomputer vendors, retailers, and mail-order houses.

Computer vendors such as IBM, DEC, Unisys, and NCR offer their line of microcomputers through a direct-sales force. IBM is also moving into the mail-order business. Buying through a computer manufacturer can have several benefits. Often, the salespeople are highly trained in the use of microcomputers for specific purposes, such as business or desktop publishing or design, and can assist you in determining which system will meet your needs. Microcomputer vendors can also provide maintenance contracts for on-site repair, and can offer replacement equipment if some part of your system should be out of order for an inconvenient period of time.

Microcomputer manufacturers also market their products through retailers such as mass merchandisers (Sears), office-supply stores (Office Depot and Office Max), warehouse stores (Sam's Club and Price Co.), and consumer electronics stores (Radio Shack). In addition, some national computer store chains such as CompUSA have built large superstores that stock a wide variety of devices and software. Keep in mind that the sales personnel at some department stores, warehouse stores, and office-supply stores may lack the knowledge you need to help you in making your choices. Small computer specialty stores are often staffed with knowledgeable people and, in most cases, have an in-house service department. You also get a hands-on pre-purchase trial there. Prices at a specialty store, however, are usually higher than at the other types of stores mentioned. Also, the salespeople may know about only the models they sell. If you are not buying through the manufacturer, be sure the reseller is authorized to pass on the manufacturer's warranty. In any case, find out who performs warranty service. (One advantage of buying at a national chain is that you have "national" coverage if you move.)

Some computers are sold exclusively through mail order, and the prices through mail-order houses can also be very good, so you may want to consider this option.

Be wary of goods sold by unauthorized dealers, described by the term *gray market*. There are two problems with such goods: Some manufacturers may not honor their products once they reach the gray market, and products sold this way may contain used or refurbished parts such as power supplies or disk drives. Although discontinued products often end up on the gray market, most products sold through the gray market come from an authorized dealer who is unable to sell all the equipment he ordered under a steep bulk discount rate.

(See 2.15 Buying by Mail; Appendix A: Popular Hardware Companies.)

2.15 Buying by Mail

Buying computers by mail may mean lower prices, but just as often, it is the convenience that attracts a mail-order shopper. So isn't it risky to order complex machines such as computers and printers by mail? Not if you deal with a reputable company, say the experts. Today, reputable companies offer high-quality machines, good service, telephone inquiries, and meaningful warranties. Many mail-order computer companies emphasize value, not price. They offer convenience and service, especially for communities that may not have a computer store.

You should be able to call a mail-order company, place an order, receive it overnight or in a matter of a few days, try out the product for 15 to 30 days, and return it cash-back, without hassle, if it is not satisfactory. You should also be able to get technical help by phone. Repair services should be timely and efficient. Warranties should be no less than a year. The products sold by reputable mail-order companies should contain exactly the chips, the memory, the drives, and so on that the system's designers thought the system should have, and advertised that it does have. (There are unscrupulous computer dealers that remove expensive components supplied by the manufacturers and insert inferior parts.)

On the down side of ordering computer equipment by mail, orders can get fouled up, and equipment that you receive can be faulty. Most companies help you fix the problems over the telephone or send replacements quickly, however. When you buy from a mail-order house, you should know exactly what you want to purchase, and feel comfortable with the knowledge you have about computers.

There are several types of mail-order dealers. Brand-name resellers generally sell the same brands of computers seen in stores, only at lower costs. Few of them offer customer support, relying instead on the manufacturers of the products to supply user help and warranty service. (Some manufacturers such as IBM and Compaq do not authorize sales through these vendors, so you may not find the products you want through brand-name resellers.) Companies that do direct-sales marketing sell products they make or package themselves. A designer-manufacturer designs and builds the equipment it sells. Examples are CompuAdd, Dell Computer, Gateway 2000, and Zeos. System assemblers buy components from various sources, and package them under their own label. House-label resellers buy products already assembled and put their own label on them.

Most of the rules of mail-ordering computer equipment are the same as those of ordering clothing, gifts, furniture, or any other products by mail. Be sure, either by reading reviews or talking to knowledgeable friends, that the company you are dealing with is reputable. You might also call the Better Business Bureau in the dealer's area for information. You can even ask the vendor for a list of customers in your area you can contact to find out about the vendor's performance. Any magazines that carry the vendor's advertisements can also tell you whether any complaints have been registered. Several computer magazines have also carried articles rating mail-order vendors and brand-name resellers. You can locate these articles through library services such as the *Readers' Guide to Periodical Literature* and computer search services.

Also, know exactly how you are planning to use the equipment, so that the equipment you order will be powerful enough to run the software you will be using, and will produce the output you need. Then adhere to the following rules while placing your order and dealing with the company:

- **Look at the advertisement to see if a full address is given.** Skip those with only a post-office box or city and state. Even check back through old issues of computer magazines to see whether, and how, the company has advertised before. Call the magazine that carried the ad to see if any complaints against the company have been registered.
- **When you call the company for information, check prices, shipping and handling costs, and the courtesy of the person you are talking to.**

- **Look for an 800 number for both sales and support.** If there is none for support, ask the company whether it has an 800 number for support. Find out if the support comes from the manufacturer or the mail-order company, if they are two different entities. Try the support 800 number before you buy. A company that uses 800 numbers most likely is healthy, and is committed to good customer support. (Some companies also provide support through fax services and electronic bulletin boards.)
- **Avoid companies that have restrictions on sales, such as "all sales final," "refunds for credit only," or "returns subject to approval."** Ask the company what is being guaranteed. Do you get all of your money back if you return the product? Do you get written assurance that you can return the product?
- **Avoid companies that reserve the right to make substitutions.** Also look for companies that replace defective parts rather than repairing them.
- **Watch for disclaimers in advertisements that say compatibility is not guaranteed.** If you are not absolutely sure that a product will work with your system, do not buy it.
- **If you are dealing with a brand-name reseller, ask about warranties, and call the manufacturer to be sure you can get support for warranty repairs.** Make sure the reseller is authorized to give you the manufacturer's warranty.
- **When you place your order, be sure to get the full name of the person taking the order.** Get an order number, a firm price, and information about when the order will arrive. Clarify everything—the model number, the make, the size, the exact components, whether parts are new or reconditioned, and so on. Have the salesperson repeat your order. Verify that your order is in stock. If the salesperson cannot be pinned down about delivery dates, perhaps it is best to cancel the order. Most reputable companies have next-day delivery, or deliver within 48 hours at the most. A seller must ship the merchandise within 30 days.
- **Follow your phone call with a letter that lists everything you have agreed to, including policies.**
- **Keep all the information about your order in a special folder, even the advertisement that prompted your order.** Include the date you placed your order.
- **Always pay by credit card.** If you deal with an out-of-state vendor, your local and state judicial system will be unable to help you if you are dissatisfied. Your credit-card company, however, can back you up if there is some

dispute, and if you have followed the credit-card company's guidelines for making a claim against the vendor. Some credit-card companies also offer extended warranty protection. Always check your credit-card statements to verify charges against your account.

- **Be leery of prices that seem too low.** You won't get a reliable system at really cheap prices. If it seems too good to be true, it probably is.
- **When the package arrives, check the condition of the cartons.** Do not sign for a package that looks as if it has been mishandled—that is, crushed or torn. Be sure that your action seems justified, however, or the vendor may not want to do business with you in the future. Open the package immediately and verify the shipment.
- **Keep the original packing materials in case you must return the products for repair or refunds.** Find out where the equipment goes if it must be returned for replacement or service. Also try the equipment to be sure it works correctly before sending in the warranty cards. (Running a game that requires intensive computer capabilities is a good test for a system.) If you send the cards in early, you may have to settle for repair rather than replacement if something goes wrong. Be aware that many mail-order companies require you to call for a return authorization number before you return any equipment.
- **Watch out for extra fees such as additional shipping or handling fees, restocking fees (for returned merchandise), or accessory costs that may not have been added to the price of the product.** Restocking fees, for example, are designed to discourage subjective returns, and may run from 10 to 15 percent of the item's price.

Some mail-order companies, as well as stores, may replace a defective part with a refurbished part. This is especially true of disk drives. Be sure you understand a company's policy about replacements. If you are as careful about buying computer equipment as you are about dealing with reputable stores or other mail-order companies, you will probably be satisfied with your products.

(See 2.13 Warranties, Service, and Legal Rights; 2.14 Where to Buy.)

2.16 Setting Up, Starting, and Shutting Down Your System

Taking good care of your computer system begins with the choices you make right after unpacking your equipment. Save the original packaging, in case you want to transport your system. Then select a clean room with low humidity for your system. Set the computer on a sturdy desk or table, away from direct sunlight, heating units, or air conditioners.

When connecting or unplugging the equipment, always hold the cable by the connector at one end, rather than holding it by the cord. Always use a grounded outlet, and never attach an adapter plug to bypass the three-pronged grounding. Do not force a connector into a socket. The cables should be firmly connected at the sockets. If the connector has screws or clamps, use them. If you cannot get the pieces to join easily, call the dealer or a technician for help. If a cable becomes frayed or otherwise damaged, disconnect it. Any time you add or remove a piece of equipment, always unplug the machines from the electrical receptacles. Avoid stretching out the cable between the computer and a peripheral. Stretching can cause strain on the connector pins, and can also result in the cable being accidentally yanked out of its socket at a less-than-opportune time.

Always follow the manufacturer's instructions for starting up and turning off your system. There is usually a small ritual of steps—to be taken in a given order—that will protect your hard disk drive and other components. Generally, turn the computer on and off as few times as possible during a day: *Once on and once off* is the rule, unless you are going to be away from the computer for more than four hours. This is because moving parts suffer wear and non-moving parts are affected by the power surge and temperature changes of start-up.

While the computer is turned on, avoid moving it or jolting it (or the table on which it sits). If you should accidentally bump the processor unit, and it has an internal (or even external) hard disk drive, the disk could contact the read/write heads and crack or break. During hard disk operation, the head does not touch the disk. If a *head crash* occurs, however, the head has scratched or burned the platters inside the drive, and you will need to replace both the head and the platters. Head crash can occur if dust gets in the system, or if you jolt the computer during operation. Most hard disks have an automatic head "parking" feature that locks the head in a safe position so that the disk will not be damaged when you transport your system. Before moving a printer, remove the ink-jet or toner cartridge to avoid leakage. Where applicable, anchor the print-head mechanism so that it does not slide back and forth in its track during transportation.

Do not block the vents on any piece of equipment. Before touching the computer, be sure to ground yourself to discharge static. Touch a metal object, for example, or use an anti-static mat under your feet at the computer. Static electricity can damage the tiny circuits in the computer. You can buy mats to use under the keyboard, and other components that help prevent damage from static electricity. Static can be a special problem when opening the system unit case for do-it-yourself tasks. Always ground yourself, and use a non-magnetic screwdriver if you install a chip or a card.

(See 2.17 Caring for Your Computer, 2.18 Surge Protectors, 5.4 Viruses, 5.9 Security Measures.)

2.17 CARING FOR YOUR COMPUTER

The key to keeping computers in good working order is to use common sense when handling them. Care should begin as soon as you purchase your computer. When transporting your equipment home or to a new location, be sure never to leave it in a hot car for an extended period of time. Before you touching your new equipment (and before every use thereafter), be sure that your hands are clean.

After every use, cover the equipment with static-free dust covers. Dust and dirt carry electric charges that can break the flow of current through the microcomputer. An accumulation of dust can also create a buildup of heat that can cause chips to fail. Debris lodged in a floppy disk drive can cause an increase in the number of input and output errors you experience. In addition, keep magnets and strong electromagnetic fields away from your computer and its storage media, or you could lose data.

Food, liquids, eraser crumbs, paper clips, and other similar materials should be kept away from the equipment. Food crumbs, eraser crumbs, and small items such as miniature paper clips can lodge between and under the keys, causing them to malfunction. Sticky materials such as soft drinks and fruit juices can cause the keys on the keyboard to jam, or worse, they can cause the electronic parts to fail. If a thin, clear liquid is accidentally spilled on the keyboard, turn off the system, turn the keyboard upside down to let the liquid drain out, and dry it for at least 24 hours. By doing this, you may avoid repair costs. If the liquid is sticky, however, you should take the keyboard to your dealer for repair. (You can buy lightweight, flexible, transparent keyboard covers that you can type through, although these may shift annoyingly if you are a speedy typist.)

Treat other equipment such as printers with the same care as you do your computer. Read the directions that come with each peripheral to see if any unusual care rules should be followed. For example, the directions that come with laser printers may recommend that you never blow on toner that has leaked from the cartridge: Blowing only spreads the toner further into the printer. Instead, wipe up the spill with a soft, slightly damp cloth. External disk drives may come with a special anti-static wrapper to cover the cable connector that plugs into the computer. The cover should be placed on the cable end if the disk drive is disconnected from the computer.

If you are leaving your computer and monitor turned on and unused for extended periods, turn down the brightness control on the screen. Otherwise, the image on the screen could "burn in" and permanently damage the screen. There are *screen-saver* programs available that remove or vary the image on the screen when the computer is turned on, but idle. Screen *blankers* black out or dim the screen, and screen *animators* display images that constantly move throughout the screen so that no one image is in a particular location long enough to burn itself into the screen. Some screen savers must be activated by a user command; others activate automatically after a particular image has been displayed for a specified time.

Before cleaning your equipment, be sure to disconnect the power cord. Most user's manuals recommend that you clean the casings of your equipment with a soft, damp (but not wet) cloth. Add a drop of liquid detergent on the cloth to remove stubborn stains or dirt. Do not use household cleansers, ammonia, powders, or solvents such as cleaning fluid, any of which can mar the finish on the casings. On new monitors, you can use a small amount of household glass cleaner sprayed on a soft cloth to wipe the screen. (Be sure to check the manuals before cleaning the monitors of computers older than five years or so.) Do not spray the cleaner directly onto the screen, however, because the liquid may drip into the interior parts of the machine and cause electrical damage. You should also clean the mouse on a routine basis. Most user's manuals will tell you how to disassemble and clean a mouse. The insides of printers can usually be cleaned to remove paper dust and bits of paper. Use a soft brush or a lint-free cloth.

Compressed air may tend to blow the dust and dirt even further into a machine's components, thus many manufacturers recommend special miniature vacuum cleaners, which can also be used on your keyboard. Your dealer or mail-order house may also stock special cleaning kits for components such as floppy disk drives. Never use attachments for your household vacuum cleaner to clean computer parts; use only vacuum cleaners especially designed for electronics.

Even though you take the greatest care, there may be times when equipment or software does not work. The problem may be simple to find. First, be sure the machine is properly plugged in, and that the connections to printers and disk drives are secure. Second, read the manual. It may give tips for some types of problems. And third, check the software by installing it in another machine able to run it. If the software does not work in a second or third machine, the problem may be with the software rather than the hardware. If these simple checks do not solve the problem, it's time to call an expert.

(See 2.18 Surge Protectors; 2.19 Caring for Your Disks; Software Review section: After Dark.)

2.18 Surge Protectors

You may wonder what would happen when your computer is turned on and the lights flicker. Perhaps there was a slight drop in power, called a *sag*. A prolonged sag is called a *brownout*. If there was a sudden drop followed by a sudden increase in power that lasts just fractions of a second, a *spike* has occurred. An increase in power that lasts somewhat longer is called a *surge*.

No community is exempt from occasional surges or drops in power, or even complete power failures, so your computer could flick off—in which case you would lose any unsaved data, and the hard disk drive could be damaged. Fortunately, protection is available.

All computers come with some surge protection built into the power supply unit, but it is a good idea to buy a separate device called a *surge protector*, also called a *surge suppressor*. This device prevents sudden and powerful electrical variations from harming your system by collecting and diffusing the excess voltage before it can reach your computer. It usually has six or more sockets into which you plug your computer, printer, and other peripherals. Surge protectors generally cost anywhere from $10 to a few hundred dollars, and may guarantee a reimbursement of $10,000 or more if your computer is damaged while the protector is in use.

Most computers can withstand prolonged voltage dips of about 20 percent, but for even greater protection, you can buy a UPS, or *uninterruptible power supply*. A UPS is a power supply with a battery that maintains power in the event of a complete power outage. The UPS maintains power, keeping the computer running for the few minutes it would take you to save data that is in RAM and shut down the system according to the manufacturer's directions. One type of UPS is the *standby power system* (SPS), which monitors the power and activates as soon as it detects a problem. By this method, there will be a few milliseconds during the switch when the computer is not receiving any power. An online UPS system avoids this power lapse by constantly providing power, even when the power line is functioning properly. Either type of UPS may cost more than a home user is willing to spend, however—$100 to $200—and offers more protection than is usually needed.

A surge protector or UPS will *not* protect your computer from lightning. Be sure to disconnect your computer from the electrical outlets (and from the telephone outlet if you use a modem) if a lightning storm is expected, or if you are leaving for a trip.

Some well-known manufacturers of surge protectors are Curtis, Proxima, and Kensington. You can buy a unit that offers protection against power surges and spikes, and also turns on all of your components in the correct sequence.

(See 2.16 Setting Up, Starting, and Shutting Down Your System, 2.17 Caring for Your Computer.)

2.19 Caring for Your Disks

Floppy disks need to be handled gently. Keep all disks away from magnets and magnetic fields that can erase or scramble the data stored on them. Magnetic items include external disk drives, monitors, printers, telephones, radios, and even paper clips that have been stored in magnetic containers. Heat can also damage disks, so store them away from sunny windows. Because automobiles can get very hot when the sun is shining, even on a cool day, avoid leaving disks in the car. Use felt-tip pens to write on labels that are already attached to the disks, and press lightly when writing. Pressing hard—or using ballpoint pens—can leave little dents on a disk's recording surface that can ruin the data. Keep the disks away from dirt, ashes, food, and liquids. Even smoke particles can affect the way the disk and drive interact. Store all disks away from heat or cold and upright in boxes designed for holding disks to prevent warping. Never store a disk in a disk drive.

The hard plastic cases that sheathe 3.5-inch disks make the disks difficult to damage. Thin metal slides, or shutters, protect the areas where the disk drive accesses the actual disk. The drive moves the metal slide before reading the disk. Do not flick these shutters back and forth, as dust and fingerprints could damage the exposed disk.

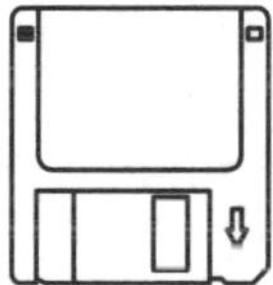

3.5-inch disks are more durable than 5.25-inch disks.

A 5.25-inch disk requires extra precautions because its jacket is flexible and parts of the disk inside are exposed. The jacket has an oval notch that allows the disk drive to read the recording area of the disk, and a small hole that helps the drive find the data and programs on the disk. Never fold or bend a flexible disk. If you do, the disk drive may not be able to get the data stored on the disk or record new data on it. Never touch any exposed recording areas of a disk, because dirt and oil from your fingers can attract dust and ruin data. Keep the disks in their paper envelopes when not in use. The envelopes protect the disks from dirt and dust that can damage the data on the disks. Do not bind them together with rubber bands or paper clips, as this could bend or crease some of the disks. Creases and scratches can cause the coating material to flake off.

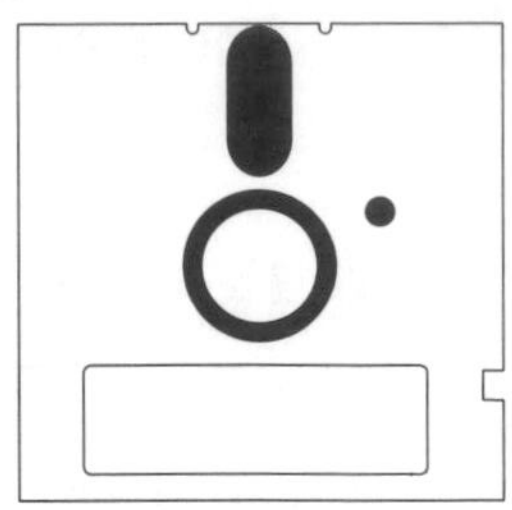

Be careful when handling 5.25-inch disks.

Before inserting a 5.25-inch disk into a drive, take it out of its paper envelope. The vinyl jacket should never be removed, however, unless you plan to throw the disk away. Either size disk should be held at the label end, so that the exposed read/write notch on a 5.25-inch disk or the shutter end of the 3.5-inch disk goes into the disk drive first. Never force a disk into the drive; slide it in gently until it clicks into place. Remember to close the drive door on your 5.25-inch drive after you insert the disk.

(See 1.24 Floppy Disks; 2.17 Caring for Your Computer.)

2.20 Getting Help: Documentation and Customer Support

When you open the packing boxes holding your new hardware or software, you will find user's manuals that tell you how to install and operate the product. These user's manuals are called *documentation*, which is the written material that tells about your equipment or software. It gives definitions, explains procedures, helps with troubleshooting, and demonstrates through pictures how a particular product works. The documentation may also include a *tutorial*, which leads you step-by-step through a typical task you can perform with the product. Some products include documentation that can be used like a dictionary, in which you look up what you need to know from an alphabetical listing of topics. You'll usually find documentation in the *help screens* of software (program information you can access on-screen through a menu) as well.

Documentation may seem to be a minor aspect of choosing computers or software, but when the documentation is poor, learning to use your system can be frustrating. And even well-written documentation may not be adequate for describing a very complex activity. When you are stumped, you should be able to call the location where you bought the product to receive help. If you can travel to the dealer's location, you can ask the dealer to demonstrate a particular task. Otherwise you will have to rely on a telephone call.

Most companies provide an 800 number you can call for *technical support*. These are often called "hot lines," and the person on the company's end of the telephone should be well-informed enough to provide you with advice and trouble-shooting tips. Note, however, that in order to compete with the lower prices their customers are demanding and still make a profit, some companies are turning off their 800 numbers. They are offering free support for the first 30 to 90 days or so after you place the first call, and then charging for technical help given thereafter. This way, they can maintain the quality of support without going broke.

Before calling a technical-support number, have your serial or registration number handy. You may need it to get past the company's automated answering system. If you do reach a live person, try to keep to the point of your call, rather than wasting time with other details of your life. Be willing to admit to your mistakes, even if the problem was a small detail you simply forgot. Be sure you are prepared with details about the problem, and about your system, too—such as the model of your computer, system information, video card, monitor, printer, and operating system version. Have a pencil and paper ready for writing the reply. Even better, call from the same room where your computer is located, so you can try out any suggestions the technician makes.

Many companies have fax-back service or toll-free voice response systems with automated answers. Some companies offer online electronic bulletin boards staffed by service technicians. If you have a modem, you can leave a message on the bulletin board and a technician will respond. You can also download software updates that correct bugs or simplify a procedure. Bulletin boards, and often the 800 numbers, are manned 24 hours a day—which can be convenient if you are working into the wee hours of the morning, or if you are in a time zone different from that of the company. Many tech-support numbers, however, are open only Monday through Friday. If you subscribe to an online information system such as GEnie or CompuServe, you may find that many manufacturers have *forums* through which products and problems are discussed. A forum may hold just the answer you need to solve your problem.

For ongoing help, you might check your local Yellow Pages or newspaper. Most communities offer at least a few classes, workshops, and seminars about using computers. The classes may address a particular computer platform such as Macintosh, a particular computer application (such as desktop publishing or word processing), or a particular software package (such as Windows or WordPerfect). If you need help on a specific aspect of computer use, or just want to get started using computers, ask your dealer for information about classes and users' groups—or check your newspaper for advertisements about coming events. Call the local schools, scout troops, YMCA, community colleges, vocational schools, colleges and universities to find out whether these organizations have any upcoming sessions that are open to the public.

(See 2.14 Where to Buy; 2.21 Magazines; 2.22 Users' Groups; Software Review section: Customer Support and Software.)

2.21 MAGAZINES

Look at any well-stocked newsstand or bookstore, and you will find a wide variety of magazines that cover computer uses, equipment, software, games, and online access. The magazines usually contain a note from the editor, letters from readers, feature articles, product reviews, tips on computer use and new products, and often a plethora of advertisements. The feature articles describe and compare a particular family of products such as printers, tell you how to make the most of a software product such as Windows, demonstrate the features of software such as word processors, discuss the use of new configurations such as multimedia, or lay out the etiquette of using online information services.

One or two sections of the magazine offer tidbits about computer use, products, care, or programming; you can graze until you find one that interests you or solves a particular problem. You shouldn't neglect the editor's note and letters from the readers; they may offer just the computing or buying tip that meets your needs. As you browse through the advertisements, you will find many of the terms we describe in this book; you will also find a variety of hardware and software products that may interest you. Most advertisers offer telephone numbers and addresses for you to obtain additional information. Before buying any products, however, you should read the product reviews, which describe the features of a particular piece of equipment or software, and outline its merits and problems. If you are considering an expensive product, you may want to check the reviews of more than one magazine.

Most computer magazines are oriented around a specific platform. For example, *PC World* and *PC Magazine* are designed for users of IBM PCs and IBM PC-compatibles. *MACWORLD* and *MacUser* contain articles and advertisements for Macintosh users. Some magazines such as *Byte* are quite technical, while others are designed for people who are just beginning to learn about computers (*PC Novice*). The online customer can buy a specialty publication called *Online Access*; users of Microsoft Windows and multimedia systems can find magazines that speak to their particular interests. Several magazines such as *PC Sources*, *Computer Monthly*, and *Computer Shopper* offer material aimed at computer buyers. A publication called *Home-Office Computing* discusses ways that you can use computers efficiently at home for both domestic and business purposes.

(See 2.20 Getting Help: Documentation and Customer Support; 2.22 Users' Groups; Appendix B: Popular Computer Magazines.)

2.22 Users' Groups

Where can a microcomputer owner go for help in getting the machine to operate? When a $150 software package will not run on the machine, who can identify the problem? Which word processing package priced under $200 works best on a certain microcomputer? Questions such as these often baffle the proud new owner of a microcomputer. One source of answers is a *users' group*. A users' group is a relatively informal group of people who own a particular brand or model of microcomputer, or a specific software package; members exchange information about hardware, software, service, and support. Users' groups may also form around applications and related topics, such as real estate, medicine, telecommunications, education, and desktop publishing.

The value of users' groups comes from the accumulation of knowledge and experience ready to be shared by members. The best evaluation of hardware and software comes from one who has purchased and used it. As software becomes more sophisticated and more hardware becomes available at prices ordinary computer users can afford, such users' groups will become even more valuable.

Since users' groups do not normally have telephones or office space, finding a local group is not always easy. Dealers who sell microcomputers usually know how to contact users' groups, however, and groups often post notices and flyers in computer stores. Information on national groups is sometimes included in the microcomputer packaging. Contacting the manufacturer directly may also yield the name of a person to contact about a local group.

(See 2.20 Getting Help: Documentation and Customer Support; 2.21 Magazines.)

Part 3 Contents Index

Software Fundamentals

Before you can find out what a computer can do, you must feed it some *software*—the programs, or sets of instructions, that tell the hardware exactly what to do. This section describes the types of software available and some programming languages used to write software.

3.1 Types of Software: System and Application

Some software manages the computer's circuits so the computer can get something from storage or put a letter or number on the screen. This software is called *system software*, and is generally grouped together as an *operating system* (OS). Other software, called *application* software, helps you do a job. Examples of application programs include Microsoft Word (a word processing program that enables you to type and edit words) and Flight Simulator (a game that lets you pretend you are flying a plane). However, you cannot use application software without the system software.

Software can be built into the machine, stored on a disk, or typed in at the keyboard. Once you know a *programming language*—a special code used to write programs—you can write your own programs. You can learn to write a program in BASIC, a common programming language for microcomputers; or copy programs that you find in computer magazines or books. Most people buy software, however; it takes too much time, study, and experience to develop your own.

Commercial software is usually stored on disks that come in packages; thus, a particular program is often called a software *package*. Each package should tell you exactly what equipment you need to run the software. For example, it may specify a particular brand and model of computer, some memory requirements, a floppy-disk drive, and perhaps a special input device such as a joystick or mouse. Once you open the package, you will also find a user's manual that explains how to use the software. When you are ready to use a program, you must put it into the computer. This operation, called *loading*, is usually done by a part of the operating system called the loader. You activate the loader on a DOS-type machine—unless you're using a GUI—after you type a special code that includes the name of the program you want to load. Loading on a Macintosh computer begins as soon as you put the disk into the disk drive. Once the icon of the program appears on the desktop, you can double-click the mouse button at the icon to *access*, or open, the program.

Most software comes with its own installation program. This feature *installs* the software by copying it from its floppy disks to your hard disk, eliminating the need to load from a floppy. To begin the installation process on DOS machines, you type a special command, usually **INSTALL**. On Macintosh machines, installation can be as simple as dragging the program's icon onto the hard disk window. Most Macintosh programs, however, require you to open the special installation program, which is generally easy to use and prompts you through the installation.

Once the software is installed on your hard disk, you still must load it into memory for use. (By the way, you should never change file names of files that appear on the screen after installation. A program needs those exact file names to access instructions during operation.)

Most software has gone through a number of revisions; both the package and the program should identify this *version number*. For example, the Macintosh System has already gone into its seventh version, called System 7.5. The latest version of Microsoft's spreadsheet software, Excel, is identified as 5.0. The number to the left of the decimal point identifies the major revision, and the number to the right of the decimal point identifies minor upgrades and improvements to the major revision. Some older versions are still available for less powerful microcomputers. Be sure your computer will run the software version you plan to purchase.

(See 3.2 Operating Systems; 3.3 Telling the Computer What to Do: User Interfaces; 3.23 General Features of Application Software.)

3.2 Operating Systems

A typical application job needs the computer, a printer, a monitor, a keyboard, and storage for data and programs. System programs, or *operating systems*, manage these components, usually without your knowing it. Some system programs are already in the ROM chips in your computer. They *boot*, or start, the activity in a computer when you first turn it on. They also tell the computer how to create what you see on your screen—for example, how to cause an *m* to appear on-screen when you press the M key.

The remainder of an operating system is stored on a hard disk. This portion of your hard disk is sometimes called the system master or the *disk operating system* (DOS, which rhymes with *boss*). The programs in the ROM chip cause the computer to get the system programs from the disk and put them in memory. Usually, only a select group of system programs are transferred to memory; the others are accessed as needed.

An operating system is written for a specific type of computer such as IBM-compatible, Macintosh, or Sun; most cannot be used on other types of computers.

Operating systems direct a computer to move data from RAM to the disk, route the data traveling to a printer, or see that data coming from a disk to the screen does not bump into the input you are typing as it travels through the circuits.

Some system programs need input from you. If you are starting with a brand-new floppy disk, for example, you will need to *format* or *initialize* (that is, prepare) it so your computer and disk drive can store data on it. *Storage* is an essential function. If you have spent your whole weekend writing a report for work or school, you certainly would not want to take a chance on something happening to your only copy. Another system program lets you make a backup copy of that report. You can also use system programs to get rid of files you no longer want, or list the files on your disk.

Most operating systems for personal computers enable one user to do one job at a time. Advanced operating systems such as OS/2 and UNIX allow one or more of the following complex configurations:

- A *multi-user* operating system allows two or more users to run programs at the same time.
- A *multitasking* operating system allows you to run two or more tasks at the same time. The task that is currently accepting input is the *foreground* task, and the task that is operating beside it is the *background* task. A background task such as print spooling (printing documents in sequence) cannot accept input while you are working in the foreground task. In *cooperative* multitasking, applications are given equal slices of time; in *preemptive* multitasking, the application that needs extra processing power gets a bigger share of the CPU.
- An operating system that offers *task switching*, on the other hand, lets you load multiple programs so that they will be available for use. Task switching does not allow two programs to be run concurrently.
- A *multithreading* operating system handles multiple threads. A *thread* is a path or theme, much as a reference theme threads through this book. In computer processing, it is a path of execution through a *process*, which in turn is an executing program that "owns" resources (such as open files and memory) while it runs. Traditional personal computers handle one thread, processing what is called a *single-threaded* application. Advanced operating systems for personal computers allow *multiprogramming* in which a process may have multiple threads. One way the OS handles multiple threads is by *time slicing*: processing time is diced into tiny equal amounts, and allocated to the various threads among which processing rotates. For example, one thread may update the screen, and another manages the user interface. While processing is rotating among the threads, some may receive priority over others—for example, when a user indicates he wants to print some material.

- An OS (operating system) engages a concept called *memory protection*—also known as *memory management*—to keep multiple programs separate in memory through the use of regions, or *partitions*. A similar situation exists with input/output devices. Two programs cannot access the same disk drive or printer at the same time.
- *Virtual memory* is an OS feature that increases the efficiency of memory usage. When a large program runs (or multiple programs run at the same time), the physical limitations of memory become critical. Virtual memory alleviates this problem. It is based on the principle that only the immediately needed portion of a program must be in memory at any given time, and the rest of the program can be kept in storage. Because only part of a program is in memory at one time, more programs can reside in memory simultaneously, allowing more programs and data to be handled within a given time interval. The programs held in storage may be broken into variable-sized blocks called *segments*, or into fixed-sized blocks called *pages*. These portions are swapped back and forth into memory as needed. Using virtual memory enables the system to treat hard-disk storage as if it were merely an extension of memory, which provides the illusion of unlimited memory.
- *Multiprocessing* requires two or more CPUs to share the processing workload. The CPUs may be linked directly in one computer, or joined through connections that link storage devices. Multiprocessing allows several programs to be executed at the same time. In contrast, multitasking techniques create the illusion that several programs are being run at the same time. Multiprocessing has only recently been used on microcomputers.
- *Plug-and-play support* is being built into new versions of operating systems. With plug-and-play, you can add hardware to a system and the system handles the configuration and driver loading automatically. (The Macintosh System has always offered support for its version of plug-and-play.)

Operating *systems* should not be confused with operating *environments*. Users run programs in the *operating environment*. The PC-DOS environment, for example, consists of all the PC-DOS commands you can use. The commands that you use to communicate with PC-DOS are called the *command language*; these include such commands as DIR (for directory), COPY, and DEL (for delete). Several software products—including DESQview X by Quarterdeck Office Systems and Microsoft Windows 3.1—provide alternative operating environments for PC-DOS. These products enable you to put several applications on the screen at once, each in its own window; you can switch among them as needed. Some products also perform some memory-management functions and multitasking. Operating environments are sometimes called *control programs*.

(See 3.1 Types of Software: System and Application; 3.3 Telling the Computer What to Do: User Interfaces; 3.6 DOS Versions; 3.7 ProDOS; 3.8 System 7.5; 3.9 Microsoft Windows; 3.10 OS/2; 3.11 UNIX.)

3.3 Telling the Computer What to Do: User Interfaces

Before you can do anything with your computer, you must learn how to communicate with it. A message telling a computer what to do next is called a *command*. Some methods of entering commands involve typing in the command you want. Other methods let you choose the command by using pictures called *icons* and lists called *menus*. The set of commands and the syntax for using them is called the *user interface*, also referred to as the *front end*.

Computers that use the PC-DOS or MS-DOS operating system have a *command-line* user interface. The operating system displays a prompt that shows you that a command can be entered. The prompt may be nothing more than **>**. Normally, you type the command on one line and then press the Enter key to activate the command. Commands run the gamut from the simple, such as DIR, to the cryptic, such as:

```
COPY %1\*.* NUL > NUL
```

The reason DOS-based computers require you to type commands is that they are *text-based* (or *character-based*) systems; they need words and messages to carry out functions. Character-based systems can display only ASCII and extended ASCII characters. These systems treat the screen as an array of boxes arranged in rows and columns; each box can hold one character.

To use a command-line user interface, you must learn and remember a lot of commands, and then type them exactly in order for the computer to act on them. This approach makes computers seem difficult to use. To make DOS programs more user-friendly, programmers have designed *menu-driven* programs that enable you to run most of an application by selecting options from menus. Also, many programs have templates you can lay over the keyboard so you can see the key commands right in front of you. Both command-line user interfaces and menu-driven interfaces are, however, inconsistent from program to program. To address the problems of user-friendliness and consistency, software companies now sell *graphical* user interfaces and *pen-based* interfaces. These are described in the two sections that follow.

(See 2.3 Which Computer? The Platforms; 3.2 Operating Systems; 3.4 Graphical User Interfaces: The WIMP Factor; 3.5 Pen-Based Interfaces; 3.23 General Features of Application Software.)

3.4 GRAPHICAL USER INTERFACES: THE WIMP FACTOR

Graphical user interfaces such as the Apple Macintosh Finder or Microsoft Windows use the computerized equivalent of a desktop as the interface between the user and the operating system. A graphical user interface is usually graphics-based, which means the objects on the screen are displayed as *bit maps*. This approach makes many user-friendly functions available (including WYSIWYG display, so you have a clearer idea of what the document will look like when it comes out of your printer). It is also much easier to use than a text-based interface; you do not have to remember command codes.

Such a graphical user interface, or GUI (pronounced *gooey*), incorporates four elements, which are sometimes called by the rather disparaging acronym WIMP, (windows, icons, menus, and pointing device). A GUI makes use of *windows*, or boxes, that hold documents or functions. More than one of these—for example, holding two or more documents (or a document and a print-formatting function)—can be present on a screen at once. The opening window is called the Desktop on Macintosh computers or the Program Manager in Windows; it is here you see the *icons*, or pictures, that represent your documents, programs, and functions. The names of the commands appear in *pull-down menus*—which you activate, in turn, from a *menu bar* (a line that lists the general functions) across the top of the screen. Some commands are available in *pop-up windows* that appear in the middle of the screen when you request them. Normally, you use a pointing device—the mouse—to point to the option you want and select it. As you move the mouse, you will see a *pointer* symbol (such as an arrowhead or an I-beam) move across the screen.

A GUI is easy to use, and it provides a consistent means of using software. Once you have learned to use one application through the GUI, you have learned the basic computer skills needed to use them all. It also makes it easier to move data from one application to another. The Apple Macintosh was the first computer to popularize a GUI. Microsoft later introduced Windows for MS-DOS and PC-DOS operating systems. Other GUIs include Ensemble (a PC-compatible GUI), GEM (developed by Digital Research and used on Atari, as well as with some DOS programs), and Amiga's Workbench. GUIs for UNIX systems include Open Look and Motif. The GUI used with OS/2 (IBM's operating system) is called Presentation Manager. Despite the prevalence and advantages of GUIs, many experienced computer users say that using a command-line user interface is much faster; they see no need to change.

To make the most use of a GUI, you may want a 15- to 17-inch monitor; a larger screen gives you more viewing area within which to arrange the windows and other components on the screen. Fast video cards also increase the speed with which the screen changes to new displays.

(See 1.38 Mice and Trackballs; 2.3 Which Computer? The Platforms; 3.2 Operating Systems; 3.3 Telling the Computer What to Do: User Interfaces; 3.8 System 7.5; 3.9 Microsoft Windows; 3.23 General Features of Application Software; 3.24 WYSIWYG; 3.36 Graphics Software.)

3.5 Pen-Based Interfaces

Pen-based interfaces (also called *gesture-based* interfaces) are found on notepad computers. Pen-based interfaces allow direct interaction with programs and data, much as if you were writing with a pencil on a clipboard.

To input data, you use a special electronic *stylus*. The stylus emits a faint signal from its tip so the notepad can detect its presence. As you write, the screen grows darker where the stylus touches it. Some notepads use built-in *pattern-recognition* software to recognize, interpret, and change your writing (or printing) into a normal computer typeface. Other notepad systems merely store the handwriting as a graphics file, so that when you retrieve it, it is still in your handwriting rather than in a typeface.

The stylus can also act as a mouse. To make a selection or initiate an action, for example, you tap the stylus on the appropriate icon. Using a stylus as an input device eliminates the constant moving back and forth between mouse and keyboard common to GUIs. Most people still prefer the keyboard, however, for long sessions of writing.

(See 1.44 Pen-Based Computing; 2.8 Portables.)

3.6 DOS VERSIONS

The acronym DOS (for **D**isk **O**perating **S**ystem) can refer to any operating system, but it has become almost synonymous with MS-DOS and PC-DOS. PC-DOS (Personal Computer Disk Operating System) was designed for use on IBM Personal Computers, which IBM introduced in 1981. As a result of its agreement with IBM, Microsoft was able to market its own version of the operating system called MS-DOS (Microsoft Disk Operating System). Although the two operating systems are nearly identical from a user's viewpoint, IBM does hold the copyright to PC-DOS and could, in the future, change it in a way that would make it incompatible with MS-DOS. Today, more than 100 different types of IBM-compatible computers use the MS-DOS operating system.

The different versions of IBM PC-DOS and MS-DOS have been designed to run with Intel 8088, 8086, and 80286 sixteen-bit microprocessors, and with the later 80386 and 80486 thirty-two bit microprocessors. Although the earlier versions of these operating systems were arcane, newer versions are somewhat more user-friendly. DOS does have a built-in memory limitation of 1MB; to exceed the limit, you need special memory software. PC-DOS and MS-DOS are single-user, single-tasking operating systems.

The latest version of MS-DOS is 6.2, designed with state-of-the-art microprocessors in mind. It is easy to install, and will not overwrite any third-party programs that enhance the operating system already in use. MS-DOS 6.2 has another advantage: you do not need to partition your hard disk into 32MB segments. You can operate an entire hard disk—of up to 1GB capacity—as a single drive. MS-DOS 6.2 includes capabilities for managing memory (with MemMaker). It also includes greatly expanded online help and a few new commands including CHOICE, which makes interactive batch files possible; MOVE, which allows you to move a file to a different directory; and DELTREE, which enables you to delete a directory and all its subdirectories and files. SMARTDrive caches CD-ROM drives.

For version 6.2 of MS-DOS, Microsoft has licensed three programs from other companies. A virus protection program comes from Central Point Software; backup capabilities and *defragmentation* software (which gathers the pieces of a file scattered throughout a disk and stores them contiguously) from Symantec. (The licensed utilities' screens look different from those DOS offers.) MS-DOS also includes ScanDisk—which surveys the surface of a hard disk to find and fix problems or potential problems—and UnErase, which calls back a file that has been accidentally erased.

Microsoft dropped the DOS Shell as a standard DOS feature after version 5. The Shell offered an easy way to manage files, and was the only way to implement task-switching. The Shell is now on the DOS Supplemental Disk included in the OS package. The supplemental disk also contains AccessDOS, a program that can help people with disabilities to use computers.

IBM's PC-DOS 6.1 is basically the same as MS-DOS 6.0, having been completed before the shared technology agreement between IBM and Microsoft expired in late September of 1993. Unlike MS-DOS, it has some support for pen-based computing and PCMCIA cards, and offers task switching. It comes with excellent documentation and telephone support, and includes the DOS Shell. It does not include QBasic, a version of the programming language BASIC that is included with MS-DOS.

A competing OS is called Novell DOS 7, which offers the usual DOS functions and more. Functions include file compression, task switching, multitasking, a special version of Stacker (the disk-compression utility), online documentation, built-in networking, file transferring, file protection, security procedures such as passwords and anti-virus utilities, and the GEM GUI. Novell claims its DOS 7 is a better foundation than MS-DOS or PC-DOS for running Windows, but DOS 6.2 also features improved coordination between DOS and Windows. Although Novell DOS 7 is the DOS version most likely to have compatibility problems with other software, it is a very highly rated operating system.

(See 3.1 Types of Software: System and Application; 3.2 Operating Systems; 3.3 Telling the Computer What to Do: User Interfaces; 3.4 Graphical User Interfaces: The WIMP Factor; 3.5 Pen-Based Interfaces.)

3.7 ProDOS

ProDOS (Professional Disk Operating System) is the revised version of the Apple-DOS (Apple Disk Operating System) developed by Apple for its use on the Apple II computers. Apple-DOS was a simple operating system designed for the nonprofessional computer user. ProDOS is even easier to use than the earlier Apple-DOS, but it offers more functions. It contains a variety of menus that partially eliminate the need for typed command codes, and it allows a single user to perform one task at a time. ProDOS, like Apple II computers, is no longer upgraded or manufactured.

(See 3.1 Types of Software: System and Application; 3.2 Operating Systems.)

3.8 SYSTEM 7.5

Apple's Macintosh family of computers uses an operating system known simply as System 7.5, which is both easy and fun to use. Portions of the operating system are loaded into RAM from the System folder (which you see on your screen at boot time, or as needed). You will also see files for desk accessory and font programs, referred to as *resources*. *Desk accessories* include an alarm clock, a calculator, a note pad for memos, and a key caps option that lets you see optional characters in a particular font. These programs are always running, no matter what application you are using. QuickDraw, the System's drawing language that places the graphics and text on your monitor, is included in its new, speedy version, GX.

The part of this operating system visible to the user is the Finder, which serves as the interface between the Macintosh user and the operating system. The Finder refers to your on-screen working environment as the Desktop. The Desktop includes icons and pull-down menus; it requires the use of a mouse. To activate the files or functions behind the icons, you move the mouse to position the cursor over the icon, and then click the mouse button twice. The menus contain commands you can select to manipulate files, organize the desktop, and so on. The menu names are located in a *menu bar*, which is the top line of the Macintosh screen. To select an item from the menus, you use the mouse to position the pointer on the proper menu name; then you press and hold down the mouse button. As you continue to hold the mouse button down, drag the pointer to the command you want to choose. When the command you want is highlighted, release the mouse button.

System 7.5 permits virtual memory, as well as a variety of communications and access functions. A convenient feature is *interapplication communication* (IAC): information that is updated in one file is updated in all related files. System 7.5 also provides a couple of ways to link programs and documents.

In one of these methods, programs end and receive messages called Apple Events (such as Open Application, Open Document, and Print Document). This type of program linking lets you use sets of instructions from one program in another. The other method, *publish and subscribe*, lets you use parts of one program in another program. AppleScript lets you automate procedures by setting up the steps under one key command. System's *drag-and-drop* feature lets you drag a selection from one position to another in the same document, in a different document, or even in a different application. The file-sharing capabilities of System 7.5 actually make everything on your hard disk accessible to anyone on your network, so you must set access privileges to protect files you want to keep private.

If you need help, System 7.5 offers Apple Interactive Help. This on-screen help feature answers questions, provides tutorials, and offers a large dictionary of computer terms. In addition, System 7.5 offers full TrueType font support,

QuickTime capability, and 32-bit addressing (which enables it to access a lot of memory). (You can turn 32-bit addressing on and off, but you must restart your Mac for the new choice to take effect. In addition, some older software crashes under 32-bit addressing.)

System 7.5 was first released on the Centris 660 AV, Quadra 840 AV, and Power Macs. It requires at least 5MB of RAM, and includes a PowerOff utility that shuts down a Mac after a specific time of inactivity.

(See 1.55 Typefaces and Fonts; 3.1 Types of Software: System and Application; 3.2 Operating Systems; 3.3 Telling the Computer What to Do: User Interfaces.)

3.9 Microsoft Windows

Windows 3.1, by Microsoft Corporation, is a graphical user interface used with DOS. Like other GUIs, Windows enables you to use a mouse to select icons and menus, use dialog boxes, and click on special icons (*buttons*) that activate commands. It also provides limited *multitasking* capabilities, meaning you can do two or more jobs concurrently. For example, you can download files from a telecommunication connection while you use a word processing program. Windows uses extended memory; it also requires that the application you are using support extended memory. Windows also has an enhanced mode that lets you use the virtual-memory capabilities found in 80386 and 80486 microprocessors.

The central part of Windows is the Program Manager, from which any installed DOS or Windows-based program can be started. Once an application has been started and is running, it can be reduced to an icon on the screen and put aside to be used later. The File Manager lets you move, delete, and copy files simply by clicking, dragging, and dropping with the mouse. You can also use the File Manager to search for files and format disks. The Control Panel lets you set options for screen colors, fonts, printers, keyboard and mouse action, and so on. Essentially, the Control Panel lets you modify Windows to suit your personal tastes.

Windows offers applications such as a word processor, paint program, telecommunications program, and mini-database program. It comes with a variety of accessories, including a notepad, a clock, a calendar with a month-at-a-glance view (as well as a daily appointment book), and a calculator. Windows supports TrueType fonts, and lets you cut and paste information from one application to another using a Microsoft file technology called Object Linking and Embedding, or OLE. For multimedia users, Windows offers Media Player; this program lets you play multimedia files, and gives you control over devices such as CD-ROM drives. In addition, Windows' Sound Recorder enables you to record, play, and edit sound files. Windows also allows disk caching and has an online tutor.

Any software that you plan to use with Windows must be compatible with it. This includes TSRs and other small programs as well as full-fledged applications. To use Windows with the least frustration, you should have at least a 25MHz 386 microprocessor and more than the minimum requirements (2MB) for memory. Windows works best on a 486 computer with at least 4MB of RAM.

(See 1.15 RAM; 1.55 Typefaces and Fonts; 2.3 Which Computer? The Platforms; 2.10 Multimedia Standards; 3.1 Types of Software: System and Application; 3.2 Operating Systems; 3.3 Telling the Computer What to Do: User Interfaces; 3.4 Graphical User Interfaces: The WIMP Factor; 3.6 DOS Versions; 3.22 Object-Oriented Programming; 3.29 Memory-Resident Programs; 4.4 Communication Software.)

3.10 OS/2

OS/2 (Operating System 2), now in version 2.1, is a single-user operating system developed by IBM and Microsoft for use on the IBM Personal System/2 (PS/2) computers. A very powerful system, OS/2 has the ability to run two or more programs at the same time, called *multitasking*. It supports multimedia applications for studio and business graphics applications. This system is also user-friendly. It contains Workplace shell, a GUI that supports the use of a mouse, thus eliminating a lot of typing at the keyboard. It also uses small pictures called icons to represent certain functions. For example, a trash can icon represents a place for unwanted files. If you want to delete a file, you use the mouse to drag the file's icon to the trash can.

Most programs written for DOS (as well as many written for Windows) will run well under the OS/2 system—in many cases, better than they do under DOS. OS/2 also offers online help. It can be used on IBM PCs and compatibles with an Intel 80486 (or later) microprocessor chip. Of interest to corporate users, however, is that OS/2 supports connectivity to all computers, including large ones. On the negative side, OS/2 consists of almost 300 files on 21 disks, is not easy to install, and requires a great deal of hard-disk space. A new version of OS/2, referred to as OS/2 Warp, will probably address these problems.

(See 3.1 Types of Software: System and Application; 3.2 Operating Systems; 3.3 Telling the Computer What to Do: User Interfaces; 3.4 Graphical User Interfaces: The WIMP Factor; 3.22 Object-Oriented Programming.)

3.11 UNIX

UNIX, an operating system developed by Bell Laboratories, can be used on mainframes and minicomputers, as well as on microcomputers (which we know as personal computers—"mini" computers are actually closet-size, and are only small compared to big mainframes). UNIX is what you might call an "industrial-strength" operating system. Like OS/2, UNIX allows several programs to be run at the same time. It also supports remote terminals, which allow several users to share a storage device and a printer. Because AT&T gave away this system when it was first developed, there are several versions of UNIX on the market, some of which are not compatible with each other.

Although it is quite powerful, UNIX is not an easy system for a non-programmer to use. In fact, it was developed for programmers to use and remains arcane. The problems with UNIX's cryptic commands can be overcome by installing a graphical user interface such as Motif, X-Window, or the NeXT user interface, NextStep.

Because of the computer language used to write it, UNIX has the distinction of being *portable*—it is usable on any computer. It is used primarily with *workstations*, powerful microcomputers with capabilities and memory approaching those of minicomputers. Even so, versions for microcomputers include Xenix by Microsoft Corporation (for IBM PCs and compatibles) and A/UX for Macintosh computers. UNIX is also used on Amiga and NeXT computers. It is not compatible with DOS; in the microcomputer market, its competition is OS/2, which has many of its features and can run DOS programs. Industry pundits predict, however, that UNIX will be the main operating system for a quarter of the worldwide computer market, and will threaten proprietary operating systems. One reason for their optimism is that UNIX is the operating system used on the Internet.

(See 2.7 Configuration and Compatibility; 3.1 Types of Software: System and Application; 3.2 Operating Systems; 3.3 Telling the Computer What to Do: User Interfaces; 4.13 The Internet.)

3.12 Computer Program Development

Think about how you write a report, proposal, business letter, or flier. When you start, you have an idea of what you want to say. You think through the steps and make a plan—maybe an outline or just a few notes. Then you write, following the rules for spelling, punctuation, grammar, and sentence structure. You test the product by reading it to yourself (or having someone else read it) to see whether it effectively reflects what you want to say. Maybe you make some changes and test it again. Then you clean up details and fine-tune the product. Writing a computer program, a procedure called *programming*, is much the same. The rules are much more rigid, however; if something is listed in the wrong order or misspelled, the computer will not do the job the program directs it to.

The set of steps in a program is called the *algorithm*. The algorithm must be clear, and must have a definite stopping point. It can proceed in one of three basic patterns: simple sequence, selection (or decision), and loop.

- *Simple sequence* means the steps are run one after another, in the order in which they are written.
- *Selection* means the program will follow one of two or more paths, depending on the current input.
- The *loop* pattern causes a set of instructions to be run over and over as needed.

To produce an algorithm that gives the correct output, first you state the problem, then design a solution. Next you write (*code*) the program; finally you test and *debug* the program. Various types of charts can be used to show the algorithm in its planning stage before actual coding begins. An example is the *flow chart*, which uses geometric symbols and arrows to depict the flow of program execution. Another is *pseudocode*, which lists the steps in prose form in a relatively unstructured format.

Once the algorithm is determined, you select a computer *programming language*, which is a set of vocabulary, symbols, and grammatical rules for instructing a computer.

(See 3.13 Structured Programming Techniques; 3.14 Bugs; 3.16 BASIC; 3.17 C; 3.19 Pascal; 3.19 Logo; 3.20 COBOL; 3.21 4GLs; 3.22 Object-Oriented Programming; 3.46 Software for Multimedia Management: Hypertext and Authoring Tools.)

3.13 Structured Programming Techniques

Programmers have developed a set of techniques called *structured programming* for producing software that is fairly error-free. These techniques include top-down design, limited control structures, documentation, and program testing.

Top-down design refers to a method of organization that proceeds from the general to the specific. *Control structures* are the basic patterns of sequence that enable the programmer to write a program in an orderly fashion. The ongoing process of *documentation* refers to creating a written description of the program that explains what the program should do, what data are needed, how data items are defined in the program, and how output is formatted. Lastly, the program modules are tested to uncover errors before the actual coding begins.

A structured program should have these characteristics:

- A program should be easy to read and to understand.
- A program should be dependable, always giving the right output.
- A program should work under all conditions, even with incorrect data.
- A program should be easy to change.
- A program should run as quickly as possible.

One way to meet these goals is the top-down method in which programs are divided into smaller and smaller subprograms called *modules*. Other techniques include these principles: avoid too much jumping around here and there in the program; use adequate tests to check for errors; provide clear documentation.

(See 3.12 Computer Program Development; 3.14 Bugs.)

3.14 Bugs

Every program contains *bugs*—that is, errors. Some are obvious very early as you begin to use a program. For example, a program that should print multiple copies of a document may stop abruptly after the sixth copy, no matter how many copies you tell it to print. A game program may constantly go in and out of a maze, no matter what else you tell it to do. Some bugs do not surface until you are ready to do a relatively uncommon job or enter some rather obscure data. The systematic search for errors to correct—even while writing a program—is called *debugging*.

There are several types of bugs, but the most common are syntax errors and logic errors. A *syntax error* involves the grammar and punctuation rules of a particular programming language. For example, the word PRINT may be misspelled. An interpreted program with a syntax error will stop running when it comes upon the error. A compiler will flag syntax errors. A *logic error* is more difficult to detect than a syntax error, because a program with a logic error may continue to run as if everything were working fine. The computer simply returns the wrong answer. Extensive *desk-checking*, or editing, may be required to unearth the logic errors. In addition, programmers often test a program with pre-figured data to see if every function yields the expected result.

According to tradition, the use of the word *bug* in conjunction with computer programs came about because in 1945 something went wrong with the Mark II, a large calculating machine used by the U.S. Department of Defense. No one could find the problem. More searching turned up a large moth beaten to death by one of the machine's mechanical parts. The moth was pulled out with tweezers and taped to a logbook, which is now at the Naval Museum in Dahlgren, Virginia. The phrases *a bug in the program* and *debugging the program* have been used ever since.

(See 3.8 System 7.5; 3.9 Microsoft Windows; 3.10 OS/2; 3.12 Computer Program Development; 5.5 Computer Errors.)

3.15 System Software and Language Translation

The first stored programs involved the most difficult and tedious methods of programming, but used languages closest to the way the computer actually works. These were *machine languages*, the first-generation language using the 0 and 1 digits of the *binary system.* With machine language, the programmer had to "map" memory and allocate all memory locations to be used. The time requirements and costs for program development were a major obstacle to computer utilization.

Improvements resulted with the language-translator programs. The first of these programs was the *assembler*, which translated the second-generation *assembly languages* into machine language. Assembly language used familiar letters and symbols such as ST for STore and LD for LoaD, but like machine language, it still required extensive knowledge of the particular computer being used. The word *easy* could not describe assembly language.

Eventually, third-generation—or *high-level*—languages were developed that used common English words. A single high-level language instruction can stand for several machine-language instructions. This reduces the time needed for writing a program; it also makes the program shorter, as well as easier to read and change. High-level languages, however, are not all easy to learn.

The first high-level language was FORTRAN, or FORmula TRANslator. FORTRAN was designed in the mid-1950s to meet the needs of engineers, scientists, and mathematicians who wanted an efficient, concise programming language. It is a good language for handling complex math problems, and it runs rapidly. Other high-level languages include BASIC, Pascal, COBOL, Logo, and C.

High-level languages are translated into machine language by one of two types of language-translator programs: interpreters or compilers. An *interpreter* translates and runs the program a line at a time while you are working at the computer. A *compiler* translates the entire program (called the *source code*) at once; then the translated version (called the *object code*) runs as a unit. Because the object code is unique for each type of computer, many compilers are available for the same language. For example, there is one Pascal compiler for IBM PCs and another for Macintosh computers. If you plan to buy a compiler for a high-level language, you should check the speed with which the compiler translates a program, and—most important—the speed at which the resulting program is executed. Buy a compiler that is reliable, shows you what the problem is when errors occur, and is produced by a company that provides good customer service.

Most software you buy is already translated into machine language, but many operating systems include a language translator for one or more programming languages. For example, most include the language translator for some version of a language called BASIC. Additional language translators for other programming languages are sold as separate software packages. Language translators are generally considered system programs.

(See 3.2 Operating Systems; 3.12 Computer Program Development; 3.14 Bugs; 3.16 BASIC; 3.17 C; 3.18 Pascal; 3.19 Logo; 3.20 COBOL; 3.21 4GLs.)

3.16 BASIC

The first programming language that a student learns is often BASIC (Beginner's All-purpose Symbolic Instruction Code). Some operating systems—and some microcomputers—include a version of BASIC, such as QBasic in PC-DOS. BASIC is easy to learn, and can be used for solving a wide variety of problems. In fact, BASIC was originally developed in the mid-1960s at Dartmouth College by professors John Kemeny and Thomas Kurtz to help students learn how to write programs. Although BASIC has been criticized as encouraging poor programming habits, newer versions such as Visual Basic promote a structured approach to programming. Actually, some of the problems with BASIC began when simplified versions were adjusted for microcomputers, which at that time had very little memory and forced developers to create shortcuts and leave out some important features.

BASIC is a flexible and simple language. It is popular as a teaching tool because in some versions, students can interact with the computer while writing a program. These versions of BASIC translate a program into machine language line by line as it is being run, instead of requiring the translation (or *compilation*) of the entire program first. Thus, students can alternately run and program, correcting errors until the program runs properly to the end. Most other languages require students to wait while the entire program is translated, after which the translated program is run. This waiting period can discourage beginning programmers, especially when a program has many errors to fix.

Visual Basic, a new version of BASIC created by Microsoft Corporation, goes much beyond the early, student-oriented BASICs. Yet it does provide a fast, understandable way for non-technical people to develop or create prototype applications, access a database, or write a Windows program. It includes Crystal Reports, a database reporting tool, and can support OLE 2.0 applications (in which data and functions of one application are accessible by pointing and clicking on a linked word in another application.) Visual Basic compels you to design an application from the user interface down. A screen designer lets you create GUIs quickly: you place toolbars, buttons, and other components on a form, and describe their behavior through a scripting language.

(See 3.9 Microsoft Windows; 3.12 Computer Program Development; 3.13 Structured Programming Techniques; 3.14 Bugs; 3.15 System Software and Language Translation.)

3.17 C

Developed in 1972, C has become popular for both system and application programming. It has some capabilities similar to those of assembly languages; it can, for example, manipulate individual bits and bytes in memory locations. Yet it also offers many high-level language features, such as a wide variety of useful control structures, economy of expression, and many built-in functions. Therefore, it is sometimes referred to as a *mid-level* language.

C is popular for several reasons. First, it is independent of machine *architecture* (the design and arrangement of a specific machine's parts); this independence makes C programs *portable*—the same program can be run on different computers. Second, C can be implemented on a wide variety of systems, from eight-bit microcomputers to supercomputers such as the Cray models. Third, C includes many structured programming features found in languages like Pascal. And fourth, some versions include tools for *object-oriented programming*, in which instructions or data are contained in modules that can be reused in new ways. A currently popular version of C is C++.

C was designed by Dennis Ritchie at Bell Laboratories. One of its first uses was in the rewriting of Bell Laboratories' UNIX operating system. Today, many of the latest microcomputer manufacturers and software developers use C for system programs, utility programs, and graphics applications.

(See 3.12 Computer Program Development; 3.13 Structured Programming Techniques; 3.14 Bugs; 3.15 System Software and Language Translation; 3.22 Object-Oriented Programming.)

3.18 Pascal

The programming language Pascal was named for Blaise Pascal, the inventor of the Pascaline (a seventeenth-century mechanical calculator). Pascal was designed to teach programming; it was the first major programming language to implement the ideas and methodology of structured programming. In fact, Pascal programs must be written by highly structured rules, or they will not run. Each Pascal program consists of modules called *procedures* that can be nested within one another. This methodology facilitates organized programs that are easy to follow.

Because it is so highly structured, Pascal is popular in high schools and colleges where teachers want students to learn good programming habits. It is easy to learn, yet powerful enough to use for designing computer art and solving complex math problems. On the down side, it is not standardized, and some experts believe it has poor input/output capabilities. Two popular compilers for Pascal are Turbo Pascal for PCs and Think Pascal for the Macintosh.

(See 3.12 Computer Program Development; 3.13 Structured Programming Techniques; 3.14 Bugs; 3.15 System Software and Language Translation.)

3.19 Logo

Logo is a programming language designed for students as young as five years old. The name *Logo* is taken from the Greek word *logos*, which means *a word*. Logo lets you define new words called *procedures* by using a basic set of words the language already understands. For example, here is a new word, SQUARE, that uses the Logo words TO, REPEAT, FORWARD, RIGHT, and END:

```
TO SQUARE
REPEAT 4 [FORWARD 50 RIGHT 90]
END
```

The procedure SQUARE will draw the image of a square. It also becomes a new word that can be used later.

Turtle Graphics, a common use of Logo in schools, allows children to make pictures by directing a turtle that leaves tracks on the screen. The turtle is a triangular cursor or other small symbol. Its tracks show the design the programmer has in mind.

Logo was developed by Seymour Papert and the Logo group at MIT in the late 1960s. Its main attraction is that it enables children and adults of all ages to begin programming in a very short time. It allows you to draw images, color them, and animate them using very simple instructions. It is *interactive*, meaning you can alternately run and write programming *statements* (instructions) until your program runs correctly. Logo is a very structured language, and helps to develop good programming habits. Although Logo might seem easy, learning every part of it can be difficult. It can be used for many jobs, including handling long lists of data, making music, working with tough math problems, and teaching a variety of subjects—including geometry, language, physics, and architecture.

(See 3.12 Computer Program Development; 3.13 Structured Programming Techniques, 3.14 Bugs; 3.15 System Software and Language Translation.)

3.20 COBOL

In 1960, COBOL (COmmon Business-Oriented Language) was designed for business use. It is well suited for handling large amounts of data, a common business task. A COBOL program consists of sentences and paragraphs, much like a report written in English; it is easy to understand and change. This feature is also a disadvantage of COBOL, because programs can get very wordy.

Although experts have been predicting its death for many years, COBOL remains the dominant language in use today by businesses and the federal government. No matter how many more efficient, easy-to-use, or faster-running languages are introduced, COBOL hangs in there, receiving periodic updates to incorporate newer programming methods and ideas. Because it is a standardized language, a firm can switch computer systems with little or no rewriting of existing COBOL programs. Such a large number of business programs have been developed using COBOL that to switch to a different language now would mean an enormous expense in labor and time.

(See 3.12 Computer Program Development; 3.13 Structured Programming Techniques; 3.14 Bugs; 3.15 System Software and Language Translation.)

3.21 4GLs

Very high-level programming languages are also known as *fourth-generation languages* or *4GLs*. These languages still require an exact syntax, but are much easier to learn and use than most other programming languages. Even if you are not a professional programmer, you can use a 4GL to develop applications. With a 4GL, you can specify what needs to be done without having to specify how it can be accomplished. Once the problem has been defined, the 4GL determines what program instructions are required to solve the problem. 4GLs are usually associated with database software.

Typically, 4GLs contain three tools that can be used in the development of an application program. These include query languages, report generators, and application generators. In addition, some 4GLs include a database manager. The *query language* portion of the language requires you to construct statements to extract and manipulate data in the database. The *report generator* portion of the 4GL enables you to designate the format of reports that display the data you have extracted and manipulated. *Application generators* give you a simplified method of developing a program that can be used to enter and manipulate data within the database. You can design screens into which data are input, for example, or you can designate verification rules to be performed on the data entered.

Fourth-generation languages are so named because of the progression of computer languages from first-generation languages (*machine language*) to second-generation languages (*assembly languages*) to third-generation languages (*high-level programming languages*). 4GLs are the computer languages closest to natural languages. In fact, some query languages are referred to as "natural languages," though special syntax rules must still be followed. They are used primarily to access databases. The de facto standard for query languages is *SQL* (Structured Query Language, pronounced *sequel*), a language most often used on minicomputers and mainframes, although available in some capacities for microcomputers.

(See 3.12 Computer Program Development; 3.13 Structured Programming Techniques; 3.14 Bugs; 3.15 System Software and Language Translation; 3.34 Data Managers.)

3.22 Object-Oriented Programming

Object-oriented programming, or OOP, is a type of programming technique that places a program's data and functions into a single unit, or *object*. In the past, programs were written with a particular function in mind. To perform a particular task, the programs would use large sections of code that were very similar to sections in other programs, but not exactly the same. Only particular types of data could be manipulated in each program, and chunks of code could not easily be transferred from one program to another without modifications.

OOP programs improved on this situation. They define both the data types and the functions, so that a collection of elements (that is, objects) can be combined to accomplish a particular task. The properties that distinguish an object are as follows:

- **Encapsulation**. An object is a self-contained structure, but it can also contain other data types—and even the functions used to act on those data types. For example, a document can have text and images, and thus includes functions for changing both. You do not need to know how an object works to use it, and you will not see everything that an object includes when you use it.
- **Inheritance**. An object can transfer characteristics to other objects. For example, if you have a document template for preparing a résumé, you can use characteristics of that template to create another template for a document such as a questionnaire.
- **Polymorphism**. Objects can respond differently when given the same command. In a draw program, for example, if you give two objects the command to draw to the screen, one may create circles and the other may create squares.

Blocks of computer instructions (or other items) with these characteristics will be treated as objects that any application can use. Changes to a particular job can be made to the object rather than to a file, and any project that uses that object benefits from the change. If you are working on a document in a word processing program, for example, and click on a graph within that document, the functions change operations from word processing to graphing—all in response to a simple click.

Objects can also "be anything" in a GUI interface. For example, the icons in the Macintosh Desktop are objects. The Trash can opens, just as a file does, when you double-click on it; to delete a file, you drag a file icon to the Trash can. Its function changes, however, when you drag a floppy disk's icon to it; this action ejects the floppy disk from the floppy disk drive.

For a program to support objects, the operating system must support objects. In the latest version of OS/2, functions open as you work on different parts of a document. Microsoft Windows offers *OLE*, or Object Linking and Embedding, in which you can link data in one program with that created in another program. OLE updates any linked data that is changed. When an icon (or object) is embedded in a program, you can click on it and have access to the functions of the program with which you created the object. For example, if you embed spreadsheet data into a word processor document, you can manipulate the spreadsheet data from within the word processor document. Apple's upcoming OpenDoc technology is closer to object-oriented programming than either the OS/2 or Windows technologies. A document opened in OpenDoc displays basic file functions such as Print and Copy. When you click on a block of text, the text-editing functions appear; if you click on a graphic, options for Image, Crop, Color, and Background appear, and so on. OpenDoc will be designed so that any software tool can be plugged in and utilized.

The object-oriented approach saves a great deal of memory space. Instead of having a dictionary for every application, for example, every application would use one dictionary. Instead of separate graphing applications for spreadsheets and databases, only one would be needed. Essentially, you can make new programs out of small application components. This saves writing similar code over and over in various programs, and also makes programs easier to change. Popular object-oriented languages are C++, Smalltalk, and object-oriented versions of Pascal.

(See 3.8 System 7.5; 3.9 Microsoft Windows; 3.10 OS/2; 3.12 Computer Program Development; 3.17 C.)

3.23 General Features of Application Software

Application software that is hard to use can be frustrating. Thus, programmers have developed several features that make software easier to use, less frustrating, and more organized-looking than much of the early software. These features are often common from package to package, so you learn to expect them.

Windows are outlined rectangular areas on the display screen. They can contain a variety of information, such as menus or files. For example, each file or program you have on-screen has its own window; each window has its own title bar so you know what it holds. Split windows help you deal with long files. If you want to compare information at the beginning of a file with information that appears later in the file, you can split the window into two sections and scroll the display in one section until you find the information you need for comparison. Many programs enable you to display two or more windows, each containing a different file in that program. Some operating systems let you display and use windows of two or more programs at once. *Tiled* windows are those you position side by side; *cascading* windows overlap onscreen so that only their title bars show. When you want to use a window that is partially hidden under another window, you put the pointer within the window you want to use and click the mouse button. This is called *popping*.

You can expand a small window to fill the screen by clicking in the window's *zoom box* (also called its *Maximize button*).

Most of today's applications also have *dialog boxes*, which contain information that guides you through a program. Dialog boxes generally require input from the user. For example, in Microsoft Word for the Macintosh, menu choices followed by an ellipsis (**...**) result in a dialog box. When you choose **Character...** from the **Format** menu, a dialog box appears in which you can specify the size and look of characters—boldfaced, underlined, shadowed, and so on. *Alert boxes* signal that something is about to happen, and may contain warnings about potentially damaging operations, such as deleting files. You may need to click a mouse button or press the Enter key to acknowledge an alert box and make it go away. The areas on boxes that cause something to happen when you point and click—such as canceling the box or starting an operation—are called *buttons*. The buttons may be rectangular with rounded corners, or *radio buttons* (small circles in which dots indicate selection).

A *menu* is a list of commands or options appearing on the display screen; from it you choose the item or data file you need. A menu on a word processing package, for example, might ask whether you want to create a new document, edit an existing document, print a document, or quit the program. There are three general ways you pick items from menus. The first is to type the letter or number that identifies the menu item. (For example, a menu may list the four items above as 1, 2, 3, and 4, or A, B, C, and D. If you want to edit an existing document, you type 2 or B, whichever appears beside the item.) The second method is to use arrow keys or the mouse to move a lighted bar to the desired item, and then hit the Enter key (or release the mouse button) to register your choice. The third method is to click in a *check box* alongside the option. An X appears in the box you have selected. Menus with check boxes usually allow you to select multiple options.

When you load some programs, the loading process ends at a full-screen menu from which you can choose the job you want to do. Other programs show a *menu bar*, or horizontal menu, across the top or bottom of the screen. Usually each option has its own menu that appears when you make a selection from the menu bar. *Pull-down menus* appear from a menu bar that is located at the top of the screen. *Pop-up menus* appear in the middle of the screen after you select from another menu. Either type of menu appears in its own window, and either type usually disappears as soon as you make your selections. A program that you use primarily by choosing from menus is called a *menu-driven* program, as opposed to a *command-line* program that requires you to type commands. A special type of menu is the *toolkit*, (also known as a *toolbox* or *toolbar*), which is an array of icons or patterns from which you make a selection by pointing and clicking. For example, in a graphics program, you may find icons for drawing lines, filling shapes, and picking patterns for different types of shading. The jobs depicted by the icons are usually called *tools*.

Very important to user-friendliness is the *undo feature* common to most software packages. This feature lets you reverse or cancel the last previous operation. For example, if you delete a paragraph by mistake, you can recover it by pressing the keys that activate the undo feature. On the Macintosh, you press the **flower** (or **Apple**) key, with the **Z** key. (This key combination lets you toggle between the change and the original, but does not let you roll back through previous changes.) Some programs enable you to retract five or more operations by pressing the undo feature's key repeatedly, but most require you to undo a mistake immediately after you make it. The undo feature can let you try unfamiliar commands at little risk, because you can return to the previous state. In some software, the Esc (Escape) key may also have an undo function; usually it lets you cancel the menu you just opened or the job (such as printing) you just started. Normally the program determines how this feature functions.

Most programs let you edit anything you have typed. *Editing* means changing an item by inserting or deleting characters and moving or copying items. You can edit single characters or use block operations. A *block* is a chunk of on-screen information—text, database fields, or spreadsheet cells. When you select a block, it appears highlighted on the screen to distinguish it from other information. When you have the program do something to the block, the job is called a *block operation*. Blocks can be moved, copied, modified, or deleted.

Most programs have *default settings*—that is, values the program selects automatically if you do not specify otherwise. In word processing programs, default settings apply to margins, line spacings, page lengths, and other formats. For example, the default line spacing may be single spacing and the default justification may be left-justified.

(See 2.3 Which Computer? The Platforms; 3.1 Types of Software: System and Application; 3.3 Telling the Computer What to Do: User Interfaces; 3.4 Graphical User Interfaces: The WIMP Factor; 3.25 Evaluating Software; 3.28 Files.)

3.24 WYSIWYG

Most older versions of word processors and other *productivity software* (work-oriented programs) enabled you to insert a wide variety of formats for printing, but you couldn't see how a document would look until you actually printed it. You only knew that the formats were there because you could select a mode that showed the embedded commands that indicated various formats. Many of today's programs, however, show on the screen how a document will look when printed; this feature is called *WYSIWYG*. Pronounced *wizzywig*, the acronym stands for What You See Is What You Get. This feature is invaluable for desktop publishing.

From the beginning, Apple's Macintosh computers embodied the WYSIWYG concept because they have always been graphics-based. Increasingly, however, users of IBM computers and compatibles are demanding WYSIWYG. To compete with the Apple standard, software manufacturers have included WYSIWYG as a special feature that can be activated or deactivated in the formatting function of productivity programs.

Some programs have a feature called *print preview* that lets you see how a document will look before it is printed. Generally, this feature must be selected as an option; editing cannot be done while the screen is in the print preview mode.

(See 3.23 General Features of Application Software; 3.31 Word Processors; 3.33 Desktop Publishing.)

3.25 EVALUATING SOFTWARE

Experts generally agree that you should choose the software before you buy the hardware; the software determines the hardware needs. This is good advice when you are first purchasing a system. Thus the primary question you should ask yourself is "What do I want to do with my computer?" Once you know what you want to do, you can pick software that fits your needs.

To choose the best software package, you should educate yourself by talking with a knowledgeable friend, joining a users' group, or reading software reviews in computer magazines. You should test several programs of the type you are considering, and try more than one platform. For example, try programs on the IBM PC platform and on the Macintosh platform.

Be sure there are no problems with compatibility between the software you ultimately choose and the system you decide to buy. Much software is *backwardly compatible*, meaning that it is compatible with earlier versions of the same product, and can use files produced by the earlier version. Also, be sure the software will handle the amount of data you will be entering. For example, check the number of records a data manager can support, the number of pages of text a word processor can work with, or the number of columns and rows that a spreadsheet can support.

Be sure the software can grow as your needs and abilities expand. A good program will enable you to run the program using only the basic commands needed to accomplish the application, but provide more sophisticated commands as you need them.

Make sure the organization of the screen display is clear and logical, and that the help screens are truly helpful. Evaluate your comfort level with the command style, often called the *look and feel*, of the program. Although menus and GUIs are helpful to novices, experienced users may find that these slow down the input and processing stages. So ask yourself a few questions. For example: How easy is the program to use? How much time do you want to spend learning how to use a program? Will you be learning many different programs, or just one or two? Do you want a menu-driven program, or do you want to learn all the commands with no menus available? Do you want menus with the option of using key commands? Would you feel more comfortable with a GUI?

Check the clarity of documentation such as user's manuals and tutorials. Be sure the tutorials guide you through the basics before inundating you with a flood of complex commands and features geared toward experienced users. Look for on-screen help you can call up as needed. (Some help screens are described as *context-sensitive*; the help they offer is applicable to the operation you are trying to perform.)

Not essential, but very helpful, is the program's ability to use *macro* commands. A macro command enables you to string together several commands or keystrokes and define them as one-key command. Once you have recorded a macro, you need only press its key sequence; the macro executes the designated set of commands or keystrokes immediately. For example, you could create a macro that would enter a difficult spelling that you use often; another macro might enter your Social Security number instantly.

Because much of the software you buy will be *upgraded* (improved) as time goes on, you will want to purchase a computer that has more capabilities than the minimum your chosen software requires. More-than-adequate capabilities will also make it easier to add to your software library. When you choose software after buying your computer, always be sure its specifications match those of your system. These include your system's microprocessor number, microprocessor speed (if necessary), version number of the operating system, amount of RAM (random-access memory), memory-managing capabilities, and size of the hard disk drive, as well as its graphics standard. Other important factors include the new software's compatibility with other programs you own (such as Windows or HyperCard), and whether it requires specific hardware (such as a mouse or sound card). For example, a package might require a Macintosh Performa or higher model (i.e., with faster chips), 4MB of RAM, System 7.0 or later, and a hard disk drive. If you own an IBM-compatible, you might find a list such as this on your software package: VGA or better graphics standard, CD-ROM drive, 80286 or better microprocessor, 4MB RAM, mouse, hard disk with 8MB of storage space free, DOS 3.1 or higher operating system, and Windows 3.1 or higher as an operating environment.

(See 2.20 Getting Help: Documentation and Customer Support; 3.23 General Features of Application Software; 5.11 Copyright and Piracy.)

3.26 Public-Domain Software, Freeware, and Shareware

Computer bulletin boards, commercial online services, users' groups, and even bookstores are sources of public-domain software, freeware, and shareware. *Public-domain software* falls outside copyright protection, and is therefore available for unrestricted use. Normally this occurs when the author decides not to protect the copyright interest and publishes the software with that stipulation. Software developed with public or grant funds may also be contractually transferred into the public domain. Such software is frequently found via electronic bulletin board systems, in magazines, or through users' groups. With *freeware*, the programmer retains the copyright on the files and can prohibit for-profit distribution. This software is intended to be used free of charge.

Shareware is copyrighted material; although it is obtainable without charge, it is not considered to be in the public domain. The ethics of using shareware demand that anyone who uses a shareware program pay a *registration fee*, often $25 to $50. The philosophy behind shareware is that users are in the best position to judge the value of a program—and that authors, if they know their fees depend upon it, will produce a high-quality product. Some magazines list and review shareware programs, and often the ratings are very high.

(See 2.21 Magazines; 2.22 Users' Groups; 3.25 Evaluating Software; 4.12 Bulletin Board Systems; 4.14 Online Services.)

3.27 Installing Software

Most software today is used from a hard disk rather than from a floppy disk (as in the past). Thus, it must be *installed* before it can be used. The software comes on floppy disks or a CD-ROM disk. Before installation can begin, you must insert the disk into the appropriate drive. Generally, you will see a *READ ME file*. Do read the file; it may contain important information that is not in the paper documentation included in the package.

You install your software onto a hard-disk drive either by activating a special installation program or by dragging the program's icon into the hard drive's window or icon (only operating systems with a GUI can support this latter method). When you use a command-line user interface like that of DOS, you must enter a command such as **INSTALL** and wait for further instructions. If you use a GUI such as Windows, you double-click on the Install program's icon, after which a window appears with further directions. Follow the directions until installation is complete.

Some software packages instruct you to make backup copies from the originals and install the program from the backup copies. You also may need to deactivate your anti-virus software before carrying out the installation. In addition, you may need to answer questions during the installation process; some ask you to indicate where you want the program installed, and others ask whether you want a "quick" or customized installation.

Although some programs come on CD-ROM disks from which they are installed onto a hard drive, many software products treat CD-ROMs as virtual hard disks. This carries the advantage of conserving hard disk space. The CD-ROM may contain a special access program that installs itself on the hard disk automatically. Be aware that you may need to delete such access programs to avoid incompatibility problems later.

Problems often occur with installing and running software on IBM-compatible computers when there is not enough memory to run the program. In such a case, you may need to create a special *boot disk* from which you restart the computer, so that only the minimum operating system functions are loaded. On Macintosh computers, you want to be sure you do not copy an extra System Folder, which is included in its entirety on some program disks. (Boot disks are useful when running "memory-hogging" programs such as games and graphics programs. For normal use, however, loading only the minimum functions of an operating system can result in less-than-optimal performance from the software.)

(See 1.24 Floppy Disks; 1.25 Hard Disks; 1.27 CD-ROMs and Optical Storage; 3.2 Operating Systems; 3.29 Memory-Resident Programs; 3.30 Utilities.)

3.28 Files

An application such as a word processor, the documents you create, drawings, or a spelling dictionary are all kept in files. A *file* is a set of data grouped under the same name (called a *file name*). Each file must have a file name; normally you give a file its file name when you create it. Thereafter you use the file name to tell the computer to duplicate the file, save it to disk, or send it to the printer for a paper copy. (In the DOS environment, the term *document* generally refers to a text file; in the Macintosh environment, files made by any application are called documents.)

There are usually specific rules for naming files. For example, you may be limited in the number of characters you can use, and some characters—such as the colon (:) on the Macintosh—cannot be used in a file name. Existing files can be opened, or accessed, by typing the file name or by selecting the file's icon. On MS-DOS and PC-DOS systems, the files are listed in directories. Any time you want to open or manipulate a file, you must type its name exactly. The file name may include a period and three additional characters called the *file-name extension*, which tells what kind of file it is. In some cases, you may type an entire *pathname*, which tells the exact location of the file—that is, the disk drive and the directory, as well as the file name and the extension. As you can see, using files can be quite complicated.

On Macintosh computers, the files are shown on the Desktop as icons with the file names beneath. Collections of files can be kept in *folders*, the Macintosh term for directories. If you give a file a name that already exists, the computer will ask whether you want to replace the existing file with the new file. This gives you a chance to change the file name before the computer erases the old one. You can easily manipulate the files using the mouse. For example, pressing the mouse button twice quickly in succession (called *double-clicking*) after you have selected a file icon opens that file.

Most programs have a status line, or status area, which shows you where you are in a file. In a word processing file, for example, the *status line* may show which page, line, or column you are in. It may also show how you formatted the appearance of characters.

To use a file in any program, you must be able to see all the material in the file. Thus, as text or database items fill the screen, you can move, or *scroll*, the text up or down the screen to make room for more. As a new line appears at the bottom of the screen, for example, the other lines move up one row and the top line disappears. Vertical scrolling moves material up and down; horizontal scrolling moves material to the right or left. Many programs that show files in windows contain *scroll bars* at the right side of window and often at the bottom of the window. These let you see where you are in a file, in relation to the whole file; within the scroll bar is a tiny square that indicates your position. If you are in the middle of a document, the square is about halfway down the bar. If you are three-quarters of the way into a document, the square is about three-quarters of the way down the bar, and so on. This feature is valuable for viewing an entire document, which in most cases is too long to be viewed all at once. Scrolling is usually independent of cursor movement, although you can move the cursor to a new spot in a file after you have scrolled. When you use the arrow keys to scroll, the cursor moves along with the scrolling.

(See 3.6 DOS Versions; 3.8 System 7.5; 3.9 Microsoft Windows; 3.23 General Features of Application Software.)

3.29 Memory-Resident Programs

Without a special operating system, most computers will not let you use two programs at once. You cannot run a word processing program and a spreadsheet program at the same time, for example. Unlike regular applications, however, *memory-resident programs* can run while you are working in almost any program. Memory-resident programs remain in memory even if an operating system is swapping portions of other programs in and out of memory. For example, if you are blind, you can use a *screen reader* program, which makes off-the-shelf software "talk." (To use a screen reader, you may need to add a *voice synthesizer* to your computer system.) Usually, you do not interact with this type of memory-resident program while you are working on an application. This type of memory-resident program is also called a *terminate-and-stay resident* program or *TSR*.

A variation of memory-resident programs requires you to press a key (or key combination) that activates the program. The keystroke is called the *hot key*. When you call up a memory-resident program, the application you are working on is temporarily suspended while you use the memory-resident program. After you are finished with the memory-resident program, it either disappears on its own or you press another key to quit it. Then the other program is active again, ready for your input. Using this type of memory-resident programs eliminates the time-consuming process of exiting one program in order to open another. This variation is sometimes called a *pop-up utility*.

Spelling checkers and thesauruses belong in this variation of memory-resident programs. So do calculators, calendars, time planners, address books, and notepads that are offered in some *personal information management* software such as Sidekick by Borland International Corp. *Contact management* software—which helps you maintain lists of names, addresses, telephone numbers, and sales activities—is also available as memory-resident software. You may need to load some programs such as spelling checkers before you can access them with the hot key.

Memory-resident programs are sometimes referred to as *RAM-resident*. Memory-resident programs reduce the amount of memory available for other jobs, and not all react well with each other. When you load so many memory-resident programs that you cannot access your application, you have achieved a condition called *RAM cram*; a message may announce "insufficient memory."

(See 1.15 RAM; 3.32 Writing Aids: Thesauruses, Spelling and Grammar Checkers; Software Review section: After Dark, Key Watch, inLARGE, Monologue, outSPOKEN, SideKick.)

3.30 UTILITIES

Utilities are programs that do specific jobs usually related to managing system resources, or "housekeeping," as some call these jobs. Often, they are tools that make using a computer's operating system easier. Operating systems contain a variety of utility programs that manage printers and disk drives or provide sorting capabilities. Other utilities enable you to recover programs you might have deleted accidentally, save your files automatically as you work, and lock files you want to keep confidential. A *defragmenting* utility, sometimes called a *disk optimizer*, gathers all the pieces of a file and collects them into one place on the hard disk. This is helpful because an operating system normally starts writing in the first empty spot it finds when you activate the save function. If there isn't enough room in that spot for all the material, the OS jumps to another empty spot and continues writing. A file that is changed and saved many times has fragments in numerous spots on the disk. Other utilities include screen savers, macro generators, and virus-protection programs.

Printer utilities enable the printer to scale fonts, emulate a LaserJet printer, shrink pages, or print a file while you are doing some other task at the computer. Some utilities are especially designed for the problems of notebook computers. For example, utility programs enable you to transfer files from the notebook to a desktop, once you link the two with the correct cables. They also keep track of remaining battery power by displaying a "fuel gauge" that tells you how much battery power is left (an alarm sounds when battery power is low).

Unlike application programs, which are large and complex and do a variety of functions, utilities are usually small, simple, stand-alone programs that do one job each. They are often installed as memory-resident programs. Collections of utility programs are often sold as one software package. Two popular utility packages are Norton Utilities from Symantec Corp. (for IBM-compatibles) and Now Utilities from Now Software, Inc. (for the Macintosh). To the cynical, utilities make up for the jobs the programmers left out of your operating system; as operating systems improve, there may be less need for utilities.

(See 2.8 Portables; 2.17 Caring for Your Computer; 3.2 Operating Systems; 3.23 General Features of Application Software; 3.29 Memory-Resident Programs; 5.4 Viruses; Software Review section: After Dark, inLARGE, Key Watch, KidDesk, LinksWare, Monologue, Norton Utilities for Macintosh, On Cue II, outSPOKEN, PC-Kwik Power Pak, QEMM-386, SideKick, Suitcase II, Symantec AntiVirus for Macintosh, Untouchable DOS, XTree Gold.)

3.31 Word Processors

A *word processor* program can sometimes seem less scary than a blank sheet of paper simply because words and sentences can be erased easily from the computer screen. If you find a misspelled word on page 2 of a report, you do not have to scratch it out and write in the correct word. You can correct it at the computer and print out a new page 2. If you find that you misspelled a name you used often, you can search for it and correct every error automatically. With a word processor, you can add, erase, copy, scramble, and experiment with words without worrying about neatness.

You might wonder what you would do with a word processor. If your writing consists mostly of personal letters, then you may not need one. If you are involved with a club, have school-aged children, do freelance writing, or keep a journal, then a word processor could help you create good-looking documents easily. Word processors are used in businesses for correspondence, reports, brochures, memos, legal documents, instructional and training materials, newsletters, catalogs, and other important written material.

To do word processing, you need a computer, a compatible word processing program, a printer, and (optionally) a mouse. Word processing consists of two basic operations: *text editing* and *print formatting*. In the text editing process, you enter text (that is, words) into a computer by pressing the appropriate keys on the keyboard. As you type, you see the words appear on the display screen. The little cursor that moves along as you type tells you where you are on the screen. If you see a mistake, you can hit the Delete or Backspace key to erase the error and then type the correct letter. You can reposition the cursor in another sentence or paragraph to delete or add some words. As the text is being entered, you can save it, or store it, on a hard disk or floppy disk.

Cursor positioning is an important part of text editing because it enables you to position the cursor at different locations to edit the text. In most word processors, you can move the cursor directly to the beginning or the end of a document, to the next or previous screenful of text, to the next or previous paragraph or sentence, or to the next or previous word.

If more characters are typed on a line than the margin allows, the program forces the cursor to the next line—carrying with it, if necessary, the word you have not finished typing. This is called automatic *word wrap*, or a *soft return*. This feature lets you keep typing without pressing the Enter key (also known as the Return key, as it performed the carriage return on an electric typewriter) at the end of the line. If you want to end the line before it reaches the right margin—at the end of a paragraph, for instance—simply press the Return key for a *hard return*.

With the word processor, you can add or delete characters, words, sentences, and paragraphs. (The add feature is usually called *insert.*) You can also move or copy text within a document or to another document; sometimes this process is called *cut-and-paste*. During cutting, the text is transferred to a temporary holding area called a *buffer* or *clipboard*. Any text you have selected to move or delete is called a *block* of text. Operations that involve selecting a block of text are called *block operations*. In some word processors, you must be in a certain *mode* to move, delete, or insert text. This means a command acts like a toggle switch to change the program's functioning. You would issue a command, for example, to enter the insert or move mode, do the job that needs to be done, and then exit the mode via a similar command. After any insert, delete, or move function, the word processor adjusts the text automatically to fit the lines and margins.

Search-and-replace is another helpful editing feature. If you used the name of your club's vice president several times in a report when you meant to use the president's name, you can engage a search that finds and changes all instances of the wrong name. There are three types of searches: finding only, finding and replacing on a per-word basis, and finding and replacing all instances of the offending word.

You can also specify options such as upper- or lowercase match, in which only the name *Leader* would be found even if there are occurrences of the word *leader*. Some word processors have a *wild card* match that lets you find any words containing specified characters in a specified location in a word. For example, if * were a wild card character, searching for **re*** would find *report*, *retread*, *rehire*, and so on.

In addition to modifying a document's content, you can use *print formatting* features to determine the way a document will look when it is printed. You will often see a *ruler* at the top of the screen that helps with formatting options such as setting margins, tabs, and line spacing. In addition, most word processors let you adjust margin settings, character appearance (plain text, boldface, or italics), line spacing (single, double, or triple), and underlining. They also provide automatic page breaking and page numbering options (called pagination). Text can be *justified*—lined up along a margin—or it can be centered. Text justified on the left margin is called *flush-left*; justified on the right, it is called *flush-right*. The opposite of flush is *ragged*; flush-left text is *ragged right* and flush-right text is *ragged left*. If both margins are evenly aligned, the text is *fully justified*. There are default settings—that is, values used by the program when not instructed to use any others—for the format of a document. The defaults usually include plain text, single spacing, and left justification.

Some word processors enable you to choose from a variety of *fonts* (consistent character designs). Most let you place *headers* or *footers* on each page, meaning that one or more lines of text appear at the top or bottom of the page for identifying a chapter title, a page number, a date, and so on. Once you have determined the format for one type of document, you can save it as a *style sheet* to use in the future. Some word processors come with preset style sheets for common types of documents such as business letters.

A number of other features distinguish the different word processing packages. Word processors usually offer a *mail-merge* option that enables you to generate *form letters*; each letter is printed with its own recipient's name and address, *imported* (brought in) from database files. Some word processors let you do *redlining*, marking text you have edited or changed so the next reader knows what you have done. The redlining is easy to remove once everyone has seen the changes. Some word processors have a *draft mode* for fast data entry and a *graphical mode* for setting up a document's appearance. Many word processors offer some sort of graphics capabilities. Some merely let you insert graphics into a document you have already created using the word processor. Others let you edit graphics you have imported from another program. Still others contain graphics tools that let you create pictures from within the word processor itself.

An *executive* word processor offers the basic functions; one that offers additional features (such as a spelling checker, thesaurus, fonts, headers, footers, pagination, macros, merges, windows, and page layout) is called *full-featured*. Special word processors are designed for legal, academic, and scientific uses. They let you insert footnotes and generate tables of contents, indexes, and other reader helps by culling together the words you have identified with special hidden marks inserted for the purpose designated.

Besides considering the functions you want to perform, you should consider a few other factors when buying a word processing program. Check to see how easy it is to do the basic editing functions such as moving and searching. Find out what the scrolling speed is; notice whether the cursor keeps up with your typing. Check to see which models of printer the program supports.

(See 1.36 Cursors; 1.37 Keyboards; 1.46 Monitors; 1.49 Printers; 1.55 Typefaces and Fonts; 3.1 Types of Software: System and Application; 3.23 General Features of Application Software; 3.24 WYSIWYG; 3.25 Evaluating Software; 3.32 Writing Aids : Thesauruses, Spelling and Grammar Checkers; 3.33 Desktop Publishing; 3.36 Graphics Software; 3.41 Suites and Integrated Software; Software Review Section: AmiPro, ClarisWorks, JustWrite for Windows, MacWrite II, Microsoft Word for the Macintosh, Microsoft Works, WordPerfect for Macintosh, WriteNow.)

3.32 WRITING AIDS: THESAURUSES, SPELLING AND GRAMMAR CHECKERS

Although using a word processor may not make you a better writer, it certainly makes it easier to improve a report or letter. A number of programs, however, can actually help you improve your writing performance. Among these are thesauruses, spelling checkers, and grammar checkers. Most word processors include spelling checkers and thesauruses, but you can also purchase separate software for these tasks. Grammar checkers usually are separate packages.

Writers need to choose their words carefully, and often turn to a *thesaurus* —a book that lists words and their synonyms—for help. An electronic thesaurus is often faster, and enables you to request a synonym for any word it contains. If the word is not in the thesaurus, the program tells you so, or lists words that you might have meant. Some programs let you add a new word to the thesaurus with the appropriate synonym.

A *spelling checker* is an electronic dictionary that helps detect incorrectly spelled words. Many packages allow you to customize the dictionary by adding special words such as technical terms and names. When you activate the spelling function, the computer will locate and highlight misspelled words, as well as words that do not appear in the dictionary. In most packages, you make the correction manually, although you can activate a "suggest" feature that lists correctly spelled words from which you can choose a replacement for the incorrect one. A spelling checker does not eliminate the need for careful proofreading, however. If you type *there sales* instead of *their sales*, the checker will not highlight *there* as a misspelled word.

Grammar checkers are designed to help you use the correct syntax of your language. They may flag a point where the noun and verb do not agree, highlight double words, or locate incomplete sentences. Before you buy a grammar checker, try it out by entering errors in a sample document. Include such items as missing verbs, incorrect capitalization, sentence fragments, and agreement errors with the wrong tense or the incorrect pronoun for an antecedent.

(See 3.29 Memory-Resident Programs; 3.31 Word Processors; Software Review section: Correct Grammar for Windows, Grammatik.)

3.33 DESKTOP PUBLISHING

Desktop publishing (DTP) enables you to create documents that incorporate a number of graphics features you would commonly see in a newsletter, magazine, book, or brochure. The heart of desktop publishing is *page-composition*, or *page-layout*, software. This software allows you to import material from word processing software and graphics programs, place it all on the same page, and manipulate it—although, of course, all the software packages you use must be compatible.

Page-composition software usually retains formats you set up with your word processing program, such as tab settings and basic type styles (boldface, italics, and so on). Then you can add a variety of fonts, multiple columns, lines of varying widths and lengths, boxes, symbols, and pictures. You can request the program to hyphenate words at the ends of some lines so characters in the line do not stretch out across the page too much. You can include various *elements*—parts such as headlines, logos, scanned photographs, captions, cartoons, and text that make up the page. You can rotate words for special effects. Figures, tables, and other ancillaries may be numbered automatically, and changed automatically if you delete one. You can use the software to generate tables of contents and indexes by inserting special hidden marks beside the words you want to include. And there are footnoting options. The resulting document can be of near-typeset quality when you use a laser printer. (For even better results, you can purchase a style book that helps you with the aesthetic design of a page.)

Desktop publishing is commonly used for creating company newsletters, advertising brochures, proposals, and reports. This can result in significant savings for organizations that would normally send documents out to be typeset. You will need the computer, a compatible program, as much computer memory as you can afford, at least an 80MB hard disk drive, a high-resolution graphics monitor, a mouse, a scanner, a laser-quality printer, and software to produce drawings and spreadsheets as needed.

Professional-looking results can be achieved using a Macintosh computer, one of the Apple LaserWriter printers, and Adobe (Aldus) Corporation's Pagemaker page composition software. Because of the great number of options and the expense of high-end printers, however, costs can run as high as $12,000 for a high-powered system. Children and teenagers, however, can enjoy creating their own newsletters and fliers using a microcomputer with an inexpensive dot-matrix or ink-jet printer and The Newsroom or Print Shop software. In addition, many word processing programs also have some page-composition capabilities—enough to be called *document-preparation* packages.

Although sophisticated word processing programs have page-composition capabilities, customarily some features appear only in programs designed for desktop publishing. For example, you will be able to scale art to fit a given page, crop pictures, wrap text around pictures in several ways, and use kerning and leading capabilities:

- *Scaling* means you can increase or decrease the size of a graphic image by percentage without distorting its proportions.
- *Cropping* is the term that describes cutting away parts that detract from the primary subject of a graphic image.
- *Wrapping* text refers to how text aligns itself around a picture. A *rectangular* wrap means that words are forced into a narrower space to the left or right of a rectangular picture inserted into a column of text. An *arbitrary* wrap follows the shape of the image. An *irregular* wrap wraps the text around the image in whatever manner you choose.
- When text is *kerned*, either manually or automatically, the distance between each letter is adjusted to make the word look proportional. The distance is equal between any two letters in unkerned text. Kerning is sometimes called *microspacing*. It is often used when text will be justified on both the left and right margins.
- *Leading* refers to the distance between lines of text. In most word processing programs, leading is preset to single, double, and triple spaces. Some DTP programs offer adjustable leading. Although the screen may show the results of kerning and leading, generally you need a high-quality printer to see those same results in *hard copy*—that is, on paper.

The WYSIWYG features of page-composition software are more complete and more accessible than those of word processors. You can usually use a mouse to manipulate the page's elements—headlines, graphs, text, and pictures. Most page-composition packages also contain drawing and graphics tools for creating pictures, boxing text, or embellishing titles or headlines. The thickness and texture of lines can be varied, for example. You can use a preset style, called a *style sheet*, for designing headlines, boxes, or general page layout.

In addition, you may find the program includes a variety of small drawings; you can insert this *clip art* into your documents without worrying about copyrights (publishers usually prohibit the use of clip art in products designed for sale). Illustrations include art for specific subjects such as sports, Christmas, nineteenth-century costume, locomotives, animals, food, and tools. Very small pieces of clip art you can use beside headings and subheadings (e.g., stars, check marks, fat pencils, pen points, and so on) are called *dingbats*. (Clip art can be purchased in separate software packages that often include dingbats.)

(See 1.33 Resolution; 1.34 Pixels; 1.38 Mice and Trackballs; 1.41 Scanners; 1.46 Monitors; 1.49 Printers; 1.50 Print Quality; 1.54 Page-Description Languages; 1.55 Typefaces and Fonts; 3.23 General Features of Application Software; 3.24 WYSIWYG; 3.25 Evaluating Software; 3.31 Word Processors; 3.36 Graphics

Software; 3.38 Paint and Draw Programs; Software Review section: Adobe Type Manager, Adobe (Aldus) Pagemaker, The New Print Shop, PFS: Publisher for Windows, Publish It!, QuarkXPress for Windows, Ventura Publisher for Windows.)

3.34 Data Managers

Schools, hospitals, governments, and almost every type of business need to store a lot of data. At one time, these records were kept on paper or microfilm in file cabinets. Finding information about one person or event was easy; a clerk would simply look under a key word or number, such as a name or a Social Security number. But it was hard to make a list of people or events that had several things in common. Imagine shuffling through a county's tax records to find all the people who were delinquent on paying property taxes *and* who lived in another state. Surely there must be an easier way to find the data.

Instead of searching through all the paperwork, you could use a special program called a *data manager* for handling the data. A data manager (also called a *database management system*, or *DBMS*) lets you use a computer rather than filing-cabinet drawers and folders to enter, store, and retrieve data. The data is stored on tapes or disks.

Traditionally, the data is organized in a hierarchy from the field to the record to the file. A *field* is one data item, such as a student name, an insurance policy number, or an invoice number. A field can be *numerical* (such as a cost), *character* (such as a name); or *logical* (such as Y or N for yes or no.) A group of related fields form a *record*. An employee record might contain fields such as the employee name, home address, telephone number, Social Security number, work schedule, and so on. A *file* is a group of related records. For example, all the employee records in a business make up one file. All the equipment information might make up another file.

Many data managers enable you to restrict the kind of data you can enter. If you set up a numerical field, then the program will not let you enter letters. If you determine that a field should have only four characters, then the program will not let you enter five characters. Some programs let you set up a *memo* field that overcomes these restrictions.

Using a data manager, you can usually manipulate the data in these ways:

- Add or delete data within a file.
- Search a file for certain data.
- Update or change data in a file.

- Sort data into some order, such as alphabetically or by ZIP code.
- Print all or part of the data in a file in some form of report.
- Perform mathematical calculations, such as totaling the data in a particular field.

There are two types of data managers: flat-file databases and relational databases. *Flat-file* managers store data in two-dimensional tables similar to spreadsheets. The columns of a table represent fields, and the rows represent records. In some less sophisticated programs, only one file can be accessed at a time, and data cannot be drawn from two files into one report.

Flat-file databases do have a problem with data *redundancy*, which is the repeating of data in different files. Since multiple files cannot be accessed at the same time, individual files may repeat data held in other files in order to be complete. If you have to change an address, it must be changed in all files in which it appears. You cannot make the change once and have it reflected in every affected file.

Relational databases solve the problem of duplicate data, and the related problem of keeping one piece of information (such as an address) current. In a relational database, you can open and use data from several files at once. An item that is changed in one file is changed in all the files in which it appears. This is because the files are linked through one or more shared relations. A *shared relation* is data that is common to all the files—that is, a common field or fields. An employee name could be the common field, for example. Since the files are linked, an employee's salary file would not need to include an address and telephone number; that information would already be in the general employee file.

Once a file is created, you can *query* (question) it to find particular information. For example, a baseball card file could be queried to find all players between specific years who come from the state of Ohio. Queries might be stated in terms of operators such as OR, AND, NOT, =, +, SELECT, and so on. You also include a *key*, which indicates which field you want to find. (An *index* keeps track of one or more *key fields* you might want to sort by, such as last name or ZIP code.)

The queries can be written so that the program prints a report containing the answers you need. The report function of a data manager is often called a *report generator*. In database programs, the query and reporting functions can become quite complex, requiring the use of a special *query language*. In fact, some sophisticated relational databases include a programming language that enables you to construct complex systems that link many steps and data.

The exact definition of the term *relational* in reference to databases is under debate. For minicomputers and mainframes, the term *relational* means a lot more than merely accessing data in multiple files. As many as thirteen rules have been developed for defining relational databases. For microcomputer users, however, a relational database is simply a database that can draw information from more than one file at one time.

Data managers are popular software packages for home use. They can be used to create and organize addresses, collections such as stamps or baseball cards, or recipes. In businesses, databases are used to maintain employee records, inventory, and lists of suppliers and customers. Data managers are often used with word processors to create personalized form letters for the individuals or organizations found on mailing lists. They supply the names and addresses that are inserted at specific points in the letters.

(See 3.1 Types of Software: System and Application; 3.21 4GLs; 3.23 General Features of Application Software; 3.25 Evaluating Software; 3.28 Files; 3.31 Word Processors; 3.41 Suites and Integrated Software; Software Review section: Approach, ClarisWorks, dBASE IV, File Express, FileMaker Pro, Microsoft Works, PackRat for Windows, Paradox, PC-File, SuperBase4.)

3.35 Spreadsheets

An electronic *spreadsheet* program lets you record numbers and solve math problems. You can use a spreadsheet program to budget your money, compare costs of computer equipment for your company, and keep track of scores for your softball league. Spreadsheet programs are the most up-to-date means for businesses to keep track of numbers. Most businesses and other organizations use these programs to predict what could happen in the future when some numbers on a spreadsheet are changed.

Before computers and software existed, people used paper spreadsheets to record financial data. These spreadsheets, or ledger sheets, were the model for the form of the spreadsheet you see on-screen: columns and rows identify where the numbers and descriptions are written. These columns and rows keep the numbers and words in line so you can find and understand them easily.

Suppose the Jones family keeps track of their income and expenses with a paper spreadsheet. There are entries for wages, interest income, housing, car payments, utilities, insurance, food, gas, clothing, taxes, entertainment, savings, and so on. Now suppose the Joneses finish paying for their car, and Mrs. Jones starts working full-time instead of half days. Two of the Jones children are getting braces on their teeth, and the youngest will begin advanced training in gymnastics. Quite a lot of numbers in the budget would have to be changed, and new totals must be figured. This would take a fair amount of time using a pencil, paper, and calculator. Now suppose that a big corporation uses a paper spreadsheet to keep track of its budget. Can you imagine the many more numbers that would have to be changed each time there were new types of costs or income?

With an electronic spreadsheet program, keeping a budget takes less time to use and makes changes easier. You see the spreadsheet on the computer screen rather than on paper, and you use the keyboard rather than a pencil to enter your numbers and descriptions. You do not need a calculator at all; once you enter the formulas that tell the program what to do, it does all the figuring for you.

The spreadsheet consists of a table of rows and columns used to store and manipulate any kind of numerical data. The point in a spreadsheet where a particular row and column meet is called a *cell*. Each cell is a unique location within the spreadsheet. A cell is identified by its *coordinate* or *address*, which consists of a letter for its column and a number for its row. For example, the cell located in column C, row 15 would be identified as cell C15. The cell you are working in currently is called the *active* cell. A block of cells is called a *range*.

Cells can contain values, labels, and formulas. A *value* is a number that can be used in calculations. A *label* is a string of alphanumeric characters (such as **COSTS** or **TEST4**) that identifies what a value means. *Formulas* are mathematical expressions that can use values from other cells. If a number used in a formula is changed, the program recalculates automatically, using the new number. Formulas can usually be set up with special preset *functions* for sums, averages, minimums and maximums, and rounding. Values and results of formulas can be formatted as integers, dollar amounts, or floating-point numbers. A *floating-point number* is a real number—that is, one that can contain a fractional part, which is expressed as a decimal value or as scientific notation (a shorthand method of expressing very large numbers).

The use of formulas is what makes spreadsheets powerful. A formula can be applied to the contents of specified cells to obtain a result. For example, you could calculate the amount of monthly payments on a loan, depending on the interest rate being charged. It would also be a simple matter to determine how much the monthly payments would be if you varied the length of payment time—say, 36, 48, or 60 months. This capability—altering variables within the spreadsheet to see what happens to those values, and how those effects depend upon the variables—is a useful tool. The type of analysis it enables you to do is called *what-if analysis*; you use the formulas to "ask" the spreadsheet *what* would happen to certain figures *if* certain other figures were changed. For example, what happens to your income tax rate if you take on a part-time job, or take a job working on commission rather than salary? How will your income be affected if interest rates decrease to 3.5 percent? Could the PTA earn more money if it sold candy rather than gift wrappings? A what-if analysis is sometimes called a *forecast*.

Once you have created a spreadsheet file (also called a *worksheet*), you can do a variety of things—for example, lock cells so the values cannot be changed, copy groups of cells to another location in the worksheet, sort the data alphabetically or numerically, or change the width of the columns. Some packages let you take data from several worksheets and consolidate it into a new worksheet. The package you are using may also let you draw graphs using data from the spreadsheet. Types of graphs used most frequently include *pie charts*, *bar graphs*, and *line graphs*. Many programs are going far beyond simple graphs and including features that enable you to create *presentation graphics* dressed up using different fonts, colors, lines, borders, clip art, and drawings.

Spreadsheet programs are used mostly in businesses. Since an important part of running any business is managing money, goods, and employees, a spreadsheet program can be invaluable. The what-if aspects of a spreadsheet can help you plan the best way to use your company's resources for maximum efficiency. Spreadsheets can also be handy for managing household finances, however; you might find them useful for keeping track of scores for Little League baseball, bowling, and other sports. If you do not have a data manager program, you can even use a spreadsheet program as a database to collect, store, and search for data.

(See 1.21 Add-ins and Add-ons; 3.1 Types of Software: System and Application; 3.23 General Features of Application Software; 3.24 WYSIWYG; 3.25 Evaluating Software; 3.36 Graphics Software; 3.37 Presentation Graphics; 3.41 Suites and Integrated Software; Software Review section: Excel for Windows, Lotus 1-2-3 for Windows, Quattro Pro for Windows, WingZ for Windows and OS/2.)

3.36 Graphics Software

Early *graphics* software, at its best, drew simple bar graphs and funny little people made up of squares. Today's computer graphics are so advanced that it is hard to tell if a picture was made by computer or by trick photography. You see examples of computer graphics in commercials and sports broadcasts on television. Videos and movies make use of computer graphics for special effects and cartoons. Businesses use programs that turn numbers into bar graphs and pie charts that are easy to understand. Special graphics packages can help engineers and architects design cars, machines, buildings, and sports shoes. And you can have fun drawing pictures with a paint program.

Microcomputers do not yet have the power to create certain types of advanced, surreal graphics, but they are getting close. Already there are programs by which you can manipulate scanned photographs and design homes and complex machine parts. In order to run most graphics programs, you need the graphics software, a computer system with plenty of memory (and at least a 40MB hard disk drive), a high-resolution graphics monitor, a printer that can print graphics, and a mouse. For heavy-duty graphics work, you might also want these options: a *video accelerator board* to make your computer run faster, a scanner, a color laser printer, a plotter, a graphics tablet, and a video camera and digitizer. (The *digitizer* transforms the video image into digital data the computer can handle.)

There are two basic types of graphics software: presentation graphics and paint and draw programs. You would use a *presentation graphics* program to create charts, graphs, and other images for business presentations. *Paint and draw* programs enable you to create and edit pictures. Some presentation graphics capabilities are often built into spreadsheet and database programs to facilitate the creation of images that show the results of calculations and summaries. A word processing program might include a simple *draw module* that allows you to create pictures from within the program. A program that includes graphics components is said to *support* graphics.

Some graphics programs provide animation capabilities that let you create cartoon-like movement of the graphics images. Most animation packages are based on *vector graphics* and are used for engineering purposes, but there are also programs children can use to create cartoons and other types of video productions. Animation can also be useful in the help features of an application program or an operating environment.

Be aware that there are several file formats for representing graphics images—including BMP (used by Windows), GIF (used by the information service CompuServe), PCX (developed by ZSoft for its PC Paintbrush software), TIFF (Tagged Image File Format, the standard file format for storing images as bit maps), and PICT (developed by Apple Computer and used for almost all graphics programs that run on the Macintosh). Be sure that the file format of the graphics software you want to use is compatible with the remainder of your software (such as desktop-publishing programs), but remember that there are conversion programs that change graphics from one format to another.

(See 1.23 Video Boards; 1.33 Resolution; 1.34 Pixels; 1.35 Gray Scaling; 1.40 Graphics Tablets; 1.41 Scanners; 1.46 Monitors; 1.49 Printers; 1.50 Print Quality; 1.56 Color Printing; 1.57 Plotters; 3.1 Types of Software: System and Application; 3.23 General Features of Application Software; 3.24 WYSIWYG; 3.33 Desktop Publishing; 3.35 Spreadsheets; 3.37 Presentation Graphics; 3.38 Paint and Draw Programs; 3.39 Moving Pictures; 3.41 Suites and Integrated Software; 3.45 Multimedia Applications.)

3.37 Presentation Graphics

Presentation graphics are used primarily to make an impression on an audience, for example, the company's customers or its employees. A presentation may be used to persuade customers to buy a new product, to justify a recent product price increase, or to introduce a new employee pension plan or a change of suppliers. The graphs and charts accept numerical data (whether imported or entered) and translate it into a summary that shows a pictorial relationship between the various numbers as follows:

- **Bar graphs** are made up of vertical or horizontal bars that compare the performance of several items in a given time. Each bar represents the value of one subject. For example, a bar chart could represent the money a town's organizations raise for a new community recreation center; each organization's effort would be represented by its own bar.
- **Line graphs** show the direction of change as an item's performance is studied over time. Several line graphs can be superimposed over each other to compare the performance of several items. The line representing each item connects points that show the item's value at one particular time. A line graph could show the monthly sales of Pike's Pizza Shop, with the second line showing last year's volume.
- **Pie charts** show a picture of a whole subject divided into parts. The chart looks like a circle divided into wedges like slices of pie, and it shows the relationship among the sizes of the wedges and the whole pie, which represents the total. A pie chart could break down the total shoe sales of Flibber Athletics Supply into the specific types of shoe: running, tennis, golf, bowling, aerobic, and multipurpose. An exploded pie chart bursts out specific wedges for emphasis.
- **Pictographs** show values in terms of pictures, with each individual picture representing a fixed number of the subject being studied. For example, a picture of an athletic shoe could represent 1,000 shoes sold; ten such pictures would stand for ten thousand shoes. Thus, a pictograph could be used to show the number of athletic shoes sold by Flibber's versus those sold by its competitor, The Dooley Shoe Store.

Presentation graphics software offers a variety of functions that help dress up a chart—including various fonts, colors, drawings, arrows, boxes, clip art, and dingbats. It provides a method of creating the *legend*, or explanation, of the elements in the graph. It may enable you to simulate three-dimensional displays.

As long as the software is compatible with desktop-publishing software, you can send the graphics to your page-composition document. Some programs also provide capabilities for creating *slide shows* using the images displayed on the computer screen. They may let you create transitions from one image to the next by fading out the first, or by peeling it down from one corner until the new picture is exposed.

For large group presentations, you can purchase very large monitors or use large-screen televisions to display the graphics. For less money, you can buy projector panels that mount on overhead projectors. Once you connect a panel to your microcomputer, you can use the overhead projector with a movie screen to display your presentation.

(See 3.35 Spreadsheets; 3.36 Graphics Software; 3.41 Suites and Integrated Software; Software Review section: Adobe (Aldus) Persuasion, ClarisWorks, CorelDRAW! for Windows, Freelance Graphics for Windows, Microsoft Works.)

3.38 Paint and Draw Programs

Paint and draw programs enable you to create your own pictures. Usually a paint program is simpler to use than a draw program. The *paint* program is based on bit-mapped graphics, while a *draw* program may be based on vector graphics. Bit-mapped graphics enable you to control each individual pixel on the screen, and vector graphics translate your entries into geometric formulas. Because of the complexity of draw programs, paint programs should be your choice if you are choosing graphics software that children can use.

With a paint program, you can use a variety of *tools* to create an image. You select these from a set of icons (also called a *palette* or a *toolkit*). For freehand painting, for example, you would select the brush icon. Most paint programs provide different shapes of brushes you can use with the texture and color of your choice. To draw lines, select the pencil icon and a pencil width. The spray paint (or airbrush) function gives a line soft edges rather than the hard edge of a brush or pencil line. The paint bucket (or fill) icon lets you dump "paint" into an entire outlined area. The eraser icon enables you to delete selected areas of your drawing or the entire picture. The marquee icon lets you select a rectangular section of a picture and copy it, move it, or delete it. A lasso icon tightens around the shape of the selected image so that you move or copy only the image, but none of the background. (A "grabber" lets you move a selection once it is chosen.) You can also select icons that let you draw circles, straight lines, ovals, and rectangles. Other features of paint programs enable you to rotate, flip, enlarge, or flatten an image. Most paint programs let you type numbers and letters of various fonts, as well. If you want to see a close-up portion of your picture, you can choose the zoom function, which displays the portion enlarged as if you were looking at it through a zoom lens on your camera.

Many of the features of paint programs (such as the line and brush variables, the shape options, rotating, zooming, and so on) are available in draw programs. A draw program that uses vector graphics, however, enables you to *scale* images to different sizes without sacrificing the smoothness of the image. The higher the resolution of the monitor, the better the vector-drawn image looks. A draw program also may let you draw freehand Bézier curves, which you can edit by controlling points along the curves. Another option is *dithering*, in which you simulate gray scaling with dot patterns. Some programs let you use *filters* that simulate bright ness, sharpness, blurriness, and contrast through a series of math calculations. If you want to convert a bit-mapped image imported from a paint program (or scanned into your computer), you can use an *autotrace* program. The autotrace option also smooths out curved lines.

Draw programs are also called illustration or design software; advanced draw programs are called *computer-aided design (CAD)* software. Most draw software is used for drafting and engineering purposes, and requires high-quality graphics monitors, as well as light pens or digitizers for drawing, and special printers or plotters.

(See 1.33 Resolution; 1.34 Pixels; 1.35 Gray Scaling; 3.36 Graphics Software; 3.40 CAD/CAM; 3.41 Suites and Integrated Software; Software Review section: Adobe Illustrator, Adobe (Aldus) Freehand, Arts & Letters Apprentice, Color It!, ColorMe, CorelDRAW! for Windows, KidPix, KidWorks2, MacDraw Pro, Painter, PC Paintbrush IV Plus, SuperPaint, Windows Draw.)

3.39 Moving Pictures

What next? Now you can watch movies on your computer screen. You can play these "movies" with QuickTime, the Apple Computer multimedia graphics standard. QuickTime is a low-cost, low-resolution type of video that provides dynamic, *time-based data*—that is, animation, video clips, and sound, rather than *static data* such as words and graphics. With QuickTime, you can play, pause, fast-forward, rewind, and advance frame-by-frame *dynamic data* (also called *movies*). Microsoft offers Video for Windows for use on IBM-compatible PCs. Both programs perform virtually the same functions; the only difference is the *codecs* (algorithms for compression/decompression) that accompany the programs. QuickTime offers Apple Video Compression, and VFW uses Microsoft Video 1; both are similar in performance. Two other video codecs—Intel's Indeo, and SuperMac's Cinepak—are available for both QuickTime and Video for Windows.

Video files are compressed; to run the movies as smoothly as possible, you need a fast Macintosh with at least a 68020 microprocessor, 5MB of RAM, and System 7. QuickTime skips frames if necessary to keep a movie synchronized with sound as the frames are decompressed and displayed from CD-ROM. Video for Windows requires at least a 386 microprocessor with a speed of 33MHz or higher, Windows 3.1, 4MB RAM, a hard drive with 50MB free space, an audio board compatible with Windows 3.1, 256-color or greater video display, video capture board and device driver, and a video source.

MPEG (pronounced *em-peg*), another compression standard that is gaining popularity, is named for the Motion Picture Experts Group of the International Standards Organization. MPEG was developed in order to provide full-screen, full-motion video. While the image is of very high quality, it requires a dedicated chip to perform the decompression. The most recent version of QuickTime, version 2.0, includes MPEG-1 playback. This feature, when used with an MPEG decompression board, enables the Macintosh to display TV-quality video. (Early releases of QuickTime supported pictures that were only about 2 inches square.)

In reality, MPEG is not true full-screen video. Rather, it is an expanded quarter-screen video, in which every other pixel has been dropped. As decompression occurs, the picture expands and interpolates to fill the missing spaces. You may see *jaggies*, lines with the stair-step or checkerboard look, because some information is lost. The first appearance of MPEG was on the ReelMagic decompression board released in late 1993 from Sigma Designs, and it is drawing rave reviews. It is supported in the Compton's Interactive Encyclopedia, Dragon's Lair, and Return to Zork CD-ROMs.

In order to edit, cut, copy, paste, record, and play dynamic data, you'll need a *video editing program*. You also will benefit from a *video capture card*, which accepts analog signals and translates them into digital data. For more elaborate productions, you will also need a sound digitizer, and even a camcorder from which you can download your movies into your computer system.

What happens when you insert a movie into a document (for example, a report written on a word processor) is unlike conventional graphics. You paste a still image from the movie into the document. This is called a *poster*, and it retains a *pointer* to the appropriate movie. By this method, the document's file doesn't become huge, but instead gains only about 10KB or so. The document can then access and play the movie as long as the movie file is readily available on a hard disk drive. Some word processors already support movies, and many more packages will do so in the future.

(See 3.36 Graphics Software; 3.45 Multimedia Applications; Software Review section: LinksWare, MacDraw Pro, Microsoft Word for the Macintosh, WordPerfect for Macintosh.)

3.40 CAD/CAM

One of the fastest-growing areas of microcomputer use in industry is *computer-aided design (CAD)*. CAD allows the engineer to design, draft, and analyze a prospective product using computer graphics. A detailed image of an object may be configured in three dimensions and rotated to display all sides. The object may be drawn in layers, as if there were plastic overlays showing a back, the insides, and a front view. The designer, working with full-color graphics, can easily make changes and test many (virtual) versions of a product before the first prototype is ever built. CAD can also analyze designs for poor tolerance between parts and stress points. This technique can save companies a great deal of money by eliminating defective designs before the money is spent to build a product. Boeing even has a three-dimensional design system that includes its own human model, a figure that crawls into images on the screen and shows the difficulty a real person might have in reaching a particular area of a jet that needs repair.

Computer-aided design is often coupled with *computer-aided manufacturing (CAM)*. The combination is referred to as *CAD/CAM*. Using CAD/CAM, the engineer can analyze not only the product but also the manufacturing process. Once the rough design of the product has been entered into the computer, the engineer can have the computer system simulate any manufacturing step needed to build the product. For example, if the product must be drilled, the engineer can use a computerized drill that can be guided (either by the engineer or the computer), to simulate the actual drilling process. This simulation can be helpful in two ways. First, it indicates major problems that may be encountered on the assembly line before it is even set up. Second, the computer records exactly how the tool moved, and stores that information on magnetic media. If the factory uses robots and numerically-controlled machinery, this stored information can be used to guide the actual machines used to manufacture the product. In this way, CAD/CAM can take the engineer from idea to final product.

Although CAD/CAM programs usually run on high-end computers with plenty of memory and 32-bit addressing, some CAD programs will run on less powerful machines. Graphics tablets (digitizers) and lightpens are common accessories for CAD software.

(See 1.39 Joysticks and Light Pens; 1.40 Graphics Tablets; 3.36 Graphics Software; 3.38 Paint and Draw Programs.)

3.41 SUITES AND INTEGRATED SOFTWARE

How frustrating it can be to use three or four software packages for managing a small business or an organization, and find that commands for doing the same type of operation are different—or that data cannot be transferred readily among the applications. For example, you may want to use a word processor to write a report, but find that the data you want to use from your data-manager program is not compatible with your word processing program. So you print out the data and read from the paper copy to type data into the report you created with the word processing program.

Integrated software attempts to maximize both command and data compatibility. Basically, integrated software is two or more *stand-alone* (usually separate) application programs that work together in the same software package, allowing easy movement of data between the applications. These packages are called *suites*. If there is a difference between integrated software and a suite, it lies in the fact that integrated software is developed as such; a suite may be a manufacturer's compilation of existing programs.

In general, all the applications in a particular integrated package or suite use a common group of commands, although the differences in the programs require specialized commands for each. For example, the command used to block off a section of text in a word processor is the same command used to block off a section of rows and columns in a spreadsheet. The spreadsheet, however, will have its own specialized command for formatting cells into dollar amounts, something the word processor doesn't need to do.

Common suites include various components; these include such capabilities as data management, spreadsheet analysis, word processing, graphics, and communications. The data formats match in the different parts or *modules*; the mailing list in the data manager can be used by the word processor, the financial data in a spreadsheet can be turned into a graph by a graphics program, and the graph can be embedded into a report produced on the word processor. In many suites, you can put two or more modules on the screen at the same time. This is convenient when you are transferring data from one module to another. Any such data is kept in a special holding area called a *clipboard* during the transfer.

(See 3.23 General Features of Application Software; 3.31 Word Processors; 3.34 Data Managers; 3.36 Graphics Software; 3.37 Presentation Graphics; Software Review section: ClarisWorks, Lotus 1-2-3 for Windows, Microsoft Works, Novell GroupWise, WordPerfect for the Macintosh.)

3.42 Groupware and Other Business Aids

A variety of software exists that facilitates groups working together, helps people plan their schedules, and keeps a project on target. Among the types of packages are groupware, personal information managers, and project management software.

A new type of software called *groupware*, typified by Lotus Notes, provides tools for groups of people to work together via computer rather than committee. Groupware is actually a combination of software products, and it enhances the productivity of groups in a number of ways. For example, how much time do you spend setting up a committee meeting? Rather than argue, committee members can activate a groupware component that schedules meeting times by accessing the computerized calendars of all the people involved. Another groupware component sends members a reminder for the meetings and the agenda; yet another is used to exchange information among members. The software sets up the connections with the participants, then keeps track of contributions to the session by identifying specific terminals with their users. An advantage of a groupware computer conference is that all participants can enter their contributions at the same time. This function requires extensive communication and file-management capabilities.

Although groupware is endorsed for its efficiency, it can increase the volume of information that is distributed. In addition, without face-to-face communication, it has the potential of slowing the decision-making process even more than is common to a stereotypical committee. Companies can reduce the adverse effects of using groupware by preparing their employees to expect changes in the way they communicate.

A *personal information manager (PIM)* helps you organize your day by integrating notepads, calendars, telephone numbers and addresses, and lists of things to do. A PIM lets you break a project into easily-handled tasks, set priorities for things to do, set alarms for deadlines and meetings, and use its calculator. Some packages keep track of the time and money you've spent on a project. A PIM's scheduling capabilities usually let you enter recurring events (such as a monthly board meeting or a weekly status meeting) once. Thereafter, the software places the meeting on the proper day and time automatically, and notifies you of schedule conflicts.

Project management software is based on the need for setting up long-term plans. It enables you to divide projects into respective tasks, schedule people and materials, and calculate money and time spent on the projects. Project management software uses the *Critical Path Method (CPM)* to divide a project into tasks that can be easily handled and completed. Under CPM, each task is listed with its projected time frame and required resources. *Dependencies* specify the relationship among tasks, such as whether two tasks need to be completed on the same day, or whether one task must be finished before another can be started. CPM is usually represented by *PERT charts*, standing for Program Evaluation and Review Technique. A PERT chart is much like a flow chart in that it shows the sequence of tasks with boxes and lines. It also shows the *critical path*—that is, the shortest distance through the project to completion. A *Gantt chart* also pictures a project's duration. On the right side of the chart, the tasks are related to a time scale; on the left side of the chart, the tasks are described. Project management software should also be able to print *progress reports*.

(See Software Review section: MacProject Pro, Project Scheduler 5, CA-SuperProject for Windows.)

3.43 Expert Systems

Results have been disappointing in *artificial intelligence*, the field of developing techniques whereby computers can be used to solve problems that appear to require imagination, intuition, or intelligence. Thus, the term is being used less frequently; present efforts in this field are described as *applied intelligence* instead. One of the products of applied intelligence is the *expert system* that covers knowledge in only one field, such as medicine or geology.

An expert system is software that evaluates, draws conclusions, and makes recommendations based on a huge database of information (the knowledge base) in the particular field. A medical diagnosis expert system, for example, could make cross-references among such bodies of data as the history, symptoms, and test results of a patient, correlate these with the data in its database, and come up with possible diseases the patient has. This helps the doctor diagnose a puzzling case and set up a plan of treatment. The expert system includes a set of rules for reasoning designed to mimic the decision-making processes of human experts in a narrowly defined field, based on what is known of the human thought processes.

Most expert systems are used in professional fields. One such system is MYCIN, which is used to diagnose infectious diseases and recommend appropriate drugs. Oncocin advises physicians on the best treatments for cancer patients, and Caduceus II holds information about hundreds of diseases and symptoms. Prospector is an expert system that helps geologists in locating mineral deposits, and Taxadvisor, developed by R. Michaelsen at the University of Illinois, helps users with estate planning. American Express uses an expert system to authorize questionable charges. Increasingly, businesses are using expert systems; people who use various online resources can activate expert systems that help them find information. You can even buy an *expert system shell* such as VP-EXPERT with which to develop your own expert system.

Expert systems are used in many fields: law, medicine, engineering, business, geology, financial analysis, and tax analysis, among others. They perform such functions as recommending strategies, diagnosing problems (such as illnesses), analyzing structures, and training personnel. Expert systems can cut costs, boost quality, and improve productivity, and they have the potential of functioning better than any single human expert in making judgments within their own areas of expertise.

(See 3.44 Educational Software; 3.47 Virtual Reality; 5.19 Automation and Applied Intelligence.)

3.44 Educational Software

Back in the 1960s, one of the trends in education was to use programmed learning to instruct and drill students. Today, programmed learning has been modified for use with microcomputers. It is now called *computer-assisted instruction*, or *CAI*, which in its limited definition consists of drills and tutorials. Computers are used for far more than drilling and tutoring students in today's classrooms, however; a wide variety of educational software also entertains for home use. In fact, when well done, the entertainment aspect of educational software encourages students to work independently and explore a topic further. Software for education falls in one of the following categories:

- *Drills* for quizzing students on routine facts
- *Tutorials* for introducing new material and skills, and testing students' understanding of the material
- *Simulations* that imitate real-world situations, allowing students to learn through experience and induction without having to take actual risks
- *Games* for learning new concepts and practicing new skills
- *Problem-solving software* that encourages exploration and application of previous knowledge
- *Multimedia* experiences and productions

Computers can be used with very young children; there are talking programs that help a non-reading child learn a variety of concepts such as shape recognition, counting, letter identification, simple math, and drawing. Older children and teenagers can hone math skills, practice logic skills, and study spelling. They can play adventure games that teach them about history or geography. They can create their own cities and worlds, and try to achieve a balance between nature and civilization.

Typing tutors teach students how to type, a skill that helps decrease the frustration of using computers. *Shells* and *authoring programs* enable students to use their own knowledge to make original programs for CAI. Students may make word games and build puzzles or create a set of questions for a school assignment. High-school students can even buy programs that help them study for college-entrance exams such as the SAT. They can use educational software to learn foreign languages. Much of the software helps students increase their attention spans and develop skills for problem-solving and critical thinking.

Students can also learn by using word processors, spreadsheets, databases, and paint programs to create newsletters, learn math skills, track information, and make drawings. Programming languages such as Logo help students learn by discovery the principles of computer programming—as well as skills in math, algebra, geometry, and engineering. Going online with an information service expands the range of available material, and teaches some research skills.

Educational software is not just for children, however. Anyone can use any of the types of programs just mentioned for fun and enjoyment as well as for learning. Your software will never call you stupid, or embarrass you for taking a long time to learn a task. It is infinitely patient; if you have chosen well, it will not be dull or patronizing.

Education programs should hold a child's interest and be easy enough to use that the child is not frustrated by fumbling through the directions. (At school, your child may use computers readily with less-than-appealing software that wouldn't hold his or her attention for long at home.)

Programs should teach new skills, but be flexible enough to allow a child to master basic levels of learning before progressing to more difficult tasks. They should provide helpful and constructive feedback, and they should give children a sense of control (although parents should continue to monitor the subject matter). Most educational packages contain recommendations for appropriate age levels. Child experts recommend that you monitor the amount of time per day your child spends at the computer—limiting children under 4 or 5 years of age, for example, to half an hour per day, and other children to no more than two hours, depending upon their project. You can also encourage book reading by setting aside a special time (before bed, for example) during which your family reads.

(See 3.25 Evaluating Software; 3.45 Multimedia Applications; 3.46 Software for Multimedia Management: Hypertext and Authoring Tools; 3.47 Virtual Reality; 4.1 Telecommunications; 4.11 Telecommuting; 4.14 Online Services; 5.12 Computer Literacy and School Curriculum; 5.13 The Computer as Teacher; 5.14 Kids and Computers: At Home and Online.)

3.45 Multimedia Applications

Multimedia applications cover the entire range of multisensory, interactive experiences by combining sound, animation, video, photo-quality images, text, and graphics with interactive computer functions. They make extended use of *optical disk* technology, which enables the storage of large databases of graphic images, text, and sound.

Multimedia can often be useful for training workers and students. For example, multimedia systems that simulate driving conditions are used to train truck drivers. Businesses can use multimedia to make sales presentations that retain a prospective client's attention. Medical students can use multimedia systems to learn about anatomy and treatments. Encyclopedias and other resources are also available in multimedia form; a compact disc or videodisc contains the illustrations and audio portions of the material. Using such a resource, you could read information about the Civil War, choose a Civil War song, put the music score on the screen, and see reproductions of old photographs showing the battlefields on your screen. Children would enjoy multimedia applications that enable them to make up their own stories, draw maps, locate places in the world, and use a dictionary that defines objects in terms of text, pictures, and sound. High-school students can learn biology, chemistry, and history through multimedia.

You may see the term *hypermedia* used in conjunction with multimedia applications. Some experts make a distinction between the two—citing multimedia as several media used separately but all on one topic, and hypermedia as several media combined into one doorway through which you can explore information in whatever direction you want.

(See 1.27 CD-ROMs and Optical Storage; 2.10 Multimedia Standards; 3.44 Educational Software; 3.46 Software for Multimedia Management: Hypertext and Authoring Tools; 3.47 Virtual Reality; 3.48 Applications for Home Management and Personal Use; Software Review section: Compton's MultiMedia Encyclopedia.)

3.46 Software for Multimedia Management: Hypertext and Authoring Tools

A special type of database system used to create dynamic links among the components, or objects, of a multimedia system is called an *authoring tool* or *authoring system*. An authoring tool is sometimes called *hypertext*, useful for browsing through large commercial databases. In fact, it is really a special way that a database management system organizes information (as opposed to a flat-file system or a relational database).

Examples of authoring tools include HyperCard and HyperStudio for the Apple IIGS and Macintosh computers. Authoring tools enable you to create scripts for automating a presentation by linking together the *objects*, such as written text, a graph, a drawing, music, and sound effects. They usually support many hardware devices and file formats so you can build productions with multiple elements. They also provide a framework by which someone else can interact with your production.

Software created by an authoring tool (or hypermedia program) is called a *stack*. The individual screens in the stack are called *cards*. You can link any card—or object on a card—to any other card, or to hardware and software outside the stack. Thus, as you select one object, you can access, or interact with, any other objects linked to it. For example, if you are studying the history of rock 'n' roll, you could put text and reproductions of photographs showing early rock stars on your screen, while choosing popular songs that will be played or that will appear as a musical score on the screen. A rock 'n' roll multimedia application might also include sound effects that add realism to the concerts. The icons you select in order to let the user view or hear these components are called *hypertext links*, or *buttons*. In many programs, you can hide the buttons behind clip art, text, or areas of an illustration.

Although some authoring tools are easy enough that children can learn to create hypermedia/multimedia productions, it is helpful to lay out a plan ahead of time, perhaps in the form of a flow chart that shows all of the elements and the links. Study a simple stack that comes with your program, and start with a simple design for your first project.

(See 2.10 Multimedia Standards; 3.44 Educational Software; 3.45 Multimedia Applications.)

3.47 Virtual Reality

The ultimate in multimedia technology is *virtual reality*, in which three-dimensional images—delivered through special goggles and gloves bristling with wires—create the illusion of being inside and moving through a scene. Inside the goggles, two slightly different views of a scene are projected on tiny liquid-crystal screens. Because neither eye perceives the scene from exactly the same perspective, a three-dimensional effect is produced. Moving your head changes the view, just as in real life. The *data glove*, a Lycra glove loaded with sensors and optical fibers, enables you to manipulate the virtual objects. "Virtual" means "being so practically but not actually"; in a virtual-reality application, you are "in essence" manipulating an object or experiencing a situation, though "actually" you are not.

Virtual reality delivers multisensory information, particularly sound and touch, and it is interactive. These characteristics make it ideal for training or learning experiences. Virtual reality has been used by pilots-in-training to learn how to fly and land airplanes. Caterpillar is testing virtual-reality models of its earthmovers to improve the performance and visibility of the real equipment. A homeowner could "walk through" a virtual model of the plans for a new kitchen and family room. Already, Nintendo users can pull on Mattel Power Gloves and play virtual handball on a virtual court with a virtual opponent.

(See 3.44 Educational Software; 3.45 Multimedia Applications.)

3.48 Applications for Home Management and Personal Use

There is such a wide variety of software available for managing home functions and organizing your personal life that you hardly know where to begin. Want to map out a career path? Plan your finances? Balance your checkbook? Find recipes that use the ingredients you have on hand? Organize a busy schedule? Play games? Then there's surely a program out there for you.

Some software helps you identify your talents and choose a career that suits your background and abilities. It may help you write a résumé and guide you through a simulated interview—complete with questions and pay negotiations. Other software gives you a platform for balancing your budget and keeping track of the money you spend. You can also find programs that help you figure your income tax or make out a will. If you want to learn more about diseases and diagnoses, you can buy an electronic medical encyclopedia.

If you like collecting recipes and preparing food, you might be interested in a program that files your favorite recipes and lets you search through the recipes for that one dinner that uses specific ingredients—for example, that zucchini and those tomatoes that are crowding the refrigerator.

If you are planning a party or organizing a fund-raiser, look for a program that lets you produce flyers, labels, invitations, business cards, and so on. Such a program will offer a variety of fonts and special design effects, including calligraphy, that help you create professional-looking results.

(See 3.23 General Features of Application Software; 3.25 Evaluating Software; 3.29 Memory-Resident Programs; 5.18 Computers for People with Disabilities: Meeting Special Needs; Software Review section: Diet Analyst, Doctor Schueler's Home Medical Adviser Pro, The Family Doctor, It's Legal, MacInTax, Mayo Clinic Family Health Book, Micro Cookbook 4.0, Quicken 4.0.)

PART 4 CONTENTS INDEX

Communication

You may have heard about those people who sit for hours in front of a computer playing games, writing programs, and experimenting. You may think those people lose a sense of reality. Yet these computer hobbyists may have been using their computers to keep touch with a greater variety of people and events than you would ever have imagined. This contact with "the real world" occurs through telecommunications, not over the back fence. Not only are there a variety of commercial information services to tap into, but there are also many private electronic bulletin boards that anyone can access, as long as they have the correct equipment and software. This section describes telecommunications and many of the commercial information services that are available.

4.1 Telecommunications

How can a reporter quickly send a story about the state championship basketball game back to the home newspaper? How can a salesperson send a report from a hotel in Peoria, Illinois, to the main office in Chicago? How does your local police officer get information about criminals, license plate numbers, or fingerprints? The answer is through a pathway called a *communication channel*. This pathway can be a telephone line, a communication satellite, or a laser beam. Using computers with these channels is called *telecommunications*.

Telecommunications can take place as near as the next room or as far away as overseas. Take, for example, the *Sports Illustrated* or *TIME* you get at the newsstand or in the mail. The news is sent from the main office by satellite to regional stations, to be printed and sent to newsstands or to your home. Via telecommunications, computers are also used for handling a variety of electronic transactions that include banking, shopping, and trading stocks.

Banks use communication channels to link central computers to computers at branches two blocks away, in the next town, or in the next state. A number of computer applications make it possible for banks to transfer funds via communication between computers. This approach is known as *electronic funds transfer (EFT)*. As one example, the Social Security Administration offers an option under which the monthly checks can be deposited automatically into their recipients' bank accounts. Similarly, many companies also offer a direct-deposit option for employee paychecks. Depositors can authorize banks to pay certain bills (such as electric or telephone bills) automatically, by transferring funds from the customers' accounts to those of the utilities. Some banks are expanding these services by making it possible for customers to use personal computers (and sometimes touch-tone telephones) to enter and authorize EFT transactions from home.

Just as customers can use computers to access their bank accounts from home, they can also make airline and hotel reservations and go shopping through a computer shopping network. These services may be available through a commercial online information service such as CompuServe, as described later in this chapter. Some high school and college courses are available over computer networks, as well; users can work on a degree program at home.

Telecommunications opens many possibilities for exchanging information. For example, the company you work for may have an electronic mail system. Electronic mail, or *e-mail*, allows reports and messages to be sent from one computer to another in a matter of seconds. Telecommunications has also created a new workplace right at home. People who *telecommute* work on their computers at home. They can link their computers with the computer at the office to get the data they need or to send their work to the office. Telecommuting helps parents with small children, people with physical disabilities, and people who just like to work at home.

You can use telecommunications at home with your computer, too—if you have the right equipment and software—to access a commercial database, take a college course, or communicate with friends over an electronic bulletin board.

(See 4.2 Communication Channels; 4.3 Modems; 4.5 Computer Networks: Wide Area Networks; 4.6 Computer Networks: Local Area Networks; 4.12 Bulletin Board Systems; 4.14 Online Services; 5.3 Hacking.)

4.2 Communication Channels

The pathways over which data (in the form of electronic signals) travels from one location to another are called *communication channels*. Here are several types of communication channels in use today:

- **Telephone lines**. Standard telephone lines, known technically as *twisted pairs*, are one of the most widely used communication channels for transmitting data and voices. Twisted pairs provide *full-duplex* service, in which data can be sent and received at the same time. (Other options are *simplex* service—which permits transmission in only one direction—and *half-duplex* service, in which signals travel in either direction, but in only one direction at a time.) Voice-grade twisted pairs carry between 300 and 9,000 bits per second (bps). Data-grade, or *10BaseT*, lines are high-speed, high-quality twisted pairs; these are less susceptible than voice-grade lines to interference that can distort the signal.

- **Coaxial cables**. An alternative to standard telephone lines is *coaxial cable*. This cable is formed from insulated copper or aluminum wire. Coaxial cable reduces distortion that interferes with signal transmission on standard telephone lines, because its wires are insulated. Coaxial cables permit high-speed data transmission. A common form is *10Base2*, or *Thinnet*. "Coax" is more expensive than twisted pairs.

- **Fiber-optic cable**. A newer form of communication channel, fiber-optic cable sends light impulses (laser beams) along a clear flexible tubing approximately half the diameter of a human hair. Their small diameter makes these cables easy to install. Plus, they can carry much more data than standard wires, and they have a low error rate because they are not susceptible to electrical interference. Currently, they are being used in some local area networks, but telephone companies are also using them as replacements for standard wires in some localities. Changing over to fiber-optic from standard telephone lines will be expensive, however, and not all communities will change house-to-house wiring to fiber-optics. Most likely, schools, hospitals, and businesses will have direct fiber-optic connections, while homes will be able to connect to fiber-optic trunk lines via standard telephone wires. Using fiber-optic lines will also require the purchase of new digital telephone equipment as well as a modem-like device different from the traditional analog-to-digital-to-analog modem you may now own.

  Because of its capabilities for tremendous speed and accuracy, fiber-optic cable may bring many different types of information services to your home. Fiber-optic networks will be able to transfer very large amounts of data—such as whole books, music, and full-motion video. Through fiber-optic lines, you should be able to access network television, cable networks, movie libraries, interactive education, music-on-demand, multiplayer games, and other services.

- **Microwave links.** Microwaves carry signals through the air in much the same way as ordinary radio broadcasts, but at high frequencies—the waves are shorter and closer together than those of ordinary analog signals. As communication channels, microwaves provide high-quality links because the powerful signals are usually not affected by weather, or by other types of interference common to radio transmission. A limitation is that microwave signals travel in straight lines (sometimes referred to as "line-of-sight"). The curvature of the earth would cause the signals' target to drop out of the line of sight; they would travel into space and be lost. To be useful over long distances, microwave signals must be *relayed*, or received and retransmitted, every 90 to 100 miles. Accordingly, cross-country signals travel over a combination of communication satellites and high towers with receivers and transmitters. Telephone lines from the receiving towers deliver the signals to users.

- **Satellites.** Communication satellites make it possible to send microwave signals over thousands of miles, providing worldwide microwave communication. A communication satellite typically is put into "stationary orbit" about 22,300 miles above the earth. The satellite can then move at the same speed, and in the same direction, as the earth's rotation. This gives the satellite a fixed location over the earth, so that microwave signals can be aimed at a known target. Satellite links make extremely wide bandwidths possible; transmission rates are fast, and can run into millions of bits per second. Intensely stormy weather can, however, interrupt these signals with interference in the upper atmosphere that does not affect near-ground transmissions.

(See 4.1 Telecommunications; 4.3 Modems; 4.5 Computer Networks: Wide Area Networks.)

4.3 Modems

A modem is a piece of special equipment you need to send messages from your computer to another, or to receive messages. A modem prepares the computer's signal for transmission over telephone lines, and "translates" an incoming signal so your computer can work with it. The word *modem* stands for *MOdulate-DEModulate*. A modem changes, or modulates, the computer's on/off digital signals into *analog* signals. These are actually audio tones that telephone lines can carry. The signals are then sent over the telephone lines to another computer. The receiving computer must have a modem, too. There the tones are changed (demodulated) back into computer signals.

There are two basic types of modems: internal and external. An *internal modem* resides on an expansion board or a PCMCIA card that plugs into a slot inside the computer. If the bus is full (or nearly full), or if you will be using the modem with more than one computer, you may want to use an *external modem* that attaches to your computer by a cable.

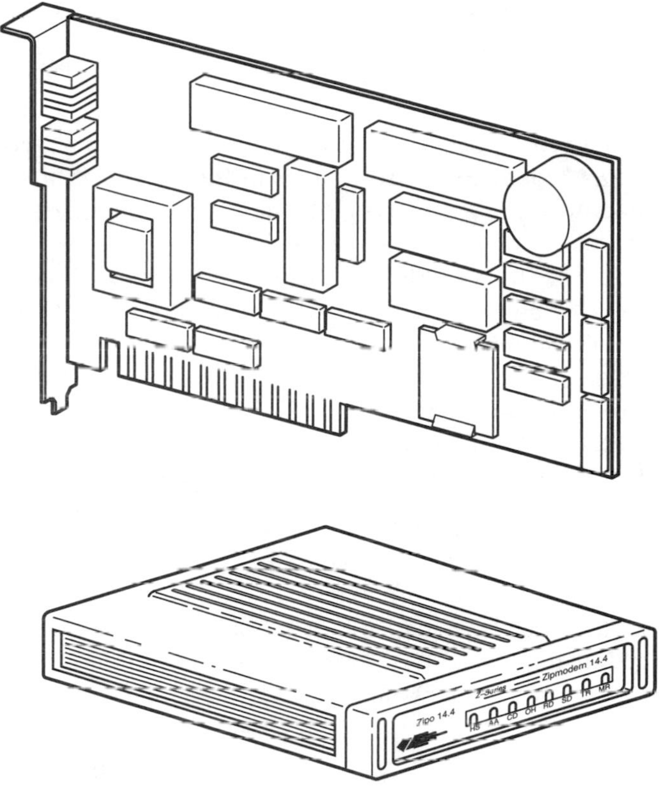

The two basic types of modems.

An *acoustic coupler* modem is an external modem that must be used with a standard contoured telephone handset. The handset's listening and speaking ends fit into cups built into the modem. These modems were popular in the 1970s, but they are no longer widely used. This style of modem has been adapted for use with pay phones and cellular phones—a handy option when you are using a notebook computer away from home. A *direct-connect* modem is an external modem that plugs into the telephone wall jack. It resides in a box outside the computer system, and is connected to the computer with a cable, which has a standard RS-232 connector. It also connects directly to the phone wall jack. External modems may have lights that indicate how they are functioning, and they can be moved to another computer easily.

Modems are identified by their speed, measured in *bits per second (bps)*; a *bit* is the smallest unit of data a computer can handle. Older modems have speeds of 300 and 1200 bps. The most common speed is 2400 bps, but 9600-bps and 14,400-bps modems are fast becoming the standard for home computer users. Since 9600-bps modems can be had for under $100, price should not be the determining factor in buying a modem. Modem speeds reach tens of thousands of bits per second. Modem manufacturers are anticipating the next speed standard for modems with *v.fast*, *v.fc* (fast class), and *v.34* modem specifications; if you see any of these, you'll know they refer to very high-speed modems. If you have a high-speed modem (9600-bps or higher), it can handle speeds less than its top speed. Online services may charge more for the use of higher-speed modems, but the cost is often offset by the shorter connect-time fees. For example, a file that includes graphics may take half an hour to transmit using a 2400-bps modem, but only seven-and-a-half minutes with a 9600-bps modem. Be aware, however, that some online services and BBSs do not fully support the newer high-speed modems.

Many modems also have a switch for choosing the mode of transmission—either half duplex or full duplex; others simply use the communications software to control these mode settings, which determine the direction the data can travel. Set at *half duplex*, a modem is capable of sending and receiving data, but only one way at a time. Half-duplex transmission is common in telephone services and networks. Set at *full duplex*, a modem can permit data to travel in both directions simultaneously.

A *fax modem* enables you to send documents as facsimiles to a fax machine, rather than to a computer. Some fax modems can also act as regular modems. Like regular modems, fax modems can be internal (called *fax boards*) or external. Fax modems are less expensive than fax machines, but only if you do not need to purchase an optical scanner to create fax documents from images on paper. They are more convenient than fax machines, however, and relay a better image quality. To be versatile, a fax modem should both send and receive faxes. Almost all notebook computer manufacturers offer fax modems with their machines. You can use your fax modem to print documents by sending them to a fax machine—a handy option if you are staying in a hotel on a business trip. Some communications software allows you to access, view, and control another PC via modem from a remote location.

If you want to transfer files between two computers that are sitting right on the same desk or table, you should use a *null modem cable* instead of purchasing two modems. You may also need communication software for the operation. Be sure to mark the null modem cable—it looks exactly like a serial cable, except the send and receive pins are reversed in the wiring. Null modems are useful when exchanging data between portable computers and larger systems. They are also handy for transferring files between two incompatible computers (for example, from an IBM PC to a Macintosh).

(See 4.1 Telecommunications; 4.2 Communication Channels; 4.4 Communication Software; 4.5 Computer Networks: Wide Area Networks; 4.6 Computer Networks: Local Area Networks; 4.12 Bulletin Board Systems; 4.14 Online Services.)

4.4 Communication Software

To link your computer with another through telephone lines, you need *communication software* in addition to a modem. This software helps your computer become a part of another computer. In effect, the software "tricks" the microcomputer into acting as an input/output device for the other computer. The software also helps the modem work. Once everything is in place, you simply dial the number of the other computer by typing it in from the keyboard, or by pressing a key that instructs the computer to do so. The modem takes care of the rest.

Most modems today are called *smart modems*, which means they come with their own software that adds special features for data-communication operations. In effect, a smart modem is a *coprocessor*—it assists the computer in performing certain operations. Many computer users like using a particular communication software package rather than the software bundled with the modem, however.

Communication software generally presents a menu that enables you to select the services you want it to perform. These include *auto-answer* (the software answers incoming calls automatically) and *auto-dial* (it dials one or more telephone numbers automatically). The modem will also transfer files or messages when the receiving computer answers the telephone. A time-delay feature allows you to set a particular time—usually at night, when rates are cheap—at which the modem calls another computer and transfers files.

In order to use functions of online services or other communications, you will need to set a number of *parameters* (or characteristics) for your modem. The parameters define the *communications protocol*, or rules, so that two devices agree on the format of the data being sent or received. The protocol includes such things as the speed of your modem in bits per second, the mode of transmission (half- or full-duplex), file transfer functions, error detection, and data compression.

Some parameters are set by flipping switches on your modem; others you set on-screen by answering *prompts*, or cues for information in your software. As noted under the topic "Modems," you may need to flip the modem switch to half duplex or full duplex to set one protocol. Then you may be required to identify the number of data bits used in each byte, *parity*, and a start or stop bit. A particular bulletin board system, for example, may require you to set your modem's parameters to

8-N-1, which means data will travel as eight data bits, with no parity and one stop bit. *Start bits* and *stop bits* occur at the beginning and end of each piece of data to distinguish legitimate data from noise.

Parity bits are one method of checking the transmission for errors. Parity can be odd or even. In *odd parity*, each byte of data will contain an odd number of bits. In *even parity*, each byte of data will contain an even number of bits. The communication software sets the parity bit to 0 or to 1 in order to make the total number of 1 bits even or odd, whichever the parity is for that transmission. Both the sending computer and the receiving computer must agree whether to use parity checking, and whether parity should be odd or even. There are other methods of error checking, including MNP and V.42 (both used on high-speed modems). MNP stands for Microcom Networking Protocol, a standard set by Microcom, Inc.; V.42 is a standard set by the European CCITT, an organization that sets international communication standards.

Data-compression capabilities enable the transmission of the same amount of data in fewer bits. A file that has been compressed is called a *packed file*. The protocols established for data compression include Class 5 of MNP (MNP-5) and V.42*bis*, set by ITU. A modem may comply with both protocols. Any compression protocols used by the sending modem must also be used by the receiving modem.

In order for you to send messages and edit documents, your communication software should have features that let you do some text editing. It should offer a variety of protocols—such as Zmodem, Ymodem, Xmodem, and Kermit—for sending ASCII or binary files and detecting transmission errors. The best overall protocol is Zmodem, which is less sensitive to glitches on phone lines; it can save partially transferred files, and if a problem occurs, it can resume transmission from where it left off.

Your communications software should also let you set up a series of shortcuts using *macros* (also sometimes called *scripts*)—sets of keystrokes or commands assigned to one word or keystroke. If you plan to link up to a mainframe with your microcomputer, the software should contain a number of *terminal-emulation drivers*, which make your computer act like a particular type of terminal that is part of a larger computer system. Terminal-emulation software enables you to use your computer to access the mainframe or minicomputer at your place of work, or at an online information service. (Terminal emulation also enables your computer to act like another computer—for example, it can let your Macintosh emulate an IBM PC. One such program is *Universal SoftPC* by Insignia.)

Many communication programs use commands set by Hayes Microcomputer Products for their modems. These commands have become the *de facto standard* for controlling modems. Thus, any modem that recognizes these commands is called *Hayes-compatible*, a desirable factor in a modem.

(See 4.1 Telecommunications; 4.3 Modems; 4.5 Computer Networks: Wide Area Networks; 4.6 Computer Networks: Local Area Networks; Software Review Section: Universal SoftPC.)

4.5 Computer Networks: Wide Area Networks

A computer *network* is the linking together of computers and other peripheral devices through a communication system. In fact, a number of small, independent networks may be linked into a very large network. The networks can be local, regional, national, or even worldwide in scope. They enable an organization to share not only data, but also computer hardware (such as expensive printers, or a modem link to an information service or public network). E-mail, *groupware* (software that enables several people to collaborate on a project and schedule meetings), and telecommuting are also popular network applications.

In a network, each point that can send or receive data—or both—is known as a *node* or *end point*. A node can be anything from a *dumb terminal* (one that has no independent computing power) to a microcomputer to a full-scale computer system. *Links* are the communication channels that connect the nodes.

Networks that cover large geographical areas are called *wide-area networks*. WANS generally consist of computers or remote local area networks (see 4.6) linked through standard telephone lines and microwave transmission. WAN links are generally provided by *common carriers*, which are organizations that have been approved by the Federal Communications Commission (FCC) to offer communications services to the public. The two largest common carriers are American Telephone & Telegraph (AT&T) and Western Union. There are also large public networks such as Tymnet, Telenet, Sprintnet, or CompuServe's network.

Although telephone lines are not the best channel for data communications, a new standard called Integrated Services Digital Network (ISDN) will increase the reliability and flexibility of sending data and video images through existing telephone lines. ISDN expands the bandwidth of conventional telephone lines, and is widely used in Europe. ISDN will eventually make the telephone system completely digital. This opens the possibility of a worldwide computer network operating by one standard. Already, we are seeing widespread communication through the Internet, a network that links at least three million computers (many of them university- and research-related) around the world.

(See 4.1 Telecommunications; 4.2 Communication Channels; 4.6 Computer Networks: Local Area Networks; 4.7 The LAN Models; 4.8 Wireless Networks; 4.9 Electronic Mail; 4.11 Telecommuting; 4.13 The Internet.)

4.6 COMPUTER NETWORKS: LOCAL AREA NETWORKS

Local area networks, or *LANs*, enable users in an organization to access and exchange information within a single office, building, or other relatively small area. The major advantage of a LAN is that users are able to share files, programs, messages, and expensive devices such as laser printers.

LAN technology has existed for several years, but many companies have not adopted it because they have doubts about its cost-effectiveness and reliability. Incompatibility among different systems and devices has also blocked the widespread acceptance of LANs. These problems are rapidly being overcome. Accordingly, installation and use of LANs can be expected to increase steadily. Although some experts predict that LANs will lead to the demise of the mainframe, others suggest that demands on the mainframe will increase with linkage to LANs. In fact, most companies will not throw out their investment in large computers; rather, they will change the way they use their mainframes.

Like other networks, LANs have nodes and links. The nodes are the usual components of a computer system: the computers, printers, and storage devices. One or more computers may be specially designated for particular jobs such as communication or network management. Nodes and links can be arranged in several different configurations, or *topologies*. One type is the *star network*, in which a series of outlying nodes are linked by separate connecting lines to a *hub*, or central switching component, forming a star, or asterisk, shape. In *ring* topology, a number of computers are connected to each other along a single, circular path. In a *bus* network, each computer plugs into a single bus cable that runs from computer to computer. Each also handles its own communications control. The bus topology is often used when just a few devices are linked.

Each computer in a LAN is equipped with a *network interface card (NIC)*, which is a printed circuit board that allows the members of the LAN to communicate with each other. The NIC plugs into an internal slot in the computer, and has a cable that connects it to the LAN. It contains the components that allow the computer to send and receive messages on the LAN. The nodes of the LAN are connected with twisted-pair wire, or with coaxial or fiber-optic cable. A variety of connectors, or plugs, link each type of cable with its appropriate devices.

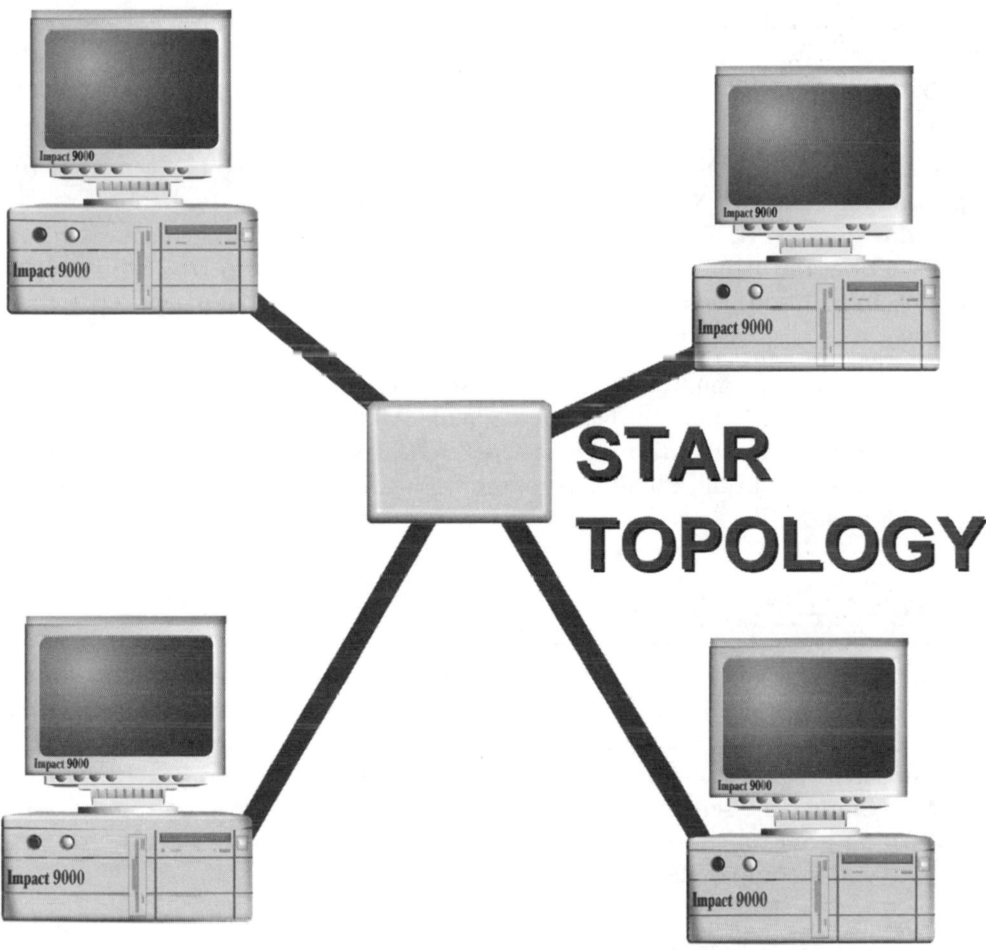

An example of a star network.

The members of a local area network must normally be positioned within 800 to 1,000 feet of each other. The strength of the transmission signal decreases as it travels; short distances enable the signal to be received properly. Multiple LANs can be joined in various ways. If similar LANs do not have the same protocol, *bridges* can connect them to other networks; *gateways* connect incompatible networks (such as a PC-based LAN to a mainframe-based network); *routers* link only those LANs that have compatible protocols.

Three standards commonly used in LANs for hardware topologies and communication channels are Ethernet, ARCnet, and Token Ring. (There are also proprietary networks, which are brand-specific and not always compatible with these standards.)

The software used to control network operations is referred to as the *network operating system (NOS)*. The NOS controls members' access to the network's shared resources. If, for example, two or more network members request access to the printer at the same time, the NOS will control the order in which printing occurs. In addition, the NOS normally includes programs that oversee network security, as well as the processing of messages (electronic mail).

(See 4.1 Telecommunications; 4.2 Communication Channels; 4.4 Communication Software; 4.5 Computer Networks: Wide Area Networks; 4.7 The LAN Models; Software Review section: Close-Up, LANtastic Network Operating System, Netware Lite, MacLink Plus/PC, Procomm Plus for Windows, Universal SoftPC, White Knight.)

4.7 The LAN Models

A *client/server* LAN is the most popular model. In this type of LAN, one or more *servers* (or "back ends") manage the sharing of peripheral devices and the database. The central server is a *dedicated* computer (used for a sole purpose); it contains the network operating system and governs operation of the LAN. In a LAN with multiple servers, each may have its own function: handling the database, controlling print functions, managing communications such as e-mail, and acting as gateways to incompatible mainframes, minicomputers, or LANs.

Most client/server LANs consist of just a few clients, but some handle hundreds. The clients (or "front ends") are the user nodes, or computers, that are connected to the server. At the client computers, the users work on applications such as word processing, payroll, or order processing, and can access the information held in relational databases on the server. Because the database server holds critical corporate data, any unauthorized access or system problem could result in disaster. That is why servers need mainframe-like programs that back up data automatically, keep unauthorized users out, and prevent system failures.

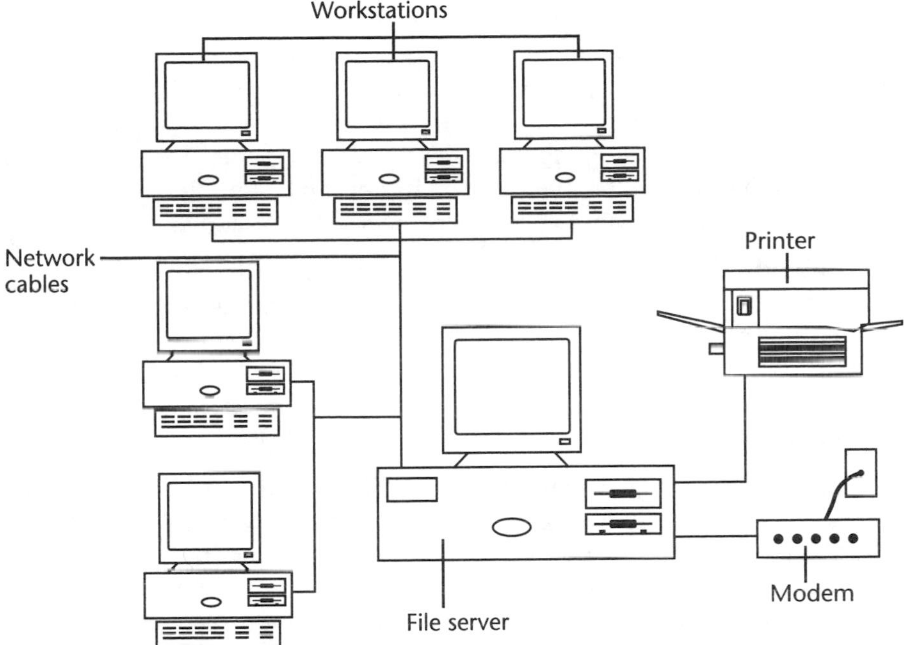

An example of a client/server local area network.

Although they have been common in the past for DOS-based systems, *peer-to-peer* LANs are gaining in popularity, and some experts even predict that they will replace client/server LANs in the near future. This type of LAN can be used in conjunction with client/server LANs. In a peer-to-peer LAN, each computer acts as a server and a client. Thus, each has the same amount of power, and no one computer controls things. Files located on any computer can be made available to other nodes along the line. Each user is responsible for the communication that takes place from his or her node, and often retains responsibility for securing data on his or her computer.

Peer-to-peer LANs are inexpensive. They are often installed in small, remote branch offices and connected over dial-up links to a corporate LAN. They work best with just a few computers, perhaps 10 or so. Peer-to-peer networks cannot, as yet, handle high-volume database work as well as client/server networks. They often bog down with heavy use.

(See 4.5 Computer Networks: Wide Area Networks; 4.6 Computer Networks: Local Area Networks.)

4.8 Wireless Networks

One of the most widely discussed technologies today is that of *wireless* networks. This is especially true now that *personal digital assistants*, or *PDAs* (usually with pen-based computing), are becoming more reliable and popular. Because of their slow speed and high cost, wireless networks will not replace wired networks, however, but they do nicely complement wired networks for added mobility.

Wireless networks do not require PDAs, but people who use wireless communication are often at locations away from their offices, and will use equipment such as notebook computers, PDAs, or electronic pagers. In wireless networks, computers communicate through radio waves or infrared links. Wireless communication generally occurs through one-way radio paging, two-way packet radio, or circuit-switched cellular systems.

One-way radio paging transmits brief messages over radio frequencies to an electronic pager. (The pager is available as a PCMCIA device.) The pager is lightweight; the messages travel rapidly, and can be received at frequent intervals. You cannot send messages through the same route, however. Instead, you place a toll-free call to an operator who transcribes and transmits your messages to the proper recipient. You can place your call through a computer modem.

Two-way packet radio sends messages in packets from the base station to the local recipient, or through a regional or national station to a base station near the receiving radio modem. The process is slow, but works with any notebook computer. Cost is based on the amount of data you send. The method provides fairly good security, but you can send only e-mail, not faxes.

Circuit-switched cellular wireless computer communication requires that your cellular telephone be connected to your cellular modem. (Circuit-switched communication is like telephone communication in which one line is linked to another for real-time, dedicated use.) The cell phone sends signals to the nearest *cell* (radio transmitter/receiver), and then the signals continue their journey along analog telephone lines. Messages sent by this method are susceptible to interference, and can be easily intercepted. In addition, cell modems work with only a few cell phones, and both the equipment and the fees for use are costly.

(See 4.3 Modems; 4.5 Computer Networks: Wide Area Networks; 4.9 Electronic Mail; 4.11 Telecommuting.)

4.9 Electronic Mail

In any business, communication is crucial. Countless messages are exchanged among company employees each day. More and more, businesses are turning to electronic mail (e-mail) to speed up the delivery of messages—and to reduce telephone, paper, and photocopying costs. *E-mail* is the transmission of text at high speeds over telecommunication facilities. It can involve text, voice recordings, or images. The "mailbox" that holds your messages is simply a computer file.

E-mail services can be public or private. CompuServe subscribers (or those of other online information services) can access *public e-mail* services through a modem. *Private e-mail* services are software packages used with a LAN.

Many companies are expanding their e-mail capabilities through the use of *electronic calendaring*. Managers and other personnel record their travel plans and appointments by computer, under the control of this application. When a special event or meeting must be scheduled, the software scans the calendars of the affected persons for acceptable schedule openings. The events can be scheduled for all parties, and e-mail can be used to notify all parties.

Both e-mail and electronic calendaring are often found in applications called *groupware*—loosely, a technology that enables people to work together on a project by sending messages and commenting on each other's work. Some groupware systems allow people to interact in real time. For example, when two individuals are editing a report, they can see each other's changes as they occur.

(See 4.5 Computer Networks: Wide Area Networks; 4.8 Wireless Networks; 4.11 Telecommuting; 4.12 Bulletin Board Systems; 4.13 The Internet; 4.14 Online Services; Software Review section: Lotus Notes.)

4.10 Fax Machines

In the past, facsimile (fax) services have played a major role in expanding the transmission of information over communication links. A *fax machine* is a desktop device that links into a dial-up telephone. The unit can scan and transmit a document, or reproduce a document received from another fax unit. To operate a fax, put the original document in the fax scanner, enter the telephone number of the recipient, and press the start button. As the document is read by the scanner, it is sent electronically over the phone lines to the recipient's fax machine. Within seconds, the recipient's machine prints a *facsimile* of the original document—a look-alike that is basically a picture of a paper document. Hundreds of thousands of fax units are in use within business organizations. Both the devices and the transmission are relatively inexpensive; the transmission is the same cost as a phone call.

Various versions of the fax machine are designed expressly for microcomputer use. For example, the *fax modem* enables you to send documents from a computer to a fax machine, rather than to another computer. You can also use a fax modem to print documents through a fax machine—handy if you are on a business trip. A computer used for faxing should be fairly powerful, with 4MB of memory and 10MB of free hard disk space.

(See 4.3 Modems; 4.11 Telecommuting.)

4.11 TELECOMMUTING

Perhaps one of the most interesting aspects of telecommunications to contemporary office workers is *telecommuting*—commuting to the office by computer, rather than in person. The system offers advantages in cities where office rent is high and mass transit systems or parking facilities are inadequate—and in businesses that do not require frequent face-to-face meetings among employees. Telecommuting provides great flexibility for working parents and employees with disabilities.

Sales representatives and journalists, who are often away from their offices, have successfully used a kind of telecommuting by taking portable computers and tiny printers with them on assignments. After entering memos, letters, stories, or reports, the employee uses a modem to send the information over telephone lines and to the office. Once the information has been received at the office, phone messages, edited copy, or other information can be sent back to the original writer. Some companies have even set up *satellite offices* in which a traveling employee spends one or two days per week and telecommutes the other three days. Telecommuting is suitable for jobs that need to be done with few distractions, such as computer programming, writing, and planning.

Telecommuting does have disadvantages, however. Some employees may not have the discipline to work away from the office. They may also fear that "out of sight is out of mind," particularly when promotions and raises are at stake. In addition, managers may worry about the amount of control they have over employees who work away from the office. Some of the wariness about telecommuting can be dispelled by implementing a hybrid plan in which the employee works at home two or three days, and comes to the office the remaining days.

Increases in telecommuting will affect both cities and business. Businesses may relocate branch offices—and even headquarters—to states with smaller tax burdens and idyllic rural areas, leaving behind the cities that have depended upon them for taxes and rental income. Current research shows that anywhere from 2 to 6.6 million people in the United States telecommute during at least a portion of the work week; experts predict the number will increase to 15 million within ten years. Businesses that provide e-mail, package delivery, and video conferencing equipment will grow.

People who telecommute, of course, need a computer and a modem or fax modem. They may also want an answering machine, an extra telephone line dedicated to modem use, and a pager or cellular service.

(See 4.3 Modems; 4.5 Computer Networks: Wide Area Networks; 4.6 Computer Networks: Local Area Networks; 4.8 Wireless Networks; 4.9 Electronic Mail.)

4.12 Bulletin Board Systems

An electronic bulletin board, or *bulletin board system (BBS)*, is a user-run service for posting messages and trading information. It can be accessed at little or no cost, unless you call long-distance. Almost anyone who has a telephone, a microcomputer system, a modem, and communication software can start a BBS. The manager of a BBS is called the *sysop*, which stands for SYStem OPerator. Some bulletin boards are tied together in larger networks, such as FidoNet, the largest such network. Through FidoNet, you can send messages to people throughout the United States and abroad. Online services also permit discussion via BBSs.

Bulletin boards are often set up for people with special computing interests, such as Apple Macintosh users, Microsoft Word users, or Lotus 1-2-3 users. Many software and hardware companies—such as WordPerfect Corp. and Toshiba America—offer in-house bulletin boards for customer support. Other bulletin boards are shared by people with special hobbies, such as sports, flying, history, or stamps. Bulletin boards designed for members of associations or professional groups usually require special information (or codes such as passwords) for access. Others are open to almost anybody. Usually, a bulletin board will limit "calls" to an hour per day per subscriber. To overcome this limit, you can use a program called an *off-line reader* (often available as shareware) that lets you sign onto the bulletin board, collect messages, and then sign off to read through the material at leisure. (You'll need to ask the sysop which off-line reader the BBS can handle.)

Some bulletin boards make *shareware* and uncopyrighted *public-domain* programs available to anyone who calls. The user simply asks the system to transmit the program to his or her computer, where it can be copied on a storage medium. Note, however, that the designers of shareware programs ask that people pay anywhere from $10 to $50 for programs they like and use. Despite its easy availability, shareware is copyrighted; if you pass it along to friends, they too should pay the fee if they use the software. *Public-domain software* is available free of charge. Shareware is often easier to use than comparable commercial software, and it may address particular problems that a number of users have been having. (You can also find public-domain and shareware software through sources other than BBSs—for example, gift stores, book stores, and other retail outlets.)

Before you sign up on a BBS, ask a friend who is a user of the service to tell you about it. You can also get a copy of *Computer Shopper* magazine, which prints a list of bulletin boards in every other issue. After signing up, remember: there are a few rules of decorum for "talking" over a bulletin board. You should announce your presence, even if you don't contribute much (not contributing at all is considered rude). Each board may have its own set of guidelines, and may squelch comments it considers illegal, libelous, or offensive. Any bulletin board that does not state *explicitly* that it is screening all notes—and blocking those that could be libelous—is not responsible for policing the notes you leave. Thus, be careful what you say—dozens of people may read your messages.

(See 4.3 Modems; 4.4 Communication Software; 4.13 The Internet; 4.14 Online Services.)

4.13 The Internet

The Internet, or simply "the Net," is more of a concept than a service or commercial venture. Loosely, it is a vast network—consisting of tens of thousands of networks, online services, and single-user microcomputers—that links users with information. There are roughly 25 million users.

The U.S. Department of Defense designed the original concept for the Internet in 1969, as an experimental project for sharing research between the military and university sources. The project, called ARPANET (Advanced Research Projects Agency), was designed to sustain communication in case of nuclear war. It consisted of a plan called *dynamic rerouting*, which would reroute traffic automatically to another link if one network link was disrupted by enemy attack. Beginning in 1980, traffic increased on ARPANET because universities were linking up thousands of workstations, rather than single large computers. Shortly thereafter, the National Science Foundation built their own (much faster) network, NSFNET, which connected a number of regional networks. By 1990, so much traffic had moved to the more efficient NSFNET that ARPANET shut down. NSFNET continues to operate the large network, which remains non-commercial and self-governing.

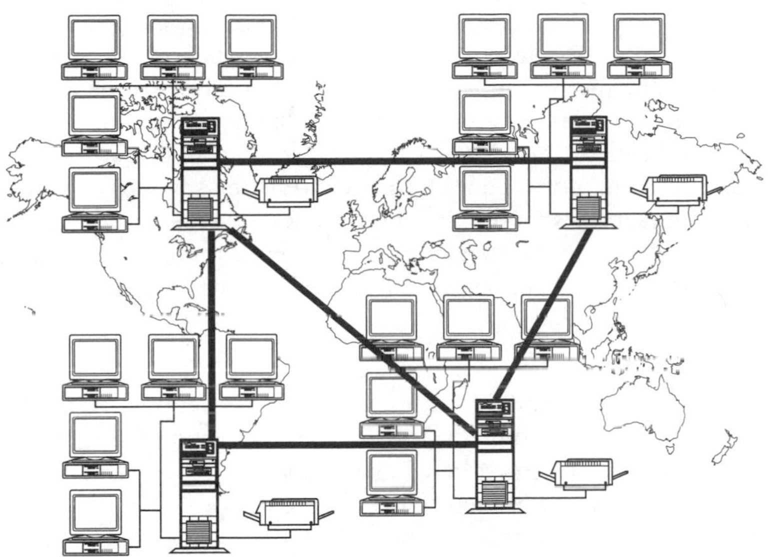

When you use the Internet, you can connect with computers all over the world.

The Internet is a cooperative, user-supported system; there is no control center or managing corporation. Accessing the Internet puts you in touch with millions of people and thousands of institutions around the world. The most frequently used functions on the Net are e-mail, news, remote login to libraries or other resources, and public discussion forums. The Internet also offers options for real-time *chatting* (Internet Relay Chat), weather information, satellite pictures, and games. Descriptions of some common Internet features follow.

- **E-mail**. The Net's e-mail services let you exchange messages with other people. The difference here is the network's scope: as long as you know the address of the recipient, you could communicate with literally millions of people all over the world. An easy way to get involved with e-mail is to join a *mailing list*, through which you receive mail on a specific topic. There are many mailing lists on a wide variety of topics. The most well-known one is LISTSERV, an application found on BITNET. BITNET (Because It's Time Network) is an academic network linking educational institutions. It uses a protocol different from that of the Internet, but can send e-mail through an Internet *gateway* (a connection in which *protocol conversion* takes place).

- **USENET**. A popular activity is the "Net" news exchange, or USENET, which works a lot like bulletin board services—users post messages and collect responses. The public messages are classified into various newsgroups—of which there are hundreds—ranging from technical subjects to social and recreational topics to regional interests. Hobbies and jokes also are popular topics. There are more than 7,000 USENET newsgroups. One of these, "alt.internet.services," contains the Internet Services Frequently Asked Questions (FAQ) list, and Scott Yanoff's "Special Internet Connections List" (which lists hundreds of services available on the Internet).
- **Remote login**. Both e-mail and USENET are available throughout the Net. If you want to use remote login and anonymous FTP, however, you must go through a system directly connected to the Internet proper. *Remote login* lets you *log in* (access or connect) to one Internet system from another remote Internet system. This practice is also known as *telnet*, which is the name of both the application and the protocol (command) that provides this function. It lets you browse through databases and card catalogs.
- **FTP**. Anonymous *FTP (file transfer protocol)* is similar to remote login. It enables an organization to set up a limited account and place in it files and archival information that the organization is willing to distribute freely. FTP is both the name of the program and the name of the command used to transfer files. Through FTP, you can have access to government documents such as Supreme Court decisions, works with expired copyrights, works that are in the public domain (or are specifically written for the Internet community), libraries' card catalogs, and software (including games). There are directories that list services available through anonymous FTP. Not all files listed in the directories are accessible to every user, but there is more than enough information to keep one person busy.

A number of tools help you find what you want on the Internet, but they are not always easy to use. As time passes, more GUIs and menu-driven tools will be available for accessing the Internet. The following list describes several of these tools.

- **Archie** is a search tool developed by McGill University. To search the FTP archives for files that hold topics of interest, you type *text-strings* for words that might be found in the file names or file descriptions. You access Archie by logging on to the computer running the Archie application or by e-mail.
- **Gopher** is a menu-based system that works much like a card catalog when you are searching for information. It lets you use the cursor and Return (Enter) key to search. It was developed at the University of Minnesota (home of the Golden Gophers) to enable campus network users to access information without the need for training. If you locate something of interest on the menu,

the Gopher gets it by using FTP, or by starting a Telnet session; you don't have to go through the mechanics of finding the resource's address and accessing it yourself.

- **WAIS (Wide Area Information Servers)** is both the program and the protocol for full-text word searches on more than 400 databases. You select the database sources, enter the word or words to be used for the search, and WAIS does the searching.
- **World-Wide Web** (or **WWW**, also "the Web") relies on *hypertext links*, in which documents are linked by association. In other words, you can select a word or topic in the original document to activate a link to another related source. WWW documents can include graphics, sound, and video. The Web was developed at CERN, a European high-energy physics laboratory in Geneva, and made available to the public in 1991.
- **Veronica** is a search tool used within gophers. This tool makes it easier to search for resources available to gophers.
- **Mosaic** is the current "killer app," or the most popular interface on the Internet today. Developed by NCSA (the National Center for Supercomputing Applications), it is a graphical user interface that allows point-and-click as the navigation device. Its competition includes Cello (an IBM-PC corporation GUI to the World-Wide Web), and MacWeb, for Macintosh computers.

Most servers attached to the Internet use the UNIX operating system. Since you most likely are using an operating system other than UNIX, you will need to go through an intermediary connection. To use the Net, you need a computer, a modem, an online Internet *account* (from Delphi or one of the hundreds of *service providers*), a word processing program that uses ASCII, DOS, or text format, and a telecommunications software program to access the intermediary connection.

You can tap the Internet in a variety of ways. Students at universities and colleges usually have "free" Internet accounts. Even if you are not a student or employee, you can sometimes use a university's access for a monthly fee. Your place of employment may also have a feed to the Internet. Most frequently, however, you will need to access an intermediary connection. For example, some commercial providers—such as CompuServe and America Online (see the next section)—sell access to the Internet. Delphi (also in the next section) and The WELL (Whole Earth 'Lectronic Link) offer full access to the Internet. Some bulletin board services may allow access to the Net's e-mail service, through which you can also get Archie. In addition, you could link through MCI Mail, Fidonet, or eWorld. You could also have a direct connection—TCP/IP, or Transmission Control Protocol/Internet Protocol—installed professionally on your computer.

Several software packages are available that facilitate your trip through the Internet. Among them are VersaTerm-Link from Synergy Software, and TCP/ Connect II from InterCon Systems Corporation—both for the Macintosh—as well as two packages for IBM-compatibles: Internet Chameleon from NetManage, and O'Reilly's and Spry's Internet in a Box.

The Internet is probably the most open network in the world. Approximately two million computers are linked to the Internet. More are being added every day, with services such as America Online now offering e-mail gateways. The added traffic presents a problem with Internet etiquette. Veteran users have already established sets of customs and manners for using the net. Among the most common breaches of etiquette is asking questions that are already answered in the *FAQ (frequently asked questions)* files. New Internet users should read the information in the FAQ files before posting questions. In addition, "newbies" can grasp the gist of interesting-sounding newsgroups by reading the contributions for a couple of weeks before adding their own opinions. While on the Internet, do not "crack" into bank computers or other private information accounts. Keep messages to a reasonable size, and keep comments relevant to a group's topic and current "thread" of discussion. Read the "read-me" files found in special mailing lists and newsgroups.

For further information, you can browse through the many books available about the Internet. Several magazines are devoted to various aspects of online activity, and you can always ask someone in a user's group to help you get started. To find a dial-up provider near you and get more information about the Internet, call InterNIC Information Services at (619) 455-4600.

(See 4.3 Modems; 4.5 Computer Networks: Wide Area Networks; 4.9 Electronic Mail; 4.12 Bulletin Board Systems; 4.14 Online Services; 4.17 Delphi; 4.25 The WELL; 5.2 Computer Crime; 5.3 Hacking; 5.11 Copyright and Piracy; 5.20 Depersonalization Versus "Telecommunity.")

4.14 Online Services

You can use a modem with a telephone and microcomputer to connect (*log in* or *log on*) to an online information service. Such a service is also called a commercial database, an information utility, or an information network. *Online* means "connected directly to a computer," so your computer will be hooked up—through a variety of communication channels—to a computer at the service's place of business. As the words *information* and *database* suggest, the service offers news or information.

The word *commercial* implies that the service is a business, and you pay to use it through membership fees and hourly *connect rates*. (Some services offer a few hours of free trial so you can see what is available before becoming a member.) Basic membership fees run anywhere from nothing to over $100. Hourly rates usually begin at around $4, and can go as high as $300. These often vary with the time of day you are connected, and the type of information you want to access. Some services also charge a separate fee per search. If you are calling long distance, you also must pay telephone bills; in some communities, telephone companies also charge customers for connecting a modem to the phone lines.

To reduce the costs of accessing expensive databases, practice the following conservation techniques:

- Study the manual that comes with your subscription.
- Read the information about the charges carefully. Be aware of hidden costs.
- Plan your "visit" so you know what is in each database—and what you are looking for—before you log on. Check your local library first; use the online service for information you can't find there.
- Be sure to know, ahead of time, how to use the operators such as AND, OR, and NOT to expand or limit your search.
- Use the *macro*, or *scripting*, functions of your software to set up certain procedures before logging on, so that you won't spend so much time typing responses to prompts.
- Have your lists of commands readily available. That way you won't waste time hunting for a command while your computer is connected to one of the databases. Be sure your communication software is capturing and saving messages (and other items that you can download) as they come in.
- Never hang up or shut off your computer without formally terminating service. Otherwise, you will be charged for connect time—possibly a large amount of it—from which you actually did not benefit.

These tips apply to any online service, and should save you time and money. Some services also offer practice sessions with brief versions of their databases, which give you a chance to master the access functions before wasting money on full searches. Although using an online service sounds expensive, the value to the user lies in time savings; online database references are faster and more convenient than traditional library research.

A subscription to a service can provide news, movie reviews, sports news, weather reports, and other information. Most also offer *forums*, discussion groups for special interests. (If you see the acronym **SIG** in connection with an online service, you should know that it stands for Special Interest Group, another term for forum.) Many services provide a number of activities and forums especially for kids, including homework help and resources. Some of the most popular activities online services offer involve *interactivity*—game-playing, real-time conferences, and *messaging*. Many companies that manufacture computer hardware and software also provide product support through online services.

For each online subscription, you get a *password* and/or an identification number. These help prevent someone else from using your subscription while you pay for it. Once you connect to the service's computer (commonly referred to as the *host computer*), you can browse through the files and *download* (transfer to your computer) anything you want to study at more length. (Some items cannot be downloaded.) If you want to download items from an online service, you should check the protocol used—such as Xmodem, Xmodem-1K, Ymodem, Kermit, and Zmodem.

A number of specialty online services carry databases that cater to particular interests. For example, the database called Horse (from Lexington, Kentucky) carries information about pedigrees, breeding records, race records, and earnings of thoroughbred horses in North America since 1922. Dun's Electronic Yellow Pages provides names, addresses, and telephone numbers for over 8 million companies in the United States. Coffeeline contains abstracts and other literature covering a wide variety of topics about coffee, from growing coffee plants to considering the health effects of drinking coffee. Baseline prints the weekly box-office receipts of 35,000 films, biographies of thousands of people in the entertainment industry, and contacts for many of the celebrities. If you want to read about bills recently introduced in the U.S. House and Senate, you should access Billcast Legislative Forecasts. This service also predicts the change of each passing stage of the approval process. Investext gives a full text of economists' analyses on public companies.

AMA/NET has four different databases that provide medical personnel with information on drugs, diagnosing, medical legislation, and public health issues. CORIS, a product of Thompson Financial Networks, provides fast, efficient access to top business information sources for a variety of users. DataTimes gives you the full texts of various national and international newspapers.

You can buy print guides to database services, but they are expensive. For example, an annual subscription to *The Directory of Online Databases* from Cuadra/Elsevier in New York costs $175 for two issues and two supplements. A subscription to *Database Directory* from Knowledge Industry Publications in New York costs $395, and includes a monthly newsletter. Current magazines frequently describe the various services, and where to get further information. Check the Yellow Pages for a city near you, or an 800-number directory, for company telephone numbers. Ask a friend or users' group to help you get started.

(See 4.1 Telecommunications; 4.2 Communication Channels; 4.3 Modems; 4.4 Communication Software; 4.5 Computer Networks: Wide Area Networks; 4.6 Computer Networks: Local Area Networks; 4.12 Bulletin Board Systems; 4.14 Online Services; 4.15 CompuServe; 4.16 GEnie; 4.17 Delphi; 4.18 America Online; 4.19 PRODIGY; 4.20 eWorld; 4.21 DIALOG; 4.22 BRS/After Dark; 4.23 Dow Jones News/Retrieval; 4.24 Mead Data Central; 4.25 The WELL; 4.26 Exec-PC; 4.27 WESTLAW; 5.1 Criminal Conduct and Ethics: Responsibility for Computer Actions; 5.2 Computer Crime; 5.3 Hacking; 5.11 Copyright and Piracy; 5.20 Depersonalization Versus "Telecommunity.")

4.15 CompuServe

CompuServe Information Service; 5000 Arlington Center Boulevard; P.O. Box 20212; Columbus, Ohio 43220; (800) 848-8199; (614) 457-0802; initial fee of $39.95; basic package per month $9.95 for unlimited use of 50 basic services and surcharges of $8 to $16 per hour for most other services and forums.

CompuServe is one of the largest information services available to individual and family users—with over 2,000 different forums, services, and departments. In fact, it bought its biggest competitor, The Source, and added even more capabilities. Hourly connect rates vary depending on the day and time of day you use the service and the type of modem you have. Some of CompuServe's special services (such as stock price and dividend information) may have additional charges. The company also publishes *CompuServe* magazine, which provides helpful information on using the firm's services. (For parents' information, members can send a written request blocking certain forums from the account.)

To get started with CompuServe, you will need a CompuServe membership kit, which you can get at a local computer store, or by calling CompuServe's 800 number. The kit includes a user's manual, a password, a user identification number, and detailed instructions for accessing the service. Otherwise, you can use any computer, any modem, and any communication package to access CompuServe. (CompuServe does offer its own software for DOS/Windows and Macintosh computers. This software can significantly decrease the connect time required to access information or send a message.) Once you are a member, you can merely dial CompuServe's phone number in your locality.

To access and navigate through CompuServe, you simply need to type the required information at the *prompts*, which are cues that tell you what kind of information you should enter. CompuServe uses both the menu-choice and the word-search approaches. *Menu-choice* enables you to access desired information by selecting a topic from a *menu* (list) and entering the number printed beside your choice. *Word-search* lets you enter a word or topic at the appropriate prompts; on the basis of what you type, the CompuServe computer looks for the related information. You will usually type the word **GO** and the name of your topic at the prompt in order to bypass the menu. A new user interface called the CompuServe Information Manager (WINCIM) makes using the service in Windows easy.

The CompuServe Information Manager (WINCIM) interface for Windows.

CompuServe offers many computer games, and allows you to shop at home by browsing through an "electronic mall"—which includes J.C. Penney, Dial-a-Mattress, and Crutchfield, to name a few. You can send messages to other subscribers by using CompuServe's E-MAIL command. In addition to the Associated Press wire service and *U.S. News and World Report*, you can also access newspapers such as the *St. Louis Post-Dispatch*, the *Middlesex Daily*, and the *Washington Post*. CompuServe also has a wide variety of services for business users. It also links together special-interest and professional groups. Each group shares a common interest such as music, IBM PCs, entrepreneurship, or law. Subscribers can communicate their comments and suggestions directly to CompuServe; these may be used to add new services. CompuServe is always changing and adding to its resources. One interesting form of interactive online communication is the CB simulator, which imitates the style of communication found on citizen's band radio.

This online service also provides weather information, travel services for airline and hotel reservations, electronic shopping, market information (through D&B

Dun's Market Identifiers and Disclosure 11 Reports), brokerage services, multiplayer games, lifestyle information (about health issues, religion, hobbies, automobiles, and so on). Educational resources include *Grolier's Academic American Encyclopedia*, U.S. government information, Peterson's college database, dissertation abstracts, and the Science and Math Education Forum. Among the kids' features are the Student's Forum, Science Trivia Quiz, and games.

CompuServe's IQuest provides a gateway through which you can access over 900 additional databases, many of which are drawn from other online services such as DIALOG and BRS. There are additional fees for using IQuest, however, many of which can run quite high.

(See 4.14 Online Services, 5.2 Computer Crime; 5.3 Hacking; 5.11 Copyright and Piracy; 5.20 Depersonalization Versus "Telecommunity.")

4.16 GENIE

GE Information Service; 401 North Washington Street; Rockville, Maryland 20850; (800) 638-9636; (301) 251-6415; basic rate per month $8.95 and $3 to $12.50 per hour in non-prime time.

GEnie, which stands for General Electric Network for Information Exchange, offers hundreds of products and services for personal computer users. It is gaining more interest every day, and is becoming a serious competitor for CompuServe. It provides local access numbers in the United States, Canada, and Japan. You need your own communication software to access GEnie.

GEnie is organized into a menu structure, which includes a main menu that you use to access submenus. To use the menu, you can enter a *keyword* or a page number, which both appear on the menus. You can also enter just the number of the menu choice. If you want to look at a previous menu, you type **P** at the prompt. GEnie provides upon request an easy-to-use GUI called Aladdin.

GEnie is well known for its bulletin boards and forums called RoundTables. These include topics such as personal computing for a number of brands of microcomputers, programming, professional services (for fields such as law, medicine, writing, photography, and education), and computer products. The RoundTables also cater to such special interests such as genealogy, aviation, history, trains, motorcycles, comics, and electronics. In a more businesslike vein, GEnie offers a variety of financial services such as the Dow Jones News/Retrieval, an electronic investment advisor called VESTOR, and stock-and-securities quotations. (Some areas of GEnie are restricted to certain age groups, unless special admittance is requested. In the kids- and teens-only areas, use of profanity and vulgarity is strictly prohibited.)

One unusual service that GEnie provides is a Genealogy KnowledgeBase that helps you find materials or organizations that will aid your own genealogy research. There are a number of other products that provide movie reviews, soap opera summaries, travel services, and multiplayer or single-player games (such as Cyberstrike or GemStone III). In addition, you can use GEnie electronic mail and CB simulator functions. GEnie's shopping services are very complete; you can shop over 35 stores to buy Florida fruit, Tiffany products, computer equipment, coffees, Godiva confections, flowers, Orvis products, and spirits, to name a few possibilities.

(See 4.14 Online Services; 5.2 Computer Crime; 5.3 Hacking; 5.11 Copyright and Piracy; 5.20 Depersonalization Versus "Telecommunity.")

4.17 DELPHI

Delphi Information Systems, Inc.; Three Blackstone Street; Cambridge, Massachusetts 02139; (800) 695-4005; (617) 491-3342; sign-up fee of $49.95 and $13 to $23 connect charges per month. Per-hour fees vary considerably, based on time of day.

Delphi, like CompuServe, was a pioneer in telecommunications. It is known for its user-friendly atmosphere, and seems more like a BBS than a formal online service. It has one of the quickest response times of any of the services, and navigation through it is clear and easy to understand. Delphi is run by General Videotex Corporation, and can be accessed through BT Tymnet, Telenet, or direct dial. In addition to its own features, it also offers full access to the Internet. You need your own communication software to access Delphi.

Delphi offers hints and software for computer users, trivia areas, games, and information services such as news wires, business information, travel information, shopping, electronic mail, and *real-time conferencing*—that is, conferences or chat areas in which you talk with other users and receive immediate responses. Online conferencing occurs in groups such as the Clubhouse, the Forum, the Color Computer Group (for users of the Tandy Color Computer), Macintosh ICONtact Group (for Macintosh users), Tandy PC Group (for Tandy personal and business computer users), and the Science Fiction group (for readers, writers, and fans of science fiction). There is also a professional translation service for translating text to and from Spanish, French, German, Italian, Portuguese, and other languages.

One unique feature is that Delphi gives its members a chance to act as a sysop (system operator) for a bulletin board system called a Custom Forum under its auspices. Any Delphi member in good standing can establish a Custom Forum.

This person becomes the host, who manages access to the forum by other members. Members can leave messages, or "talk" through a conference feature. Sysops and forum hosts enforce Delphi's policies discouraging profanity and abusive language.

(See 4.14 Online Services; 5.2 Computer Crime; 5.3 Hacking; 5.11 Copyright and Piracy; 5.20 Depersonalization Versus "Telecommunity.")

4.18 America Online

Quantum Computer Services, Inc.; 8619 Westwood Center Drive; Vienna, Virginia 22182; (800) 827-6364; (703) 448-8700; basic fee is $9.95 per month, with $3.50 per hour connect fee beyond 5 hours of use per month.

America Online began as AppleLink Personal Edition, an offshoot of AppleLink, Apple's corporate and developer bulletin board and electronic mail service. It is an attractive, bold-looking service, available to users of Apple II, Macintosh, and IBM PC computers. AOL does require you to use its own communication software, but the program is easy to use—provided you have a mouse—and its graphical user interface makes navigation easy. AOL can be accessed through Telenet and BT Tymnet, as well as by direct dial, and setting up the file transfer protocols is easy. The service also provides access to two Internet features, USENET and Gopher. The reasonable charges include a monthly membership fee and an hourly rate.

America Online (AOL) enables you to access bulletin boards called *message centers* for special interests, as well as very complete and up-to-date software libraries (with both public domain and shareware programs, games) and forums for real-time "chitchat." (AOL prohibits profanity and vulgarity, and offers parental controls for locking out certain "chat rooms" and other similar types of activities.) Its libraries are extensive, including *Compton's Encyclopedia*, and its forum leaders carefully watch discussion to be sure participants stick to the subject. One of its most innovative features is Center Stage, a mass-audience conference; the audience can ask questions of the moderator, and "whisper" to other participants. AOL also offers a new high-resolution graphics interactive game from TSR, Inc., called *Neverwinter Nights*. Play requires the installation and registration of additional software.

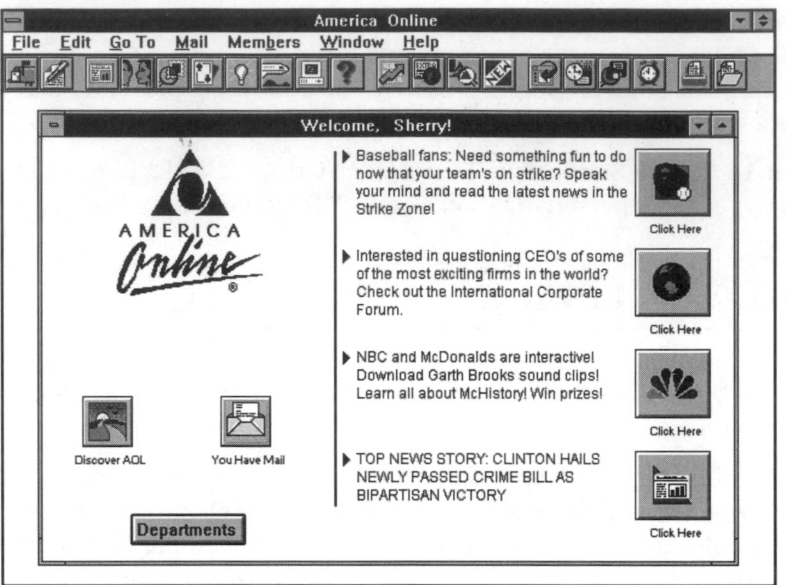

America Online's GUI is easy to use.

Much of AOL's news is drawn from *USA Today*, and it has the usual financial and market information. The service does offer shopping and reference services (though these areas are less extensive than those of other online services). AOL offers plentiful services for computer professionals and hobbyists. For children, there are Disney Adventures, Scholastic KidsWorld Sampler, TIME Magazine for Kids, and many games.

AOL and Tribune Company are cooperating on the first local online service for Chicago-area personal computer users. The service is called Chicago Online; Tribune's Chicago-area businesses—the *Chicago Tribune*, WGN radio, WGN television, and the Chicago Cubs—participate in its development.

(See 4.14 Online Services; 5.2 Computer Crime; 5.3 Hacking; 5.11 Copyright and Piracy; 5.20 Depersonalization Versus "Telecommunity.")

4.19 PRODIGY

Prodigy Services Company, 445 Hamilton Avenue; White Plains, New York 10601; (800) 776-3449; (914) 993-8000; $29.95 initial fee, $14.95 per month and $3.60 per hour connect fee.

A relatively new competitor—but currently able to boast the largest number of members in the information-service market—is PRODIGY, a joint venture between Sears and IBM. Geared to individuals and families, PRODIGY is a menu-driven, very user-friendly service that allows subscribers to shop at home, perform banking tasks, make airline reservations, and access a wide variety of news and entertainment information. Besides using menus, you can navigate in PRODIGY using the JUMPwindow and JUMPword features of the service. To use this feature, you merely access the JUMPwindow, where the prompts for jumping appear, and enter the JUMPword (that is, keyword) that indicates the topic you are interested in. There is a JUMPword dictionary that lists the key words and topics available.

A look at PRODIGY's opening screen.

The bulletin boards are watched carefully for subject matter and gossip. (Parents can lock out any board that seems unsuitable for their children.) There's a Just Kids area that includes Babysitter's Club and Online Sesame Street. Adults can access Home Life bulletin boards, Close Up for discussion about current events, and ESPNET for sports fans. There are no real-time "chats," but the service is planning to add chats. Though it has no software libraries, PRODIGY does offer a wide variety of shopping services, through which you can buy just about any product you wish. The service also serves as an advertising medium for about 200 companies. These companies pay for advertising on the PRODIGY system on the basis of how many times an advertisement is accessed by subscribers, and also by the number of products sold to subscribers. The advertising is controversial, however, because parents may not want their families to be subject to the constant sales pitches.

Prodigy Services believes it can be successful by appealing to a large number of home computer users at an inexpensive price (the advertising makes this lower price possible). PRODIGY has a monthly fee, and allows unlimited use of services for that price. You will need to install PRODIGY software, however, rather than using general communications software. (Kits are available through software dealers.) In addition, you cannot upload or download files, except in a few limited areas of the system.

(See 4.13 The Internet; 4.14 Online Services; 5.2 Computer Crime; 5.3 Hacking; 5.11 Copyright and Piracy; 5.20 Depersonalization Versus "Telecommunity.")

4.20 eWorld

Apple Computer, Inc., P.O. Box 4493, Bridgeton, Missouri 63044-9718; (800) 428-5331; no sign-up fee; $8.95 per month; $4.95 to $7.90 per hour beyond two free hours of use per month during evenings and weekends.

Designed for Macintosh users inside and outside the United States, eWorld is arranged somewhat like a community. In the opening window, you'll see a set of buildings. When you click on one, another window appears, offering you a choice of things to do. Among the buildings are the Arts & Leisure Pavilion for information and discussion about the arts, television, and sports, as well as interactive adventure games. The Marketplace offers shopping services; the e-mail Center lets you communicate with other people. The Newsstand provides information from news services around the world. The Community Center is where you'll find the interactive forums. The Learning Center provides reference materials in the form of books, encyclopedias, and dictionaries, and the Computer Center is a source of information about computers, as well as technical support and software demos. The Business & Finance building offers business and financial news that can help businesses, as well as your personal investments. (The buildings are also listed in the Places menu.)

To use eWorld, you need the eWorld program, a modem, and a Macintosh computer with system software version 6.07 or later, as well as at least 4MB of RAM. eWorld will link Newton, Internet, and AppleLink users. By the end of 1994, eWorld will replace AppleLink.

(See 4.13 The Internet; 4.14 Online Services; 5.2 Computer Crime; 5.3 Hacking; 5.11 Copyright and Piracy; 5.20 Depersonalization Versus "Telecommunity.")

4.21 DIALOG

Dialog Information Services; 3460 Hillview Avenue; Palo Alto, California 94304; (800) 334-2564; (415) 858-3785); start with the $35 fee to the Knowledge Index.

DIALOG began in 1963 as a Lockheed Missiles and Space Company research and development program. In 1972, it was established as a commercial search service. Its first customers were scientific and technical libraries, but business users soon followed. In 1981, DIALOG became a wholly-owned subsidiary of Lockheed Corporation. As individuals—such as business executives, scientists, teachers, doctors, and investors—began using personal computers, they became interested in the types of research services DIALOG presented. In turn, DIALOG expanded the number of its databases. Today, DIALOG is part of Knight-Rider's Business Information Services Division.

DIALOG contains more than 425 databases, for which it represents itself as the "World's Largest Online Knowledgebank." Its comprehensive Information Retrieval Service includes coverage of virtually every area of study—including art, music, humanities, business, aerospace, biology, chemistry, physics, and zoology. The service offers full-text news wire services such as Associated Press, UPI, and Knight-Rider Financial News. It also contains the text of other publications such as journals, patents, books, and trademarks, and lists information about more than 12 million companies, using sources such as Dun & Bradstreet and Standard & Poor. Plus, you can access the service through simplified approaches such as the DIALOG Business Connection (for business users) and DIALOG Medical Connection (for health professionals). DIALOG also offers the KNOWLEDGE INDEX, which presents over 90 popular DIALOG databases at reduced rates after 6:00 p.m. on weekdays and during most of the weekend. The number of available databases is limited, but each provides easy access that requires no special training.

DIALOG's scope is worldwide; it culls customers from around the world as well. Employees at government agencies, universities, libraries, and other research organizations tap into DIALOG databases. Students also use DIALOG, as do professionals such as lawyers, engineers, medical personnel, and information brokers.

Customers pay an annual service fee and a connect-time charge, which ranges from $.25 to $2.75 per minute. You can use any standard communication software to access DIALOG, but the company also offers its own links for IBM-compatibles and Macintosh machines. DIALOG offers customer training to teach you how to search its databases. Subscribers also receive a monthly newsletter called *Chronolog*.

(See 4.14 Online Services; 5.2 Computer Crime; 5.3 Hacking; 5.11 Copyright and Piracy; 5.20 Depersonalization Versus "Telecommunity.")

4.22 BRS/AFTER DARK

Maxwell Online, Inc.; 8000 West Park Drive; McLean, Virginia 22102; (800) 468-0908; one-time subscription fee of $75 and $12 per month minimum usage fee.

A low-cost database service that operates during evening and weekend hours is BRS/After Dark. This service is a subset of BRS/Search system, also an information service. The letters BRS stand for Bibliographic Retrieval Services, and the service provides nearly 100 databases.

To get started using BRS/After Dark, you must contact Maxwell Online Inc. Your fees include a one-time subscription fee and minimum monthly usage fee. The database charges include *access charges* (for accessing a particular database) and *display charges* (for viewing a citation), and there are differences in charges among the various databases. As these charges may be surprisingly high for one citation, be aware of these charges before accessing the material. Although some charges may seem high, overall BRS/After Dark offers some of the cheapest access rates of any online database service.

The system is available between the work-week hours of 6:00 p.m. and 6:00 a.m. (your time zone) Monday through Thursday, and between the weekend hours of 6:00 p.m. Friday through 6:00 a.m. Monday. You can access BRS/After Dark through Telenet (U.S. SprintSPRINTNET) and BT Tymnet, as well as through regular long-distance lines.

(See 4.14 Online Services; 5.2 Computer Crime; 5.3 Hacking; 5.11 Copyright and Piracy; 5.20 Depersonalization Versus "Telecommunity.")

4.23 DOW JONES NEWS/RETRIEVAL

Dow Jones & Co.; P.O. Box 300; Princeton, New Jersey 08543-0300; (800) 522-3567 ext. 69; (609) 452-1511; rates vary depending on the amount and type of information retrieved (some are as much as $2.85 per minute).

The Dow Jones News/Retrieval Service is designed with business information in mind; its primary users are business professionals and individuals interested in business. There are various user levels—Standard, Corporate, and Blue Chip—available with varying membership fees. Connect rates per hour also vary, depending on the time of day, speed of communication, and database accessed. Some databases also include extra charges per citation or document viewed. Dow Jones News/Retrieval uses a menu approach to its services, but also offers training programs in major cities to teach users how to make the best use of the databases for the most reasonable charges.

The system provides information on every company listed on the New York and American stock exchanges, as well as some selected companies whose stock is traded over the counter. You can get historical stock market quotes, and current information that is only fifteen minutes behind that action on the exchange floors. The service also gives corporate earnings estimates, and price/volume data. With a Dow Jones News/Retrieval subscription, you also can get UPI summaries of local and national news, news stories from various financial newspapers and magazines such as *The Wall Street Journal*, and access to the *Grolier's Academic American Encyclopedia*. The service offers an archive of publications, too, which includes the contents of *The Wall Street Journal*, the *Washington Post*, *Forbes*, and many others. It also has movie reviews and weather information, and allows you to shop from home.

Three software packages are available with which you can record and manipulate information from the News/Retrieval databases. The Market Analyzer performs 17 analytical functions and charts the results. The Market Microscope ranks companies and industries by 68 financial indicators. The Market Manager monitors and updates investment portfolios. Dow Jones will be introducing a new easy-to-use user interface for searching the system and using the archives. It is also studying ways to reduce and simplify its rates.

(See 4.14 Online Services; 5.2 Computer Crime; 5.3 Hacking; 5.11 Copyright and Piracy; 5.20 Depersonalization Versus "Telecommunity.")

4.24 Mead Data Central

Mead Data Central, Inc. (Subs. The Mead Corporation); 9443 Springboro Pike; Dayton, Ohio 45342; (800) 227-4908; (513) 865-6800.

Mead Data Central is one of the oldest online-service companies selling searches of unique databases. It includes LEXIS—a computer-assisted research service for the legal professions—that includes cases, regulations, laws, and decisions in the United States, England, and France, as well as other legal materials from Australia, New Zealand, Ireland, and Scotland. Mead's other major database is NEXIS, a service that contains general and business news. NEXIS provides more than 750 news sources in full text, including the *New York Times*, the *Washington Post*, *Business Week*, *Fortune*, *U.S. News and World Report*, and others—as well as the AP, UPI, and Reuters news wires. There are also more than 2,000 sources of abstracts. NEXIS is used primarily by professionals in business, banking, advertising, public relations, law firms, libraries, and news companies.

Mead Data also offers a financial information service, a patent research service, a law database, a medical service, Medline (a bibliographic database produced by the National Library of Medicine), a library of annual reports, and other corporate information.

(See 4.14 Online Services; 5.2 Computer Crime; 5.3 Hacking; 5.11 Copyright and Piracy; 5.20 Depersonalization Versus "Telecommunity.")

4.25 The WELL

The WELL (Whole Earth 'Lectronic Link); 27 Gate Five Road; Sausalito, California 94965; (415) 332-4335; monthly fee of $15 and hourly charge of $2.

The WELL was designed by Whole Earth and Network Technologies (NETI) to be an online meeting place. It includes over 200 conferences—of which some are computer-specific, some are entertainment-oriented, and some are based on current issues and events. The WELL also includes an electronic mail function. It charges a monthly fee and an hourly rate. If you use a credit card for payment, you will also be required to place an advance payment. The service is accessible by a phone call, as well as through the CompuServe network.

Conferences in education and business include discussion about desktop publishing, home ownership, the stock market, the future, word processing, and other topics. There are conferences on social and political issues such as AIDS, Central America, drugs, parenting, peace, psychology, and spirituality. The arts, recreation, and entertainment subjects include boating, comics, flying, eating, games, gardening, movies, and a wide variety of other pursuits. There are also computer-specific conferences for people who use Macintosh computers, HyperCard, UNIX, IBM PCs, and other computer technologies. The WELL is connected to the Internet, but is protected by a gate such as a password or credit card number.

(See 4.13 The Internet; 4.14 Online Services; 5.2 Computer Crime; 5.3 Hacking; 5.11 Copyright and Piracy; 5.20 Depersonalization Versus "Telecommunity.")

4.26 Exec-PC

Exec-PC; P.O. Box 57; Elm Grove, Wisconsin 53122; (414) 789-4200; seven hours a week for $60 per year.

Exec-PC began as an electronic bulletin board service, and is still run by a couple who hire no other employees. It offers a huge library of MS-DOS public-domain and shareware software. Old titles are rarely deleted from the collection, however, so this service remains a place to look at early software. Exec-PC is simple; a variety of menus guide you through the system. Help is available by typing the question mark (?), and a tutorial can be downloaded if you need further assistance.

The software is grouped into seven major collections, including the Free Collection; collections for Apple Macintosh, Commodore Amiga, Atari ST, and UNIX/XENIX-running computers; the Mahoney Collection (collection of the sysop, Bob Mahoney); and the California PC-SIG collection. Most of the titles in the Mahoney Collection are contributed by subscribers. There is also a message system.

(See 4.14 Online Services; 5.2 Computer Crime; 5.3 Hacking; 5.11 Copyright and Piracy; 5.20 Depersonalization Versus "Telecommunity.")

4.27 WESTLAW

West Publishing Company; 50 W. Kellogg Blvd.; P.O. Box 64833; St. Paul, Minnesota 55164-9752; (800) 937-8529

WESTLAW is a research service for attorneys and judges. WESTLAW helps legal professionals keep current; they can also find relevant information in the accumulated cases of many years past—a job impossible by normal means. The service has in its databases the full texts and *headnotes* (brief explanations) of all opinions of the United States Supreme Court from 1925 to date, the United States Court of Appeals from 1945 to date, and the United States District Courts from 1950 to date. The full text and headnotes of all reported opinions of the state courts are available from 1967 to the present. Both state and federal cases are added to the database as decisions are reported. Besides finding specific cases, the system can also find references to specific judges, witnesses, products, companies, medical terms, and unusual legal terms. Items such as these are not usually indexed in law books. A simplified search mode—which allows you to avoid formulating (and typing in) a complicated Boolean query—has recently been introduced as part of the WESTLAW service. WIN (WESTLAW is Natural) lets you describe your search in simple, plain-English sentences, or in lawyers' jargon.

WESTLAW also offers over 400 legal periodicals online. It has a gateway, or connection, to Washington Alert, the online service of Congressional Quarterly Inc. Washington Alert tracks the full text of every bill through each stage of Congress, and includes a variety of other information about voting, calendars, schedule changes, the *Congressional Record*, and committee notes. Via gateways, WESTLAW can also access 140 databases from DIALOG and the Dow Jones News/Retrieval Service.

(See 4.14 Online Services; 5.2 Computer Crime; 5.3 Hacking; 5.11 Copyright and Piracy; 5.20 Depersonalization Versus "Telecommunity.")

Part 5 Contents Index

ISSUES AND CHALLENGES

The invention of computers made work a lot easier for many people, but it also fostered problems. Computers made it possible for almost anyone to root around in data we once thought private, or at least restricted in some way. Restricted data became one more area for creative criminals to explore. Computers also made more trouble for people through sometimes-gargantuan errors. And now there is a faint suspicion that working at a computer all day long may not be good for your health.

On the other hand, computers have created a wonderful way for people with some types of disabilities to communicate with family and friends. They have provided students with a way to cut down on the practice of boring, tedious arithmetic facts and spelling, and to use their knowledge more in problem solving and simulations. They have enabled industries to use robots for dangerous work. Many people can benefit from the invention of computers; the technology has also brought with it some characteristic troubles. In this section, we present some of these problems and benefits in greater detail.

5.1 CRIMINAL CONDUCT AND ETHICS: RESPONSIBILITY FOR COMPUTER ACTIONS

When you were in school, were you ever tempted to copy someone's homework for the next day's class, or sneak a look at someone else's answers during an exam? Have you ever been tempted to take something from a store without paying for it? At work, did you ever want to claim credit for someone else's suggestion, or peek at files that held confidential information about other employees? Did you ever try to place the blame for a mistake on a coworker? What you actually did in response to these temptations depended on your code of *ethics*, the morals on which we base our behavior. Ethics are standards by which we tell the difference between right and wrong and act accordingly.

Ethics apply to our behavior around computers, too. Have you ever heard anyone brag about using a computer and telephone lines to break into the main computer at a hospital, school, or business? Have you ever wanted to copy a friend's software disk so you would have a program without paying for it? Have you ever been tempted to look at confidential computer files at your place of employment? How hard would it be to convince you that it would be okay to get into a university's database to change your grades, or access a bank's computer to change your credit rating? If you have a strong code of personal morals, you probably would choose to do the right thing in each case. Your conscience would tell you to follow a code of *computer ethics* based on your other beliefs of right and wrong. Computer ethics are the standards by which we judge the correct uses of computers.

Unfortunately, an act may seem less serious when it occurs at a computer than it would seem in front of other human beings. This is because people see a computer as an impersonal machine. The pain felt by a victim of thieves is not so obvious when the theft occurs by hitting a few keys rather than by mugging someone on the street. In addition, finding the computer criminal—or even the crime—is sometimes very hard.

Attempts to govern computer activity present problems as well. Some computer experts believe that any limiting of access to any type of computer activity constitutes a violation of free speech and access to information. Even so, the content of messages sent over computer networks must be protected from prying eyes and censorship.

Bulletin board systems (BBSs), especially, can fall prey to misuse. Although users should be able to express personal opinions freely, they should not be able to post access codes to company computers, describe methods of building weapons, or insert programs called *viruses* that could destroy other users' software and data files. Yet, when the Secret Service attempted to shut down dozens of computer bulletin boards in order to stop a group of youthful computer enthusiasts suspected of trafficking in stolen credit-card numbers, telephone access codes, and other similar information, their actions raised a free-speech issue. Civil libertarians hold that those bulletin boards should be fully protected by the Constitution.

To safeguard the potential of free and open inquiry—and yet limit criminal activities such as those just mentioned—there must be adequate (but not repressive) legislation in place. The law has yet to catch up with the technology. Even so, civil libertarians will be active in finding ways to protect individual rights in *cyberspace*—that universe occupied by audio and video signals traveling across state and national borders at nearly the speed of light.

In addition, computer users must assume responsibility for their own actions; any standards will be meaningless if people cannot (or will not) govern their own behavior. If you use bulletin boards or electronic mail frequently, for example, you should never send something you don't have the nerve to say to someone face to face. Assume that someone other than the intended receiver is "listening"—that is, reading. Your words may be recorded for posterity.

(See 5.2 Computer Crime; 5.3 Hacking; 5.4 Viruses; 5.6 Privacy Issues; 5.9 Security Measures; 5.11 Copyright and Piracy.)

5.2 Computer Crime

Computer-related crime is more of a problem than most people realize. Americans are losing billions of dollars every year to high-tech thieves whose activities often go undetected and unpunished. Estimates of losses range from at least $2 billion to more than $40 billion per year. No one really knows how much is being stolen, but the total appears to be rising rapidly.

The term *computer crime* covers two types of activities: using a computer to commit crime, and damaging actual hardware, software, or data. The criminal may change computer input or programs in order to get money, data, or even merchandise. He may steal computer time or software from an employer or a school. Sometimes the criminal destroys the hardware or software. The basic categories of computer crime are outlined here:

- **Theft of services** includes using a government's or company's computer for activities that involve personal gain. For example, a politician might use a city's computer to conduct campaign mailings, or a professor might sell university data to outside businesses.
- **Theft of property** occurs when a person steals merchandise from a company whose orders are processed by computer. These crimes are usually committed by internal personnel who have the knowledge of the operations. Through record manipulation, dummy accounts can be created that direct a product order to be shipped to an accomplice outside the organization. Two other common property crimes are the theft of computer equipment itself, and software piracy (which is the topic of section 5.11).
- **Financial crimes** are those committed when a person uses a computer to make out multiple checks to the same person, or to reroute checks to false addresses. Another financial crime is *round-off fraud*, in which the thief collects fractions of cents from customers' bank accounts each time interest rates are figured. These fractions are then stored in an account created by the thief. The theory is that fractions of cents collected from thousands of accounts on a regular basis will someday yield a substantial amount of money. Another financial crime involves creating favorable (but false) credit histories for profit.
- **Sabotage** results in the damage of computer hardware, programs, and data. Although it can occur through physical means, it also happens when someone introduces a virus into the system. A *virus* is a set of software lines that makes something happen to a computer system, without the owners and users knowing it until it's too late to prevent disruption or damage.

Most crimes covered by the term *computer crime* are called *white-collar crimes* because they are committed by professional people or office employees who have easy access to computer systems and data. For example, an angry programmer may leave a little "present" in the form of a few programming lines that destroy data months after he is fired. A data-entry clerk may stumble on a way to siphon off a few cents from the interest on all the savings accounts in a bank. An accountant may copy a company's expensive spreadsheet and database software for her own use at home.

Even people who use online information services or electronic bulletin boards may be tempted to commit computer crime. More and more people are using telecommunications to call online information services. Problems occur when people do not pay for these services, or when they misuse the data they get. Accessing an online information service without paying the fees is illegal. In addition, users must be careful about using data they can download from the service. *Downloading* means moving data from a remote computer to the user's computer for later use. Most users scan the data, and download material for teaching and research. They do not want to pay connection fees for long periods of use, when they can print or store the data for leisurely study. The problems with this practice arise when large amounts of data are downloaded and claimed as the user's own original material. Misuse of data from online databases is hard to detect, however; the final use of that data still depends on the user's code of ethics.

State computer-crime laws have become the principal weapon used by prosecutors against illegal acts. In their quest to provide an adequate deterrence against computer crime, most state legislatures have enacted extremely broad and harsh statutes. In the state of Ohio, for example, it is a felony to "approach a computer system with the intent to do anything that is unauthorized." Individuals convicted under this statute would receive sentences approximating those received by criminals committing an equivalent crime armed with weapons. Juries have a difficult time understanding the justification for any unauthorized access to computer files; defense is difficult in such cases. As a result, most such cases have resulted in plea bargains—often adverse to the defendant—to avoid a trial.

(See 5.1 Criminal Conduct and Ethics: Responsibility for Computer Actions; 5.3 Hacking; 5.4 Viruses; 5.6 Privacy Issues; 5.9 Security Measures; 5.11 Copyright and Privacy.)

5.3 HACKING

Hacking is the activity of computer enthusiasts who are challenged to explore every potential of a computer. Although it originally had a positive connotation, describing hardworking and persistent programmers, it is now commonly used to describe unsavory activity. (The term *cracker* now refers to a hacker bent upon malicious activity, as opposed to the hacker merely obsessed with cybernetic curiosity.)

Whether hacking or cracking, the activity often includes breaking computer security measures designed to prevent unauthorized access to a particular computer system. Hackers do this with a number of goals in mind. Sometimes they do it to find out about different types of operating systems, or simply for the challenge. Less benign goals include gaining access to confidential data, getting illegal computer time, and using services (such as long distance calling or online information services) without charge. Regardless of motivation, some types of hacking are criminal acts prohibited by state and federal statutes.

One example of computer hacking made national headlines when a group of high school computer buffs in Milwaukee were discovered accessing numerous information systems—including those of banks, hospitals, and the defense research center in Los Alamos, New Mexico. The students reportedly gained access by using each system's password. Some of the passwords had not been changed for years, and others were obtained from public sources. After being caught, the students stated they had not seen any classified information, but that they had accidentally erased some files. The same group of students had also accessed a computer used to monitor 250 cancer patients in a New York cancer center; the students' activity caused the computer to fail for a short time. Questioned about why they behaved this way, the group said they did not know it was a crime, and that it gave them something to do in the evenings.

A major purpose of criminal hacking is, of course, to get an access code, and access codes are at the heart of a major problem for businesses: telephone *toll fraud*. The culprits use telephone credit card and account numbers to make long-distance calls. They even gain access to 800-number accounts, tying up a company's 800 number and sticking the company with bogus calls. Hackers often get access to a company's long distance telephone account by using *autodialers*, computer programs that repeatedly do the dialing and punch in the access codes until access is established. (In the United States, you can legally redial only up to 15 times.)

Companies that use PBX systems are particularly vulnerable if they take advantage of *direct inward system access* (DISA). This capability allows traveling employees to call the home office and enter a code that (in turn) enables them to make long distance calls on the company's account. To protect themselves against this type of phone fraud, companies that use PBX systems should ask the telephone company to disable remote-access features, or limit their use to business hours. They could also install a *call-back modem system*, in which the user calls the system, enters the access code, hangs up, and waits for the system to call him back. Most call-back modem systems can also require the user to phone only from authorized locations.

Access codes are not always discovered through computer programs, however. Many are acquired from telephone company employees, company dumpsters, the airwaves (from cellular phone use), and at public telephones. Those who use binoculars or video cameras (or simply good eyesight) to spy on people making telephone-credit-card calls at public phones are called "shoulder surfers." Although hackers often use these access codes, the big-league "telecrooks" are organized crime and drug dealers. Some may even set up store fronts as locations for "customers" to "buy" long-distance calls.

Having access codes also enables hackers to enter and wreak havoc in a voice-mail system. This happened to International Data Group, Inc., a publisher and trade-show operator with publications such as *PC World*, *Network World*, and *Computerworld*. In September 1990, company employees using their voice-mailboxes found that instead of the normal greetings and messages, there were vulgar messages, bomb threats, and gibberish. The problems kept on happening for weeks. The hackers, a couple of teenage boys from Staten Island, were angry because a poster they'd ordered through the company's *GamePro* magazine had never arrived. They received little punishment from authorities.

Some states have enacted laws against hacking; at the federal level, the Computer Fraud and Abuse Act of 1986 provides protection against computer abuse in a few areas. For example, an individual is prohibited from knowingly accessing a computer without authorization to obtain information that is protected by the Right to Financial Privacy Act of 1978, or information contained in the file of a consumer reporting agency. An individual is also prohibited from knowingly accessing a government computer or the computer of a financial institution and using, modifying, destroying, or disclosing information stored in the computer, or interfering with the regular use of the computer.

More recently, concern has focused on abuses during the actual transmission of data. This concern led to the drafting of the Electronic Communication Privacy Act of 1986, which prohibits outside interception of data communications—for example, of electronic mail—by a third party such as police, a government, or an individual without proper authorization. The act also makes it illegal for a provider of electronic communications services to knowingly divulge the contents of a communication, except to the intended parties. This law does not protect e-mail transmitted within one company, however.

(See 4.12 Bulletin Board Systems; 4.14 Online Services; 5.1 Criminal Conduct and Ethics: Responsibility for Computer Actions; 5.2 Computer Crime; 5.4 Viruses; 5.6 Privacy Issues; 5.9 Security Measures.)

5.4 Viruses

There has been at least one instance of commercial software being infected by a virus. Aldus Corporation unwittingly made thousands of copies of a graphics software package named Freehand that was contaminated with the so-called "Peace" virus. On March 2, 1988, a universal message of peace was displayed on the screens of several thousand Macintosh computers when they were turned on. The viral program then deleted itself.

Some of the recent viruses are not as innocuous as the Peace virus. Two brothers in a computer store in Lahore, Pakistan, sold cut-rate software that they infected with a virus. When the software disk was inserted into a computer, the virus would copy itself into the computer's memory, where it would later be copied onto other disks placed into the machine. It would then scramble the contents of these disks. The brothers said they created the virus to punish purchasers of bootlegged software.

So what is a *virus*? It's a program that can change the way a computer operates, or change the programs or data files stored on the computer, without the knowledge of the computer's owner or user. The virus copies itself onto another program by adding itself to the program, or by overwriting some of the code in the program. Its primary task is replication.

Examples include Stoned, which displays the message, "Your PC is stoned—LEGALIZE MARIJUANA" while at the same time destroying the information that makes it possible to access files on your disk. The Cascade virus makes all characters on the screen collapse to the bottom of the display, ruining the information. The Joshi virus is a *bomb* (any computer virus triggered by a date, time, or event), as is Jerusalem-B, which erases any program you try to run on any Friday the 13th, and writes black boxes to your screen (blotting out your data).

Another variation on the virus is the *worm*, a self-contained program that works its way through computer systems. In early March 1988, a computer-science graduate student released a worm that ultimately jammed 6,000 computers around the United States. Within 24 hours, it had spread to approximately 100,000 computers. The worm was passed through the Internet, a network tying together a large number of university and government computer systems. The worm wound itself through the computers, using up valuable computer time and memory space. Fortunately, this was a relatively "benign" worm that did not destroy data—but it did cost a fortune in computer time, as personnel spent hundreds of hours cleaning up their infected systems. Another variation of the virus is the *Trojan Horse*—a useful program that hides a destructive program. When triggered, it causes damage such as erasing a hard disk. At least it does not replicate like a virus.

To compound the difficulties, a new generation of highly destructive "stealth" viruses appear to be spreading into some systems. Their authors have designed them to avoid detection by antivirus software, much as a Stealth bomber is designed to avoid radar detection. These viruses are also difficult to remove once found. They demonstrate that virus writers are becoming more skilled at hiding their work from detection. The most successful virus has no symptoms, but you may suspect a virus if any of the following problems occur:

- Changes in program length
- Slow operation
- Unexplained disk activities
- Unexplained reductions in memory or disk space
- Unusual screen activity or error messages
- Changes in times or dates
- Failure of a program to execute

Some of these problems may be due to factors other than viruses, but if your system has more than one such symptom, scanning for viruses is a good idea.

Viruses and their variations are difficult to avoid because many microcomputer users use a variety of disks and networking systems. For example, electronic bulletin boards may contain infected public-domain software that users download and use on their microcomputers. It is easy for the authors of viruses to insert them into such programs; potentially the virus can infect any computer used to download the software. It is estimated that only about 7 percent of viruses enter a system through a modem, however. Instead, most users get viruses from using shared floppy disks that contain legitimate programs or demo programs.

About 180 companies in the United States alone are in the business of marketing computer security products and services to prevent virus problems. International Data Corporation, a research company, estimates that the market for these products is about $3 billion annually. Products include *antivirus* programs designed to detect and ward off viruses, and *password generators* that create new passwords automatically to keep ahead of hackers who try to break into a system using stolen security codes.

Antivirus programs can scan new software to block incoming viruses, or can ferret out established viruses. They identify viruses by searching a system for program-code patterns unique to each known computer virus. They can identify where the virus resides—in memory or in a file, for example, or in the special start-up area of a disk (known as the *boot sector*)—and then destroy the virus. Most antivirus programs have a *terminate-and-stay resident* module that stays in RAM and monitors your system constantly for viruses. Other antivirus programs simply inform you when an unauthorized program is being copied into your computer's main memory. A problem with antivirus software, however, is that often it is not updated frequently enough to deal with new strains of viruses.

One antivirus program is Norton AntiVirus (or for the Mac, SAM—Symantec Antivirus for the Macintosh) from Symantec in Cupertino, California. Both versions check drives for infections; they also help delete or repair infected files. FluShot Plus, from Software Concepts Design, New York City, checks for viruses each time a program is executed. A program called Checkup, written by Richard Levin of Philadelphia, compares files to see if they have been changed. Other programs include the Viruscan series from McAfee Associates, Certus International's Novi, Disinfectant by John Norstad, and Virex from Datawatch Corporation. Ontrack Computer Systems produces Dr. Solomon's Anti-Virus Toolkit, another popular and effective antivirus program. Some antivirus programs are available through a BBS run by Computer Virus Industry Association, and some software manufacturers include virus blockers and detectors with their software packages.

John Norstad's Disinfectant anti virus program is free. You can get it from most online services and MUGs, or send a self-addressed, stamped envelope and an 800K floppy disk to John Norstad, Academic Computing and Network Services, Northwestern University, 2129 Campus Drive North, Evanston, Illinois, 60208.

Most computer professionals believe that the best protection for the average user is common sense. Here are some points they make:

- Back up data files frequently; use recommended antivirus software to scan files and programs regularly for viruses.
- If you use a repair program after discovering a virus, always rescan; the first virus may have hidden another virus.
- If you do find a virus on your computer, be sure to check all of your floppy disks for the virus after you have "disinfected" your system.
- Be careful who you allow to use your computer. Use only your own disks. If there is a chance that someone else will be using your computer without your knowing it, consider purchasing a *password-protection program*.
- Don't buy a software package that looks like the shrink-wrap has been changed or tampered with. If at all possible, scan any new software with your antivirus program before you install it.

- Access networks, bulletin boards, and databases with caution. You cannot get a virus by logging onto a BBS or by leaving messages, so before using any programs or data from a system, ask the bulletin board sysop whether all programs available for downloading have been checked for viruses. If you see that a BBS contains pirated copies of commercial software, beware. Viruses often travel on bootleg programs. Commercial online information services are generally virus-free, and the majority of system operators (sysops) of bulletin boards are also conscientious about checking for viruses.
- If you do download a program from a BBS, test it from a floppy disk if you can. If you must use the hard disk, put all other program files in their own subdirectory to isolate them. The virus may affect only the current directory or subdirectory. Never install untested software of any kind in the root directory. If a program does not list the author's name, address, and telephone number, do not run it.
- Do not copy programs from friends or business associates. This is one of the most common ways that viruses are passed between microcomputers. Even computer technicians can pick up a virus from one customer and pass it along to another on a disk.
- Do not buy bootlegged software.
- Watch your system for signs of trouble, such as unusually slow loading or processing times, or unusual error messages.

Following these rules will go a long way toward preventing most viral infections.

(See 5.2 Computer Crime; 5.3 Hacking; 5.9 Security Measures; Software Review section: Symantec AntiVirus for Macintosh, Untouchable DOS.)

5.5 Computer Errors

Everyone has heard stories about massive computer mistakes. These stories seem to be favorites of newspaper and broadcast journalists. A classic concerned the man who was declared dead because of a computer error. Social security payments stopped, pension benefits ceased, and the infamous red tape began. "So sorry, but if the computer claims you are deceased, you *are* deceased. Computers do not make mistakes... ." Of course, computer errors do happen. Some can be funny, but others are downright annoying. If you are affected, you want to know who was responsible for the mess.

Barring hardware breakdown, computers do not make errors—but incorrect software can certainly wreak havoc. Greater sophistication and increased complexity can also mean a more vulnerable program. Software is measured in *lines*, each of which instructs the computer to carry out a specific task. Ten years ago, a long program contained a few thousand lines of code. Today, a word-processor program can contain 50,000 lines; the software for a jumbo jet may use well over a million lines. You can see that the potential for errors is tremendous. Even *hard-wired software*—that is, software built into chips—is not exempt from error. A recent example is a design problem in the Intel Pentium chip, which has caused certain rarely performed division calculations to deliver the wrong answer.

Software failure costs the nation more than a billion dollars each year. An example of a massive failure is the AT&T snafu in January of 1990 that left 65 million calls unconnected. A single misplaced line—among the three million lines of computer instructions designed to handle phone calls—shut down the company's long distance service for nine hours. Computer errors can produce questionable election results, allow customers to withdraw unlimited amounts of cash from automatic teller machines, or instruct a machine to deliver fatal doses of radiation during cancer therapy. The problem is that it would take years to run through every conceivable contingency to see if a particular large program will fail.

By far the most common type of mistake is *input error*, the so-called *garbage in, garbage out (GIGO)* principle. If information going into a computer contains mistakes, the information coming out cannot be correct. Incorrect input comes from two main sources: errors in source information or keyboard-entry mistakes.

An offbeat example shows how computers can magnify human error. An order from Army offices near Colorado Springs, Colorado, resulted in a shipment of a ship's anchor to a landlocked U.S. Army base. A maintenance unit at the fort ordered a $6.04 incandescent lamp, and wound up with a $28,560 anchor, probably built for use on a destroyer or light cruiser. The anchor's journey began in early March, when the lamp was requisitioned via computer. Instead of keying the correct order number, 2040-00-368-4972, a clerk entered 2040-00-368-4772, the order number for "anchor, marine fluke." Because the order number did correspond with an available item, the computer validated the order. The anchor was shipped from Sharpe Army Depot in Lathrop, California, and arrived at Fort Carson on March 25. Someone astutely observed that it was not a lamp.

Another cause of computer errors is that the program does not anticipate every possibility. For example, if a program does not take into account the possibility that this year may be leap year, a bank's customers could lose one day's interest.

A third type of error occurs when the input is right and the program is right, but the answer is wrong. These errors can be generated by a failure to consider the limitations of real and integer arithmetic or by physical causes such as a power surge or a damaged disk. Theoretically, even cosmic rays can interfere with computer operations, but that possibility is extremely slight.

A fourth way to generate a computer error is to design a program—unintentionally—that does not give the same response as a person would in a similar situation. A prime example of this type of error involved a stop-payment order on a check. A corporate customer of a large bank ordered a stop payment on check number 896, drawn on account number 02042178315, dated February 27, for $1,844.48. The actual amount of the check, however, was $1,844.98. When the computer processed the check, it noted the 50-cent difference, and issued payment. The error resulted in a lawsuit in which the judge ruled that, because a human operator would not have issued the payment on the check, the bank was liable for the amount.

A fifth kind of error involves hackers who enter a system and change data, or introduce some programming code. Errors can range from a few cents siphoned from accounts in a bank to altered dosages of drugs or radiation treatment for patients in a hospital.

Although computer errors are often obvious, figuring out who is responsible is not. Is the programmer personally responsible for errors that are written in a program? Or does the company using the program assume responsibility when it purchases the program? Should the data-entry operator be held responsible for input errors? Or is it management's responsibility to check the information once it is captured? There is, for that matter, little legal guidance in dealing with computer mistakes. Can an organization be ruled "not responsible" for an error made because a hacker entered the computer system and changed or erased data? Or does the organization have a responsibility to keep backup data and check its validity often? And how often is "often"? Can computers really be expected to act as human beings would?

The probability of failure has become, justifiably, a major area of concern and serious study. For example, it is known that a complex system with 1,000 components, each 99.9 percent reliable, has a 50 percent probability of failure at any given time. The rule of thumb: Anything that can fail, will. Thus, part of the planning for development and use of any computer system should include creation of scenarios that picture potential failures. This process has been called "constructive worrying." Constructive worrying should be used when programs are designed to automate jet flight or run traffic control systems. It must be used to create realistic backup plans and ways to soften the blow of inevitable failures and intrusions. It can result in fail-safes ranging from simple office practices to the duplication of entire systems in case a disaster does occur.

(See 5.3 Hacking.)

5.6 Privacy Issues

A California woman could not rent an apartment because her name was in a computer database of renters who had caused trouble with previous landlords. A woman in Illinois failed to get an appointment with the doctor of her choice because the doctor she called checked a service called Physicians' Alert. This service lists patients who have filed civil suits against doctors, and sure enough, the woman's name was there. A man in New York could not get a job after trying for months. Finally, he got a notice for dishonorable discharge from the army—but he had never been in the army. That was when he realized that a former college roommate was using his name and Social Security number. The roommate had racked up jail records and bad credit ratings, all of which were attributed to the New York man without his knowledge.

Computers are the main means by which businesses and governments collect and store information about people. Thus, many people face problems like these when their names get into databases, often without their knowledge. Their privacy is invaded when things are happening to their personal information of which they are unaware.

Privacy is simply the right to be left alone. It means people have a right to decide what, when, and how personal data may be shared with others. It includes the right to have personal information protected from abuse. Computers, however, make it so easy to get information that privacy is often forgotten. When all this data was kept on paper files, it was harder to access it; outdated paper files were often destroyed to make room for new ones. Computer storage, however, has made it much easier to keep large amounts of data for longer periods of time.

If you are an average U.S. citizen, data about you appears in 39 federal, state, and local government databases, and in 40 private files. Computers have made the collection and storage of this data easier, and have made the exchange of this data quick, easy, and cheap. In fact, collecting and storing data by computer is so easy that organizations collect far too much—including data they do not really need. The federal government is the largest collector of data. The government's databases hold information about anyone who has served in the armed forces, had a physical or mental disability, had a driver's license suspended, committed a crime, received Social Security benefits, owned a boat, traveled to foreign countries, or completed an income tax return.

The schools you attend and the companies you work for are also finding it easier to use computers for storing files. These files are probably the most complete records kept about you. Information entered into the files may include school grades, standardized test scores, behavior evaluations, work records, results of psychological and physical exams, stays in hospitals and clinics, transfers, personal references, and disciplinary actions. Other organizations collect data, too—banks, credit agencies, insurance groups, and hospitals. So you can see that it would be hard for you to keep track of who has data about you.

Concern about the unauthorized use of data was highlighted by a fracas over Lotus MarketPlace. This product is a database on CD-ROM that provided detailed demographic data on households and businesses in the United States. After a deluge of protests from people who feared the product would violate their privacy, Lotus canceled MarketPlace just before its release.

The problem was not the availability of data; most of it was already maintained on mainframes and minicomputers. Rather, the concern focused on the fact that the data could be accessed and used easily and cheaply—in effect, by "just anyone." Thus, the major concerns about the issue of privacy can be summarized as follows:

- Too much personal data about individuals is collected and stored in computer files. This data is too easy to access and share, and too difficult to challenge and change.
- Organizations often make decisions based solely on the contents of these files.
- Much of the personal data collected about individuals may not be relevant to every purpose for which it can be used.
- The accuracy, completeness, and currency of the data may be unacceptably low.
- The security of stored data is a problem.

Despite the problems involved in creating and keeping data collections, organizations do need data. Using computers to store data can save time and money, alert organizations to risks, and help in making decisions by providing the most current information. Businesses need it for choosing employees and deciding how to spend money. Schools need data in order to check the progress of students and improve teaching methods. Hospitals need data to be able to treat patients properly, and to get paid for their services. Companies need data so they can make decisions about new products and the effectiveness of advertising. The government benefits from data by finding abusers of government services, which in turn benefits taxpayers. Consumers want their credit-card purchases approved quickly and want to be able to cash checks anywhere, so they voluntarily provide personal information whenever they fill out forms for warranties, health-care providers, credit-card applications, and club memberships.

(See 5.3 Hacking; 5.5 Computer Errors; 5.7 Privacy Legislation; 5.8 Data Vendors; 5.9 Security Measures; 5.10 Employee Monitoring Systems.)

5.7 Privacy Legislation

How can we deal with an organization's need for information and still protect each person's privacy? Several laws have been passed that address this question. For example, the Fair Credit Reporting Act of 1970 protects people against false information about their credit histories. Sometimes files contain errors that prevent people from getting credit cards or taking out a loan for a new home. The law lets people see their credit histories so that they can challenge and correct errors.

The most sweeping federal legislation is the Privacy Act of 1974. This act gives people the right to see information kept about them by federal agencies, and gives people the right to correct inaccurate information. Under this law, the government cannot keep records about a person's religious or political beliefs. A big part of the Privacy Act limits how a government agency can use data. A government agency must tell a person if it wants to use personal information for purposes other than those originally planned. It must also safeguard the contents of files and databases, but there is a loophole: if an agency wants data for "routine use," little notice is needed. The loophole allows government agencies to cross-check the files of different agencies. These cross-checks, sometimes called "computer matching," let the government find people who do not pay off student loans or keep up their child-support payments. The government can also help to locate people who get unlawful government funding, or who pay too little in income taxes.

Other federal privacy legislation includes the following:

- The Freedom of Information Act (1970) allows individuals to have access to data about themselves that was collected by federal agencies. (A lawsuit may be necessary to get the data, however.)
- The Family Education Rights and Privacy Act (1974) regulates access to computer-stored records of grades and behavior evaluations kept by public and private schools.
- The Right to Financial Privacy Act (1978) limits federal government access to the customer records of financial institutions.

Many state laws are patterned after the federal laws. They are generally similar to each other, varying mostly in how each state defines a particular term or violation. Some state laws address the unlawful access to databases in even more detail than federal laws. For example, South Dakota has a provision that prohibits the disclosure of passwords. In Hawaii, all unauthorized computer use is considered a felony. Idaho laws, on the other hand, make a distinction between accessing information (a misdemeanor) and altering information (a felony).

Much still needs to be done about guarding data. There are many loopholes and ambiguous parameters in existing privacy laws. Both states and the federal government need to pass effective legislation—and to prosecute offenders just as effectively. One such effort was the Computer Matching and Privacy Protection Act of 1988, which sets up procedures (and exceptions) for the computer matching of federal data.

Even with current legislation, however, relatively few cases of information and privacy violation have been litigated. One problem of privacy violation is that data is transferred and disclosed without the knowledge or consent of the subjects; people are not likely to know how data about them is used, and may not realize they have a claim to take to court. Furthermore, privacy litigation is somewhat contradictory in concept. By taking claims to court, litigants may expose private aspects of their lives to a far greater extent than did the initial intrusion.

(See 5.3 Hacking; 5.5 Computer Errors; 5.8 Data Vendors; 5.9 Security Measures; 5.10 Employee Monitoring Systems.)

5.8 DATA VENDORS

If you own a business and want to hire a receptionist and a couple of production workers, what can you ask the people who apply for the jobs? The information you can legally require varies from state to state, but may include the following:

- Convictions for crime
- Performance at previous jobs
- Moving violations and accidents
- Workers' compensation claims
- Medical history

You cannot ask an applicant about these items:

- Marital status
- Age
- Citizenship
- Race
- Religion
- Lifestyle

- Children
- Arrest record, with no convictions

Today, however, many employers want as much information as they can get about prospective employees; businesses face rising costs from thefts and other crimes committed by workers. Often, previous employers are afraid of libel suits, and refrain from giving negative references. Polygraphs in the workplace are illegal, too, and questioning applicants can be a legal minefield if employers ask the wrong questions.

If employers can't get the information they want from the applicant or from the previous place of employment, they may turn to *data vendors* such as Equifax and Apscreen. Through these vendors, they can get credit files, school records, driving violations, insurance claims, purchasing habits, and assorted other information they feel would help them decide whether to hire an applicant.

Once upon a time, all the records were on paper, and after a period of years, many files were destroyed to make room for more. Today, however, disk storage makes it possible to keep records much longer, meaning that employers can learn about events that happened years ago. Figures show that the additional information has reduced theft and turnover by weeding out potentially problematic employees.

Getting data is so popular that the data-vending industry has grown to $1 billion per year. The largest data vendors generally have reputations for thoroughness and accuracy. Most do remind customers that their data should be just one aspect of the pre-employment investigation. Getting data from such a source may be expensive, however, running anywhere from $100 to thousands of dollars for each applicant. Thus, some employers resort to cut-rate dealers in data. These dealers compile data from courthouses, motor-vehicle departments, credit bureaus, and other sources. The problem is that some of the data from the cut-rate dealers cannot be used legally when hiring someone.

(See 5.1 Criminal Conduct and Ethics: Responsibility for Computer Actions; 5.6 Privacy Issues.)

5.9 Security Measures

The amount of security needed for any system is based on four factors:

- The value of the hardware
- The value of the software
- The cost of replacing the hardware, software, or data
- The cost of the security controls

Most security problems are accidents: errors, omissions, fires, and so on. With careful planning and proper training, companies and individuals can avoid these problems—often at little cost. If you own a small business or use your company's data files on your computer at home, you may want to follow a few simple steps to avoid problems:

- Be sure to make backup copies. (Some experts like to present the topic of backup as "restoration" in order to stress that, rather than a chore, backing up data is an important individual or company priority.) In the case of important data, keep copies at a location other than your home, and be sure these copies are updated frequently.
- Use a password program if you do not want other people using your computer without your knowledge.
- Attach a surge suppressor to your system to prevent problems caused by uneven delivery of electrical power.
- Use hard disk drives you can remove or lock up.

The problem of computer crime, however, is hard to control completely. The list that follows suggests some ways that organizations can deal with theft, privacy, and piracy. These methods can be adapted even for small, home-based businesses:

- Set up procedures for acquiring and registering software. Log all resources, and conduct regular audits to review the whereabouts of the resources.
- Define ethical behavior for all employees, and set standards for hiring and training. (Sample codes are available from the Software Publishers Association in Washington, D.C., at 202-452-1600.)
- Deal with misuse immediately.
- If you use a password system, change the passwords a few times per year.
- Watch for careless behavior, such as taping passwords to drawers or throwing out important printouts without shredding them.
- Lock the computer room, if necessary.
- Scramble sensitive data.
- Use dial-back measures to guard telephone access. Dial-back requires the user to telephone the computer, give a password, and then hang up. If the user and password check out, the computer calls the user back and allows access. The user must also call from the correct location.
- As one method of protection against viruses, restrict employees from using their own software on company machines.

In order to stop crime, some large organizations have combined several security measures. Access to a computer is granted only after users pass several tests. In such a test, a user may be required to supply the following:

- Something known, such as passwords.
- Something given, such as fingerprints, nose prints, or even a picture of eyeballs.
- Something done, such as writing signatures.
- Something owned, such as magnetic cards or electronic keys.

The equipment used to evaluate the test may be too expensive for small, home-based businesses. In addition, many security measures can still be overcome by a smart technician. In the end, you must depend on the ethical behavior of your colleagues.

(See 5.1 Criminal Conduct and Ethics: Responsibility for Computer Actions; 5.2 Computer Crime; 5.3 Hacking; 5.4 Viruses.)

5.10 Employee Monitoring Systems

Once you hire people, how do you keep track of their work? Use a discreetly placed surveillance camera? Listen in on telephone conversations with customers? Monitor by computer the number of keystrokes an employee types?

Often, reservation clerks and people who take orders from catalog customers are monitored for voice, manner, and accuracy. Some companies mount fish-eye cameras behind pinholes in walls to check on employees suspected of crime. There are even special chairs that can record how much an employee fidgets, implying that a fidgeter is not working. Employers justify the practices on the grounds that they need to know if a worker is being accurate and polite over the phone, if a worker is walking away with company property in her lunch box, or if an employee is wasting company time.

In defense of employers, a company can be liable for a worker's crimes or negligence on the job if an applicant is not screened properly for potential problems. A company also needs to track thefts that occur once applicants are hired. The key is to avoid being sloppy about how surveillance, questioning, and information-gathering is done. Within legal bounds, a company can protect itself by videotaping or checking employees' lunch boxes, but it may want to have employees sign waivers for such surveillance, and distribute copies of search policies.

The company should follow the policies closely, and even inform employees that surreptitious snooping may occur, and that refusal to permit it may get an employee disciplined or fired. By no means should a company say one thing and do another. For example, a company that implies e-mail messages are private should not be monitoring those messages. Before implementing any surveillance measures, however, a company should check the current laws and legal guidelines that prevent it from abusing an employee's right to privacy and freedom from harassment. In addition, employers should be aware that a system that assumes ill behavior on the part of employees can have adverse effects. In fact, such a system can lead to outright confrontation. Companies interested in fostering higher productivity and ethical behavior may find setting a tone of cooperation much more effective than setting up a surveillance system.

(See 5.9 Security Measures.)

5.11 Copyright and Piracy

Software is protected primarily by the U.S. Copyright Act of 1978. The creator of an original work possesses a copyright from the moment the work is fixed in some tangible medium, such as hard copy or disk storage. Since March 1, 1989, when the United States became a member of the International Berne Copyright Convention, most formal requirements of registration and identification have become optional.

Because of numerous legal advantages and relatively minor cost, however, authors should register their works with the Copyright Office and place a copyright notice on all copies of their works. (A *copyright notice* includes the sign ©, the word *copyright* or the abbreviation *copr.*, along with the name of the copyright owner and the year of the work's first publication.) Once a work is copyrighted, it is against the law to copy it for any purpose other than archival use. *Archival copying* covers the backup copy that you make of purchased software in case something happens to destroy the original copy.

It is critical to understand that ownership of a software copyright does not always belong to the programmer. If an employee develops a program using either the resources of the corporation or trade secrets derived from employment, the corporation is the owner of the copyright. If you are planning to create either software or databases for commercial purposes and the ownership issue is unclear, consult legal counsel for guidance. A parallel concern is the concept of *joint copyright*, where more than one individual or corporation contributed to the creation of the program. Copyright protection relates to the expression of the idea; in the case of software, only the program code and screen designs are protected by copyright—whereas the purpose, concept, or methodology of the program are not.

If the idea behind the software or database is unique and novel, its creator should consider patent protection, despite the significant cost ($3,000 to $5,000).

Software piracy is the illegal copying of copyrighted software. It includes making copies of copyrighted software for resale to a friend or other person, and copying software that belongs to a friend or a business for personal use. Most current legal cases about copyrights involve illegal bulletin board uses, corporate misuses, and the sale of pirated software. With estimates of losses being in the $10-billion range each year worldwide, these cases are being heavily investigated and prosecuted.

A current focus is on China, where Microsoft, Lotus Development, and Autodesk are filing suit against Chinese retailers they claim are selling—both in China and as exports—computers loaded with pirated programs. In the United States, a company can be held liable for piracy even if the copying is done without a manager's knowledge. In contrast, individuals who copy software for personal use will probably not be caught, but they are breaking the law nonetheless. Their behavior becomes a matter of personal ethics. Because they listen to their consciences, most people will not make copies of their software for a friend's use, and they would not dream of selling pirated programs. In addition, most computer users know that if they use pirated software, they also run the risk of getting a virus, compliments of the pirate.

Some software manufacturers do not rely solely on copyright law to protect their software. They protect their software with codes that make copying disks hard, or that destroy some data when a disk is copied. This practice became less popular after 1983, when the major software companies decided to "unlock" their disks because of the inconvenience of copy-protection codes. The codes prevent users from making an archival copy (which is legal), and may also prevent the use of the software with hard disk drives. Manufacturers of game and entertainment software may still use a form of off-disk copy protection that requires you to type a special number, word, or code that you find on a special card that you cannot photocopy, or on a page selected at random in the user's manual that comes with the software.

Most people never think about what to do with software they can no longer use because it doesn't work on their current computer, or because newer and better editions are available. Actually, when you buy software, you don't own it; you merely have a license to use it. In addition, the registered user has the legal right to use the software on one computer at a time, and normally this right covers only one user at a time. (This is important if, for example, you are using a local area network in your business; the restriction can be overcome by obtaining a *site license* that permits multiple users of the program on the network.) Accordingly, when you are finished with the software, you cannot legally sell it. Many software manufacturers will, however, suggest that you donate it to a school or other nonprofit organization. Software upgrade packages may include instructions about disposing of the old versions being replaced.

So far, we have discussed copyright as it pertains to entire programs. What do copyright laws have to say about using portions of a work? In most cases, you must have the permission of the author to use portions of a work; however, the law grants you *fair use* of a work. Most generally, this exception gives you the right to quote excerpts in a review or criticism to make a point, or in a scholarly work to support or illustrate a point. In addition, some authors give you permission to use material as long as you acknowledge the source in your work. For example, CorelDRAW! 4.0 includes 18,000 pieces of clip art on a CD-ROM. You cannot resell the clip art, but you can use it in newsletters or other publications as long as you say who produced the clip art. Some people feel that if you change an image such as clip art or a photograph, then you can claim it as your own. In fact, manipulating a copyrighted image makes it a *derivative work*; by copyright law, only the original authors can create derivative works.

(See 3.26 Public-Domain Software, Freeware, and Shareware; 5.1 Criminal Conduct and Ethics: Responsibility for Computer Actions; 5.2 Computer Crime.)

5.12 Computer Literacy and School Curriculum

One trend in education is the belief that every student should be able to use a computer. Some futurists believe that one day almost every type of job will require employees to use computers. Education will certainly change through computer use and access to databases. Most transactions will take place via computers and telecommunications. People with little computer experience will be profoundly affected because they will not be able to access a database, instruct a computer to do a task, or qualify for a job that requires a great deal of computer use. Therefore, some educators are pressing for extensive computer education in schools, a curriculum categorized as *computer literacy*. A course teaching computer literacy includes technical knowledge about computers, computer programming, using computers to solve problems, and awareness of how computers affect society.

There is a problem with trying to define computer literacy in terms of specific objectives: the objectives themselves change continuously to keep pace with developments in technology. Perhaps in no other industry in history have changes occurred as rapidly as in the computer field. As technology changes, the life experiences of members of society change; the definition of what is and is not important also changes.

This point can be illustrated by reviewing the approach to computer literacy in schools in the last 10 years. Early attempts at teaching computer literacy focused on computer history, terminology, and internal operations. Although that information is still recognized as important, the focus has changed from how a computer works to how a computer can help solve problems. The emphasis has moved from circuitry to applications. Literacy courses also examine the effects of computers on society. Knowing the history of computers, being able to give examples of current usage, and projecting future trends are all important to understanding how computers are changing our lives. More recently, in response to some forms of computer abuse, literacy courses are also including discussions on computer manners and ethics. Some states such as Texas, Tennessee, and New York are adopting objectives for computer literacy that indicate a student should reach a specific level of expertise by a specified point in his or her school career.

On the other hand, other researchers believe that computer education per se is largely overrated as a prerequisite for jobs. They say that only a small percentage of jobs will require actual knowledge of technical areas involving electronic circuits, computer programming, and hardware. Rather, they believe that reading and thinking skills and general knowledge will distinguish those who will be successful from those who will not. If computers are to be used, they must become tools for learning these skills. Any computer experience that non-technical jobs require can be easily taught to receptive learners. Even so, many educators, parents, and other adults—many of whom did not grow up comfortable with computer technology—have seen the computerization of the workplace and realize there is no turning back. They believe schools cannot be allowed to ignore computers, as the machines have radically altered jobs, entertainment, and home lives.

(See 3.44 Educational Software; 5.13 The Computer as Teacher; 5.14 Kids and Computers: At Home and Online.)

5.13 The Computer as Teacher

A question asked frequently during the 1980s centered on whether computers would replace teachers. The answer is a resounding "maybe." Common sense tells us there will be employment for teachers for many years to come. Problems with education and advances in computer software indicate, however, that computers will play a greater role in future education; some believe they will replace teachers to a great degree.

Computers can help teachers with their work, supporting such activities as self-paced student learning, preparation of grade reports, and development of tests and other instructional materials. As with educational films and television, computers can help link multiple schools into an integrated learning system. Use of videodiscs and CD-ROMs increases the amount of information available to students.

In the past, programs aimed at computer-assisted instruction have suffered from a common problem. Hardware has been ready—and often purchased and installed—before the software needed for its use could be completed and made available. As a result, many forward-looking schools that rushed into the purchase of computers in the late 1970s and early 1980s suffered frustrating setbacks. While they waited for additional software for use of their equipment, hardware manufacturers brought out more advanced hardware. When software came to market, much of it could not run on the computers previously purchased. Currently, the situation is improving. Millions of computers have been installed in elementary and secondary schools. More teachers are learning, both in their college preparation and at their places of employment, effective uses of computers in the classroom.

How could computers do a better job than some teachers? First and foremost, computers enable a student to progress at his or her own pace. Many programs enable students to learn new material through a series of guided exercises, or practice old material in computer drills. Second, computers are patient and do not give derisive feedback, such as "hurry up," "you'll never learn this," or "wrong." They enable students to go back and review material that is difficult without fear of being taunted about their slow speed. Third, each student has an opportunity to participate in an activity and to receive feedback about his or her work, something that is often lacking in classrooms with 30 or more students. Fourth, computer programs can help students learn boring-but-essential basic arithmetic tables, spelling, grammar, and other disciplines in an entertaining atmosphere. Fifth, software provides experiences that many students would not have in a structured classroom:

- Some programs simulate real-world events, allowing students to learn through experience and induction, without having to take actual risks such as blowing up the science lab or crashing a plane.
- Problem-solving software encourages exploration and application of previous knowledge.
- Multimedia enables students to learn material through several senses, and also to create their own multimedia presentations.
- Productivity software—word processing, database, desktop publishing, and so on—lets students organize and present their work, just as it helps adults be productive.
- Computers equipped with modems can link students with other students, teachers, and lessons from around the world.

Computers and programs hold great promise for assisting students and teachers in two essential areas: establishing expectations for achievement, and applying the discipline needed to acquire basic educational results. If a student lacks (as many do) the willpower to set personal expectations (or to form the study habits needed to follow through), a computer can help by being a hard taskmaster. It presents expectations and acts as a scorekeeper of student performance, providing an element of discipline while at the same time not deriding the student's efforts. Computers challenge students partly because they do not represent a threat or an authority; each student can deal with a computer on an individual basis. Beating a computer can also represent a challenge akin to that of beating a pinball machine or video game.

Although students respond well to computers in the classroom, the same has not been uniformly true for educators. Some classroom teachers see computers as threats. Other teachers denigrate the use of computers for drill and practice purposes. Still others resent the element of entertainment that is inherent in many educational programs, and that has inspired the term *edutainment*. There is room, however, for many uses of computers in the classroom; in reality, they will not be replacing teachers in the near future. Educators need to be aware that different learners have different levels of expectations and different tolerances for discipline; computers can serve as tools that help bring out the best in each. In addition, most teachers recognize the need for careful review of software to be sure the programs are accurate and worthwhile. The challenge for use of computers in education is to serve the students; in meeting that challenge, educators should believe that learning can be the most entertaining thing a person does in a lifetime.

(See 3.44 Educational Software; 5.12 Computer Literacy and School Curriculum; 5.14 Kids and Computers: At Home and Online.)

5.14 Kids and Computers: At Home and Online

We have all read the articles admonishing parents and teachers to expect high performance and competitive behavior from children, and we have read the opposite: Let children set their own pace and do not expect the moon. Computer literacy just provides one more arena for disagreement. How much should we push children toward using computers, and how important will knowing about computers be for their future? Perhaps the best approach is a balance between expectations and performance—a balance that encourages a child to explore the computer and learn to use it as a tool for further learning, rather than as an end in itself. Most parents handle such "balances" well, but they still may have specific questions about their children and computers. Some examples follow.

IF MY CHILD DOES NOT HAVE A COMPUTER AT HOME, WILL HE OR SHE LAG BEHIND AT SCHOOL?

You probably have read about the "haves" and the "have nots" in regards to knowing how to use computers: Those who have computer experience will advance much further in school and work than those who have not had computer experience. Some parents may be concerned that their children do not get to use computers often enough in school, yet feel they cannot afford even a low-end computer, much less the latest multimedia machine.

Although some statistics show that people with computer knowledge do advance more quickly in their work, what is overlooked is that people who are computer literate are often well educated in other areas as well—and their parents probably spent a lot of money for educational items. It is more important that children be able to read well, think clearly, and know where to look for answers to their questions. An inability to do these things will put a child far behind his or her grade level.

On the other hand, computer experience is important, and many students prepare school assignments with computers. If you cannot afford to buy a computer for your child, look for places such as public libraries or neighborhood computer centers where your child can use a computer for short periods of time. Perhaps you can afford a fairly recent used computer, or perhaps your child is willing to help earn some money toward the purchase of a computer.

HOW OLD SHOULD MY CHILD BE TO USE A COMPUTER?

Children vary in the speed of their development, so the ages of computer "readiness" also vary, though children can use computers at very early ages. Very young children can make things happen on-screen by using a touch screen or a mouse. At age 2 1/2 to 3, children recognize symbols; they may be able to use a very simple program with a little help from parents, though they may remain interested for only a few minutes. By ages 4 and 5, children can use a computer independently and remain interested for half an hour or longer. Parents can also encourage their children simply by using computers themselves.

WHAT TYPE OF SOFTWARE SHOULD I BUY?

With so many different educational and entertainment packages on the market, it is difficult to choose. Most reviews and recommendations, of course, cater to what the parent or educator thinks is "good" for children. To give children some control over purchases, take cues from what your children like to do. Children who paint and draw may like a painting program. Children who like music may want a program that helps them create songs. Software that does multiple jobs or lets a child create a product may retain the child's interest longer than software that does only one job. For example, many children enjoy using word-processing, graphics, and desktop-publishing programs. Try one of the high-quality children's versions of these programs, or let your child try an easy-to-use adult version. Many children will enjoy multimedia and CD-ROM applications; just be sure the program is easy to use, and appropriate for the child's age. Children should feel that they are in control of the programs they use. Guidance can be in the form of questions such as "What if?" rather than direct instruction.

How do we handle going online?

Just as you worry about your child playing in the neighborhood and going to the mall, you should be concerned about your child's welfare online. A child working unsupervised at a computer can get into trouble—both from what he or she does at the computer, and from the expense involved.

Online services such as CompuServe and America Online can provide children with many positive educational and entertainment activities and resources. These services provide references, magazines, games, chatting, and messages. Some online material may be profane and vulgar, however, and some new online "friends" may have hidden agendas. Here are a few guidelines to follow:

- Remind your children that people they meet online are strangers; they should never provide personal information such as home address, telephone number, or even home city with the child's full name. Discuss appropriate responses to uncomfortable situations or requests for personal information.
- Explore the online service or bulletin board with your child.
- Watch for changes in behavior or attitude, such as trying to hide something or surly answers to questions.
- Set up an online budget, and make sure your child understands the penalties such as paying out of an allowance—for exceeding the budget.
- Check the rules and parental controls on the online services in which you are interested. For example, America Online lets the master account (the parent) bar other individuals on the account (the child) from chats and conferences.

CAN A CHILD SPEND TOO MUCH TIME AT THE COMPUTER?

Yes. Not only can computer games be just as addictive as other electronic games, but the many online activities can be extremely enticing, too. Some children are so drawn toward computer activities that they neglect homework and shut out friends and other activities. Just as you set up a budget for computer expenses, set up a time budget for your children.

(See 5.12 Computer Literacy and School Curriculum; 5.13 The Computer as Teacher.)

5.15 COMPUTER-ENHANCED GRAPHICS: WHAT'S REAL AND WHAT'S NOT?

Remember the TV commercial that asked, "Is it live or is it Memorex?" Or the more recent AT&T ad transmitting Whitney Houston's voice? With the widespread use of very powerful computer capabilities, you might wonder what's real.

In the area of entertainment, you have probably seen music videos, movies, and special effects in which real events mingle with computer-generated events. Some studios use computers to "colorize" old black-and-white movies, which can give new viewers a mistaken impression of the original. Recent popular movies blur reality and unreality to a greater degree. In 1993, the producers of *Jurassic Park* used complex and highly developed graphics-modeling software to achieve realistic dinosaurs. In *Terminator 2*, a chrome blob changed into a metal creature, and then into actor Robert Patrick, while emerging from a blazing fire. In scenes from another recent movie, *Forrest Gump*, the main character appeared to be shaking hands and talking with John F. Kennedy and Lyndon B. Johnson, both long dead. Another film, *The Mask*, presented one elaborate digital illusion after another. We all know that the movies are fantasies, but what we trust as the truth can also be altered digitally. What about the digital manipulation of a photograph? In 1994, a newsmagazine was heavily criticized for its digitally altered cover picture of O. J. Simpson as dark and brooding. Can opinion be influenced? Can history be altered? What is the truth and what is contrived?

A similar question can even be asked of evidence used in a courtroom. A videotape taken by a passerby rallied much of the nation to take the side of Rodney King in a Los Angeles incident involving the question of police brutality. The tape presented a live event, and though it did not depict the action from the beginning, eyewitnesses supported its truthfulness.

Consider, however, a 1991 case in Corte Madera, California, in which Jim Mitchell drove to the home of his younger brother and business partner, Artie, and shot him. The district attorney did not believe that the killer shot eight times in self-defense. Because there were no eyewitnesses, the prosecution persuaded the judge to let the jury watch a video of the shooting. Rather than actual footage, however, the video was a simulation of the event, using bullet trajectories and created with the help of computer-aided design software after the evidence found at the scene was analyzed. The video did convince the jury that Jim was guilty, but an appeal is in the works, in part because the defense attorney claims the contrived video had no place in a court of law. One problem with the tape is that the figure who was shot did not brandish his beer bottle in a threatening manner, which might indicate that the older Mitchell needed to defend himself. The case raises a question: Can such a graphics simulation be used fairly in a courtroom? Can it accurately illustrate everything that happened?

Just as statistics can be manipulated to support almost any position, videos and photographs can be altered to suit almost any agenda. Just as we have learned to question the statistics behind the reasoning, we must learn to differentiate images that have been altered for entertainment from those designed to support (or distort) the truth.

(See 5.1 Criminal Conduct and Ethics: Responsibility for Computer Actions.)

5.16 Ergonomics

To most people, ergonomics is a relatively new science, but the idea of changing the work environment to suit the worker has been around since the 1940s. The term *ergonomics* is derived from an ancient Greek word meaning "work." Ergonomics first became an established science during World War II. During the war, fliers were crashing planes because the instrument panels and controls were too difficult for them to master. The situation improved after ergonomists redesigned the controls, making them easier to use.

Following the war, the specialists continued streamlining aircraft controls. Gradually the same principles used in aircraft design were applied to other areas. Currently, ergonomics is being applied to a vast array of products. The brake light now mounted in the rear window of all new cars is the culmination of a battle between ergonomists and designers. Designers find the placement of the light aesthetically offensive; ergonomists feel it catches the eye of other drivers better than traditional brake lights, thereby improving the safety of new cars.

Ergonomists are very much needed in the computer industry, and the number of full-time ergonomists in the United States has been steadily increasing. Their importance is evidenced with the first Apple II microcomputer. This computer, the machine for which the term *user-friendly* was coined, was famous for its "non-user-friendly" keyboard. The machine had the Reset key located next to the Return key. When pressing Return (the same as Enter), users often pushed the Reset key at the same time by mistake, causing an immediate loss of all data in memory. The problem was corrected on subsequent machines. Since the early days of the Apple mistake, ergonomists have spent a great deal of time designing keyboards that really *are* user-friendly. Some of the improvements include standardizing symbols and layout, sculpting keys for easy touch, and making keyboards detachable. There are many other computer features that were designed with ergonomic principles in mind, such as the Apple mouse and the Hewlett-Packard touch screen.

The primary concern of ergonomists working in the computer industry today, however, is the worker in the automated office who spends the entire day in front of a *video display terminal (VDT)* or monitor. Studies have shown that the stress resulting from extensive computer use is related to absenteeism and a high annual turnover rate. In addition to creating stress, working at terminals for prolonged periods of time may cause physical problems. Back problems make up 25 percent of the workers' compensation claims made by office executives, and *repetitive-motion injuries* (also called repetitive-strain injuries or RSIs) like Carpal Tunnel Syndrome are on the rise. It pays to examine environmental conditions and machine design in the office.

There are four major problem areas computer users face: eyestrain, aches and pains, excessive fatigue, and stress.

EYESTRAIN

The typical distance between the eye and printed material for ordinary desk work is from 14 to 16 inches. People using monitors usually have a viewing distance of about 25 inches. Some workers must continually refocus from paper to monitor, and others spend long periods of time looking only at the screen. The *refresh rate* of many screens is slow, and this constant flicker adds to eye irritation. The size of characters that appear on the screen, as well as the screen contrast, can also contribute to eyestrain. Then there is screen glare from fluorescent lights and nearby windows. Some recent research has shown that workers in their 20s and 30s using computers need reading glasses long before they would under normal circumstances. The long-term effects of these eye changes are under investigation, but although eye fatigue is annoying, there is no evidence that indicates permanent damage.

Aches and Pains

Lower-back pains are common among computer users because of the rigid posture associated with staring at the screen for long periods of time. The position most workers use is even more fixed than that of typists, because typing requires more body movement. Because of poor posture and work habits, some people end up with repetitive-strain injuries (also known as cumulative trauma disorders) that may manifest themselves as Carpal Tunnel Syndrome (a nerve-compression injury), tendonitis (irritation of the tendons), and other assorted wrist, neck, shoulder, and elbow problems. Even using excessive force during keystrokes can contribute to such disorders. Carpal tunnel problems can result from keeping the elbows elevated, bending the wrists, resting the wrists on the edge of the desk top, and striking the keys hard. When the wrist is bent, for example, finger motion generates friction—and therefore injuries—because the ligaments passing through the carpal tunnel rub against one another.

Excessive Fatigue

Many employees who use computers have a generalized feeling of depression and tiredness. Eyestrain and poor posture contribute to the problem. Yet, for many employees, the ever present computer screen is a constant reminder to continue working.

Stress

Stress is something all workers face, but employees who use computers find the tireless nature of the computer a constant challenge that is impossible to keep up with. Stress also comes from the real or imagined need to keep up with coworkers and please bosses who can easily monitor computer output.

Ergonomists suggest number of solutions to alleviate problems with computer use in the office and at home. The primary recommendation is easy and cheap: take frequent rest periods (ideally, a short stretch every half hour, but a minimum of 15 minutes every two hours) to help alleviate excessive fatigue and stress. In addition, correct posture can eliminate many of the problems that are often attributed to furniture or computer design. The following topics deal with other solutions to the physical problems resulting from computer use.

MONITOR POSITION

The center of the monitor should be about 20 degrees below the eye level so that the eyes are gazing slightly downward at it but the neck is not bent. (This puts the top of the screen even with your forehead.) The distance between the eyes and the screen should be about 24 to 28 inches.

Once you are looking at the screen, you should train yourself to blink often in order to rest your eyes. This practice occurs naturally when you are reading a newspaper or book, but somehow stops when you begin using a computer screen.

GLARE AND RESOLUTION

When screen filters are used to reduce glare, there is an increase in contrast, creating less eyestrain. Be sure, however, that an antiglare filter does not interfere with the clarity of the screen display. Many new VDT screens are being manufactured with matte finishes to reduce glare. The monitors may also come with tilt-and-swivel options so you can adjust them for lighting. Screen resolution is being improved, so the contrast of characters is sharper. The resolution should be the same as the resolution on a printed page. High refresh rates (70Hz to 72Hz or higher) on monitors can also reduce eyestrain. Hard-to-read, green-on-black screens are being replaced by those with black characters on white or near-white backgrounds—a good option to choose in programs that let you customize screen colors.

LIGHTING

Office lighting can help reduce glare from a screen, as well. The best lighting is indirect and natural. If you are setting up your system near a window, be sure you will not be looking at the window in order to see your screen display. Similarly, sunlight coming from directly behind you can cause glare from the screen display. Position your work area so that the window is beside you, or use blinds or curtains to soften the light coming in. If natural lighting is unavailable, the next best option is incandescent lighting, particularly Chromalox bulbs, which almost replicate natural daylight. If a small focused lamp is used, however, it should not aim direct light on the screen, nor should it shine directly into your eyes. Rather, it should shine sideways on papers, and should not produce glare on the computer screen. Using a document holder can help eliminate some glare from papers you are reading in conjunction with your computer work.

Keyboards

Generally, a desk designed for pen or pencil writing is too high for comfort when typing on a computer keyboard or even looking at the monitor. You can buy desks especially for computer use, but be sure the computer components will be positioned according to ergonomic recommendations. The keyboard should be placed on a surface a few inches lower than the desk (which is normally about 30 inches high). A keyboard support—such as that on a specially built computer desk, or a pull-out keyboard tray built into your desk—should be between 23 and 28 inches from the floor. Your forearms should be neither raised nor lowered in order to reach the keyboard. If you hold your elbows at a ninety-degree angle and your arms and hands are parallel to the floor, the keyboard should be about where the thumb joints are. At the least, the wrists should be straight. For most typing purposes, your hands should "float" above the keyboard, rather than resting on it. (Some keyboards are designed so that you can rest the palms of your hands comfortably on them during lulls in typing.) *Wrist pads*, foam pads that are placed directly in front of the keyboard, have recently been introduced to relieve pressure on the wrist while keying. The mouse or trackball should be at the same height as the keyboard. When sliding the mouse around on the desktop, use your arm rather than simply pivoting the wrist.

A number of companies have experimented with keyboard design. Most ergonomic designs position your palms toward each other somewhat, which is more natural than palms-down. Some fit across your lap. Others rest on the chair arms or on the desk. Most of these special keyboards are decidedly more expensive than the standard ones.

The Chair

Manufacturers of office furniture have taken suggestions from ergonomists, and have begun designing chairs to help combat lower-back pain. Some of the features incorporated into a well-designed chair include controls that allow you to adjust the height of the seat from the floor—as well as the height and angle of the back with the touch of a lever. A chair should also cushion the curve of the lower back. Some workers use backless kneeling chairs, which redistribute weight from the lower back and backside to the knees. You should adjust the chair so that your feet rest flat on the floor or comfortably on a foot rest. Either way, your thighs should be parallel to the floor.

After all of this advice about ergonomics, remember that one of the best ways to relieve the stresses and strains of computer use is to get up frequently and walk around for a few minutes. Vary your work position, too—put the keyboard in your lap for a while. Stand up while on the phone. Sit at another table for paperwork and reading.

(See 1.37 Keyboards; 1.47 Evaluating a Monitor; 5.17 Safety Issues.)

5.17 Safety Issues

If you are spending a great deal of time in front of a computer monitor, will the emissions from the monitor harm you? Recently, scientists have been seeking answers to questions about the possible health effects of long-term exposure to *extremely low-frequency (ELF)* and *very low-frequency (VLF)* electromagnetic fields. ELF fields emit at a rate of 1Hz to 1,000Hz; for VLF fields, the figures run from 1,000Hz to 400,000Hz. One area of concern, for example, has been to study the relationship between VDTs and miscarriages (results are, as yet, inconclusive).

The issue of safety encompasses electrical wiring, televisions, hair dryers, microwave ovens, and other household appliances in addition to computer monitors. Even wireless communications are being examined. The general consensus at this time is that the electrical and magnetic fields produced by computer monitors do not pose a great health risk. However, you should be aware that the emissions are stronger at the backs and sides of the machines.

European countries such as Sweden and Germany have already taken the initiative and passed legislation to protect workers' health. For example, in Sweden, the government has recommended that VDT workers spend no more than four hours a day at a terminal. Some European countries are regulating VDT construction and usage as a precaution against the danger of emissions from the VDTs, even though the alleged dangers associated with VDT emissions have not been substantiated by research.

Some cities and states are considering passing laws that would reduce many of the problems VDT operators face. These states are attempting to control the design of VDTs and keyboards. They also want to require rest periods for VDT workers. In 1990, the city of San Francisco led the way by passing the first legislation to mandate ergonomics guidelines for VDT operators. Undoubtedly, similar laws will one day exist around the country. Corporations will benefit from the legislation in the long term through increased worker health and productivity.

For now, monitor manufacturers are beginning to produce low-radiation monitors, so look for a monitor that adheres to the MPR II guidelines established by the

Swedish National Board for Measurement and Testing. A more recent Swedish standard—developed by TCO, the country's office-workers' union—is even more stringent on limits, and requires that measurements be taken closer to the monitor than MPR II standards. The United States Energy Star program also requires power-saving features that help reduce emissions.

If you are still using an older monitor, you can avoid the emissions by staying an arm's length away from the front of the monitor; electromagnetic fields decay within that distance. Try to stay at least five feet away from the back and sides of your neighbor's monitor at work. In addition, as the prices decrease in the future, consider using an *active-matrix LCD* instead of a *CRT-based* video display to eliminate the emissions problem.

Another emission that concerns computer users is ozone gas, which can be a mild to severe irritant. This gas is given off in detectable levels by almost all laser printers and photocopier machines. Ozone is an unstable substance that is produced only when the printer is printing; the gas quickly breaks down to oxygen.

In laser printers, the primary source of ozone is the *corona wire*, used to produce an electrical discharge that makes the toner powder adhere temporarily to the print drum just before the paper passes over the drum. Laser printers that use a corona wire have special filters to control the level of ozone emissions. If your laser printer has a corona wire (you can find out from the service provider), the ozone-emission control system should be checked—and the ozone filter should be replaced—every 50,000 pages. Check your owner's manual for specifics.

You can also take a few precautionary measures at home to control exposure. Be sure your printer is located in a well-ventilated place. Keep the area dust-free to avoid dirty filters. Be sure the printer's exhaust fan blows away from you.

(See 5.16 Ergonomics.)

5.18 Computers for People with Disabilities: Meeting Special Needs

Computers have opened an entirely new world for people with special needs. The equipment ranges from special software to special adjustments for people with limited motor control. Some autistic people have begun to communicate using specially designed computer programs. Entire computer systems have been designed to enable even the most physically limited people to communicate using a puff of air, an eye twitch, or a chin movement.

Special keyboards have large keys for those with motor-control difficulties. Others are miniature keyboards for people who can use only one hand, or who must use a typing stick to press the keys. For these people, special *sticky-key* programs are also available; these turn the Shift, Control, or Alt keys into toggles so users can type any commands or characters that require pressing two keys. For example, if the Shift key is pressed once, the next key pressed is the shifted character on the key. The second time the Shift key is pressed, it locks. The third time releases the Shift. Some sticky-key software can also disable the repeating function of keys, so that people with spastic hand movements can use the keyboard more easily. An example of this type of software is HandiShift by MicroSystems Software. (Macintosh computers have Easy Access built in. This program adapts keystrokes and mouse clicks for one hand or single-switch use.)

Macro generator software can help physically challenged people, too, because several characters can be assigned to one key, thus reducing the amount of typing needed to accomplish a task. *Word prediction* software also reduces the amount of typing; it tries to guess the words that are being typed. If a *g* is typed, the software begins listing words that start with the letter g. Although the list usually begins with the most common words, it could be quite long, so the user can narrow the choices by typing two or three more letters, then picking the desired word. Some word prediction software includes subject-verb agreement when listing its suggestions. Usually predictors are also smart enough to know which words you use most frequently, and will move these words closer to the top of the list. Two popular word predictors are Brown Bag Software's MindReader and Microsystems Software's HandiWord.

Other innovations enable even the most seriously disabled to use a computer. The user uses a simple tool or switch to enter a selection from a menu into the computer. The switches have been designed to work with any muscle that is controlled by the user. Joysticks with fire buttons are the most common of these switches. Lever switches activate with head motion, and leaf switches are used with the elbow, under the chin, or in the mouth. Brow-wrinkle switches are attached to the forehead with a sweatband. Even for people who can only breathe, sip-and-puff straws enable them to use blowing and inhaling to activate the switch.

There are two ways selections can be displayed for use with these various types of switches. One is an alphanumeric scanner on the screen, continuously highlighting a set of letters and numbers, one after another. By activating the switch for the appropriate highlighted letter, the user can build up words, write programs, and run software. The other type of system simply displays the keyboard or menus on the screen, and works with a point-and-shoot device. Usually, this device moves a cursor (like a mouse), and is mounted on the head. The user points at a selection, and then enters the selection by activating a switch or puffing a breath. The switch or puff straw is usually attached to the headset. This type of data entry is time-consuming, but it works. Most of these systems can be used with word prediction software to eliminate some of the time-consuming selections.

The ultimate in technology for people with disabilities is the Eyegaze Computer System from LC Technologies of Fairfax, Virginia. This system substitutes light for touch. It operates by detecting the retinal reflection produced when light enters the eyeball. This phenomenon is called "bright eye." The user just focuses his gaze on the monitor. A low-power infrared light, mounted below the monitor screen, illuminates the eye. The beam is reflected off the cornea and then is picked up by image-processing software on the monitor that continually computes where the user's gaze is directed on the screen. A longer-duration gaze (actually only a fraction of a second) makes the selection. As the user becomes more proficient with the system, the duration time of the gaze can be reduced to speed up the process. The monitor can display a virtual keyboard or menus; these enable the user to control the environment or communicate with people.

Other systems have been designed that rely on spoken commands. Two of the companies associated with voice recognition are Dragon System, Inc. and Kurzweil Applied Intelligence, Inc. Generally, a voice-recognition system with a large vocabulary must be "trained" to recognize the speaker's voice. The speaker must speak clearly, and pause between each word and the next. Voice-recognition systems not only enable a person with a disability to use a computer, but also to control his or her environment; the user can actually tell the computer to turn off the lights, for example, or to turn on the oven.

Voice-recognition systems are suitable for those with vision impairment; other, less expensive systems are available that magnify letters and numbers up to three inches high. Usually these systems can be added to popular off-the-shelf computers. A hardware-based system has a video add-on card, a large monitor, and a special joystick or mouse with which to move the cursor. Software-based systems enable the user to vary the magnification. Some systems show a window with regular-sized print beside or above the magnified print. This window can be used for watching cursor movement. An example of this type of software is ZoomText by AI Squared of Atlanta, Georgia.

Blind people can use computers that can synthesize Braille characters or speech. They can also buy Braille printers, Braille displays (with which they can feel the output in the patterns made by the Braille dots), and Braille keyboards. They do not have to rely on Braille devices, but instead can purchase *speech synthesizers* for use with optical-recognition software. These systems—used either with microcomputers or as stand-alone configurations—scan printed material and produce output as synthesized speech. The actual speech synthesizer is an add-on board. It turns letters into phonemes, the smallest units of speech, and produces the output as speech through a speaker located outside the computer.

Another type of system for the blind is the *screen reader*, which directs all keyboard input and screen text to the speech synthesizer. The speech system is usually what is referred to as *terminate-and-stay-resident* software. Once the speech program is loaded, another program can be loaded on top of it. This way, popular off-the-shelf software can be used without any special preparation by its manufacturer. Henter-Joyce's screen-reader software, Job Acquisition with Speech, can drive synthesizers that are compatible with DOS machines; outSPOKEN by Berkeley Systems is a screen reader for the Macintosh. The CD-ROM will revolutionize computer systems for the blind. One CD-ROM can hold an entire reference work, and thus eliminate the expense and volume of Braille reference works. The CD-ROM can be used with many speech synthesizers.

People who are deaf usually have no problems using computers, but they most likely cannot hear the various beeps and clicks a computer makes. They can, however, purchase software that converts the sounds to video format; it displays the word **Beep** or flashes the screen display.

As development of input/output technologies continues, the speed, accuracy, and effectiveness of data-processing operations will improve. As a result, microcomputers can be expected to provide a wide variety of new and innovative applications for people with special needs. Legislation (such as the Technology Related Assistance Act of 1988 and the Americans with Disabilities Act of 1990) is speeding along the drive to help users with disabilities enrich their lives.

An adjunct to the discussion of adaptations for people with special needs is the extent to which employers are required to accommodate employees with disabilities. Effective July 26, 1992, companies with 25 or more employees were required to make reasonable accommodations for employees with disabilities, provided the accommodations do not create an undue hardship on the company. The new law covered businesses with 15 or more employees as of July 26, 1994.

Although some may consider such requirements may an unjust burden, they may actually serve people that we never knew were in need. For example, the curb cuts designed to help individuals in wheelchairs also aided people pushing young children in strollers, bikers, and the elderly. In addition, companies should remember that blanket adaptations may not serve individual disabled people; each worker with a disability may need his or her own solution. Often the solutions are not that expensive. They may include such simple ideas as a particular type of mouse, a trackball instead of a mouse, a special keyboard, or a sticky-key program. Business owners should remember that new laws do not mean they must hire unqualified workers, only that they should give qualified people with disabilities an equal opportunity for employment.

(See 1.38 Mice and Trackballs; 1.43 Speech Recognition; 1.58 Voice Synthesizers; Software Review Section: inLARGE, Monologue, outSPOKEN.)

5.19 Automation and Applied Intelligence

The term *number-crunching* was born in the vacuum-tube era of computers, when mathematicians, scientists, and engineers used the machines to handle huge amounts of equations and numbers. Even today, number-crunching is what computers do best, but computer scientists are working on building computers and software that have even greater powers—the powers of *artificial intelligence (AI)*. They want to give computers capabilities that are like human thinking. For example, they want computers to have common sense, to learn from experience, and to make decisions. Many people call the new level of computer power the *fifth generation*.

Because of the disappointments associated with AI research, the term is being used less frequently to mean "artificial" intelligence; instead, efforts in this field are described as *applied intelligence*. To use applied intelligence, scientists will need faster computers with new designs. The question is, how will applied intelligence affect people and their jobs? Will the benefits outweigh the problems?

Advances in applied intelligence and voice recognition will lead to further automation in the workplace. Just as Jacquard's loom replaced skilled weavers, voice-recognition devices could replace skilled typists. Customers could use a voice-recognition/voice-output system to order items they want at a store or over the phone. Other types of smart machines could do many other jobs that typists and clerks do now. For example, smart computers could read books, newspapers, journals, and magazines, and write summaries of the material. They could scan mail and sort all letters but those with the most illegible handwriting. Are the benefits of applied-intelligence devices great enough to make up for the problems in unemployment? How will such devices affect the social relationships that now occur during everyday transactions?

One area of applied intelligence whose output has the potential to do better work than human beings can is the *expert system*—software that covers knowledge in only one field, such as medicine or geology. These systems evaluate, draw conclusions, and make recommendations based on a huge database of information in that field. A medical-diagnosis expert system, for example, could make cross-references among various bodies of knowledge. It could coordinate the patient's history, symptoms, and test results with the data in its own database, and come up with an assessment of the possible diseases the patient has. This helps the doctor make a diagnosis and set up a plan of treatment. Two such programs are Oncocin, which advises physicians on the best treatments for cancer patients, and Caduceus II, which holds information about hundreds of diseases and symptoms. Other types of expert systems include Prospector, which is an electronic geologist, and Dipmeter Advisor, which helps oil companies find good locations for drilling.

Expert systems are not true applied intelligence; they cannot deal with change, or use new information to do better work. They can, however, enable people to keep up to date in their fields, and can flag potential problems that may occur when a particular course is followed. The question is, can an expert system provide better output than a human being can? Will an expert system replace the valuable training a person receives while preparing for a particular profession? Will the expert systems become crutches instead of tools?

Another area of applied intelligence that fascinates many people is that of *robotics*. You may dream of a robot that could mow the lawn, wash the dishes, or clean the bathroom, but such a convenience is still futuristic. Today's robots are limited in vision, touch, mobility, and intelligence; they cannot do these jobs. Robots will change as applied intelligence develops, and these changes will affect jobs.

Already in some cases, one robot can do the job of six workers. Factory owners say robots produce the same high-quality work over and over. In Japan, robots are being used for construction work, such as assembling steel girders, smoothing concrete slabs, and spray-painting walls. Field robots are being used to clean up commercial nuclear power plants, inspect rigs for the oil industry, and dispose of bombs. For example, a 77-inch long Rosa robot snakes through the steam-carrying tubes adjacent to the nuclear reactor in a power plant serviced by Westinghouse. In one hour, it can inspect the pipes and make more—and better—welding repairs than entire squads of human repairmen (who must rush into the area and then out again after only 45 seconds, for safety's sake). Robots such as Rosa are controlled remotely by human operators. So how many more workers will be replaced when smarter robots are used? Will these workers be retrained for other jobs such as building and maintaining robots? Will those who remain in the factories feel like mere button-pushers with no real responsibilities?

Some experts say that robots and other forms of automation are needed to help the United States compete with other countries in manufacturing. With automation, they reason, factory owners can keep jobs in the United States that might otherwise go to factories in poorer countries with lower wage levels. In addition, there are many jobs that are just too dangerous for human beings to do. In the future, for example, the U.S. nuclear industry will need many robots to help decommission and mothball approximately 100 old nuclear power plants. In addition, the Energy Department will need robots to help decontaminate hundreds of millions of cubic feet of nuclear-weapons waste that is buried at 31 sites. The temperature of up to

300 degrees Centigrade—as well as the lethal level of radiation—will make it impossible to use people for the job.

There are no easy answers. Future applied intelligence is bound to result in smarter automated machines and more effective expert systems. Applied intelligence and the changes it creates could improve the quality of our lives, but many problems still need to be solved.

5.20 Depersonalization Versus "Telecommunity"

One of the major fears associated with computer use is that the computer makes exchanges between humans machine-like and impersonal. Rather than chatting with colleagues during an office break, you communicate through e-mail. Rather than listening to the friendly voice of a company's receptionist, you hear a voice synthesizer or a recording instructing you to enter any of 10 or more different numbers to reach the proper department. Rather than greeting the bank teller while making a transaction, you punch in a few numbers at an automatic teller machine. Rather than going to work at the office every day, you phone in your work over a modem from home. Computers seem to take the informal human contact out of everyday transactions.

In fact, a number of studies have indicated that employees' behavior changes when they use e-mail. In a normal personal social context, a person's behavior is controlled by (and receptive to) body language and other social factors. When people use e-mail, this control is lacking; they are more self-centered and less worried about status and making a good impression. People also exhibited more antisocial, confrontational, and extreme behaviors in the absence of face-to-face human contact.

People expressed the same fears of depersonalization after the invention of telephones and television, but somehow we have survived the widespread use of these technologies. Just as telephones and televisions widened our scope of the world, computers can enable people to make contacts they never might have initiated otherwise. Couples meeting over computer bulletin board systems end up exchanging wedding vows a year or so later. People with disabilities who might have seemed fated to spend their lives in an uncommunicative state can use computers to talk with their families and express their feelings. Via modem, they can access a number of individuals and services. People who shy away from interaction with others may find that communicating through computers decreases their discomfort and helps them make friends. Some of the same studies that found antisocial behaviors in communication by computer also found that people were more honest and revealing about themselves when they weren't worried about appearances.

Computer experts hope that eventually the use of fiber-optic cables can bring a wide variety of services into our homes, so that we can access the stacks of far-away libraries by computer. We can hold conferences with experts in a field, and bring the world into our living rooms. Our neighbor may live in the Himalayas or Greenland, rather than next door to us in Gary, Indiana. Thus, the social effect of computers lies in their use, rather than in the technology itself.

(See 4.9 Electronic Mail; 4.12 Bulletin Board Systems; 4.13 The Internet; 4.14 Online Services.)

Part 6 Contents Index

Communications

Databases

Desktop Publishing

Education

Games

Graphics

Home and Personal Use

Word Processing, Grammar and Spelling Checkers, and Thesauruses

Software Reviews

Wouldn't it be a boring world if everyone liked the same car? Instead, some want an expensive, red sports car with lots of "bells and whistles." Others like a modestly priced, modestly performing car. Still others want a smooth, luxurious car. Software is the same. Even if all of the word processors or data-management programs or even games seem similar on the surface, there are differences, and many of those differences are tailored to suit the "driver." Some people want an expensive, do-it-all program whether they use all of the features or not. Others want to pay only so much for a particular kind of program, and that's that. In addition, the "look and feel" of different packages varies. Read about several programs and try them out to discover which one is right for you—whether you are shopping for a productivity package, an educational program, or a game.

You will notice that each software review begins with a numerical rating from 1 to 5; worst is 1, best is 5. We have made every effort to include software reviews that are rated 3 or above—we feel they are the best of what's available. Great care has also gone into criteria used to select the packages. Software was evaluated based on its reliability, accuracy, value, and overall user-friendliness. You will find a sample review of almost any category of software of interest to you.

You'll get an idea of what products are available, but remember to "test drive" the ones you are interested in—especially the ones that cost a lot. The programs generally come on CD-ROM disks or 3.5-inch floppy disks, although some are still available on 5.25-inch floppy disks. As such, you need to know the type of disk your computer can handle in order for you to run or install the program. Note that the system requirements are minimum: Games, for example, may run slowly—to the point where you don't enjoy them—with these minimal specifications. In addition, you will need a floppy disk drive in order to load or install every program, even though a hard disk drive is required to run the program. All programs require a computer, a monitor, a keyboard, and at least one floppy disk drive. Most also recommend a printer. When using the software for the first time, review the README files included on the disk for updates to the user's manual.

A Word About Software and Customer Support

Many software companies take pride in the quality of their technical support. Their technicians are usually friendly and knowledgeable. Any frustration you may experience will usually be because of the long waits to reach a technician, once you have gotten through without a busy signal. The documentation that comes with the software will tell you how to reach this help through an 800 number, a 900 number, or the company's regular listed telephone number. Some companies have separate telephone numbers for technical support and customer service. Call the technical support number if you are having problems performing a particular task in the software. Call customer service if the program will not load or run, or if an element of the software package is missing.

The 800 numbers are often called "hot lines," and the person on the company's end of the telephone should be well-informed enough to provide you with advice and troubleshooting tips. There is no charge for the technician's time, and the free help may last indefinitely. In order to compete with the lower prices that customers are demanding and still make a profit, some companies are discontinuing their 800 numbers. They are offering other types of support designed to decrease costs and maintain the level of quality of technical support. For example, you may receive a limited time—say, 30 days—after your first technical help phone call during which you receive free technical support. After that, you must pay for additional help, often through 900 numbers. When calling technical support, be sure that you are near your computer, have written down information about your system, including the serial number of the program and the difficulties you have been experiencing, and you have pencil and paper readily available.

Other technical support options include fax-back, MCI mail, or an in-house electronic bulletin board system. If you belong to an online information service, look for forums about the software you are using. Ask at the store where you bought your software for help or for information about pertinent users groups. You can even post a message on an informal bulletin board that you access to see if anyone else experiences the same problems or has a tip that will help you solve your particular problem. Check your bookstore for a book written specifically about your software.

Most educational software is straightforward and fairly simple to use, and you probably will not have questions about how to use it. For this reason, companies that provide educational software may not advertise their technical support and customer service in the same manner as companies that sell productivity software. In fact, the only telephone number you may find in a package's documentation is the company's regular telephone number. Yet, you will get some sort of help, even if you must pay for the call.

A

Most questions you will have about entertainment software will be about how to win the game. Unlike the answers to questions you have about how to print a word processor document or how to copy information from one spreadsheet to another, the answers to gaming software will be less specific—just hints. You will generally get these hints by calling a special "hint line" that is a 900 number rather than by calling a technical support number. The customer or technical support telephone number should be used only in cases when the program will not load or run, or when an element of the software package is missing.

Many companies provide hint, or clue, books for their complex adventure software. They may also have an in-house bulletin board that you can access for help or clues. If you belong to a commercial online information service, you may find that it offers a forum about a particular game. Other computer users may also have some hints. Some adventure games are so complex, you may even wonder how to get started. You may have to try several options and restart the game several times before you know how to play. If the software offers a tutorial, be sure to use it—especially if you're a novice at adventure games.

If you are having trouble with a particular package or don't think that the software is operating the way it should, check a few things before calling the company. Be sure that the equipment you are using matches the requirements of the package. Read the manual and check out any troubleshooting sections. If you still have problems, then you should seek outside help.

A.D.A.M.: The Inside Story

Publisher: A.D.A.M. Software, Inc.; (800) 755-2326

System Requirements: Macintosh (68030); 8MB RAM; 5MB hard disk space; System 7; CD-ROM drive

Suggested Retail Price: $79.95

The Program

A reference guide to the human anatomy, A.D.A.M. is not only educational but also entertaining. This interactive program for ages 10 and up contains illustrations with layers of color details, as well as animations that show the cause-and-effect of common body functions. All is interspersed with lay person's terms and humor.

ACES OF THE PACIFIC

Publisher: Dynamix, Inc. (a part of the Sierra family; P.O. Box 485, Coarsegold, CA 93614); 99 W. 10th, Suite 224; Eugene, Oregon 97401; (503) 343-0772

System Requirements: IBM or compatible with 25MHz 386SX or better; 2MB RAM; VGA graphics; hard disk drive; 1.2MB 5.25-inch or 1.44MB 3.5-inch floppy disk drive; DOS 5.0 or higher

Suggested: Mouse or joystick recommended (joystick best); second joystick for specific flight control; supports yokes, pedals, and Thrustmaster Flight Control System or Weapons Control System (both of which are similar to joysticks in operation, but have more capabilities); supports Ad Lib, Thunderboard, SoundBlaster, and Roland MT-32/LAPC-1/CM-32L sound cards

Documentation: Documentation for this game includes a 240-page manual that contains a detailed history of the Pacific Theater and the war, complete with photos, maps, pilot profiles, tactics, and color aircraft illustrations. This manual also describes flight instructions, maneuvers, and combat tactics; it includes a glossary and selected references for further reading. There is also a quick reference card that lists game commands, view controls, and information needed to run a joystick or yoke with the program. A technical supplement tells how to install the program. Despite the extensive manuals, the documentation needs more information about how to actually play the game.

Support: Most Sierra games have clue books available and an automated telephone hint line with a 900 number. You can also get hints from Sierra's online bulletin board system, and often a commercial information service may offer hints for Sierra games. For technical help, you can call or write to the company's customer support department.

Suggested Retail Price: $69.95

THE PROGRAM

In this story of World War II combat, here's your chance to show what you would have done if you had been flying a warplane in the Pacific. You can decide to fly an historic mission, a dogfight with a famous flying ace, a squadron fight, a fighter sweep, or an anti-shipping strike. You can also choose such specifics as the number of planes, pilot abilities, type of planes, and conditions such as Sun Blind Spot, Realistic Weather, Engine Burnouts

Allowed, and Limited Fuel. If you like war games and enjoy World War II items, then you will probably like this game and its manual. Both are designed to be historically accurate. The program contains greatly detailed and realistic simulation; realistic assessment of the planes' abilities includes flaws that could get you into trouble. Sound effects even match the individual sound characteristics of each plane.

Address Book Plus 3.0

Publisher: Power Up! Software Corporation; 2929 Campus Drive; San Mateo, CA 94403; (415) 345-5900; (800) 851-2917

System Requirements: IBM PC, XT, AT, PS/2, PS/1 or compatible; 512K RAM; one floppy disk drive; DOS 2.1 or higher

Suggested: Hard disk drive; HP LaserJet Plus or Series II/III and compatible laser printers or HP DeskJet series; most dot-matrix printers

Other Platforms (not reviewed): Macintosh

Documentation: The documentation includes a quick reference card with keyboard commands and screen descriptions. The user's manual is well organized, delineating topics clearly.

Support: The documentation contains a guided tour that helps you learn to use the program. Technical help is available on weekdays between 8:00 a.m. and 5:00 p.m. Pacific Standard Time for the cost of a toll call.

Suggested Retail Price: $79.95

The Program

Address Book Plus is designed for storing and handling addresses. You can use it to create address pages, rotary-file cards, labels for correspondence, envelopes, and phone lists in any custom size. The program will use the stored telephone numbers to place calls through your modem. You enter information through predefined data-entry screens, and you can format the screens with the program's included fonts. You can use the Address Book Plus to organize all lists, and then use these lists for mail-merging with popular word processing programs. You can use the search-and-sort functions to find any information you need. Address Book Plus also allows you to import and export ASCII files. Convenient, predesigned formats are compatible with most popular organizers (such as Day-Timer and Day Runner).

Adobe (Aldus) Freehand 4.0

Publisher: Adobe Systems, Incorporated; 1585 Charleston Road; P.O. Box 7900; Mountain View, CA 94039-7900; (415) 961-4400

System Requirements: IBM PC or compatible (80286 or better); 2MB RAM; EGA or Hercules; 80MB hard disk drive; mouse or other pointing device; Windows 3.0 or higher

Suggested: 80386 or faster microprocessor; 4MB RAM; high-resolution graphics

Other Platforms (not reviewed): Macintosh

Documentation: The documentation for this program is good. It includes color charts and extensive information on color separations and other printing topics.

Support: The package includes an online tutorial that demonstrates the program's features. There is free technical support at an 800 number for 90 days; thereafter, you purchase more time or use the 900 number.

Suggested Retail Price: $595

The Program

This program is a serious drawing tool for people who need precision. Originally produced for the Macintosh, it is comfortable to use (as are most Macintosh programs), and the IBM-compatible version can swap files with the Macintosh version. It comes with Adobe Type Manager and some standard typefaces (Times, Helvetica, Symbol, and Courier). The program has the usual drawing tools, line styles, and fill patterns. Freehand also has new page-design and text-editing features. This complex and versatile package is suitable for a variety of professional uses, including color separation for professional printing.

Adobe Illustrator 5.5

Publisher: Adobe Systems, Inc.; 1585 Charleston Road; P.O. Box 7900; Mountain View, CA 94039-7900; (415) 961-4400

System Requirements: Macintosh Classic, II, LC, PowerBook, or Quadra; 2MB RAM; hard disk drive with at least 4MB free space; floppy disk drive; System 6.0.3 or later; PostScript-capable laser printer

Other Platforms (not reviewed): IBM PC or compatible; 386 (or higher) processor

Support: If you need help with this program, the technical support department is easy to reach.

Suggested Retail Price: $595

The Program

This program lets you do a number of graphics tasks, ranging from fine art to business-oriented graphics. You can scan and edit drawings or import digital artwork. You can use the autotrace tool to smooth and enhance bit-mapped images. You can use a number of drawing tools such as freehand draw, pen, rectangle, oval, blend, scale, rotate, and reflect to create your own illustrations. The program also offers sophisticated features for type handling and font editing. Adobe Illustrator is for serious graphics professionals; it takes some time and dedication to learn, and its special features are geared toward professional graphics.

Adobe (Aldus) PageMaker 5.0

Publisher: Adobe Systems, Incorporated; 1585 Charleston Road; P.O. Box 7900; Mountain View, CA 94039-7900; (415) 961-4400

System Requirements: 80286 IBM PC or compatible; 2MB RAM; Microsoft Windows 3.0 or higher; DOS 3.0 or higher; floppy disk drive; 20MB hard disk drive; EGA or Hercules graphics adapter; mouse; printer

Suggested: 80386 or higher microprocessor; 4MB RAM; 40MB hard disk drive; VGA graphics

Other Platforms (not reviewed): Macintosh; IBM PCs with OS/2 operating system

Documentation: The manual is well written, including a detailed index and good illustrations.

Support: The company offers 90 days of free support from the first phone call, after which there are a number of options for phone support, including 900-number service.

Suggested Retail Price: $895

The Program

PageMaker has long been considered the most elegant, easiest-to-use desktop publishing package. It contains a full array of layout, text editing, and graphics tools, with a drawing-board feel—there's room beside the publication page to hold graphics or scraps of type until they are needed. PageMaker's menus are logically organized and complete. It lets you create detailed indexes and generate a table of contents; it also has a table editor and a word processing editor. A number of ready-made templates speed up operation and help the beginning user make design decisions.

PageMaker takes text from all major word processors. This version's new features enable you to enter, edit, and spell-check text without leaving the program. It also imports graphics easily from a large number of graphics file formats. PageMaker has good kerning and color-separation functions. You can use its color selection menu to change the color of your document's elements, choosing from color charts such as Pantone (the printing-industry standard). A magnifying feature helps you create details on a page, and PageMaker is very good at handling long documents. Despite its hefty price, however, it does not have precise capabilities for rotating graphics and text.

PageMaker is bundled with PageAhead, a program that enables you to link it to database management systems, from which you can then query, retrieve, and format data.

Adobe (Aldus) Paint & Publish

Publisher: Adobe Systems, Inc.; (206) 622-5500

System Requirements: Macintosh Plus; 2MB RAM

Suggested Retail Price: $89.95

The Program

This graphics-and-design bundle combines Aldus HomePublisher and SuperPaint. You can use it to enter and format text, create art, and develop professional-looking documents with ease. Home Publisher is a powerful word processor complete with 50 templates, 12 TrueType fonts, and nearly 100 clickart images. Its versatile graphics program, SuperPaint, offers easy-to-use painting and drawing tools in one program.

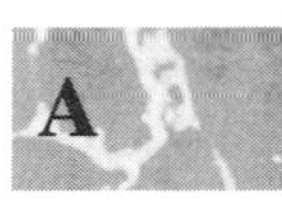

Adobe (Aldus) Persuasion 3.0

Publisher: Adobe Systems, Incorporated; 1585 Charleston Road; P.O. Box 7900; Mountain View, CA 94039-7900; (415) 961-4400

System Requirements: Macintosh Color Classic or greater; 4MB RAM; hard disk drive with at least 3.2MB free; one 800K floppy disk drive; System 7 or later; accelerated for PowerMac

Suggested: Printer

Other Platforms (not reviewed): IBM with Windows

Suggested Retail Price: $495

The Program

You can use this presentation-graphics program in conjunction with files from spreadsheet or database programs to illustrate your data. You can produce organization charts, for example, as well as tables and graphs (pie, bar, or line). Any of these items can be combined in a set and used as the basis for 35mm slide shows and overhead projections. Persuasion's improved interface makes this version easier to use. A major advantage is its very strong charting capabilities; the Chart Module offers 84 chart types and many ways to modify them. The program supports QuickTime and contains a number of built-in design templates, but you can also use the program to create or import logos, technical diagrams, and other illustrations.

Adobe (Aldus) SuperPaint 3.5

Publisher: Adobe Systems, Incorporated; 1585 Charleston Road; P.O. Box 7900; Mountain View, CA 94039-7900; (415) 961-4400

System Requirements: Macintosh Classic, Quadra, PowerBook, LC, or Macintosh II; 1MB RAM; two 800K floppy disk drives, or one hard disk drive with at least 2MB free space and one 800K floppy disk drive; System 6.0.2 or later

Suggested: 2MB RAM; hard disk drive with at least 2MB free space; computer with color monitor option

Documentation: Though short, the manual is clear and concise; it contains informative illustrations.

Suggested Retail Price: $149.95

The Program

With SuperPaint, you can edit both bit-mapped (paint) and vector-graphics (draw) art. You can draw smooth geometric shapes in the draw mode, and then switch to the paint mode to add details and shading. The program includes an autotrace option for creating line art from bit-mapped graphics. The program's tools include freehand Bézier curve, text and object rotation, airbrush, dash patterns, many textures and gradient fills, and support for up to 16.8 million colors. You can use the RGB, HSB, or CMYK models to define your colors, and save custom palettes for future use. You can preview your work in color and (with the proper printer) print in color.

Adobe Type Manager 3.6

Publisher: Adobe Systems, Incorporated; 1585 Charleston Road; P.O. Box 7900; Mountain View, CA 94039-7900; (800) 521-1976; (415) 961-4400

System Requirements: Macintosh with 1MB of RAM and System 7 or greater; hard disk drive; one floppy disk drive needed for installation; accelerated for PowerMac

Suggested: Printer

Other Platforms (not reviewed): IBM PC or compatible in both DOS and Windows

Support: Technical support for Macintosh users is available on weekdays from 6:00 a.m. to 6:00 p.m. (6:00 a.m. to 2:00 p.m. on Friday) Pacific Standard Time. Registration gets you free support and free product updates for 90 days.

Suggested Retail Price: $99.95

The Program

This program manages fonts. Easy to install, Type Manager works with word processing, page-layout, spreadsheet, and graphics applications. (Some word processing packages include it.) You can see your results on-screen and on hard copy. Adobe Type Manager improves jaggies, and enables even inexpensive printers to print PostScript-language fonts with a crisp, smooth appearance. The program can use scalable fonts and bit-mapped fonts. It supports Type 1 font formats and gives you access to thousands of fonts from dozens of companies.

The Adventures of Willy Beamish

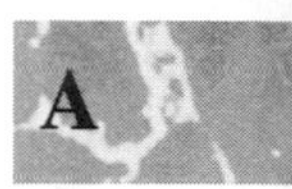

Publisher: Dynamix, Inc.; 99 W. 10th, Suite 224; Eugene, Oregon 97401; (503) 343-0772 (a part of the Sierra family; P.O. Box 485, Coarsegold, CA 93614)

System Requirements: IBM PC or compatible with a 286 or better microprocessor; 640K RAM; hard disk drive; floppy disk drive; VGA graphics

Suggested: Mouse; supports Thunderboard, Pro Aud Spectrum, Ad Lib, Roland MT-32/LAPC-1/CM-32L, SoundBlaster

Other Platforms (not reviewed): EGA DOS and Tandy

Documentation: This package contains the Sierra game manual (with generic instructions for all Sierra games), a set of Willy stickers, a pizza menu from Slice of Life Pizzarama (also containing technical instructions for using the program), and a Willy Beamish notebook full of simulated childhood drawings and notes. To understand what the program is all about, however, you'll have to start to play by trial and error.

Support: Most Sierra games have clue books available, as well as an automated telephone hint line with a 900 number. You can also get hints from Sierra's online bulletin board system; often a commercial information service may offer hints for Sierra games. For technical help, call or write to the company's technical support department.

Suggested Retail Price: $69.95, $59.95 (EGA and Tandy)

The Program

Here's your chance to relive your childhood over again, only this time you can be positively unmanageable and precocious. You, as Willy, get into trouble with teachers, Mom and Dad, the babysitter, and just about everyone else. You also meet a ghostly grandfather back from the grave, and uncover a plot to blow up the city's sewer system. The program uses takeoffs on familiar celebrities and brand-name products as part of its humor structure. Although the package design would appeal to children, the program is designed with adult players in mind.

After Dark 3.0

Publisher: Berkeley Systems, Inc.; 2095 Rose St.; Berkeley, CA 94709; (510) 540-5536; (800) 877-5535, fax (510) 540-5115

System Requirements: Mac Plus or greater; 1MB of RAM

Suggested: Color Monitor (to get the full effect of the vivid color graphics)

Other Platforms (not reviewed): Windows version for IBM PCs and compatibles

Documentation: The first section of this manual—written in a clean, organized fashion—is directed toward the typical user. The second section is written for those of you in programming. It guides you through the creation of your own screen-saving module, which you could enter in Berkeley's annual contest. Those lucky enough to have their images chosen could receive discounts, gifts, and inclusion of those images in the next release of the program.

Support: Technical support is available by mail or telephone, or through online bulletin boards on CompuServe and America Online.

Suggested Retail Price: $49.95

The Program

You can choose from more than 30 entertaining modules designed to prevent screen burn-in. Many modules include sound; virtually all can be modified using the interactive demo module. For example, you can also determine the speed at which the items in the module cruise across the screen, as well as the volume of the accompanying sound. The message module allows you to key in a variety of messages. A logo module allows you to paste your company logo into the program (it appears on-screen when the program engages). After Dark lets you determine how soon the program should engage when there is no activity at the computer. The SystemIQ feature monitors your computer's activity so that After Dark will not slow down database sorts, backups, or other lengthy operations. A password-protection feature allows you to thwart unwanted access when your computer is left on and unattended. This is an extremely entertaining and essential program.

Agent DA 2.0

Publisher: Team Building Technologies; 836 Bloomfield Avenue; Montreal, Quebec H2V 3S6 Canada; (514) 278-3010; fax (514) 278-2874

System Requirements: Macintosh Plus or greater with System 6.0.7 or later

Suggested: Printer

Documentation: The user's manual for this program is clear and straightforward.

Support: If you call for technical support, expect good help.

Suggested Retail Price: $99

The Program

If you need to organize your appointments and be reminded of them at the appropriate time, this easy-to-use calendar program might be suitable for your needs. It has extensive display options. You can also create a recurring event from day to day, week to week, month to month, or year to year. You can choose to see how often you want to be reminded of the event. The reminder is an alarm function with both sound and a reminder box on-screen. Once an activity is finished, you can check it off the calendar. You can also issue a command that finds activities not checked off, or a Find command that searches for any activity. Agent DA is very flexible and simple, and does everything a calendar program should do. For its type, however, it is quite expensive.

Alge-Blaster Plus! (ages 12 and up)

Publisher: Davidson & Associates, Inc.; P.O. Box 2961; 19840 Pioneer Ave.; Torrance, CA 90509; (310) 793-0600, (800) 545-7677; fax (310) 793-0601

System Requirements: IBM PC/Tandy or compatible; VGA, MCGA, Tandy graphics, EGA, CGA, or Hercules graphics; 512K RAM (Tandy graphics require 640K); DOS 2.11 or higher; 3.5-inch or 5.25-inch floppy disk drive

Suggested: Installable on a hard disk; supports Ad Lib and SoundBlaster Music cards; printer and mouse are optional

Other Platforms (not reviewed): Macintosh and Apple II series

Curriculum Areas: This program helps a student learn pre-algebra and algebra fundamentals.

Documentation: The manual contains a quick-start summary inside the front cover, descriptions of the objectives and skills to be mastered in each activity, teaching tips for reinforcement, and instructions for using the program with each platform. The steps are clearly outlined, and the menu options are listed. The manual also includes a troubleshooting guide and an index.

Support: There are hints and on-screen help for this program. For answers to technical questions, you can call customer service at an 800 number on weekdays.

Suggested Retail Price: $49.95 ($59.95 for Macintosh)

The Program

Alge-Blaster Plus! gives the student practice at skills needed to study algebra. The student controls the pace and can review any steps at any time. The fun part is that while playing a challenging graphing game, you are defending a space station against asteroids as you master skills. For example, you can use coordinates to draw "space webs" that keep an asteroid from reaching the station, or use the slope of a line to blast an asteroid.

The game offers a step-by-step, interactive tutorial approach. You can get hints and on-screen help and can access an editor for adding your own problems to the game. The program also contains an on-screen student record-keeping system. To use Alge-Blaster Plus!, your child should have already mastered the four basic math operations—addition, subtraction, multiplication, and division—using whole numbers, fractions, and decimals. Make sure your child understands that he or she should take notes while using this program; information provided on one screen may not be available later on when it is needed. (Younger children may need to be reminded from time to time.)

This program is also available as Alge-Blaster 3 for Windows. In this version, you learn to solve algebraic equations in the Challenger mode in order to help your alien friends defend Planet Quadratica, use your skills to translate enemy messages in Decoder, blast the invaders out of the sky with Simulator, and sharpen your graphing skills in the arcade-style game Red Alert!

Ami Pro for Windows 3.1

Publisher: Lotus Development Corporation; Word Processing Division; 5600 Glenridge Drive; Atlanta, GA 30342; (800) 831-9679

System Requirements: IBM PC or compatible (80386 or higher); 2MB RAM; EGA, VGA, or higher graphics card; hard disk drive with 8MB available; floppy disk drive; Windows 3.1 or higher

Suggested: Mouse, printer

Other Platforms (not reviewed): IBM PC or compatible; Windows version for IBM PCs; OS/2 version 3 for IBM PCs

Documentation: The documentation is well organized and thorough.

Support: The package contains a Quick Start Tutorial for beginners, as well as short, animated lessons on stylesheets, frames, and tables. Help is context-sensitive and accessible at any time. The company offers free 24-hour support.

Suggested Retail Price: $495

The Program

With this version of Ami Pro, Lotus has produced a word processor that challenges the competition. In addition to the usual word processing functions, the program includes a number of improved formatting features—and does it all at a faster speed than the earlier versions. Ami Pro features a spelling checker, grammar checker, thesaurus, and Adobe Type Manager. It provides drag-and-drop editing (you use the mouse to select and move blocks of text), and offers charting and equation-editing features (for use in business and scientific documents).

Like a few other word processing programs, Ami Pro has a SmartMerge option that leads you step-by-step through the creation of form letters. It has an on-screen, Rolodex-style database for use during mail merge. The program can merge from dBASE, Lotus 1-2-3, Excel, Paradox, DIF, or ASCII data. For other data-linking functions, Ami Pro supports the Object Linking and Embedding (OLE) functions of Windows. Ami Pro is tightly integrated to other Lotus programs such as 1-2-3 and Freelance; if you use other Lotus software, the program should be very attractive to you.

Andrew Tobias' Managing Your Money 11.0

Publisher: Block's Financial Software; 55 Walls Dr.; P.O. Box 912; Fairfield, CT 06430; (800) 288-6322; (203) 255-1441

System Requirements: IBM PC or compatible; hard disk drive; 512K RAM; DOS 2.0 or higher

Suggested: Printer

Other Platforms (not reviewed): Macintosh

Documentation: The documentation is straightforward and helpful. Each module of the program is fully described in its own section. A section on troubleshooting covers problems you may encounter and offers possible solutions.

Support: There is an online tutorial that teaches you everything you need to know about the program in 20 minutes. Context-sensitive help screens are available at the touch of a key. Technical support technicians are available if you place a toll call.

Suggested Retail Price: $219.98

The Program

A personal financial manager, Managing Your Money incorporates eight different programs into one easy-to-use, fully integrated package. The Money module is the heart of the program. You record any checks written on your account, and your checkbook is balanced automatically. As transactions are entered, Managing Your Money updates the information automatically throughout the program. This module also helps you budget and forecast available cash, as well as generate reports. The Tax module allows you to estimate the coming year's tax liability. The Analyze module helps answer questions regarding refinancing, saving for your children's education, buying or leasing a car/home, and planning for retirement.

Other modules deal with stocks and bonds; another helps you keep an up-to-date balance sheet on your personal worth. Asset Allocation allows you to map out long-range financial goals with the least possible risk, and build the strategy to achieve them. Managing Your Money also provides for electronic, check-free payment of bills utilizing your existing checking account. With the additional ability to keep track of appointments, vital information on friends, family, and clients, and print personalized letters, Managing Your Money has more functions in one package than you'll probably ever use.

APPROACH FOR WINDOWS 3.0

Publisher: Approach Database Division, Lotus Development Corporation; 800 El Camino Real West; Mountain View, CA 94040; (415) 335-2200

System Requirements: 286 IBM PC or compatible, able to use Windows 3.1 or higher; hard disk drive; floppy disk drive needed for installation

Suggested: At least a 386 microprocessor, printer

Documentation: Documentation for this program includes a Quick Start Reference booklet that summarizes everything you need to know for constructing and using simple flat-file databases. The reference manual is long, but you need it for the complex functions of this relational database package.

Suggested Retail Price: $399

The Program

Approach for Windows is a relational database package that does not require a great deal of learning to begin using. To begin using this package quickly, however, you'll need to understand fields, records, search functions, sorting functions, reporting, and forms. For most functions, you can use the menus or the icons on a vertical bar displayed right below the pull-down menus. Novices can use it to create flat-file databases, design layouts, and generate reports. Defining reports, forms, and mailing labels is easy, as is browsing through files, finding items, and adding or deleting records. The program features a built-in macro facility that lets you combine several jobs into one command.

Approach is compatible with dBASE, Paradox, and Oracle SQL database files. You can also use it as a front end to access existing databases. It can import files from Q&A, Microsoft Works, and FoxPro, among others. It also offers a few other sophisticated features. First, it has a Join command you can use to interrelate fields in two to ten database files, and fill fields in a new database automatically. Second, Approach accepts OLE (object linking and embedding) objects—though you cannot use the feature to carry objects from Approach into another OLE-savvy program. Being medium-priced, Approach offers a few more features than the inexpensive data-manager programs. Though it is within many budgets, it lacks some high-end tools.

ARITHMETIC CRITTERS (AGES 5 TO 7)

Publisher: MECC; Brookdale Corporate Center; 6160 Summit Drive North; Minneapolis, MN 55430-4003; (612) 569-1640; (800) 685-6322; fax (612) 569-1551

System Requirements: Apple II Series; 64K RAM; 5.25-inch floppy disk drive

Curriculum Areas: This program provides practice in adding single digits and subtracting numbers less than 18. It introduces other simple number tasks, such as measuring and counting, and teaches number recognition through 99.

Documentation: The manual is a loose-leaf notebook that includes disks in a plastic pocket. It describes learning objectives, additional activities, and follow-up options.

Suggested Retail Price: $39.95

The PROGRAM

This lively program provides addition practice in Animal Addition adding two groups of up to nine identical animals. Fowl Play gives practice in subtracting one to nine birds from a group of up to 18 birds. Unit Worm lets you work on lengths and perimeters with caterpillars as measuring units. Egg Plant requires you to count from 10 to 99 crates of eggs being shipped from an egg factory and then write the correct numerals. The program offers instructive feedback when you make an incorrect response. The first feedback is a message telling you to try again, the second is a hint, and the third is the correct answer. After every set of 10 problems, a scoreboard appears, describing your performance. This drill-and-practice program also offers teacher options for controlling the difficulty and appropriateness of the program. The menu of options is reached by using a command given in the teacher's manual but not shown on the screen.

ARTS & LETTERS APPRENTICE 1.0

Publisher: Computer Support Corporation; 15926 Midway Road; Dallas, TX 75244; (214) 661-8960

System Requirements: IBM PC or compatible with a 286 microprocessor; 2MB RAM; 9MB of hard disk space; Windows 3.0 or higher

Suggested: A 386 microprocessor or greater is highly recommended.

Documentation: The program requires a great deal of learning; it should have better documentation.

Support: The documentation contains a short, basic tutorial. There are also mini-lessons online, which are self-documenting drawing files that allow the user to practice concepts.

Suggested Retail Price: $169

The Program

This draw program is a stripped-down version of the high-end, expensive Arts & Letters Graphics Editor. It enables you to create drawings, and it has good charting abilities for area, bar, line, pie, and point charts (for which you enter your data on a spreadsheet-like grid). It includes lots of good clip art in many categories (symbols, food, holidays, nature, people, cartoons, maps); the clip art is resizable and can be accessed quickly.

The program includes a superb set of line- and Bézier curve-drawing tools for freehand drawing tasks. You can use a number of stretch, move, shrink, slant, flip, rotate, and duplication tools and rotate, bend, reshape, and resize elements proportionally. Fill patterns include gradient fills. You can use a wealth of colors from 14 palettes, and can mix colors to create more. You can also perform color separations, a capability that even some high-end packages do not have. The program offers 26 typefaces, scalable from 4 to 3200 points, for which you can choose a style, alter kerning, and select a fill pattern. You can make text follow a path or shape, and edit the text once it is placed on the curve. Despite its many features, this program has one element that could be a problem, depending on your needs: It lets you import from only one graphics format (.WMF).

The version of this program for children is called Picture Wizard, which is basically the same except the clip art is geared toward young people. It costs $89.95.

Atlas Pack

Publisher: Mindscape; 60 Leveroni Court; Novato, CA 94949; (415) 883-3000

System Requirements: Macintosh with 2MB RAM and System 6.0.2 or later; CD-ROM drive; 7MB hard disk space

Suggested: Color display available

Other Platforms (not reviewed): Diskette versions are also available.

Documentation: Separate manuals describe the U.S. Atlas and the World Atlas; these list the vast sources of statistical information contained in the atlases.

Support: Registered users can call or write the company's technical support group. E-mail and fax services are also available.

Suggested Retail Price: $ 59.95 for each program

The Program

This set of atlases lets you explore the U.S. or the world via maps. You point and click your way through the maps, indexes, and statistical information. The programs have audio help, and also play anthems of countries and states. Once you have selected a general map, you can zoom in for a closer view of the specific map. Maps are also available that illustrate statistical information (such as topography, government, people, health, education, and crime), which is also available in text form. The U.S. atlas contains city maps as well as state maps. Information included in this program can become outdated quickly. The program also limits the amount of detail found in the maps.

Audioshop

Publisher: Opcode Systems, Inc.; 3950 Fabian Way, Ste. 100; Palo Alto, CA 94303; (415) 856-3333; fax (415) 856-3332

System Requirements: Macintosh 68030 or greater; 4MB RAM; hard disk drive; Sound Manager 3.0; QuickTime 1.6; System 7.0 or later

Suggested: CD-ROM disk drive

Suggested Retail Price: $149.95

The Program

Audioshop is a sound editor for managing audio files. It displays sound as a continuous graph. You can use functions such as sequence, play, record, pause, stop, fast forward, rewind, and track select. You can achieve a variety of effects with the sound such as repeat, pause between, and so on. The program has volume controls, a choice of playback rates, and both mono and stereo capability. You can cut, paste, copy, and fade in or fade out any part of the sound, and use special effects such as echo, vibrato, and reverse. You can play from a computer sound file or an audio CD in a CD-ROM drive. The program can read or write a number of sound formats, including HyperCard and QuickTime, though its editing functions are limited compared to more expensive programs. The program includes some sound effects and music produced by Earwax Studios of San Francisco.

Backgammon, by George! 1.3

Publisher: Graphics Software Labs; P.O. Box 6247; Huntington Beach, CA 92648; (714) 960-6361

System Requirements: IBM PC or compatible; hard disk drive; floppy drive needed for installation

Suggested: Mouse

Documentation: The documentation for this game assumes you already know how to play backgammon. It could use a section on strategy.

Suggested Retail Price: $39.95

The Program

In this program, you play backgammon against the computer. There are three levels of play; once you are a reasonably good player, you can beat the program in the two lower levels. Beginners can use the Suggest Move menu command that recommends a reasonable move for your next play. You can also set up and practice specific situations. There is no option for more than one player.

Bank Street Beginner's Filer (ages 7 to 11)

Publisher: Sunburst Communications; 101 Castleton Street; Pleasantville, NY 10570; (914) 747-3310; (800) 628-8897

System Requirements: Apple II series; 48K RAM; 5.25-inch floppy disk drive; blank disks for storing files

Suggested: Printer

Other Platforms (not reviewed): Commodore 64

Curriculum Areas: This program helps a child with gathering and organizational skills in addition to writing and reading strategies. It teaches the concept of a database.

Documentation: The manual consists of a tutorial for teachers, a teacher's guide for using the program in the classroom, classroom activities and lessons, activity sheets, and a reference section that tells about the program by topic. It is clearly written and bound in a loose-leaf notebook.

Suggested Retail Price: $79

The Program

Bank Street Beginner's Filer is a simple flat-file database program for young people and novice database users; it is a simplified, easy-to-use version of a larger program, Bank Street School Filer. The program helps you collect, organize, locate, and report information. With its options (located in a menu bar at the top of the screen), you can enter information, browse among files, find information, sort information, make a report, change report format settings, and set up printer options. You can create up to 50 records, each with a maximum of ten fields. Although the program is good for introducing the concepts of computer filing programs, it can be quickly outgrown because of these limitations on file size. The package includes a Beginner's Database Disk with several files you can use for practice in some of the database operations (or as examples for creating a new database, if you are teaching).

Barbie PC Fashion Design and Color

Publisher: ATI; 12638 Beatrice Street; Los Angeles, CA 90066; (800) 955-5284; (310) 823-1129

System Requirements: IBM PC or compatible; 640K RAM; EGA graphics; floppy disk drive; DOS 3.2 or higher

Suggested: VGA graphics; hard disk drive; mouse or joystick; printer

Documentation: The documentation is in a leaflet of brief, explicit instructions.

Support: If you have questions, you can call the customer service number between 3:00 p.m. and 5:00 p.m. Eastern Standard Time, or write to the technical support department.

Suggested Retail Price: $30

The Program

If your child is a Barbie fan and also wants to learn how to use a personal computer, this program will make the learning painless. It lets you create a

Barbie look from hundreds of outfits that fit one of the following themes: Barbie Steps Out, Barbie on Vacation, or Barbie at the Fashion Show. You select each item of clothing separately, and color it as you please. You also can choose various accessories such as shoes, and even change Barbie's hair style. A Save feature lets you keep your favorite designs. You can also print out black-and-white pictures to color.

The program is easy to use and provides hours of fun for Barbie fans of all ages. It offers 120 colors on its palette and has a zoom feature that lets you color details. While working, your child learns to select options from a menu, use a toolbox type of menu, enter a number of simple commands, and use devices such as a mouse and a printer. This program is more for entertainment than education, but it can motivate children to learn how to use a computer.

Battle Isle

Publisher: UBI Soft/Electronic Arts; 1505 Bridgeway; Suite 105; Sausilito, CA 94965; (415) 332-8749

System Requirements: IBM PC or compatible; EGA/VGA; floppy disk drive; DOS 3.2 or higher

Suggested: Hard disk drive; mouse or joystick; supports Ad Lib and compatibles

Other Platforms (not reviewed): Amiga

Documentation: Documentation consists of several little booklets: a quick-reference-and-quick-start folder, a booklet that explains the background of the situation, another that explains the machines and weapons of war, and a third that explains other things you need to know. These topics include the game, the battle commands, the buildings, the terrain, combat formations, helpful hints, and other useful information for playing the game. Although the material seems extensive, the manuals could be more helpful about actual game play.

Support: The program lacks a tutorial, which would help beginners understand what is involved in play. The company sells an add-on scenario disk that features 25 new one-player maps and 9 new two-player maps. If you have technical questions, you can write to the company's technical support division, or call the tech support number on weekdays between 8:30 a.m. and 4:30 p.m. Pacific time.

Suggested Retail Price: $49.95

The Program

Two can play this war simulation with its excellent graphics and realistic digital sound. The game is suitable for novices at war gaming, but it is difficult to master. The game takes place on the planet Chromos, where a deadly conflict rages between the humanoid forces of the Druller and the computer-controlled androids of their enemy. The Druller need help quickly and are looking for a true strategist, who happens to be you. To play, you control over 23 playable war elements and use more than 32 maps. There are also two "secret map" missions. It may take several hours to play a single map, so the program enables you to save games for later play.

BizPlan Builder 4.1

Publisher: JIAN; 127 Second St.; Los Altos, CA 94022; (415) 941-9191; (800) 346-5426

System Requirements: Mac 512 or greater; word processor (including Microsoft Word 3.01 or later, MacWrite 4.5 or later, MacWrite II, WordPerfect, Microsoft Works, WriteNow 2.0 and later, and most others); spreadsheet processor (SYLK-compatible full-function)

Suggested: Hard disk drive

Other Platforms (not reviewed): IBM PCs and compatibles; 512K RAM; hard disk drive

Documentation: The manual is very extensive. The first half walks you through the creation of a complete business plan. The second half is a reference guide that covers, in detail, the fundamentals of finance, management, and marketing.

Support: Technical support is available for the cost of a toll call, Monday through Friday, between 9:00 a.m. and 5:00 p.m. Pacific Time. As an extra service, JIAN has a national network of professional consultants who have worked with their software and have expressed interest in assisting JIAN's customers to build businesses. After registering your software package with JIAN, you will receive a free copy of the *JIAN Consulting Associates Directory*.

Suggested Retail Price: $129

The Program

BizPlan Builder uses your own word processor and spreadsheet program to create an effective business plan. The program provides you with over 90 pages in the most popular format already organized into a working outline. All you have to do is key in the information specific to your particular needs. Financial spreadsheet cells are already defined with formulas that calculate totals automatically. You need only load the BizPlan Builder files onto your hard disk or open them directly from the backup copy. As you open the files, they will become available automatically in your word processor or spreadsheet program. If you are in need of capital for a new venture, BizPlan Builder will be a very useful tool.

The Boars Tell Time (Ages 5 to 7)

Publisher: Pelican (A Division of Queue, Inc.); 338 Commerce Drive; Fairfield, CT 06430; (800) 232-2224; (203) 335-0906

System Requirements: Macintosh with 512K RAM

Suggested: Color monitor, printer

Other Platforms (not reviewed): Apple II series with 64K RAM and 5.25-inch disk drive

Curriculum Areas: The program offers practice in telling time, using both analog and digital clocks.

Documentation: The manual is clearly written, with suggestions for further learning activities.

Support: You can select a help option that displays game instructions on the screen.

Suggested Retail Price: $39.95

The Program

In three different types of activities, this program helps you practice telling time using both analog and digital displays. In Telling Time, you set a digital clock to the equivalent time shown on an analog clock. In Setting the Clock, you set the analog clock to the time shown on a digital display. In playing Game Time, you are actually taking a test; after you are finished, you can print a certificate that shows how many correct answers you had. Other reinforcement in the program includes music and animation. There are four levels of difficulty: hours, half hours, quarter hours, and five-minute increments.

The program is easy to use, and makes use of just a few keys. It requires less reading than MECC's ClockWorks, but ClockWorks gives practice in reading and understanding time in written-out form. One problem noted with the Macintosh edition we reviewed is that the help screen tells you to double-click on an activity to activate it—but if you do, you also choose the activity in the next menu that is right under the spot where you clicked. A single click is all that is needed to make each choice. The company also produces The Boars' Store, which helps a child with counting coins and making change.

Buck Rogers XXVc: Matrix Cubed

Publisher: SSI (Strategic Simulations, Inc.); 675 Almanor Avenue, Suite 201; Sunnyvale, CA 94086; (408) 737-6800

System Requirements: IBM PCs and compatibles; 640K RAM; hard disk drive with 2MB free space at minimum; one floppy disk drive needed for installation; EGA or VGA graphics or Tandy graphics; DOS 2.1 or later

Suggested: Ad Lib, SoundBlaster, and Roland sound cards; mouse or joystick

Other Platforms (not reviewed): Amiga

Documentation: Documentation consists of a Rule Book, a Log Book, and a leaflet containing general operation instructions. The Rule Book lists the menu options, and the Log Book contains descriptions of every game element.

Support: If you have trouble solving the puzzle, you can call a 900 number for hints, or buy one of SSI's cluebooks. For answers to technical questions, call the technical support team between 11:00 a.m. and 5:00 p.m. Pacific Standard Time on weekdays, except holidays. Support and hints are also available through several commercial online services.

Suggested Retail Price: $69.95

The Program

Sequels seem to be popular in computer games as well as movies and television shows, and the Buck Rogers XXVc programs are no exception. This science fiction role-playing game is a sequel to Buck Rogers XXVc: Countdown to Doomsday. You can even transfer characters from Countdown to this game.

The object is to rescue scientists who can build the Matrix Device, which can change any substance into pure energy. The Matrix Device is the only hope left for an Earth that has been devastated and enslaved. To find the scientists, you travel throughout the universe. Your characters gain skills and levels as they explore the dangerous universe of the twenty-fifth century. This game is quite involved in the number of skills, weapons, and combat options available. It is designed for people who enjoy complex role-playing games and intend to spend up to 100 hours or more solving the puzzle. The copy-protection scheme requires you to look up words in the Rule Book or the Log Book.

This company, the producers of the Dungeons and Dragons games, also has created such games as No Greater Glory: The American Civil War, Gettysburg: The Turning Point, and Tony La Russa's Ultimate Baseball.

Business Card Maker Deluxe

Publisher: IntraCorp, Inc./Capstone Software; 7200 NW 19th Street, Ste. 500; Miami, FL 33126; (800) 468-7226; (305) 591-5900; fax (305) 591-5633; BBS (305) 471-8962

System Requirements: IBM PC or compatible; DOS 2.1 or higher, or Windows 3.0 or higher; 640K RAM; EGA graphics

Suggested: Mouse, VGA graphics

Other Platforms (not reviewed): Business Card Maker is available for Macintosh, Amiga, Atari ST, and Apple II.

Documentation: The manual is divided into two sections, one for DOS and one for Windows. It clearly describes the operations and tools of this program.

Support: Registered owners can call an 800 number for technical assistance on weekdays between 10:00 a.m. and 6:00 p.m. Eastern time. A company bulletin board system is available 24 hours a day.

Suggested Retail Price: $49.95

The Program

Use this program to design and print your own business cards at home. The program contains 16 typefaces in multiple sizes, and paint features such as air brush, fill patterns, lines, circles, boxes, freehand drawing, cut and paste, invert, rotate, and so on. Templates and logos are also included. The program supports WYSIWYG, along with a magnifying mode for editing. Stock for continuous-feed and laser printers comes with the box, and you can order additional stock from the company. Business cards aren't the only kind of document you can create with this program: Try making badges, name tags, and place cards, too.

CA-Cricket Graph III 3.0

Publisher: Computer Associates International, Inc.; One Computer Associates Plaza; Islandia, NY 11788; (516) 342-5224; (800) 225-5224

System Requirements: Mac Plus or greater; hard disk drive; System 6.07 with 1MB free memory; or 2MB for System 7

Documentation: The User's Guide is well organized, and complete with helpful illustrations throughout the instructional material. Appendixes explain the calculations CA-Cricket Graph III uses to determine specific data, and define and give examples of popular mathematical functions used in graphing.

Support: The built-in online help is extensive. After you register your purchase, technical support is available for the cost of a toll call. If you choose, an 800 service is available for $35 a year.

Suggested Retail Price: $195

The Program

If you need professional graphs with a minimum of effort, CA-Cricket Graph III is a good choice. CA-Cricket Graph III enables you to create high-quality graphs and charts using business, scientific, and engineering data. There are 12 chart types: Scatter, Quality Control, Stacked Bar, Pie, Double T, Polar, Column, Line, Area, Stacked Column, Bar, and Text charts. Graphs are appropriate for scientific, business, and educational use. Data can be imported from word processor, database, or spreadsheet programs, or you can enter it directly into the program. In addition, graphs can be exported in PICT format for use in desktop presentation applications.

CA-Cricket Graph III features the hot-linking of data that updates any change in data automatically for all graphs in which the data appears. The program allows text to be formatted using multiple fonts, styles, and sizes. It also offers extensive page layout capabilities and a drawing toolbox that includes text, zoom, hand, Bézier, rectangle, rounded-rectangle, ellipse, polygon, arc, line, and diamond. Editing graphs you've created using CA-Cricket Graph III is as easy as pointing to the element, clicking the mouse, and making your changes in the dialog box that appears. For scientific uses, CA-Cricket Graph III includes your choice of polynomial, logarithmic, simple, or exponential curve fits.

CA-Super Project for Windows

Publisher: Computer Associates International, Inc.; One Computer Associates Plaza; Islandia, NY 11788; (516) 342-5224; (800) 225-5224

System Requirements: Any 286, 386, or 486 PC or compatible; Windows 3.0 or higher; 2MB RAM; EGA or higher-resolution monitor; enhanced mode or standard mode

Documentation: Documentation is extensive, and includes a Getting Started pamphlet, User Guide, and Reference Manual for CA-Super Project—as well as a User Guide and two Reference Manuals for CA-Realizer, a complete application-development environment capable of producing and running professional applications using a superset of BASIC. The Network Activator Guide describes the ACTIVATE Program, which installs CA-Super Project on a local area network.

Support: CA-Super Project includes Project Manager's Assistant, an online feature that allows you to toggle back and forth between it and your project, providing a step-by-step guide through the procedure of project management. In addition to online help and a tutorial, an Assist mode displays help for the current field automatically when activated. Technical phone support is free for the first 90 days, thereafter you are charged a per-minute fee (or you can purchase CA's Support Plan for $195 a year).

Suggested Retail Price: $895

The Program

CA-Super Project is designed to satisfy a wide range of project-management needs and experience levels. It allows you to define every task type, relationship, and date constraint, and it provides an outline for tasks, resources, and even account codes. Including probability fields allows you to determine your chances of finishing the project within a certain time frame. CA-Super Project also allows you to assign consumable material resources, define variable resource loads and cost-related factors, and use overtime cost-and-availability factors. If necessary, you can view more than one project at a time, each in a separate window. Projects can be linked with the ability to view resource conflicts and level them. Comprehensive import/export capabilities—including a variety of formats, options, and file types—are an attractive feature. CA-Super Project has full DDE and DLL support.

CA-Realizer is also included in the package, offering a complete development language and most of the tools needed for developing, editing, and running applications. This is a stand-alone package unrelated to CA-Super Project.

Calendar Creator Plus 4.0

Publisher: Power Up! Software Corporation; 2929 Campus Drive; San Mateo, CA 94403; (415) 345-5900

System Requirements: IBM PC, XT, AT, PS/2, PS/1, or compatible; 512K RAM; two floppy disk drives; DOS 2.1 or higher; graphics card required for optional page previewing (CGA, EGA, VGA, MCGA, Compaq, and Hercules graphics); HP LaserJet Plus and Series II/III and compatible laser printers, or HP DeskJet series; HP PainterJet; most dot-matrix printers

Other Platforms (not reviewed): Macintosh

Documentation: Documentation for this program includes a quick reference card and a user's manual. The user's manual includes suggestions for designing your calendars, an explanation of pertinent DOS information, and information you need to run the program to its best advantage.

Support: Online help and a tutorial are available to help you understand the program, but in case of questions, technical support is available on weekdays between 8:00 a.m. and 5:00 p.m. Pacific Standard Time.

Suggested Retail Price: $69.95

The Program

This program enables you to create calendars in any size and any style in the following formats: daily, two-day, weekly, monthly, and more. You can enter fixed events (such as appointments), recurring events (such as staff meetings every Monday), and floating events (such as a board meeting the first Tuesday of every month). You can create personal and business calendars and merge them into a master calendar. The program supports popular organizers such as Day Runner, Day-Timers, Lefax, and others.

Calendar Creator offers a number of features for designing your calendar. For example, fonts are scalable from 6 to 72 points. The package includes two typefaces, but Power Up's add-on, Express Fonts, is available for more. You can use PCX images with events on calendars and put graphics at the top of a calendar. You can use scanned images or cut-and-paste one of the more than 40 clip-art images included in the package. You can shade items to highlight holidays or weekends. Some RAM-resident programs will not work with Power Up programs. This program does, however, support expanded memory.

Cartoon Maker

Publisher: IntraCorp, Inc./Capstone Software; 7200 NW 19th Street, Ste. 500; Miami, FL 33126; (800) 468-7226; (305) 591-5900; fax (305) 591-5633; BBS (305) 471-8962

System Requirements: IBM PC or compatible with an 80286 or better microprocessor; 640K RAM; 3MB free hard disk space; DOS 3.3 or higher; EGA graphics

Suggested: VGA graphics, mouse, and printer are optional, but recommended.

Documentation: A single manual explains the system requirements, trouble-shooting problems, keyboard shortcuts, and the "canvas."

Support: If you cannot solve a problem by using either the online help or the troubleshooting sections of the manual, call the company.

Suggested Retail Price: $34.99; additional cartoon images (Political Figures, Meet the Pickleberrys, or Screen Screams) are available by mail at $4 each plus shipping and handling.

The Program

Use this fun program to create cartoon graphics for memos, faxes, posters, flyers, invitations, birthday greetings, children's coloring books, and original cartoons. The program contains over 200 clip-art characters, objects, and backgrounds with dozens of facial expressions and poses for each character. You can color items and add captions to thought and speech bubbles. Then print out the results, using almost any printer.

The interface for this program is easy, being mostly point-and-click. Change the posture of a character using the Body option, or change the facial expression at the Face option. With the Write option, you can put text in a speech or thought balloon, and you can also select the Talk option to make a character appear to talk. Other options include Think, Dagger (to express anger or jealousy), Smoke (to show fire or anger), Dizzy (to show light-headedness), Pain/Star(s) (to show pain or stars in the sky, Musical Notes, Z's for sleep), and others. With this program, you can save your work as PCX, TIFF, or BMP files for export into other software applications. The program is fun to use, but depends upon clip art for successful execution.

Castle of Dr. Brain

Publisher: Sierra, Sierra On-Line, P.O. Box 485; Coarsegold, CA 93614; (800) 326-6654; (209) 683-4468

System Requirements: IBM PC or compatible with a 286 or better; 640K RAM; hard disk drive; VGA graphics

Suggested: Mouse; supports Thunderboard, Pro Audio Spectrum, Ad Lib, Roland MT-32/LAPC-1/CM-32L, SoundBlaster, and Sound Source

Other Platforms (not reviewed): EGA DOS and Tandy

Documentation: The documentation consists of the generic Sierra game manual that explains installation, the icons and cursors, saving games, sources of hints, problems, and instructions for a boot disk (which you may need in order to play the game if your computer does not have enough memory otherwise). A small brochure discusses the game specifically, and displays a secret decoder grid that helps you get into certain doorways once you have earned the secret password. The package contains a *Fantastic Book of Logic Puzzles* that you use without your computer.

Although the documentation explains what you need to know to play the game, you must work your way through this game by trial and error. Each Sierra game *should* tell exactly how to access the program in its manuals; not all its games follow the directions given in the basic "Sierra-generic" manual, and the prompt gives you the startup information only the first time you install the program. This game, for example, is not accessed through its initials (as the manual indicates it should be); instead, you type the word **brain** in a pathname that includes the drive and the directory.

Support: Most Sierra games have clue books available, and an automated telephone hint line with a 900 number. You can also get hints from Sierra's online bulletin board system, and often a commercial information service may offer hints for Sierra games. You can call the company's technical support number for technical help, or write to the customer support department.

Suggested Retail Price: $49.95

The Program

This adventure game has puzzles you must solve to progress through the castle. The puzzles include math puzzles, point-and-click games, 3-D (or four-level) mazes, word puzzles, and a jigsaw room. There are time experiments, astronomy puzzles, robotics, codes and ciphers, and logic, too. You may find yourself confronted with a math puzzle in which you insert numbers so that each column, row, and diagonal equals the same sum. Maybe you will have to figure out how to shut off an alarm clock while at the same time figuring out how to get time cards so you can punch in at another clock. Try all the doors, drawers, cupboards, knobs, and other objects to see if they help you solve a puzzle. The three levels of difficulty are easy (novice), medium, and "brain-blasting."

Although the puzzles may take a while to solve, there is a lot to do in The Castle of Dr. Brain, and you will be entertained by the rock 'n' roll soundtrack while you are thinking. The packaging is designed to appeal to children, but the program is actually designed for a wide range of ages, from 12 to adult.

Castles (Ages 12 and Up)

Publisher: Interplay; 3710 S. Susan, Suite 100; Santa Ana, CA 92704; (800) 969-4263; (714) 549-2411

System Requirements: IBM PC or compatible; CGA and EGA graphics; sound card; floppy disk drive

Suggested: VGA or MCGA graphics; mouse; supports most popular sound cards

Curriculum Areas: This program is based on historical facts, so it builds authentic information about castles while it encourages strategic thinking.

Documentation: The manual describes the world as it was during the time period portrayed, but most children won't have the patience to read this part of the manual. The manual also tells how to load and play the game.

Suggested Retail Price: $59.95

The Program

The year is A.D. 1280 as you start the game; you select your title as Ruler of Albion from the beginning menu. You must stay in power by defending your conquests against warring neighbors, labor accidents, and treacherous family members. Your success depends on your ability to design and build castles.

You pick a site and design the towers, walls, doors, and battlements. You also must plan to hire a certain number and kind of workers, obtain food, and get troops for defense. There always seems to be unrest among the locals, so it is important to keep your workers working and figure out which workers seem to work harder. If you design a complex building, the local people may tear down your walls before you are finished. If you run out of money, you unfortunately must raise taxes among the people, and this may cause even greater unrest. You have achieved success when your castle can withstand an attack. The level of difficulty starts with Peasant, at which time the castle is partially built, and you have unlimited funds.

You can save and resume sessions, a necessary feature because this can be a time-consuming game; failure can result, however, in as little as 15 minutes. A sophisticated program with minimal typing, Castles also requires a lot of reading. A new program called The Northern Campaign is designed to be used with Castles and expand the scope of play. It is a new campaign with new combat features, troop training, and a new plot, including the economics of buying and selling grain and other commodities.

Circus Math (ages 7 to 8, grades 2 to 3)

Publisher: MECC; Brookdale Corporate Center; 6160 Summit Drive North; Minneapolis, MN 55430-4003; (612) 569-1640; (800) 685-6322; fax (612) 569-1551

System Requirements: Apple II series; 48K RAM; floppy disk drive

Suggested: Printer

Curriculum Areas: The program can be used in conjunction with arithmetic. Students should know about place values of numbers before tackling the program.

Documentation: The loose-leaf-notebook manual includes the disks in a plastic pocket. As do the other MECC programs, this manual also offers descriptions of the games, options for teachers, and a variety of additional activities.

Suggested Retail Price: $59

The Program

This program offers practice in whole-number addition with up to four digits and three addends. Each of the games—Clown Maker, Clown Car, High Wire, Cannon Shoot, and Elephant Walk—provides a different combination of addends and number of place values; you can practice a wide variety of addition problems. The rewards for correct answers include making a clown face, making a small figure walk a high wire, shooting a figure out of a cannon, picking up clowns in a clown car, and watching "your elephant" shoot "the computer's elephant" with water. The rewards are not related to the task, although they are fun. The graphics can be turned off so that the practice can be used as remedial work for older students. The teacher has options for changing the timing on some games, comparing the students' scores, and using the printer. The code for reaching the teacher options is in the manual, not on the screen.

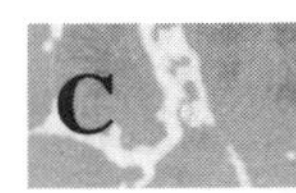

This program is one of a seven-part Mastering Math series. Other programs are Early Addition, Addition Logician, Space Subtraction, Subtraction Puzzles, Multiplication Puzzles, and Quotient Quest. Problems and rewards are similar in nature to those in Circus Math. These programs maintain an educational flavor, and offer an entertaining platform for students who need drill-and-practice work. Students who enjoy arcade games, however, may find these exercises a bit slow.

Civilization

Publisher: MicroProse; 180 Lakefront Drive; Hunt Valley, MD 21030-2245; (410) 771-1151; (800) 879-7529

System Requirements:M PC/XT/AT/PS2/Tandy and most compatibles; 640K RAM; EGA, VGA, MCGA, Tandy graphics; DOS 3.0 or higher

Suggested: Mouse; sound cards supported include IBM, Roland, Ad Lib, SoundBlaster, and Tandy Sound

Other Platforms (not reviewed): Macintosh

Documentation: The documentation consists of a technical guide and a game references guide. The technical guide, well-organized and readable, contains installation and running procedures, key commands, a terrain chart, and a special resources chart. The game references guide is an extensive manual with information about civilizations in general and information required for this game in particular.

Support: An online "Civilopedia" includes information about items of significance in the game. The company will answer technical questions over the telephone through its Customer Service Department weekdays from 9:00 a.m. to 5:00 p.m. Eastern time.

Suggested Retail Price: $69.95

The Program

This program challenges you to create "an empire that stands the test of time." In order to build this empire, you find and manage cities while advancing in technology. You start at the dawn of recorded history (4000 B.C.) and nurture your society toward the Space Age. In the beginning, you must fight to survive by discovering new technologies and fending off barbarians. The program has great flexibility for playing, but you must respond successfully to forces that shaped the past.

Play proceeds in a series of turns, during which you make a number of decisions for your civilization. The computer then takes the turn for the other civilizations. At the beginning of a turn, a disaster can occur unless the target city has prepared ahead of time for the disaster. After each turn, your civilization is evaluated as to advancement, happiness of the people, power, size, and wealth.

You communicate with the game by pointing and clicking the mouse at the various menus and icons. You can save a game for later play. During play, however, you are interrupted by the copyright-protection scheme, which requires you to type answers to questions that appear on the screen. You'll find the answers in the user's manual. This occurs after every 50 turns, which, admittedly, take a while to complete.

A game ends if you choose to quit, if you retire (at which time your civilization score is shown), if you are destroyed, if a spaceship from any of the colonies reaches the Alpha Centauri star system, or if you have conquered the world. For scoring purposes, all games end automatically by a certain date on the timeline, if they haven't ended sooner for other reasons.

ClarisWorks 2.1

Publisher: Claris Corporation; 5201 Patrick Henry Drive; Santa Clara, CA 95052; (408) 727-8227; (800) 554-8554

System Requirements: Macintosh; 1MB RAM (2MB required if using System 7 and 2MB RAM and hard disk drive required for communications usage); two 800K disk drives; System 6.0.5 or later

Suggested: Hard disk drive

Other Platforms (not reviewed): IBM PCs with Windows 3.1 or greater

Documentation: The documentation for this program is generally very good and clear. It could use more examples and more information about some of the specific features.

Support: You can get built-in help online or by using the HyperCard-based tour of the program. The technical support phone lines are often busy, but the help is free except for the toll call.

Suggested Retail Price: $249

The Program

ClarisWorks is an integrated software package (suite) with a smooth interface that consists of word processor, spreadsheet, database, graphics (draw only), and communication modules. The spreadsheet module includes charting with seven chart types, among them 3-D and exploding-pie charts. The charts are updated when the spreadsheet is updated. All modules are adequate on all counts: The communications module is the weakest one, but it does perform the basic communications functions. There is seamless integration among the modules. The program can read and write to other popular file formats including PICT, MacWrite II, and Microsoft Works.

This package is exceptional in its use of frames to integrate the elements of the modules. *Frames* are somewhat like using a program within a program; when a frame is used in any document, it becomes part of that file. The frame appears over text; the text does not wrap around the frame. In any document, a frame can access another module; you can open a spreadsheet frame, for example, while you are in a word processing document. When you click in the frame, the spreadsheet tools become instantly accessible, and program's menus change to spreadsheet from word processor.

The program uses the standard Macintosh techniques, and is easy to learn and use. A spelling checker and thesaurus are available from the different modules. You have full access to drawing tools from the word processor, spreadsheet, and database modules. Although you can insert automatic footnotes into a document, there is no outlining capability and the macro-making capabilities are limited in editing functions.

ClarisWorks is useful with the 20MB Macintosh PowerBooks. From each module, you can easily move up to Claris's full-featured programs (MacWrite II, FileMaker Pro, Resolve, and MacDraw Pro) if you need greater capabilities.

ClockWorks (Ages 5 to 8, Grades 1 to 3)

Publisher: MECC; Brookdale Corporate Center; 6160 Summit Drive North; Minneapolis, MN 55430-4003; (612) 569-1640; (800) 685-6322; fax (612) 569-1551

System Requirements: Apple II Series; 64K RAM; 5.25-inch floppy disk drive

Curriculum Areas: The program consists of four parts that teach and review time in analog and digital forms.

Documentation: The manual is bound in a loose-leaf notebook with the disks in a plastic pocket. It lists learning objectives and offers preparation suggestions for the teacher as well as follow-up activities for the students.

Suggested Retail Price: $59

The Program

This drill-and-practice program gives practice telling time. The What's the Time option requires you to read the time shown on an analog clock and select the correct time from four possible choices. In Set the Clock, you are given the time on a digital clock and must set that time correctly on an analog clock. Digital Drill is similar, except that you set a digital clock, given time expressions in words or the time on an analog clock. If you make a mistake, you can try twice to enter the correct answer, after which the program shows the answer. The program does not offer clues or help.

For fun, you can select Clock Factory and design your own alarm clock; you select features such as the shape of the clock, the type of numerals on the clock face, and the time the alarm will go off. When the alarms on the clocks you build go off, there is a wide range of consequences.

Options for the teacher or parent are reached through a command shown only in the teacher's manual. By using the options, you can set the time intervals for hours, half hours, quarter hours, or five-minute increments. ClockWorks also offers the option of turning off the sound; the program can be used in school situations without the alarm being heard. A child should be able to read at second-grade level in order to use the program independently.

Close-Up 4.01

Publisher: Norton-Lambert Corp.; P.O.Box 4085; Santa Barbara, CA 93140; (805) 964-6767; fax (805) 683-5679

System Requirements: IBM PC, XT, AT, PS/2, or 100-percent compatible; DOS 3.0 or higher; Hayes and all popular modems (including h-speed modems running V.32, V.32*bis*, V.42, and V.42*bis*); monochrome through VGA monitors; up to 244K RAM, depending on function

Suggested: Mouse; Windows 3.0 or higher (optional); usable on network

Documentation: Documentation for this program consists of two spiral-bound manuals that are well-organized and well-designed. One is for the Support/ACS (Remote Side); the other is for the Customer Terminal. Each book has a "Getting Started" chapter that lets you set up and use your program quickly; the remainder of each book is filled with specifics about using the program. The illustrations in both books could be improved.

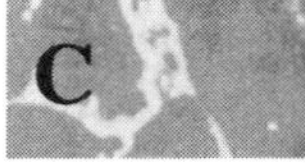

Suggested Retail Price: $199 (dual pack: host and remote site)

The Program

With Close Up you can control another computer remotely via modem. One practical use is to enable two people to work together on spreadsheets, databases, accounting, and word processing programs. To do this, you need both programs of the package, the Customer/Terminal and the Support/ACS. (The customer program can communicate with another customer program, but only to exchange data. The support program cannot communicate with another support program.)

For terminal communications, you would use the Customer/Terminal program to access information systems, bulletin boards, and time-sharing larger computers. In addition to sending e-mail, you can send and receive items at the same time you are working on another application. For automated communications, you would use the ACS part of the support program to exchange files with computers outfitted with Customer/Terminal programs; no other user needs to be at the other end. This means these operations can be done automatically at night, when telephone rates are low. You can also print remotely.

The program includes virus protection, multi-level password security, a Dial Back facility (to check whether a call is legitimate), and a chat window for conversing remotely. The program includes support for both Windows and DOS. It has a fast, easy-to-use interface with pull-down menus and optional mouse operation.

Code Quest (Grades 4 to 7)

Publisher: Sunburst Communications; 101 Castleton Street; Pleasantville, NY 10570; (914) 747-3310; (800) 628-8897

System Requirements: Apple II series; 48K RAM; 5.25-inch floppy disk drive

Suggested: Color monitor

Other Platforms (not reviewed): Commodore 64, IBM PC, PS/2, Tandy 1000

Curriculum Areas: The program is excellent for developing problem-solving strategies and improving skills in reading comprehension.

Documentation: The documentation is in a loose-leaf notebook with a three-ring plastic pocket for disks. It offers hints for solving codes and tells how to use the program on each platform.

Suggested Retail Price: $65

The Program

Code Quest presents a mystery object and clues for guessing what it is. The catch is, the clues are coded; you must break one of several codes before you can understand the clues. A help option offers hints; a test option lets you enter a set of known letters (for example, your name) that the computer arranges in the same code format as the original clue.

There is no time limit to solve the puzzle. You can enter a guess after you have deciphered the first clue; however, if you guess wrong, the game is over and you can start a new mystery search. In addition, you must type the answer correctly; a misspelling is counted as a wrong answer and ends the game. If you guess correctly, you have the option to enter your own mystery object and set of six clues.

Code Quest helps you hunt for critical information, look for patterns or sequences, analyze information, and use trial-and-error strategies or a process of elimination. You can customize the program to fit a specific subject area such as history or geography. The graphics are somewhat dated, but if your child likes puzzles and codes, this program presents a number of well-designed challenges.

Color It! 2.3

Publisher: Timeworks International, Inc.; 625 Academy Drive; Northbrook, IL 60062; (708) 559-1300

System Requirements: Macintosh Classic or greater; 2MB RAM; hard disk drive; System 6.0.5 or later (System-7-compatible); 32-bit QuickDraw

Suggested: Gray-scaled or color monitor; 8-bit video card

Documentation: The User's Manual for this program contains both tutorial and reference sections including a large number of illustrations; printed page tabs let you locate items quickly. The glossary could be more complete.

Support: The well-constructed tutorial uses files already included with the program. The program supports Balloon Help in System 7. To receive technical support, you must have registered your program.

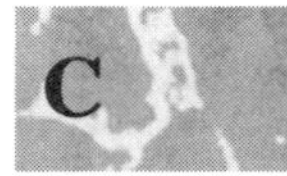

Suggested Retail Price: $299.95

The Program

Color It! is both a 32-bit color paint program and an image-enhancement program. Designed for novices as well as professional artists, its easy-to-learn user interface has a toolbox, a color palette, pattern tools, menus, and dialog boxes with buttons and checkboxes. You can edit the toolbox to suit a particular task. It offers 16 million colors and almost every tool you can imagine. You can use the program to superimpose one image on another, colorize gray-scale images, and select fill patterns from a pattern palette. The program supports pressure-sensitive graphics tablets so you can create brush strokes that mimic traditional painting techniques.

The program enables you to crop, retouch, edit, scale, rotate, flip, stretch, grow to (snap to), slant, and distort images. You can change the perspective or the resolution of a picture. You can erase blemishes, clean up cluttered backgrounds, and adjust an image's brightness and contrast. You can blend, smudge, stamp, smooth, blur, and sharpen the edges of an object. There are antialiasing tools for rounding out the edges of text or colored objects. You can select the degree of transparency of color, or select a brush that lays down a gradient line. A scratchpad is available for testing brushes on a portion of the image before you work on the full image. Multiple undo and redo features let you back up 15 times so you can experiment and correct mistakes. You can use the masking feature to block out areas before you apply a pattern or brush. You can save files in a number of formats; a couple of add-ins make the program especially useful for work with photographs.

ColorMe (Ages 3 to 10)

Publisher: Mindscape Educational Software; Department D; 1345 W. Diversey Parkway; Chicago, IL 60614; (800) 829-1900

System Requirements: IBM PC or compatible; 256K RAM; 5.25-inch floppy disk drive; Koala Pad, mouse, or joystick

Suggested: Color monitor; printer

Other Platforms (not reviewed): Apple II series, 128K RAM

Curriculum Areas: This program helps children experiment with color and composition in drawing pictures, develop reasoning skills, and practice writing about their work.

Documentation: The manual explains how to use the program.

Support: The company provides products that extend the use of the program. ColorMe Picture Disks, for example, contain additional predrawn pictures (clip art), and the ColorMe Supply Box contains supplies for making items such as greeting cards and stickers.

Suggested Retail Price: $29.95

The Program

With this program, you can create original art or use dozens of clip-art pictures. It is known as the easiest paint program on the market, simple enough for a three-year-old to figure out, yet older children can use more challenging options. It also appeals to a wide variety of children, regardless of gender or background.

Drawing tools include different-sized crayons, different colors, four sizes of text, and two drawing styles. The user can erase a drawing by choosing a crayon color to match the background color and coloring over the drawing, a method similar to using white-out. There is also an Erase Page option. A text option enables you to add short captions or messages to your drawing.

Complete House

Publisher: Deep River Publishing; P.O. Box 9715-975; Portland, Maine 04104; (207) 871-1684; fax (207) 871-1683

System Requirements: IBM PC or compatible with a 12MHz 80386 SX or better microprocessor; 2MB RAM; Windows 3.1 or higher; DOS 3.1 or higher; 30MB hard disk drive; MPC-compatible CD-ROM drive; SVGA graphics; sound card; mouse; Microsoft CD-ROM Extensions 2.2 or later

Suggested: 4MB RAM recommended

Documentation: A flyer included in the disc case describes the program briefly, lists troubleshooting questions, and notes system requirements. A complete reference guide is included on the disc for the CAD/FP drawing package.

Support: Call or write to the company with questions.

Suggested Retail Price: $39.95

The Program

Complete House contains four major parts, as described here. House Design analyzes the relationship among the homeowner, environment, and house, and explains historic American construction techniques, plan types, and styles. Kitchen & Bath Design helps you plan kitchens and baths that work well. The Magazine of Design contains plans and photos of homes by leading architects and building companies. CAD/FP is a drawing package that includes 20 completed floor plans, but also lets you experiment with your own ideas.

Other CD-ROM titles by Deep River include Fractal Ecstacy (which contains patterns, designs, and animations), Adventures (a multimedia resource for worldwide adventure travel), Everywhere USA Travel Guide (attractions and things to do in the United States), and Great Restaurants (a multimedia guide to restaurants, wineries, and microbreweries).

The Complete Maus

Publisher: The Voyager Company; (800) 446-2001; (914) 591-5500

System Requirements: Macintosh; CD-ROM drive

Suggested Retail Price: $59.95

The Program

Based on Art Spiegelman's Pulitzer-Prize-winning novel, this program is about the Holocaust. It is a literary work that has been very well adapted to the CD-ROM format. The story is about Spiegelman's father and his life in Eastern Europe before and during World War II. Although told in comic-book format, the story is serious; it includes excerpts from taped interviews with the father. Spiegelman himself talks about his experiences writing the book, shows family photographs, and explains his relationship with his father.

Compton's Interactive Encyclopedia 2.0

Publisher: Compton's New Media, Inc.; 2320 Camino Vida Roble; Carlsbad, CA 92009; (619) 929-2500; (800) 862-2206; fax (619) 929-2600

System Requirements: IBM PC or compatible with 386SX/16 or better CPU, 4MB RAM, 256-color SVGA monitor, 30MB hard disk drive, and MIDI-compatible 8-bit sound card; floppy drive for installation; single-speed CD-ROM drive; speakers; headphones; mouse

Suggested: Double-speed CD-ROM drive; 16-bit sound card

Other Platforms (not reviewed): Macintosh; available for use with Windows 3.1 or greater

Suggested Retail Price: $395

The Program

This package consists of the 26 volumes of the 1991 print edition of *Compton's Encyclopedia* on a CD-ROM disk. It includes articles, maps, graphs, drawings, captioned photographs, recorded sounds, and speech. It has an electronic atlas, a time line, and Merriam-Webster's Intermediate Dictionary. You can access information by searching for ideas, major topics, article titles, pictures, or captions. For multimedia effects, you use the icons—for example, click on the camera to see pictures, or the headphone to hear speech, music, or other sounds. A bookmark option lets you mark a place for later reading. A notebook file can store items for later use.

The program is noted for its ease of use and more than 7,000 images. It has an icon-based tool bar, an atlas that allows "hot links" between locations on the maps and related articles, topic trees, and hypertext links from text to dictionaries. The InfoPilot feature lets you select a key article and ask the program to find four related articles. All articles are then shown in their own scrollable windows. The Merriam-Webster Online Dictionary and Ami Pro 3.0 for Windows are bundled with the program.

Compton's offers various CD-ROM reference titles. Guinness Disc of Records (UniDisc/Britannica Software), for example, is a fun resource for kids and the whole family ($99.95 for MS-DOS and Macintosh, $149.95 for MPC). Mammals: A Multimedia Encyclopedia (National Geographic Society; 17th and M Streets, NW; Washington, D.C. 20036 800/368-2728) is available for MS-DOS. The New Grolier Encyclopedia (Grolier Electronic Publishing; Sherman Turnpike; Danbury, CT 06816; 800/356-5590) is priced at $395 for MS-DOS or Macintosh.

Computer Acquire

Publisher: The Avalon Hill Game Company (A Division of Monarch Avalon, Inc.); 4517 Harford Road; Baltimore, MD 21214; (410) 254-9200

System Requirements: IBM PC or compatible; 256K RAM minimum; floppy disk drive

Suggested: Microsoft-compatible mouse

Documentation: The documentation is a little four-page leaflet, including the game rules, loading procedure, and a game glossary. To understand the documentation, it helps to have already played the board-game version of Acquire.

Suggested Retail Price: $24.95

The Program

This game is the computerized version of the classic board game Acquire, advertised as adhering to "Acquire's high standards of fun, strategy, and greed." Players buy hotels, create hotel chains, and trade stock in those chains, the object being to become the richest player in the game. Each player begins with $6000 and six hotels. The game is for two to six players, with the option of playing against human players or computer players. Games can be saved to finish later, but a typical game lasts under an hour.

The program is menu-driven, with clear, easy-to-read screens. If you don't use the mouse, you'll use mainly the arrow and Enter keys. As with other computer games of this nature, the major problem occurs when you are playing against other human players: When it's your turn, the other players should not look at the screen, but this rule is sometimes hard to enforce.

Conflict Catcher

Publisher: Casady & Greene Inc.; (800) 359-4920; (408) 484-9228

System Requirements: Macintosh Plus; System 7

Suggested Retail Price: $79.95

The Program

This utility program tracks down startup problems relating to extensions and control panel options. Automatically and systematically, Conflict Catcher disables all combinations of extensions and control panels, periodically asking you to determine whether the problem still exists. It also allows you to organize startup items so that user-specified groups of extensions and control panels can be loaded when you press specific keys during startup. The program can also disable or enable files in your startup and font folder.

Conversions Plus for Windows

Publisher: DataViz, Inc.; 55 Corporate Drive; Trumbull, CT 06611; (203) 268-0030; fax (203) 268-4345

System Requirements: IBM PC hard disk drive; VGA or better monitor; 2MB RAM; Windows 3.0 or higher; high-density floppy disk drive

Documentation: The manual is well written and clearly organized.

Support: Registered users are entitled to free technical support on weekdays from 9:00 a.m. to 6:00 p.m. Eastern time.

Suggested Retail Price: $149

The Program

This program enables you to exchange documents between popular Macintosh and PC programs, at the same time retaining document formatting specifications including embedded graphics. The extensive file-translation paths enable this feature. With Conversions Plus, you can also use Macintosh disks in your PC drive after installing the Macintosh disk-mounting utility. Then you can convert your files into either PC or Macintosh format. The interface for this program makes it easy to use: All you have to do is click on a file, and the computer does the rest.

Coordinate Math 1.1 (Grades 4 to 9)

Publisher: MECC; Brookdale Corporate Center; 6160 Summit Drive North; Minneapolis, MN; 55430-4003; (612) 569-1640; (800) 685-6322; fax (612) 569-1551

System Requirements: Apple II series; 128K RAM; floppy disk drive

Curriculum Areas The program provides practice in using grids, coordinates, and maps. It can be used in conjunction with arithmetic.

Documentation: Documentation includes descriptions of the games, additional classroom activities, and worksheets. It is written to help a teacher with learning objectives and specifics about curriculum and appropriate grade and reading levels. It is a loose-leaf notebook with disks in a plastic pocket on the inside front cover.

Suggested Retail Price: $59

The Program

Three games—Nomad, Snark, and Radar—give you practice using coordinates. In Nomad, you must move the cursor from the airport to Grandma Nomad's house (she moves around a lot)—either by entering N, S, E, and W (for North, South, East, or West), or by entering the coordinates (letter, number) of each intersection on the map. The coordinates are for first-quadrant ordered pairs.

Once you feel comfortable using the coordinates in Nomad, try Snark. Here you must find the Snark hidden somewhere on a grid. You place circular nets to snare it by specifying the center and the radius of the circle. The center is entered in the form of coordinates. Once the circle, or "net," is drawn, the computer tells you whether the Snark is inside or outside the circle. You adjust your play from there, and have 12 tries to find the Snark. You can play in any of the four x- and y-axis quadrants. There are three levels of difficulty. The easiest shows all the points you have eliminated in your search; the hardest requires you to remember the eliminated points.

Radar is a simulation in which your rescue boat must save a runaway ship. To get to the ship, you choose to work with either degrees or coordinates. To be successful, you must be able to use angles, understand the relationship between angle size and degree measurement, or be able to find and use ordered pairs in all four quadrants. If you don't arrive in time, the ship crashes.

The games have teacher options for controlling and locking out certain activities or levels, such as turning the sound on or off. The rewards are related to the task at hand, and to whether or not you accomplish it. Tasks are interesting and appropriate to the information to be learned. In use the program seemed schoolish, and ran slowly on a 128K Apple IIe.

CorelDRAW! 3.0 for Windows

Publisher: Corel Systems Corporation; The Corel Building; 1600 Carling Avenue; Ottawa, Ontario; K1Z 8R7 Canada; (800) 836-DRAW; (613) 728-8200; fax (613) 728-9790

System Requirements: IBM PC or compatible with an 80386 or better microprocessor; 4MB RAM; hard disk drive with 10MB free space (23MB for full installation and 33MB if you use everything that comes on the CD-ROM); one floppy disk drive needed for installation; graphics card that supports Windows; mouse or other pointing device; Windows 3.1 or higher

Suggested: 8MB RAM; CD-ROM drive

Support: The program includes online help. Technical support by telephone is free for registered users, but a call to Canada from the United States can be expensive.

Suggested Retail Price: $105.95

The Program

This easy-to-use drawing program is geared toward users who are preparing illustrations and designs rather than technical drawings. CorelDRAW! includes a CD-ROM with 50 animation sequences, a library of over 14,000 clip-art images, and 250 fonts (TrueType and Adobe Type 1 formats). The program also supports object linking and embedding (OLE); thus you can insert drawings into other applications (such as a Word for Windows document) or put a document such as a spreadsheet directly into a CorelDRAW! file. You can use the program for painting, charting, and multimedia presentations. It is basically a jack-of-all-trades graphics program that business users will like. Professional artists, however, may prefer specialized programs.

To use the program, you will work in one of several modules. In CorelCHART! you can create many different types of charts, including bar, pie, line, standard deviations, 3-D scatter, spectral, pictograph, and histogram. You can rotate a chart in three dimensions, and import data from popular packages. In the module called CorelPHOTO-PAINT!, you can touch up scanned or bit-mapped images, and work in color or black and white. When you are finished, you can put the images in the presentation module, CorelSHOW!; it accepts drawings, charts, sound, video, and animation for creating multimedia presentations. If you need to convert bit-mapped images into draw objects (vectors), you can use the CorelTRACE! module to edit or change curves easily. You can catalogue drawings and clip art in the module called CorelMOSAIC!

The program includes powerful text-handling capabilities with a spelling checker and a thesaurus. You can merge external text into a design, or type text directly into a drawing. Kerning and other spacing is easy; you just drag the "handles" on words or letters. You can align text on a curve, and even perform manual kerning on a curve. Available to you are 153 fonts in TrueType, which can be used in all Windows 3.1 applications. The program also supports Adobe Type 1 fonts, and offers Adobe Type Manager free to PostScript users.

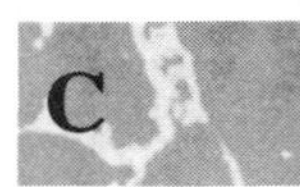

The graphics tools are easy to learn and use. You can stretch, distort, and wrap objects. You can project elements in three dimensions, and rotate objects in three dimensions. You can create multi-layer drawings and make each layer nonprintable, invisible, or locked.

CorelDRAW! 4.0 for Windows ($275.95) includes version 3, plus additional art and technical enhancements, object-oriented animation, OCR capabilities, and multi-page layouts. It has 750 fonts and over 18,000 clip-art images. CorelDRAW! 5.0 for Windows ($459.95) is speedy, offers enhanced color management, and contains 825 fonts and 22,000 clip-art images.

Correct Grammar for Windows 2.0

Publisher: Writing Tools Group, Inc.; 201 Alameda del Prado; P.O. Box 6113; Novato, CA 94948; (800) 523-3520; (415) 382-8000; fax (415) 883-1629

System Requirements: IBM PC or compatible with a 286 or better microprocessor; 640K RAM; VGA graphics; Windows 3.0 or higher; DOS 3.1 or higher; floppy disk drive; hard disk drive

Suggested: 80386 microprocessor or higher; additional RAM strongly recommended

Other Platforms (not reviewed): Macintosh

Documentation: Documentation is adequate, though it could use more and better illustrations. You can use a separate Technical Reference Manual while learning to use the rule-writing language and the compiler.

Support: On-screen tutorials offer examples and clarify the problem at the error being flagged.

Suggested Retail Price: $99

The PROGRAM

This grammar checker contains a 135,000-word spelling checker. It does a good job of catching errors, and it provides context-sensitive suggestions for changes. It gives advice and explanations specifically about the error being flagged. It also checks readability. The program installs easily, and operates with menus and well-labeled buttons. When an error is flagged (by highlighting), you can choose among the response buttons, including Check/Change, Ignore, Tutorial, Quiet, and Edit.

Correct Grammar also contains nine style sheets that can use or ignore specific grammar rules for particular kinds of writing. For example, business writing and technical writing stylesheets will not allow certain types of clichés, but may be less rigid than the legal stylesheet. Creative writing is quite relaxed. You can customize your own stylesheet, and create your own rules using the program's rule-writing language and compiler. The program works with any Windows application that can read the Clipboard; it has special links for use with programs such as Ami Pro, WordPerfect for Windows, and Word for Windows.

CROSSTALK FOR WINDOWS

Publisher: Digital Communications Assoc.; (800) 348-3221; (404) 442-4000

System Requirements: PC; Windows 3.1

Suggested Retail Price: $179

The PROGRAM

CrossTalk is a communications software package that offers a bevy of features, including very powerful scripting capabilities. Automating keystrokes is a breeze with QuickPads that allow you to create buttons and icons for common online activities. QuickBar allows you easy access to frequently used functions.

THE CRUNCHER (AGES 10 TO ADULT)

Publisher: Davidson & Associates, Inc.; P.O. Box 2961; 19840 Pioneer Ave.; Torrance, CA 90509; (310) 793-0600; (800) 545-7677; (800) 556-6141; fax (310) 793-0601

System Requirements: Macintosh LC, II, Performa, Centris, or Quadra series; System 7.0 or higher; 2MB RAM; 8MB hard disk space

Suggested: Memory and free disk space quoted are minimums—more is recommended; printer

Other Platforms (not reviewed): IBM PC, Tandy, and PC compatibles; 286 CPU or higher; Windows 3.1 or higher; VGA; hard disk drive; sound card suggested

Curriculum Areas: This program can help a student learn about spreadsheets as well as about planning ahead, analyzing finances, and communicating results. The spreadsheet can be used to set up various types of math problems unrelated to money, too.

Documentation: The manual is well written and easy to comprehend; it includes a "how-to" Quick Reference. Appendixes list menus, preset projects, and tutorials, as well as offering troubleshooting hints and a glossary.

Support: The manual contains a troubleshooting appendix, and the program has online tutorials as well as online help. Customer Support Technicians can be reached by telephone on weekdays from 7:00 a.m. to 6:00 p.m., by fax 24 hours every day, or by mail.

Suggested Retail Price: $59.95

The Program

The Cruncher is a spreadsheet program with enough features to do almost any school or home project. All options are available through pointing and clicking at the menu bar or other areas of a worksheet. Highlight a cell, click on the sound icon, and the computer will read aloud the contents of the cell you have selected.

You can also create stickers to illustrate or highlight an important point. A sticker may contain a preset image, a sound, a frame, and text. You can import your own art through the Clipboard, or create your own sticker sound if your machine has a microphone.

The program's preset functions are sum, average, median, mode, maximum, and minimum, plus two sets of advanced functions—some of which are trigonometric. Ten preset projects are ready to recieve your data; these include Can We Get a Pet?, Travel Planner, Party Planner, Baseball Statistics, and others. Opts for charting are bar, line, scatter, and pie. An online notebook can be used for special notes about a spreadsheet, and data in a particular note can be locked.

This program is colorful, fun to use, and easy to use. It is the first of Davidson's new Power Tools series—a set of educational programs "designed to empower students age 10 to adult to think, analyze, and communicate in the Information Age."

dBASE for DOS 5.0

Publisher: Borland International, Inc.; 100 Borland Way; Scotts Valley, CA 95066-3249; (800) 682-9299; (408) 431-1000; fax (408) 431-4123

System Requirements: IBM PC, XT, Personal Computer AT, PS/2, or 100-percent compatible; Compaq Portable II, III, DeskPro 286 and 386, SystemPRO, or compatible; 4MB RAM; hard disk drive with 9MB minimum available space; one 1.2MB (high-density) 5.25" floppy disk drive or one 720K 3.5-inch floppy disk drive required for installation (360K low-density 5.25-inch format is also available); monochrome or color graphics (CGA, EGA, or VGA); DOS 3.1 or higher

Suggested: 8087 or 80387 math co-processor; mouse; supports a wide range of dot-matrix, laser, and ink-jet printers

Other Platforms (not reviewed): Version 5.0 for Windows has just been released, and it lets you develop applications visually.

Documentation: Documentation for this program consists of a four-inch-thick stack of manuals and reference booklets. It includes a Quick Reference Guide, a Getting Started manual, a user's manual, a programming manual, and a language reference guide.

Support: The Getting Started manual includes a tutorial that uses sample files provided on the disks. The documentation material also addresses the most frequent questions that Tech Support receives. The package includes keyboard templates you can lay on your keyboard while using the program. The company also offers a publication called *TechNotes* for "power users," at $40 for 12 issues. This magazine includes mostly programming items for dBASE application development, with usage tips, utilities, applications and programming tips. A Hot Line is open from 6:00 a.m. to 5:00 p.m. Pacific Standard Time, or you can write to the company. You can also access CompuServe and BIX forums for help. Technical help is available only for registered users.

Suggested Retail Price: $795

The Program

This relational database program is very popular in PC-based businesses. It is usable without programming knowledge, though it does provide programming capabilities. You can create databases by just filling in the blanks on the database-design screen, or use automatic tools for developing applications to make use of the data. You can see at a glance any data files, data-entry forms, reports, labels, queries, and applications. dBASE enables you to manage single and multiple related tables, custom forms with data validation, flexible report formats for printing labels, free-form reports, and tabular reports. Its applications generator enables you to develop your own applications with minimal programming; it has a programming language for developing custom applications suited to a specific business.

The Query By Example (QBE) feature lets you set up queries that display selected information from one or multiple files. You mark fields you want to see with conditions you set up by using simple formulas and expressions. IQ! (Index Query optimizer) enables QBE to select automatically the fastest method for retrieving your data. If you are a more advanced user or a professional application developer, you can use the dBASE language, the Template Language, and SQL (Structured Query Language). The dBASE language has more than 460 commands and functions; it includes advanced relational capabilities of SAA-compliant SQL.

Relational databases use SQL; with dBASE, a user can operate on data as relations or as tables, and choose to do all operations on these tables. A compiler provides control of generated code; a symbolic debugger and editor help in the development of applications. With the applications already within the dBASE program, however, you can perform one or more database-management tasks. The program allows multiuser access to data and applications on LANs, with file-locking and data-security measures.

There's a great deal to learn about dBASE; if you have never used a database before, you may want to start with a simple program or get experienced help before you begin using this program.

D-Day: The Beginning of the End

Publisher: Impressions Software, Inc.; 222 Third Street, Ste. 0234; Cambridge, MA, 02142 (617) 225-0848

System Requirements: IBM PC or compatible with an 80286 or better microprocessor; 640K RAM; VGA graphics; DOS 3.0 or higher; hard disk drive; Microsoft-compatible mouse

Suggested: 80386 or better microprocessor recommended; supports SoundBlaster or compatible sound card

Documentation: The manuals include a Quick Reference Card, a Strategic Operations Handbook, a Tactical Operations Handbook, a Technical Supplement and Tutorial, and An Overview of Overlord. Also check the README.TXT file included with the program.

Support: Using the Quick Start Tutorial will help you learn to play the game. The Technical Support and Tutorial manual contains troubleshooting solutions, but if you still have problems, you can call the company's technical support line on weekdays from 9:00 a.m. to 5:30 p.m. Eastern time. Help can also be reached through the company's BBS system, or through several online services such as CompuServe, GEnie, and PRODIGY.

Suggested Retail Price: $ 69.95

The Program

Aficionados of World War II will enjoy this strategy game in which you can elect to play on either side of the conflict. You can customize the starting conditions for the game and select from among difficulty options. For example, for an easier game (unless starting conditions have been altered), play the Allied side, select the Easy Mode, and turn off the Supply option so you do not have to pay attention to the supply levels of your troops. Using the Personality option makes for a more difficult game, because you have to worry about distinct personality traits of your generals, which can complicate strategy. At the Campaign level of play, you get your bearings, move into position, and engage the enemy. At the Micro Miniatures level, you can control just about every aspect of each battle as it occurs. D-Day: The Beginning of the End requires intensive reading and study to play well. Be prepared to spend a lot of time playing.

Dabbler

Publisher: Fractal Design; (800) 297-2665; (408) 688-8800

System Requirements: Macintosh II; 4MB RAM

Suggested Retail Price: $99

The Program

This paint program is actually simulated art in action. Select the medium on which you choose to work (paper type) and the tool you want to use (crayon, chalk, pastels), and you're ready to create. You can apply a number of special effects to your creation, including brush strokes to give your art a painted look. Dabbler can teach you to draw or further refine your artistic abilities.

The Dagger of Amon Ra (A Laura Bow Mystery)

Publisher: Sierra, Sierra On-Line; P.O. Box 485; Coarsegold, CA 93614, (800) 326-6654; (209) 683-4468

System Requirements: IBM PC or compatible with a 286 or better microprocessor; 640K RAM; 256-color VGA or 16-color EGA (for Tandy, VGA only); hard disk drive; floppy disk drive

Suggested: Mouse; 386 or better microprocessor, supports Thunderboard, Pro Audio Spectrum, Ad Lib, Roland MT-32/LAPC-1/CM-32L, and SoundBlaster sound cards

Documentation: The documentation consists of several booklets. The game manual provides generic instructions for all Sierra games. In addition, The Dagger of Amon Ra includes a museum leaflet you can use as a map. The Museum Guide contains answers to some questions you may be asked, lists some sources if you are interested in Egyptology, and provides the background behind this mystery (as well as information about other museum exhibits). The package includes an additional Instructions leaflet that walks you through a game to help you get started.

Support: Most Sierra games have clue books available, and an automated telephone hint line with a 900 number. You can also get hints from Sierra's online bulletin board system, and often a commercial information service may offer hints for Sierra games. For technical help, you can call or write to the company's customer support department.

Suggested Retail Price: $69.95

The Program

Laura Bow, as a cub reporter for a major New York newspaper, is trapped in a museum in the dead of night with various socialites, miscreants, thieves, and a murderer. She must uncover the secret of the Dagger of Amon Ra, an ancient

Egyptian artifact, and find out why it was stolen. Using the point-and-click interface, you'll take her through hidden passages and rooms containing secrets and suspects. Click on one of the icons in the icon bar, and you can ask questions of the other characters, write down answers in Laura Bow's notebook, look at something in a drawer or behind a door, or do any of the other actions needed to solve the mystery. The story line is complex and multi-layered; several endings are possible.

The program is set in the 1920s, and includes period music, costumes, and cars. Sierra artists used hand-painted scenes to generate the digital background art. The characters' lips even move during conversations, though the lip sync doesn't quite match the words. Laura Bow is also featured in The Colonel's Bequest, a typical murder mystery with a fortune and a murder victim.

Dashboard 2.0 for Windows

Publisher: Borland International; (800) 533-0004

System Requirements: 286 CPU or higher; 1.5MB hard disk space; Windows 3.1 or higher

Suggested Retail Price: $99

The Program

Dashboard provides you with a set of on-screen buttons and icons that can be customized to suit your needs. The controls help make working with Windows user-friendly, and are visible in a pop-up window that can be positioned anywhere on the screen. Some functions include quick launch (which allows you to open applications and files with one click of the mouse), a clock and calendar with alarm features, and extended screens that allow you to move easily among programs.

Datebook & TouchBase Pro

Publisher: Adobe Systems Inc.; (619) 558-6000

System Requirements: Macintosh; 4MB RAM; 2.5MB hard disk space

Suggested Retail Price: $149.95

The Program

Datebook & TouchBase Pro has great organizational tools. The bundle offers a calendar and contact manager with multiple features. These include scheduling, projects, to-do lists, and alarms, as well as database storage of names, addresses and phone numbers. The bundle allows you to print custom formats of calendars, envelopes, mailing labels, address books, and file cards. TouchBase can dial the phone number of a personal contact, and DateBook lets you view your schedule without even opening the applications.

Decimal Concepts (Ages 8 to 11)

Publisher: MECC; Brookdale Corporate Center; 6160 Summit Drive North; Minneapolis, MN 55430-4003; (612) 569-1640; (800) 685-6322; fax (612) 569-1551

System Requirements: Apple II series; 128K RAM; floppy disk drive

Suggested: Printer

Curriculum Areas: This program focuses on giving students practice with recognizing and using decimal numbers, using estimation, and comparing decimal numbers.

Documentation: The loose-leaf-notebook manual describes activities, types of teacher preparation needed, and teacher options for adjusting the program for specific student needs. The disks are in a plastic pocket inside the front cover of the notebook.

Suggested Retail Price: $59

The Program

The activities in this program are more directly related to the math problems than are those in Circus Math and others in the Mastering Math series. You can practice using decimal numbers in three games that concentrate on place values, ordering and comparing decimal numbers, rounding decimal numbers, and exploring the relationship between decimals and fractions. In Maze Runner, you negotiate an invisible maze. After you are successful at running the maze, the entire maze appears; your time and "distance" traveled give you practice in reading and writing decimal numbers. You may also be required to compare the value of two or more decimal numbers. Decimal Duel is a target game in which you try to get as close as possible to a decimal-number goal without exceeding it. In Decimal Bounce, you guide bouncing numbers to their proper locations on a number line. This game combines the use of decimals and fractions; for example, a ball containing the number 0.52 bounces from the top number line (printed in decimal increments) toward the bottom number line (printed in fractional increments). You must guide the ball to the correct location.

Decimal Concepts is menu-driven and easy to use. Feedback about your performance is immediate: you may be told to try again, or (if you make a mistake) you may see an explanation for the correct answer. When play is complete, you see a summary of your performance.

Using the code printed in the manual, you can access the teacher's options menu, from which you can change the content level, the number of problems, and the speed of play. You can also view records of student performance. There is a printer option.

This game program is one of ten in MECC's Conquering Math set. The other programs are Fraction Concepts, Fraction Practice Unlimited, Conquering Whole Numbers, Conquering Fractions, Conquering Percents, Conquering Ratios and Proportions, and two Conquering Decimals programs.

Desert Storm: The War in the Persian Gulf

Publisher: Warner New Media, a Time Warner Inc. Company; 3500 W. Olive Avenue; Burbank, CA 91505

System Requirements: Macintosh Plus or later; 1MB RAM; System 6.0.5 or later; Apple-compatible SCSI CD-ROM drive

Suggested: Color capability; 2MB RAM

Other Platforms (not reviewed): IBM PCs and compatibles

Documentation: A flyer briefly describes the history of Desert Storm. Otherwise, all information is online.

Support: Open the README file online for further information.

Suggested Retail Price: $39.99

The Program

This disk presents a series of correspondents' reports, speeches, sound effects, photographs, and interviews of Desert Storm. You track the war week by week, and learn about personalities and countries involved in Desert Storm. Also included are weapons summaries, maps, charts, and key documents designed to make the war seem real from a correspondent's viewpoint. The program is presented from material in the TIME archives, and reflects TIME reporting and vantage points.

DETROIT

Publisher: Impressions Software, Inc.; 222 Third Street, Ste. 0234; Cambridge, MA 02142; (617) 225-0848; (800) 545-7677

System Requirements: IBM PC or compatible, with an 80286 or better microprocessor; 640K RAM; MS-DOS 3.0 or later; VGA graphics; hard disk drive; Microsoft-compatible mouse

Suggested: Sound card; 80386 or better microprocessor

Documentation: The manuals include a brief reference card, a Cheat Card with game hints for best figures to choose, The Open Road: A History of the Popular Car, and an Owner's Manual. In addition, a Technical Supplement and Tutorial lists strategic hints and technical tips. Playing the simulation well requires a lot of reading in all the manuals.

Support: Call the company on weekdays between 9:00 a.m. and 5:30 p.m. Eastern time for technical support. A company BBS provides product information, software patches, and updates. Other help may be found through CompuServe, GEnie, and PRODIGY.

Suggested Retail Price: $59.95

The PROGRAM

Detroit is a simulation of automotive history; you start in the year 1908 with a single factory, one sales office, $60,000 in capital funds, and a design for a car. From this beginning, you build your empire by making marketing decisions, building and modernizing factories, hiring (or firing) employees, and creating better cars. Features include newsflashes that describe current events that could be of interest to your company, sets of car types, reports and charts of your progress, and unexpected strikes by unhappy workers.

The game is played in turns; you compete with three other players (which can be played by the computer). Time and Money are the important components of the game, and you will have to choose wisely to come out ahead. The game is complex, and offers many options; it is wise to play the Quick Start Tutorial offered in the Technical Supplement and Tutorial manual. Simulation games take time; you can save your games and resume where play left off.

Diet Analyst

Publisher: Parsons Technology, Inc.; One Parsons Drive; P.O. Box 100; Hiawatha, IA 52233-0100; (319) 395-9626

System Requirements: IBM PC or 100-percent compatible; 512K RAM; monochrome or 80-column color monitor; two floppy disk drives; DOS 2.11 or higher

Suggested: Hard disk drive, with one floppy drive needed for installation

Documentation: The manual is easy to read and well organized. Any important notes or cautions are placed in shaded boxes.

Support: Online help is available. Technical support is available through the company's fax or over the technical support telephone lines on weekdays from 8:30 a.m. to 9:00 p.m. and on Saturday from 9:00 a.m. to 1:00 p.m., Central Standard Time. Also look on the CompuServe forums.

Suggested Retail Price: $59

The Program

Use this program to calculate calories, track nutrients, check cholesterol, and monitor exercise. Diet Analyst helps you create a personalized plan for weight control, and plan a diet for specific foods or nutrients around your particular dietary needs. You can sort and display foods according to nutrient content, and enter what-if queries to consider food substitutions or changes in exercise plans. The program analyzes the foods you ate on a particular day or for a particular meal, and lists nutrients for 13 fast-food restaurants. You can request a calorie break-out for protein, carbohydrates, and fats; you can monitor any of 24 nutrients, as well as sodium, saturated fat, and caffeine. The Program also lists foods for optimum vitamin and mineral intake, and has a recipe database for analysis, to which you can add your own recipes. It even offers a password feature for secrecy.

DiskDoubler 4.0

Publisher: Symantec; (800) 441-7234; (504) 291-7221

System Requirements: Macintosh Plus; 4MB RAM; System 7.0; (accelerated for Power Mac)

Suggested Retail Price: $79.95

The Program

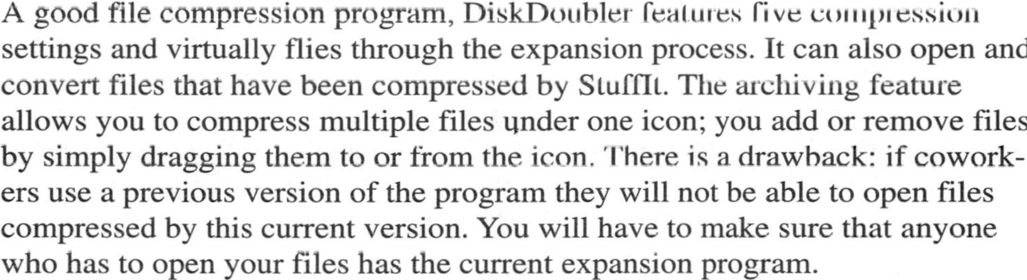

A good file compression program, DiskDoubler features five compression settings and virtually flies through the expansion process. It can also open and convert files that have been compressed by StuffIt. The archiving feature allows you to compress multiple files under one icon; you add or remove files by simply dragging them to or from the icon. There is a drawback: if coworkers use a previous version of the program they will not be able to open files compressed by this current version. You will have to make sure that anyone who has to open your files has the current expansion program.

Doctor Schueler's Home Medical Advisor Pro

Publisher: Pixel Perfect, Inc.; 10460 S. Tropical Trail; Merritt Island, FL 32952; (800) 788-2099; (407) 779-0310; fax (407) 777-0323

System Requirements: IBM PC or compatible; 512K RAM; EGA (256K) or VGA; hard disk drive; DOS 3.0 or higher; CD-ROM drive

Suggested: Mouse

Other Platforms (not reviewed): The program is available for Windows and for Windows with CD-ROM drive.

Documentation: A very basic user's manual contains the minimum of program instructions: keyboard commands, introduction, and installation procedures. Otherwise, it contains mostly medical information that is helpful while browsing through the computer files—such as general health information about taking temperatures and pulses, using cold and hot compresses, and reading a height-weight chart. The manual also describes the fields of various medical specialists and has a 500-word medical glossary.

Support: After you send in your registration, you can get program updates at a cost of $5; these are advertised as becoming available every eight to 10 months. Free technical support is available by phoning.

Suggested Retail Price: $69.95

The Program

This up-to-date encyclopedia is a database of information. It lists and describes over 1,400 common complaints or symptoms, diseases, and injuries, as well as over 800 prescription and over-the-counter drugs, poisons (from toilet-bowl cleaner to Rato sassafras tea), and medical tests. As a medical expert system, it offers 450 diagnoses, 1,000 color pictures, and 100 video clips. In the poisons section, it lists non-toxic items as well as poisonous substances, and gives recommended actions to take after contact with each substance.

The program seems complete. Its purpose is to help you make an informed choice, be aware of preventive care, and seek physician care for earlier, rather than later, diagnosis. It should help you provide your physician with the information needed to make a diagnosis. The program does contain a warning that it should not replace your physician, and instructs you to call your doctor immediately if your symptoms show fever over 103 and diarrhea, for example, and you are in danger of becoming dehydrated.

To use Dr. Schueler's Home Medical Advisor, you enter a general symptom (usually the key complaint), and the program will ask a number of questions that can lead to a specific "diagnosis"—that is, a specific discussion of the problem you may have. Information is not always organized logically, and you may need to scroll through long lists of keywords to find the information you need, though scrolling is quick. Also available is a medical records section in which you can record surgical procedures, allergies, vaccinations, and so on.

Dragon's Lair

Publisher: ReadySoft Incorporated; 3375 14th Avenue, Unit 7 & 8; Markham, Ontario, Canada L3R 2L6; (905) 475-4801, fax (905) 475-4802

System Requirements: IBM PC or compatible, with 80386 or better microprocessor; 4MB RAM; VGA graphics; CD-ROM drive

Suggested: Joystick and sound card; 486DX CPU; local bus or accelerated video; 8MB RAM

Documentation: A flyer included in the disc case describes the program briefly.

Support: Call or write to the company with questions.

Suggested Retail Price: $59.95

The Program

The purpose of this game is to rescue the Fair Princess who is being held captive by Singe the Evil Dragon. You must survive the dangerous journey into the castle and caverns below, defeating your numerous foes. Flashing items indicate danger or the direction in which you are to move. Just be careful not to act to early—or too late—or your adventure may end. The scenes include End of Corridor, Snake Room, Pool of Water, the Goons, Sliding Stairs, and more. You must help Dirk, the hero, to escape safely from the danger each scene holds. The game emphasizes strategic play; each room you travel through requires many attempts to master.

Earthquest Explores Ecology

Publisher: Earthquest Inc. (distributed by Davidson and Associates, Inc.); 125 University Avenue; Palo Alto, CA 94301; (415) 321- 5838

System Requirements: Macintosh Plus/Classic or greater; 1MB RAM, System 6.0.5 or later; System 7 compatible; hard disk drive

Suggested: 2MB of RAM recommended (when used with System 7, you should have at least 2.5MB of RAM for smooth and complete operation of the program)

Other Platforms (not reviewed): IBM PC/Tandy or compatible

Documentation: The instruction booklet is not extensive, but it explains all the parts of the program and the icons. Play is somewhat trial-and-error at first.

Suggested Retail Price: $59.95

The Program

This game helps you learn about vital relationships and cycles that sustain life. It includes 15 interactive games, six biosphere simulations, dozens of ecology topics, and an in-depth trek through the Brazilian rain forest. You'll hear the sounds of animals and birds, too. Some of the games do not require knowledge, nor do they offer any new insights; for example, the matching game merely requires you to remember which picture is under which tile. A Workshop feature lets you expand the program by designing new screens and animating small objects on them.

The program works with HyperCard, which is included in the package if you don't already have the current version installed on your hard drive. The program explores many valuable facts and relationships, providing lots of information to read. The rain forest information is particularly interesting. The simulations lack depth, however, and the animation in most cases is not instructive but merely ornamental. In the games, some of the animal sounds are hard to differentiate, unless you have memorized the originals from the Rainforest part or the EcoSimulator part.

EcoQuest: The Search of Cetus

Publisher: Sierra, Sierra On-Line; P.O. Box 485; Coarsegold, CA 93614; (800) 326-6654; (209) 683-4468

System Requirements: IBM PC or compatible with 286 or better microprocessor; 640K RAM; VGA or EGA graphics (for Tandy, VGA only); hard disk drive; floppy disk drive

Suggested: Mouse; supports Thunderboard, Pro Audio Spectrum, Ad Lib, Roland MT-32, SoundBlaster, and Sound Source sound cards

Other Platforms (not reviewed): IBM PC/Tandy or compatible

Documentation: The documentation for this game includes the usual Sierra game manual that provides generic instructions for playing all Sierra games. There is also a game sheet called "Adam's EcoNews" about this particular game, and a book on 55 fun ways to help save the planet.

Support: Most Sierra games have clue books available and an automated telephone hint line with a 900 number. You can also get hints from Sierra's online bulletin board system, and often a commercial information service may offer hints for Sierra games. For technical help, you can call or write to the company's customer support department.

Suggested Retail Price: $49.95

The Program

In EcoQuest, you start off on an undersea adventure with Adam and Delphineus, the dolphin, to find the great whale, King Cetus. On the way, you encounter toxic waste, oil spills, deadly drift nets, and other hazards. While you play these challenging and educational ecological puzzles, you acquire some knowledge about how individuals can make a difference in ecology. (Sierra does its part by donating a portion of the proceeds from the sale of each EcoQuest game to the Marine Mammal Center, Marine Headlands, Golden Gate National Recreation Area, Sausalito, CA 94965.) This game shows the research and attention to detail that are Sierra's standards. The scene backgrounds are hand-painted and then digitized into the game; the soundtrack is stereo.

Encyclopedia of Sound Volume 1

Publisher: CDRP, Inc., publishers of Chestnut CD-ROMs; P.O. Box 360; Cambridge, MA 02141-0004; (616) 494-5330; fax (617) 494-6094

System Requirements: IBM PC or compatible with Windows 3.1 or higher, with Sound Recorder or Media Player installed; CD-ROM drive; sound card

Documentation: A "Getting Started" flyer is enclosed in the disc case.

Support: Call or write the company for help.

Suggested Retail Price: $29.95

The Program

This CD-ROM contains 211 sound effects in 8-bit and 16-bit WAV format. It also includes eight full-length musical scores and 13 WAV music clips. The items on the disk can be used only for non-commercial, non-profit purposes. Sounds include CB radio, two people clapping, dog barking, doorbell, sneezing, snoring, sobbing, and many more.

This company also produces Encyclopedia of Sound Volume 2, MIDI Master Collection (a collection of Festival Music, American Pop, Movie Classics, Cartoon Classics, and Composers Across Time—complete with graphics and text), Insane Impersonations, The Legal Guide Team's Complete Home and Office Legal Guide, and HIV-AIDS Resource Guide.

Excel for Windows 5.0

Publisher: Microsoft Corporation; One Microsoft Way; Redmond, WA 98052; (206) 882-8080

System Requirements: IBM PC or compatible with an 80286 or better microprocessor, or PS/2 computer; 4MB RAM; hard disk drive, with 15MB needed for installation and 22MB needed for a complete installation; one floppy disk drive; graphics monitor with EGA, VGA, or Hercules capabilities; DOS 3.1 or later; Windows 3.1 or higher

Suggested: 80386 or better microprocessor; 6MB to 8MB RAM; mouse

Other Platforms (not reviewed): Macintosh; OS/2 1.1 or higher version for IBM computers

Documentation: The documentation for this program is good, but technical. It consists of almost 1,000 pages.

Support: The program's online help menu gives you access to two tutorials. One provides a quick overview of the basics, a summary of new features, and an introductory lesson for 1-2-3 users; the other provides 11 lessons that help you learn to use the package. There is also a standard Windows help button in almost every dialog box. You can call a 24-hour automated telephone number or use the fax-back service. If you want to talk with a real person, the technical support phone lines are available from 6:00 a.m. to 6:00 p.m. Pacific Standard Time on weekdays. Support is free to registered users, for the cost of the toll call. It is reasonably easy to reach, with knowledgeable technicians on the company end. You can also access a forum on CompuServe or receive the newsletters and regular notices of updates from the company.

Suggested Retail Price: $495

The Program

Excel, the excellent spreadsheet program for Macintosh computers, is also available in a Windows version for IBM PC or compatible. Almost all of the same features and formats have been transferred to the Windows version, except for the specific online help system and the method of linking documents. The program offers a large number of formatting options and a full range of what-if variations and statistical features. It provides many charting options including 3-D surface area charts, 3-D bar charts, and polar charts. It has been described as "one awesome spreadsheet."

The program is easy to install; the screen layout is attractive; the interface and operation are smooth and intuitive. You can work with multiple documents and 3-D pages. The graphics and charting capabilities are large and varied, the macro language is powerful, and the program has strong auditing capability. The page-publishing features are almost the quality of desktop publishing. For formatting your worksheet, you can select typefaces, type sizes, bold and italic styles, borders, patterns, and colors, or even go the shortcut route by choosing one of 14 standard stylesheets, ranging from conservative to trendy-looking.

Besides outlining capability and a spelling checker, this program contains a Scenario Manager that lets you assign names to specific sets of assumptions. This feature is useful for what-if analysis. With the OLE feature, you can link any information with files in another program that supports linking. If you have moved to Excel from Lotus 1-2-3, the 1-2-3 Macro Interpreter can run most 1-2-3 macros from version 2.01 and earlier as is.

A number of features make this program easy to use. The program supports an excellent use of icons and buttons. There are nine predefined toolbars; you can customize each, or build your own. You can use the right mouse button to get easy access to frequently-used operations, at which time a context-sensitive menu quickly leads to a dialog box. The status bar at the bottom of the screen shows short summaries of what the tools and menus will do for you.

The program offers IntelliSense, a feature in which the computer does a great deal of your work for you. For example, with Drag and Plot, the computer updates charts automatically when you select new data and drag it into an existing chart. With PivotTable, you can use drag-and-drop for analysis functions. The Wizards feature guides you step-by-step through unfamiliar tasks such as creating a chart and developing a data cross-tabulation table from an Excel database. An autofill option enables you to put the same formulas or labels in adjacent cells. As you can see, Excel offers a large assortment of varied features. Choose it for its number-crunching capabilities and for the Analysis ToolPak if you need to do serious statistical analysis.

THE FAMILY DOCTOR

Publisher: CMC (Creative Multimedia Corporation); 514 NW 11th Avenue, Ste. 203; Portland, OR 97209; (503) 241-4351; fax (503) 241-4370

System Requirements: For Macintosh: Macintosh Plus or higher; System 6.0.5 or later; 1MB free RAM; CD-ROM drive

For IBM with Windows: 386SX or greater IBM PC and compatibles; Windows 3.0 with multimedia extensions or Windows 3.1; 2MB RAM; hard drive with 500K or more free space; VGA or greater; CD-ROM drive

For DOS: DOS 3.1; 500K RAM; VGA; CD-ROM drive

Suggested: For Macintosh: 8-bit color with 32-bit QuickDraw

For IBM: sound capability recommended

Documentation: A leaflet explains installation. Otherwise the program is easy to use; instructions are on-screen.

Support: Online help is available by long-distance phone call on weekdays from 8:00 a.m. to 5:00 p.m. Pacific Standard Time. The company also offers 24-hour BBS service.

Suggested Retail Price: $79.99

The Program

This program offers medical advice about nearly 2,000 commonly asked medical questions. It includes illustrations for anatomy, body processes, diseases and injuries, medical procedures, and social and health issues. Also included are descriptions about more than 1,600 prescription drugs, resources and support groups, and a glossary. The material is basically what you might expect to find in a book, except for the audio pronunciation of the names of body parts and functions. You can browse your way through by selecting from lists of topics, illustrations, and so on.

Fetch

Publisher: Adobe Systems Inc.; (206) 622-5500; (800) 685-6636

System Requirements: Macintosh Classic; 4MB RAM

Suggested Retail Price: $295

The Program

An image- and sound-cataloging program, Fetch allows you to browse and retrieve sound and art images in one common visual database. You can search for items by keywords, or simply view them in a miniaturized catalog format. Other features include find, sort, copy, preview, play, print, and place.

File Express 5.1

Publisher: Expressware Corporation; P.O. Box 1800; Duvall, WA 98019; (800) 753-3453

System Requirements: IBM PC or compatible; 512K RAM; hard disk drive; floppy disk drive needed for installation; CGA, EGA, VGA, or Hercules video cards; DOS 2.0 or higher

Support: The program has good context-sensitive help messages available at a keystroke.

Suggested Retail Price: $99

THE PROGRAM

This character-based data manager program is functional, speedy, and easy to use. It has a logical menu structure and clearly designed input screens. Its search option lets you hunt for information even if you don't know how to spell the word or words you are looking for. It has good built-in reporting capabilities with programmed templates for common formats such as columnar reports, individual reports, and so on. Its text editor lets you merge information from a file into a single-page document, an option that is useful for form letters. If you need a basic data manager without sophisticated database, database language, and formatting options, this one might serve your purposes.

FILEMAKER PRO 2.1

Publisher: Claris; 5201 Patrick Henry Drive; Santa Clara, CA 95052; (408) 727-8227

System Requirements: Macintosh Classic or greater; 1MB RAM; hard disk drive; System 6.0.3 or later

Suggested: Printer

Other Platforms (not reviewed): IBM PC or compatible in both DOS and Windows 3.1 or higher

Documentation: Includes a Quick Reference Guide, a Getting Started manual in which Chapters 1 through 5 are tutorials, and a well-organized User's Guide complete with appendixes that list calculation formulas and keyboard shortcuts.

Support: A series of professionally designed templates are included which you can customize for your use. Filemaker Pro includes an interactive help system which allows you to switch back and forth between Help and your file by clicking the window you want to make active.

Suggested Retail Price: $399

The Program

This is a basic flat-file data manager program; it is fast, simple, and logical. It lacks the high-end features, but it has an easy-to-use interface with which you can create and adjust the layouts for data input and reporting. You create layouts by simply choosing options from menus, but you also make use of standard Macintosh techniques such as grabbing hold of a field with the mouse and stretching it, or dragging it to resize or reposition it. You can use these features to enhance data forms and reports with type options and illustrations, and can import logos and other pictures for this purpose.

Filemaker Pro allows you to add, change or remove fields within a particular layout without losing data. You can set variable-length text fields, and use the extensive security features to guard your data. Easy-to-use scripts and graphics buttons allow you to automate routine tasks and menu operations without programming. Utilizing the layout feature, although a somewhat tedious procedure, lets you create merge letters. The program offers a number of templates. You can use its ScriptMaker to automate tasks by picking items from a macro list and associating them with buttons you put in the forms. Filemaker Pro allows importation of SLYK, DBF, DIF, BASIC, and WKS files. The program is System 7-compatible and supports multimedia.

Flying Colors (ages 8 to adult)

Publisher: Davidson & Associates, Inc.; P.O. Box 2961; 19840 Pioneer Ave.; Torrance, CA 90509; (310) 793-0600; (800) 545-7677; (800) 556-6141; fax (310) 793-0601

System Requirements: 256-color Macintosh with System 6.0.5 or later; 4MB RAM with 2.2MB free; 2.5MB available hard disk space; 3.5-inch floppy disk drive

Suggested: Printer

Other Platforms (not reviewed): IBM PC with Windows 3.1 or greater

Documentation: The manual is well organized and easy to read. It describes the windows and menus graphically, and contains keyboard shortcuts for various actions. It does, however, lack an index.

Support: The manual contains a troubleshooting appendix and tutorials in the manual, and the program has online help. Customer Support technicians can be reached by telephone on weekdays from 7:00 a.m. to 6:00 p.m., by fax 24 hours every day, or by mail.

Suggested Retail Price: $59.95

The Program

This color paint program includes most common paint tools: mover, brush, eraser, text, bucket fill, colors, spray, eyedropper, zoom, shrink, and rotate, as well as shapes (for example, oval, rectangle, and polygon). Flying Colors also includes a stamp tool with an extensive library of images that can be added to the predrawn "canvases" (or to your own creation). The stencil tool (similar to the eyedropper option in other paint programs) allows you to change selected parts of a painting while protecting other parts. You can work behind images, selectively erase portions, or change colors. A unique color cycling option produces animation, and a symmetry tool creates kaleidoscopic effects. The program also includes 101 possible gradients and 148 patterns. There are three levels at which to work in Flying Colors. In Small Kids Mode, text is entered one letter at a time by pointing and clicking, and some tools are hidden. In Basic mode, most tools and features are available; in Advanced mode, the stencil, opacity control, and other advanced features are available.

FoxPro 2.6

Publisher: Microsoft Corporation; (206) 882-8080

System Requirements: Macintosh (68030); 4MB RAM; System 7 (accelerated for Power Mac)

Suggested Retail Price: $495

The Program

This relational database is very fast and easy to use, thanks to its graphical tools and Macintosh interface. It offers compatibility with both its DOS and Windows versions. The Screen Builder allows you to build a data entry screen in minutes; you can use its graphical tool set to import graphics and add buttons to enhance the screen. Microsoft Graph is included in the package for quality charts to accompany the not-so-impressive reports it generates. The package also includes a developer's guide and language reference for those who are interested in modifying the applications to use its full power.

Fractal Design Painter 3.0

Publisher: Fractal Design; 335 Spreckels Drive, Suite F; Aptos, CA 95003; (408) 688-8800; fax (408) 688-8836

System Requirements: Macintosh LC or II series; color monitor; 32-bit QuickDraw; 8-bit color card; 2.5MB RAM; hard disk drive; 800K floppy disk drive needed for installation; System 6.0.5 or later (System 7-compatible)

Suggested: 24-bit color card; 4MB to 5MB RAM; pressure-sensitive stylus

Other Platforms (not reviewed): IBM PC with a 386 or higher microprocessor

Documentation: Documentation for this program is brief but well done. It offers tips and tricks for using the features of the program.

Support: The program includes no tutorial or online help, but technical support is friendly, knowledgeable, and available with a toll call.

Suggested Retail Price: $499

The Program

Fractal Design Painter lets you simulate the textures and behavior of natural media such as chalk, pastels, charcoal, pencils, pens, crayons, felt-tipped markers, airbrushes, oils, and watercolors. In fact, one of its tools is water, so you can adjust the transparency of the "paint." The program offers a variety of brushes and an eraser. A Library of Image Hose patterns (a special-effects paintbrush) is new to this version. The Gradient Composer creates color ramps. Stroke by stroke, you can control the amount of color a brush takes up and the bleed of the paint (how much paint seeps into surrounding lighter colors). If you want to imitate fine art, you can select settings to simulate the brush strokes of a particular artist such as Van Gogh. The program not only imitates the medium, it also simulates the texture, or graininess, of a variety of canvases and papers. It is especially remarkable when paired with a pressure-sensitive graphics tablet, which makes it easier to imitate the pressure you might apply with a real brush or pencil.

The basic palette of this program is simple: It offers Brush, Zoom, Grabber, Ink Dropper, and Selection Rectangle, but all tools can be zoomed to provide more tools. You can also use a frisket, which simulates the mask used on artwork to shield areas during painting or air brushing. A tracing paper option enables you to trace over a scanned or original image with new paint tools. The program also offers multimedia and animation features, as well as all the features needed for photo design (such as color separation and photo compositing). The program does have a number of limitations, but these are to be expected; it was designed as an ancillary tool for use with other programs for presentation, art, and page-layout purposes. It does not support text, and it takes up a lot of memory, so if you want smooth performance, you should have a speedy machine and lots of hard disk space.

Fractal Design has released a similar program called Sketcher for gray-scale work when you want to simulate black-and-white drawings. This program is economical at $79. Fractal Design Dabbler, also economical at $99, is designed to be educational. It is an easy-to-use, natural-media, draw-and-paint program.

Freelance Graphics for Windows 2.1

Publisher: Lotus Development Corporation; 55 Cambridge Parkway; Cambridge, MA 02142; (800) 343-5414

System Requirements: IBM PC or compatible with a 286 microprocessor; 2MB RAM; hard disk drive with minimum of 10.5MB free space; Windows 3.0; floppy disk drive; mouse

Suggested: 386 microprocessor; 4MB RAM

Documentation: The documentation for this program is adequate.

Support: Freelance Graphics includes an on-screen tutorial and context-sensitive online help. If you need help from the company, you can call its customer support 800 number from 8:30 a.m. to 8:00 p.m. on weekdays. The line is often busy, but the technicians are helpful and knowledgeable.

Suggested Retail Price: $495

The Program

This presentation graphics program has traditionally been one of the best, and now it is available for use with Windows. It lets you create high-quality slides, overhead transparencies, and other visuals for presentations. The program is easy to use; you can take SmartIcon shortcuts and customize the palette of command icons. You can also use drag-and-drop to move items. In addition to its own features, Freelance Graphics has powerful links to other applications.

The program includes 500 clip-art images and a palette of 16 million colors. It contains 64 SmartMaster template sets, or page layout designs. The program lets you create 16 types of charts including two- and three-dimensional bar graphs, line graphs, pie charts, and scatter graphs. Within each, it is easy to edit legends, labels, colors, and other elements. You can also import graphics in a variety of formats. The program supports OLE (object linking and embedding), and offers both improved support for workgroups and Notes/FX 1.1 support.

GeoJigsaw (All Ages)

Publisher: PC Globe, Inc.; 4440 South Rural Road; Tempe, Arizona 85282; (602) 730-9000; fax (602) 968-7196

System Requirements: IBM PC/Tandy or compatible

Curriculum Areas: This program integrates history and geography.

Suggested Retail Price: $39.95

The Program

This program is considered by some critics to be the best computerized jigsaw puzzle. It consists of twelve map pictures that integrate history and geography in sets such as the Ice Age, U.S. Acquisitions, Animals of Africa, and Buccaneers of the Caribbean. The program breaks the picture into as many as 294 pieces. The main window in the middle of the screen is where you construct the puzzle. You see the pieces reduced in size in a window at the bottom of the screen. Just as you expect with a cardboard or wooden jigsaw puzzle, the clues to solving the puzzle are in the shape and colors of the pieces. When you finish the puzzle, the picture animates. You can save puzzles in progress to finish later.

Glider 4.0

Publisher: Casady & Greene, Inc.; 22734 Protola Drive; Salinas, CA 93908; (800) 359-4920; (408) 484-9228; fax (408) 484-9218

System Requirements: MacPlus or greater; System 6.0.2 or later (System 7-compatible); floppy disk drive; mouse

Suggested: Color monitor; hard disk drive

Documentation: The manual is a booklet, rather informally written. It describes most of what you need to know without spoiling the surprises for first-time users. The manual includes a STOP warning at the point where any surprises might be revealed.

Support: Read the online help before starting this program; it offers information not covered in the manual. You can see part of the online help between games on the opening screen. Call the company's technical support if you have technical questions after you have read the troubleshooting tips in the manual.

Suggested Retail Price: $49.95

The Program

If you've ever shot paper airplanes in school, here's the ultimate computer program to test your skill. In Glider, you fly your paper airplane through an eerie mansion with lots of rooms, tables, cupboards, lights, and drips. The object is to get through all 60 rooms and fly out of the house. If you master the game, you may be ready to try building your own rooms; the second half of the manual contains more specific information about the rooms and the objects in them. The graphics are great; the glider emulates the drifts, tips, and flutters of a real paper airplane, and even casts its shadow on the floor. You can choose from several control options: two keyboard options, the mouse, and a joystick. If you're a first-time user, you may have better control using the keyboard option.

Glider Pro is now available, in which you search for the Magic Star Wand. In this game, your glider flies over meadows and rooftops, in and out of mailboxes, and even underground. Glider Pro requires System 7. Casady & Greene, Inc. produces a number of other games—including Crystal Quest with CritterEditor (a popular Mac game in which you collect crystals while avoiding mines, bullets, and other "nasties"), and Sky Shadow (a bombing-raid arcade game).

Global Conquest

Publisher: MicroProse Software, Inc.; 180 Lakefront Drive; Hunt Valley, MD 21030-2245; (410) 771-1151

System Requirements: IBM 286, 386, 486, or compatible; 640K RAM; DOS 3.0 or higher; floppy disk drive; high-res EGA (will not run in MCGA)

Suggested: Hard disk drive; mouse (although it supports a joystick); supports IBM and Ad Lib sound cards

Documentation: Despite the extensive game documentation, with game background and information on game elements, playing the game requires a great deal of trial-and-error.

Support: The documentation contains a very informally written tutorial that helps you see what happens when you perform certain operations. The company produces an official strategy guide that contains hints, five custom-designed tutorial scenarios, and winning scenarios from a Global Conquest tournament.

Suggested Retail Price: $39.95

The Program

Global Conquest is a game of strategy and exploration to discover and conquer the world (and the forces lined up against you). The game board is different each time around, increasing the longevity of the game. A feature called cloaked terrain obscures all the board's characteristics at the beginning of each game. As your playing pieces move around, they remove the cloaked terrain to reveal the actual world beneath in a process called "discovering the world." Your playing pieces are infantry, armor, submarines, battleships, aircraft carriers, airplanes, and two special pieces called the spy and the command center (Comcen) that have special capabilities. The object of the game is to be the last Comcen alive. There are always four opponents, human or computer.

As you play, you may encounter a number of unforeseen revolts, monsoons, terrorist attacks, and so on. There are also wild-event cards such as trench fever, fitness craze, time warp, and others. You can form alliances with enemies to beat a common foe, but these "friends" may betray you during the course of the game. The game includes three levels of difficulty and a variety of game options. You need to learn a great deal to play the game, but people who enjoy combat strategy games will like it.

Grammatik 5.0

Publisher: WordPerfect, The Novell Applications Group; 1555 N. Technology Way; Orem, UT 84057; (801) 225-5000; (800) 451-4151; fax (801) 228-5377

System Requirements: IBM PC or compatible with a 386 or better microprocessor; 640K RAM; hard disk drive with 1.6MB free space; DOS 3.0 or later; Windows 3.0 or later; floppy disk drive

Suggested: Printer

Other Platforms (not reviewed): Macintosh

Documentation: Grammatik's documentation is good, but unnecessary.

Support: This program's online help is context-sensitive. If you have technical questions, you can call the company's toll line on weekdays from 7:00 a.m. to 5:00 p.m. Pacific time.

Suggested Retail Price: $49.95

The Program

This program detects most common usage errors, including double negatives, doubled words, and slang. It points out too-frequent use of a phrase or a sentence beginning, and checks the readability of your text by length of sentences, number of sentences per paragraph, and word count. Its spelling dictionary is not as large as Word or WordPerfect's, but you can add to it.

When Grammatik flags an error, it provides a selection of corrections. Sometimes it misses errors; at other times it finds mistakes where there aren't any (it always flags "accept" and "except," for example). You can, however, edit, ignore, or add rules to suit your style. In addition, you can set the program to apply to the writing style most suitable for the document you are currently writing. There are more than 30 different styles, including technical writing and fiction.

You can use Grammatik within a word processing program. It works with Word for Windows, WordPerfect, Ami Pro, and others. (It does not support Word for Windows 6.0 file formats; instead it converts documents to Rich Text Format before checking them. It does not change the files back to Word files when finished.)

Grandmaster Chess Deluxe Edition

Publisher: IntraCorp, Inc./Capstone Software; 7200 NW 19th Street, Ste. 500; Miami, FL 33126; (800) 468-7226; (305) 591-5900; fax (305) 591-5633; BBS (305) 471-8962

System Requirements: IBM PC or compatible with a 386 or better microprocessor; 640K base memory, and 1MB extended memory; VGA graphics; MS-DOS 3.3 or higher; CD-ROM drive; 5MB free hard disk space; mouse

Suggested: 486 microprocessor; double-speed CD-ROM drive; SoundBlaster or compatible sound card

Documentation: The manual explains requirements, troubleshooting, changing configurations, the game screen, the menus and keyboard shortcuts, and play.

Support: On-screen help and play analysis gives you hints as needed. Check the troubleshooting section before calling Customer Support.

Suggested Retail Price: $59.95

The Program

You can play chess against another person or against the computer (you choose black or white) in this high-tech chess game. You can also watch the computer play both black and white. This option is a useful learning tool, especially if you set one side to play stronger than the other, and study the corresponding moves between the two sides. You can set the computer's playing skill to Beginner, Novice, Intermediate, Expert, or Grandmaster. The computer can also be set as Balanced (in which the computer attacks and retreats with equal consideration), Active (in which the computer emphasizes capturing pieces and attacking your King), and Passive (in which the computer plays defensively, protecting its pieces). The time-control option lets you set the computer for 60 moves in five minutes or 60 moves in 15 minutes. Of course, the more time it has, the better the computer will play. Other options include an assortment of chess sets, boards, and backgrounds, as well as board rotation, blindfold play, and an opening-moves library of hundreds of classic starting positions.

The disc also contains a bonus chess game called Terminator 2: Judgment Day Chess Wars, which puts play into a futuristic battleground with 3-D animated graphics and digitized sound. The game is based on the movie *Terminator 2: Judgment Day*, and utilizes the movie's characters as chess pieces. Playing strength and playing style are similar to the Grandmaster Chess game, but time control provides nine options. At the end, the computer rates your play based on U.S. Chess Federation ratings. For people who like strategy games and board games, this program provides all the ingredients. IntraCorp also produces the strategy game Corridor 7, an alien-invasion scenario.

Harvard Graphics 3.0 for Windows

Publisher: Software Publishing Corp.; (800) 336-8360

System Requirements: 386 PC; 4MB RAM; 9MB hard disk drive; Windows 3.1; VGA monitor; mouse

Suggested Retail Price: $289

The Program

Harvard Graphics is not only a presentation package, but also an interactive multimedia package. Features include charting, screen shows, and multimedia. There is plenty of assistance offered with this program. The Five-Minute Coach includes an overview of the program's features in short, easy tutorials. With Advisor, a context-sensitive help screen, you are given step-by-step advice, including design tips, while creating your presentation. Data from word processors and spreadsheets can be imported easily into Harvard Graphics.

Headline Harry and the Great Paper Race (Ages 10 and up)

Publisher: Davidson & Associates, Inc.; P.O. Box 2961; 19840 Pioneer Ave.; Torrance, CA 90509; (310) 793-0600; (800) 545-7677; fax (310) 793-0601

System Requirements: IBM PC/Tandy or compatible; 640K RAM; 256-color VGA graphics and MCGA; DOS 3.3 or higher; hard disk drive; 5.25- or 3.5-inch high-density floppy disk drive

Suggested: Minimum of 8MHz; supports Ad Lib, SoundBlaster, Tandy, and PS/1 sound devices

Other Platforms (not reviewed): Macintosh (supports System 7 and QuickTime)

Curriculum Areas: The program is suitable for use in reviewing miscellaneous events in history, sports, art, entertainment, and science. It encourages the elements of good journalism.

Documentation: Documentation for this program is written in the form of a newspaper or newsletter, with the information in article form. This format is a bit confusing at first (you may not see the information you need at a glance), but it should appeal to students. For example, the answers to some questions appear in the form of Dear Gabby columns. The documentation lists the menu options, the reporting tools, troubleshooting tips, and the stories by decade. The installation procedures are written inside the front cover in a format normally used for this type of instruction.

Support: You may need to play this game a few times before you are accustomed to its requirements. If you need technical assistance, you can call Customer Service at an 800 number on weekdays.

Suggested Retail Price: $59.95 for DOS or Macintosh versions

The Program

In this program, you become a cub reporter for *U.S. Daily Star* and must get the scoop on stories before your dishonest competitor, Marvin Muckracker, does. Before you play, you choose the geographic area you want to explore, and then Headline Harry, your editor, tells you what your assignment will be. Well, not exactly. He will give you a few clues about where to start and what to look for, but he won't tell you what the real story is. That's your job: You must determine which event is the story and collect the date, year, key events, key people, and key locations of the main event.

The goal of this game is to teach the importance of getting at the truth and having a conscience as a reporter. You also learn the elements of good journalism, including the who, what, when, where, and why of a story. This program requires you to analyze information because you must discern the correct story despite the red herrings, blind alleys, lying informants, and unethical tricks of the competition. You can save an unfinished story; the program will return to exactly where you left off the next time you open the program.

The program has sound effects, music, digitized speech, and beautiful graphics. It includes historical events in the recent past (1950-1990) of the United States. The Macintosh version uses QuickTime video clips and animation of the actual events. Stories are about the arts, sports, science, entertainment, history, and geography. The maps include regional information. This game is harder than the Carmen Sandiego games, but once you have played completely through, the game displays the same sets of clues each time you restart the game.

History of the World

Publisher: Bureau Development, Inc.; 141 New Road; Parsippany, NJ 07054; (201) 808-2700

System Requirements: Macintosh Classic or greater with System 6.0.4 or later; 1MB RAM; CD-ROM drive supporting ISO-9660 standards; 32-bit QuickDraw; monitor capable of 640 × 480 resolution with 256 colors or shades of gray

IBM PC XT and compatibles or greater; DOS 3.1 or later; 640K RAM; CD-ROM drive supporting ISO-9660 standards; Microsoft Extensions 2.0 or later

Suggested: Hard disk drive; VGA and speakers or headphones for IBM; 2MB RAM and color monitor for Macintosh; printer

Documentation: The manual includes instructions for both Macintosh and IBM platforms. It lists activities for students and teachers, as well as major works represented on the disk.

Support: Registered customers can call the company for the cost of the phone call.

Suggested Retail Price: $125

The Program

This disk presents the history of the world by title, theme, region, and time period (from origins of civilization to the present). It contains over 600 illustrations, maps, photos, tables, speeches, and eyewitness accounts. Material is accessed through menus. You can request a search or simply browse, or scroll, through the titles list. Although there are many materials and resources on the disk, some people might prefer to browse through the library for similar materials. The program's strength is the wide variety of sources used, many of which would not appear in local libraries.

The Home Series (Kitchen, Home, Bathroom, Deck, and Landscape)

Publisher: Autodesk Retail Products; 11911 North Creek Parkway South; Bothell, WA 98011; (206) 487-2233; fax (206) 485-0021

System Requirements: IBM PC, XT, AT, PS/1, PS/2, or compatible; 640K RAM; hard disk drive; floppy disk drive needed for installation; two- or three-button mouse; Hercules color or monochrome, MCGA, CGA, EGA, or VGA graphics; DOS 3.0 or higher; Epson dot-matrix printer or 100-percent compatible; HP LaserJet or 100-percent compatible

Suggested: 2MB expanded memory; math coprocessor; VGA graphics

Documentation: Documentation for these programs includes a Quick Start card that explains installation, running, menu choices, and function key commands. The user's manual gives tips for various design problems you may have. It is clearly written, but requires study unless you are already familiar with the subject matter.

Support: It is helpful to use the tutorial included with each program, because using these programs requires dedicated study. Technical support is free, except for the toll call, and is available on weekdays from 7:00 a.m. to 6:00 p.m. and on Saturday from 9:00 a.m. to noon, Pacific Standard Time.

Suggested Retail Price: $59.95 each

The Program

The Home Series consists of five separate programs for designing, remodeling, or building ideas. Each differs from the others in its symbols. Each includes standard-sized, pre-drawn symbols for such things as different-sized cabinets, doors, sofas, sinks, windows, electrical outlets, tubs, deck lumber, and so on. Within each category of symbols, there are a number of variations. The door selection, for example, contains right- and left-opening doors, bifolds, and sliding doors, as well as five types of garage doors. Landscape includes a large variety of symbols for lawn furniture, courts, pools, trees, ground cover, shrubs, sprinklers, and so on. In Kitchen, Bathroom, Deck, and Landscape, the program automatically generates a shopping list of items needed to do the job.

This set of programs most resembles a draw program or a CAD (computer-aided design) program used by architects. You can move and rotate items, and can generate different views from your entries. You can use the snap-to feature to fill out a required space, and can zoom in and out of a drawing by specifying a particular portion with a window. You also can label items with text and dimensions. Each program is menu driven, but that makes it easy to use only for those of you who know about measurements and room proportions.

Each program includes sample drawings, which are helpful especially for people who are not sure about using technical drawings of this nature. It requires using measurements of your existing spaces. It draws to scale, so you can create professional looking prints that can be used as blueprints. The drawings you create can be used with other Home Series programs; it may be helpful to start with a one-room program. The actual Home program, however, contains all the tools needed for the other programs. The programs are in the same format as the program Generic CADD, a popular professional design system for which hundreds of stock plans are available.

INLARGE 2.0

Publisher: Berkeley Systems, Inc.; 2095 Rose Street; Berkeley, CA 94709; (510) 540-5535; (800) 877-5535; fax (510) 540-5115

System Requirements: Macintosh Plus or greater; 1MB RAM; set for 256 colors only, unless you are running in black and white; System 6.0.5 or later; System 7-compatible

Documentation: The manual is clearly written in large print (21 points). There is also a version on disk for on-screen display. It includes information on the compatibility of this program with some other popular programs and hardware.

Suggested Retail Price: $195

THE PROGRAM

This memory-resident program enlarges the display on the screen so that visually impaired people can use a computer. It magnifies from two to 16 times, and can invert the standard display so that light print appears on a dark background, rather than the default of dark print on a light background. The program can enlarge the entire screen or just the portions you wish to access. You can also supplement the standard Macintosh pointer to a full frame crosshair that may be easier to see. The program has a number of other user-definable options.

IT'S LEGAL

Publisher: Parsons Technology, Inc.; One Parsons Drive; P.O. Box 100; Hiawatha, IA 52233-0100; (800) 223-6925; fax (319) 395-1002

System Requirements: IBM PC or 100-percent compatible; 512K RAM; two floppy disk drives; DOS 2.11 or higher

Suggested: Hard disk drive; mouse; printer

Documentation: Documentation for this program is good, with an easy-to-read design. It marks notes well with a boxed, gray background. The notes tell exceptions, warnings, instances when state laws may vary, and so on.

Support: The package includes an online reference guide and glossary. Technical support is available through registration and is free and unlimited (except for the toll call) on weekdays from 8:30 a.m. to 9:00 p.m. and Saturday from 9:00 a.m. to 1:00 p.m. Central Standard Time.

Suggested Retail Price: $69

The Program

This program, designed by a team of attorneys for home and small business use, helps you create your own legal documents, agreements, and letters. Documents include simple wills, general and special powers of attorney, revocations of powers of attorney, certificates of guardianship, promissory notes, living wills, and durable health-care power of attorney. There are various legal agreements. These include residential, commercial, and equipment leases, as well as agreements for consulting, independent contractors, and bills of sale. Letters include credit and collection letters, and letters of consumer complaints; employment packages help you offer, confirm, and accept employment. There is even a form for board minutes. It's Legal is menu-driven and easy to use. This package warns you that laws may have changed since the program was produced, and also that a particular circumstance may require the services of an attorney.

Parsons also produces Personal Advocate, designed to help you write letters for reasons such as disputing your credit card statement or complaining about a product. This related program covers alimony and child support, as well as a range of consumer, credit, and government issues that include Medicare, Social Security, and requests for birth, death, and marriage certificates. The program also describes what you might expect as a result of sending such a letter. It is priced at $69.

JFK Assassination: A Visual Exploration

Publisher: Medio Multimedia; (800) 788-3866; (206) 867-5500

System Requirements: IBM PC; Windows; CD-ROM drive

Suggested Retail Price: $59.95

The Program

Create your own version of history with this compilation of actual evidence in the JFK assassination. Available are the backgrounds of the people involved, autopsy notes and photos, diagrams of the parade route in Dallas, film footage, and 3-D computer-animated re-enactments of the shootings. The program does not draw any conclusions. Instead it invites you to compare the facts with what you have heard in the various media versions.

Jimmy Connors' Pro Tennis Tour

Publisher: UBI Soft; 15 Atwood Avenue; Sausilito, CA 94965; (415) 571-7171; (415) 332-8749

System Requirements: IBM PCs or 100-percent compatible, or Tandy 1000 family; 640K RAM; EGA, VGA, CGA, or Tandy 16-color; floppy disk drive; DOS 3.2 or higher

Suggested: Joystick; hard disk drive; supports Ad Lib and SoundBlaster sound cards

Other Platforms (not reviewed): Amiga

Documentation: The manual, though complete enough for you to play the game, is geared toward the joystick user.

Support: If you have technical questions, you can write to the company's technical support address or call the tech support number on weekdays between 8:30 a.m. and 4:30 p.m. Pacific Standard Time.

Suggested Retail Price: $49.95

The Program

This program lets you play tennis and tennis tournaments, or use a programmable ball machine for practice. You create and save your own players. Your options include selecting up to four male or female players, specifying the kind of play, assigning a level of play, and choosing the kind of court. The game takes some practice to play because it requires timing the swing. It's also hard to play when your character changes sides, hitting the ball toward you. The off-disk copyright-protection scheme requires you to type a code from the code table in the manual; you are allowed three attempts at the correct code.

JustWrite for Windows 2.0

Publisher: Symantec Corporation; 10201 Torre Avenue; Cupertino, CA 95014; (408) 253-9600; (800) 441-7234; fax (408) 252-4694

System Requirements: IBM PC or compatible with a 286 or better microprocessor, 2MB RAM, Windows 3.0 or higher, DOS 3.1 or higher, hard disk drive, floppy disk drive

Suggested: Printer

Documentation: The documentation, though adequate and well-organized, should include more tutorial help.

Support: Technical support, although not toll-free, is free, prompt, and knowledgeable. Symantec has a BBS you can use for getting help, too.

Suggested Retail Price: $199

The Program

This word processing package aims for the user who does not need a powerful package like WordPerfect or Microsoft Word. It doesn't take up as much space on hard disk, nor does it operate as fast as some other word processors. The package includes a word-count feature, grammar checker, fast spelling checker, and thesaurus that contains definitions of words. It does lack macros and redlining capability, however.

This program has a number of features designed to increase user-friendliness. It has an option for automatic, timed file saving. It has a flexible toolbar that can be customized. Using special program functions, you can create footnotes, multiple columns, a table of contents, and an outline. The program allows for some simple arithmetic (sum, average, minimum, and maximum) in tables. It lets you import and export data easily, and can merge data from Q&A, dBASE, Paradox, or ASCII data. It also supports OLE links (object linking and embedding).

Key Watch 2.0

Publisher: Micro Logic; P.O. Box 70; Hackensack, NJ 07602; (201) 342-6518; fax (201) 342-0370

System Requirements: IBM PC or compatible; 10K RAM; DOS 2.0 or higher

Documentation: A small manual accompanies the program.

Support: If you need help, you can place a toll call to the company's technical support line.

Suggested Retail Price: $29.95

The Program

This program creates macros automatically by watching your keystroke patterns. It signals you audibly, beeping to indicate it has detected and remembered a pattern. It then assigns that pattern to a single key. You can play back the pattern any time with a single keystroke, until a new pattern is detected. As you continue work and Key Watch detects a new pattern, it replaces the old pattern with the new one. (The action-key command is **Alt** and **F5** pressed together.) You can set your own sequence to the key command, change the action key command, or lock the macro so it won't be replaced automatically. The program recognizes a pattern such as a set of numbers—101, 102, 103… upon which you press the **Alt** and **F5** keys to make the computer continue typing the sequence automatically. Key Watch also lets you change and set the Caps Lock and NumLock keys on your computer.

Kid Cad (Ages 7 and up)

Publisher: Davidson & Associates, Inc.; P.O. Box 2961; 19840 Pioneer Ave.; Torrance, CA 90509; (310) 793-0600; (800) 545-7677; (800) 556-6141; fax (310) 793-0601

System Requirements: IBM PC or compatible with an 80386 or better microprocessor; Windows 3.1 Enhanced Mode; 256-color SVGA; 4MB RAM; 9MB free hard disk space; 3.5-inch floppy drive

Suggested: 25MHz and above CPU recommended; SoundBlaster or other sound card; printer

Documentation: The manual is logically organized, illustrated, and easy to read.

Support: Online help is available. The manual contains a troubleshooting appendix, as well as a quick reference for the demolition and building tools. Customer Support technicians can be reached by telephone on weekdays from 7:00 a.m. to 6:00 p.m., by fax 24 hours every day, or by mail.

Suggested Retail Price: $49.95

The Program

Kid Cad is a 3-D building-and-design studio for creating houses, forts, gazebos, and all sorts of structures with built-in electronic building blocks. (It resembles an electronic Tinkertoys, Erector Set, or Lego set.) Not only can you create a building, you can also add an assortment of people, pets, furniture, and ferns. Paint tools let you color your design with solid colors and "wallpaper" patterns. You can zoom in or out to see a close up or a bird's-eye view of your creation, or circle around to check out all angles of your building using the Camera function of Kid Cad. The program also contains an amazing assortment of demolition tools all complete with sound effects. Other features include rotation, a hide tool that makes objects disappear so you can see what is behind them, and a linking tool that joins or separates objects when you make changes to your structure.

You can begin with the tutorial, advance to sample designs, and then go on to the Design Studio where you build your own creations. The program lets you design structures in any of three landscapes: a farm, a town, and a big city. This program has been highly rated, but may take adult supervision for the youngest users.

Kid Keys (ages 4 to 8)

Publisher: Davidson & Associates, Inc.; P.O. Box 2961; 19840 Pioneer Ave.; Torrance, CA 90509; (310) 793-0600; (800) 545-7677; (800) 556-6141; fax (310) 793-0601

System Requirements: Macintosh Classic or greater; System 6.0.7 or later; 2MB RAM (1MB free) for black and white; 4MB RAM (2MB free) for color; hard disk drive with 9MB free space; 3.5-inch, high-density floppy disk drive

Suggested: Printer

Other Platforms (not reviewed): 12MHz 286 or faster IBM PC or compatible

Curriculum Areas: Children can learn the alphabet, simple three- and four-letter words, location of letters on the keyboard, and the correct fingers to use on the keyboard.

Documentation: The manual is concise and easy to read.

Support: The manual contains a troubleshooting appendix. Customer Support technicians can be reached by telephone on weekdays from 7:00 a.m. to 6:00 p.m., by fax 24 hours every day, or by mail.

Suggested Retail Price: $49.95

The Program

Kid Keys is a playful, colorful program with three activities designed to help young children learn to type and build early reading skills. The type is large and easy to read; accuracy is stressed over speed. This program is very elementary and indeed is suitable for young children, with the most difficult levels requiring them to type only simple three- and four-letter words. The digitized speech, music, animation, and sound effects make what can be a chore—learning to type—fun and interesting for children with short attention spans.

Kid Pix 2 (Ages 4 to 12)

Publisher: Broderbund Software, Inc.; 500 Redwood Boulevard; P.O. Box 6121; Novato, CA 94948-6121; (415) 382-4400; (800) 521-6263

System Requirements: IBM PC with 640K RAM; hard disk drive; mouse; Windows 3.1; VGA graphics, floppy disk drive

Suggested: Sound card (SoundBlaster, Tandy Digital Sound, or Disney Sound Source); any of the popular printers

Other Platforms (not reviewed): Macintosh

Curriculum Areas: This program provides wonderful art fun, but it also lets you explore symmetry, shadowing (or gradation), and 3-D art design. In addition, you can add songs and use writing skills to enrich your drawings.

Documentation: The User's Guide shows all of the features. A Teacher's Guide (available for $10) will help you select a project that is appropriate for a particular age or grade level.

Suggested Retail Price: $39.95

The Program

The program repackages the original Kid Pix and the Kid Pix Companion. It provides normal paint tools, including a variety of line widths, rectangles, ovals, erasers, pens, and brushes, but adds to them in unusual ways. For example, the Wacky Brushes option lets you paint in 28 different patterns, including Leaky Pen and Drippy Paint. The Electric Mixer tool changes the drawing in a variety of fun and silly ways, such as shattering a picture into broken pieces. Erasers don't just delete what you've drawn—they may suck it into a black hole or explode it like fireworks. As you work, you can hear sound effects for different painting tools. For example, the Undo option says "oops," the Rubber-Stamp option goes *kachunk*, and the paint glugs out of the bucket.

Entering text is easy any way you do it, but an option for young children lets you point to the Letter tool, after which letters pop up and you click on the ones you want. The program's ability to record sounds and support AVI movies (which you can paste into paintings or create from a Kid Pix Slide Show) keep children and even pre-teens interested. There are also 25 pictures to color, but the 36-color limit of the program is a drawback to coloring activities. Although even adults will enjoy this program, older children will eventually graduate to "adult" paint programs that have more editing tools.

KidDesk

Publisher: Edmark Corporation; 6727 185th Avenue, NE; P.O. Box 3218; Redmond, WA 98073-3218; (206) 556-8484; fax (206) 556-8998

System Requirements: IBM PC/Tandy or compatible; 640K RAM; hard disk drive; one floppy disk drive; EGA graphics; mouse; DOS 3.1 or higher

Suggested: VGA graphics; sound card (sound input requires SoundBlaster or SoundBlaster Pro); printer

Other Platforms (not reviewed): Macintosh

Documentation: The manual is concise and well organized, explaining both the Kid Section and the Adult Section. It also offers suggestions for using parts of the desktop as learning devices.

Support: Technical support is available by telephone.

Suggested Retail Price: $39.95 (educational version, $49.95)

The Program

Ever imagine your children punching a few keys and wiping out your important contacts file and the latest version of that important presentation that's due tomorrow? This program lets your children launch their own programs and files without accessing yours.

Installation is highly customizable. You can choose to have KidDesk run automatically when your computer is turned on, for maximum protection of your data and applications. Once you are in the program, you can enter the Adult section by holding the **Ctrl** and **Alt** keys while pressing **A**. For extra security, you can add an adult password for entering this section. Here you set up a desktop for each child that will be using your computer. There are six desktop designs from which to choose. Applications that can be accessed from the desktop are shown as colorful icons on the desktop. When you click on other special items on the desk, you can do a number of tasks. The desktops are so delightful that you may even want to set up one for yourself.

KIDS COLLECTION

Publisher: IntraCorp, Inc./Capstone Software; 7200 NW 19th Street, Ste. 500; Miami, FL 33126; (800) 468-7226; (305) 591-5900; fax (305) 591-5633; BBS (305) 471-8962

System Requirements: IBM PC or compatible with an 80286 or better microprocessor; 640K RAM; MS-DOS 5.0 or later; CD-ROM drive; EGA graphics; SoundBlaster-compatible sound card

Suggested: VGA graphics; mouse or joystick; printer

Documentation: The box contains manuals for all three games. The Coloring Book also includes a Learning Guide that provides ideas for learning activities based on ideas in the Coloring Book.

Support: Online help is available, as is a 1-2-3 Classic option that lets you see the familiar DOS version's menus.

Suggested Retail Price: $19.95

THE PROGRAM

Kids Collection contains three Capstone children's games: An American Tail, Trolls, and Rock-A-Doodle Computerized Coloring Book. An American Tail features Fievel from the movies *An American Tail* and *An American Tail: Fievel Goes West*. The game is based on a point-and-click interface through which Fievel can talk to characters, pick up objects, access inventory, or ask for hints. As Fievel moves through the program, he must play and win a number of games in order to move on. In Trolls, you play arcade games at seven different levels. Levels can be completed in any order, but all must be completed to win the game (that is, to enter the large wooden door on the third level). In the Rock-A-Doodle Coloring Book, you can create a picture by selecting from sets of backgrounds, figures, and colors. The program also contains a Print option with which you can print a hard copy of your picture. This collection of programs has something for everyone: puzzle challenges, fast arcade games, and art work.

KidWorks2 (Ages 4 to 12)

Publisher: Davidson & Associates, Inc.; P.O. Box 2961; 19840 Pioneer Ave.; Torrance, CA 90509; (310) 793-0600; (800) 545-7677; (800) 556-6141; fax (310) 793-0601

System Requirements: IBM PC/Tandy or compatible, at least 8MHz; VGA, MCGA, EGA, or Tandy graphics; 640K RAM; DOS 3.0 or higher; hard drive with at least 2MB free space; 3.5- or 5.25-inch floppy disk drive for installation; mouse

Suggested: Printer; program supports Disney Sound Source, Sound Commander, Hearsay 100, SoundBlaster, Ad Lib, Covox Speech Thing, Echo PCII, IBM PC Speech Adapter, and IBM PC ACPA

Other Platforms (not reviewed): Macintosh; CD-ROM version supports both Macintosh System 7.0 or higher and Windows 3.1 or higher

Curriculum Areas: This program supports reading, writing, and drawing. It helps beginning readers make the connection between symbols and the printed word.

Documentation: The manual moves you through an example, then describes each activity and all of the icons. It includes tips for teachers and parents, troubleshooting, a list of icons, and an index. The tutorial is good.

Suggested Retail Price: $59.95 for Macintosh, DOS, Windows, and CD-ROM versions

The Program

With this exciting program, you can create stories in Story Writer, using a combination of words, icons, and drawings. You can use the icons provided by the program, or create your own in Icon Maker. When you paint a picture to go with your story in Story Illustrator, you can choose from a variety of colored backgrounds, picture stamps, and painting tools (such as draw, fill, erase, and spray). Add a few sound effects, and then you can hear your story read back to you in Story Player, though the speech is not great without special sound capabilities. Once you are finished, you can print out your story and picture.

The user interface consists of icons and buttons; a control panel enables you to turn program components on and off, adjust speech capabilities, and resize text. The program does offer spoken instructions for some tasks. The program has a few limitations: you cannot use the icons in your picture, and the spoken pronunciation of a word may not match the correct pronunciation. The program does have a "sounds like" option in which you can change the pronunciation of a word to its phonetic spelling, however. It may take some practice to get used to meanings of some of the icons, too. The icons for nouns and verbs can be the same. In addition, the icons for concepts (found in the Descriptions/Locations icon box) can easily be mistaken for an object or an action.

Besides offering the fun of writing stories and creating art, this program encourages you to use punctuation such as periods and commas, because without it, the "voice" reads straight through with no natural breaks. You soon learn that if you want a story told well, there must be punctuation. You also will be learning sequencing, as you write your story in a logical order.

King's Quest V: Absence Makes the Heart Go Yonder

Publisher: Sierra, Sierra On-Line, P.O. Box 485; Coarsegold, CA 93614; (800) 326-6654; (209) 683-4468

System Requirements: IBM PC or compatible with a 286 or better microprocessor; 640K RAM; VGA graphics; hard disk drive

Suggested: Mouse; supports Ad Lib, PS/1, Game Blaster, Roland MT-32/LAPC-1/CM-32L, and SoundBlaster sound cards

Other Platforms (not reviewed): The program is available in a CD-ROM version, with enchanting music, varied voices, and high-quality graphics.

Documentation: The documentation introduces the story of the game, including the background of the previous King's Quest games (I through IV), but it is not much help as far as starting the game is concerned. You're on your own as you look and make choices from the screen.

Support: Most Sierra games have clue books available and an automated telephone hint line with a 900 number. You can also get hints from Sierra's online bulletin board system, and often a commercial information service may offer hints for Sierra games. For technical help, you can call or write to the company's customer support department.

Suggested Retail Price: $69.95

The Program

In this installment of the King's Quest series, you set out with King Graham to find the missing royal family of Daventry. This is an interactive adventure story; you must look everywhere, explore carefully, draw a map marking each area you visit (and the objects and dangers you find), get objects you think you need, and use these objects to solve problems. Backtracking may be necessary as you try to solve the mystery, and it helps to save your game often. The characters are highly developed and the graphics are detailed. The music is an original stereo soundtrack. The interface is simple point-and-click, requiring no typing.

LANtastic Network Operating System 4.0 Starter Kit

Publisher: Artisoft, Inc.; Artisoft Plaza; 2202 N. Forbes Blvd; Tucson, AZ 85704; (800) 846-9726; (602) 293-6363; fax (602) 670-7101

System Requirements: DOS-based IBM PC or compatible; 24K RAM for each workstation; 50K for a server

Other Platforms (not reviewed): Macintosh

Suggested Retail Price: $699 (A more economical program is Simply LANtastic at $299.)

The Program

This program enables you to set up a local area network (LAN). It is a peer-to-peer system rather than a dedicated-system server. The kit includes two AE-2 network adapter cards, 25 feet of RG-58 coaxial cable, and the operating system for handling up to 300 nodes. The program supports the company's adapter cards, but Artisoft also sells an Adapter Independent version that serves other company's network cards. For a 386 or higher machine, the program can also be loaded high, using an extended memory manager.

The LAN will serve three network wiring schemes. You can configure all connections, sharing of resources, and disk and printer options. You can also use its very fast disk-caching program (called LANcache) for all three types of memory. The program offers password security and access control features. A CHAT feature enables you to send messages to people on the network; the program also has an e-mail feature. For $99, you can buy an adapter for sending voice mail. If you are setting up a small LAN, this program may fit your needs. It costs much less than a LAN designed to serve large numbers of workstations.

Last Chance to See

Publisher: The Voyager Company; 578 Broadway, Ste. 406; New York, NY 10012; (212) 431-5199; (800) 446-2001; fax (212) 431-5799

System Requirements: Macintosh LC or larger; 2MB RAM (4MB for color); 8-bit video card or 24-bit video and QuickTime; CD ROM drive; System 6.0.7 or later

Suggested: Headphones or speakers

Documentation: A booklet included in the disc case describes the program briefly, lists troubleshooting questions, and notes system requirements.

Support: Registered users can receive phone support and notification of updates.

Suggested Retail Price: $59.95

The Program

Last Chance to See visits endangered species in their natural habitats, and teaches about the efforts being made to save these animals. This program closely follows the original book by Douglas Adams and Mark Carwardine. Douglas Adams is the narrator throughout the program, and you hear him read when you open any chapter or section. As you navigate through the program, you can use links to explore topics further. Use these by clicking on small pictures that appear when a link is available. You can set a number of parameters, including sound volume.

Lemmings

Publisher: Psygnosis Limited; 29 St. Mary's Court; Brookline, MA 02146; (617) 731-3553; fax (617) 731-8379

System Requirements: IBM PC, XT, AT, PS/2 or compatible, Tandy, Amstrad PC; VGA, EGA, Tandy 16-color; 512K RAM; 3.5- or 5.25-inch floppy disk drive; joystick and keyboard options

Suggested: Mouse highly recommended; Ad Lib and SoundBlaster supported

Other Platforms (not reviewed): Amiga; Macintosh; Atari ST (These versions allow two-player games.)

Documentation: The documentation is very basic, and at times you wish it contained more information. It explains installing or loading for various computers, describes the icons, and offers some tips for playing.

Suggested Retail Price: $49

The Program

Lemmings are the creatures that supposedly herd themselves into the sea to destruction as a means of controlling their population. With this program, you can save some lemmings from propelling themselves to their death. To keep them safe from cliffs, boiling water, lemming-eating mechanisms, and so on, you can give special abilities to some of the lemmings. For example, a lemming can be a blocker to stop others in their march to a cliff—or a lemming can build a bridge, dig through the earth, climb, or float. Once you get your lemmings safely to an exit, you receive a password that enables you to go on to the next level. (Remember this password, and you can continue where you left off when you start play again at a later time.) Each new level presents a puzzle that you solve by giving certain lemmings the right abilities. The abilities used successfully in one puzzle may be useless in another puzzle. The lemming options are shown in a bar of icons at the bottom of the screen.

The game has good animation and sound, with an excellent music track. Critics have liked this game well enough for it to have won some awards as the best game of the year, and it is popular enough that the company has produced another package, Oh No! More Lemmings, with 100 more puzzles.

LINKS 386 Pro

Publisher: Access Software; 4910 West Amelia Earhart Drive; Salt Lake City, UT 84116; (800) 800-4880

System Requirements: IBM PC or compatible or Tandy with a 16MHz 386SX microprocessor; 2MB RAM; SVGA with 1MB memory and a compatible monitor; mouse

Suggested: 4MB RAM

Other Platforms (not reviewed): Macintosh (*Links Pro Macintosh*)

Suggested Retail Price: $69.95

The Program

If you have a 16MHz 386SX or better microprocessor in your computer, you might try this golf program. It has excellent graphics and realistic perspective. Choose your clubs and head for the golf course. So that you can see where to aim on the greens, the program uses a pole to mark the target. It also indicates the difference between the pole and the point where the player strikes the ball. Putting is not easy with this game, but this is true of most golfing programs. You do have a chance to practice the program's unique swinging method by hitting balls on the driving range and the chipping green. The program also includes an option for tournament play. If you don't have the required system for this game, Access produces Links Championship Course for less powerful computer systems.

LinksWare

Publisher: LinksWare Corporation; 641 Lily Street; Monterey, CA 93940-1631; (408) 372-4155; fax (408) 646-9104

System Requirements: Macintosh Plus or greater; 2MB RAM; System 6.0.5 or later; some features require System 7

Suggested: Hard disk drive strongly recommended

Other Platforms (not reviewed): Apple IIgs

Documentation: Documentation for this program is a small manual with instructions, tips, and hints. You actually have to set up a link to understand exactly what this program is about.

Support: Technical support is available to registered users at the company's address or telephone number.

Suggested Retail Price: $189

The Program

This program is used to create hypertext or hypergraphics links among your word processor and graphics files. It is compatible with Microsoft Word, MacWrite, and many others. Using it requires no programming; the directions tell you to just click on a word or graphic area. The program works with files stored on read-only media such as CD-ROM, and can be used with QuickTime movies, sound, graphics, and word processor files. It shows the links on the screen, but you can access the linked words and files through the main menu. It does not use HyperCard, and it displays documents without the need for the original application program. The program does not change files, but you can add links, remove links, show links, and expand links so that every word which had ever been linked is active. The actual links are stored in a separate file. If you create multimedia presentations, you will appreciate the simplicity of this program.

Living Books Series

Publisher: Broderbund Software; (800) 521-6263; (415) 382-4400

System Requirements: Macintosh; 4MB RAM; CD-ROM drive; 256-color monitor

Suggested Retail Price: $37.00

The Program

This series of books contains colorfully animated, interactive stories for three-to-eight-year-olds. Text displayed on the screen is read aloud to children by character voices while the story is simultaneously acted out. Children are guided through their options, including playing in the pages of the book and listening as the book is read aloud. Music and sound effects make the stories even more entertaining. Some of the books include *Ruff's Bone*, *The Tortoise and the Hare*, *Little Monster at School*, and *Just Grandma and Me*.

Lost in L.A. (Parental Discretion Advised)

Publisher: Accolade; 5300 Stevens Creek Blvd., Suite 200; San Jose, CA 95129; (408) 985-1700

System Requirements: IBM AT or 100-percent compatible with recommended speed of 10MHz or higher; MCGA, VGA; 640K RAM; hard disk drive; high-density floppy disk drive

Suggested: Mouse

Documentation: The instructions leaflet imitates a newspaper.

Support: A clue book is available, but you can also call the company's hint line over the telephone, or access a bulletin board for Accolade. For technical help, you can call a customer support number on weekdays between 8:00 a.m. and 5:00 p.m. Pacific Standard Time, or write Accolade Customer Support at the address given above.

Suggested Retail Price: $59.95

The Program

This is a Les Manley animated-graphics adventure. In this game, Les must find out who is kidnapping the most popular stars in Hollywood. Les is invited to California by Helmut Bean, the world's smallest man (his old friend from Search for the King). Before he can get there, Bean disappears. Les must find Bean while not falling victim to the temptations of the Southern California lifestyle. As you guide Les through this adventure, the program pokes fun of the L.A. lifestyle of lifeguards, "beach bunnies," celebrities, and talent agents. In some scenes you cannot move Les because you are seeing the scene from his point of view. The game can be saved to resume later, a good thing to do before you make Les take any risks.

Accolade has worked hard to present high-quality graphics. The artists created digitized photos—and footage using real actors and models—to portray the characters in the program. The characters were then superimposed upon backgrounds digitized from matte oil paintings of real Southern California locations. The music is rock 'n' roll, appropriate for the plot and the humor of the program.

Like many other companies, Accolade has worked out an off-disk copy-protection scheme so you can make archival copies of your disks. This one requires you to rotate a set of cardboard disks to the specifications listed on the screen in order to enter the 4-digit code number you see when the disks are aligned properly. Unfortunately, there is just as much chance that something will happen to the cardboard wheel as to the computer disk. If you lose it, you can get a new one for $15; if it is destroyed, Accolade will replace it free, as long as you send in its remains.

Lotus 1-2-3 for Windows 4.01

Publisher: Lotus Development Corporation; 55 Cambridge Parkway; Cambridge, MA 02142; (617) 577-8500; (800) 343-5414

System Requirements: IBM PC or compatible with an 80386 or better microprocessor; 4MB RAM for Windows version; Windows 3.1 or higher; DOS 3.3 or higher; CD-ROM drive

Suggested: 6MB RAM; 80486 microprocessor

Other Platforms (not reviewed): Macintosh; DOS version for IBM PCs and compatibles

Documentation: The manuals include one that explains the SmartIcons, an Adobe Type Manager user's guide, a Quick Start manual, and a Solver Guide for using what-if situations in the spreadsheet. The main User's Guide is well written, and it is easy to find the topics you want.

Support: Online help is available, as is a 1-2-3 Classic option that lets you see the familiar DOS version's menus. A CD-ROM is necessary for the Learning Tools, a 40-minute guided tour with animation and sound. The QuickMovie animation illustrations steps in difficult procedures, and you can toggle between the movie and the worksheet.

Suggested Retail Price: $495

The Program

This program does everything a spreadsheet program should do, and more. It has functions and tools for charting, drawing, editing, and formatting elements of a spreadsheet. You can edit directly in a cell. You can move, open, and close almost every element of the worksheet. You can modify menus to include what you use the most, without leaving the worksheet. The charting options include rotating your text and changing the colors of elements. The program has a print preview mode, though you cannot edit elements in that mode. The presentation tools are limited in comparison to some other spreadsheet programs, but this program is a workhorse, enabling you to view and work with up to 256 worksheets simultaneously. It also has graphics and some simple flat-file database-management capabilities.

This program also has a few unique features that make it especially attractive. It has three-dimensional organization through the Worksheet Tabs. The Scenario Manager features let you set up and save scenarios (situations) that juggle data to help you visualize the business consequences that arise from various conditions. Its interface has user-programmable SmartIcons. With Lotus Annotator, you can create and embellish multimedia notes in Windows applications. With Lotus Media Manager, you can add sounds and video to a worksheet. Version Manager is a workgroup feature used to keep track of changed scenarios without making multiple copies of files or overwriting existing information.

The company also produces a package called Lotus 1-2-3 for Home (created specifically for home use), and Improv for Windows 2.1, an open-ended spreadsheet program that eliminates the basic row/column structure of worksheets and enables more direct cell work.

MacDraw Pro 1.5

Publisher: Claris Corporation; 5201 Patrick Henry Drive; Santa Clara, CA 95052; (408) 727-8227; fax (408) 987-7440

System Requirements: Macintosh Plus or greater; 2MB RAM; one 800K disk drive; hard disk drive; System 6.0.5 or later; System 7 or later (to use publish-and-subscribe and Balloon Help); Finder 6.1.5 or later; 32-bit QuickDraw 1.2 (not required for System 7, but supplied with MacDraw Pro 1.5 for System 6 users); 2MB RAM and hard disk drive required for communications usage

Suggested: 4MB RAM if using System 7 or color

Documentation: Documentation includes a quick reference guide, a New Features Guide, a Color Guide, a Getting Started Guide, and a User's Guide. The manuals are easy to use and understand; the information you need is easy to find.

Support: Technical support for registered users is available from 6:00 a.m. to 6:00 p.m. weekdays, and Friday from 6:00 a.m. to 2:00 p.m. Pacific Standard Time.

Suggested Retail Price: $399

The Program

This 32-bit color drawing program focuses mainly on offering a number of color options. It has three color systems: HSL, RGB, and CMYK. Thus, the program can be used for documents you will print using traditional ink printing systems. It also offers a number of color palettes through which you choose the colors you need, including the Claris Colors and Pantone matching system colors.

The program provides the normal draw features: pen, fill with tile patterns, gradient fill, different shapes, and different widths and textures of lines. You can move objects, scale an object to a certain size by percentage, change the order of stacking objects (that is, whether objects are in front of or behind each other), and smooth objects. You can select a shape that overlaps another, and treat it as a single unit not affecting the other unit. The zoom feature lets you zoom in and out on a specific area (fractional zooming), and use zoom to work on matching your printer's resolution. You can edit complex curves and polygons, and use gradient shading in objects. If you create several layers of a picture, you can sift through them using arrows located at the bottom of the screen. There are a number of charting options.

MacInTax

Publisher: ChipSoft Inc. (a subsidiary of Intuit); 6330 Nancy Ridge Drive, Suite 103; San Diego, CA 92121-2246; (619) 453-8722; (800) 964-1040; fax (800) 374-7057

System Requirements: Macintosh Plus or greater; 1MB RAM; System 4.2 or later; hard disk drive, one 800K floppy drive needed for installation; printer

Other Platforms (not reviewed): The program for Windows and DOS is called TurboTax.

Documentation: The User's Manual includes information about all the tax forms and the menus, as well as tips, error messages, and information about using data from other files or applications.

Support: Documentation includes online context-sensitive help and an EasyStep feature to guide you through the steps. You can also call up the TaxHelp feature for detailed information about the topic you are having problems with. Technical support is free (other than the toll call) to registered users on weekdays from 8:30 a.m. to 5:00 p.m. Pacific Standard Time, with extended hours during the heavy tax season, January 13 through April 15.

Suggested Retail Price: $69.95 with each state supplement at $39.95

The Program

This program could help you save money at tax time. It prepares almost a hundred federal tax forms, with the state forms available separately, and every form is WYSIWYG. The explanations are good, and the program does all the routine calculations and repetitious filling-in of blanks for you. The program *should* be good; this company also produces a full line of tax software for use by professional accountants and CPAs. Be aware that you will need a new program every year because the government issues new forms and revised regulations annually. If you decide to use the program, be sure to read the README file first: There are tax updates in it, plus it gives corrections to the manual and tells more about importing files. Then use the Quick Tour, which gives an overall view of all of its features.

MacInTax checks for inconsistencies and errors among the data you enter, and also flags things that could trigger an audit. A Deduction Finder helps locate places where you might have missed items that could be entered as deductions. There is also a section called Personal Tax Issues that discusses aspects of taxation such as having your office in your home or being the sole proprietor of your own business. The package offers an option for filing electronically through a data-entry service.

Other good tax-preparation programs include Andrew Tobias' TaxCut 1040 for DOS at $89.95, from MECA Software, Inc., P.O. Box 912, Fairfield, CT 06430-0912, (800) 288-6322; it has 13 state programs available. Also good is EasyTax at $79.95, from Timeworks, Inc., 625 Academy Drive, Northbrook, IL 60062, (800) 323-7744; it has 24 state tax programs available.

Macintosh PC Exchange

Publisher: Apple Computer, Inc.; 20525 Mariani Ave.; Cupertino, CA 95014; (408) 996-1010

System Requirements: Macintosh; 3MB RAM; hard disk drive; one SuperDrive floppy disk drive; System 7 or later

Suggested Retail Price: $79

The Program

With this program, you can transfer PC files to Macintosh applications. You can work with files stored on 3.5- or 5.25-inch floppies formatted with either DOS or Microsoft Windows. After a transfer has taken place, the files and subdirectories appear as standard Macintosh documents and folders. A control panel lets you create links between DOS files and Macintosh applications. For example, if you have a Lotus 1-2-3 file in DOS, you can click on the icon on the Macintosh desktop and it will open Lotus 1-2-3 for the Macintosh; that is, as long as you have the program on the hard disk drive. The application program you use must be able to read that DOS file's format. The program is compatible with all Macintosh applications, as well as many leading DOS and Windows applications.

MacLinkPlus 8.0

Publisher: Data Viz, Inc.; 55 Corporate Drive; Trumbull, CT 06611; (203) 268-0030; (800) 733-0030; fax (203) 268-4345

System Requirements: Mac Plus or greater; hard disk drive; System 6.0.3 and later

Documentation: The documentation is as well organized and easy to use as the program itself.

Suggested Retail Price: The program has three MacLinkPlus/Easy Open Translators. The basic Translator is $109 for people who already have access to PC files through networks, and so on. The Translator Pro ($149) adds Mac PC Exchange so you can use DOS disks in a Macintosh. The MacLinkPlus/ PC Connect ($199) includes an 8-foot serial cable and communication software for sharing files.

The Program

A file-transfer-and-translation program that includes communications software and a cable, MacLink Plus is easy to use. It exchanges a wide variety of text, database, spreadsheet, and graphics files between Macs and PCs. It includes a DOS-mounting software which allows PC disks to be accepted by a Mac SuperDrive and displayed on the Mac desktop. When you work with word processing documents, MacLink Plus retains text-formatting elements (such as footnotes, headers, underlines, print styles, indents, and tabs) during translation for a seamless transfer. You can easily and accurately import text or data created on any computer system into any Mac spreadsheet or database application, or convert to another spreadsheet or database format. Regardless of which computer a graphics file was created on, MacLink Plus translators provide you with a fully modifiable file, and also save a copy of the file to the Mac clipboard, which allows easy pasting. You can use the enclosed cable or a modem as a physical means of transferring files. A new "drag-to-translate" feature allows you to convert a file by dragging it over the MacLink Plus icon. Designate the settings in terms of mode, translators, and communications, and you're ready to transfer files in either direction. The current library allows 600 file-transfer combinations between Mac and PC applications.

MacProject Pro 1.5

Publisher: Claris; 5201 Patrick Henry Drive; Box 58168; Santa Clara, CA 95052-8168; (408) 727-8227; fax (408) 987-7440

System Requirements: Mac Plus or greater; one 800K floppy drive and a hard disk drive; 2MB RAM (4MB for System 7); System 6.0.5 or later; or A/UX 2.0 or later

Suggested: LC or greater

Documentation: Documentation is exceptional. A Getting Started manual walks you through the installation process and includes a tutorial for first-time users. The User's Guide is well organized, complete, and easy to read. It also provides step-by-step instructions for completing tasks in MacProject Pro. A Quick Reference card includes keyboard shortcuts and effective project-management tips.

Support: MacProject Pro offers excellent online help; concise step-by-step instructions for specific tasks and dialog box options. Sample documents and perspectives are included to offer ideas, or to use as templates for your projects. Be sure to register your software, as you are entitled to the following benefits: unlimited technical support, software updates, and specially priced upgrades, as well as newsletters and other product information from Claris.

Suggested Retail Price: $599

The Program

MacProject Pro is a versatile management tool that allows you to plan, track, control, and present projects of any size. The main focus of the program is on tracking three project elements: tasks, timelines for completion, and resources. The built-in Outline feature gives you a fast, easy way to brainstorm and record ideas. The program assigns legal-style outline numbers automatically to each entry; it also lets you move entries around, change their hierarchical orientation, delete them, or expand them. The outliner, however, is limited to 25 hierarchical entry levels.

MacProject Pro can meet a broad range of needs: if you are an experienced project manager you will appreciate the 11 graphic charts and tables, including Gantt and PERT; if this is your first experience with project management, the outliner offers flexible and easy-to-use data entry.

MacUSA (Ages 8 and up)

Publisher: Broderbund Software, Inc.; 500 Redwood Boulevard; P.O. Box 6125; Novato, CA 94948-6125; (415) 382-4400; (800) 521-6263

System Requirements: Macintosh Plus or greater; 1MB RAM; hard disk drive; System 6.0.4 or later; supports System 7; one 800K floppy disk drive (needed for installation)

Suggested: 2MB RAM; color monitor

Other Platforms (not reviewed): IBM versions are PC USA and PC Globe 5.0.

Curriculum Areas: This program supports geography, civics, and history through its maps and charts that reveal land forms, demographics, and important tourist attractions.

Documentation: The manual explains installation and features of the program. Once installed, however, the program is easy to explore, even without the manual. Although the manual is complete, it does not tell you which icon to double-click on to open the program.

Support: Technical support is available for the cost of the toll call. To receive annual updates, you must have mailed in your registration card.

Suggested Retail Price: $49.95

The Program

MacUSA provides maps and statistics on just about anything from the lands acquired in the Treaty of Paris to the rate of violent crime per 100,000 people. This program is great for exploration; it can also help students collect information for a report, or learn how to read maps and charts. If you buy MacUSA, be sure to purchase the annual updates to maintain the usefulness of the program.

Each state has its own individual map, complete with four different modes: Base Map, Cities Map, Elevation Map, and Features Map. In each of these views, you can also double-click on the map to access (for example) a chart about population, minerals, and tourist attractions. (Once you enter a chart, you can return to the map by clicking in the **Close** box on the chart window.) The comparison maps use color (or pattern, on black-and-white Macs) to show how each state ranks in a variety of categories (such as demographics, vital statistics, economy, government, crime, highways, education, voting, minerals, and products). The interface for this program is so user-friendly that you merely point-and-click your way through the mass of information.

The company also produces MacGlobe, a similar program with maps and statistics for the entire world. Like MacUSA, MacGlobe is easy to use, and offers a myriad of facts. The one criticism of this program is that many of the smaller countries are hard to find, and once you have found them, they are too small to reveal the patterns used in the comparison maps.

MacWrite Pro 1.5 v2

Publisher: Claris; 5201 Patrick Henry Drive; Box 58168; Santa Clara, CA 95052-8168; (408) 727-8227; (800) 987-7000; fax (408) 987-7440

System Requirements: Macintosh with System 7.0 or later; 1MB RAM; hard disk drive; one 800K disk drive; accelerated for PowerMacs

Suggested: Printer

Documentation: Documentation includes a quick-reference card, a Getting Started manual that is a tutorial, and a User's Guide. The User's Guide is well-designed; you can easily find what you need. It explains all menu options and procedures, and lists keyboard commands if you want to bypass the mouse.

Support: This program has excellent and extensive on-screen help. In addition, when you register your program, you receive regular issues of Technical Solutions, the Claris newsletter that contains product news, helpful hints, and other information. If you have questions, you can make a toll call to the company's technicians on weekdays from 6:00 a.m. to 6:00 p.m. (6:00 a.m. to 2:00 p.m. Friday) Pacific Time.

Suggested Retail Price: $249

The Program

MacWrite Pro contains the usual word processing options, including mail merge, a thesaurus, and a spelling checker, plus some good formatting options including table generation and style sheets. It is powerful enough for creating documents ranging from memos and brief reports to business proposals, multi-column newsletters, and 1,000-page manuscripts. It enables you to import and export files using a number of other popular word processing programs including WordPerfect. The program also offers spreadsheet and graphics support.

MacWrite Pro is easy to use; it provides a clean, uncluttered interface. The menus and dialog boxes are clearly laid out and easy to follow. MacWrite Pro is compatible with both the publish-and-subscribe and alias feature. It supports the QuickTime, PowerTalk, and AppleScript functions of System 7. You can store dictionary, translator, help, and automatic stationery files in a different location, and then access them through aliases placed in the application, Claris, or system folder.

Mangia

Publisher: Upstill Software; (800) 568-3696; (510) 486-0761

System Requirements: Macintosh Plus; 1MB RAM

Suggested Retail Price: $49.95

THE PROGRAM

This cookbook program allows you to organize recipes by taste preferences, regions, etc., in a realistic-looking recipe-card file box. Over 300 recipes are included; Mangia allows you to enter your own creation easily with a feature called QuicFill. The recipe cards are simple, easy to read, and rate each dish by nutrional value and ease of preparation (you can change the ratings if you don't agree). The program prepares a shopping list to print and take along to the grocery; if you have entered what you have on hand, it will calculate only the amount of an ingredient you actually need to purchase.

THE MANHOLE

Publisher: ActiVision; 11440 San Vicente Blvd; Los Angeles, CA 90049; (800) 477-3650; (310) 207-4500

System Requirements: IBM PC or compatible with a 16MHz 286 or better microprocessor; CD-ROM drive; DOS 3.3 or greater; 640K RAM; EGA graphics or better; Sound Blaster and Roland MT-32 supported

Suggested: Windows 3.1; 4MB RAM; VGA graphics; mouse or joystick supported

Other Platforms (not reviewed): Also in floppy disk format; Macintosh version available

Documentation: An introductory flyer is included in the disc case.

Support: Technical support is available by calling the company weekdays between 9:00 a.m. and 5:00 p.m. Pacific time.

Suggested Retail Price: $59.95

THE PROGRAM

In this award-winning fantasy exploration, you visit a magic land where you meet fantastic characters. The Manhole contains more than 600 linked screens where you can scale a beanstalk or explore a shipwreck. Any activity is accompanied by sound effects; the Dragon roars, the starfish sing, and characters talk. The Manhole is not a game you play to win, but rather an adventure. By pointing and clicking on objects, you can see what they will do. Click on characters and they will talk. Click on locations to move around. Although this program is designed for children, adults will have fun exploring the Manhole with its wacky characters and sound effects.

MasterCook

Publisher: Arion Software, Inc.; (800) 444-8104

System Requirement: Macintosh; 2MB RAM; 3MB hard disk space

Suggested Retail Price: $29.95 (Windows); $39.95 (Mac)

The Program

You can search for recipes by ingredients you have available in your kitchen, or scan the list of provided recipes for something that strikes your fancy. MasterCook enables you to build a shopping list from selected recipes, and then print the list with ingredients organized by where they might appear in the grocery. Conversions are available for increasing ingredients, and you can enter your own recipes. The MenuMaker feature helps you plan meals up to a month in advance, and lists the nutritional values of MasterCook's 1,000 recipes.

Math Rabbit (ages 4 to 7)

Publisher: The Learning Company; 6493 Kaiser Drive; Fremont, CA 94555; (800) 852-2255; (510) 792-2101; fax (510) 792-9628

System Requirement: Color Macintosh with System 6.0.7; 2MB RAM for System 6.0.7, or 3MB RAM for System 7; 11MB disk space

Other Platforms (not reviewed): IBM PC or compatible; Deluxe version with CD-ROM for both Macintosh with System 7 or higher, and Windows 3.1 or higher.

Curriculum Areas: This program helps build counting and number-identification skills. It also introduces the child to simple addition and subtraction, number relationships (greater than and less than), and concepts of equality and inequality.

Documentation: The manual is well written, explaining the options clearly.

Support: On-screen help is designed to tell the child how to play the game, but not how to do the problems.

Suggested Retail Price: $59.95

The Program

Using digitized voices, music, and a dancing rabbit, this program presents math concepts in a format that is appealing to both boys and girls. The program has four major parts. The Calliope Counting Games let you create tunes by moving up and down a 0 to 8 scale; the Tightrope Show has you match sets of objects, numbers, or math problems; the Sea Lion Show has you answer add-and-subtract problems; the Balloon Matching Game has you match pairs of objects, numbers, or math problems as you pop balloons.

Math Rabbit is suitable for your child once he or she knows the digits and is able to count small groups of objects. The program displays clear sight-and-sound cues in case of a mistake, but does not offer specific help for reaching the right answer. The rewards for correct answers are tickets that can be cashed in for on-screen "prizes" such as a gumball machine, a smiling shark with sunglasses, or other animations and sounds. The program can be adjusted for difficulty, speed, math operations used, and the numbers that will be shown. The games can be toggled between using objects and using numbers for the various exercises.

Math Shop (ages 10 and up)

Publisher: Scholastic Software; 2931 East McCarty Street; P.O. Box 7502; Jefferson City, MO 65102; (800) 541-5513

System Requirements: IBM PC or compatible 256K RAM needed floppy disk drive EGA or VGA color graphics card

Other Platforms (not reviewed): Macintosh, 1MB; Apple II, 64K

Curriculum Areas: The program requires the child to work with math concepts such as basic computation, decimals, ratios, and beginning algebra.

Suggested Retail Price: $29.95

The Program

Teachers love this program. In addition to providing practical work with the concepts of math, it requires children to think about how to solve problems, and to think about the relationships between numbers as well as what they can do. To play, you become a shopkeeper in a mall, selecting to work at just one shop or all ten at once. Each store has a different set of problems. For example, at the Boutique Shop, you must make change. At the Pharmacy, you use addition with fractions and percentages to fill prescriptions. In the All

Shops option, any delays in your work can cause waiting customers to give up and leave. When you do poorly enough that 50 customers leave the mall, the game ends.

The program helps you see how math is used every day. You might want to talk with your child about the skills required for each shop so that child can start at an appropriate level. Without a manual, it is sometimes hard to discern exactly what you are supposed to do in each shop. The make-believe aspects of the program are attractive, but it is a slow program. Not being an arcade-style program, it is a long time before rewards are evident. The computer offers hints only, not correct answers. Younger children (ages 6 to 9) might enjoy the Math Shop Jr. program produced by the same company. It requires you to count change, use the basic four operations, work with odd and even numbers, and estimate results.

The Math Zone (ages 4 to 10)

Publisher: Milliken Publishing Company; 1100 Research Boulevard; St. Louis, MO 63132; (800) 643-0008

System Requirements: IBM PC or compatible; CGA, EGA, VGA/MCGA, Tandy 16-color, or Hercules graphics; 512K RAM; MS-DOS 2.0 or higher; floppy disk drive

Suggested: Hard disk drive required to use the sound and voice features (sound effects available if using the 3.5-inch disk); mouse; supports Covox Speech, Tandy 1000, Ad Lib, Sound Blaster, The Sound Source, and IBM Speech Adapter sound cards; printer; 640K RAM required to generate and print worksheets

Curriculum Areas: This program is suitable for number readiness and arithmetic operations.

Documentation: The package includes a User's Guide and a Help Manual for addition and subtraction. Both are well organized, and adequate to meet the needs of most users. The User's Guide shows the sequence of levels in number readiness, addition, and subtraction. The Help Manual provides instruction in addition and subtraction that cannot be obtained from the program. Older children will be able to read it, but younger children will need a parent's help with the tips.

Support: When the Help button is shown, on-screen help is available to guide a child through the problems. The program will work through the regrouping steps in addition and subtraction.

Suggested Retail Price: $49.95

The Program

The Math Zone is an offshoot for the home from the popular school program Math Sequences; this program provides practice in counting, addition, and subtraction. It offers immediate reinforcement; rewards for correct answers are sound effects and colorful graphics. You enter your answer when a large, flashing question mark appears on the screen. If the number entered is incorrect, you are given a second chance to answer correctly. If the second attempt is incorrect, the program shows you how to solve the problem step by step. Once you have achieved a certain percentage of correct problems at a certain level, you can advance to the next level. If, however, you answer three problems in a row incorrectly or your percentage of correct problems drops below 50 percent, the program drops you to the previous level of difficulty. The program keeps track of your progress and displays it on a bar chart.

Mathematica 2.2

Publisher: Wolfram Research; (217) 398-0700

System Requirements: Macintosh; 5MB RAM; 8MB hard disk space; System 7 (accelerated for Power Mac)

Suggested Retail Price: $595

The Program

This symbolic mathematics program includes every possible aspect of modern mathematics; it includes a Function Browser for the new user (or poor typist). You can scroll through the list of operations with corresponding descriptions, choose one, and then paste your choice into your Notebook for immediate, accurate use. The quintessential mathematics and science program.

Mayo Clinic Family Health Book 1.2

Publisher: IVI Publishing; 7500 Flying Cloud Drive; Minneapolis, MN 55344-3739; (800) 952-4773

System Requirements: Macintosh LC or greater; 4MB RAM; System 6.0.6 or later; mouse and 12" color monitor; CD-ROM drive; hard disk drive; QuickTime 1.6.1 (can be installed from CD-ROM disk)

Suggested: Additional RAM

Other Platforms (not reviewed): 386SX or greater IBM PCs and compatibles with Windows 3.1 or later and DOS 3.1 or later

Documentation: There are no manuals except for a small leaflet explaining setup and running instructions.

Support: Guided Tours online help you learn to navigate through the text, illustrations, and animations.

Suggested Retail Price: $69.95

The Program

The Family Health Book is a comprehensive and straightforward resource. It contains information about over 1,000 medical conditions, first aid, prevention, and more. Topic sections include LifeCycles, The World Around Us, Keeping Fit, Human Disease and Disorders, and Modern Medical Care. You can easily click on certain text for hypertext links to further information, including animated illustrations with voice-over commentary. Symptoms are discussed, but the program is not intended as a diagnostic tool; it can help you learn preventive measures, or be prepared for certain diagnostic procedures.

Mayo Clinic Family Pharmacist

Publisher: IVI Publishing; 7500 Flying Cloud Drive; Minneapolis, MN 55344-3739; (800) 952-4773

System Requirements: 25MHz 386SX (or greater) IBM PC or compatible, with Windows 3.1 and DOS 5.0 or later; 4MB RAM; CD-ROM drive; 256-color VGA+ with 640 x 480 resolution; stereo headphones or speakers; 5MB free hard disk space; mouse minimum MPC-Level 1 sound card

Suggested: 33MHz 386SX or greater; 8MB RAM; double-speed CD-ROM drive; 10MB free hard disk space

Documentation: Unlike the documentation for other programs in the series, the instruction leaflet contains information about using the interface, the toolbars, and the program features.

Support: The Overview—as well as animated and indexed online help—enable you learn to navigate through the text, illustrations, and animations.

Suggested Retail Price: $69.95

The Program

The latest in the Mayo Clinic series provides information about more than 7,600 prescription and over-the-counter medications in understandable language. In the Personal Profile section, you can record and print personal medical profiles for you and your family. Question-and-answer segments help you select non-prescription medications. Step-by-step animations illustrate important first aid techniques such as CPR. The program contains 68 videos and animations, 1,600 photographs of medications, and 50 minutes of audio material.

Mayo Clinic: The Total Heart

Publisher: IVI Publishing; 7500 Flying Cloud Drive; Minneapolis, MN 55344-3739; (800) 952-4773

System Requirements: Color Macintosh LC or greater, with 4MB RAM and System 6.0.6 or later, or System 7; CD-ROM drive; hard disk drive; QuickTime 1.6.1 (can be installed from CD-ROM disk); HyperCard 2.1 with 3MB RAM; mouse

Suggested: 5MB or more of RAM; 13-inch monitor

Other Platforms (not reviewed): 386SX (or greater) IBM PCs and compatibles, with Windows 3.1 or later and DOS 3.1 or later

Documentation: There are no manuals except for a small leaflet explaining setup and running instructions.

Support: Guided Tours online help you learn to navigate through the text, illustrations, and animations.

Suggested Retail Price: $59.95

The Program

Mayo Clinic: The Total Heart goes into great detail about heart disease, EKGs, reducing risk for heart problems, and what to do in cardiac emergencies. It also lists drugs for various circulatory ailments. Easy to use and understand, the program includes graphics and sound, along with 48 videos or animations, 145 color illustrations, and 60 minutes of audio material.

Mickey's 123s: The Big Surprise Party
Mickey's ABCs: A Day at the Fair
Mickey's Colors and Shapes: The Dazzling Magic Show (all for ages 2 to 5)

Publisher: Walt Disney Computer Software, Inc.; 500 S. Buena Vista St.; Burbank, CA 91521-6740; (800) 688-1520

System Requirements: IBM PC, PS/2, or compatible, with 512K RAM (or Tandy 1000 with 640K RAM); floppy disk drive for 3.5-inch disks, or two floppy disk drives for 5.25-inch disks

Suggested: The Sound Source (Disney's own add-on sound card) is recommended. Without a sound capability, the words are not spoken. A printer and color monitor are also recommended. The program can be installed on a hard drive.

Curriculum Areas: The programs develop reading and number readiness, as well as recognition of shapes and colors. The child should begin to see the relationship between letters and words.

Documentation: The manuals offer suggestions for different ways to use the programs and extend learning activities.

Suggested Retail Price: $49.95

The Programs

In a trio of programs for preschoolers, Mickey Mouse helps you count, learn beginning letter sounds, and recognize colors and shapes. Mickey's 123s begins when Mickey wakes up and remembers that he must get ready for his big surprise party. In helping Mickey make all of the arrangements, you make choices that involve entering numbers. For example, you choose how many balloons to buy, how much food to serve each guest, how many invitations to send out, and so on.

In Mickey's ABCs: A Day at the Fair, you press a key on the keyboard, and Mickey Mouse runs around the house or travels through the fair, highlighting objects that start with the letter you pressed. There are over 80 different animated responses with speech and sound effects. The letters you press and the names of the objects are spoken and also displayed on the screen.

In Mickey's Colors and Shapes: The Dazzling Magic Show, Mickey is a magician who does tricks. The package contains a flexible overlay for the keyboard that helps you select the shapes and colors Mickey will use in his show. There are three acts in the performance. In act one, Mickey juggles the items chosen; in act two, Mickey creates a picture; in act three, Mickey locates an animal. The program contains over 150 animated actions and more than 130 objects. This is the best of the three Mickey programs.

Young children will probably need your help to begin any of these programs, as the off-disk copy-protection scheme is difficult to use. It involves a sheet of Mickey characters from which you must match a picture to a number displayed on the screen. The pictures on the sheet are hard to see. Look for the expanded versions of these programs, such as Mickey's ABCs Enhanced for 256-color VGA graphics.

Mickey's Crossword Puzzle Maker (ages 5 to 11)

Publisher: Walt Disney Computer Software, Inc.; 500 S. Buena Vista St.; Burbank, CA 91521-6740; (800) 688-1520

System Requirements: IBM PC or compatible, with 512K RAM; 5.25-inch floppy disk-drive; blank disks for saving puzzles

Suggested: Printer and color monitor

Other Platforms (not reviewed): Also available for Apple II with 128K RAM and Macintosh with 1MB, color monitor and mouse recommended for both ($39.95 each)

Curriculum Areas: The program encourages independent vocabulary and spelling growth, and teaches reading and writing skills.

Documentation: The manual is extensive, with suggestions for continued use.

Support: The menus are in pictures, and there is step-by-step on-screen instruction for using each of the four main menu choices in the form of a New User Keyboard Help screen. Help is also available by pressing the question-mark key.

Suggested Retail Price: $44.95

The Program

You or your child can use this program to create personalized crossword puzzles; there are also ready-made puzzles at three levels of difficulty. You can play on your own or against a Disney character. Clues and hints pop up on the screen in case you need help. When a game is finished, the winner's name appears in fireworks over the Disney graphic of Cinderella's castle.

Mickey's Crossword Puzzle Maker is simple to use; to use the program independently, however, a child should be reading at the third-grade level, and even then may require help while learning the keys and the menus. The range of possibilities is wide enough that the program can be easy or challenging, and provide fun and learning on a long-term basis. Older children may want to turn off the Disney graphics and just use words. As in the other Mickey programs described in this section, the off-disk copy-protection is in the form of a hard-to-see sheet of Mickey Mouse images.

Micro Cookbook 4.0

Publisher: Pinpoint Publishing; P.O. Box 1359; Glen Ellen, CA 95442-1359; (707) 523-0400

System Requirements: IBM PC or 100 percent compatible; 384K memory

Suggested: Hard disk drive; RAM disk; 640K memory; printer

Documentation: Documentation for this program consists of a well-organized booklet that explains some things you need to know about DOS, too.

Support: If you are a registered user and have questions, you can call the Technical Support team from 9:00 a.m. to 5:00 p.m. Pacific Standard Time.

Suggested Retail Price: $59.95

The Program

This particular program is a hefty one, suitable for professional use in schools, bed-and-breakfast operations, resorts, and companies, as well as the home. It will let you adjust a recipe from six portions to eight, or for a crowd. From among 1,000 recipes, the program will spew one out that fits the ingredients you feed in—a handy option when you don't want to make one more trip to the store for something you forgot. It prints recipes on pin-feed recipe cards so you don't need to keep your computer near the simmering spaghetti sauce in case you need to check what to add next. Micro Cookbook manages recipes, creates shopping lists, and provides lots of useful information (such as ingredient substitutions, nutrition charts, and food storage tips). It also provides pre-fabricated menus for entire meals.

The program is menu-driven. The program is fairly easy to use, but setting up your printer is rather complicated, and you may need your printer manual for help. In addition, you must remember to use the Switch option when moving from one recipe file to another; otherwise the indexes of the two might get mixed up. The program does offer a few utilities, such as Clean Up, which reclaims space in a recipe file from which a recipe has been changed or deleted. This package includes 350 tested recipes, with an option to add your own. The company also produces additional recipe disks, with a total of over 3,000 recipes.

MicroBridge Companion

Publisher: Great Game Products; 8804 Chalon Drive; Bethseda, MD 20817; (800) GAMES-4-U; (301) 365-3297

System Requirements: Any Macintosh; System 7 compatible

Suggested Retail Price: $59.95

The Program

If you like to play bridge, or want to learn more about the game, this program is for you. It has options for both rubber play and duplicate play. The major mode is Bridge Baron V where all the card playing occurs. Here the program is a good bidder and card player. Bridge Baron V has a nice graphical interface with point-and-click options for the mouse. The menus show shortcuts and play options, and matches can be saved. It can show you exactly how and why it makes each bid, and describes options for playing your hand. It can be used by just one person or serve as a fourth for three human players. There are four skill levels.

Other modes are Bridge Match (the program sets up a tournament for duplicate players), Bridge World Challenges (the program presents 24 challenging hands), and Personal Play Library (you can save interesting hands for replay). Bridge World Challenges is particularly educational; you must play the hands correctly or the program will not accept your plays.

Microsoft Bookshelf

Publisher: Microsoft Corporation; (800) 426-9400; (206) 882-8080

System Requirements: PC; Windows; CD-ROM drive or Macintosh; CD-ROM drive

Suggested Retail Price: $79.95

The Program

This disk contains Roget's Thesaurus, the American Heritage Dictionary, an encyclopedia, an atlas, a book of quotations, a chronology, and an almanac. The parts are linked so you can shift from reference work to reference work to find complete information about your topic. If you are looking up a topic in the encyclopedia, for example, you can double-click on a particular word to find its meaning in the dictionary.

Microsoft Flight Simulator 4.0

Publisher: Microsoft Corporation; One Microsoft Way; Redmond, WA 98052; (800) 426-9400

System Requirements: IBM PC or compatible; 640K RAM; floppy disk drive

Other Platforms (not reviewed): Macintosh

Documentation: Documentation for this game includes information on an additional 130 airports and their altitudes, runway lengths and directions, and latitudes and longitudes.

Suggested Retail Price: $64.95

The Program

This program is realistic enough to be played by someone who is interested in actually learning to fly. While playing, you learn to taxi, take off, cruise, and land your choice of several planes. You must take into consideration such variables as speed, sound, weather, time of day, and season. The graphics are good, with realistic first-person perception of the flight. The program includes 23 of the nation's leading airports' runway maps. Several airports have replicas of actual cities near them. Microsoft also sells an additional program that enhances the graphics (which are already excellent), and adds a Boeing 747 to the choice of planes.

Although Microsoft Flight Simulator has been the quintessential flight program, it is a flight *simulator*, not a game. There are some fighter-plane game programs you might want to try. For example, a very realistic program for IBM PCs and compatibles called F-117A Nighthawk Stealth Fighter 2.0 lets you fly in a variety of combat situations, and challenges you to make a safe landing. It costs $79.95 from MicroProse, 180 Lakefront Drive, Hunt Valley, MD 21030, (301) 771-1151.

Another realistic program that allows two players to compete via modem is Falcon 3.0 at $79.95 from Spectrum Holobyte, 2061 Challenger Drive, Alameda, CA 94501, (800) 695-GAME. Its system requirements are high: a 12MHz 286 microprocessor, 1MB RAM, DOS 5.0, and a VGA monitor (a 33MHz 386 with math coprocessor is recommended). Falcon 3.0 is at its best when played at a single computer. Also try Chuck Yeager's Air Combat at $59.95 from Electronic Arts, 1450 Fashion Island Boulevard, San Mateo, CA 94404, (800) 245-4525 or (415) 571-7171 for an easy-to-use, dogfighting air-combat game.

Microsoft Word for the Macintosh 6.0

Publisher: Microsoft Corporation; One Microsoft Way; Redmond, WA 98052-6399; (206) 882-8080; (800) 426-9400

System Requirements: Macintoshes with CPUs greater than 68000; 4MB RAM; 8MB on PowerMac; 5MB-20MB hard disk space; one 800K disk drive; System 7.0 or later

Suggested: Printer

Other Platforms (not reviewed): Windows version for IBM PC or compatible

Documentation The Getting Started Manual leads you step by step, with clear illustrations, through most of the program's features. The user's manual, though large (over 1,000 pages), is well organized and thorough.

Support: Word includes excellent online help. Although not free, Microsoft's phone help is courteous and knowledgeable.

Suggested Retail Price: $495

The Program

For beginners and experts, Microsoft Word offers all the tools necessary to make creating even the most complex documents easy. The menus and dialog boxes are arranged to reduce the time required to learn all the features, yet you can activate many of the functions by using key commands instead. If you need to move words, use drag-and-drop to select text and drag the mouse to move the text to its new location. You can access the spelling checker, thesaurus, grammar checker, and a wide variety of formatting features to finish your document. In fact, Word offers many of the features of desktop publishing programs.

This version of Word provides toolbars for almost every function. The dialog boxes are big and busy, with tabs that act as gateways to additional options. You can customize the dialog boxes, however, and create customized menus that supplement (and even replace) the existing ones. Many functions—including kerning, figure-numbering, caption generating, and cross-reference—are automatic. The AutoCorrect function catches some common typing errors as you work. Word also allows multiple undos and redos, and provides good revision tracking (which you can toggle on or off) by underlining new text and drawing lines through deleted text. It allows multiple columns of uneven width on a single page, and offers good graphics capabilities.

Word has excellent outlining and indexing capabilities. If you need to arrange information in table form, the program offers outstanding table-generating capabilities; you can also edit complex equations right within the program. When you must work with personalized form letters, Word walks you through the entire process, step by step. For those of you interested in multimedia productions, Word supports QuickTime movies and allows the importation of voice and sound. This program is very RAM-intensive, but over all, it offers a bevy of features you can use or ignore, balanced with an incredible ease of use. It is highly recommended by critics.

Microsoft Works 4.0

Publisher: Microsoft Corporation; One Microsoft Way; Redmond, WA 98052; (206) 882-8080; (800) 426-9400

System Requirements: Macintosh Plus or greater, System 6.0.2 or later, accelerated for Power Mac

Suggested: HyperCard 1.2.2 or later (to utilize the tutorial); modem for communications

Other Platforms (not reviewed): IBM PC or compatible with Windows

Documentation: Documentation for this program is clear, complete, and well organized.

Support: The tutorial that comes with this program is very good. Online help comes in the form of WorkWizards, which are step-by-step instructions for items such as greeting cards, certificates, and newsletters.

Suggested Retail Price: $99.95

The Program

Microsoft Works is a solid, basic set of applications in an integrated package. It offers word processing, mail-merge, spreadsheet, database, drawing, and communications capabilities. It is, however, integrated only in the ability to cut and paste information between modules using the drawing-tools palette. This capability is usually found between nearly any two Macintosh applications. If you have a low-end hardware system or a notebook computer, do not need sophisticated capabilities in any of these applications, or have limited funds, this program is worth investigating.

The word processor includes a thesaurus, a fast and efficient spelling checker, and a word-count function. A new toolbar contains formatting commands on pop-up menus. Multiline headers and footers are available in any of the modules, as is a drawing-tools palette in all but communications. The drawing module allows for multipage layout; buttons allow you to move elements easily from one frame to another. Special paint options include blur, emboss, and trace edges. The spreadsheet module includes line, bar, stacked-bar, or combination charting functions. You can use the AutoStart Stationary templates for starting new documents, or create your own templates. The program also contains a table-making tool, a calendar, and an address book component. You can use macros to automate procedures such as telecommunications activities.

Microtype: The Wonderful World of Paws (Grades 3 to 9)

Publisher: South-Western Publishing Company; 5101 Madison Road; Cincinnati, OH 45227; (800) 543-7972

System Requirements: Macintosh

Suggested: Printer

Other Platforms (not reviewed): Apple II series, which contains both spoken and written instruction; IBM PC or compatible

Curriculum Areas: The program teaches typing skills.

Suggested Retail Price: $69.50

The Program

Learning to type can be tedious. South-Western has produced a little relief for that problem in the character Paws, an amiable cat who helps you improve keyboarding accuracy and speed and even shows how to place your paws—er, fingers—properly on the keyboard. The program has 13 different lessons, offering practice sessions and a challenging speed drill. You have the option of reviewing the previous lessons before proceeding with new ones. An Open Screen option (like a word processor) lets you test how many words per minute you can type and also lets you type, edit, and print original text. Reinforcement for correct work is a smiling Paws; when you make a mistake, Paws frowns and the correct key is highlighted in the on-screen keyboard. At the end of each session, you can get a report about how well you performed.

In a classroom setting, each student can use a password option that prevents others from opening his or her files. The teacher can turn off the option of using the Delete key, which should encourage accuracy rather than speed only, and can also turn off the speech option that pronounces the names of the keys. In addition, you'll find options for reporting student progress, including the Technique Guide Sheet, which shows areas in which students need to improve.

Might and Magic III: Isles of Terra

Publisher: New World Computing, Inc.; 20301 Venture Blvd., Suite 200; Woodland Hills, CA 91364; (818) 999-0606; (800) 325-8898

System Requirements: IBM PC or 100-percent compatible; 640K; VGA, MCGA, EGA, or Tandy graphics; hard disk drive; floppy disk drive

Suggested: Supports Roland, Ad Lib, Sound Blaster, and Tandy 3-Voice DAC sound cards

Other Platforms (not reviewed): Amiga version available

Documentation: Documentation for this game includes an imaginary map in poster form; a reference card (listing installation procedures, gaming instructions, important places to visit, character creation, and character statistics), and a booklet that tells the story of the game.

Support: The company provides a clue book at $19.95 that gives tips and guides you through the game. For technical support, you can place a toll call to the company's customer support department on weekdays from 9:00 a.m. to 5:00 p.m. Pacific Time.

Suggested Retail Price: $59.95

The Program

In this fantasy and role-playing game, you lead a party of hand-picked adventurers to a rendezvous with the legendary wizard Corak. According to his journal, you must stop the evil Sheltem from destroying the Isles of Terra. As you travel, you meet bizarre and interesting characters. You find blacksmiths that help you buy, sell, and fix items; you stop at taverns where you buy food and listen for rumors and tips. Maybe you will run into guilds where you learn spells, or stop at the bank where you can safely store excess gold and gems and earn interest. The game involves combat, too.

The object of this game is not obvious from the manuals or from the game's beginning plays. There are several on-screen indicators, however, that help you in your adventure. They tell you what skills are engaged, what spells are in effect, when a party is in danger of being attacked, and so on. The game screen is really quite well designed. Once you get started, this is an entertaining and challenging game.

Mike Ditka Ultimate Football

Publisher: Accolade; 5300 Stevens Creek Blvd.; San Jose, CA 95129; (408) 985-1700

System Requirements: IBM AT or 100 percent compatible with recommended speed of 10MHz or higher; MCGA, VGA, EGA; 640K RAM (570K free RAM); hard disk drive; high-density floppy disk drive

Suggested: Joystick or mouse

Documentation: Documentation for this game includes a manual and a "control card." The manual contains game instructions and troubleshooting tips. The control card lists a summary of options for all input devices, the formations and plays, designated player, passing, hints and reminders, and other items needed for play.

Support: The game offers a practice session for field goals, kickoffs, passing, and running plays. The program also contains a demo where you relax and the computer does the work.

Suggested Retail Price: $54.95

The Program

This computer football program lets you customize each contest to match your skill level. This arcade-style game is realistic, with good graphics, animation, and sound effects. You can modify existing plays or create new ones. You assign responsibilities to the main players, and draw patterns for them on the screen in "chalkboard" play editing. The play generally proceeds according to standard, conservative football.

Although the game is very playable and easy for beginners to manage, the off-disk copy-protection scheme is complex. It includes a three-layered code wheel that you manipulate to find the info you need to type at the prompt in order to play. This is an 8-step procedure, but you get three chances to type the correct number before you are kicked back into DOS.

Millie's Math House (ages 2 to 6)

Publisher: Edmark Corporation; 6727 185th Ave. NE; P.O. Box 3218; Redmond, WA 98073-3218; (206) 556-8484; (800) 426-0856; fax (206) 556-8998

System Requirements: Macintosh Plus or greater; hard disk with 5.5MB available during installation); 1MB RAM for black and white, and 2MB RAM for color in System 6.0.7 or later; 2MB RAM for black and white, and 4MB RAM for color in System 7 or later.

Suggested: Printer, sound-input device, TouchWindow (a removable touch screen available through the company for $335.00)

Other Platforms (not reviewed): IBM PC or compatible, with DOS 3.1, 286 CPU, 540K RAM, 8MB hard disk space, sound card; version also available for Windows 3.1

Curriculum Areas: The program helps develop math and reading readiness with numbers, shapes, and counting. It stresses geometry skills and patterning abilities needed for equations and algebra.

Documentation: The manual is short, well oganized, and well illustrated; it suggests activities that parents can do with children to reinforce the skills learned.

Support: A Parent's Notebook on screen explains the skills being taught and gives suggestions for activities that reinforce learning. The sections of this notebook are Game Play, Learning Goals, Ideas for School Play, Ideas for Home Play, and About Kids. Call the company if you have technical questions.

Suggested Retail Price: $49.95

The Program

Start this program and you find yourself in Millie's Main Room. From here, you enter a number of rooms, each of which stands for a particular activity. In Mouse House, you work with shapes such as circles, triangles, and squares to build houses or machines. In Build-a-Bug, you see numerals and hear them spoken as you pick a quantity of eyes, ears, legs, and other attachments to put on your caterpillar. You learn size words and concepts by picking little, medium-sized, and big shoes to fit a family of three creatures in Little, Middle, & Big. Bing & Boing lets you make repeating sound patterns. In the Number Machine, you count from 0 to 10 critters that come out of a drawer. In the Cookie Factory, you make things happen by clicking on parts of a cookie-making machine.

Each game has two modes: Explore and Discover and Question and Answer. There is an option for keeping records of your child's play. You can customize the program in several ways, such as allowing or disallowing printing, or turning the music on or off. The program provides delightful activities for open-ended and playful learning. It is definitely more fun with color. It is slow while switching activities, however, unless you are working on a speedy machine.

The Milliken StoryTeller (ages 3 to 8)

Publisher: Milliken Publishing Company; 1100 Research Boulevard; St. Louis, MO 63132; (800) 643-0008

System Requirements: IBM PC or 100-percent compatible; 512K RAM; CGA, EGA, VGA/MCGA, Tandy 16-color, or Hercules graphics; MS-DOS 2.0 or higher; floppy disk drive

Suggested: Mouse; supports Covox Speech, Tandy 1000, Ad Lib, Sound Blaster, The Sound Source, and IBM Speech Adapter sound cards; printer

Other Platforms (not reviewed): Apple IIGS, Macintosh

Curriculum Areas: This program helps children acquire reading-readiness skills.

Documentation: The package includes two User's Guides: one for the stories and one for the activities. Both are adequate for using the programs, which actually require little instruction. Both include a number of activities that stretch the life of the program.

Suggested Retail Price: $49.95

The Program

The Milliken StoryTeller reads aloud and shows pictures for six children's classics, three to a package. The package reviewed contained Henny Penny, The Ugly Duckling, and a nonviolent version of Little Red Riding Hood in which the wolf wants to eat not Little Red Riding Hood, but the goodies in her basket. A separate package consists of Jack and the Beanstalk, Aladdin and the Magic Lamp, and Peter Rabbit. Each story has from 21 to 23 screens with a picture on the top and the story or a question about the story in an area at the bottom of the screen.

It is easy to load and play the program. Young children will quickly learn which selections to make to keep the program moving. The voice that reads the stories is human, not computer-generated, and the program contains an option to go through the story without the question screens. Once the story is finished, you can use the activities program, which includes coloring and writing options. The package also includes a set of four crayons that can be used with a printout of a blackline drawing of four story screens.

Young children should enjoy the story and the activities, as they learn to follow the words with the voice and use the computer at the same time. Older children may quickly outgrow the somewhat primitive animation and the graphics (which, although colorful, are not detailed enough for much discussion about the pictures). Although the program has a number of features that prepare a child for reading and writing, it is no substitute for buying well-illustrated, well-told book versions of the same stories, and sitting and reading with your child in a comfortable chair.

Mixed-Up Mother Goose (ages 4 and up)

Publisher: Sierra; Sierra On-Line; P.O. Box 485; Coarsegold, CA 93614; (800) 326-6654

System Requirements: IBM PC/compatible 286 or better; 640K RAM; VGA or EGA graphics; hard disk drive; floppy disk drive for installing the program

Suggested: Mouse recommended; sound card strongly recommended (The program supports Thunderboard Pro Audio Spectrum, Ad Lib, Roland MT-32, Sound Blaster, and Sound Source.)

Other Platforms (not reviewed): The program is available for Macintosh, Apple II series, Apple IIGS, and Amiga. The Apple II edition is slow and awkward to operate. There is a high-quality CD-ROM version for IBM PCs or compatibles.

Curriculum Areas: The object of this game is to teach early reading skills and computer skills.

Documentation: The two manuals are a parent guide (which explains items specific to this Sierra game), and the generic game manual Sierra includes in most of its games. The generic manual explains installation on the hard disk drive and basic instructions on playing Sierra games. The package includes a color map of Mother Goose Land; little paper doors open to reveal pictures.

Support: This program offers a walk-through (in the parent guide) for first-time players so they will have an idea of what is required of them to complete the game. You can also select the help icon on the screen for additional instruction. There is phone-in support for the cost of the toll call if you have technical questions.

Suggested Retail Price: $39.95 for IBM PC ($29.95 for the other platforms)

The Program

Little Bo-Peep has lost her sheep, Old King Cole can't find his pipe, Mary Quite Contrary has misplaced her watering can, and Peter Pumpkin Eater has lost track of his wife. And that's not all—characters from up to 18 popular Mother Goose nursery rhymes have similar losses. In this children's adventure game, your job is (first) to select the character you want to be, and (second) to find characters or items that have been misplaced. There are more than 40 colorful screens to search. To win the game, you must remember where these characters live, because you must pick up the lost item and return it to the correct owner. A map is included as help. Any objects you pick up can be used to trade for a needed object.

game fun to play over and over.

The program's user-friendly interface features icons for actions such as look, walk, action (for picking up an object), talk, and so on. Icons specific to this game include those for the map, the score, inventory (lists the objects you have picked up), stop, speed, and volume. The menus are easy to use, and you can save games to resume later. This program encourages exploration; the random location of objects and characters throughout the scenes make the game fun to play over and over.

MONOLOGUE

Publisher: First Byte Inc.; 19840 Pioneer Avenue; Torrance, CA 90503; (800) 523-2983

System Requirements: IBM PC or compatible; 384K RAM; DOS 3.0 or higher

Suggested: 640K RAM; sound adapter such as Sound Blaster or Covox Speech Thing recommended

Suggested Retail Price: $149

THE PROGRAM

This program is a text-to-speech synthesizer that can read highlighted passages or entire documents out loud. It can help you customize a computer system for a visually impaired user. It can also be used for proofreading (detecting missed words and so on), reading numbers to double-check a spreadsheet, helping students practice reading, and other creative uses. The program is rule-based, so it guesses at words it doesn't know. Some guesses can be almost unrecognizable, but the program is customizable; you can teach it the correct pronunciation of commonly used words. It is a memory-resident program.

MULTILEDGER 4.0

Publisher: Checkmark Software; (800) 444-9922; (303) 225-0522

System Requirements: Macintosh Plus; 1MB RAM

Suggested Retail Price: $199

The Program

This complete, integrated accounting package offers comprehensive General Ledger, AR/AP, Inventory and job costing, Income Statements, and Balance Sheets. It can also display multiple reprort windows, and allows the user to define pop-up lists of shipping methods and custom aging periods. Multiledger also has built-in multi-user capabilities. A companion package, Payroll 5.3, integrates seamlessly.

Multimedia Workshop

Publisher: Davidson & Associates; (800) 545-7677; (310) 793-0600

System Requirements: Macintosh; CD-ROM drive

Suggested Retail Price: $79.95

The Program

For ages 10 to adult, this multimedia program offers you the tools to create a paper, project, or presentation. Three easy-to-use modules—writing workshop, paint workshop, and video workshop—can be used together or separately. Predesigned templates accompany the word processor, as well as a spelling checker and thesaurus. Video Workshop allows graphics, movies, and text to be combined into an animated story. Paint Workshop includes both the basic art tools and special tools such as a water-drop tool that smears and smudges the color on the page. A CD-ROM is also included that contains over 300 photogtraphs, 75 QuickTime movies, 200 sound effects, 40 music clips, and 500 clip-art images.

Mum's the Word Plus

Publisher: Terrace Software; P.O. Box 271; Medford, MA 02155; (617) 396-0382

System Requirements: Mac Plus or greater; System 7 and earlier compatibility; accelerated for PowerMac

Suggested: Hard disk drive

Documentation: The manual is comprehensive, straightforward, and easy to use.

Support: The disk has a sample garden included; the manual walks you through a tutorial in which you learn all you need to know to design your garden with Mum's the Word Plus.

Suggested Retail Price: $119

The Program

Mum's the Word Plus is an integrated landscape-design program. It combines a database with information on over 650 plants, object-oriented graphics, and clip art to help you create and maintain a beautiful, customized landscape. Flowers and plants can be selected on the basis of color, bloom season, height, uses, type, hardiness zone, exposure, soil, and drought tolerance; a compatible and healthy garden is easy to design. The program allows you to add your own plants, edit furnished information, and change the symbols. Those who enjoy landscaping but have limited knowledge about plants (and limited time to investigate) will find Mum's Plus a very useful, affordable, and easy-to-use program.

The Mutanoid Math Challenge (Ages 7 to 14)

Publisher: Legacy Software; 9338 Reseda Boulevard, Second Floor; Northridge, CA 91324; (800) 532-7692; (818) 885-5773

System Requirements: IBM PC or compatible; 512K RAM; CGA, EGA, and VGA graphics display; floppy disk drive; DOS 3.0 or higher

Suggested: Hard-drive installable; mouse; supports Sound Blaster and Roland compatible sound devices

Other Platforms (not reviewed): Macintosh

Curriculum Areas: This program provides practice in developing math skills.

Documentation: It is provided, but the program is easy to use without it.

Suggested Retail Price: $49.95 (school edition costs more), $59.95 (Macintosh)

The Program

If you want to drill in math facts or like arcade-style practice, this program is not for you; it makes you think about number relationships, and builds deductive reasoning and estimation skills. To play, you work with equations so they intersect on a game board somewhat like words in a game of Scrabble. The fun comes from the graphics, sound, puns, and wisecracks. You choose an opponent from a menu of 15 bizarre aliens called mutanoids. The mutanoids hoot and wisecrack when you do well, wishing you worse luck next time. You control difficulty of the game by choosing how many different operation signs you want to include in your equations (+, -, x, and /). As you win games, you move up in rank, so that the puzzles are different. There are hints if you get stuck. The program is well worth the effort and price if you want a challenge. The company also offers Mutanoid Word Challenge.

M.Y.O.B. 4.0

Publisher: Best!Ware; 300 Roundhill Dr.; Rockaway, NJ 07866; (800) 322-6962; (201) 586-2200; fax (201) 586-8885

System Requirements: Macintosh Plus or greater; 2MB RAM; 3MB hard disk space; System 6.0 or later (System 7 compatible)

Suggested: Printer; 2 MB RAM

Other Platforms (not reviewed): IBM PC or compatible with Windows

Documentation: The manual is fairly easy to read.

Support: Online help is extensive. Telephone support is free and unlimited for the first 30 days. After that, you can subscribe for $79 per year.

Suggested Retail Price: $199.95 ($99.95 without Payroll)

The Program

This money-manager program is an alternative to Quicken. It is suitable for small businesses, and requires no bookkeeping knowledge. It is a business accounting package that combines checkbook management with general ledger, sales and receivables, purchases and payables, inventory management, invoicing, and calendar. It includes a card file that keeps track of customer, vendor, and employee information automatically, and can produce mailing labels and mail-merge letters.

The program has an automatic prompt feature to remind you to make recurring payments (such as credit card payments) or tax deposits on time. It features a To Do list that alerts you automatically to overdue receivables and payables, inventory that needs to be reordered, recurring payments that need to be made, and merchandise needing to be shipped. Those without accounting backgrounds can follow its structure easily. The user enters data by using the program's attractive forms and scrollable lists of options. M.Y.O.B. includes a Payroll module, but can be purchased without the module. There are more than 80 management reports.

Myst 1.04

Publisher: Broderbund Software; (800) 521-6263; (415) 382-4600

System Requirements: 386 CPU; 4MB RAM; 3 to 4MB hard disk space; DOS 5.0; Windows 3.1; CD ROM drive; mouse

Macintosh; 2.5MB RAM; 3MB hard disk space; System 7.0.1; CD-ROM drive; QuickTime 1.6

Suggested Retail Price: $59.95

The Program

Myst is an adventure/simulation game where the player is encouraged to explore unknown, fantasy lands—and solve sometimes-difficult puzzles to unlock doors to other lands—all in hopes of solving the mystery. The graphics as well as the plot are captivating. The musical soundtrack and integrated action sounds—combined with the moving-picture scenery and 3-D animation—give this game a fantastical, dreamlike quality. Part of the mystery is deciding your purpose in this fantasy land, and what you should do next. You'll descend staircases to deeper parts of the island, explore a library with strange books, examine the controls in an observatory, and try to get on a sunken ship or a spaceship, both near the island.

NetWare Lite

Publisher: Novell, Inc.; 122 E. 1700 South; Provo, UT 84606; (800) 429-7000

System Requirements: IBM PC or compatible; DOS 3.0 or higher; 27.5K RAM at each workstation; about 49K RAM at the server

Other Platforms (not reviewed): Macintosh, UNIX, and OS/2 environments

Suggested Retail Price: At $99 per node, this program sounds inexpensive, but it can get quite expensive once the LAN extends to over 10 users.

The Program

This DOS-based local area network (LAN) supports a great number of network interface cards; it is very easy to install and work with. It has both menu-driven and command-line interfaces for setting up the sharing and the use of network services. Its caching system is not really good, however, and the copy-protection scheme forces you to install the program from a different disk for each computer. Thus, you must keep track of which disk goes with which computer. Novell is a well-known LAN company, especially for its NetWare software.

New Math Blaster Plus! (ages 6 to 12)

Publisher: Davidson & Associates, Inc.; P.O. Box 2961; 19840 Pioneer Ave.; Torrance, CA 90503; (310) 793-0600; (800) 545-7677; fax (310) 793-0601

System Requirements: IBM PC/Tandy or compatible; VGA, MCGA, EGA, CGA, Tandy graphics, or Hercules graphics; 512K RAM (Tandy graphics require 640K); DOS 2.1 or higher; 3.5- or 5.25-inch floppy disk drive

Suggested: Can be installed on a hard disk; supports Ad Lib and Sound Blaster Music cards; printer and mouse optional

Other Platforms (not reviewed): Windows and Macintosh versions available; the Windows 3.1 or higher version is called Math Blaster: In Search of Spot

Curriculum Areas: This program provides practice in the fundamental arithmetic operations in a variety of number situations.

Documentation: The documentation contains both a quick start-up summary and detailed instructions. Clear, easy-to-read, and well-organized, it includes the major screen menus, parent/teacher tips for further math activities, troubleshooting tips, and an index. There are also review lessons, a test maker, supplementary activity books, and a chart with appropriate grade and skill levels.

Support: The program provides online help, and includes a record- or score-keeping facility. For the answers to technical questions, a customer service is available through an 800 number on weekdays.

Suggested Retail Price: $49.95 for the IBM PC version; $59.95 for the Macintosh and Windows versions

The Program

New Math Blaster Plus! is a classic drill program. Its drills cover addition, subtraction, multiplication, and division facts, as well as techniques like reducing common fractions, adding and subtracting fractions, finding percentages, renaming improper fractions, multiplying decimals, and figuring fraction/percentage equivalents. The drills are incorporated into four game modes, each of which features the animated Blasternaut. There is no connection between the math content and the space activities; the activities are vehicles for entertainment instead of integral to the math content. Only one mode—the Number Recycler—focuses on problem-solving. The graphics are attractive and play is exciting, however, and the interface (which uses menus) is easy to learn.

For each level of perfect scores, a graphic or text "certificate of excellence" can be printed out. In the editor mode, you can enter your own set of math problems to extend the life of the product and customize it for particular needs. Every file of math problems may be viewed, which helps teachers or parents see that a student is working on the appropriate level. Before your child begins play, he or she should be able to recognize the digits from 0 to 9 and read at the first-grade level. The youngest children will need help.

Davidson also produces Math Blaster Mystery, a program that helps you learn to solve arithmetic word problems by breaking them down into steps that are easy to understand. Using the program can help you to reason and solve problems; the program offers excellent hint screens when you make a mistake.

The New Oregon Trail (Ages 10 and Up)

Publisher: MECC; Brookdale Corporate Center; 6160 Summit Drive North; Minneapolis, MN 55430-4003; (612) 569-1500; (800) 685-6322

System Requirements: IBM PC or compatible; 512K RAM; floppy disk drive; CGA or EGA graphics

Other Platforms (not reviewed): Macintosh with floppy disk drive or CD-ROM drive

Curriculum Areas: This program can be used in conjunction with American history. It teaches reasoning and strategy skills; your child will also build his or her vocabulary.

Suggested Retail Price: $49.95 (CD-ROM version $69.95)

The Program

You are embarking on a 2,000-mile cross-country journey in a covered wagon in 1848. Before starting out, you must purchase oxen and provisions for the trip. You decide quantity of supplies, the route to take, the time of travel, and other details. Remember that you can supplement your supplies by hunting or trading along the way. You are successful if you arrive at your destination before all the supplies run out, the oxen or travelers die, or the weather turns severe. You get more points for each traveler arriving in good health and each supply still available at the end of the journey. If you make a mistake, the wagon may turn over or you may lose your food. If you die from typhoid or starvation, you may see your name in an epitaph on the screen.

The role you choose at the beginning of the game—banker, carpenter, or farmer—determines the difficulty of the game, how much money you start off with, and how well you fare along the way. This is a true simulation, rather than an entertaining story. Each trip is different. In order to play well, you must pay attention to other travelers' stories and make wise decisions while trading. This game works well with a small group of students.

The New Print Shop (ages 6 and up)

Publisher: Broderbund Software, Inc.; 500 Redwood Boulevard; P.O. Box 6121; Novato, CA 94948-6121; (415) 382-4400; (800) 521-6263

System Requirements: IBM PC or compatible; 512K RAM with 640K for color; 3.5- or 5.25-inch floppy disk drive; color monitor; printer

Suggested: Color printer; mouse

Other Platforms (not reviewed): Apple II series; 128K RAM (An older version called The Print Shop is available for the Apple Macintosh and the Commodore 64.)

Curriculum Areas: The program teaches writing and design skills, as well as elements of using a word processing program. To use the program independently, a child should be at third-grade reading level.

Suggested Retail Price: $59.95, $49.95 for Apple II family version

The Program

The New Print Shop is basically a desktop publishing program that elementary-school-aged children can use to create banners, signs, greeting cards, calendars, letterhead, and certificates. It includes 8 type styles, with choices of solid, outline, or three-dimensional characters that can be used in three sizes. There are 12 fonts, 9 border designs, and 100 pieces of clip art. Different fonts can be used on the same page. Graphics and text can be put anywhere on a page, resized, moved, flipped, or centered. You can import other graphic images, including those from Broderbund's own sets. These include a school and business library, a collection suitable for parties, and a sampler of various subjects. There is also a print preview mode.

The program is easy to use through menus. You can see the menu options along with the screen you are creating, in a split-window format. You have the option of using the mouse or the keyboard. When you are ready to insert names into an invitation or a certificate, you can create a name file that merges the data with the documents. A calendar feature enables you to create calendars in daily, weekly, monthly, or yearly formats, in various sizes. Posters can be enlarged up to 9-feet-by-6.5-feet. There are some preset templates for posters, banners, and certificates.

The Norton Utilities for Macintosh 3.0

Publisher: Symantec Corporation; 10201 Torre Ave.; Cupertino, CA 95014; (408) 253-9600; (800) 441-7234; fax (310) 829-0247

System Requirements: Macintosh Plus and greater; 2MB RAM (3MB for System 7); hard disk drive; one floppy disk drive needed for installation; System 6.0.4 and later; accelerated for PowerMac

Other Platforms (not reviewed): IBM PC or compatible

Documentation: The user's manual is characterized by excellent design and good organization; the information you need is easy to find in the book. Documentation includes a reference guide, a guide for the network administrator, and a description of how software affects the disk operation.

Support: If you have questions, you can make a toll call to the company's technical support technicians on weekdays from 7:00 a.m. to 5:00 p.m. Pacific Standard Time.

Suggested Retail Price: $149

The Program

This package, called NUM 3.0 for short, is actually a set of programs that include the following: The Norton Disk Doctor is used to repair damaged hard disks, floppy disks, and data. The Norton Disk Editor enables you to explore and edit the structure and contents of files and disks. The Volume Recover restores accidentally erased or crashed hard disks. The UnErase modules let you recover trashed or lost files. The FileSaver gives you a record of critical disk information for fast and easy data recovery. Norton Backup allows scheduled backups to floppies, removable cartridges, and network drives, but not to tape drives. (It does not erase old versions of backups; you can simply update the backup with recent files.) For data security, use the Wipe Info module, which lets you erase all traces of confidential information from a disk. You can encrypt files with DES (Data Encryption Standard) or Norton's proprietary format. Directory Assistance lets you sort, access, list, find, and create new folders without returning to Finder. The Fast Find option enables you to find files rapidly, because it speeds disk access. This package also includes functions for data compression, data verification, error correction codes, and defragmenting files (disk optimization). It lets you create, manage, and protect disk partitions.

The Norton Utilities are also available at $179 for the IBM platform, which requires 512K and DOS 2.0 or later. Its disk optimizer capabilities are rated highly. Another utility library for IBM PCs is PC Tools (MacTools for the Mac) from Central Point Software, Inc., 15220 N.W. Greenbrier Parkway #200, Beaverton, OR 97006, (800) 445-4208 and (503) 690-8083 (fax); at $179. PC Tools requires 640K RAM and DOS 3.0 or higher.

Novell GroupWise (WordPerfect Office) 4.2

Publisher: WordPerfect Corporation; 1555 N. Technology Way; Orem, UT 84057; (800) 451-5151; (801) 225-5000

System Requirements: IBM PC, AT, XT, or higher and compatible; or PS/2 computer; hard disk drive; floppy disk drive; DOS 2.1 or higher

Suggested: Printer

Other Platforms (not reviewed): Macintosh

Documentation: The documentation for this program is complete and varied. It includes installation instructions right in the packets with the disks. There is a quick-reference leaflet for key commands; a small getting-started manual contains installation instructions and basics. The actual reference manual is over 800 pages long; its appendixes (from A through N) cover macros, error messages, troubleshooting, and other information. There is also a fairly detailed index. GroupWise is well organized by program (i.e., Calculator, Calendar, Editor, and so on), showing exceptions and specific instances of special cases.

Support: Program help is accessible through the F3 function key. A workbook has lessons that take you step-by-step through the functions of the program. There are also lessons on integration with the WordPerfect, DataPerfect, DrawPerfect, and PlanPerfect applications. Screen dumps are included. The Notebook file in the actual software contains additional support information. If you need technical help, you can call the company's 800 customer support number on weekdays between 7:00 a.m. and 6:00 p.m. Mountain Time, or access the company's forum on CompuServe by entering **Go WP files**.

Suggested Retail Price: $149

The Program

This program contains an office shell for keeping your computer organized. It makes applications readily available, and it can automate tasks in (as well as between) your applications. You use it through a menu system. You can create lists, phone directories, and other similar information with the Notebook program, a simple database. The Calendar program helps you keep track of appointments, meetings, and other events, with priorities at the top of to-do lists. You can also use the module to write memos to yourself and schedule routine appointments for weeks, months, or even years in advance.

The GroupWise File Manager is designed for organizing directories and files, using the delete, copy, rename, search, and view functions. You can also create directories with this module. Use the Editor program for defining and editing WPCorp application macros, or for writing program code, editing ASCII text, and modifying binary files. The Calculator program enables you to perform financial, programming, scientific, and statistical calculations. This program is also available in a LAN version that has a Mail program for electronic mail and a Scheduler for planning office functions.

Now Contact 3.0

Publisher: Now Software; (503) 274-2899

System Requirements: Macintosh Plus; 1MB RAM; System 7 (accelerated for Power Mac)

Suggested Retail Price: $99

The Program

Now Contact is a database designed especially for recording names, addresses, phone numbers, and other information about the people with whom you come in contact. The information can then be arranged in custom formats using specified fonts. Sorting by field is as easy as clicking on a column heading. The Detail window allows you to view and edit information on a single contact; in the text box you can view notes and calendar events associated with that contact. Contacts can be categorized and sorted by category. If you use the mini word processor and mail-merge feature, you can prepare correspondence to send to your contacts. Now Contact also has a linking feature that allows you to attach documents created in other Macintosh applications to contact records. You need only click on the linked document; if the application resides on your Mac, the file opens.

Oceans Below

Publisher: Mindscape; 60 Leveroni Court; Novato, CA 94949; (415) 883-3000; fax (415) 883-3303

System Requirements: Macintosh with 256-color, 13-inch monitor or greater; 4MB RAM with 2.5MB available; System 6.0.7 or later; CD-ROM drive with 150KB-per-second speed or faster

Other Platforms (not reviewed): IBM PC or compatible with a 386DX-33 or better microprocessor (486DX-33 CPU recommended); 4MB RAM; 5MB available hard disk space; SVGA graphics; mouse or other pointing device; MPC-rated CD-ROM drive and sound card; speakers or headphones; DOS 5.0 or later; Windows 3.1 or later; Microsoft CD-ROM Extensions 2.21 or later

Documentation: The program contains online guidance and tours.

Support: Contact the company by telephone or fax.

Suggested Retail Price: $49.95

THE PROGRAM

If you ever wanted to experience scuba diving without the risk, this program is for you. It contains over 200 video clips and 125 photographs of marine life, plant life, and undersea sites such as shipwrecks or plane wrecks. You can learn about relics of the past when you discover one of the 68 sunken treasures hidden throughout the program. Narration and original music complete the picture.

The program demonstrates recreational diving, and provides information on scuba equipment, water temperature, currents, and marine life. From maps, you select the locations you want to explore; the program takes you there, offers specific information about the site, and provides hints for diving there. The icon bar at the bottom of the screen offers total control of navigation through the program.

In addition to this high-rated simulation, Mindscape also produces a well-known and high-rated CD-ROM program called Capitol Hill. In this program, you act as a member of the House of Representatives. The program is easy to use, entertaining, and educational, as you learn just how Congress operates. The company's Multimedia Encyclopedia is easy to use and educational, complete with movies, animations, sound effects, voice narration, and photographs.

OMAR SHARIF ON BRIDGE

Publisher: Interplay Productions; 3710 S. Susan, Suite 100; Santa Ana, CA 92704; (800) 969-GAME (4263); (714) 549-2411

System Requirements: IBM PC or compatible; 640K RAM; DOS 2.1 or higher; CGA, EGA, VGA, Tandy graphics; floppy disk drive

Suggested: Mouse; hard drive installable; supports Ad Lib, Sound Blaster, Roland, and Pro-Audio Spectrum as well as Tandy's sound

Other Platforms (not reviewed): Macintosh II series

Documentation: The documentation explains the game of bridge, introducing the topics of bidding, scoring, and strategy, as well as describing the technical aspects of loading and playing the game.

Support: There is an on-disk tutorial for beginners that shows the correct play if you make a mistake, and also explains why the recommended play is best in a particular situation.

Suggested Retail Price: $49.95, $59.95 (Macintosh)

The Program

This program teaches you how to play contract bridge, a game that is difficult to simulate with a computer. This is a good program, usable by one to four people. It has a novice mode, but also challenges advanced players.

To make bids, you use a mouse to make selections from a bidding chart on the screen that displays all possible bids. The computer prevents you from making an illegal play, and will also suggest a play for you. You can take back a play if you make a mistake (or if you just want to see what would happen if a different card were played). You can also design your own hand, recreate exciting games, or set up situations you might find in a newspaper column or book. The program lets you save games in progress to resume later; you can print a hand, the bidding, or any other aspect of the game, either to a printer or to the disk. A unique feature of the program is that it uses Omar Sharif's digitized voice for the comments.

On Cue II

Publisher: ICOM Simulations, Inc.; 648 South Wheeling Road; Wheeling, IL 60090; (708) 520-4440; fax (708) 459-7456

System Requirements: Macintosh; 1MB RAM; System 6.0.2 or later

Documentation: The spiral-bound documentation is well organized, but page footers do not tell you what chapter you are in.

Support: Technical support is available for registered users.

Suggested Retail Price: $99.95

The Program

If you want more control over the desktop in your Macintosh computer system, On Cue provides you with personal file and application managers. With it, you can launch any application or file without going through layers of folders, and launch any file from the keyboard. You can also return to work on a recently used file. The program provides various ways to search for files—for example, by file name, file format (TIFF, PICT, etc.), creator application, dates created or changed, file size, or a combination of these criteria. On Cue does file management from within any application, and ensures fast access by tracking the files and folders used most recently. It offers good search capabilities.

Operation Neptune (Ages 9 to 14)

Publisher: The Learning Company; 6493 Kaiser Drive; Fremont, CA 94555; (800) 852-2255; (510) 792-2101; fax (510) 792-9628

System Requirements: IBM PC or compatible; 512K RAM (640K for Tandy); CGA, EGA, MCGA, or VGA, or Tandy 16-color; DOS 2.0 or higher

Suggested: VGA recommended; Ad Lib, Sound Blaster, or Roland LAPC-1 sound card recommended

Other Platforms (not reviewed): CD-ROM version for DOS or Windows

Curriculum Areas: You work with math fundamentals and problem-solving skills to play the game.

Documentation: The manual is well written and straightforward.

Suggested Retail Price: $59.95

The Program

The purpose of this arcade-style game is to recover undersea wreckage and solve the mystery of a failed secret space mission. You must find cannisters with information about the flight, and recover the capsule before it releases a toxic substance that could destroy all life. You are in a small submarine, and have only so much oxygen to use while maneuvering underwater. Periodically, you receive requests from the command ship that require you to solve a math word problem in order to proceed. If you answer incorrectly, your oxygen supply decreases. To complete the mission, you must travel through five zones, each with three sectors. Each sector has its own supply station, but you must break the security code to refuel. You must also break codes to see what is in each cannister. This is done by completing a number pattern on the screen.

There are two levels: voyager and expert. As you play, the math problems and mazes become increasingly difficult and complex. You learn to watch for certain kinds of patterns as you navigate through the maze of undersea trenches filled with dangerous sea creatures. The problems are interesting and relevant to the task. There are hints if you are having difficulty, and you can also choose to use an optional on-screen calculator. The word problems tend to lack variety, and the sound and music are not as great as the graphics, but the game is fun to play and makes you think about all the ways you can manipulate numbers.

OUTSPOKEN 1.7

Publisher: Berkeley Systems, Inc.; 2095 Rose Street; Berkeley, CA 94709; (510) 540-5535; fax (510) 540-5115

System Requirements: Macintosh Plus or greater; 1MB RAM; System 6.0.5 or later; compatible with System 7, but does not recognize balloon help; floppy disk drive

Suggested: Hard disk drive

Documentation: Documentation for this program explains a bit about the Macintosh, as well as describing the outSPOKEN program. It is available in book form, on cassette tape, and on Braille sheets. The Braille sheets include sample copies of the desktop display, menu bar, and dialog boxes. The manual offers a number of tips that help you use the program to the best advantage with other types of applications (such as spreadsheets, communications, and word processing programs).

Suggested Retail Price: $495

THE PROGRAM

This memory-resident program reads out loud the items that appear on the screen. You control it through the numeric keypad. You can control scanning and reading, and do it letter by letter, word by word, line by line, or in columns (as well as other options). You can have the computer announce where the pointer is on the screen, or spell the current word. The Find option can be used in a variety of ways.

Because outSPOKEN pronounces words according to a set of phonetic rules, some words may not be pronounced correctly. You can change the pronunciation of a word through the outSPOKEN dictionary (you may have to enter a different spelling of the word). You can set a number of custom options for speaking style, oral feedback as you type words, and punctuation. The program customizes a computer system for use by a blind person. It also provides a method for certain types of proofreading and reading practice.

PACKRAT 4.0 FOR WINDOWS 4.0

Publisher: Polaris Software; 17150 Via Del Campo, Ste. 307; San Diego, CA 92127; (619) 674-6500

System Requirements: IBM PC or compatible with a minimum 286 microprocessor; floppy disk drive; hard disk drive; Windows 3.1 or greater

Suggested: 386 or better microprocessor (for making the best use of Windows)

Suggested Retail Price: $395

The Program

PackRat is a special type of database called a contact manager or personal information manager. It enables you to store the types of information you might need for running a business or managing an office. These include addresses and phone numbers, meetings and appointments, lists of things to do, phone logs of past and pending calls, flexible reports, project scheduling and resource allocation, financial-account status and history, and the amount of time devoted to particular projects. The program divides the screen into a series of windows for each kind of information, and lets you use a set of icons to flip through to other displays. Entering and storing new information is easy, and access to any information is fast. You can run this program while working in other applications, since it operates under Windows. This is a specialized program for people with particular needs. Its price may require you to examine your needs carefully before deciding to buy it (rather than using a data manager, for example, to store similar information).

Paradox 5.0 for Windows

Publisher: Borland International, Inc.; 100 Borland Way; Scotts Valley, CA 95066-3249; (800) 682-9299; (408) 431-1000; fax (408) 431-4123

System Requirements: IBM PC or compatible with 6MB RAM; 15MB hard disk space; floppy disk drive; Windows 3.1 or later

Suggested: Mouse; VGA graphics; printer

Documentation: The program has tutors called Interactive Coaches and online Experts; these guide you, step by step, through the process of creating forms.

Suggested Retail Price: $495

The Program

The current version of this object-based database program is much faster than earlier versions. Paradox is compatible with dBASE tables and SQL data; it does everything database programs should do, but a number of features give it its own character.

The ProjectViewer is a quick-launch interface to tables, queries, reports, scripts, and other elements. It offers a number of new field types, including autoincrementing, logical, and time fields. Paradox is compliant with DDE and OLE 2.0; you can embed objects within forms and fields, and put Paradox tables in other documents. It supports publish-and-subscribe functions for workgroup and mail items, allows you to set weekly or monthly updates, and lets you lock individual records. There are more than 300 new Methods and Properties to help you develop ObjectPAL Windows applications.

Paradox offers a new way to handle inquiries when it is used on a network. When most database programs are used on a network, you cannot query a file if someone else is updating it. Usually, in such a circumstance, the program abandons the query and you must start over. If a lot of updating is going on, you might have to wait quite awhile for your information. With Paradox, you can turn off this restriction and view a file until you are finished. If updating is occurring at the same time, however, some of the information may become obsolete quickly.

Patent It Yourself

Publisher: Nolo Press; (800) 992-6656; (510) 549-1976

System Requirements: PC; 4MB RAM; Windows 3.1; VGA Monitor; mouse

Suggested Retail Price: $229.95

The Program

This patent-law program asks you appropriate questions about your invention, prepares the legal forms and searches for previous patents. It also helps you evaluate your product's commerical potential. Quite a savings over a $3,000-to-$5,000 attorney fee.

PC-File 6.5

Publisher: ButtonWare Inc.; P.O. Box 96058; Bellevue, WA 98009; (800) 528-8866; (206) 454-0479

System Requirements: IBM PC or compatible, with an 80286 microprocessor or better; 450K RAM; hard disk drive with 1MB free; high-density floppy disk drive needed for installation; graphics monitor required for graphs; DOS 2.0 or higher

Suggested: Mouse

Documentation: Includes a substantial User's Manual with tutorial and Getting Started guides. Unlimited-call technical support is offered for 30 days at no cost. After that, you can telephone a 900 number or pay $49.95 for one year of technical support.

Suggested Retail Price: $150 ($450 for LANPACK)

The Program

This flat-file data manager is powerful and capable, but not very fast. It has superb graphics and multi-file handling capabilities, as well as good report, label, and mail-merge features. PC-File is compatible with dBASE III Plus files. If you want an easy-to-use program with pop-up menus at a reasonable price (and don't need the sophisticated features of database programs), you might try PC-File.

PC-Kwik Power Pak 2.12

Publisher: Multisoft Corp.; 15100 S.W. Kill Parkway; Beaverton, OR 97006; (800) 274-5945; (503) 644-5644

System Requirements: IBM PC or compatible; 128K RAM; DOS 2.0 or higher

Documentation: The documentation for this program is thorough and outstanding.

Support: The program includes online help, but for assistance from experts, you can call the company's technical support number or reach its forum on CompuServe.

Suggested Retail Price: $129.95 (caching software available as Super PC-Kwik at $79.95)

The Program

You can control almost every aspect of this disk-caching program. The cache is adjustable for every application, but experimenting with the amounts may take some time. The program operates with conventional, expanded, or extended memory, and with Windows 3.0 and DESQview 386 as well. This is a popular program, but not the easiest utility to use.

Under DOS 5.0 or DR DOS 6.0, this program loads itself into upper memory automatically. Operation is invisible, but you can see on the screen how much help the program is giving you. If necessary, the program can lend other functions some of the memory it's using as a cache.

PC-Kwik Power Pak offers a number of features that improve the operation of your system. One important new option is PowerWrite, which buffers disk writes. (Some programs and systems can't use PowerWrite, and the company does give some guidelines about this limitation in the documentation.) A screen accelerator moves video BIOS from ROM into memory, but this is only effective on text displays. The program has a RAM-disk option for fast access to files, and until files are placed in it, it doesn't use up any space at all. The print spooler can handle two printers at a time. The program also offers data compression, a keyboard and screen speed-up utility, and a command-line editor. (The data compression cannot be used with PostScript files or soft fonts.)

PC Paintbrush IV Plus

Publisher: ZSoft Corporation; 450 Franklin Road, Suite 100; Marietta, GA 30067; (404) 428-0008

System Requirements: IBM 286 PC or compatible; 640K RAM; hard disk drive with 1MB free; graphics monitor; mouse; DOS 3.0 or higher

Suggested: 386 microprocessor recommended

Suggested Retail Price: $199

The Program

This program has long been the graphics standard for the IBM/DOS platform. It offers paint and draw tools, and can be used for image enhancement and photo retouching. As such, it allows scanning directly into the program.

Before you retouch images, you can scale them from 25 percent to 400 percent of the original size. While editing images, you can blend (or smudge), lighten, darken, and change tints. You can also create three-dimensional effects and a variety of textures. The toolbox on the side of the screen includes scissors (for cutting and moving), text (for entering text into an illustration), paintbrush, paint roller, spray can, the hand (for grabbing and moving the drawing), and the eraser—as well as drawing tools such as line, box, ellipse, and polygon. For creating or editing details, you can use the variable-zoom feature for up to 16 times the size of the image. For ease of use, PC Paintbrush includes pull-down menus for a variety of options. It supports up to 8MB extended memory and virtual memory, up to 880-by-600-pixel screen resolution, and up to 256 colors or shades of gray.

Personal Law Firm 1.1

Publisher: BLOC Publishing Corporation; 800 S.W. 37th Avenue; Miami, FL 33134; (305) 445-0903

System Requirements: 256K IBM PC or compatible; two 5.25-inch or 3.5-inch floppy disk drives; monochrome, CGA, EGA, VGA, or Hercules graphics; DOS 2.1 or higher

Suggested: Hard disk drive; printer

Documentation: The package has very good documentation, which includes a glossary of legal terms, explains the documents, gives samples, and tells you how to run the program.

Support: Support for registered users is free (except for the toll call) and unlimited, on weekdays from 9:00 a.m. to 6:00 p.m. Eastern Standard Time.

Suggested Retail Price: $100

The Program

This program is an easy-to-use, fill-in-the-blank method of preparing 30 legal documents for business and personal matters. It is the largest, most comprehensive legal program available; the package does warn, however, that the program should not replace legal counsel.

The forms are well explained on the screen and in the manual. The program also helps you decide when you might need a legal document or other action to protect your interests—for example, if you invent something or hire someone to help with your business. The documents include Commercial Real Estate Lease, Promissory Note, Trade Secret Protection, License of Intellectual Property, Bill of Sale, Notice of Contract Assignment, Warranty Agreement, Work for Hire agreement, and Work for Hire contract. This program also helps you prepare certain personal documents such as the Will, Living Will, Power of Attorney, Child Guardianship Consent Form, Living Together Agreement, Pre- and Post-Nuptial agreements, and Marital Settlement Agreements.

PFS: Publisher for Windows 1.0

Publisher: Spinnaker Software Corporation; 201 Broadway; Cambridge, MA 02139; (800) 323-8088; (617) 494-1200; fax (617) 494-1219

System Requirements: IBM PC or compatible, with a 286 or better microprocessor; 1MB RAM; hard disk drive; floppy disk drive; printer; Windows 3.0 or higher

Suggested: 386 or better microprocessor

Other Platforms (not reviewed): The DOS counterpart is PFS: First Publisher.

Documentation: The manuals for this program are very good.

Support: The package includes a thorough tutorial that walks you through the process of creating a newsletter.

Suggested Retail Price: $149

The Program

This program provides an easy way to create professional-looking documents. You build boxlike frames and pour text into them. There are 50 preset templates for common publications such as order forms, invoices, and multicolumn pages; you may not have to create your own design at all. In addition, there are paragraph style sheets. When you must create your own document design, you can set up master pages with rules, logos, and other elements that repeat on every page of your document. Each file can use documents of up to 99 pages. The package includes Atech's Publisher's Power Pack, with 12 scalable font outlines and support for Windows 3.1 TrueType fonts. (Power Pack is incompatible with PostScript printers.) The package also contains about 200 pieces of routine clip art, a built-in word processor, a thesaurus, and a spelling checker.

The program accepts text in a variety of popular formats, and generates an index and table of contents. You can crop graphics, draw (though the drawing tools are limited), and wrap text around pictures. There is support for OLE. Using multiple columns and adding pages requires a lot of manual work with this program. When you make changes or add graphics, the screen-redrawing operation is rather slow. There is little control over type, such as kerning or leading, and no support for color output.

PFS Résumé & Job Search Pro

Publisher: Spinnaker; 201 Broadway; Cambridge, MA 02139-1901; (800) 323-8088

System Requirements: IBM PC or compatible

Suggested: Printer

Documentation: The package includes an easy-to-understand manual that contains a variety of tips for writing effective résumés and keeping track of your correspondence while job-hunting.

Suggested Retail Price: $59.95

The Program

This program is designed to help you prepare an effective résumé, a cover letter, and other job-hunting correspondence. It is easy to use, and assumes you know nothing about the résumé-writing process. It suggests paper selection, résumé length, and other factors that may influence whether your résumé gets attention. The program's excellent samples are categorized into nine types such as Quick & Easy, Student, and Business. Once you have chosen the type you want, the program asks you for the information it will use to complete your résumé.

The program has a word processor with a spelling checker. You can also address envelopes, keep a record of contacts with potential employers, and keep track of your appointments. There's a mail-merge feature that helps you save time while preparing mailings. Although suitable for preparing your documentation for almost any kind of job, this program's basic approach is best suited to entry and mid-level positions.

PhotoDisc Multimedia Sampler

Publisher: PhotoDisc, Inc.; 2013 4th Avenue, Ste. 200; Seattle, WA 98121; (800) 528-3472; (206) 441-9355; fax (206) 441-9379

System Requirements: IBM PC or compatible with an 80286 or better microprocessor; 2MB RAM; DOS 4.1 or higher; 40MB hard disk drive; EGA graphics

Macintosh II; 4MB RAM with an Adobe Photoshop plug-in compatible application (otherwise 8MB RAM); 20MB free hard disk space; System 6.0.7 or later

Suggested: For IBM: 80386 or better microprocessor recommended; Windows 3.0 or later; 4MB RAM; 80MB hard disk drive; high-resolution graphics adapter card with 512K video memory; mouse

For Macintosh: Mac IIci or greater; 20MB RAM; 100MB free hard disk space; Storm Technology JPEG decompression board; System 7; 24-bit color

Documentation: Off-line documentation is simply a flyer that explains the system requirements and the groups of images.

Support: You can call the company for the price of the phone call.

Suggested Retail Price: $69.00

The Program

This disk contains more than 1,000 stock, low-resolution TIFF images from selected PhotoDisc Volumes, including Business & Industry, People & Lifestyles, Backgrounds & Textures, and Science, Technology & Medicine. The company's LIGHTBOX feature provides an image-retrieval utility for key-word search, preview, and placement into other programs. The program is compatible with leading desktop publishing, presentation, and multimedia programs.

The material on the sampler disk can be used for in-house proofing and presentations to clients. You must, however, purchase a volume to use an image for reproduction—and be sure to read the licensing agreements before using the images. Upon purchase, you are granted a license for placement of images in advertising, newsletters, brochures, corporation communications, and media presentations. You may not use the images in products designed for resale (such as calendars, posters, greeting cards, and so on). The company continues to produce collections of photographs, including the new volume, World Commerce & Travel.

The Playroom (Ages 3 to 8)

Publisher: Broderbund Software, Inc.; 500 Redwood Boulevard; P.O. Box 6121; Novato, CA 94948-6121; (415) 382-44001; (800) 521-6263

System Requirements: IBM PC/Tandy or compatible, with 512K RAM and floppy disk drive

Suggested: Sound card; color monitor; printer; mouse

Other Platforms (not reviewed): Macintosh and Apple II (The Macintosh version lets you add your own sounds if your Mac has sound-input capabilities.)

Curriculum Areas: The program is designed to help a child learn letters and numbers, keyboarding, problem-solving, and time. There are a number of matching problems; the child also learns to distinguish relevant from irrelevant clues.

Documentation: The manual offers follow-up activities for each program segment. Don't lose it, by the way.

Suggested Retail Price: $44.95 for the IBM PC version

The Program

This program presents an inviting playroom in which you can make an object do something just by pointing at it and clicking the mouse. A fish might do somersaults, for example, or a drawer fly open to release balloons. Some objects, however, take you out of the playroom for other types of exploration. The Mousehole, for example, takes you to a board game on which you roll electronic dice to advance, using counting and strategy skills. The character in The Playroom is a white mouse named Pepper; if you make a mistake, Pepper guides you to the right answer.

This game is easy to operate; no reading ability is required, so it is suitable for preschoolers. You can intuitively figure out what the on-screen cues mean. You use cursor keys, a joystick, or a mouse to point at an object, and press the Enter key (or click the mouse or joystick button) to make things happen. Most activities have multiple levels of difficulty, and though the work is structured, there is plenty of room for free play. The copy-protection code can be aggravating, however, and young children may require your help. You must match a code that appears on the screen with one that is on the back of the manual, and you know what that means: you must keep track of the manual and not let the dog chew it.

Also available is The Backyard, in which the adventures and activities take place in a garden, sandbox, or pool of a backyard. The program is imaginative and rated highly, just as The Playroom is.

Pick and Pile

Publisher: UBI Soft/Electronic Arts; 1505 Bridgeway, Suite 105; Sausilito, CA 94965; (415) 332-8749

System Requirements: Tandy, IBM PC, XT, AT or compatible; floppy disk drive; DOS 3.2 or higher; 512K RAM; CGA, EGA, VGA, and Tandy graphics

Suggested: Mouse; hard disk drive; supports Ad Lib sound card and compatibles

Other Platforms (not reviewed): Apple IIGS; Macintosh

Documentation: The documentation explains the minimum needed to run the game. It could explain the game elements a bit better, and could use art that describes the on-screen graphics images. It also should explain that most of the menu items are toggle switches; you don't need to pick items unless you want to change one of them.

Support: Technical support is available by writing to the company's technical support address, or by calling the technical support telephone number on weekdays between 8:30 a.m. and 4:30 p.m. Pacific Time.

Suggested Retail Price: $39.95

The Program

The object of Pick and Pile is to make the multitude of colored balls falling from the "sky" disappear. Once the initial objects have descended, they form columns along the bottom of the screen. When two or more balls of the same color end up in the same column, they disappear. Some will fall into the same column and disappear right away. The remainder you must move into an empty space or exchange with another object. If you end up with only single balls of different colors, you can command the program to release more balls and objects from the "sky." If you get all of the balls to disappear before time runs out, you win.

Different things happen if other objects disappear in the same column as a group of like balls. When an hourglass disappears with a column of balls, for example, the time that remains to finish a screen is increased by 200 counts. Bombs, flames, flowerpots, walls, and death's-heads can help or hinder your play. When a column with a sum of more than 1,000 points disappears, a diamond appears at the top of the column. You can put the diamond in your storehouse. When diamonds in the storehouse reach across the screen, your score increases. The game is simple, once you know what each on-screen item does. Good reflexes help you play better, but are not essential to winning.

Picture It! Italian

Publisher: Penton Overseas, Inc.; 2091 Las Palmas Drive, Suite A; Carlsbad, CA 92009-1518; (619) 431-0060; (800) 748-5804; fax (619) 431-8110

System Requirements: IBM PC, XT, AT, PS/2 or compatible; hard disk drive; one 3.5-inch floppy drive; 640K RAM, EGA or VGA graphics

Suggested: Sound Blaster sound card and Microsoft Mouse, or a sound card and mouse that are 100-percent compatible with these brands

Other Platforms (not reviewed): Windows 3.0 or higher; Macintosh

Curriculum Areas: This program reviews foreign-language vocabulary.

Documentation: The documentation contains suggestions for using the program. The manual could be organized better, and there's no index. Be sure to read the README file upon installation.

Support: The Help option lists on-screen help; the Notes option tells you on-screen how to use the program.

Suggested Retail Price: $69.95

The Program

This interactive program is a foreign-language bilingual picture dictionary; you experience the word in three forms: text, sound, and graphic. You can expand or customize the picture dictionary to include additional vocabulary you might wish to learn. You can also create your own tutorial session, using words you find most problematic. There is quick access to the translation and definition of any word. The program is very routine in conception, and is strictly a drill-and-practice exercise. Although the program is menu-driven, using all the options takes some getting used to. The program is available in Spanish, French, German, and Japanese.

Planet's Edge: The Point of No Return

Publisher: New World Computing, Inc.; 20301 Venture Blvd., Suite 200; Woodland Hills, CA 91364; (818) 999-0606; (800) 325-8898

System Requirements: IBM PC and 100 percent compatibles; 640K; VGA, MCGA, EGA, or Tandy graphics; hard disk drive; floppy disk drive

Suggested: Supports Roland, Ad Lib, Sound Blaster, and Tandy 3-Voice DAC sound cards

Documentation: Documentation for this game consists of a poster map of the solar systems, a U.N.F.A (United Nations First Approach) Contact Manual and the reference guide. The Contact Manual lists the chronology of the events that lead to the disappearance of the planet Earth, and describes crew members, ship systems, weapons, and other useful information for playing the game. The reference guide gives information about installation, menus, key commands, playing, and more details about the crew, the warehouse, and other gaming elements.

Support: It is helpful to read both documentation booklets before playing; they include hints about starting the game. There is no tutorial, however, so you have to plunge into the game to discover how to play it. The company provides a clue book at $19.95. If you have technical questions, you can call the company's customer support line on weekdays from 9:00 a.m. to 5:00 p.m. Pacific Time.

Suggested Retail Price: $59.95

The Program

The object of this game is to follow a path of clues across the cosmos on a quest to return the Earth to its own space-time continuum. While doing so, you explore solar systems with planets that have their own unique inhabitants and environments. This game offers real-time combat options, but also requires strategy to play. You maneuver throughout the game by making selections from menus and palettes of icons. Play involves solving story puzzles, which often have more than one solution, encouraging experimentation and replay. Many puzzles involve finding a particular object and delivering it to the right place, but there are also cryptograms, logical deductions, and other types of puzzles. The graphics, animations, and sound effects are good, though the graphics are not state-of-the-art. The game is time-consuming, with challenging puzzles and a huge environment in which to play.

Police Quest 3: The Kindred (parental discretion advised)

Publisher: Sierra, Sierra On-Line, P.O. Box 485; Coarsegold, CA 93614; (800) 326-6654; (209) 683-4468

System Requirements: IBM PC or compatible with a 286 or better microprocessor; 640K RAM; VGA graphics; hard disk drive; floppy disk drive needed for installation

Suggested: Mouse; supports Thunderboard, Pro Audio Spectrum, Ad Lib, Roland MT-32/LAPC-1/CM-32L, and Sound Blaster sound cards

Other Platforms (not reviewed): EGA DOS platforms and Tandy programs are sold separately.

Documentation: Documentation consists of the basic game manual (with generic instructions for all Sierra games) and a "procedures and operations manual" for the Lytton Police Department. This latter manual includes definitions, military time, traffic-officer guidelines, basic police procedures, and the background for this story.

Support: The Procedures Manual contains a "first day briefing" that helps you get started playing the game. In addition, most Sierra games have clue books available, as well as an automated telephone hint line with a 900 number. You can also get hints from Sierra's online bulletin board system, and a commercial information service may offer hints for Sierra games. For technical help, you can call or write to the company's customer support department.

Suggested Retail Price: $69.95

The Program

In this third installment in the PoliceQuest series, you are a policeman, but after your wife is stabbed by Jesse Bains's brother, you find it hard to keep your cool and be professional about solving the crime. The program is an accurate simulation of police action, and in addition, requires you to solve the mystery "by the book" while directing forensics and the crime lab. The cases are based on some real police cases. This is the most realistic of the PoliceQuest series of games. The characters in the game are input from videos of human actors, so action is lifelike and realistic, as are the sound effects. The soundtrack is by Jan Hammer, who wrote the music for *Miami Vice*. The easy-to-use point-and-click interface requires no typing.

Power Chords 1.0

Publisher: Howling Dog Systems; Box 80405; Burnaby, BC; Canada, V5H3X6; (604) 436-0420; fax (604) 436-0425

System Requirements: IBM PC or compatible; MIDI-compatible sound card

Documentation: The documentation is adequate.

Suggested Retail Price: $84.95

The Program

This is a songwriting program that can be used with a sound card that provides MIDI capabilities. With it, you can create chord progressions and pattern-plucked, stringed-instrument sounds (such as guitar, drums, a bass line, and a melody). It is convenient for writing and playing songs, but it is not designed for sequencing or synchronizing.

PowerMenu

Publisher: Brown Bag Software; 2155 S. Bascom Avenue, Suite 114; Campbell, CA 95008; (408) 559-4545

System Requirements: 256K IBM PC or compatible or IBM PS/2; 256K RAM; one 5.25- or 3.5-inch floppy disk drive

Suggested: Hard disk drive

Documentation: The documentation is good; finding what you need to know is easy.

Support: The program includes online help. The support line is free for one year, with the cost of the long distance phone call. It is easy to reach.

Suggested Retail Price: $49.95

The Program

PowerMenu is a DOS-shell program with an intuitive graphic interface you can use to organize and manage everything on your disks. It is a good program if you must transfer from application to application often and quickly. The program includes a menu system, a disk manager, a system manager, and a security system. It can run up to 10,000 programs from pop-up menus. Each menu contains up to ten choices; each choice can lead to up to 10 more choices, down through four layers of submenus. Installation of this program is easy. You can change the AUTOEXEC.BAT file to put the main menu onscreen automatically each time your computer is turned on.

Prince of Persia 2: The Shadow and the Flame (Parental Discretion Advised)

Publisher: Broderbund Software; 500 Redwood Boulevard; Novato, CA 94948-6121; (415) 382-4400

System Requirements: Mac Plus or greater; 2MB RAM (2.5MB of RAM for System 7 and 4MB for color under System 7); hard disk drive; System 6.0.2 or later (System 6.0.5 for color)

Other Platforms (not reviewed): Apple II with an optional joystick

Suggested Retail Price: $49.95

The Program

In this animated adventure game, you progress among 12 mazelike levels. In each, you must find the exit and open it by pressing a trigger hidden somewhere in the level. Obstacles in your path include guards with swords, deadly spikes, poisoned potions, and razor-edged gates.

If you play using the keyboard, you must be able to recall keyboard commands quickly to advance in the game. If you press the wrong key while dangling out of a window, you could fall to your death. A high tolerance for frustration is required for this game; you may need to try quite a few times before you can advance. In addition, each time you die, you must start at the beginning of the level again. If you pass a level, you should save the game so you don't have to start all over at the next computer session.

The game has superb graphics, animation, sound effects, and music. The drawings are detailed, with colorful backgrounds. Actually, the graphics may be too realistic for young children; a lot of blood is spilled when characters die. Like many current computer games, however, this one has an off-disk copy-protection scheme: here you must look up a key word in the manual and then find a magic potion on the screen that is labeled with the first word of the key word in order to start the program.

Princeton Review's: SAT, LSAT, GRE, GMAT

Publisher: Princeton Review; (800) 255-6226

System Requirements: Mac SE/30; 1.5 MB RAM; 3MB hard disk space

Suggested Retail Price: $29.95

The Program

These computerized diagnostic exams allow you to take sample tests and have them scored by the program. It analyzes your test-taking abilities, pointing out strengths and weaknesses. Timed sections give you practice in answering questions similiar to those on the actual exams. Your progress is charted on easy-to-read reports.

Procomm Plus for Windows

Publisher: Datastorm Technologies; 3212 Lemone Blvd.; Columbia, MO 65205; (314) 443-3282

System Requirements: IBM PC or compatible with a 286 or better microprocessor; hard disk drive; floppy disk drive for installation; Windows 3.0 or higher

Suggested: 386 microprocessor or better

Other Platforms (not reviewed): IBM PCs with DOS; Macintosh

Support: Online support is available by pressing **Alt+H**.

Suggested Retail Price: $149

The Program

This communications software gives you precise control over a communications session. It installs easily, is easy-to-use and flexible, and has a good Windows interface. The program uses icons; it has an Action Bar for modem, dialing, and speeding up common jobs.

This program has 34 different terminal emulations, including DEC VT series and IBM 3101. For emulations, it lets you redefine any key on your keyboard. It offers many common communications protocols (including Zmodem, Kermit, and CompuServe CIS B+). Procomm Plus includes the ASPECT programming language for customizing the program, and supports linking with other applications.

Project Scheduler 5

Publisher: Scitor Corporation; 393 Vintage Park Drive, Suite 140; Foster City, CA 94404; (415) 570-7700; fax (415) 570-7807

System Requirements: Macintosh Plus, Classic, LC, Portable, II series; System 6.0 or later; 1MB RAM

Suggested: 2MB RAM; hard disk drive; printer; color monitor; plotter

Documentation: Reference and tutorial manuals are included with the program. The reference manual contains detailed information for installing and using the program; the tutorial provides a step-by-step guide to learning the program.

Support: Scitor provides unlimited technical phone support—you call a toll number between 8:00 a.m. and 5:00 p.m. (Pacific Time)—as well as access to the Project Scheduler Bulletin Board System. They also offer fee-based training courses and project-management consulting services.

Suggested Retail Price: $695

The Program

Project Scheduler 5 is a project-management software package with powerful workgroup support and multi-project management tools. The program is intended for corporate project managers who must coordinate resources and labor to complete projects within a budget and on time. Individual workgroups can create separate files related to a particular project; these files can then be merged into one central project. The project-integration feature allows any updates and dependencies to be carried over to all related subprojects. The program is able to identify conflicts that may arise as changes are made to a subproject that may affect another subproject. Project Scheduler 5 also has the ability to create Organizational and Work Breakdown Structure charts automatically.

Project Scheduler 5 allows for formatting of text in report fields and flexibility in terms of headers. You cannot create your own reports—you only edit the program's existing reports—and there is no way to import graphics to enhance the appearance of charts and reports. The program's interface is very awkward, especially to Mac users. The program does, however, offer the ability to exchange files between your Mac and other platforms, making it a good choice for environments that use different platforms. Project Scheduler 5 does not support System 7's publish-and-subscribe or Balloon Help features;

it also lacks in-depth context-sensitive help. If you need to merge subprojects into one project and coordinate cross-project resources, Project Scheduler 5 could be a program worth investigating.

Publish It! 3.0

Publisher: Timeworks International, Inc.; 625 Academy Drive; Northbrook, IL 60062; (708) 559-1300; (800) 323-7744; fax (708) 559-1399

System Requirements: IBM PC, XT, AT, PS/1, PS/2, or compatible; 1MB RAM; one 5.25- or 3.5-inch floppy disk drive; hard disk drive; IBM CGA/EGA/VGA, Super VGA, Hercules, or AT&T Monochrome; DOS 3.0 or higher

Suggested: 2MB RAM; mouse; printer

Other Platforms (not reviewed): Publish It! Easy for the Macintosh

Documentation: Documentation for this program includes a Reference Guide brochure with options and key commands and the User's Manual. The well-developed User's Manual contains a Getting Started Section; a Reference Section tells how to use the program, and gives an alphabetical summary of all its elements. Another booklet describes the program's library of clip art and templates.

Support: The Getting Started Section contains a tutorial called the Quick-start Mini-manual that helps you practice using the program's features. Online help offers simple, not detailed, explanations. Technical support is free for registered owners, for the cost of a toll call on weekdays from 9:00 a.m. to 5:00 p.m. Central Standard Time. (For an annual fee of $50, you can use the 800 number.) The company also sends newsletters periodically about its programs and services. It sells clip-art and font-accessory packs to complement this program.

Suggested Retail Price: $249.95

The Program

This desktop publishing program is easy-to-learn and full-featured; it offers almost every feature seen in the expensive packages. It runs under GEM graphics environment (a windowed environment with icons, menus, dialog boxes, and mouse use), and uses the GEM graphics file format. Some functions include quick-access buttons so you can do many tasks with a click of the mouse. The program has a built-in word processor, an 80,000-word spelling checker, a built-in graphics tool box, over 100 ready-to-use sample layouts, over 150 high-resolution clip-art illustrations, and 20 typefaces you can adjust in a variety of ways. It also supports extended and expanded memory.

With Publish It!, you can select from a number of excellent style sheets, and develop paragraph styles, and design your own document. The PowerText feature lets you rotate or skew (slant) your text, or fill outline text with patterns. The program also has leading and kerning abilities. Publish It! lets you import graphics from (but not export them to) a number of popular graphics programs. A number of drawing tools help you edit imported graphics and draw your own pictures. You can scale, crop, and edit imported bit mapped images, but not line art from vector drawing programs. The program supports some color printing of PowerText items and imported color line art.

QEMM-386 7.0

Publisher: Quarterdeck; Quarterdeck Office Systems; 150 Pico Boulevard; Santa Monica, CA 90405; (310) 392-9851

System Requirements: IBM PC or compatible with a 386 or better microprocessor; DOS 3.0 or later; can be used with Windows 3.1 or later

Suggested Retail Price: $99.95

The Program

This memory-manager program adjusts your system so that memory becomes available in whatever form you need for a particular application. The operation is performed automatically, unlike DOS 5, in which you need to allocate memory manually and reboot the machine for each change. The package also includes Quarterdeck Manifest, an analysis program that tells you what's going on inside your computer—for example, what memory is allocated to what use.

QuarkXPress for Windows 3.3

Publisher: Quark, Inc.; 1800 Grant Street; Denver, CO 80203; (800) 788-7835; (303) 894-8888; fax (303) 894-3399

System Requirements: IBM PC with an 80486 processor or better; 2MB RAM; Windows 3.1 or higher; hard disk drive; high-density floppy disk drive

Suggested: More than minimum RAM is suggested for such programs.

Other Platforms (not reviewed) Macintosh (accelerated for PowerMac)

Documentation Documentation for this program is very good.

Support Initial 90-day, unlimited-call, telephone support. Subsequent pay service: $25 for 30 days of unlimited calls, or one-year plan at $195 (including upgrades and newsletters).

Suggested Retail Price: $895

The Program

This desktop publishing program has been popular and powerful for the Macintosh, and now it available for Windows and the IBM platform. The program is known for its precision, and does almost every desktop publishing function required. It features precise numerical positioning, text rotation in one-degree increments, and excellent printing capabilities. With it, you can link and unlink columns of text at will. It performs flawless alignment of columns and text within tables. You can scale, crop, and adjust the contrast of imported graphics. It supports three major color printing standards: Pantone, Focoltone, and Trumatch, but it also has great support for gray-scale printing. You can create gradations of tone or color. Its features are ideal for accurate creation of color separations for commercial color printing.

Not only is QuarkXPress a terrific DTP program, it also has sophisticated text-editing features and includes a spelling checker. In addition, you can import text from most common formats. Its major drawback for most users is its cost.

Quattro Pro for Windows 6.0

Publisher: Borland International, Inc.; 100 Borland Way; Scotts Valley, CA 95066-3249; (800) 682-9299; (408) 431-1000; fax (408) 431-4123

System Requirements: IBM PC with 386 or better microprocessor; 4MB RAM; 10MB hard disk space; high-density floppy disk drive needed for installation; Windows 3.1 or higher

Suggested: SVGA graphics; mouse; printer

Other Platforms (not reviewed): DOS 2.0 or higher version for IBM computers

Documentation: Documentation includes a number of manuals: a spiral-bound quick-reference guide, a Functions and Macros Guide; a Getting Started manual, and a large User's Guide. The manuals are unified by the use of one color along with black-and-white, good organization, and lots of tables. The User's Guide contains a printer setup guide, error messages, a glossary and large index.

Support: The Getting Started manual contains a tutorial; the User's Guide contains a large questions and troubleshooting section. Online help includes experts (which give you step by step guidance) and coaches (Borland's name for its interactive tutorials). The package also includes a leaflet describing common questions and troubleshooting which you should read before panicking and calling technical support. There is also a product support Hot Line, as well as bulletin-board support on CompuServe, BIX, GEnie, and a company BBS. To talk with a real person, you can call the technical support phone number from 6:00 a.m. to 5:00 p.m. Pacific Time on weekdays. There is also a fax number. Technical support requires registration.

Suggested Retail Price: $495

The Program

This spreadsheet program emphasizes organization and simplicity. All on-screen elements (ranges, column headings, title bars, and so on) can be manipulated directly with a mouse. You can use the drag-and-drop function to move cells. Clicking the right mouse button at an object calls up an activity known as "property inspection": you get a dialog box that lists all the options available for that object (such as a title bar). The toolbar is dynamic; it displays different tools depending on the operation you are performing. If you select editing, for example, the toolbar changes to display the editing options.

The program also has a three-dimensional structure that enables you to work across a number of worksheets. The program supports in-cell editing and OLE 2.0. It offers more than 360 Analytical Tools, a Scenario Manager, a Data Modeling Desktop for viewing data, and a Consolidator for merging data and making summary reports.

Quattro Pro's graphics package rivals dedicated graphics programs. You can create illustrations, charts, and slide shows. There is a full range of drawing tools, including layering, colors, and a scalable grid. The program also integrates seamlessly with Borland's two database packages, dBASE IV and Paradox. The program gives you direct access to database files and has extensive file-linking capabilities.

QUICKEN 5.0

Publisher: Intuit, Inc.; P.O. Box 3014; 155 Linfield Ave.; Menlo Park, CA 94026; (800) 624-8742; (415) 322-0573

System Requirements: Mac Classic or greater; 1MB of RAM

Other Platforms: Quicken for Windows CD-ROM Deluxe Edition requires the IBM platform with a CD-ROM drive. It includes the three Quicken add-ons. With Quicken Quotes, you can log onto CompuServe and download stock-market information; with Tax Estimator, you can track the amount of taxes you might owe; with Home Inventory, you catalog your possessions and their worth.

Quicken is also available for DOS and Windows without a CD-ROM drive.

Documentation: The User Manual is well organized, offering instruction for the first-time user in the form of a Quick Tour. There are chapters written specifically for business and home users. Icons, Quicken Tips, and screen dumps interspersed throughout make the manual visually pleasing as well as instructional.

Support: Tech Support is free and unlimited for as long as you use Quicken. Quicken also provides on-line help. Specific information about a task being performed is available by pressing _ - ?. Pressing the same key sequence and clicking on Topics provides a list of help topics. Click on a boldface term, and more information about that term is provided on the screen. The online tutorials are called QuickTours.

Suggested Retail Price: $69.95

THE PROGRAM

Quicken is a single-entry bookkeeping software program appropriate for both personal and small business finances. A built-in print capability allows you to print checks; you can use checks preprinted by Quicken, or you may choose to pay bills electronically by modem through the CheckFree Service at additional cost. Quicken tracks spending, saving, and tax deductibles. It gives you the results in preset automatic reports for budget, cash flow, itemized categories, net worth, tax summary, transaction detail, and summary. In addition, the business section offers customizable reports for accounts payable, accounts receivable, balance sheet, payroll, job/project, and income statement. The Billminder option enables you to set Quicken to remind you when checks need to be printed, payments need to be transmitted, or transactions groups are due. Quicken also allows exporting of data to tax software such as MacInTax for use in preparing tax forms.

The Deluxe edition includes the Quicken Companion, which tracks home inventory, estimates taxes owed, and provides the full text of 20 U.S. government documents about finances and money (as well as articles from *The Wall Street Journal*). It also contains The Wall Street Journal Video Guide to Money and Markets.

QuicKeys 3.01

Publisher: CE Software; (515) 221-1801

System Requirements: Macintosh; 4MB RAM; System 7

Suggested Retail Price: $169

The Program

This macro-building utility enables you to create your own set of useful keyboard shortcuts; it includes 12 sets of ready-made macros to be used with many of the popular applications on the market. The Record features allow you to develop personalized macros by recording only your keystrokes, or keystrokes plus any pauses (deadtime) between them. The QuicKeys Editor has a full set of menus that enable you to edit new or existing macros.

QuickMail 3.0

Publisher: CE Software; (515) 221-1801

System Requirements: Macintosh Plus (user), Macintosh SE (server), hard disk drive

Suggested Retail Price: $199 (1 user), $449 (5 user)

The Program

QuickMail is a comprehensive, cross-platform e-mail package available for up to 100 users. Each package includes server and administrative software, clients (Mac, Windows, DOS), and customizable forms. It also includes a remote feature to send and receive messages on the road, and bridges to connect to AppleLink, CompuServe, and MCI Mail—as well as spell-checking, managing, and searching capablilities.

Reader Rabbit I (Ages 3 to 6)

Publisher The Learning Company; 6493 Kaiser Drive; Fremont, CA 94555; (800) 852-2255; (510) 792-2101; fax (510) 792-9628

System Requirements: IBM PC or compatible; floppy disk drive

Suggested: VGA graphics recommended for maximum appeal

Other Platforms (not reviewed): Apple IIGS and Macintosh; Deluxe CD-ROM version for both Macintosh and Windows

Curriculum Areas: This program teaches pre-reading and early reading skills; it helps a child acquire reading-readiness skills, counting and number recognition, and skills in recognizing mathematical patterns.

Documentation: The manual has good explanations of the program and its goals.

Suggested Retail Price: $49.95

The Program

Through the pictures, moving graphics, and music of this program, you match shapes, images, and words in Matchup, and practice reading and spelling three-letter words in Labeler. In Word Train, you build word "trains" so that each successive word differs from the previous word by a single letter (cat, hat, mat, sat, and so on, for example). In Sorter, you sort words by their first letter, their last letter, or middle letter. You both see and hear the letters and words you work with. Although this program is somewhat like school, it is still entertaining. There are multiple difficulty levels, and the program gently focuses on arriving at the "right" answers. You can return to the program where you left off the last time you played.

Reader Rabbit 2 (for ages 5 to 8) consists of four games: In Word Mine, you build words; in Vowel Pond, you identify and sort words of the targeted vowel sound; in Match Patch, you use rhyming, homonyms, and antonyms; in Alphabet Dance, you place names of animal characters in alphabetical order. In the related product Writer Rabbit, you identify kinds of information and work on sentence parts, while helping Writer Rabbit make refreshments for his parties.

Return to Zork

Publisher ActiVision; 11440 San Vicente Blvd; Los Angeles, CA 90049; (800) 477-3650; (310) 207-4500

System Requirements: Macintosh with a 25MHz 68030 or greater CPU; System 7.0 or higher; 4MB RAM with 2,500K available; double-speed CD-ROM or Apple CD 300; 256-color (8-bit) graphics, with 640-x-480 resolution; 13-inch or larger color monitor; 3MB free hard disk space

Suggested: 68040 or better microprocessor; 8MB RAM

Other Platforms (not reviewed): IBM PCs and compatibles for DOS and DOS CD-ROM

Documentation: The manual describes the game interface, guidelines for the first-time adventurer. The Encyclopedia Frobozica describes the characters, places, treasures, and tools (and spells by topic alphabetically, just as an encyclopedia would).

Support: Customer service is available by phone, as well as through CompuServe, PRODIGY, GEnie, and America Online. You can also call a 900 number (a hint line) when you are frustrated by play. Charges are 95 cents per minute, and callers must be 18 years old or have parental permission in order to call.

Suggested Retail Price: $79.95

The Program

Compared with the first text-oriented version of Zork, Return to Zork is a world away: It contains great graphics, a point-and-click user interface, over 180 original orchestral compositions, and more than one hour's worth of spoken dialogue. While playing, you can use the map, camera, photo album, and tape recorder, and keep track of your inventory of objects that you pick up along the way. You can talk with characters by engaging them in conversation or by playing Question and Answer. The conversations may provide clues that help you in your journey through the Underground Empire, which you must save from the forces of evil. The puzzles are fascinating, with various levels of difficulty and well-placed clues that help new players learn how to play. The most challenging puzzles keep even veteran game players interested. It helps to save your game often in case you "die." Then you can return to the last point you successfully reached.

Reunion 4.0

Publisher: Leister Productions; (717) 697-1378

System Requirements: Macintosh

Suggested Retail Price: $99.95

The Program

Tracking your family history and creating genealogy charts is as easy as "filling in" an on-screen card for each family member. Scanned photos and legal documents can be added to embellish the charts. The program also automatically creates family and personal histories, mailing lists and labels, and birthday calendars. Although Reunion is easy to use, it includes a tutorial and user's guide.

Richard Scarry's Busiest Neighborhood Ever (Ages 3 and up)

Publisher ActiVision; 11440 San Vicente Blvd; Los Angeles, CA 90049; (800) 477-3650; (310) 207-4500

System Requirements IBM PC or compatible with a 25MHz 386 or better microprocessor; 1MB RAM; 6MB free hard disk space; 150K/sec CD-ROM drive; VGA graphics with color monitor; MS-DOS 5.0 to 6.2; sound card

Suggested: Mouse

Other Platforms (not reviewed): Macintosh with CD-ROM drive

Documentation: A Parent Guide is included, which explains play.

Support: A flyer in the disc case explains installation, files, and troubleshooting. For comments and answers to questions, you can call the company between 9:00 a.m. and 5:00 p.m., or use one of the following online services: CompuServe, PRODIGY, GEnie, or America Online.

Suggested Retail Price: $39.95

The Program

This program provides a surprise-filled journey through Busytown. It is based on characters and places from Richard Scarry's books. You begin with a "map" of the town, and use the Star to navigate to a location of your choice. Press the Action button (mouse button) when you see something you want to explore. Children can play several games in Busytown; these include matching cookie shapes at the Bakery and helping Doctor Bones perform a checkup. The program helps build skills in music appreciation, creative discovery, problem-solving, and memory. A Small Kids mode enables you to lock the program and protect your hard disk drive from damage that may occur when children play at your computer.

A similar game, Richard Scarry's Best Neighborhood Ever, won the Gold Cindy Award in the Interactive Video and Multimedia Competition. Requirements, age group, and price are the same as for Busiest Neighborhood Ever; children who play can begin to develop strategy, build memory and concentration skills, and begin basic reading of the signs found in Busytown.

Robinson's Requiem

Publisher: ReadySoft Incorporated; 3375 14th Avenue, Unit 7 & 8; Markham, Ontario, Canada L3R 2L6; (905) 475-4801; fax (905) 475-4802

System Requirements: IBM PC or compatible, with 80386 or better microprocessor; 4MB RAM; VGA graphics; mouse

Suggested: 486 CPU recommended; supports Sound Blaster sound card

Other Platforms (not reviewed): Macintosh; CD-ROM versions for both IBM and Macintosh

Documentation: The manual provides a summary of the game, its actions, and icons. The AWE White Booklet is your "pretend" reference manual.

Support: Call the technical support telephone number in case of technical problems.

Suggested Retail Price: $69.95

The Program

This game is a survival/adventure simulation in which you are to escape from an alien planet—even if you have to amputate one of your own limbs to do so. As you play, the program manages more than 100 variables such as stress, fatigue, pain, disease, and hallucination. Your "prison" is a three-dimensional world, complete with canyons, hills, waterfalls, and caves. Here you must hunt and gather food, find water, make your own clothes and weapons, fight off predators, and more to get off the planet. To play the game, you can take a number of actions such as examine the map, consult the computer, use an object, dress, eat, sleep, and so on. The screen shows the objects you have, the compass, and your state of health. This game is time-intensive, and requires a number of times through before you can play well.

The Rocketeer

Publisher: Walt Disney Computer Software; 500 S. Buena Vista St.; Burbank, CA 91521-6740; (800) 688-1520

System Requirements: IBM PC or compatible, with 10MHz 80286 microprocessor or better; 640K RAM; EGA or VGA; floppy disk drive

Suggested: Hard disk drive; mouse or joystick; supports Ad Lib, PS/1 Audio Card, Roland MT-32/LAPC-1, Sound Blaster (386 required, MCV not supported), Tandy Sound, and The Sound Source sound cards

Suggested Retail Price: $29.95, $69.95 (bundled with sound source)

The Program

This game is patterned after the Disney movie, *The Rocketeer*, except here, you are the Rocketeer, racing in planes at Bigelow's Air Circus and fighting the Nazis. Although primarily an arcade game, the program also has elements of an adventure game. It is fast-paced, with good graphics and exciting sound, although the dialogue is somewhat stiff and predictable. The graphics simulate a 1930s airfield with realism and clarity. It is hard to advance through the levels of difficulty, and you can't save your games. You can, however, skip earlier episodes once you have mastered them.

The Rosetta Stone

Publisher: Fairfield Language; (703) 432-6166

System Requirements: Macintosh, 2700K of RAM, CD-ROM drive, 8-bit color

Suggested Retail Price: $395

The Program

Although the library includes several foreign languages, we reviewed the Spanish version. The program teaches both vocabulary and grammar, using a combination of pictures, text, and spoken words. The interface is somewhat clumsy; it has no control-key combinations, and options are indicated by icons. A book corresponding to the lesson plans is included in each language version, but there is no online help.

Rusty & Rosy (Ages 3 to 7)

Publisher: Waterford Institute; (800) 767-9976

System Requirements: DOS; 286; 12MB hard disk space; sound card; 386SX; Windows; 12MB hard disk space; sound card

Suggested Retail Price: $49.95

The Program

This reading series is designed for three-to-seven-year-olds. Volume II, Read with Me, teaches sound/word recognition and gives the children ten games to play. While playing, they learn to match words, shapes, and letters. Also included is a nursery-rhyme video that contains some 25 songs for reading and vocabulary building.

Sea Rogue

Publisher: MicroProse; 180 Lakefront Drive; Hunt Valley, MD 21030-2245; (410) 771-1151

System Requirements: IBM PC 286 or greater, or compatible; 640K RAM; high-resolution EGA; DOS 3.3 or higher; hard disk drive

Suggested: Mouse recommended; supports IBM, Roland, Ad Lib, and Sound Blaster sound cards

Documentation: Documentation includes a technical reference card that describes installation and key commands, a game book that explains game elements, and a long list of wrecks and their locations (over 270).

Support: The package includes tutorials that guide you through your first wreck adventure and your first combat; both tutorials include hints for successful gaming. For technical support, you can call the company's customer service number on weekdays from 9:00 a.m. to 5:00 p.m. Eastern Time.

Suggested Retail Price: $14.99

The Program

Sea Rogue takes you on an international quest for sunken treasure. On the way, you'll encounter drug smugglers, claim jumpers, hijackers, sharks, barracudas, storms, shifting ocean currents, and Evil Eddy. You begin as a novice equipped with a trawler; at this game level, there are no combat options. At the intermediate level, the combat options are limited. At the professional level, you are the captain of the super submarine *Sea Rogue*, and must deal with tough combat and increased competition for wreck sites. Interaction with the game generally consists of checking things on a menu. For example, you will assign skills to your crew of five by selecting from a menu. The identification of wrecks, not the value of wrecks, leads to the highest overall score.

The graphics are not state-of-the art, and there is not a lot of depth in the role-playing and simulation encounters, but there is a wealth of information about wrecks and treasure. With its shipwrecks and controlled combat situations, this program will appeal to someone who is interested in shipwrecks, or someone who is just starting adventure-and-combat computing.

Search for the King 1.1 (Parental Discretion Advised)

Publisher: Accolade; 550 South Winchester Blvd, Suite 200; San Jose, CA 95128; (408) 985-1700

System Requirements: IBM PC, XT, AT, or compatible, with an 8MHz or faster microprocessor, or Tandy 1000 series; MCGA, VGA, EGA, CGA, or Tandy 16-Color; 640K RAM; hard disk drive; high-density floppy disk drive

Suggested: Mouse; supports Ad Lib, CMS, Tandy 3-Voice, Roland MT-32, and other MIDI-based sound cards

Other Platforms (not reviewed): Amiga 500, 1000, 2000

Documentation: The instruction manual tells you how to play the game, and describes Les.

Support: At the end of the manual is a walk-through that will help beginners start to play the game. A clue book is available. For technical help, you can call a customer support number on weekdays between 9:00 a.m. and 6:00 p.m. Pacific Time, or write Accolade Customer Support at the address shown.

Suggested Retail Price: $59.95

The Program

This is not—we repeat, not—a search for a medieval king in some adventure game with knights, dragons, and castles. Instead, it is a role-playing adventure in which you, as Les Manley, set out to find Elvis. To play, you must tell Les what to do: look around, pick up something, check things out, and so on. You move Les around using the keyboard or the mouse. The animation is lifelike, and the program contains engaging puzzles. To help you remember where you've been and what you've done, draw a map of the places you visit; mark the dangerous situations, locations of objects, or landmarks along the way.

The company's off-disk copy-protection scheme consists of a sheet with red spatters that cover up pictures of electronic parts and their prices. You use the enclosed pair of cardboard "official decoder" glasses (with red lenses) to block out the splatters and read the information. Even with the red glasses, however, it is hard to see the pictures and the prices. But when you are asked for prices of these electronic parts, you must do your best to match the parts and see the numbers.

The Secret Codes of C.Y.P.H.E.R.: Operation Wildlife (ages 8 and up)

Publisher: Tanager Software Productions; 1933 Davis Street, Suite 208; San Leandro, CA 94577; (510) 430-0900; fax (510) 430-0917

System Requirements: Macintosh Plus or greater; 1MB RAM; System 6.0.2 or later; supports System 7

Suggested: 256-color monitor; 2MB RAM; hard disk drive

Other Platforms (not reviewed): IBM PC or compatible

Curriculum Areas: This program encourages exploration of the characteristics and "lifestyles" of mammals, and is suitable for enrichment activity in science or biology classes. Users also develop logic and language skills by decoding the messages.

Documentation: The manual, in pamphlet form, gives the minimum information needed to use the program. You will need to play through one "mission" to really understand how the program works. The School Edition and Lab Pack versions include a Teacher's Guide with educational objectives, blackline masters and their uses, classroom activities, glossary, and references. The blackline masters can help students with decoding, as well as with interpreting data about the animals.

Suggested Retail Price: $59.95; School Edition: $69.95; Lab Pack version: $139.95

The Program

In this game, you become a C.Y.P.H.E.R. (Courageous Young Partners in Hush-hush Electronic Radiotelegraphy) agent. The organization provides its clients with a confidential message-delivery system. The message, called a CYPHERGRAM, is coded and broken up into pieces before being sent to the client's city. As an agent, you must locate the CYPHERGRAM pieces, and then decode and deliver the message to your client.

In order to receive the pieces of the message, you must follow a trail of mammal clues obtained from your contacts in Discovery City. You must also confirm your identity through the C.Y.P.H.E.R. main computer, secretly accessible through the Wildlife Park Information System. If you make a mistake, you may find yourself up against Loathsome Underhanded Rotten Krooks (L.U.R.K.), a group of crooks just waiting to steal the codes and sell them for profit. As you get the information, it is stored away in your Microscan Watch, a portable wrist-top computer. Through this watch, you can review all the clues or look in the FunCyclopedia, a reference that contains a variety of facts about the 87 mammals. Once you have correctly received the entire coded CYPHERGRAM, you are ready to begin decoding. You can use the Hints button and information about the client's background to help you crack the code.

There are 18 clients to choose from. You can play a series of 10 games with each client. There are four levels of difficulty, and five decoder alphabets (English, American Sign Language, Braille, Morse Code, and Semaphore). Each time you start the program, you must use an off-disk copy-protection scheme that includes a set of two cardboard wheels upon which you match patterns and decode a set of three symbols. The program moves slowly—it took two hours to move through the entire set of games with one client—but you can click on some of the screens to make them move faster. You might wonder whether this is a decoding program with mammals information on the side, or a mammals program with decoding on the side. Either way you look at it, the codes and clients have nothing to do with the mammals: their function is to provide a fun and exciting reward for learning information about animals in their natural habitats.

The Secret of Monkey Island II: LeChuck's Revenge

Publisher: LucasArts Games; P.O. Box 10307; San Rafael, CA 94912; (415) 721-3333

System Requirements: IBM PC with a 286 processor or better; 640K RAM; hard disk drive; VGA graphics; floppy disk drive needed for installation

Suggested: Ad Lib, Roland, Sound Blaster, or SoundMaster II sound card

Suggested Retail Price: $59.95

The Program

In this interactive adventure game, you are Guybrush Threepwood, a pirate engaged in uproarious adventures. In a previous adventure, you defeated the pirate LeChuck and rescued your sweetheart, Elaine Marley. Now LeChuck is out for revenge. This entertaining, funny program has excellent cartoon graphics and animation, with interesting attention to details. For example, people gesture as they talk, and the lighting in a room looks like the artist paid attention to the way real lighting behaves. The music fits the action or mood you choose. You use the mouse to select your actions from a menu at the bottom of the screen that lists items such as talk to, look, open, and so on.

Seven Days in August

Publisher: Time Warner Interactive; (800) 482-3766; (818) 955-9999

System Requirements: PC with DOS and CD-ROM drive, or Macintosh with CD-ROM drive

Suggested Retail Price: $59.99

The Program

This program brings to life the opening week of the Cold War, and presents various perspectives of the construction of the Berlin Wall. The disk contains documentary films, interviews of people who lived through the historic week, and backgrounds of the people who played critical roles in the event. An interesting aspect of the program is that a timeline presents a Mickey Mantle home run, a JFK cruise around Martha's Vineyard, and other innocuous events in the United States occurring simultaneously with the construction of the Berlin Wall, which shut off the East from the West for nearly 30 years.

The 7th Guest

Publisher: Virgin Interactive Entertainment; (800) 874-4607; (714) 833-1999

System Requirements: PC with DOS and CD-ROM drive, or Macintosh with CD-ROM drive

Suggested Retail Price: $99.99

The Program

The 7th Guest is an interactive horror story that takes place in an old mansion. The player is given some 50 puzzles to solve, ranging from easy to intense, while becoming thoroughly entwined in its complex story line. This is a spooky program that entraps you literally in the on-screen house, and figuratively in the addiction to spectacular full-motion graphics and engrossing secrets. A long-awaited sequel, The 11th Hour, is due for release soon; it boasts double the amount of video of 7th Guest, as well as a new twist: a love story.

Shanghai II: Dragon's Eye

Publisher: ActiVision; 11440 San Vicente Blvd; Los Angeles, CA 90049; (800) 477-3650; (310) 207-4500

System Requirements: IBM PC or compatible with a 25MHz 386 CPU; Windows 3.1 or later; MS-DOS 5.0 to 6.2; mouse; 4MB RAM; 3MB free hard disk space; 16 or 256-color VGA with 640 x 480 resolution or higher; SoundBlaster-compatible sound card

Other Platforms (not reviewed): Macintosh and DOS versions available, as well as Sega

Documentation: The manual explains use of the program, describes the eight tile sets, strategy hints, tournament playing, and the 12 animals of time. A resource card describes installation setup and troubleshooting.

Support: Comments and questions can be directed to the company through a customer representative by phone, or through online services (CompuServe, PRODIGY, GEnie, and America Online) or the Internet.

Suggested Retail Price: $49.95

The Program

If you enjoy strategy and tile games, this game may be for you. The game is based on the ancient game, Mah-Jongg. The object is to snap off matching pairs of tiles until you run out of pieces, run out of possible moves, or run out of time. Very addictive.

To be removed, a tile must have nothing on top of it and must be slid to the left, to the right, or both. Thus, both matching tiles must be free. The default layout is Shanghai with the Mah-Jongg tiles. Thirteen layouts and eight tile sets are available. The layouts match the 12 animals of time as well as Shanghai. They are categorized in Easy, Advanced, and Master levels. The tile sets include the traditional Mah-Jongg set, sports, playing cards, alphabet, fantasy world, flags of the world, animals, and hanafuda.

A bonus game is the Dragon's Eye, in which two "players" vie. (You can be both players, but the game can also be played by two players.) The Dragon Slayer tries to remove tiles from the Dragon layout, especially from the heart and limb spaces. The Dragon Master tries to build the Dragon to full strength. This game is for experienced players. Tournaments can be played with both the Dragon's Eye and the Shanghai options.

SideKick 2.0

Publisher: Borland International, Inc.; 1800 Green Hills Road; P.O. Box 660001; Scotts Valley, CA 95067-000; (800) 331-0877; (408) 438-8400

System Requirements: IBM PC, PS/2, or compatible; 512K RAM; hard disk drive with 3MB free space for installation; floppy disk drive needed for installation; DOS 2.0 or later; program can use expanded memory; modem needed for built-in dialer; program supports network use

Suggested: Mouse; printer

Documentation: The documentation is organized into sections that describe each SideKick part.

Support: The documentation includes a question-and-answer section for troubleshooting, but for help you can log on to Borland's forum on CompuServe, or write or call the Technical Support Department. You must be a registered user to get technical support. The technical support telephone line is available from 6:00 a.m. to 4:45 p.m. Pacific Standard Time on weekdays.

Suggested Retail Price: $99.95

The Program

This program is a memory-resident desktop organizer. It has a user-friendly interface with Windows, menus, dialog boxes, and mouse support. You can set up an address and telephone number database, and use the program's built-in dialer to call someone. The program also includes communications for placing calls to get data from another computer, and it allows password protection of your files. You can create scripts for calling a specific computer. The Time Planner lets you set up calendars with a variety of time increments, appointment books, schedules, to-do lists, and alarms as reminders of your appointments. The program's four different calculators—Simple, Business, Scientific, and Programmer—all have a tape-printer option. This program offers cut-and-paste integration with other programs. It also has a small word processor for writing notes and ideas, with spell-checker and thesaurus capabilities.

SimAnt

Publisher: Maxis; 2 Theater Square, Suite 230; Orinda, California 94563; (510) 254-9700; (800) 336-2947

System Requirements: Macintosh; 1MB RAM for monochrome, 2MB for color; hard drive required for color; System 6.0.2 or higher

Suggested: Hard drive recommended for monochrome use

Other Platforms (not reviewed): IBM/Tandy or compatible, Amiga

Documentation: Both the program and the manual contain basic information about ant behavior; the manual also contains strategy tips for playing the game, a glossary, an index, and a tutorial.

Support: The tutorial lets you run through the program options before starting a game.

Suggested Retail Price: $59.95

The Program

SimAnt is a computer-simulated ant farm, so if you drop the box it comes in, you won't have released hundreds of little ants into your tidy nest. You, as the player, become a black ant. You control environmental events and ant behavior to encourage or discourage the success of a colony of ants. You can decide to hoard food or attack red ants. In order to accomplish any of these tasks, you must manage the ratio of workers to soldiers, as well as that of males to queens. Your options include entering or leaving the safety of the colony, searching for food, making new tunnels, and acquiring new territory. Your obstacles include a competing colony of red ants, predatory bugs, downpours, lawn mowers, humans, and that house at the far end of the backyard. And if you wonder how reliable the information is about ants, you can relax: the authors drew on the 1990 Pulitzer-Prize-winning book *The Ants*, by Bert Hölldobler and E. O. Wilson, who are biologists at Harvard University.

For ages 7 to adult, the game provides fun on a simple level, yet it is complex in the way ants function in their real world. The two modes allow a quick game and a more complex, full game. Playing this game can also lead to playing the more complex SimCity and SimEarth games.

SimCity 2000

Publisher: Maxis; 2 Theater Square, Suite 230; Orinda, California 94563; (510) 254-9700; (800) 336-2947

System Requirements: IBM 386 PC; VGA; 640K; 5.25-inch or 3.5-inch floppy disk drive; DOS 2.1 or higher; Windows 3.1 or higher

Suggested: Second floppy disk or hard disk; mouse or joystick; printer; supports Ad Lib and Sound Blaster

Other Platforms (not reviewed): Macintosh. A version called SimTown (on CD-ROM for DOS, Mac, or Windows) is available for children.

Documentation: The documentation includes a system-information-and-reference card that gives basic information and key commands. This card also contains a chart that shows how the factors of city life and growth are related (helpful to use while you are "building" a city). The manual explains the most important commands and the menus and options, as well as the editing options, budgeting options, and maps. It explains the scenarios, describes the factors that influence the chance of your city's survival, and gives you tips for building your city. Also included are a short history of city planning, comments on types of planning, and a troubleshooting guide.

Support: The manual includes a tutorial that runs you through a sample simulation. Maxis also publishes a newsletter twice yearly.

Suggested Retail Price: $49.95 (Windows version: $59.95; Macintosh color version: $79.95)

The Program

In this simulation game, you become both the mayor and the city planner; you create a city of your choosing, or manipulate an existing city. The goal is to run the city well enough for it to grow and prosper. In doing so, you must consider human factors and economic factors and have strategies for dealing with disasters, crime, and pollution, and political factors.

The game includes eight scenarios, with an unlimited number of ways to win or lose. Each scenario is a victim of horrible planning, or is about to be a victim of a disaster; you have a limited time to correct or repair the problems. It illustrates relationships among these elements: city planners, civics, politics, budgets, taxes, and public opinion. To be successful, you must be sensitive to costs, the amount of funds available, and the feelings of the residents. Throughout play, you get information from maps. A number of tools enable you to use the mapping systems for planning your city.

Although the program is recommended for children as young as seven, it is complex, and parents will want to help the child get started. It takes patience to play, and may not appeal to people who like computer games with a lot of action. Adults will enjoy playing the game and comparing its features to their own towns or cities. Being successful at building a city may require a few attempts, but this game is not as complex as the SimEarth simulation by the same company. For an additional price, you can have a group of famous actual or would-be disasters; these include Hurricane Andrew in Homestead, Florida, and a make-believe riot.

SimEarth

Publisher: Maxis; 2 Theater Square, Suite 230; Orinda, California 94563; (510) 254-9700; (800) 336-2947

System Requirements: IBM AT, PS/1, PS/2, Tandy or 100-percent compatible; VGA, MCGA, EGA, Hercules, or Tandy Graphics; 640K RAM; hard disk with at least 1.5MB free space; DOS 2.1 or higher

Suggested: Mouse and printer optional; supports Ad Lib, Sound Blaster, Sound Master and Tandy sound cards

Other Platforms (not reviewed): Macintosh

Documentation: The documentation for this game is extensive, with lots to read and learn. It explains game play, lists the windows and menu options, contains reference material you'll need while playing, and provides a tutorial. It also contains an introduction to earth science. The package does include a quick-start manual that summarizes the minimum material needed to play. A teacher's guide is available at extra charge for classroom use.

Support: In addition to the tutorial section in the user's manual, the game includes online help functions and an online tutorial.

Suggested Retail Price: $59.95

The Program

With SimEarth, a planet-simulator game, you develop a planet from the moment of creation to an advanced technological age. The game is based on James Lovelock's Gaia theory, which suggests that we look at our planet and the life on it as a whole, rather than as separate areas of study. (This theory is controversial, and not an accepted truth in all scientific circles.) The program treats a planet as a whole; life, climate, the atmosphere, and the planet itself all affect each other.

The game provides a number of rules and tools that describe, create, and control a system. The rules are based on chemical, geological, biological, and human factors, but you can customize the simulation by changing the rules. While creating and managing your planet, you can refer to maps, charts, and reports for information and evaluation of your progress. The program offers a

wide range of feedback mechanisms to help you distinguish the relationship between events that occur because of user intervention and events that result from natural change on the planet. The program relies a great deal on the use of energy. In the experimental game mode, you are given unlimited amounts of energy. In the game mode, you try to develop, manage, and preserve your planet within allotted energy budgets.

You communicate with the program through menus and dialog boxes; you can use multiple windows that overlap each other (and can be sized smaller or larger). Although the interface is user-friendly and the game mode has three levels of difficulty, SimEarth is still very complex. You must learn a lot to play. The program offers seven scenarios you can play through before starting your own; it's a good idea to use at least a couple of them. Although the age range starts at 7, young children playing the game will probably need an adult's help. Accompanying books that Maxis sells are *SimEarth: The Official Strategy Guide* and *The SimEarth Bible*. The latest edition to this Maxis family of programs is SimLife, an "artificial life" program, in which you attempt to recreate many of life's processes.

SimTown

Publisher: Maxis; (800) 336-2947

System Requirements: DOS with Windows, or Macintosh (68030 or greater microprocessor, with a speed of 16MHz or greater); 4MB RAM; CD-ROM drive; 256-color monitor

Suggested Retail Price: $34.95

The Program

This scaled-down version of the popular SimCity is designed for eight-to-twelve-year-olds. It allows the player to design a neighborhood from a collection of buildings, trees, and other items. The people who inhabit the neighborhood are created complete with personalities and their choice of pets. As the neighborhood grows, resources are consumed, and garbage is produced—giving kids a lesson about everyday life and its impact on the environment.

Sleeping Gods Lie

Publisher: ReadySoft Incorporated; 30 Wertheim Court, Suite 2; Richmond Hill, Ontario, Canada L4B 1B9; (416) 731-4175

System Requirements: IBM PC or compatible; EGA or VGA graphics; 640K RAM; DOS 2.0 or higher; floppy disk drive; can be installed on a hard disk

Suggested: Mouse or joystick

Other Platforms (not reviewed): Atari ST and Amiga

Documentation: The documentation booklet explains the minimum information needed to play the game. It tells a background of the story, and briefly describes the kingdoms, weapons, armor, and ammunition you'll be using as you play the game. It also gives the key commands, loading procedures, and a few tips.

Support: The program could probably use at least a brief tutorial to acquaint beginning gamers with an approach to game playing techniques.

Suggested Retail Price: $49.95

The Program

In this game, you must save Tessera by finding and waking N'Gnir, an Old God rumored to slumber in one of the farthest-flung of Tessera's eight kingdoms. An interesting aspect of this role-playing game is its first-person perspective; movement through the game somewhat resembles that of a flight simulator or car-driving program. Mouse or joystick control, rather than keyboard control, will enhance this perception. As you walk or run through the landscapes, you'll see a variety of items along the way. If you walk over an item, you automatically pick it up. You can monitor your progress by watching several elements on the screen. For example, a compass will give you direction. Pie charts will show the amount of stamina and magical presence you have remaining. A text window shows your score, your weapons and ammunition, and clothing.

Solving with NIM (Grades 3 to 8)

Publisher: MECC; Brookdale Corporate Center; 6160 Summit Drive North; Minneapolis, MN 55430-4003; (612) 569-1640; (800) 685-6322; fax (612) 569-1551

System Requirements: Apple II series, 128K RAM, 5.25-inch floppy disk drive

Curriculum Areas: This program encourages the development of strategies related to concepts of mathematics.

Documentation: The documentation includes descriptions of the games, additional classroom activities, worksheets, and strategies for winning two versions of Nim. It also includes information on thinking skills, on the origin of Nim, and on cooperative learning. It is written to help a teacher with learning objectives and specifics about curriculum, as well as appropriate grade and reading levels. Its loose-leaf-notebook format includes disks in a plastic pocket inside the front cover.

Suggested Retail Price: $59

The Program

This excellent strategy game requires the manipulation of on-screen objects to find a solution. In Nim games, a certain number of objects are arranged in some discernible manner. Each player takes turns removing up to a specified number of objects; the player taking the last object either wins or loses, depending upon how the game is set up in the teacher options. This program allows you to play with another person or against the computer. Although the graphics in this program are somewhat dated looking, the program is very good—in fact, sometimes frustrating. There are options to turn off any games, change the number of objects, and allow students to access the settings.

Nim is easy to play, but hard to master. Mathematical concepts and strategies for winning two of the games are described in the manual. In Fish Nim, each player's fish "eats" up to a set number of dots. The mathematical concept behind Fish Nim involves division and remainders. In Space Nim, each player blasts asteroids, using strategy that requires knowledge of binary concepts. In Calculator Nim, the players either add single-digit numbers to reach (or avoid) a target value, or subtract single-digit numbers to reach (or avoid) zero. There are six ways to play. In Moonlight Nim, each player turns off a given number of adjacent lights in a house.

MECC has begun to release products that focus on learning, but also feature entertainment. The Nim program is one of these. Others include The Secret Island of Dr. Quandary, Hero by Night, SnapDragon, and Storybook Weaver. The company also produces the Science Inquiry Collection, which includes a diverse range of other titles.

Space Quest IV: Roger Wilco and the Time Rippers

Publisher: Sierra, Sierra On-Line; P.O. Box 485; Coarsegold, CA 93614; (800) 326-6654; (209) 683-4468

System Requirements: IBM PC or compatible, with 286 or better microprocessor; 640K RAM; VGA graphics; hard disk drive

Suggested: Mouse; supports PS/1, Game Blaster, Ad Lib, Roland MT-32/LAPC-1/CM-32L, and Sound Blaster sound cards

Other Platforms (not reviewed): Programs for EGA DOS platforms and Tandy are sold separately.

Documentation: Documentation for this game includes the game manual (with generic instructions for all Sierra games) and the Space Piston Magazine, which describes this particular game.

Support: A clue book is available, and you can call an automated telephone hint line with a 900 number. You can also get hints from Sierra's online bulletin board system, and often a commercial information service may offer hints for Sierra games. For technical help, you can call or write to the company's customer support department.

Suggested Retail Price: $69.95

The Program

In this humorous installment in the popular Space Quest game series, Roger Wilco is an intergalactic sanitation engineer (or janitor), and a hero. Hot on his trail are the Sequel Police, deadly cross-time assassins who want to put an end to Roger and his nonsense. The game has a rock 'n' roll soundtrack, realistic animation, and a point-and-click interface that requires no typing. Basic play includes looking everywhere, opening doors and drawers, talking with characters, and picking up objects you think you might need. While playing, you should draw a map that shows places you've been, objects you might need, and obstacles or dangers. Be sure to save your game often, and be alert for surprises.

Space Shuttle

Publisher: Mindscape; 60 Leveroni Court; Novato, CA 94949; (415) 883-3000

System Requirements: Macintosh with CD-ROM drive

Documentation: The program is easy to use, with minimal documentation. For the Macintosh, just pop in the disk and follow the on-screen directions.

Support: Registered users can call or write the company's technical support group. E-mail and fax services are also available.

Suggested Retail Price: $49.95

The Program

This disk presents over 50 authentic NASA missions, in which you can meet the crew and get basic information before you blast off into space. While in space, you get a chance to do such activities as monitor the delivery or maintenance of a satellite, take an untethered space walk, and perform space experiments for weightlessness and other factors. The program contains a narrated video of NASA footage, photographs, schematic diagrams, and full-motion video.

Spectre

Publisher: Velocity Development Corporation; 2161 Union Street; San Francisco, CA 94123; (800) 856-2489; (415) 776-8000

System Requirements: Macintosh Plus or greater; 1MB RAM; System 6.0.3 or later

Suggested: Mac with a later microprocessor than 68000; 2MB RAM; color monitor

Other Platforms (not reviewed): Pack for LANs; Spectre VR CD-ROM (for PCs equipped with Windows and CD-ROM, as well as Macintosh equipped with CD-ROM)

Suggested Retail Price: $59.95

Support: The game includes demos for levels 1 to 50 to give you an idea of how to play.

The Program

This arcade-style game calls for battle strategy and high-speed eye-to-hand coordination. The object is to collect flags located around an arena. You do this by driving a vehicle over the flags. To advance to the next level, you must collect all the flags. While doing so, however, you could get shot at by an enemy vehicle, and may be destroyed. To protect yourself, you can run away or shoot back. As the levels advance, the number, strength, intelligence, and aggressiveness of the enemy vehicles increase, but you also have more weapons. You can lob grenades at the enemies, destroying more than one at a time, and you can look at a radar screen that can help you detect flags and enemies. Windmills and other objects can be strategic because they offer protection from enemy fire.

The game has an infinite number of possible levels; the first few can be achieved rather quickly. With the right machine, you'll experience smooth animation and three-dimensional simulation. You can choose the perspective you want: bird's-eye, a view positioned slightly above your tank, or a cockpit view. You also get to choose the characteristics of your vehicle—for example, its speed and ammunition levels.

Spell It 3 (Ages 6 to Adult)

Publisher: Davidson & Associates, Inc.; P.O. Box 2961; 19840 Pioneer Ave.; Torrance, CA 90509; (310) 793-0600; (800) 545-7677; (800) 556-6141; fax (310) 793-0601

System Requirements: 12MHz 286 or higher IBM PC or compatible; DOS 3.3 or higher; VGA; 640K RAM; 5MB free hard disk space; 3.5-inch floppy disk drive

Suggested: DOS 5.0, Sound Blaster or other sound card; mouse; printer

Other Platforms (not reviewed): Spell It Plus for Macintosh and Apple

Curriculum Areas: Students learn to spell words at a number of levels of difficulty.

Documentation: The manual is illustrated and easy to follow. It contains the word lists, as well as tips for parents and teachers.

Support: The manual contains a troubleshooting appendix. Customer Support Technicians can be reached by telephone on weekdays from 7:00 a.m. to 6:00 p.m., by fax 24 hours every day, or by mail.

Suggested Retail Price: $59.95

The Program

This "talking" spelling program contains 3,600 words, ranging in difficulty from Junior to Grand Master. You navigate through the program via menus; the five gaming activities are represented on the main screen. Bayou Word Preview helps you learn to spell the words, and includes any applicable general spelling rules. Leap to Complete requires you to correctly finish spelling words with missing letters. Frog Crossing is a crossword-puzzle game. Midnight Correction requires you to edit sentences, with rewards courtesy of the Froggy Band. The Bullfrog Log Game requires you to pick a correct spelling from four choices. For all but the junior lists, you can take a spelling test in the Spelling Bee.

You can create your own list of spelling words using the built-in Editor, which also lets you adjust pronunciation and use a Foreign Language font for Spanish, French, Italian, or German lists. The program is fun for kids and can be challenging for adults.

Spin Doctor

Publisher: Callisto Corp.; (508) 655-0707

System Requirements: DOS or Macintosh; 1MB hard disk space

Suggested Retail Price: $59.95

The Program

Players maneuver a spinning wand through a grid of dots and mazes by reversing the wand's direction, spinning it, flipping it, or bouncing it off a nearby dot. There are a total of 106 environments that require increasing dexterity and thought—but decreasing time limits—with each level. Built-in obstacles and traps are encountered all along the way, but a number of resources can help you make your moves. The colorful graphics allow no mind to wander from the playing field.

Sports Illustrated CD-ROM Sports Almanac

Publisher: Time Warner Interactive Group; 2210 Olive Avenue; Burbank, CA 910506-9959; (800) 482-3766

System Requirements: Macintosh with System 6.0.5 or later (some Macs require System 6.0.7 or System 7 to run this program); 2.2MB RAM; CD-ROM drive

Suggested: 4MB RAM recommended

Documentation: A flyer included in the disc case describes the program. The README file on disc contains requirements and other technical information.

Support: Call or write to the company with questions.

Suggested Retail Price: $59.95

The Program

This disc contains sports information about a multitude of sports—including archery, baseball, boxing, college football, pro football, gymnastics, swimming, horse racing, and others. Comprehensive information about all sports is included; results of World Series, Super Bowls, and other major sporting events are listed in detail. Also of interest are the profiles, 1991 sports highlights, athletic awards, public opinion polls, quotations from major figures in sports, and color photos. The program is easy to navigate; it is all point-and-click.

Sports Illustrated 1994 Multimedia Sports Almanac

Publisher: Starpress Multimedia; (415) 274-8383

System Requirements: 386SX, Windows 3.1, CD-ROM drive

Suggested Retail Price: $59.95

The Program

This almanac features an entire year of the magazine, including articles and photos. It focuses on major league baseball, as well as basketball and football (college and professional). An additional thirteen other sports include hockey, tennis, swimming, and soccer. The program offers a narrated video clip of each sport, as well as photos, stats, and memorable moments from November 1992 to November 1993.

Star Wars: Rebel Assault

Publisher: LucasArts Entertainment; (800) 782-7927; (415) 721-3300

System Requirements: PC with Windows, or Macintosh; CD-ROM drive; joystick

Suggested Retail Price: $79.95

The Program

Pit yourself against Darth Vader and his Imperial cronies in the action-packed video game. The onslaught of invaders is relentless as you find yourself confronting the TIE fighters or Imperial Walkers sent out to destroy you.

Stickybear Town Builder (ages 6 to 9)

Publisher: Weekly Reader Software/Optimum Resource, Inc.; 10 Station Place; Norfolk, CT 06058; (800) 327-1473; (203) 542-5553; fax(203) 542-5685

System Requirements: Apple II series; 48K RAM; 5.25-inch floppy disk drive

Suggested: Color monitor; joystick

Other Platforms (not reviewed): IBM PC or compatible; Commodore 64

Curriculum Areas: The program introduces and builds map skills; it also teaches the use of map symbols, directions, distances, and relative distance. Map skills can be used in both arithmetic and social-studies curriculum areas.

Suggested Retail Price: $49.95

The Program

Although the graphics may not seem as captivating as those of more recent programs by this company, Stickybear Town Builder is effective in its purpose: teaching the design and reading of maps. The three options are Build a Town, Take a Drive, and Find the Keys. In the first option, you construct a town; you borrow from the cache of 30 buildings stored in the program, and insert roads, parks, and bridges. In the second option, you use your original map to drive through the town, making as many stops as possible before running out of gas. In Find the Keys, you must locate 12 keys hidden in the town, also before running out of gas.

The program helps build skills about direction. The child, not the computer, is in charge of the activities here. Other packages in the Stickybear series include Stickybear Word Problems, Stickybear Reading Comprehension, Stickybear Music, Stickybear Math, and Stickybear Reading.

SUITCASE II 2.1.4

Publisher: Fifth Generation Systems, Inc.; 10049 N. Reiger Road, Baton Rouge, LA 70809; (504) 291-7221; (800) 873-4384

System Requirements: Macintosh 512SE or greater; 800K floppy disk drive; System 4.1 or later (for beep sounds, System 6.0 or later); System-7-compatible

Suggested: Hard disk drive

Documentation: Documentation for this program is well organized and well designed. It took a while to understand the program and its advantages, but this was probably due to the nature of the program rather than the documentation.

Support: If you have questions, you can call toll-free 24 hours a day, seven days a week (except major holidays).

Suggested Retail Price: $79

THE PROGRAM

The Macintosh is so easy to use that sometimes resources located on your hard disk drive may be disorganized and hard to find when you want them. If you'd like more control over the files or fonts in your Mac system, you might try this best-selling, award-winning utility program. It lets you manage fonts, desk accessories, FKEYs, and sounds—without installing them in the System file. Suitcase II is particularly useful when you have a large number of resources that need to be available at all times.

The name of the program comes from the little suitcase icons the Mac uses to represent files that contain one or more resources. The program manages fonts when conflicts occur among them. It aids in file transfer; you can take a document to another Macintosh computer and be sure the fonts will be the same as you originally intended. You can also view any font, in any point size, quickly. You can also choose preferences to customize Suitcase options to suit your needs; for example, you can choose where a Suitcase desk accessory is located on your Menu.

Super Munchers… The Challenge Continues (Ages 8 and up)

Publisher: MECC; Brookdale Corporate Center; 6160 Summit Drive, N.; Minneapolis, MN 55430-4003; phone (612) 569-1500; (800) 685-6322; fax (612) 569-1551

System Requirements: Mac Plus or greater; 1MB of RAM

Suggested: Color monitor

Other Platforms (not reviewed): Apple II series; IBM PC or compatible

Curriculum Areas: The program helps develop word-recognition and categorizing skills, as well as vocabulary and knowledge in social studies, science, music, and popular culture.

Documentation: The manual is short, simple, and straightforward, but the online instructions are so complete that the manual is hardly necessary.

Support: Technical support is available by telephoning an 800 number. The technicians are very courteous, and enjoy their products.

Suggested Retail Price: $49.95

The Program

The color graphics are vivid; the sound effects and music set the pace for this fast-moving game. Your ultimate task is to move the muncher around a grid-like playing board, making it eat the items that match the "target rule" or subject area displayed at the top of the screen. There are seven subject areas; they include animals, sports, famous Americans, food and health, geography, and music. Within these subject areas there are over 4000 facts in 130 categories, at three levels of difficulty: Beginner, Advanced, and Genius.

You move munchers around the playing board by clicking the mouse in a chosen cell or by using a variety of keys on the keyboard, including the up-down arrows. You get the muncher to eat an item by clicking on it or by pressing the Spacebar. Points are earned for each correct item eaten. When an incorrect item is eaten, or a muncher meets up with a Troggle, the muncher is lost. The game ends when there are no munchers in reserve.

A password-protected management-option menu allows you to customize Super Munchers to meet particular educational needs. The only option not available that would be of use is the ability to determine your own set of data, including target rules, categories, and items. Children enjoy this fast-paced educational game. The company offers two other programs in this trilogy: Number Munchers and Word Munchers.

Super Solvers: Outnumbered! (Ages 7 to 14)

Publisher: The Learning Company; 6493 Kaiser Drive; Fremont, CA 94555; (800) 852-2255; (510) 792-2101; fax (510) 792-9628

System Requirements: Macintosh; 512K RAM

Other Platforms (not reviewed): IBM PC or compatible

Curriculum Areas: This program offers practice in math and problem-solving skills.

Suggested Retail Price: $59.95 (for IBM PC: $49.95)

The Program

In this arcade-style game, you search each of five rooms to find the Master of Mischief before he takes over Shady Glen's television station and airs boring programs. As you search the rooms, you solve math problems and collect clues. The two obstacles are Telly (a robot) and LiveWire (a hot electric wire). You may have to zap them with your zapper, but be careful: Telly has clues you need to solve the problem. Each time you find the Master, your rank improves, and you move to a more difficult level.

Most math problems are drills and are irrelevant to the game. Some educators criticize the fact that the program develops more skills in playing arcade-style games than skills in math; the child may not need to solve very many math problems to play the game. There is an on-screen calculator, and you can customize the drills to fit what your child is studying or having trouble with in math.

Super Solvers: Treasure Mountain (Ages 5 to 9)

Publisher: The Learning Company; 6493 Kaiser Drive; Fremont, CA 94555; (800) 852-2255; (510) 792-2101; fax (510) 792-9628

System Requirements: IBM PC/Tandy or compatible; floppy disk drive

Suggested: VGA and mouse recommended

Curriculum Areas: This program develops reading and thinking skills.

Suggested Retail Price: $49.95

THE PROGRAM

The Master of Mischief has stolen the magic crown of Treasure Mountain, and is using its powers to steal gold from the Mountain. You must get it back by collecting all the mountain's remaining treasures and locking them up in the castle on top of the mountain. To do your job, you must search the mountain trails; mischievous elves may help or hinder you in your search. You must capture elves with your net and solve their riddles in order to get clues or magic coins that identify where the treasures are.

The riddles require you or your child to apply language arts, arithmetic, and science skills. Any question that is answered incorrectly is repeated up to three times during the game, while the incorrect answers are eliminated. You may also need to integrate several answers to find where a treasure is located. As your skill increases, the game gets harder, but the treasures become more valuable. This game provides your child with reading practice and logic problems in an arcade format. It is lots of fun, but requires thinking and reading skills. Games can be saved and resumed later.

Other Super Solvers puzzles include Midnight Rescue! and OutNumbered!; both are for ages 7 to 10 ($59.95 for the Macintosh version, and $49.95 for the IBM PC group). In addition, Challenge of the Ancient Empires is available for ages 10 to adult (IBM PC or compatible, $49.95) and Super Solvers Spellbound! is available for ages 7 to 12 (IBM PC or compatible, or CD-ROM version). All the games are equally entertaining, educational, and user-friendly.

SUPERBASE4

Publisher: Software Publishing Corporation; 8404 Sterling Street; Irving, TX 75063; (800) 562-9909; (408) 980-0729

System Requirements: IBM PC 386 or compatible; 640K RAM minimum; Windows 3.0 or higher; hard disk drive; high-density floppy disk drive needed for installation

Suggested: VGA graphics; printer

Documentation: The documentation is adequate, but the program is so easy to use that the limitations of the manual do not pose much of a problem.

Support: Online help is available, but limited.

Suggested Retail Price: $695

The Program

This database program is extraordinarily easy to use, but, on the other hand, it can handle very complex queries. You can easily create a new file, and use the palette and button toolkit for editing and formatting jobs. SuperBase4 is visually attractive, fast, and it supports the popular database file formats. Its built-in communications facility checks for errors during file transfers. It has a powerful SQL facility, within which you can save and print queries in standard formats. It also has an extensive programming language to which you will quickly adapt if you are an experienced BASIC user.

Symantec AntiVirus for Macintosh (SAM) 4.0

Publisher: Symantec Corporation; 10201 Torre Ave.; Cupertino, CA 95014; (408) 253-9600; (800) 441-7234; fax (310) 829-0247

System Requirements: Macintosh Plus, SE, Classic, SE/30, II series, Portable, or LC; hard disk drive; one 800K floppy disk drive needed for installation; System 6.0 and Finder 6.1 or later; MultiFinder- and System-7-compatible

Documentation: The user's manual is well written, clear, and well organized, with well-placed illustrations and definitions of the viruses.

Support: A Getting Started tutorial in the user's manual guides you through various aspects of the program. As new viruses are always being invented, you can obtain new virus definitions by calling the 24-Hour Virus Newsline or the Symantec Virus Bulletin Board. From the BBS, you can download the new virus definitions to automatically update your copy of SAM.

Suggested Retail Price: $99; $45 per year for updates

The Program

This antivirus program rates high as a protective measure against viruses and Trojan Horses, as well as for its detection capabilities (and for file repair after a virus has been detected). Common Macintosh interface guidelines make the SAM programs easy to install and use. When running under System 7, SAM provides Apple events and Balloon Help. The SAM antivirus programs can be configured to suit your particular situation and provide macro capabilities for a number of tasks. The SAM Intercept Jr. program enables you to have virus protection on computers with limited memory or disk space. SAM can slow

down your system startup and application launches; sometimes it gives too many alerts for suspicious activities. Even so, it is effective and complete.

Tesserae 1.04

Publisher: Inline Design; 308 Main St.; Lakeville, CT 06039; (203) 435-4995; (800) 453-7671

System Requirements: Macintosh Plus or greater; System-7-compatible; automatically configures itself to match the color capabilities of your computer

Documentation: All documentation is online, with interactive instructions.

Suggested Retail Price: $49.95

The Program

This clever strategy game requires you to clear the game board of colored tiles by jumping one over another in as few moves as possible. The color of the tiles is important to play; it governs which tiles you can jump, and where you can land after jumping. The primary tiles are red, yellow, or blue; secondary tiles such as orange and green are blends of primary colors; and tertiary tiles are gray. (In the black-and-white mode, the tiles are differentiated by pattern.) One hint is to make sure there are no stranded tiles left on the board.

TETRIS

Publisher: Spectrum Holobyte (A Division of Sphere, Inc.); 2061 Challenger Drive; Alameda, CA 94501; (415) 522-3584

System Requirements: Macintosh; 512K RAM; floppy disk drive; (Mac II version requires 256-color capability)

Other Platforms (not reviewed): IBM PC or compatible; Apple IIGS; Amiga; Atari ST; Commodore 64

Documentation: The small booklet is adequate for loading or installing the program; the strategy you must figure out yourself.

Support: Customer support is available by writing to the company or calling its technical support telephone number, (510) 522-1164 on weekdays from 9:00 a.m. to 5:00 p.m. Pacific Time.

Suggested Retail Price: $39.95

The Program

This game is a fast-action puzzle requiring quick eye-to-hand coordination. Play takes place in a "pit," which is actually a box on the screen. Geometric shapes, each made up of four blocks in different patterns, drop toward the pit. You must flip, rotate, and scoot the blocks so they settle into empty spaces and form solid lines. A completed line, or layer, disappears from the screen, allowing more room to maneuver incoming pieces more easily. After you complete a certain number of layers, you advance to the next level, in which the pieces fall faster. You get points each time a piece settles into a line, with extra points for positioning your piece quickly and more points for completing a layer. When your pieces reach the top of the pit, the game ends.

Folk music plays while the pieces descend, with different tunes for different rates of speed. You can turn the sound off, if you wish, and choose other options as well. For example, you can engage a preview mode called Next that lets you see the next shape and plan for it. Using the Next option reduces your score, however. There are ten levels, but you can speed up play by toggling on the advance mode. You can also choose among five different heights from which to begin. A tournament mode enters the scores of up to six players, and includes a time option for limiting the maximum length of time each player's game can last.

This company also produces Super Tetris for Windows and Super Tetrix for Macintosh; play is slightly different, but just as maddening. Other games include WellTris (a similar game in three dimensions), Faces (you form complete faces from face parts), and WordTris (you create words from letters falling on the screen).

Thinkin' Things 1.0 (Ages 4 to 8)

Publisher: Edmark Corporation; 6727 185th Ave. NE; P.O. Box 3218; Redmond, WA 98073-3218; (206) 556-8484; (800) 426-0856; fax (206) 556-8998

System Requirements: Macintosh Plus or greater; hard disk drive; System 6.0.7 or later.

Curriculum Areas: The program helps develop memory, critical thinking, and problem-solving skills. It also encourages creativity.

Documentation: The manual is short, well organized, and well illustrated; it provides suggestions for activities that the parent can do with children to reinforce the skills learned.

Support: An adult's section on-screen explains the skills being taught, and gives suggestions for activities that reinforce learning. Call the company if you have technical questions.

Suggested Retail Price: $59.95

The Program

This high-rated program has six learning activities that help children develop thinking skills. In Oranga Banga, an orangutan with a drum set challenges children to develop auditory and visual discrimination and memory. In the Fripple Shop, children help a series of comical customers select Fripples with specific characteristics such as curly hair or purple stripes. Children learn to use Boolean logic relationships (AND, OR, and NOT). Feathered Friends enables children to create birds with the right characteristics to finish a series. Children improvise musical patterns in Toony Loon, using some unusual xylophones. Each of these activities has a Create mode and a Question & Answer mode (in which the program adjusts the level of difficulty automatically).

Children develop spatial awareness while they select shapes and set them into motion in the two remaining activities, Flying Spheres and Flying Shapes. Ideally, Thinkin' Things promotes thinking skills and entertains at the same time.

Thunder 7 1.5.3

Publisher: Baseline Publishing; (901) 682-9676

System Requirements: Macintosh Plus; 1MB RAM; hard disk drive

Suggested Retail Price: $99.95

The Program

Thunder is a stand-alone spelling-checker-and-thesaurus program that interactively monitors your keystrokes (no matter what application you are using) and alerts you to possible errors as you are keying. In this interactive mode, you are given the option to accept the program's suggestion of override it for a choice of your own. Multiple dictionaries are available; you can add unknown words to any dictionary you choose to use. The program expands any shorthand abbreviation you key into the full word or phrase, as long as you have previously keyed it into the glossary. You can analyze text for reading

level—as well as number of characters, words, syllables, sentences and paragraphs—with the Statistics option. The 40,000-word thesaurus includes definitions, synonyms, and antonyms; it also specifies compared, related, and contrasted words.

Time Treks

Publisher: Earthquest Inc. (distributed by Davidson and Associates, Inc.); 125 University Avenue; Palo Alto, CA 94301; (415) 321- 5838

System Requirements: Macintosh Plus/Classic, SE, Se/30, LC, II series; 2MB recommended; System 6.0.5 or later; System 7-compatible; hard disk drive

Suggested: When using this game with System 7, you should have at least 2.5MB of RAM for smooth and complete operation of the program.

Other Platforms (not reviewed): IBM PC/Tandy or compatible

Documentation: The manual provides enough information to install and play the game, but you may need to pick up some of the more puzzling aspects of the game by trial and error.

Suggested Retail Price: $59.95

The Program

A brilliant archaeologist develops a Time Machine for probing the past. Unfortunately, in doing so, he has allowed several ruthless tyrants from the past to escape into the present. It is your job to put the tyrants behind bars. The game consists of a board of 30 time doors, each of which is covered by a Time Tile. You must gain control of at least 16 of these time doors to put a tyrant in jail. To control a door, you must complete the challenge that the Time Tile presents. Some of the more difficult challenges provide an opportunity for you to close more than one door at once. There are a number of puzzles, quizzes, matching games, and—yes—boobytraps. As you control one set of time doors, you progress to the next level, where another tyrant is on the loose.

There are two sources for answers to the history questions. One is the Archives—a time line broken down into 176 pieces that display dates for events, inventions, and other world topics. The other is a Themes section that categorizes historical facts into topics such as wars, religion, science, continents, time, and communications. Thus, you can explore history by century or by topic. Each challenge is timed; as you progress to higher levels, the time decreases. If you have forgotten much of your history, you should browse through the Archives before playing, to pick up information that will help you play faster. It is also helpful to know exactly what is covered under each of the Themes.

While playing the game, keep a piece of paper handy so you can jot down a word or two about each question—because once you travel to the Archives or some other aspect of the game, the question disappears. The program provides valuable experience in using and reading a time line. Once you have played the game a time or two, you become familiar with some of the more eccentric features of the program.

Timeslips III

Publisher: Timeslips Corp.; (508) 768-6100, (800) 285-0999

System Requirements: Macintosh; 1MB RAM

Suggested Retail Price: $299.95

The Program

Timeslips is a complete timekeeping-and-billing package. The desk accessory, TS Timer, allows you to easily enter time and job information. The report feature extracts information, and can generate invoices and reports in a wide variety of formats. Timeslips can handle 3,000 clients and 128 jobs per client. The program is designed with the freelancer in mind.

Tony LaRussa's Ultimate Baseball

Publisher: Strategic Simulations, Inc., distributed by Electronic Arts; 1820 Gateway Drive; San Mateo, CA 94404; (800) 245-4525; (408) 737-6800

System Requirements: IBM PC or compatible, floppy disk drive

Other Platforms (not reviewed): Macintosh

Documentation: The documentation is easy to understand and the program is easy to install.

Suggested Retail Price: $49.95

The Program

Good graphics, realistic action, and fluid animation characterize this baseball computer program. As you play, you'll see the players pitching, sliding into base, diving for the ball, and reaching up for spectacular catches. The simulation is excellent, but allows a split-second delay after a hit, so that the defenses can register the hit. The game makes the ball's flight path genuinely random. The various ball parks included have different fence distances, wind conditions, and turf.

The game lets you manage the game and concentrate on statistics and strategy (such as defensive assignments, pitching rotations, batting lineup, and signal-calling). You make your decisions through pop-up menus and bull-pen screens. For a real challenge, you can let the computer play and manage the opposing team, or you can play against a real person.

Treasure Cove! (Ages 5 to 9)

Publisher: The Learning Company; 6493 Kaiser Drive; Fremont, CA 94555; (800) 852-2255; (510) 792-2101

System Requirements: IBM PC or compatible, with a 25MHz 386 or better microprocessor; 1MB RAM; DOS 5.0 or higher; double-speed CD-ROM drive; 100K free hard disk space; 256-color VGA; Sound Blaster or compatible sound card

Suggested: Mouse; Windows 3.1, running in Standard or 386 Enhanced mode

Curriculum Areas: Children learn reading, math, and thinking skills involved in reasoning and drawing conclusions. Arithmetic skills involve addition, subtraction, multiplication, division, and numerical reasoning.

Documentation: The disc case contains a folder explaining requirements, starting the program, and troubleshooting problems for both platforms. A User's Guide explains the program in detail.

Support: If you need help after checking the User's Guide and the troubleshooting sections, you can call the company 800 number or the regular telephone number.

Suggested Retail Price: $59.95

The Program

Another Super Solvers and Master of Mischief program, this game requires students to stop the Master of Mischief from polluting Treasure Cove. The

Puzzler games help you earn clues. They ask questions from among more than 300 riddles that can be read or heard through the voice option. As you accumulate clues, you can look for sea animals that answer the clues. If you select the correct animal, you'll find a gem or a puffer fish. Use the puffer fish to stuff the Goobie hole in each area of Treasure Cove, and return the gems to the elves on the mainland. You have completed the game when the elves have enough gems to rebuild the bridge across the cove.

This game increases in difficulty as you progress through it. Spoken messages, hints, and feedback help beginning players and non-readers. The game is typical of The Learning Company's games: fun, educational, and challenging.

Treasure MathStorm! (Ages 5 to 9)

Publisher: The Learning Company; 6493 Kaiser Drive; Fremont, CA 94555; (800) 852-2255; (510) 792-2101

System Requirements: For Macintosh: Macintosh with System 7 or later; color monitor; double-speed CD-ROM drive; 4MB RAM

For IBM PCs and compatibles: 25-MHz 386 or better; 256-color SVGA or 16-color VGA; double-speed CD-ROM drive; 4MB RAM; Windows 3.1 or later; Windows-compatible sound card (mouse optional)

Curriculum Areas: Children learn math concepts, including addition, subtraction, multiplication, telling time, making change, counting, equality, and pattern recognition. Children also learn strategy as they plan a course through the game.

Documentation: The disc case contains a folder explaining requirements, starting the program, and troubleshooting problems for both platforms. A User's Guide explains the program in detail.

Support: If you need help after checking the User's Guide and the troubleshooting sections, you can call the company's 800 number or the regular telephone number.

Suggested Retail Price: $59.95

The Program

This math-learning program is based on a story of the Master of Mischief. You must foil his plan to steal the crown by collecting treasures and filling up the treasure chest. Activities include the Store (you learn to count money), the

Time Igloo (you learn to read time on a dial clock), the Gold Room (you solve equations by moving weights on a scale), and the Crystal Cave (you learn groupings of ones, tens, and hundreds). As you solve problems, you collect items that are useful in moving through the game. As you progress through the game, the game increases in difficulty. The difficulty levels of each game can be reset through the Customization menu. This game includes a perky little mountain tune, and is fun to play.

The Treehouse (Ages 6 to 10)

Publisher: Broderbund Software, Inc.; 500 Redwood Boulevard; P.O. Box 6121; Novato, CA 94948-6121; (415) 382-4400; (800) 521-6263

System Requirements: IBM PC or compatible with 640K RAM; 3MB hard disk drive; EGA display or better; DOS 3.0 or higher; floppy disk drive

Suggested: Mouse recommended; supports Tandy Digital sound, Sound Blaster, Disney Sound Source, IBM PC PS/1 Sound Card

Other Platforms (not reviewed): Macintosh

Curriculum Areas: This program is a variation of The Playroom for older children. It introduces math, science, music, and writing.

Documentation: There are two clearly-written guides, a program guide, and an activity guide for reinforcement. Some of the activities include building your own musical instrument and going outside to learn about animals.

Suggested Retail Price: $59.95

The Program

In The Treehouse, you choose either the boy or the girl "awesome possum" as your electronic playmate; you'll see the possum family picture, a blackboard, a radio, a synthesizer, toys, and more. There are activities for everything you can click on. You can explore a music maze and a music synthesizer, and compose your own songs. The program also offers 24 melodies, including "Clementine," "Camptown Races," and the "Russian Dance" from *The Nutcracker Suite* by Tchaikovsky. You can also choose from a variety of instruments and sounds. An included audio cassette has a child's tour of the symphony (The Rhapsody in Rap), which can just as easily appeal to adults. In the theater, you can create scripts that come to life—and choose the characters to act them. A road-rally game teaches coin values. The Animal Album consists of over 90 animals common to North America. All these activities have attractive graphics, sound, and topics.

TRUMP CASTLE 3

Publisher: IntraCorp, Inc./Capstone Software; 7200 NW 19th Street, Ste. 500; Miami, FL 33126; (800) 468-7226; (305) 591-5900; fax (305) 591-5633; BBS (305) 471-8962

System Requirements: IBM PC or compatible with an 80386 or better microprocessor; 640K RAM; 12MB free hard disk space; DOS 5.0 or later; CD-ROM drive; EGA or greater graphics; Sound Blaster or compatible sound card; speaker

Suggested: Double-speed CD-ROM and memory manager recommended; mouse optional; boot disk

Documentation: The user's manual explains the setup, the interface, the games, and methods for playing over networks or modems.

Support: Online help is available for the how-tos of playing the games. Registered owners can call Customer Support on weekdays between 10:00 a.m. and 6:00 p.m. Eastern Time. A bulletin board is available 24 hours a day for questions, upgrades, and other company information.

Suggested Retail Price: $59.95

THE PROGRAM

Trump Castle 3 offers casino-gambling simulations for blackjack, roulette, Baccarat, Keno, craps, slot machines, four types of poker (5-card draw, 5- and 7-card stud, and Texas Hold'em), as well as video poker. (Keno is available only in VGA or SVGA.)

The interface includes an option bar and menus. You begin your stay at Trump Castle in the lobby, from which you travel to the game you want to play. The Options Menu allows you to select sound, music, PopUps (asking whether you want to play Keno), game animations, characters, Save Game, Load Game (to load a previously-saved game), and Play Editor (which lets you create a unique face for each player). The options bar lets you load a player, create a new player, exit the Player Editor, get help, remove a player, delete a player, and so on. An ATM machine lets you get cash. Options are available for playing over a network or via modem. The program is fun for anyone who enjoys casino-type games.

Typing 101

Publisher: Parsons Technology, Inc.; One Parsons Drive; P.O. Box 100; Hiawatha, IA 52233-0100; (319) 395-9626

System Requirements: IBM PC or 100 percent compatible; 128K RAM free space; monochrome or 80-column color monitor; DOS 2.11 or higher

Suggested: Hard disk drive, printer

Documentation: The documentation contains a good introduction, with well-laid-out pages and easy reading.

Support: Technical support is available on weekdays from 8:30 a.m. to 9:00 p.m. and on Saturday from 9:00 a.m. to 1:00 p.m. Central Standard Time. Fax support is also available.

Suggested Retail Price: $49

The Program

If you need to learn how to type or use the numeric keypad, this program can help you. It teaches typing basics for beginners, and offers typing-improvement techniques for those who are already touch-typists (or for those who need practice primarily on the numbers and symbols). You can set it for QWERTY or Dvorak versions of the keyboard. One program option lets you set learning goals in hours per week and words per minute. The program offers a great deal of variety in practice, so there is little chance for boredom.

This menu-driven program helps you build speed, and gives you a chance to analyze feedback on your performance. It includes Letter Blaster, an arcade-style video game that reinforces accuracy. There is an Instructor mode for teaching others, so the program is usable in schools, at home, or in offices. As an instructor, you can use the program's lessons and tests, or customize lessons and tests to a specific field such as law, science, or medicine. The program provides progress reports in accuracy and speed.

Typing 101 is geared to the adult student. Children might enjoy the program Mavis Beacon Teaches Typing, which incorporates interesting graphics, text, and a few arcade-style exercises. The Mavis Beacon program comes from Mindscape, Inc.; 60 Leveroni Court; Novato, CA 94949; (800) 234-3088. It costs $44.95, and is available for IBM, Apple II, and Macintosh platforms.

Universal SoftPC

Publisher: Insignia Solutions, Inc.; 1300 Charleston Road; Mountain View, CA 94043; (415) 694-7600; (800) 848-7677; fax (415) 694-5434

System Requirements: Mac Plus or greater; 2MB RAM under System 6 and 4MB under System 7; hard disk drive; 3.5-inch floppy drive; System and Finder 6.0 or later

Suggested: SuperDrive floppy disk drive

Documentation: Documentation for this program is readable and understandable. The notes and exceptions are marked clearly in the margins; screen dumps help explain what you should be seeing on the screen. The printing job is not crisp, however, making the words hard to read.

Support: If you have questions and are a registered user, you can call the company's "hot lines" from 8:00 a.m. to 5:00 p.m. Pacific Standard Time. As a registered user, you will receive notices of future releases.

Suggested Retail Price: $165

The Program

Universal SoftPC emulates an IBM PC/AT, and is best used when you are working with text and limited graphics programs. It basically enables you to run off-the-shelf and customized MS-DOS programs on your Mac. Copying, pasting, and printing from PC programs is supported. SoftPC also allows you to set up protocols and cables to enable your Mac's hard disks, floppy disks, CD-ROMs, mouse, serial ports, and printer port to emulate PC peripherals. The SlavePC utility allows SoftPC to access and use a floppy disk drive mounted on a PC connected to your Macintosh via a null-modem cable. (SlavePC is quite slow, however, and is not recommended for everyday use.)

Other SoftPC products include SoftPC 3.1 with Windows, an accelerated version of the original SoftPC that includes Windows 3.1 installed and ready to run (requires a Quadra or equivalent 68040 CPU, 12MB RAM, SuperDrive, and System 6.0.7 or later). A networking product, SoftPC 3.1 Professional, is designed to run DOS and NetWare applications with VGA graphics on high-performance Macs (68020 or greater with 8MB RAM, SuperDrive, and System 6.0 or later). SoftPC Professional provides access to LAN manager, Windows for Workgroups, and UNIX file servers; it integrates with all Macintosh peripherals.

UNTOUCHABLE DOS

Publisher: Fifth Generation Systems, Inc.; 10049 N. Reiger Road; Baton Rouge, LA 70809; (504) 291-7221; (800) 873-4384

System Requirements: IBM PC, XT, AT, PS/2 and compatibles; 512K RAM; hard disk drive, one floppy disk drive needed for installation; DOS 3.0 or higher

Suggested: Mouse (compatible with Microsoft and Logitech mice)

Documentation: The Quick Start Card contains directions for installation. The user's manual is well organized, but needs more illustrations. It includes a section about customizing the setup, a reference section, and a description of common PC viruses.

Support: The company offers 24-hour, toll-free support (800) 766-7283. Updates are available quarterly for $15.

Suggested Retail Price: $99

THE PROGRAM

This program is advertised as giving you 100-percent protection against known and unknown viruses. It recognizes over 1,000 known viruses, and protects itself against infection. It guarantees 100-percent recovery of any file it decides to repair, and also eliminates false alarms. It does require periodic updating to thwart certain types of viruses. Untouchable detected or intercepted a virus in all but a very few instances—but you should still perform regular backups and use common sense.

VENTURA PUBLISHER: 5

Publisher: Corel Systems Corporation; The Corel Building; 1600 Carling Avenue; Ottawa, Ontario, Canada K1Z8R7; (800) 772-6735.

System Requirements: IBM PC or compatible, with 286 or better microprocessor; 640K RAM plus 256K for Professional Extension (note that Windows alone requires a great deal of RAM); floppy disk drive; hard disk drive with 10MB free space; graphics monitor; Windows 3.0; printer

Suggested: 386 strongly recommended; 40MB free disk space on hard disk drive; mouse

Other Platforms (not reviewed): IBM PC or compatible with DOS 3.1 or higher; Macintosh; OS/2

Documentation: The manual is extensive and thorough. Included is a spiral-bound Training Guide, complete with 12 lessons to give hands-on instruction. Additional documentation includes a Quick Reference Guide; in the extensive Reference Guide, all program features are organized according to the menu hierarchy.

Support: Free technical support for the first 30 days. After that, on-demand technical support at $15 per call.

Suggested Retail Price: $795

The Program

This program does almost everything a desktop publishing package should do. It has the usual DTP features, plus it handles long technical documents (over 100 pages); you can break them into chapters but print them as a whole. You can develop huge style sheets for global application—that is, to the entire document. Ventura Publisher: now includes the company's Professional Extension (previously an expensive add-on) for indexing, handling long documents, and other specialized tasks. The program runs on the slowest of machines, too.

Ventura controls type precisely, indicating that the leading and kerning options are very good. Modifying fonts is easier than in the DOS version. It has excellent table-creating tools and many comprehensive style sheets. It works with a wide variety of word processing and graphics programs, but does not have its own spelling checker or search-and-replace option. Designed mainly for intensive and detailed work, it is an excellent program when you are using lots of technical tables and complicated illustrations in your document. Casual users will probably be deferred from purchasing it because of its high cost.

Virex 5.0

Publisher: Datawatch Corporation; Triangle Software Division; P.O.Box 13984; Research Triangle Park, NC 27709; (919) 549-0711; fax(919) 549-0065

System Requirements: Any Mac except the Macintosh 512; System 6.0.5 or later; System 7-compatible

Suggested: Compatible with MultiFinder, A/UX 2.0, A/UX 3.0, AppleShare, and most networking software

Documentation: The manual is simple and straightforward.

Support: Technical support is available by writing or calling Datawatch. Registered users of Virex receive their first upgrade free of charge, and also receive notification of new viruses and program updates. Datawatch also offers an annual Subscription Service ($75) that entitles users to viral and feature-enhancement updates as they become available. In the past two years, Virex is averaging six updates to the program per year, making the service well worth its cost.

Suggested Retail Price: $99.95

THE PROGRAM

A comprehensive anti-virus software program, Virex offers prevention, detection, and treatment of all known viruses. The SpeedScan feature makes Virex the fastest virus protection available. You can customize Virex operating procedures by selecting certain options through the control panel. Password protection is provided by Virex; you can prevent anyone from altering any changes you have made to the program settings.

Virex also has an Expert mode that includes features to help you detect the presence of an unknown virus. By periodically running the Record/Scan feature and comparing previous reports, you will be able to detect any unusual changes that might indicate the presence of an unknown virus. If you suspect an unknown virus is present on your computer, Virex would like to hear about it. Write or call them, using the phone number and address shown.

VOCABULEARN/CE SPANISH 2.0

Publisher: Penton Overseas, Inc.; 2091 Las Palmas Drive, Suite A; Carlsbad, CA 92009-1519; (619) 431-0060; (800) 748-5804; fax (619) 431-8110

System Requirements: Macintosh Plus, Se, II, or any Mac capable of supporting HyperCard; hard disk drive; HyperCard 2.1 (enclosed); System 6.0.5 or later.

Other Platforms (not reviewed): IBM PC or compatible; Windows version available

Curriculum Areas: This program helps you review foreign-language vocabulary.

Documentation: The documentation includes a vocabulary-list booklet and directions for using the program. New directions for installation on a hard disk drive were printed in an enclosure, rather than in the actual program manual.

Support: The program package includes two language tapes (90-minute stereo cassettes) you can use to improve your pronunciation and oral recognition of words.

Suggested Retail Price: $59.95

The Program

This program most resembles a set of foreign-language flashcards that you use for vocabulary drill. You have a number of options while using the program. For example, you can display or hide the answers, type answers, review the vocabulary, select a scan (or flash) rate, or add to (or otherwise modify) the existing list of words. You can also take a test of the words you think you know.

The program is basic drill, with no entertaining presentation or unusual features. It will not help you use the words in context or with correct grammar. Although it did not install as expected according to the new directions (included separately with the package), it was possible to access and use the program. The program is available in Italian, Japanese, Hebrew, French, German, and Russian.

What's My Angle? (Ages 14 to Adult)

Publisher: Davidson & Associates, Inc.; P.O. Box 2961; 19840 Pioneer Ave.; Torrance, CA 90509; (310) 793-0600; (800) 545-7677; fax (310) 793-0601

System Requirements: IBM PC/Tandy or compatible; CGA graphics or better; 512K RAM (Tandy graphics requires 640K); DOS 2.1 or later; 3.5-inch or 5.25-inch floppy disk drive

Suggested: Can be installed on a hard disk; supports Ad Lib and Sound Blaster sound cards; printer and mouse are optional

Curriculum Areas: This program helps a student learn geometry fundamentals.

Documentation: The manual contains a quick-start summary inside the front cover, as well as descriptions of the objectives and skills to be mastered in each activity, teaching tips for reinforcement, and instructions for using the program with each platform. The steps are clearly outlined and the menu options are listed. The manual also includes a troubleshooting guide and an index.

Support: There are hints and on-screen help for this program. For answers to technical questions, you can call customer service at an 800 number on weekdays.

Suggested Retail Price: $49.95

The Program

Students learn geometry skills through five separate activities. The first, GeoBoard, teaches fundamental concepts and lets students explore patterns. In GeoLife, students use geometry to solve everyday problems for characters such as Rosa the Rock Star (she needs to position lights for a concert), Changle the Carpenter, and Yvonne the Inventor. GeoConclusion enables students to practice proof and problem-solving skills. Students must unscramble the steps in mixed-up proofs in the section called GeoProofs. In GeoGolf, students use geometry skills to play a miniature-golf game. There are 60 possible holes, from which the program selects 18 at random.

Pull-down menus make the program easy to navigate. Students can keep records of their progress—and look up words in a glossary of 150 terms—while using the activities. The program displays the correct answer if students do not answer correctly after two tries. The activities are varied and challenging, and are designed to cover a year's worth of geometry.

Where in the World Is Carmen Sandiego? (Ages 8 and up)

Publisher: Broderbund Software, Inc.; 500 Redwood Boulevard; P.O. Box 6121; Novato, CA 94948-6121; (415) 382-4400; (800) 521-6263

System Requirements: IBM PC/Tandy or compatible; floppy disk drive

Suggested: Sound card; color monitor

Other Platforms (not reviewed): Macintosh and Apple II series (A deluxe edition for IBM PC computers includes graphics of the locations that look very much like photographs. The pictures were digitized from National Geographic Society slides.)

Curriculum Areas: This program can help develop reference skills and problem-solving strategies. It also develops awareness of different countries, cultures, and currencies, all of which might be studied in a geography class.

Documentation: The included manual is written well, but informally.

Suggested Retail Price: $49.95 (Apple II, $44.95)

The Program

This program sends the detective (you, the player) throughout the world to find the international thief, Carmen Sandiego and her gang. The criminals are stealing priceless national treasures such as the Statue of Liberty's torch. Each game has at least 10 agents; the clues and locations are randomly generated, thereby creating great variety. The clues involve geography and knowledge about the culture, money, and buildings of foreign countries. You must figure out the clues, figure out which routes to take, and identify the criminal in order to issue a warrant for arrest. You conduct interviews, use reference works, and take notes in order to find where you should look next. The game includes an almanac you can use to look up what the clues mean, but often as soon as you find out where to look next, the thief or her gang have moved on.

There are three levels of difficulty, and a time limit in which to operate. Children may eventually learn to track a criminal in a half hour. The program is complete with mysterious music and trench-coated figures. It is not violent—there are no injuries or blood—but playful and humorous. You can save a game in progress for continuing later. One problem with the program is that in this ever-changing world, a fact or two may go out of date.

There are other games in the series: Where in Europe Is Carmen Sandiego?, Where in the USA Is Carmen Sandiego?, Where in America's Past Is Carmen Sandiego?, and Where in Time Is Carmen Sandiego? All include a paperback resource book such as *The World Almanac* (with Where in the World...?) or *The New American Desk Encyclopedia* (with Where in Time...?) so you can find out what the clues mean. Books are useful on their own, too. The latter two Carmen Sandiego adventures are recommended for ages 12 and up.

White Knight 12.0

Publisher: The FreeSoft Company; 105 McKinley Road; Beaver Falls, PA 15010; (412) 846-2700; fax (412) 847-4436

System Requirements: Macintosh Plus; SE; II; or greater with 1MB memory; modem

Documentation: The documentation is geared to all levels of experience, and includes plenty of options for experienced users. It is a specific and complete manual, although informal in style and design. It clearly signals notes of interest, very important information, and warnings. One big plus: It shows examples of actual communications.

Support: The documentation contains tutorials and step-by-step instructions for beginners. Technical support is also available to registered users from 1:00 p.m. through 5:00 p.m., Eastern Time.

Suggested Retail Price: $139

The Program

This highly-recommended telecommunications program is user-friendly and flexible, but you must read and study the manual before beginning to use the program. It has but a single application window and a large array of menus and submenus. The program will work in background in MultiFinder. The package also includes Okyto, a Mac-to-Mac file transfer program to use with modems or AppleTalk. Without this program, file transfer requires a variety of protocol settings, modem commands, file-transfer protocols, and repetition of said items for each file transferred.

The package has a rich set of error-correcting protocols and performs terminal emulation of TTY, VT52, VT100, and VT102, with fast speed for connecting to other microcomputers, minicomputers, mainframes, time-sharing networks, laboratory equipment, bulletin board systems, and so on. It works with all modems and direct connections, supports a wide range of modem speeds, and supports all printers.

A number of features make the program easy and flexible to use. For example, you can define macros and use a powerful procedure (or scripting) language that can fully automate your communication sessions. There is also a feature called Write A Procedure For Me that watches what you do and automatically writes a procedure that matches your actions. Other features include password protection, dialing and phone-book features, text editing, and a buffered keyboard option you can use to create up to 32,000 characters before sending. An on-screen meter displays time and money spent during a communications session so you can match your work to your budget.

Willmaker 5.0

Publisher: Nolo Press; (800) 992-6656; (510) 549-1976

System Requirements: Macintosh Plus, 1MB RAM

Suggested Retail Price: $69.95

The Program

This program quickly and easily creates a will for you by asking you a designated set of questions that you respond to by using the keyboard. The accompanying manual is cross-referenced to the help screens, and is very helpful. The program also helps you prepare legal documents regarding health care and final arrangements. Final documents are legal in all states except Louisiana.

Windows Draw 3.0

Publisher: Micrografx, Inc.; 1303 Arapaho Road; Richardson, TX 75081; (214) 234-1769; (800) 733-3729 ex. 5050

System Requirements: IBM PC or compatible; 80286 or better microprocessor; 1MB RAM; EGA, VGA, 8514/A or other graphics supporting Windows 3.0; 20MB hard disk drive; floppy disk drive; pointing device; Windows 3.0 or higher; DOS 3.1 or higher

Suggested: 80386 or better microprocessor; 2MB RAM; 40MB hard disk drive

Documentation: The documentation is adequate, although some areas—such as working with curves—could include more information.

Support: A tutorial is included, and there are on-screen hints. Twenty-four hour technical support is available on weekdays, with limited hours on weekends.

Suggested Retail Price: $149.95

The Program

This program is a draw program with vector graphics. Installation is easy, and the program is easy to use. Windows Draw offers good color palettes and a large selection of tools. (The toolbar also contains the color palettes.) There are tools for pointing, drawing, entering text, viewing, and coloring. A ribbon area shows the options for a particular tool. A fill can be a gradient, a bit-map pattern, or a vector pattern. A blend option lets you blend from one object to another in the number of steps you specify. You can flow text to follow any contour or curve.

This is a large package—the entire program takes up 17MB of hard-disk space. (Much of the space is clip art.) The program supports Adobe Type Manager, and can import and export in almost every format. The program is slow with Windows, however. It can't print color separations or do autotrace (that is, trace bitmaps into vector items), and it is not suited for complicated technical drawing. If you have no need to perform these tasks, the program is well worth considering for its flexibility, ease of use, and large collection of clip art.

WingZ for Windows 3.0 and OS/2

Publisher: Informix Software; 4100 Bohannon Drive; Menlo Park, CA 94025; (415) 926-6300, (800) 331-1763

System Requirements: (for Windows) IBM PC or compatible, with an 80286 or better microprocessor; 2MB RAM minimum; 2.7MB hard-disk space; 5.25-inch or 3.5-inch floppy disk drive for installing; VGA, EGA, or 8514/A monitor; Windows 3.0 or higher; DOS 3.1 or higher

Suggested: 3MB or more RAM, Intel math co-processor, mouse

Other Platforms (not reviewed): Macintosh

Documentation: Documentation for this program is extensive. There are four separate guides: Installation Guide, User's Guide, HyperScript Manual, and Reference Manual. All are well organized, with the material explained adequately; the manual on HyperScript is extensive. The Reference Manual explains the WingZ options and specifications in a definition format. The User's Guide is basically a tutorial, but not all operations are covered in the Reference Manual. After you've read everything, you can use the Quick Reference Card to remind you of the common operations.

Support: One disk contains a Test Flight program that demonstrates WingZ. For answers to technical questions, you can call the company's technical support line, where the technicians are friendly and well informed.

Suggested Retail Price: $399

The Program

WingZ has the normal spreadsheet options, plus a broad range of advanced financial and mathematical functions and a mini word processing module. It has over 140 built-in functions, plus linking and auditing capabilities. You can open multiple worksheets and import worksheet files. The program also supports Windows Dynamic Data Exchange (DDE) to transfer data between WingZ and other applications. Within the program, you can also assign passwords to secure your data and files.

The program has excellent integration capabilities: You can integrate object-oriented graphics and word processing areas on your spreadsheet. That is, reports can contain words, numbers, charts, and pictures. The charting options include bar charts, pie charts, exploding pie charts, 3-D charts, and combination charts. The user interface consists of a menu bar with pull-down menus, dialog boxes, and a Tool Box. You can manipulate any object (chart, text field, graphic image, or button) to change its size, color, pattern, or border. You can move, copy, stack, group, and lock objects, or you can remove or hide any object. The drawing tools in this program have the power of a basic draw program.

When you are investigating spreadsheet programs, consider this one for its great graphics capabilities—and the best macro system for building custom applications.

Word Attack 3 (Ages 10 to Adult)

Publisher: Davidson & Associates, Inc.; P.O. Box 2961; 19840 Pioneer Ave.; Torrance, CA 90509; (310) 793-0600; (800) 545-7677; (800) 556-6141; fax (310) 793-0601

System Requirements: IBM PC or compatible with a 12MHz 286 or better microprocessor; DOS 3.3 or higher; 550K RAM; 5MB free hard disk space; VGA card; can run from Windows icon

Suggested: Mouse, DOS 5.0, Sound Blaster or other sound card, printer

Other Platforms (not reviewed): Word Attack Plus for Apple

Curriculum Areas: This program helps students learn definitions, usage, spelling, and pronunciation of vocabulary in a number of entertaining ways.

Documentation: The manual is illustrated and easy to follow. It includes tips for parents and teachers and the word lists.

Support: The manual contains a troubleshooting appendix. Customer Support Technicians can be reached by telephone on weekdays from 7:00 a.m. to 6:00 p.m., by fax 24 hours every day, or by mail.

Suggested Retail Price: $49.95

THE PROGRAM

This vocabulary-building program teaches over 3,200 words in the several categories. By using the program, you can begin to master definitions, spellings, and pronunciations of new words. The five activities are the Presentation Activity (a scramble game that introduces new words, gives definitions, and shows a sentence with correct usage), the Tile Game (a timed game in which you clear stacks of tiles by matching them to correct definitions), the Crossword Puzzle (you can use existing puzzles or create your own), the Maze Game (a timed game for matching definitions and words), and the Hat Game (an arcade game in which you select the word that goes with a definition).

In Word Attack, you can keep records of your progress and enter your own word list. You can also adjust the pronunciations of words you add through the Editor, and select foreign language fonts for files containing Spanish, French, or German words. The program lets you print flash cards, word-search puzzles, and crossword puzzles.

WORDPERFECT FOR MACINTOSH 3.1

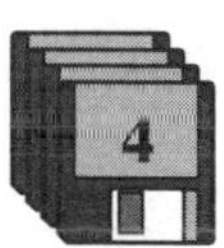

Publisher: WordPerfect, The Novell Applications Group; 1555 N. Technology Way; Orem, UT 84057; (801) 225-5000; (800) 451-4151; fax (801) 228-5377

System Requirements: Macintosh with 68030 CPU or greater; 5MB RAM; hard disk drive; one 800K disk drive; System 7.0 or later; supports System 7 Pro

Suggested: Printer

Other Platforms (not reviewed): IBM PC or compatible; Windows version for IBM PCs

Documentation: Documentation for this program includes a workbook, with which you learn to use the features of the program, and a reference guide that is arranged alphabetically by topic. The manuals are clear and well designed, with screen dumps and other illustrations.

Support: WordPerfect includes online help and (for System 7 users) supports Balloon Help. If you need technical help, the company's technicians are friendly and knowledgeable, and are available by telephone on weekdays from 7:00 a.m. to 6:00 p.m. Mountain Time.

Suggested Retail Price: $495

The Program

WordPerfect is the most widely installed word processing package for personal computers in businesses today. The latest version competes well with Microsoft Word in ease of use and capabilities. WordPerfect has a highly customizable environment and an innovative interface. It includes context-sensitive button bars and seven expandable rulers.

The table features enables you to do basic calculations within the tables, and add colors and tints to parts of a table. The indexing and table of contents functions are very good, and the hyphenation options are superb. There is no glossary function, however, and the outliner function is weak. The program's macro capabilities are strong, and the program includes a library of macros.

With its many formatting and graphics features, WordPerfect is also a good alternative to desktop publishing packages. You may need to travel through several dialog boxes just to change a few style options, however, and the styles are all document-based, rather than character-based or section-based. There are no editing options in the print preview, and this mode is the only mode that displays headers, footers, and endnotes.

For System 7 users, WordPerfect has QuickTime support; it also enables you to use the publish-and-subscribe function. It includes the Grammatik 5.0 grammar checker, as well as a spelling checker and thesaurus. It implements System 7 features of Apple Open Collaboration Environment, including PowerTalk (the client portion of the mail-enabling system), AppleScript (a system-level scripting language), and World Script (for multiple-language documents).

For those of you with less powerful computers and less available money, the company markets a scaled-down version called LetterPerfect for Mac at $199. It lacks the more sophisticated features of WordPerfect (such as style sheets, sort function, macro editor, and QuickTime support). It can be used with System 7, and it can import graphics. It also offers a spelling checker, thesaurus, and mail merge.

Write Now 4.0.1

Publisher: WordStar International; 201 Broadway, Cambridge, MA 02139; (800) 227-5609; (617) 494-1200; fax (617) 494-1219

System Requirements: Macintosh; 512K RAM; hard disk drive; one 800K floppy disk drive; supports System 7

Suggested: Printer

Documentation: The user's manual is very readable.

Support: Online support is available.

Suggested Retail Price: $119.95

The Program

This low-end word processor is for anyone who will be creating straightforward correspondence, reports, and so on. It is very easy to learn, with a friendly interface and consistent performance. In its current form, the program runs quickly, requires little memory, and supports virtual memory in System 7. For these reasons, it is a good choice for use with the PowerBooks.

The program offers solid word processing features. These include spelling checker, thesaurus, word count, footnoting capability, mail merge, and style sheets. You can also create character style sheets for individual characters when you want to format technical terms or foreign expressions. A style sheet lists everything you specify. You see documents on the screen as they will print (including columns, headers and footers, and page edges). The print preview shows a single page, facing pages, or a thumbnail view that displays as many pages as will fit on the screen.

In WriteNow, you can open and save documents in a number of other word processing programs, including Microsoft Word 5.0, WordPerfect, and Microsoft Works. You can also import and position graphics, but they cannot be edited.

The Writing Center (ages 7 to adult)

Publisher: The Learning Company; 6493 Kaiser Drive; Fremont, CA 94555; (800) 852-2255; (510) 792-2101

System Requirements: Macintosh computer (excepting 128K and 512K Macs) with 1MB RAM; System 6.0.7 or greater; CD-ROM drive; 3.2MB available hard disk space

Suggested: Color monitor; printer

Curriculum Areas: Students can not only use this program to create a product, they can also learn how to write a report using the research guide.

Documentation: Manuals include the User's Guide as well as a number of flyers (installation instructions, Ready Reference Card, and picture reference sheets). The box also contains Getting It All Together, a guide to writing a good report. Both manuals are well organized, well written, and illustrated. The User's Guide contains quick references and an extensive index.

Support: The manual contains a troubleshooting guide. A school edition of the program is available. Help is also available through the Customer Service Department.

Suggested Retail Price: $89.95

The Program

This program is an easy-to-use word processing program with a low learning curve. In addition to writing, editing, and printing, the program contains color images for picture placement, as well as a spelling checker. You can use page-layout templates for reports, letters, newsletters, and flyers, or create a custom layout. You can resize, crop, rotate, or flip images. Pictures can span multiple columns. The program accepts PICT picture files and ASCII text files. The Writing Center has been especially designed for students, families, and social groups; a number of reviewers have rated it highly. Especially helpful to students is the enclosed guide to writing research papers.

This company also produces The Student Writing Center for Windows (ages 10 to adult) and The Children's Writing & Publishing Center (ages 7 to 14) for IBM PCs and compatibles, or for the Apple II series. Both are fine programs, but may seem a bit more "businesslike" than some of the "jazzier" word processors for children. They are product-oriented rather than process-oriented.

XTree Gold 2.5

Publisher: XTree Company; Executive Systems, Inc.; 4330 Santa Fe Road; San Luis Obispo, CA 93401; (800) 634-5545; (805) 541-0604

System Requirements: IBM PC, XT, AT, PS/2, or compatible; 256K RAM; VGA display required for 256-color images; EGA, CGA, and Hercules monitors also supported; DOS 3.1 or higher; supports Windows

Suggested: Mouse

Documentation: The manual gives an excellent overview of the package before going into details about operation and files.

Support: The package provides good online, context-sensitive help, but a tutorial would help beginners get acquainted with the system. You can get support through the company's technical support telephone number (you pay the toll call) or through the company's BBS. To receive technical support, you must give the serial number of the software you bought. The technical support line is open from 8:00 a.m. to 5:00 p.m. Pacific Standard Time on weekdays.

Suggested Retail Price: $129

THE PROGRAM

If you are frustrated with the DOS method of handling files and applications, this menu-driven program keeps your hard disk in order—and lets you launch up to 13 applications from its menu tree. This program also lets you predefine batch files that associate files with applications and cover the necessary DOS commands needed to launch an application by way of the file. In the AutoView mode, you can view files in split windows; for example, you can scroll through a list of file names on one side of a split screen while viewing the contents of the file on the other side.

The program lets you view files of many different types of file formats without starting the application. Other features include a "wash" command that eradicates any evidence of a deleted file, an undelete function that lets you get back a file you deleted, and a file-compression system for ZIP archives. You also can search for key words in the text of a file, use basic file functions such as Compare, Delete, Filespec, Rename, and Print, and also Prune and Graft especially for this program. A keystroke-history function lets you save the most recent search parameters for repeat execution. The program supports many file formats, and lets you manage directories. XTree Gold may take a while to get used to. The opening screen can be unnerving to the first-time user, with its many commands and different panels of information.

The XTree Company also produces a program called AllSafe v. 1.0 ($129) you can use especially with your portable computer. It provides password protection at either the system or the file level and for file encryption. A ViruSafe module recognizes over 480 known viruses in a number of different permutations. The minimum requirements are an IBM AT, PS/2, or compatible; 256K RAM, and DOS 3.0 or higher. Purchase of an XTree package automatically enrolls you in Global ReLeaf, an environmental organization, and a tree will be planted when you return your registration form.

Your Personal Trainer for the SAT 2.0

Publisher: Davidson & Associates, Inc.; P.O. Box 2961; 19840 Pioneer Ave.; Torrance, CA 90509; (310) 793-0600; (800) 545-7677; fax (310) 793-0601

System Requirements: Macintosh SE, Classic, LC, Performa, Centris, Quadra or Powerbook; 4MB RAM; System 7.0 or later; hard drive with 4.5MB of space available

Suggested: Printer optional

Other Platforms (not reviewed): The program is available for use IBM PC or compatible, using DOS 2.11 or higher, as well as using DeskMate, the Tandy graphical user interface.

Curriculum Areas: The program provides practice in all the areas tested in the SATs (Scholastic Aptitude Tests).

Documentation: Documentation consists of two manuals. One tells you how to run the program; the other gives you tips and strategies for taking the SATs, and provides sample tests for you to take and study. The manuals are well organized and clear. They give troubleshooting tips, and show how to customize the program in minor ways.

Support: There are online hints and an online glossary.

Suggested Retail Price: $59.95

The Program

This program is designed to score and analyze your performance on sample math and verbal tests designed like the SATs. Before you work with the sample tests, you should conduct the assessment activity, in which you take a practice SAT (or pretest); the program scores this test in order to arrive at your personal training schedule. Once you have finished the preliminaries, you use the test manual to take the sample tests, mark your answers on an online answer sheet, and let the computer score it and again list areas in which you need to improve. All practice is timed; to get the most benefit from the program, you should stay within the timing requirements.

Both the program and the manual give some strategies for taking the test; they show how the SAT is structured, administered, scored, and timed. They show you how to use your test booklet for writing and figuring out answers. Many of the test-taking tips and clues to watch for are excellent. The interface is easy to use, consisting mostly of menus, icons, and buttons. This program is in competition with several paper SAT guides that are less expensive, but the detailed online explanations of the answers and the listing of areas for improvement make this program unique among SAT self-help tools. The program also charts your progress with graphs.

Zoo Keeper (Ages 6 to Adult)

Publisher: Davidson & Associates, Inc.; P.O. Box 2961; 19840 Pioneer Ave.; Torrance, CA 90509; (310) 793-0600; (800) 545-7677; (800) 556-6141; fax (310) 793-0601

System Requirements: 256-color Macintosh with System 7.0 or higher; 4MB RAM; 10MB free hard disk space; floppy disk drive;

Other Platforms (not reviewed): IBM PC or compatible with DOS 3.3 or higher; 570K available RAM; 8MB free hard disk space; VGA card; mouse; sound card optional

Documentation: The manual is logically arranged and easy to read; both the DOS and Macintosh instructions are included.

Support: The manual contains a troubleshooting appendix. Customer Support Technicians can be reached by telephone on weekdays from 7:00 a.m. to 6:00 p.m., by fax 24 hours every day, or by mail.

Suggested Retail Price: $59.95

The Program

With Zoo Keeper, children will learn what animals look like, what they eat, where they live, and how they can be protected. The program contains real-life photographs and sounds, courtesy of *ZooLife* magazine and the *ZooLife With Jack Hanna* television show. The program requires you to take over operation of a zoo with the help of the zoo helpers. The task is not easy; a band of trouble-makers are feeding the animals the wrong foods, littering the habitats, and wrecking the plant life.

While playing this educational game, children will learn about zoos and their role in increasing animal populations in the world. They will also learn to follow directions, plan ahead, gather and analyze information, and learn from mistakes. Each new game has a new challenge. The game has received a number of awards, including Best Educational Product from *Computer Game Review* and the Innovations '93 Award from Consumer Electronics Show.

POPULAR HARDWARE COMPANIES

Acer America Corporation
401 Charcot Avenue
San Jose, CA 95131

Acer (Direct)
2641 Orchard Parkway
San Jose, CA 95134
(800) 239-2237
(408) 432-6200

Adobe Systems
1585 Charleston Road
P.O. Box 7900
Mountain View, CA 94039
(800) 833-6687
(415) 961-4400

Advanced Micro Devices
17777-D Main Street
Irvine, CA 92714
(800) 248-9099
(714) 261-7878

Advanced Vision Research, Inc.
2201 Qume Drive
San Jose, CA 95131
(408) 434-1115

Agfa Compugraphic
200 Ballardvale Street
Wilmington, MA 01887
(800) 288-4039
(508) 658-5600

Altima Systems, Inc.
1390 Willow Pass Road
Suite 1050
Concord, CA 94520
(800) 356-9990

Apple Computer, Inc.
20525 Mariani Avenue
Cupertino, CA 95014
(800) 776-2333
(408) 996-1010

Atari
1196 Borregas Avenue
Sunnyvale, CA 94089
(408) 745-2000

ATI Technologies
3761 Victoria Park Avenue
Scarborough, Ontario
Canada M1W 3S2
(416) 756-0718

AT&T Computer Systems
1700 South Patterson Boulevard
Dayton, OH 45479
(800) 225-5627

BASF Corporation
Information Systems
Crosby Drive
Bedford, MA 01730
(617) 271-4000

Bitstream, Inc.
Athenaeum House
215 First Street
Cambridge, MA 02142
(800) 237-3335
(617) 497-6222

Caere Corporation
100 Cooper Court
Los Gatos, CA 95030
(800) 535-7226
(408) 395-7000

Canon USA, Inc.
One Canon Plaza
Lake Success, NY 11042
(516) 328-5960

Cardinal Technologies, Inc.
1827 Freedom Road
Lancaster, PA 17601
(800) 233-0187
(717) 293-3000

Citizen America Corporation
2450 Broadway, Suite 600
Santa Monica, CA 90411-4003
(800) 477-4683
(310) 453-0614

CMS Enhancements, Inc.
2722 Michelson Drive
Irvine, CA 92714
(714) 222-6600

Colorado Memory Systems, Inc.
800 S. Taft Avenue
Loveland, CO 80537
(800) 346-9881
(303) 669-6500

Colorocs
2805 Peterson Place
P.O. Box 1828
Norcross, GA 30071
(404) 840-6500

Commodore Business Machines
International Ltd.
1200 Wilson Drive
West Chester, PA 19380
(215) 431-9100

Compaq Computer Corporation
20555 State Highway 249
Houston, TX 77070
(800) 231-0900
(713) 370-0670

The Complete PC
1983 Concourse Drive
San Jose, CA 95131
(800) 229-1753
(408) 434-0145

CompuAdd Computer Corp.
12303 Technology Boulevard
Austin, TX 78727
(800) 627-1967
(512) 219-1800

Connor Peripherals
3081 Zanker Road
San Jose, CA 95134
(408) 456-4500

Covox
675 Conger Street
Eugene, OR 97402
(503) 342-1271

Creative Labs
1901 McCarthy Boulevard
Milpitas, CA 95035
(800) 998-5227
(408) 428-6660

C-Tech Electronics
2701 Dow Avenue
P.O. Box 2098
Tustin, CA 92680
(800) 347-4017
(714) 833-1165

Curtis Manufacturing Co., Inc.
30 Fitzgerald Drive
Jaffrey, NH 03452-1931
(800) 955-5544
(603) 532-4123

Cyrix
2703 Central Expressway
Richardson, TX 75080
(214) 234-8387

Datadesk International, Inc.
9330 Eaton Avenue
Chatsworth, CA 91311
(800) 328-2337

Dell Computer Corporation
9505 Arboretum Boulevard
Austin, TX 78759-7299
(800) 426-5150
(512) 338-4400

Diamond Computer Systems, Inc.
532 Mercury Drive
Sunnyvale, CA 94086
(408) 736-2000

Digital Equipment Corporation
MK01 2/J25, P.O. Box 9501
Merrimack, NH 03054
(800) 255-9986

Dragon Systems, Inc.
320 Nevada Street
Newton, MA 02160
(617) 965-5200

Eastman Kodak Corporation
343 State Street
Rochester, NY 14650
(800) 242-2424
(716) 724-4000

Electronics for Imaging, Inc.
950 Elm Avenue
San Bruno, CA 94066
(415) 742-3400

Epson America, Inc.
P.O. Box 2842
20770 Madrona Avenue
Torrance, CA 90503
(800) 289-3776
(310) 782-0770

Everex Systems
48431 Milmont Drive
Fremont, CA 94538
(800) 992-3839
(510) 498-1111

Focus Information Systems
4046 Clipper Court
Fremont, CA 94538
(800) 925-2378
(510) 657-2845

Forval America
6985 Union Park Center
Suite 425
Midvale, UT 84047
(800) 367-8251
(801) 561-8080

Fujitsu Personal Systems, Inc.
5200 Patrick Henry Drive
Santa Clara, CA 95054
(408) 764-9443

FWB Inc.
2040 Polk Street, Suite 215
San Francisco, CA 94109
(415) 474-8055

Gateway 2000
610 Gateway Drive, P.O. Box 2000
North Sioux City, SD 57049
(800) 523-2000
(605) 232-2000

Global Village Communication
685 E. Middlefield, Bldg. B
Mountain View, CA 94043
(800) 736-4821
(415) 390-8200

GrassRoots
8226 Mieman Road
Lenexa, KS 66214
(913) 681-3001

GRiD Systems Corporation
47211 Lakeview Boulevard
Fremont, CA 94537
(800) 222-4743
(510) 656-4700

Hayes Microcomputer Products, Inc.
P.O. Box 105203
Atlanta, GA 30348
(404) 441-1617

Hercules Computer Technology, Inc.
3839 Spinnaker Court
Fremont, CA 94538
(510) 623-6030

Hewlett-Packard Corporation
P.P. Box 58059
MS #511L-SJ
Santa Clara, CA 95051
(800) 752-0900

Hitachi America, Ltd.
Computer Division
2000 Sierra Point Parkway, MS 500
Brisbane, CA 94005-1819
(800) 448-2244
(415) 589-8300

IBM Corporation
IBM PC Direct
3039 Cornwallis Road
Building 203
Research Triangle Park, NC 27709
(800) 426-2968

Insite Peripherals
4433 T Fortran Drive
San Jose, CA 95134
(408) 946-2302

Intel Corporation
5200 NE Elam Young Parkway
Hillsboro, OR 97124
(800) 538-3373
(503) 629-7402

Irwin Magnetic Systems, Inc.
Division of Maynard Electronics
36 Skyline Drive
Lake Mary, FL 32746
(800) 821-8782
(407) 263-3500

Kensington Microware Limited
2855 Campus Drive
San Mateo, CA 95054
(800) 535-4242

Kurzweil Applied Intelligence, Inc.
411 Waverley Oaks Road
Waltham, MA 02154
(617) 893-5151

La Cie Ltd.
8700 SW Creekside Place
Beaverton, OR 97005
(800) 999-0143
(503) 520-9000

Lapis Technologies, Inc.
1100 Marina Village Parkway
Suite 100
Alameda, CA 94501
(800) 435-2747
(510) 748-1600

Leading Edge Computer Products, Inc.
117 Flanders Road
Westboro, MA 01581
(800) 874-3340
(508) 836-4800

Lexmark International
740 New Circle Road NW
Lexington, KY 40511
(800) 258-8575
(606) 232-2000

Liberty Systems, Inc.
160 Saratoga Avenue, Suite 38
Santa Clara, CA 95051
(408) 983-1127

Logitech, Inc.
6505 Kaiser Drive
Fremont, CA 94555
(800) 231-7717
(510) 795-8500

Marstek, Inc.
15225 Alton Parkway
Irvine, CA 92718
(800) 366-4620
(714) 833-7740

Matrox Electronic Systems, Ltd.
1055 St. Regis Boulevard
Dorval, Quebec
Canada H9P 2T4
(800) 361-4903
(514) 685-2630

Maxell
(*subsidiary of Hitachi Maxell Ltd.*)
22-08 Route 208
Fairlawn, NJ 07410
(201) 794-5900

Maxtor Corporation
211 River Oaks Parkway
San Jose, CA 95134
(800) 262-9867

Maynard
(*a division of Archive Corporation*)
36 Skyline Drive
Lake Mary, FL 32746
(800) 821-8782
(407) 263-3500

Media Vision, Inc.
47300 Bayside Parkway
Fremont, CA 94538
(800) 348-7116
(510) 770-8600

MicroNet Technology, Inc.
20 Mason
Irvine, CA 92718
(714) 837-6033

Micropolis Corporation
21211 Nordhoff Street
Chatsworth, CA 91311
(818) 709-3300

Microsoft Corporation
One Microsoft Way
Redmond, WA 98052-6399
(206) 882-8080

MicroSpeed, Inc.
5005 Brandin Court
Fremont, CA 94538
(510) 490-1403

Microtech International, Inc.
158 Commerce Street
East Haven, CT 06512
(800) 626-4276
(203) 468-6223

Microtek Lab, Inc.
3715 Doolittle Drive
Redondo Beach, CA 90278
(800) 654-4160
(310) 297-5000

Mitsubishi Electronics America
800 Cottontail Lane
Somerset, NJ 08873
(800) 733-8439
(908) 563-9889

Mitsubishi International Corp.
701 Westchester Avenue
White Plains, NY 10604
(914) 997-4999

Momenta Corp.
295 North Bernardo Avenue
Mountain View, CA 94043
(415) 969-3876

Motorola Codex
20 Cabot Boulevard
Mansfield, MA 02048
(800) 544-0062
(508) 261-4000

Mouse Systems Corporation
47505 Seabridge Drive
Fremont, CA 94538
(510) 656-1117

Nanao USA Corporation
23535 Telo Avenue
Torrance, CA 90505
(800) 800-5202
(310) 325-5202

NCR Corporation
1700 South Patterson Boulevard
Dayton, OH 45479
(800) 225-5627
(513) 445-5000

NEC Technologies, Inc.
1414 Massachusetts Avenue
Boxborough, MA 01719
(800) 632-4636
(508) 264-8000

NeXT Computer, Inc.
900 Chesapeake Drive
Redwood City, CA 94063
(800) 879-6398
(415) 366-0900

Nikon Electronic Imaging
1300 Walt Whitman Road
Melville, NY 11747
(800) 645-6687
(516) 547-4355

Northgate Computer Systems, Inc.
7075 Flying Cloud Drive
Eden Prairie, MN 55344
(800) 548-1993
(612) 943-8181

O.C.E.A.N. Microsystems, Inc.
11235 Knott Avenue
Suite A
Cypress, CA 90630
(800) 944-6232
(714) 898-1340

Okidata
532 Fellowship Road
Mount Laurel, NJ 08054
(609) 235 2600

Olivetti Office USA
765 U.S. Highway 202
Somerville, NJ 08876
(908) 526-8200

Omni Labs and RTM, Inc.
13177 Ramona Boulevard
Suite F
Irwindale, CA 91706
(818) 813-2630

Optima Technology Corporation
17526 Von Karman
Irvine, CA 92714
(714) 476-0515

Pacific Data Products
9125 Rehco Road
San Diego, CA 92121
(619) 552-0880

Panasonic Communications
& Systems Co.
2 Panasonic Way
Secaucus, NJ 07094
(201) 348-7155

Peripheral Land, Inc.
47421 Bayside Parkway
Fremont, CA 94538
(510) 657-2211
(800) 288-8754

Philips Consumer Electronics Co.
One Philips Drive
Knoxville, TN 37914-1810
(615) 521-4316

Princeton Graphic Systems
1100 Northmeadow Parkway,
Suite 150
Roswell, GA 30076
(800) 221-1490
(404) 664-1010

ProCom Technology
2181 Dupont Drive
Irvine, CA 92715
(800) 800-8600
(714) 852-1000

Prometheus Products, Inc.
9524 Southwest Tualatin
Sherwood Road
Tualatin, OR 97062
(800) 477-3473
(503) 692-9600

Proxima Corporation
6610 Nancy Ridge Drive
San Diego, CA 92121
(619) 457-5500

QMS, Inc.
One Magnum Pass
Mobile, AL 36618
(800) 523-2696
(205) 633-4300

Quantum Corporation
500 McCarthy Boulevard
Milpitas, CA 95035
(800) 624-5545
(408) 894-4000

Radius Inc.
1710 Fortune Drive
San Jose, CA 95131
(800) 227-2795
(408) 434-1010

RasterOps Corporation
2500 Walsh Avenue
Santa Clara, CA 95051
(408) 562-4200

Ricoh Corporation
File Products Division
5150 El Camino Real, Suite C20
Los Altos, CA 94022
(415) 962-0443

Roland Corporation
7200 Dominion Circle
Los Angeles, CA 90040
(213) 685-5141

Safari Systems
14K World's Fair Drive
Somerset, NJ 08873
(908) 302-5808

Samsung Information Systems
America, Inc.
3655 N. First Street
San Jose, CA 95134
(800) 624-8999
(408) 434-5400

Seagate Technology
920 Disc Drive
Scotts Valley, CA 95066
(408) 439-2670

Seiko Instruments USA, Inc.
1130 Ringwood Court
San Jose, CA 95131
(800) 533-5312
(408) 922-5900

Sharp Electronics Corporation
Sharp Plaza, MS One
Mahwah, NJ 07430
(800) 237-4277
(210) 529-8731

Slate Corporation
15035 N. 73rd Street
Scottsdale, AZ 58260
(602) 443-7322

Sony Corporation of America
Computer Peripheral Products Co.
3300 Zanker Road
San Jose, CA 95134
(800) 352-7669
(408) 432-0190

Spatial Data Systems
P.O. Box 550
Melhourne, FL 32902
(407) 725-3711

Star Micronics America
420 Lexington Avenue, Suite 2702
New York, NY 10170
(800) 447-4700
(212) 986-6770

Storage Dimensions
1656 McCarthy Boulevard
Milpitas, CA 95035
(408) 954-0710

Sun Computers, Inc.
1000-T E. Dominguez Street
Carson, CA 90746
(213) 538-8338

SuperMac Technology
215 Moffett Park Drive
Sunnyvale, CA 94089
(800) 541-7680
(408) 541-6100

Tallgrass Technologies Corp.
11100 W. 82nd Street
Lenexa, KS 66214
(800) 825-4727
(913) 492-6002

Tandy Corporation
700 One Tandy Center
Fort Worth, TX 76102
(817) 390-3011

Taxan American, Inc.
161 Nortech Parkway
San Jose, CA 95134
(800) 648-2926

Teac Corporation of America
7733 Telegraph Road
Montebello, CA 90640
(213) 726-0303

Tektronix, Inc.
P.O. Box 1000, MS 63-630
Wilsonville, OR 97070
(800) 835-6100
(503) 627-7111

Telex Communications, Inc.
9600 Aldrich Avenue S
Minneapolis, MN 55420
(800) 828-6107
(612) 887-5524

Texas Instruments
P.O. Box 149149, MS 2240
Austin, TX 78714
(800) 527-3500

Texel America, Inc.
1080-C East Duane Avenue
Sunnyvale, CA 94086
(800) 886-3935

3M Visual Systems Division
6801 River Place Boulevard
Austin, TX 78726
(800) 328-1371

Tidemark Company
4601 SW 34th Street
Orlando, FL 32811
(407) 841-8344
(800) 345-6530

Toshiba America Information Systems
Computer Systems Division
9740 Irvine Boulevard
Irvine, CA 92718
(800) 745-4745
(714) 583-3000

Turtle Beach Systems
Cyber Center, Unit 33
1600 Pennsylvania Avenue
York, PA 17404
(717) 843-6916

U.S. Robotics, Inc.
8100 N. McCormick Boulevard
Skokie, IL 60076
(800) 342-5877
(708) 982-5001

Verbatim
(*subsidiary of Mitsubishi Kasei Corporation*)
1200 W. T. Harris Boulevard
Charlotte, NC 28213
(704) 547-6500

Video Seven
46221 Landing Parkway
Fremont, CA 94538
(510) 623-7857

Zenith Data Systems
2150 E. Lake Cook Road
Buffalo Grove, IL 60089
(800) 227-3360
(708) 808-5000

Zeos International, Ltd.
1301 Industrial Boulevard
Minneapolis, MN 55413
(800) 423-5891
(612) 362-1234

Popular Computer Magazines

Listed here you will find just a smattering of the many publications about personal computing. Those listed have a fairly wide audience. Look in your college or university library for publications geared to business users, educators, graphics artists, engineers, and scientists.

We recommend you buy a few different publications before settling on one or two subscriptions. One magazine may be more technical or business-oriented than another; usually the publication's title will tell you whether its target market is more specialized than you need. Individual issues may include cards offering special subscription rates that are less than the prices generally charged.

Amazing Computing for the Commodore Amiga
PiM Publications, Inc.
$3.95 single copy, $29.95 per year (monthly)

For subscriptions, call (800) 345-3360 or write to the publisher at Currant Road; P.O. Box 2140; Fall River, MA 02722-2140.

For users of the Amiga computer, this magazine includes reviews, information about desktop publishing, tips for users, languages and programming, and programs you can key into your computer.

AmigaWorld
Tech Media Publishing, Inc.
$3.95 single copy, $29.97 per year (monthly)

For subscriptions, call (800) 827-0983 or (800) 734-1109, or write to the magazine at P.O. Box 50365; Boulder, CO 80321-0365.

For users of the Amiga computer, this magazine includes news about products, reviews, techniques for using the computer and software, and information about using the Amiga for graphics applications.

Atari Explorer
Jainschigg Communications
$2.95 single copy, $14.95 per year (6 issues)

For subscriptions, call (218) 723-9202 or write to the magazine at P.O. Box 6488; Duluth, MN 55806.

Articles in this magazine are a mix of topics—from games to productivity software to the technical aspects of computer use. Subjects also include programming and new hardware products. Some articles are geared to the business or graphic-arts professional. This magazine is of interest mainly to Atari computer users.

Boardwatch Magazine
Boardwatch Magazine
$3.95 single copy, $36 per year (monthly)

For subscription information, write to the magazine at 8500 W. Bowles Avenue, Suite 210; Littleton, CO 80123.

This magazine is geared to the user of electronic bulletin boards. It contains information about products, issues, international networks and coordinators, as well as national EBB systems and online services. Although the magazine contains a lot of information, we recommend buying and reading a single copy before buying a subscription; you may or may not appreciate the informal design of the layout and articles, or the extensive letters to the editor on a variety of topics.

Byte
McGraw-Hill, Inc.
$3.50 single copy, $29.95 per year (12 issues)

For subscriptions, call (800) 257-9402 (U.S. only) or write to the *Byte* Subscription Department; P.O. Box 555; Hightstown, NJ 08520.

This magazine was one of the first magazines about microcomputers. By reading the early issues, you can trace the development of the personal computer from hobby to powerful business and graphics machine. The articles are very technical; writers often assume you know computer terminology well beyond the basics (even when a term could be clarified with few extra words). The writing is very good, however, and articles are about state-of-the-art products and ideas. The magazine covers everything—from products to languages to databases. Articles usually interest users of any platform.

Compute!
COMPUTE Publications International Ltd.
$2.95 single copy, $19.94 per year (12 issues)

For subscriptions, call (910) 275-9809 or write to *Compute!* at 324 W. Wendover Avenue, Suite 200; Greensboro, NC 27408.

Compute! contains the usual articles about products and software, tips, and reviews—except its reviews include more games than most general-computing magazines do. The reviews are well written, including special lists of requirements for using the products. Each issue also includes a tear-out special section called "Getting Started With" that addresses a special subject such as multimedia or hard-disk drives, for example. Information is generally PC/DOS-oriented.

Computer Buyer's Guide and Handbook
Bedford Communications, Inc.
$4.95 single copy, $36 per year (12 issues)

For subscriptions, call (800) 877-5487 or write to the magazine at P.O. Box 318; Mt. Morris, IL 61054-9942.

This magazine contains reviews of software, computers, scanners, drives, and other products as well as how-to's for some of the products. Toward the back of each issue is a list of street prices and dealers for selected products. Information is generally PC/DOS-oriented, though other users will benefit from reading the information.

Computer Gaming World
Golden Empire Publications, Inc.
$3.95 single copy, $28 per year (12 issues)

For subscriptions, call (800) 827-4450 or write to *Computer Gaming World* Subscriptions; P.O. Box 730; Yorba Linda, CA 92686-9963.

This magazine is about gaming, with many game reviews, industry news, gaming tips, and the experiences of people who play computer games.

Computer Life
Ziff-Davis Publishing Company
$2.95 per issue, $24.97 per year

For subscriptions, call (800) 926-1578 or write to *Computer Life*; P.O. Box 55880; Boulder, CO 80322.

Intended for anyone who might use a computer at home, *Computer Life* pledges to introduce the opportunities and experiences that a computer can afford you. It includes both hardware and software reviews, including multimedia, personal productivity, and entertainment. "Buzz" offers news-and-views on upcoming and new releases, best-seller lists, and entertaining news shorts. A regular feature, "Just Do It," introduces projects you can accomplish at home with your computer. The issue we reviewed gave a step-by-step pictorial guide to giving your PC video-capture capability. It also lists everything you will need to accomplish the project and "Dos and Don'ts." "Lifelines" includes articles on multimedia news and products, online communications, and so on. There are many advertisements, but this publication has a lot to offer.

Computer Monthly
Vulcan Publications, Inc.
$1.95 single copy, $15.95 per year (monthly)

For subscriptions, write to *Computer Monthly* Subscriptions; P.O. Box 7062; Atlanta, GA 30357-0062.

This publication is a source for buyers. Topics include trends, software reviews, and a column for handicapped computer users.

Computer Shopper
Coastal Associates Publishing, L.P.
$2.95 single copy, $29.97 per year (monthly)

For subscriptions, call (800) 274-6384 or write to *Computer Shopper*; P.O. Box 52568; Boulder, CO 80322-2568.

This large volume contains ads, ads, ads—and informative articles about trends, products, technology, buying tips, and programming, as well as a technical section. It also has reviews, lists of coming events, and information about electronic bulletin boards and users' groups. Geared to people who are willing to shop by mail-order, it also targets business users, but other users can benefit from the articles inside.

DOS Resource Guide
Business Computer Publishing, Inc.
$4.95 single copy, $15.80 per year (published quarterly)

For subscriptions, call (800) 238-6580 or write to the publisher at 80 Elm Street; Peterborough, NH 03458.

This publication is handy for people who want more information about using DOS commands and files. Its policy is teaching by example, and topics include tips from readers and programming.

Electronic Entertainment
Infotainment World, Inc.
$5.95 per issue, $18 per year (12 issues)

For subscriptions, call (415) 349-4300 or write the publisher at 951 Mariner's Island Blvd., Ste. 700; San Mateo, CA 94404.

This publication is intended for the multimedia-game enthusiast. The pages are chock-full of mini news releases about software, hardware, and peripherals. The numerous reviews include great-looking screen shots and photographs. Each issue includes the "Leader Board" that lists the best-selling PC, Mac, and CD-ROM entertainment software. Features include pre-release previews of software, as well as "Guided Tours" of popular games. The screen shots in these articles are unbelievable! Games from each of the following categories are reviewed in each issue: Role-Playing, Virtual Worlds, Strategy, Simulation, Brain Drain, Action, and Sports. Again, the accompanying screen shots are incredible. The "Tech Shop" department offers information on a myriad of game-related issues; these include managing memory, reconfiguring your computer, and designing an ergonomically correct computer environment. If computer gaming is your interest, *Electronic Entertainment* is published for you.

Family PC
Family PC
$2.95 single copy, $9.95 per year (six issues, bimonthly)

For subscriptions, call (800) 413-9749 or write to the publisher at P.O. Box 400454; Des Moines, IA 50340-0454.

This magazine is designed for parents. It offers sound advice on what to buy and how to get the most from your purchases. Each issue includes information for the family on the latest issues and trends, over two dozen software and hardware reviews, shopping advice, troubleshooting tips, how-to's, and articles on bulletin boards and online services. The "Creative Computing Department" includes articles on anything from how to publish your own newsletter to designing great book covers. Each includes a handy checklist of what you'll need to complete the project. Reviewed software and hardware is family-tested by the FutureKids network of families throughout the world, claiming to be the world's largest computer school. *Family PC* articles deal with *PCs, Macs, and Multimedia*.

Home-Office Computing
Scholastic Inc.
$2.95 single issue, $19.97 per year (monthly)

For subscription information, call (800) 288-7812 or address your general questions to the magazine at P.O. Box 2511; Boulder, CO 80302.

If you operate an office from your home, this publication offers a guide to equipping your home with electronic information as well as running a business from your home. Topics include financial aspects of running a business, hints and tips for using computers, and buying products. Individuals who own their own businesses at home and use computers are often featured. No matter what platform you are using, you can benefit from reading these articles.

InfoWorld
InfoWorld Publishing, Inc.
$2.95 single copy, $130 per year (newspaper is published weekly; Christmas and New Year's weeks are combined)

For subscriptions, call (800) 227-8365 or (708) 647-7925, or write to *InfoWorld* Subscriptions; P.O. Box 1172; Skokie, IL 60076.

This newspaper contains industry news, as well as articles about innovations and competition. It reviews software and hardware, and offers comparisons of similar products. There is a nice mix of short articles and longer, in-depth articles. If you meet their criteria, you may be eligible for a free subscription. Phone *InfoWorld* and request the subscriber information card.

Internet World
Internet World
$4.95 single issue, $29 per year (10 issues)

For subscriptions, call (800) 573-3062 or write to the publisher at P.O. Box 713; Mt. Morris, IL 61054. Other requests can be directed to Internet: **info@mecklermedia.com** or CompuServe: **70373,616**.

A publication written with the die-hard Internet cruiser in mind, *Internet World* seems to focus on a particular area of online communication in each issue. The issue we reviewed focused on the chatting resources of the Internet, as well as e-mail communication. Features included articles on the evolution of USENET, e-mail relationships, and online intellectual property issues. Other regularly imparted information includes a myriad of user's guides (including tips on LISTERV), Internet news releases, book reviews, and pointers for accessing any resource available online. A comprehensive magazine, with more than anyone needs to know about life on the Internet.

Kids and Computers
Golden Empire Publications, Inc.
$2.95 single copy, $14 per year (six issues, bimonthly)

For subscriptions, call (800) 827-4450 or write to the publisher at 130 Chaparral Court, Suite 260; Anaheim Hills, CA 92808.

This magazine is designed for parents. It includes articles on developing home learning centers, connecting with networks, carrying school learning over into home activities, and using the computer for a variety of interesting and entertaining activities. A section called "Kids' View" features computer art and other creative endeavors by students. A reviews department describes the merits, problems, and requirements of software for children and teenagers. Both the reviews and the feature articles were excellent in the copy we reviewed.

Lotus
Lotus Publishing Corporation
$4 single copy

For subscription information, write to *Lotus* Subscription Department; P.O. Box 52350; Boulder, CO 80321-2350.

This publication, geared to users of the Lotus 1-2-3 spreadsheet program and other Lotus software, talks about trends and issues of computing with Lotus. Other topics include using Microsoft Windows with Lotus-compatible products, using computer peripherals with Lotus products, and learning about new products. *Lotus* also features examples of spreadsheet formulas, as well as templates for using Lotus 1-2-3.

MacUser
Ziff-Davis Publishing Company
$2.95 single copy, $27 per year (12 issues)

For subscriptions, call (800) 627-2247 or write to *MacUser* Subscriptions; P.O. Box 56986; Boulder, CO 80322-6986.

If you are a Macintosh user, this magazine is one of the few targeted directly toward you. The articles are somewhat technical, but very helpful in getting the best out of your Macintosh machine for many types of applications. Products and software are reviewed; graphics applications are often featured.

MacWorld
MacWorld Communications, Inc.
$3.95 single copy, $30 per year for 12 issues

For subscription information, call (800) 234-1038 or write to *MacWorld* Subscriber Services; P.O. Box 54529; Boulder, CO 80322-4529.

This magazine is for Macintosh users. Its topics include issues such as education, as well as the technical and practical aspects of using a Macintosh computer. It contains features such as "Bug Report," "Virus Watch," a question-and-answer column, tips for users, and reviews. Major topics include how-it-works articles, new products, and graphics how-to's. The magazine is well written; it should be useful to advanced users and new users alike.

Mobile Office
CurtCo Publishing
$3.95 single copy, $23.90 per year for 12 issues

For subscriptions, call (800) 627-5234 or write to *Mobile Office* Subscription Department; P.O. Box 57268; Boulder, CO 80323-7268.

This magazine about portable computing includes articles about appropriate software for portable computers, the notebook and subnotebook computers themselves, and information for modem users. Being about working away from your home office in general, it also includes articles about traveling, auto security, cellular phones, and other useful information for home-office computer users who are also telecommuters. Users of portable computers—any platform—will benefit from its articles.

Multimedia World
PC World Communications, Inc.
$3.95 single copy, $14.97 per year (12 issues)

For subscriptions, call (800) 281-8650 or write to *Multimedia World*; Subscription Department; 501 Second St., #600; San Francisco, CA 94107.

This magazine offers a lot of good information on the world of multimedia. Each issue includes letters from readers, coming attractions and industry updates, product reviews, and a new product feature. The issue we reviewed also included a feature article on the Reader's Choice Awards, the products *Multimedia World* chose as best in over 48 different categories. Information is available for both Macintosh and PC/DOS platforms.

NewMedia
Hypermedia Communications, Inc.
$3.95 single copy, $48 per year (12 issues)

For subscriptions, call (609) 764-1846 or write to the Customer Service Department; *NewMedia*; P.O. Box 1771; Riverton, NJ 08077-9771.

This magazine capitalizes on the interest shown in multimedia and shows you how to take advantage of your computer's sound, graphics, and video equipment. It contains buying guides and information about new products, offers articles about simulations, animation, and sound, and test drives of equipment and software. Both Macintosh and PC/DOS users will benefit from reading this publication.

Online Access
Chicago Fine Print, Inc.
$4.95 single issue, $19.80 per year (quarterly)

For subscription information, write to the publisher at 2271 N. Lincoln Avenue; Chicago, IL 60614.

If you use a modem or are planning to buy one, this magazine looks at the commercial information services available to you. Each issue features a particular information service, and may include articles about gaming online or researching tips. There are brief descriptions of a wide variety of online services other than the big information services, as well as a calendar of online events for the three months ahead.

PC Computing
Ziff-Davis Publishing Company
$2.95 single copy, $24.97 per year for 12 issues

For subscriptions, call (800) 365-2770 or write to *PC Computing*; P.O. Box 58229; Boulder, CO 80322-8229.

PC Computing contains many product reviews and articles about products relating to accomplishing a particular task, such as scanning or shopping for a notebook computer. It has a yearly round-up of best products—helpful for Christmas shopping since it occurs in the December issue. The table of contents indicates the content of each feature article in a sentence or two under each title. PC/DOS users will benefit from the articles.

PC Games
A+ Publishing
$3.95, $19.95 per year (8 issues)

For subscriptions, call (800) 343-0728 or write to A+ Publishing at MacWorld Communications; 80 Elm Street; Peterborough, NH 03458.

If you like computer games and buy a lot of them, you'll appreciate this magazine, which reviews individual games as well as clusters of games on a particular topic (such as golf or football). Its buyer's guide contains mostly MS-DOS software.

PC Home Journal
PC Home Journal, Inc.
$2.95 single copy, $17.95 per year (12 issues)

For subscriptions, call (800) 827-0364 or write to *PC Home Journal* Subscriptions; P.O. Box 469; Mt. Morris, IL 61054.

This magazine is designed for the home computer user of IBM and compatible computers, and even has items about children and computing. It has feature articles about products, tips for use, reviews, and information about using computers for such applications as home design and money management. The company also produces *Mac Home Journal*, for Macintosh users.

PC Laptop Computers Magazine
L.F.P. Inc.
$3.95 single copy, $24.95 per year for 12 issues

For subscriptions, call (818) 760-8983 or write to *PC Laptop Computers Magazine*; P.O. Box 16927; North Hollywood, CA 91615.

Describing primarily IBM-compatible machines, this magazine profiles laptop computers and their users. Its articles address multimedia, networks, software, and uses of laptops in business. There are reviews for both software and hardware, as well as a brief buyer's guide.

PCM (Personal Computer Magazine)
FALSOFT, Inc.
$3.50 single copy, $34 per year (12 issues)

For subscription information, call (502) 228-4492 or write to the publisher at The Falsoft Building; P.O. Box 385; Prospect, KY 40059-9989.

Described as "The Premier Personal Computer Magazine for Tandy Computer Users," this magazine contains articles about programs, languages, applications for personal use, and tips for using computers. Reviews list complete requirements for each piece of software or hardware. It also contains a Shareware Software Shopper. Users of IBM PCs and compatibles will also benefit from reading this magazine.

PC Magazine
Ziff-Davis Press
$2.95 single copy, $44.97 per year (22 issues)

For subscriptions, call (800) 289-0429 or write to *PC Magazine*; P.O. Box 54093; Boulder, CO 80322-4093.

Geared primarily to business users of IBM-compatible microcomputers, this magazine contains product reviews and comparisons, various question-and-answer columns, and tips for users. The table of contents gives a short sentence or so about most articles.

PC Novice
Peed Corporation
$2.95 single copy, $24 per year (monthly)

For subscriptions, call (800) 848-1478 or write to the publisher at 120 West Harvest Drive; P.O. Box 85380; Lincoln, NE 68501.

This magazine contains in-depth articles about how a computer and its peripherals work. Subjects include memory, programs, monitors, graphics, notebook computers, and so on. Each issue includes a glossary of some main terms used in the issue. There are also articles relating to specific software packages (such as WordPerfect or dBASE IV). The magazine is geared primarily to PC/DOS users, though users of other platforms will benefit from reading the articles. Although the magazine's title indicates it is designed for novices, some of the articles are quite technical and explanations are not always clear.

PC Sources
Coastal Associates Publishing, L.P.
$1.95, $16.97 per year (12 issues)

For subscriptions, call (800) 827-2078 or write to *PC Sources*; P.O. Box 53298; Boulder, CO 80322-3298.

If you are interested in a magazine primarily about hardware and software products, this magazine is designed with you in mind. Articles are arranged topically by product, often with two or more relating to a particular product. There are good checklists for evaluating and buying each type of product—and checklists to use when you call companies about their products. Reviews include short summaries and lists of product characteristics (including support, warranties, return policies, and requirements for use). The magazine also has a good product index. The information is of interest if you are using the PC/DOS platform.

PC Today
Peed Corporation
$2.95 single copy, $24 per year (monthly)

For subscription information, call (800) 424-7900 or write to the magazine at P.O. Box 85380; Lincoln, NE 68501-9815.

By the same publishers as *PC Novice*, this magazine is geared to the business user of PC/DOS platform computers. It gives the usual information about computers, peripherals, programming, and tips, all designed to help the user in his or her business. It also offers information about the effects of computers and computing. Like *PC Novice*, the publication has a glossary with terms pertinent to the current issue.

PC Upgrade
Bedford Communications, Inc.
$4.95 single copy, $22.50 per year (6 issues)

For subscriptions, call (800) 877-5487 or write to the publisher at 150 Fifth Avenue; New York, NY 10011.

For IBM PC/DOS users, this publication tells how to upgrade existing PCs—and gives information on when it pays and doesn't pay to upgrade. There is a swap-meet calendar, items for Macintosh users, build-your-own information, and street-price guides.

PC World
PC World Communications, Inc.
$3.95 single copy, $29.90 per year for 12 issues

For subscriptions, call (800) 234-3498 or write to the magazine at P.O. Box 55029; Boulder, CO 80322-5029.

This magazine contains information about trends, products, and generally all you ever wanted to know about the PC/DOS platform. It is a popular magazine, and the articles are timely and well-written.

Portable Computing
CurtCo Publishing
$4 single copy, $19.20 per year for 6 issues

Subscription information is available at (800) 682-1188 or from the publisher at the Subscription Department; 21800 Oxnard Street, Suite 250; Woodland Hills, CA 91367-9731.

For both Macintosh and PC computer users, this publication is targeted toward readers who use portable computers. It describes new products and trends, compares similar products, offers information on using Microsoft Windows with portables, and describes communications with portables. It also discusses current software, providing hints and tips on portable computer use (e.g., how to stretch battery life).

Publish!
$3.95 single copy

For subscription information, call (800) 274-5116 or write to *Publish!* Subscriber Services; P.O. Box 55400; Boulder, CO 80322.

For those of you who are working in desktop publishing, this magazine gives examples of good design in publications, graphics, animation, and multimedia presentations. Other topics include fonts and authoring software.

RUN (Commodore Magazine)
Technology Media Group, Inc.
$3.95 single copy, $24 per year (bimonthly)

For subscriptions, call (800) 827-0983 or write to the magazine at P.O. Box 50295; Boulder, CO 80321-0295.

Designed for Commodore computer users, this magazine includes programs you can enter into your computer, as well as information on new products, tips for using software, tips from users, and reviews of software.

SW (Shareware Magazine)
$2.95 single copy, $17.70 per year (6 issues)

For information about subscriptions, call (800) 245-6717 or write to *Shareware Magazine* Subscriptions; 1030-D East Duane Avenue; Sunnyvale, CA 94086.

This magazine is primarily for people who are interested in learning about and using shareware programs. Topics also include viruses, interfaces, and education.

Windows Magazine
CMP Publications
$2.95 single copy, $29.94 per year (12 issues)

For subscriptions, call (800) 284-3584 or write to the magazine at P.O. Box 58647; Boulder, CO 80321-8647.

This magazine is for users of Microsoft Windows. It includes information about new products, news about computing and companies, and articles about using Windows. It is advertised as an aid to optimizing, customizing, and maximizing your system.

Windows and DOS User's Guide
Chicago Fine Print, Inc.
$4.95 single copy, $29.70 per year (bimonthly)

For subscription information, call (312) 573-1700 or write to the publisher at 920 N. Franklin Street, Suite 203; Chicago, IL 60610.

This new magazine is designed for users of IBM PCs and compatibles. It provides practical tips, techniques, and news for readers whose skills range from beginning to advanced. It is helpful for business users, people who are interested in using multimedia, and people who want the latest in shareware. There are sections for marketplace (products), opinions, and macros.

Windows User
Wandsworth Publishing, Inc.
$2.95 single copy, $29.97 per year (monthly)

For subscription information, call (800) 627-9860 or write to the magazine at P.O. Box 56630; Boulder, CO 80323-6630.

This publication is another magazine geared to the user of Microsoft Windows. In addition to helpful hints and quick news about products, trends, and companies, it includes information about sound and add-ons that enhance the Windows pro gram, and walk-throughs of compatible software. Sometimes it is hard to tell the articles from the advertisements.

WordPerfect Magazine
WordPerfect Corporation
$3 single copy, $24 per year (12 issues)

For subscriptions, call (801) 228-9626 or write to the magazine at 270 West Center Street; Orem, UT 84057.

Yes, here is another magazine geared to a particular software product. Any WordPerfect user will benefit from reading this magazine. It contains articles describing how to accomplish particular tasks using the software. It also features articles about macros, WordPerfect Office, using peripherals with WordPerfect, tips, and news about the software. There are question-and-answer columns and reviews of compatible products.

Glossary

4GL See fourth-generation language.

8mm helical-scan cartridge Type of tape technology used in VCR tapes adapted for tape backups.

8514/A An IBM high resolution video standard found in some video boards.

accelerator board A printed circuit board that increases the speed of a certain type of computer processing, such as graphics display.

access To retrieve data, or the ability to get information by computer.

access arm The physical device that positions the read/write head of a disk or tape drive over a particular spot on the disk or tape.

access time The amount of time the disk drive needs to locate information on a disk.

acoustic coupler modem A device that connects telephone lines to the computer system; it requires that you place a standard telephone handset into its cradle.

active cell Cell in which you are working in a spreadsheet program.

active-matrix LCD A type of liquid crystal display that is refreshed often. (See also thin film transistor.)

adapter card An expansion board required to support a particular device.

add-in A component (usually a chip) that extends the capabilities of a computer or a program.

add-on A circuit board (expansion board) or a program that gives additional capabilities to a computer or program.

address A unique identifier assigned to each location within memory or storage.

AI See *artificial intelligence.*

alert box A window that contains information or a warning message, but needs no response other than acknowledgment (clicking on the OK button, for example).

algorithm The sequence of steps needed to solve a problem.

ALU See *arithmetic/logic unit.*

analog A representation that shows change in a continuous manner so that every possible infinite value is represented; term used to describe a computer, monitor, or signals in a communication channel.

animation A technique for creating image motion sequences.

anti-aliasing A software technique that diminishes jaggies (those step-like, blocky curves).

antivirus program A program that helps you thwart viruses that might invade your computer system.

application See *application software*.

application generator A tool, often found in a software package such as a database program, that helps you develop custom applications with little programming.

application software Also application program. A computer program designed to let you complete a task such as writing a document, working on a spreadsheet, or playing a computer game.

architecture The design of the electronics of a particular make and model of computer.

archiving Making copies of files for the purpose of having them available for unforeseen uses in the future; may refer specifically to compressed files.

arithmetic/logic unit (ALU) The part of the CPU that handles arithmetic and logic jobs; sometimes, together with the control unit, it is called the processor.

artificial intelligence (AI) Intelligence shown by a machine or software; the field of research that develops methods by which computers can be used for solving problems that appear to require imagination, intuition, or intelligence.

ASCII Pronounced *ask-ee*. Acronym for American Standard Code for Information Interchange. A code for representing English characters as numbers.

assembly language A low-level programming language that uses abbreviations to code instructions rather than zeros and ones or complete words.

attribute A characteristic; also, a field within a record in a computer file.

authoring system A program that enables you to write hypertext or multimedia applications, usually by combining elements such as text, music, and pictures.

autosizing In reference to monitors, accepting signals at one resolution and displaying them in another.

autotrace To convert a bit-mapped image to a vector image; a feature of some draw programs.

background task In a multitasking operating system, a job that can be executed while you are working on some other job at the computer.

backlighting A technique that increases the contrast between characters and background in flat-panel displays, thus making them easier to read; this technique illuminates the background to make the foreground characters stand out.

backup Also backup copy. A spare copy of a document or program just in case something happens to damage or destroy the first copy; "to back up" means to make such a copy in order to prevent data loss.

bandwidth The rating of a communication channel's capacity to carry data; this rating is expressed in bits or bytes per second for digital devices or in Hertz (cycles per second) for analog devices.

bay An area inside a computer set aside for installing a disk drive.

BBS See *bulletin board system.*

binary digit See *bit.*

binary numbers Zero (0) and one (1).

binary number system The base 2 number system that uses the digits 1 and 0. This system corresponds to two possible states in machine circuitry, on and off.

bit Short for BInary digiT; the smallest unit of data that a computer can handle and that can be represented in the digits (0 and 1) of the binary number system.

bit architecture The internal electronic design of a microprocessor that determines the number of bits that can be processed at a given time, for example, 8-bit architecture, 16-bit architecture, or 32-bit architecture.

bit map Graphic image formed by controlling individual pixels.

block A selected section of a document, such as a paragraph in a word processing program or a range of cells in a spreadsheet program.

block operation A feature that enables you to define a section of a document and then perform a specific operation (such as move, copy, or delete) on that section.

boot To load the start-up instructions into a computer. A cold boot occurs when you turn on the computer from the "off" position; a warm boot occurs when you reset a computer that is already turned on.

buffer A separate area of memory in which characters can be stored and retrieved; this area is often used when data is transmitted from one device to another, such as from the keyboard to memory.

bug A program error involving logic or the misuse of a programming language.

bulletin board system (BBS) Also known as an electronic bulletin board, it is a user-run service for posting messages and trading information through your modem. It's usually informal and offered at little or no cost except for telephone bills.

bus A set of wires through which data is sent from one part of the computer to another; it's usually described by its width. For example, a 32-bit bus carries 32 bits of data at one time.

bus mouse See *mouse.*

button A small outlined area in which you click to make a selection. It is found in dialog boxes in graphical user interfaces and it may be round (radio button) or rectangular with rounded corners.

byte Eight adjacent bits used to encode a letter, number, or other character and operated on as a unit.

cache memory Also known as a high-speed buffer or RAM cache. A working buffer or temporary area built into memory and used to help speed up the execution of a program. See also *disk cache.*

CAD See *computer-aided design.*

CAI See *computer-assisted instruction.*

card 1) Same as printed circuit board. 2) Each different screen in a hypermedia stack.

cartridge A removable storage medium usually encased in a hard plastic protective case; it may hold fonts or a hard disk.

cathode ray tube (CRT) A component used in monitors to produce images by moving an electron beam back and forth across the back of a screen.

CD-ROM Pronounced *see dee ROM*. Stands for compact disc read-only memory. It's an optical disk that can only be read from, not written to. CD-ROMS have a very large storage capacity and are often used for multimedia storage.

CD-ROM drive A drive used for CD-ROM disks. It uses optical technology to read the disk.

cell In a spreadsheet, the unique location where a row and a column cross. It can hold a value, a label, or a formula.

central processing unit (CPU) The circuits that act as the brain of the computer to process data. This unit has three parts: the control unit, the arithmetic/logic unit (ALU), and memory.

CGA Stands for color graphics adapter. An early color graphics system for IBM PCs and compatibles that provided limited colors and limited resolution.

channel A communications path between two devices. See also *communication channel.*

character A single letter, number, special graphics symbol, or symbol such as ?, #, &, -, /, *, or space. It requires one byte of storage.

check box A box into which you point and click with the mouse to register a command selection. Usually, an X fills the box you selected.

chip Solid-state circuitry on a tiny piece of silicon or gallium. It may contain millions of electronic components.

circuit board See *printed circuit board.*

CISC Pronounced *sisk.* Stands for complex instruction set computer. Most personal computers have this type of architecture. It may contain as many as 200 to 300 instructions.

clicking Pressing and immediately releasing a button on the mouse.

client-server network A network consisting of a central computer (server) responsible for controlling the database and other critical functions connected to a PC network (clients) which perform dedicated processing.

clip art Illustrations and symbols created by professional artists for non-artists to use in their documents.

Clipboard An area of memory where data is held temporarily during copying or moving procedures.

clock speed The rate at which a microprocessor executes instructions or an expansion bus operates, expressed in megahertz.

clone A computer that functions exactly like another, better-known product; this term can refer to software or other hardware, too.

closed architecture See *proprietary architecture.*

command A message from you to the computer that tells it what to do next. You may give a command by choosing an option from a menu, pressing a key or key combination, or using input equipment, such as a mouse or a joystick.

command language The language with which you communicate with a computer. In DOS, for example, you use the command DIR to tell the computer to list a directory's contents.

command-line user interface A user interface that requires you to type in commands in order to tell the computer what you want it to do.

commercial database See *online service.*

communication channel A pathway or medium along which data travels between sending and receiving devices.

communication software Software that makes it possible to transmit and receive data through modems over telephone lines.

compatible A term that describes software and hardware that can work together and be used together without bad effects, even though they have been produced by different manufacturers; also used as a term for computers that can act as IBM computers do, but are not IBM computers.

compiler program A program used with a high-level language to translate it into machine language.

compression See *data compression.*

compression board An add-on that automatically compresses data as it is written to the disk or decompresses data as it is retrieved. This add-on may double or triple the capacity of a disk.

computer A programmable electronic device used to accept, process, store, and get information. It can perform arithmetic and comparison operations, store information for continuing use, and carry out a series of instructions.

computer-aided design (CAD) Process of designing, drafting, and analyzing a prospective product using special graphics software on a high-end computer.

computer-assisted instruction (CAI) The use of a computer to instruct or drill a student.

computer literacy A basic understanding of computer terminology, capabilities, and issues.

computer network The linking together of computers and peripherals through a communication system.

computer programming language See *programming language*.

configuration The specifications for, or items needed to use, a piece of software or hardware.

connector The part of a cable that plugs into a port or interface to connect one device to another.

contact-management software Software that helps you keep track of addresses, phone calls, and number of contacts made in running a business or service.

context-sensitive help On-screen help that provides assistance with the activity currently being performed.

continuous-tone printer Printer that prints images in an almost unlimited range of gray levels.

controller The component used to connect a peripheral device to a bus; controls the transfer of data from the computer to a peripheral device.

control unit The part of the CPU that controls operation of the CPU and coordinates the functions of other devices within a computer system; sometimes, together with the ALU, it is called the processor.

conventional memory On DOS systems, refers to the first 640K of RAM.

convergence Refers to how accurately the three dots that make up a pixel (red, green, and blue) merge. Poor convergence results in a blurry pixel.

coordinates In a spreadsheet program, the column letter and the row number that identify a particular cell. For example, the coordinates D5 name the cell that is in column D and row 5. Coordinates can be used in formulas or in another cell to transfer a value to that cell. See *cell.*

coprocessor A processing chip that assists the CPU in doing certain types of operations. For example, a math co-processor does complex math operations.

copy A function that enables you to duplicate a block of text or cells within a program.

copy-protection code A small program that prevents you from copying a software package.

CPU See *central processing unit.*

crop To cut away unnecessary or distracting parts of a graphic image that will be reproduced in a document.

CRT See *cathode ray tube.*

cursor A symbol, such as a solid rectangle, underline bar, vertical bar, or arrow, on a computer monitor that shows your current position for working.

cursor-control key A key such as an arrow key that you can use to move the cursor. One key may move the cursor character by character and another may move the cursor to the previous screen of text.

cut and paste A feature of many programs that lets you select a block of data in a document and move it to another location in the same document or a different document.

cylinder The tracks on all disk surfaces that may be read without repositioning the access arm.

daisy-chain To link devices together in a series, as opposed to plugging each of them into one machine.

DAT See *digital audio tape.*

data The symbols used to represent facts, events, or things; the raw material of information.

database A collection of facts that are stored in a well-organized way (for example, a large database at a factory may contain files for equipment, inventory, raw materials, and so on).

database manager See *data manager.*

database software See *data manager.*

database management system (DBMS) Software that permits access to and control of information stored in multiple files by multiple application programs.

data bus The wire or wires that connect the CPU with RAM.

data compression Technique by which data is stored in a format that requires less space than usual; also called data packing.

data manager A program used to computerize the everyday jobs of recording, organizing, and storing information in a file or database. It handles the kind of information that you might usually keep on file cards or in filing cabinets.

data packing See *data compression.*

data processing A set of methods for collecting, handling, and outputting data to reach certain goals; sometimes called information processing. See *processing.*

debugging The process of finding, isolating, and correcting errors in a computer program.

decompression Method of unpacking data in order to be able to use it.

de facto standard A format, language, or protocol that has become a standard out of common usage rather than by the approval of a standards organization.

default setting A preset value that a program applies if you do not change it. For example, a default in a word processing program might set the top and bottom margins at 1 inch.

defragmenting utility A utility program that regroups files that have been broken up by multiple changes. When each file is located onto a contiguous area of a hard disk, the system can work more efficiently.

delete To remove or erase.

density The compactness of data on a disk or tape.

design software See *draw program.*

desk accessory On Macintosh computers, a utility such as a calculator that is always available no matter what program you are running.

desktop A metaphor for the user's working environment in the Macintosh user interface or in any graphical user interface, such as Microsoft Windows.

desktop model The style of computer system that consists of several separate components and resides on a desktop. It's generally not easily or conveniently transported.

desktop publishing The use of a personal computer, special software, and a letter-quality printer to typeset and lay out pages for reproduction. Software for desktop publishing lets you pick from a variety of type fonts and sizes, use decorative lines and other art, and use a printer that provides a fairly high degree of resolution for both the text and the art.

dialog box An outlined area that appears on the screen to request input. For example, you may format a character's font through a dialog box.

digital audio tape A type of tape storage enclosed in a cartridge only slightly larger than a credit card that can hold large amounts of data.

digital computer A computer that uses electronic (not mechanical) parts and that handles data in distinct units, on and off.

digital monitor A monitor that receives digital signals from the video adapter card.

digital signals Representation of data as a series of zeros and ones.

digitizer See *graphics tablet.*

dingbat A small picture such as a star, check mark, or pen tip that can be inserted into a document to draw attention to something.

DIP See *dual in-line package*.

DIP switch A tiny set of switches encased in a dual in-line package and built into a circuit board.

direct-access storage Storage from which data can be obtained in any order. An example is a disk.

direct-connect modem A device that is attached to the computer by a cable and connects the computer directly to the telephone lines by plugging into the telephone wall jack.

directory A file that contains a list of the other files on a disk. In the Macintosh interface, this is called a folder.

disk A round plate made of metal or some type of plastic used as a direct-access form of storage. The two basic types are magnetic or optical.

disk cache A portion of RAM used to speed up access to data on a disk.

disk drive The mechanical device used to record data on a disk and to read what is stored on a disk. It rotates the disk, floppy disk, or optical disk past a read/write head.

disk optimizer See *defragmenting utility.*

dithering A method of creating new colors or shades of gray by varying the pattern of dots in a pixel.

docking station A chassis into which you can plug a portable computer in order to gain more capabilities such as using a CRT-type monitor. It usually contains two slots into which you can plug a sound, video, or network adapter card; it also may contain a drive bay into which you can insert a CD-ROM drive.

document A file that contains information that you have entered into a computer via a particular program. It commonly refers to a text file produced with word-processing software.

documentation Written instructions that tell about a program or piece of equipment. It often includes definitions, explanations, charts, and changes to the program or equipment.

document-preparation package A word-processing program that is powerful enough to do many of the complex tasks found in page-composition and desktop publishing packages.

DOS Acronym for disk operating system. Although it can stand for any operating system, it is commonly used to specifically refer to MS-DOS and PC-DOS used on IBM PCs and compatibles.

dot-matrix printer An impact printer that prints characters made of dots produced when pins strike the paper and ribbon together. The pins are arranged in a matrix of rows and columns, and only the pins needed for forming a particular character are selected. (The dot-matrix formation may also be used in nonimpact printers.)

dot pitch A measurement of the distance between each pixel on a display screen.

double clicking Clicking the mouse button twice rapidly in succession.

download To transfer a program or data from a remote, or host, computer to one's own computer or from a computer to a peripheral device.

dpi Acronym for dots per inch. Indicates the resolution of images.

draft mode A printing mode that prints fast with reduced quality; also used to describe a mode in a word-processing program in which you can enter text quickly without regard to WYSIWYG.

dragging Moving the mouse while holding down the mouse button in order to move an icon or block of data to a new location on the screen.

DRAM Pronounced *dee RAM*. See *dynamic RAM.*

draw program Also illustration or design software. Application program used to create vector and bitmap graphics images.

driver A program that controls a device.

DTP See *desktop publishing.*

dual in-line package (DIP) A type of rectangular chip casing with two rows of connecting pins on either side.

Dvorak keyboard A type of keyboard designed for speed typing with the keys used most often located in the middle, or home, row of keys.

dynamic RAM (DRAM) A type of RAM used in most personal computers. It must be refreshed constantly or it will lose its contents.

EEMS See *expanded memory specification.*

EEPROM See *electrically erasable programmable read-only memory.*

EGA Stands for enhanced graphics adapter. A graphics display system for IBM PCs and compatibles that provides better resolution and more colors than CGA, but less than VGA.

electrically erasable programmable read-only memory (EEPROM) A PROM chip that can be erased using an electrical charge.

electroluminescent display A type of flat-panel display that works with a thin film of phosphorescent substance between two plates.

electronic bulletin board See *bulletin board system.*

electronic mail (e-mail) A system for sending messages at high speed over communication channels.

electronic thesaurus See *thesaurus.*

e-mail See *electronic mail.*

embedded command A command that is inserted into a document, but that is invisible unless you enter a special mode that lets you see all the embedded commands. Examples of this kind of command are the commands that designate the beginning and end of boldfaced text.

EMS See *expanded memory specification.*

emulation The ability of a program or device to imitate another program or device.

EPROM See *erasable programmable read-only memory.*

erasable optical disk See *magneto-optical disk.*

erasable optical disk drive The drive used for erasable (magneto) optical disks.

erasable programmable read-only memory (EPROM) A form of read-only memory that can be erased through use of ultraviolet light and then reprogrammed.

ergonomics The field of researching and designing hardware, software, environment, and procedures to enhance employee productivity and comfort.

executive word processor A word processor that provides only the basic word processing capabilities.

expanded memory See *expanded memory specification.*

expanded memory specification (EMS) A technique by which a DOS-based computer uses more than 1MB of RAM. This technique consists of extra physical memory and the driver, or software, that enables the computer to access the extra memory. Improved versions include EEMS and EMS 4.0.

expansion board Also expansion card. A printed circuit board that you can insert into a computer to give it additional capabilities.

expansion bus A set of wires and components that enable you to insert printed circuit boards into your computer.

expansion slot See *slot.*

expert system A form of artificial intelligence software designed to imitate the decision-making processes of experts in a certain field.

exporting Transferring data that has been formatted so that it is usable in another program.

extended memory (XMS) Memory beyond the 1MB of RAM that DOS supports.

external modem A modem in a self-contained casing outside the computer.

facsimile See *fax system.*

fax modem A modem with facsimile capabilities that is usually installed in an expansion slot.

fax system A system of transmitting documents of pictures and text over telecommunications lines in which an original document is digitized at the sending end and reproduced at the receiving end.

FDHD See *SuperDrive.*

fiber-optic cable A communication channel that consists of multiple thin threads of glass that carry signals as light waves.

field The part of a record that stores one characteristic of the person or thing that the record is about (for example, an address file might include a ZIP code field for each record).

file A group of related records stored together (for example, all of the records about the software packages in a school's computer lab would be listed in the Software file). Also, a specific unit of data stored on a disk or tape, such as a database or a word-processing file.

file format A method of storing data in a file.

file name A name given to a file for storage and retrieval purposes.

file server A device that contains the master files and main network programs on its hard disk.

file transfer program A program that provides for the sending of files from one computer to another.

firmware Instructions or programs encoded into ROM (read-only memory) chips.

fixed pitch A description of a typeface in which every character has the same width. Also called monospace.

flash memory A type of EEPROM that can be rewritten while it is in the computer. See also *electrically erasable programmable read-only memory.*

flatbed scanner A scanner with a flat surface upon which you place the page to be scanned.

flat-file database A simple filing system in which each database is contained in a single file. The system is quickly being replaced by the more efficient *relational database.*

flat-panel display A thin, flat screen that shows images using one of three basic technologies—liquid crystal display, gas plasma, or electroluminescense. This kind of display is used on portable computers.

floating-point number A real number. It can contain a fractional part and has no fixed number of digits before or after the decimal point. Floating point numbers are often used in conjunction with spreadsheet and statistical packages.

floppy disk The nickname given to a plastic, flexible disk coated with a magnetizable substance upon which data is stored; also called diskette.

floppy disk drive The drive used to read from, write to, and erase a floppy disk.

floptical disk drive A type of drive that uses both magnetic and optical technologies.

flow chart A picture in which symbols stand for the flow of operations, data, and equipment of a program or system.

folder A device represented by an icon on the desktop that can hold documents, applications, and other folders. It's used to organize the desktop and symbolizes a directory.

font A set of alphanumeric characters in a particular typeface, size, and style.

font manager A program that lets you manipulate fonts.

footprint A term used to describe the amount of space a computer takes up on a desktop.

forecast A plan that helps you predict what will happen to some numbers when other numbers change. An electronic spreadsheet lets you quickly try out a lot of numbers in a forecast so that you can see what action is needed to achieve the results you want.

foreground task The immediate task that you are working on in a multitasking system, such as Microsoft Windows.

format 1) To prepare a disk so that data and programs can be stored on it by a particular operating system and computer equipment. 2) A specific method by which files are stored by a particular computer program. 3) To design the way text or numbers will appear on paper or on the screen.

form feed Printer feature that lets you advance paper one full page length.

formula A math expression, or equation; values result from formulas that have been calculated.

fourth-generation language (4GL) A high-level technique that makes it possible to assemble a series of query commands as an operational program. This technique enables users to develop programs directly and is associated most often with databases.

freeware Programs that are protected by copyright law but intended to be used free of charge.

friction feed Method of feeding paper into a printer in which the paper is grabbed and pulled into the printer by the sheet.

full-duplex transmission Communication that permits transmission in both directions along a communication channel simultaneously.

full-featured word processor Word-processing program that offers extra features such as a spelling checker, grammar checker, thesaurus, macros, page-layout capabilities, and so on.

full-page scanner A scanner that can read an entire page at once.

function A formula or logical operation that is already built into a spreadsheet program. It is a shortcut that saves typing long formulas and that can be used in a formula. Values result from functions that have been calculated.

function keys Special keys on the keyboard, usually labeled F1, F2, and so on, that enable you to do different jobs depending upon which program you are running.

garbage in, garbage out (GIGO) A phrase used to illustrate that the usefulness of computer output depends on the accuracy and relevancy of the data fed into the computer.

gas plasma display A flat-panel technology that uses electric current to cause gases to glow.

GB See *gigabyte.*

gigabyte (GB) Approximately 1 billion bytes (or characters); 2 to the 30th power bytes.

GIGO See *garbage in, garbage out.*

grammar checker A program that enables you to find syntax errors in a text document.

graphical user interface (GUI) A user interface that provides icons (or pictures), menus, and dialog boxes through which you can use a mouse to communicate with the computer. It enables you to avoid using complex command languages. Sometimes referred to as a transparent user interface.

graphics board A circuit board installed within a computer to process images. See also *video adapter board.*

graphics mode Setting in which the screen becomes an array of pixels so that unlimited shapes and fonts can be displayed. In contrast, the screen becomes an array of blocks, each of which can hold one ASCII character, in text mode.

graphics software Software that produces images such as charts and illustrations.

graphics tablet An electronic pad on which you can draw with a puck or a stylus in order to produce images on the screen. It lets you bypass the keyboard.

gray market Dealer that sells products unauthorized by the manufacturer that made them.

gray scaling Using many shades of gray to create an image.

GUI Pronounced *gooey*. See *graphical user interface.*

hacking Experimenting with a computer. The term is often used to connote mischievous or illegal intent, such as breaking security codes.

half-duplex transmission Communication that permits transmission in both directions along the same communication channel, but in only one direction at a time.

half-page scanner See *hand-held scanner.*

hand-held scanner A scanner small enough to fit in your hand, which you must physically move across a page, scanning only part of the page at a time.

hard card A printed circuit board that contains a hard-disk drive.

hard copy Output that is printed on material such as paper or film.

hard disk A rigid disk, usually made of metal such as aluminum, encased in a hard-disk drive or in a plastic case or cartridge. It's used in most microcomputers as a storage medium.

hard-disk drive The machine that rotates and reads the hard disk.

hardware The physical parts of a computer system—keyboards, printers, monitors, and so on.

hard-wired Description of a device onto which program instructions are recorded permanently so that content cannot be changed or deleted by other stored-program instructions or lost when a computer is turned off.

head crash A disk drive malfunction in which the head has scratched the disk.

help screen See *online help.*

hexadecimal number system A base 16 number system commonly used when printing the contents of memory to aid programmers in detecting errors. It consists of 16 unique symbols—the numbers 0 to 9 and the letters A to F. Every byte can be represented as two hexadecimal digits.

high-end system Along the range of computer systems ranked according to capabilities, a system with the most capabilities and speed.

high-level language A language that is geared more toward you than toward the computer system. High-level languages contain English words such as READ and PRINT and must be translated into machine language by a compiler before the programs can be run.

high memory In DOS-based systems, the first 64K of RAM above 1MB.

host computer The central computer in a network that is accessed by a user in a remote location.

hot key A key sequence that activates a memory-resident program.

hypermedia Another term for multimedia.

hypertext A method of linking objects in a database.

icon A picture or graphic symbol used to represent such things as an application, document, folder, or disk in a graphical user interface.

illustration software See *draw program.*

impact printer A printer that forms characters by striking an inked ribbon, paper, and raised character or pins together.

importing To use data from another program.

information network See *online service.*

information service See *online service.*

information utility See *online service.*

initialize The same as format—to prepare a disk to accept data in a particular computer system.

inkjet printer A nonimpact printer that sprays fine streams of charged ink onto paper to form dot-matrix characters.

input To enter data into the computer; as a noun, the data that is entered into the computer.

input device A piece of equipment used to enter data into a computer system.

insert To put in or add text or data within the body of an existing document.

installation Act of putting a program onto a hard-disk drive or a component into a computer.

instruction A command.

instruction set Rudimentary instructions built in to the computer for performing arithmetic, comparison, and storage and retrieval operations.

integrated circuit (IC) Another name for chip; circuitry whose parts are etched together on a tiny chip made of silicon or other semiconductor material.

integrated software Two or more application programs that work together, allowing easy movement of data among the applications.

interface Something that connects two separate components.

interlaced monitor Monitor in which the electron guns draw only half the horizontal lines on one pass down the screen and draw the other half on the next pass. It's designed to increase resolution while holding down costs.

interleaving A method of organizing the sectors of a disk with the purpose of making the drive more efficient.

internal modem A modem on a printed circuit board that fits into a slot inside the computer and connects directly to the wall telephone jack.

internet A conceptual network consisting of tens of thousands of networks, online services, and single-user microcomputers linking users with information.

interpreter A program used with small computer systems to evaluate and translate program statements as the program is executed, one line at a time.

I/O Short for input/output.

jaggies Steplike projections on curved lines where there should be smooth lines.

joystick A lever or handle attached to a base and used as an input device to control the movement of the cursor on the screen.

justification Even alignment of text along the left or right margin or both.

KB See *kilobyte.*

kerning Adjusting the spaces between characters for a more attractive and readable look.

key The unique identifier or field of a record; used to sort records for processing or to locate specific records in a file.

keyboard An input device that usually consists of keys similar to those on a typewriter that are pressed to enter letters, numbers, special characters, and commands into the computer.

keyboarding The term used to describe typing at a computer.

keystroke The pressing of one key on the keyboard.

kilobyte (KB) 1,024 bytes, often rounded to 1,000.

label A word or other information in a cell that tells about another cell, a group of cells in a row or column, or the entire spreadsheet.

LAN See *local-area network.*

landscape Term that describes the orientation of a monitor or a printed page when it is wider than it is tall.

language-translator program A program that changes a computer code made up of words and symbols into a two-digit code a computer can use.

laptop computer A portable computer that weighs 8 to 12 pounds and contains special batteries, a keyboard, a flat-panel display, a hard-disk drive, and a 3.5-inch floppy-disk drive.

laser beam A beam of very concentrated, high-energy light used to read optical disks.

laser disk An optical disk that can be read by a laser beam.

laser printer A nonimpact printer that generates images through use of a laser beam that passes over the surface of a xerographic drum.

LCD See *liquid crystal display.*

leading Refers to the amount of vertical space between lines of text.

legend Text that explains the meaning of colors, shading patterns, or symbols used in a graph.

light pen A pen-shaped input device with a photoelectric cell at its end that enables you to work directly on the screen (for example, to draw and change designs shown on the monitor, to move objects around, and to point to a choice on a menu). It lets you bypass the keyboard.

line feed A printer feature that enables you to advance paper one line at a time.

liquid crystal display (LCD) A method used to display images by applying electrical currents to flat crystal surfaces.

load To put a program into a computer's memory from a disk or other storage medium.

local-area network (LAN) A system that uses communication channels to connect computers in the same general physical area, allowing them to share peripheral devices and information.

local bus Bus upon which the CPU sits.

log on To gain access to a network system by entering the correct identification items. Finishing a session is called logging off.

logic error An error in program design that produces incorrect information when the program is executed.

loop A control structure that causes a specified set of instructions to be run over and over until certain conditions are met or as long as certain conditions remain constant.

low-end system Along the range of computer systems ranked according to capabilities, a system with the least capabilities and speed.

low-level language A machine-oriented programming language such as an assembly or machine language.

luggable See *transportable.*

machine language The only language that a computer can run directly. It codes the computer's electrical states in combinations of ones and zeros.

macro A sequence of keystrokes that you assign to a single command that often involves only two or three keystrokes. For example, you might assign a set of commands for formatting a character, or a frequently used phrase, two keystrokes that you activate when you want the computer to input the sequence.

macro generator A program that lets you create your own macros or commands.

magnetic disk See *floppy disk* and *hard disk.*

magnetic tape See *tape*.

magneto-optical disk An optical disk that can be written to, read from, and erased.

mail merge A feature of many word-processing programs that enables you to combine a form letter with a list of names and addresses from a database so that you can generate individualized copies of the letter without having to retype a letter for each recipient.

mainframe computer A large computer that can handle very large amounts of data very quickly and support many users, programs, and peripheral devices in the same time frame.

mass storage Storage that lets you retain large amounts of data outside the computer, includes tapes, floppy disks, optical disks, and so on.

math coprocessor See *coprocessor.*

MB See *megabyte*.

MDA Stands for monochrome display adapter. The monochrome video standard for IBM PCs and compatibles.

mean time between failures (MTBF) An indication of the life, or sturdiness, of hard-disk drives and printers. It's measured in hours.

megabyte (MB) Represents 1,048,546 bytes, or approximately 1 million bytes (or characters).

megahertz(MHz) One million cycles per second.

memory Internal physical memory that consists of chips. It holds instructions, data, and intermediate and final results during processing. Also known in the past as internal storage, main memory, primary memory, and primary storage.

memory board A printed circuit board that contains memory chips and is designed to boost RAM.

memory cache See *cache memory.*

memory-management software Program designed so that DOS-based computers can better use memory.

memory-resident program Program that stays in memory even though you are working on another program. It will not be swapped in and out of storage.

menu A list of choices displayed on the screen from which you choose a command or data to enter into the computer.

menu bar A set of options for user selection arranged horizontally across one or two lines.

menu-driven program A design under which access to functions and services of application programs is controlled through lists from which options are selected.

MHz See *Megahertz.*

microcomputer A computer that uses a single microchip as its processor. Most microcomputers are small enough to be placed on a desk, but some are small enough to be put into a briefcase. Also called a personal computer.

microfloppy Term for a 3.5-inch floppy disk.

microprocessor A processing unit (placed on a silicon chip) that does the computing and logic work of a computer. It can be programmed to do many different jobs and thus is used in microcomputers, calculators, and microwave ovens and for many other applications.

microspacing Adjusting text with variable-sized spaces in order to make justified text more attractive and readable.

MIDI Acronym for musical instrument digital interface. This interface enables you to connect instruments such as synthesizers to your computer and input and output music.

minicomputer An intermediate, or scaled-down, version of a mainframe computer; a computer sized between a mainframe and a microcomputer.

MIPS A million instructions per second. A measure for a computer's speed and power.

mnemonics Symbolic names or abbreviations used in assembly language.

mode A setting or state of a device or program.

modem Short for MOdulate/DEModulate. A device through which a computer can send and receive data over telephone lines. It prepares the computer's signals so they are compatible with communication facilities and allows linkage with another computer.

module An independent part or segment that does only one job in a program; a term used in structured programming and also in integrated software.

monitor A video display device or screen for showing computer output.

monochrome monitor A computer monitor that shows one color (such as amber, green, white, or black) on a black, gray, or white background.

motherboard The main circuit board of a microcomputer.

mouse An input device that you roll on a smooth surface to move the cursor, or pointer. The movement of the pointer on the display screen corresponds to the movement of the mouse on the desktop. It is shaped like a small box and has a ball bearing roller underneath it that senses motion. It lets you bypass the keyboard. Bus mice are attached through a card interface to the computer, and serial mice are plugged into a serial port.

mouse cursor The cursor, such as an arrow or I-beam, that shows the movement of the mouse, as opposed to the cursor that shows the movement of keys.

mouse pad A square piece of dense foam-like material with a smooth surface that provides an even tracking surface for a mouse.

mouse pen A pen-shaped device with a ball bearing roller in its tip that has the same function as a mouse, but can be moved like a pen.

move A feature of a program that enables you to relocate data within the same document or to another document.

MPC Multimedia PC.

MTBF See *mean time between failures.*

multifrequency monitor Monitor that is capable of accepting signals at a select number of different frequency levels.

multimedia Computer applications that combine audio and video components with interactive applications.

multiscanning monitor Monitor that automatically adjusts to the frequency of the video adapter board to which it is connected.

multisync monitor See *multiscanning monitor.*

multitasking Running two or more programs on a computer at once.

multi-user operating system An operating system that allows more than one terminal, and thus more than one user, to use the computer at the same time.

music synthesizer See *synthesizer.*

nanosecond A billionth of a second.

natural language A programming language based on the type of English we would normally speak or write rather than upon a more rigid code. It's designed to be user friendly and is often used to access data in a database.

network See *computer network.*

network interface card (NIC) An electronic circuit board added to a computer that allows it to send and receive signals through network cabling.

network operating system (NOS) The software that directs and controls a LAN.

NIC See *network interface card.*

nondestructive read/destructive write The feature of computer memory that permits data to be read repeatedly without being erased until it is written over by new data.

nonimpact printer A printer in which the printing process involves heat, laser, or photographic methods of making images. Because there is no hammering or striking, this kind of printer creates little noise.

non-interlaced monitor Monitor in which the electron gun draws each line on every pass.

NOS See *network operating system.*

notebook computer A portable computer that weighs less than 8 pounds and easily folds up and fits into a briefcase; contains a keyboard, hard-disk drive, floppy-disk drive, RAM, a flat-panel display, and special batteries.

notebook printer A portable printer that is easy to carry around.

notepad computer See *pen-based computing.*

null modem cable A cable that enables you to connect two computers to each other through their communication ports.

numeric keypad The section of a keyboard designed in the format of calculator keys and meant to be used as you would use a calculator. Most keys in this section have alternate functions if the Num Lock option is turned off.

object code A sequence of machine-executable instructions derived from source-program statements by a language-translator program such as a compiler.

object-oriented programming (OOP) Method of programming in which program modules are usable with different objects, or elements, rather than having to be recoded for each different type of use.

OCR See *optical-character recognition.*

off-disk copy protection Method of copy protection by which you are required to enter something into the program from a manual, a special paper wheel, or a list that has been included in the software package. The idea is that only one user will have this paper item and thus a pirated program will be essentially useless.

online Directly connected to a computer.

online help A help system built into a program that enables you to find information about using a particular feature of the program.

online information service See *online service.*

online service A business that offers information through communication channels and modems to paying subscribers with computers and modems.

online UPS system An uninterruptible power supply system that constantly provides power so that if a power outage or some other problem occurs, the computer can continue to function.

on-screen help See *online help.*

OOP See *object-oriented programming.*

open architecture An architecture that enables you to connect the system to devices and programs made by manufacturers other than the manufacturer of your computer. This architecture is possible because the computer's specifications are made public.

operating environment The environment in which you run programs.

operating system A collection of programs used by the computer for managing its own operations. It provides a link between the user, the application program, and the computer hardware.

optical-character recognition (OCR) An input technique that involves light-sensing recognition of characters in print form.

optical disk A large-capacity storage medium on which data is stored and retrieved by laser.

optical scanner See *scanner.*

optical storage See *optical disk.*

outline font A scalable font in which the outline of each character is geometrically defined and can be sized to any possible requirement.

output To send data to the user or output device or information that comes from the computer as a result of processing.

output device A device that presents information from a computer.

overlay See *template.*

packing Compressing a file.

page Material that fits in one page frame or fixed-size physical area in memory; a fixed amount number of bytes.

page-composition software A set of programs that lets you create and assemble finished pages suitable for publication.

page-description language A language used to define the layout and contents of a page.

page-layout software See *page composition software.*

pagination The process of dividing a document into pages and numbering the pages.

paint program An application that enables you to create bit-mapped images.

palette A set of colors, patterns, or drawing tools in a graphics program.

palmtop A small, limited computer that fits in your hand and weighs less than a pound.

paper-white monitor Monitor with high-contrast output that looks almost like black ink on white paper.

parallel port An interface that can be used for communication in which transmission occurs more than one bit simultaneously.

parameter A characteristic.

parity The characteristic of being odd or even. It's used in a method that adds an extra bit to each byte of data handled by the computer, seeking either an even number or an odd number of bits in order to detect incorrect transmission of data.

PC card A card only slightly larger than a credit card that may contain extra memory or capabilities for a computer. It's used primarily in notebook computers.

peer-to-peer LAN A local area network in which each workstation has the same capabilities and responsibilities.

pen-based computing A type of computing which makes use of notepad, or slate, computers, small tablet-like devices on which you write with a stylus and also see your output.

peripheral device A device that is attached to the computer and aids in input, output, or both.

personal computer Another name for the microcomputer.

phase-change inkjet printer A high-resolution inkjet printer.

pin-feed paper Paper with tear-off margins that have holes designed for computer printers that pull the paper through by tractor action.

piracy The unauthorized copying of a copyrighted software program or hardware design.

pitch The number of characters printed per inch. Also the spacing between pixels on a monitor.

pixel Short for picture element. An individual point of light on a display screen; it can be lit or unlit. It's also sometimes called a graphics dot.

platform The basic hardware and software for a system.

plotter An output device that uses pens to make graphic images from computer data. The hard-copy graphics output may include maps, charts, and drawings. Plotters come in two types: flat-bed and drum.

pointer Also pointer symbol. A small symbol such as an arrow that moves as you move the mouse.

pointing and clicking The act of moving the mouse pointer to the item you want and then clicking the mouse button to accomplish a task.

pointing device Device with which you control a pointer. A mouse is an example of such a device.

pop-up menu A menu that appears when you select an option from another menu.

pop-up utility See *memory-resident program.*

port An interface on your computer where you can connect a peripheral device.

portable The characteristic of a program that can be run on many different computers with minimal changes.

portable computer A computer that is easy to carry around. It can weigh from 1 to 20 pounds and includes transportables, laptops, notebooks, sub-notebooks, and palmtops.

portrait Refers to the orientation of a monitor or a printed page horizontally so that it is taller than it is wide.

power supply The component that distributes power to the computer.

presentation graphics Software that enables you to create a number of stylized charts and graphs (such as pie charts, line graphs, 3-dimensional bar graphs, pictographs, and so on) that can be used to make an effective impression on an audience.

printed circuit board A board that holds chips and circuit paths and that can be inserted into a slot on the motherboard of a computer for the purpose of adding some feature to the computer, such as more memory or greater graphics capability. See also *add-on.*

printer A machine that prints characters or other images on paper; may be categorized as impact or nonimpact.

printer fax Printer that can act as a receiver for faxed documents.

printout Hard copy from a printer.

print spooler A device or software that uses a portion of RAM to store print data until it is needed. When used as a background task, it permits you to continue with another job on the computer while a document is being printed.

privacy The right of an individual to be left alone. As related to data processing, the right of an individual to have personal data protected (that is, left alone) from unauthorized use.

procedure Routine or function.

processing The action of a computer on data, such as sorting, calculating, classifying, summarizing, or storing. It results in information.

processor The term used for both the control unit and the arithmetic/logic unit together as part of the CPU. See also *microprocessor.*

program A set of step-by-step instructions that tell a computer exactly how to do a certain task. There are two types of programs: application and system. Also called software.

programmable read-only memory (PROM) A form of read-only memory that can be programmed only once, either by the manufacturer or the user, with special functions that meet the unique needs of the user.

programmer A person who writes computer software.

programming The act of writing a computer program.

programming language A code in which a computer program is written.

PROM See *programmable read-only memory.*

prompt A symbol, message, or cue that indicates that the computer is ready for input. User-friendly prompts guide you during computer processing. They tell you what input is needed, what might be wrong in case of an error, or how you can ask for help.

proprietary architecture Design of a computer that makes it difficult to connect components of another manufacturer.

protected mode A use of memory on Intel 80286 and higher microprocessors that parcels out specific memory to each program, utilizes extended and virtual memory, and provides multitasking capabilities.

protocol The description of rules for the format of data when transmitting and receiving data.

pseudocode A listing of steps to be executed by a program that is written in structured English statements that are understandable to users and usable as guides for programming.

public-domain software Programs unprotected by copyright law for free, unrestricted public use.

pull-down menu A menu that drops down from a menu bar when you make a selection.

query by example A method of searching a database that involves entering conditions.

query language A set of commands that can be used to retrieve information and execute processing commands through direct user access to a database.

querying Requesting information from a database.

QWERTY Term used to represent the standard layout of the keys on a keyboard. It stands for the first six letters from the left in the row of keys above the home row.

radio button A round button in a dialog box in which selection is indicated by a large, centered dot. Radio buttons are often arranged in groups in which only one can be selected.

RAM See *random-access memory.*

RAM cache See *cache memory.*

RAM disk A software concept in which RAM is configured to simulate a disk drive. The purpose is to improve speed for programs that require frequent disk access.

random-access memory (RAM) An array of chips used to build memory within the computer's CPU into which instructions and data can be directly read, written, or erased. Temporary memory that is erased when the computer is turned off. The contents may be changed many times during processing, but they also may be read over and over during processing.

read To access (for example, to detect what is written in random-access memory, in read-only memory, or on a disk or tape).

read-only memory (ROM) The form of memory that holds items as circuitry patterns that can be read but not erased or changed by normal computer input. Memory that is built into the chips.

read/write head The component of a tape or disk drive that records (writes) data onto a disk or tape and detects (reads) data from a tape or disk.

read/write notch An oval cutout in the jacket of a floppy disk that lets the disk drive access the actual disk.

record In a file, all of the information about one person, animal, thing, or event. A collection of information stored together that relates to a single unit (for example, in a Software file, there might be a record for *Microsoft Word*).

redlining Method of marking text that has been changed or added during editing. This method is useful when two or more people review a document.

reduced instruction set computer (RISC) Pronounced *risk*. An architecture in which the CPU uses a limited number of instructions.

refresh To recharge. The rate of refresh for a monitor is expressed in hertz. RAM is also refreshed.

register Special storage area on the microprocessor that receives data, holds it, and transfers it rapidly as directed by the control unit.

relational database In its microcomputer form, a database that is stored in multiple files and that allows you to open and use data from several files at one time.

remote network A system that uses telecommunication channels to connect computers separated by great distances.

report generator A program feature that gleans information from one or more files and presents it in a specified format.

resolution The sharpness or clarity of displayed characters or images.

RGB monitor A monitor that uses three color signals (red, green, and blue) to display high-resolution text and graphics in color.

RISC See *reduced instruction set computer.*

robotics The science that deals with the construction, capabilities, and applications of robots.

ROM See *read-only memory.*

run To operate or execute a program.

scalable font A font that is defined in shape but not in size, and that can be sized to suit the document. See also *outline font.*

scaling Increasing or decreasing the size of an entire graphic image by percentage without destroying the proportions of its contents.

scanner A device that electronically senses information on a graphic document and transmits the images to a computer for processing.

screen saver A program designed to either blank out the monitor screen or set up an animated sequence in order to prevent any one image from being permanently etched into the screen.

script A list of commands that can be executed without interacting with the computer.

scroll To move text or images on and off the screen, either up and down or right and left.

scroll bar A narrow rectangle, usually running down the right side of a window, that uses a small square to show where you are in a document.

SCSI Pronounced *scuzzy*. See *small computer system interface.*

seamless Unnoticed by the user.

search and replace A feature that enables you to find a designated string of characters in a document and replace it automatically with other keyed-in text, if desired.

sector A specific section in the shape of a wedge on a floppy disk or hard disk.

sector aligning hole An opening on a floppy disk jacket that enables the floppy-disk drive to locate a particular sector, or wedge, on the disk.

seek time The amount of time a program or device takes to locate a data item.

semiconductor Substance such as silicon or gallium whose conductivity is poor or improved depending upon the addition of another material or energy such as light.

sequential-access storage Storage from which data must be read in a fixed sequence without skipping any data until the needed data is located. An example is magnetic tape.

serial mouse See *mouse.*

serial port An interface that can be used only for serial communication in which data is transmitted only one bit at a time.

server See *file server.*

shared relation A field that is common to several files in a database.

shareware A program that is distributed to the public. The author retains the copyright with the expectation that users who find the program helpful will reimburse the author a specified (usually small) amount.

sheet-fed scanner A scanner with a mechanism that pulls a new page through as the last one is scanned and slipped out the other end.

sheet feeder A molded plastic mechanism on a printer that permits the automatic feeding and stacking of individual sheets of paper.

shell Another term for user interface.

SIG Acronym for special interest group. People who are interested in a particular subject and discuss it via an online service.

SIMM Acronym for single in-line memory module. A small circuit board that can hold up to 9 RAM chips.

simple sequence A control structure in which one statement is executed after another in the order in which they appear in the program.

simulation A computer program that you can use to imitate a real-world situation. The model can project what will happen when conditions (or variables) in that situation are changed.

SIP (single in-line package) Chip housing that connects to a circuit board with a single row of connector pins.

slot An opening and connector inside a computer that allows for the installation of extra memory or other options; also called expansion slot.

small computer system interface (SCSI) A parallel interface standard used by Macintosh computers and some IBM computers that enables you to daisy chain devices.

smart modem A modem with its own built-in programming that can automate communication functions including telephone calling and answering.

snap-to-grid A feature of draw software in which an image can be sized up or down to fit an existing frame on the screen.

soft copy A temporary display of machine output (for example, a display that appears on a monitor or screen, or voice output).

soft font A font that can be downloaded into printer memory from the computer. In contrast, a resident font is built into the printer or a font cartridge that is inserted into the printer.

software Programs, or instructions, used to direct the computer in solving problems and overseeing operations.

software package A set including a computer program or programs, procedures, and manuals needed for a certain computer job.

sound card A printed circuit board that gives sound capabilities to a computer.

source code The program instructions in their original programmed form.

speech recognition See *voice recognition.*

speech synthesizer See *synthesizer.*

speed-doubling chip A chip that increases the speed of a computer's operations, although it does not necessarily double it.

spelling checker An application, usually found in word-processing programs, that checks words in a document against words in a dictionary file. It's used to detect misspellings.

split window Technique that separates one window into two areas so that two sections of the same document can be displayed on the screen at one time.

spreadsheet A computer program that looks like a table (divided into rows and columns) and is used for working out budgets and studying numbers; also called electronic spreadsheet.

SPS See *standby power system.*

SQL Pronounced as the word *sequel.* See *structured query language.*

SRAM Pronounced *ess RAM*. Stands for static RAM, a form of memory that is faster and needs to be refreshed less often than DRAM.

stack A set of cards in a hypermedia presentation.

standard A format, program, or protocol that has been approved by a recognized standards organization or is accepted as a de facto standard by the industry.

standby mode A state of a battery-powered computer in which the computer consumes power at a very low rate in order to conserve battery power until you are ready to work.

standby power system (SPS) A form of uninterruptible power supply that monitors the electrical line for problems and kicks into battery power when it detects a problem.

stand-alone program A self-contained application program that serves one purpose.

status area See *status line.*

status line A line or group of lines that gives format information and tells you where you are in a document or other program.

storage A term used to refer to an area external to the CPU in or on which data is held, such as a hard disk or a floppy disk; also referred to as secondary, external, or auxiliary storage.

storage media The material on which data is stored, such as magnetic disks, magnetic tapes, or optical disks.

stored-program concept The idea that programs can be stored in a computer's memory and can be changed electronically rather than by resetting switches and rewiring the computer.

structured programming A collection of methods for developing a well-designed, less error-prone program. Structured programming methods emphasize the top-down modular approach, thorough documentation, and program testing to improve programmer productivity and program clarity.

structured query language (SQL) A language for requesting information from a database.

style sheet A set of recommendations for creating a professional-looking document. It may contain specifications for font, borders, titles, headers, and so on.

stylus One term for the penlike instrument used for on-screen, graphics tablet, or notepad input.

sub-notebook computer A type of notebook computer that weighs from 3 to 5 pounds.

supercomputer The fastest, most expensive type of computer, able to do billions of calculations per second and process huge amounts of data. It is distinguished from the mainframe mainly by its incredibly fast processing power in doing one job rather than by the number of users it can support to do many jobs.

SuperDrive Stands for floppy drive high density. A 3.5-inch disk drive for the Macintosh that can use double-density or high-density disks and can read DOS-formatted floppy disks.

Super VGA (SVGA) A graphics standard with greater capabilities than VGA.

surge protector (surge suppressor) A device that prevents sudden and powerful electrical current from harming a computer or another electrical product.

suspend/resume mode See *standby mode*.

swapping In virtual memory, the process of transferring the required portion of a program from storage (that is, virtual memory) into RAM.

syntax error A violation of the rules of a programming language that makes a program unusable.

synthesizer A device used to imitate sounds of a voice or an instrument and to create other sounds not represented by any instrument.

sysop The SYStem OPerator of a bulletin board system.

system software Programs that manage the operation of computer circuitry and act as a link between the computer's internal circuitry and the application software. They do the background jobs of a computer's operation.

tape A narrow plastic strip with a magnetizable coating on which data can be recorded as magnetized spots. It provides sequential-access storage. Magnetic tape is wound on reels and is similar to the tape used in sound recording.

tape drive A machine that moves magnetic tape past a read/write head.

task switching Capability of an operating system or environment that enables you to have two or more programs open at the same time so that you can work back and forth between or among them.

telecommunication The combined use of computers and communication channels such as telephone systems.

telecommute To work at home and on the road and communicate with the office or send data to the office via electronic machines and telecommunications channels.

template A master form that contains the format and setup for a document such as a business letter or a spreadsheet worksheet. Also a paper or plastic overlay for the keyboard that summarizes the commands in a particular program, such as *WordPerfect*.

terminal-emulation driver Program that enables you to access a mainframe computer or bulletin board system with your computer.

terminate-and-stay-resident program (TSR) See *memory-resident program.*

text Strings of words.

text cursor A pointer that shows where the next typed character will appear.

text mode A state or setting in which only text can be entered at the computer. See also *graphics mode.*

text wrap Term used to describe the flow of text around an image embedded in the text.

thermal printer A printer that forms impressions on heat-sensitive paper with heated pins placed in a matrix format.

thesaurus In reference to computers, an electronic book of words and their synonyms, found in advanced word processing software.

thin film transistors A type of LCD screen in which each pixel has three separate transistors, one each for red, green, and blue. It provides better resolution than a conventional LCD.

time-sharing system An arrangement by which a central computer divides its resources among many users, each at a separate terminal, so that each user receives what seem to be simultaneous results. Also known as "time-slicing."

title A name for a commercial multimedia program.

toggle A switch or command that enables you to go back and forth between two states or settings.

tool A feature that enables you to accomplish a task in a program; for example, in a graphics program, the brush tool lets you lay down certain types of lines.

toolbar A defined area on the display screen where the icons of tools are kept.

toolkit See *toolbar.*

top-down design A method of designing a solution, starting with a big problem and breaking it into smaller, more detailed units.

touch screen A computer screen equipped for detecting the point at which you touch it. It lets you bypass the keyboard.

tower configuration A computer in which components such as the power supply, motherboard, and various drives are stacked in a case on top of each other vertically.

track One of series of formatted concentric circles on the surface of a magnetic disk.

trackball An input device in which a ball resting on top of a base is spun to move the cursor on the screen. An advantage of a trackball over the mouse is that the trackball does not need space to roll around on. It lets you bypass the keyboard.

tractor feed Paper feed in which teeth on the printer catch into the holes in the continuous fan-fold paper and pull it through as printing occurs.

transistor A device that controls electric current flow without using a vacuum tube. There are millions of transistors on a single computer chip, but early transistors were solid-state devices that were large enough to see.

transportable A portable computer that weighs more than 17 pounds, but is still small enough to be carried around. It usually requires an external power source.

trigger The button on a joystick.

TSR See *terminate-and-stay-resident program.*

typeface The shape (design) of type.

undo feature A feature that cancels, or retracts, a command that had just been performed. Depending on the program, you can usually undo from 1 to 5 operations, and occasionally many more.

uninterruptible power supply (UPS) A battery-operated power supply used for running your computer for a few minutes in order to save files in case of a power outage.

unpacking Decompressing files.

upgrade To install hardware in an existing computer with the purpose of giving it additional capabilities or speed.

upper memory Memory that consists of the remaining 384K of RAM in DOS after 640K has been designated as conventional memory.

UPS See *uninterruptible power supply.*

user friendly Description of hardware and software features that promote ease of use and lessen frustration among computer users.

user interface The set of commands, menus, or icons with which you communicate with a program.

users group An informal group of people with a particular microcomputer, software package, or computer interest who meet to exchange information about hardware, software, service, and support.

user's manual The type of documentation included in a software package or hardware package that explains how to install and use the item.

utility program (or utility) A program that performs a specialized function having to do with actual computer operations rather than with completing a task such as preparing a document or reading a file.

value In a spreadsheet, a number that is entered into a cell. A value can be a specific number or a variable number that results from a calculation.

variable A value that can change during processing.

VDT See *video display terminal.*

vector graphics Technique for creating line images on computers.

very high-level languages Fourth-generation languages that are designed to be user friendly.

VGA Stands for video graphics array. A graphics display system for IBM PCs and compatibles that uses analog signals and has a high degree of resolution and over 200,000 colors.

video accelerator board A printed circuit board that enables graphics display to occur rapidly.

video adapter board A printed circuit board that gives a computer graphics capabilities; also called video board.

video display terminal (VDT) A terminal with a keyboard and monitor that can receive output from a remote computer and send input to the remote computer.

video RAM (VRAM) Pronounced *vee RAM*. Memory chips used to increase graphics capabilities; can be accessed by two devices simultaneously.

virtual memory A technique in which portions of programs not being used are placed on the hard disk until needed, giving the impression that memory is unlimited.

virtual reality A computer arrangement including hardware and software that enables a person to experience and manipulate a three-dimensional world that exists only in projected images.

virus A troublesome computer program that can disrupt a computer's operations or destroy the contents of a hard disk or floppy disk.

virus-protection program See *antivirus program.*

voice recognition The ability of a computer to recognize and act upon commands spoken by users.

voice-response unit A device that allows you to "train" the computer to understand your voice so that you can input information orally. It lets you bypass the keyboard.

voice synthesizer See *synthesizer.*

volatile Characteristic of memory that loses its contents when the computer is turned off.

waveform sound Sound represented in continuous wave form rather than in digital form.

"what-if" analysis A planning technique that uses spreadsheet software to project consequences of assumed future conditions.

wide area network A computer network that covers a large geographical area.

wild-card match A search in which you can specify a special symbol that stands for variable characters in a character string. * stands for any number of characters; ? stands for just one character. For example, if you searched for SP?N, the result would find SPAN, SPIN, and SPUN. If you searched for SP*N, you would also find SPAWN, SPERMATOZOON, and SPHAGNUM.

Winchester drive Another name for hard-disk drive.

window A frame that displays all of or a portion of a file or message on the screen.

word processor A computer program designed for the preparation of text that enables you to enter, edit, format, print, save, and retrieve text.

word size The number of bits that the computer can manipulate at one time.

word wrap The feature by which the cursor is automatically moved to the beginning of the next line when the current entry line is full. If a word goes past the right margin, it is automatically moved in its entirety to the next line. Also called wraparound and automatic word wrap.

worksheet A single spreadsheet.

workstation A high-end microcomputer; also a member of a local-area network (LAN) where work on applications takes place.

WORM disk See *write once, read many.*

write/enable, or write/protect, notch A notch that is used to prevent accidental erasure or overwriting of the contents of a floppy disk. On a 5.25-inch disk, you cover the notch with tape. On a 3.5-inch disk, you slide up a tiny square inside the notch.

write once, read many (WORM) disk An optical disk that can be written to just once, but read from many times.

write The term used to describe the electronic recording of data into random-access memory or onto a storage medium such as a disk or tape.

WYSIWYG Pronounced *wizzywig*; short for "what you see is what you get," a phrase that identifies a program's capability to display text on the screen much as it would appear when printed on paper.

XGA Short for extended graphics array, a high-resolution graphics standard from IBM.

XMS See *extended memory.*

INDEX

SYMBOLS

A

B

C

D

E

F

G

H

I

M

N

O

P

Q

R

S